Foreword

This book has been prepared for Medicare benef. relatively thorough explanation of the Medicare program with particular emphasis on services covered in institutional settings and services provided by physicians and suppliers.

Published annually, this book includes changes made by law and regulation amendments and by updates to program manuals issued by the Centers for Medicare and Medicaid Services (CMS). This edition includes changes issued during 2015 that affect Medicare beneficiaries and providers in 2016.

The 2016 highlights are as follows:

Medicare Part A (hospital insurance). For 2016, the inpatient hospital deductible will be $1,288 per each beneficiary "spell of illness," an increase from the $1,260 inpatient deductible in 2015. Patients are responsible for a coinsurance amount for each day after the 60th and through the 90th day per spell of illness, and in 2016 daily coinsurance amounts will be $322 for the 61st through 90th day of hospitalization. When Medicare patients use their lifetime reserve days in 2016, their coinsurance will be $644 per day. When Medicare patients are patients in skilled nursing facilities in 2016, their coinsurance will be $161 for the 21st through 100th day of skilled nursing facility care (see ¶ 220, ¶ 224, ¶ 242).

Medicare Part B (supplementary medical insurance). Most people with Medicare Part B will be "held harmless" from any increase in premiums in 2016 and will pay the same monthly premium as 2015, which is $104.90. The Part B premium for beneficiaries not subject to the "hold harmless" provision, i.e., those not collecting Social Security benefits, those who will enroll in Part B for the first time in 2016, dual-eligible beneficiaries who have their premiums paid by Medicaid, and beneficiaries who pay an additional income-related premium, will be $121.80.

Income-adjusted premiums for 2016 are as follows: Individuals with modified adjusted gross income (MAGI) greater than $85,000 but less than or equal to $107,000 and couples with MAGI greater than $170,000 but less than or equal to $214,000 will pay a monthly premium of $170.50. Individuals with MAGI greater than $107,000 but less than or equal to $160,000 and couples with MAGI greater than $214,000 and less than or equal to $320,000 will pay a monthly premium of $243.60. Individuals with MAGI greater than $160,000 but less than or equal to $214,000 and couples with MAGI greater than $320,000 and less than or equal to $428,000 will pay a monthly premium of $316.70. Individuals with MAGI greater than $214,000 and couples with MAGI greater than $428,000 will pay a monthly premium of $389.80. The rates are modified slightly for beneficiaries who are married and lived with their spouse at any time during the taxable year but file a separate tax return from their spouse (see ¶ 320).

For 2016, the Part B deductible will be $166 (see ¶ 335).

Beginning January 1, 2016, at the discretion of the beneficiary, annual wellness visits include advance care planning services, including discussions about future care decisions that might need to be made, how the beneficiary can let others know about care preferences, and an explanation of advance directives that may involve the completion of standard forms (see ¶ 369).

Physician reimbursement. The physician fee schedule payment amount for a service is determined by a formula that takes into consideration the relative value unit for the service, the conversion factor for the year, and the geographic adjustment factor for the service. Through 2014, the conversion factor update for a year was based in part on changes in expenditures for physicians' services, measured by using the Sustainable Growth Rate (SGR), which produced negative updates requiring annual legislation to update the conversion factor. The Medicare Access and CHIP Reauthorization Act of 2015 (MACRA) (P.L. 114-10) repealed the SGR effective April 16, 2015, and changed how the conversion factor is updated (see ¶ 855).

Medicare Part C (managed care plans). The special needs plan (SNP) program, which covers managed care plans for individuals with special needs, has been extended through 2018 (¶¶ 400).

Medicare Part D (prescription drug plans). For 2016, beneficiaries in standard prescription drug plans (PDPs) will be subject to a $360 deductible. In 2016, beneficiaries in the coverage gap will continue to receive a 50 percent discount on brand-name drugs. PDPs also must pay another 5 percent, providing Part D beneficiaries with total coverage of 55 percent in the donut hole (see ¶ 507).

For 2016, the national average monthly bid amount for a PDP will be $64.66, down from $70.18 in 2015. The 2016 base beneficiary premium is $34.10, up from $33.13 in 2015. High-income beneficiaries are subject to income-adjusted premiums for Part D, just as they are for Part B. For 2016, the income-related monthly adjustment amount for a PDP premium will be $12.70 for an individual with MAGI greater that $85,000, but not more than $107,000; $32.80 for an individual with MAGI greater than $107,000, but not more than $160,000; $52.80 for an individual with MAGI greater than $160,000, but not more than $214,000; and $72.90 for an individual with MAGI greater than $214,000. In the case of a joint tax return, the MAGI dollar amounts are doubled (see ¶ 505).

Quality of care. A number of quality of care initiatives will continue to be implemented by CMS in 2016, many of which will affect provider and facility reimbursement.

MACRA consolidates and replaces the electronic health record meaningful use program, Physician Quality Reporting System, and the value-based payment modifier into the new Merit-Based Incentive Payment System (MIPS) program. MACRA will sunset the three programs at the end of 2018. Starting in 2019, the amounts paid to individual providers will be subject to adjustment through one of two mechanisms, depending on whether the physician chooses to participate in an Alternative Payment Model (APM) program or MIPS (see ¶ 855).

As a part of a restructuring of the quality improvement organization (QIO) program in 2014, CMS introduced two new phases aimed at improving patient care and health outcomes and saving taxpayer resources. The first phase of the restructuring allows two Beneficiary and Family-Centered Care (BFCC) QIOs to review and monitor the program separately from the traditional quality improvement activities to ensure consistency in the review process. In the second phase of the restructuring, CMS will award contracts to Quality Innovation Networks (QIN) QIOs that will work directly with providers and communities on data-driven initiatives (see ¶ 710).

Inpatient hospitals that do not submit required quality data on specific quality indicators to the Medicare program each year will have their applicable hospital market basket percentage increase reduced by 2 percent. Similarly, Medicare payments to hospitals can be reduced under the Hospital Readmissions Reduction Program, and hospitals can earn incentives under the Hospital Inpatient Value-Based Purchasing Program (see ¶ 810).

Outpatient hospitals that fail to report on quality measures in 2016 will have their payments reduced by 2.0 percent in calendar year 2018. To ensure that hospitals are accurately reporting quality of care measures for chart-abstracted data, CMS may validate one or more measures by reviewing documentation of patient encounters submitted by

2016
Medicare
Explained

Wolters Kluwer

Managing Editor
Paul Clark
Assistant Managing Editor
Kelly J. Rooney, J.D., M.P.H.

Contributing Editors

Kathryn S. Beard, J.D.

Melissa Mitchell, J.D.

Sheila Lynch-Afryl, J.D., M.A.

Patricia K. Ruiz, J.D.

Lawrence D. Smith
Production

4025 W. Peterson Ave.
Chicago, IL 60646-6085
800 344 3734
wklawbusiness.com

Printed in the United States of America

ISBN: 978-1-4548-7403-4

SUSTAINABLE FORESTRY INITIATIVE

Certified Sourcing
www.sfiprogram.org
SFI-01028

selected participating hospitals. CMS requires outpatient hospitals to achieve a minimum 75 percent validation score based on this validation process to receive the full update (see ¶ 820).

Other Wolters Kluwer publications:

Further details on the topics covered in this book, together with the texts of pertinent laws, regulations, policy guidelines, court decisions, etc., may be found in Wolters Kluwer's MEDICARE AND MEDICAID GUIDE. The GUIDE is available as a six-volume, loose-leaf print product as well as electronically on the Internet. Other electronic databases, including the full text of the CMS program manuals and the codes and complete descriptions contained in the physician fee schedule, are offered as part of Wolters Kluwer's electronic Health Law Library. Wolters Kluwer also has an easy-to-read electronic reporter specializing in Part B issues entitled the PHYSICIANS' MEDICARE GUIDE. Wolters Kluwer also offers, in print and electronic form, a comprehensive guide to the landmark health care reform legislation passed in 2010, entitled LAW, EXPLANATION AND ANALYSIS OF THE PATIENT PROTECTION AND AFFORDABLE CARE ACT (2014 UPDATE), VOLUMES 1 AND 2.

Finally, Wolters Kluwer publishes the following related paperback books:

2016 Master Medicare Guide

2016 Social Security Benefits (Including Medicare)

2016 Social Security Explained

To find out more about these publications, call 1-888-224-7377 or visit www.WKLawBusiness.com.

A note about the citations in the text:

Throughout the text, statements are documented, when possible, by citations to the law, regulations, and program manuals issued by the federal government. In the interests of simplicity and conservation of space, citations generally have been made only to the highest authority available for the statement in the text, although, when appropriate, multiple citations (i.e., citations both to a law provision and its implementing regulation) are included. In some instances, when there is no clear ranking of authorities, only the most widely available source is cited.

January 2016

Table of Contents

Detailed Table of Contents

Chapter 1—Introduction

Chapter 2—Medicare Part A—Hospital Insurance

Eligibility and Enrollment

Inpatient Hospital Services

Nursing Home Services

Home Health Services

Hospice Care

Chapter 3—Medicare Part B—Supplemental Insurance

Eligibility and Enrollment

Benefits

Chapter 7—Administrative Provisions

Chapter 8—Payment Rules

Chapter 9—Claims, Payments, and Appeals

Topical Index

Chapter 1- INTRODUCTION

[¶ 100] Introduction to Medicare

As part of the Social Security Amendments of 1965, Congress established two new programs to cover the cost of medical care for the elderly and disabled. The first of these programs, largely financed through the hospital insurance taxes, provides basic protection against the costs of inpatient hospital and other institutional provider care. Officially, this program is called "Hospital Insurance Benefits for the Aged and Disabled," although it includes much more than hospital benefits. Unofficially it is sometimes called "basic Medicare," "hospital insurance," or "Medicare Part A" (because the authorization for the program is Part A of Title XVIII of the Social Security Act).

The second of these programs is a voluntary program covering the costs of physician and other health care practitioner services and items and supplies not covered under the basic program. It is financed through monthly premiums from enrollees and contributions from the federal government. Officially, this program is called "Supplementary Medical Insurance Benefits for the Aged and Disabled," but unofficially it is called "supplementary Medicare," the "medical insurance program," or "Medicare Part B."

A third Medicare program that expands managed care options for beneficiaries who are entitled to Part A and enrolled in Part B was created under the Balanced Budget Act of 1997 (BBA) (P.L. 105-33) and expanded under the Medicare Modernization Act of 2003 (MMA) (P.L. 108-173); it is now commonly referred to as "Medicare Part C" or "Medicare Advantage." Since January 1, 1999, beneficiaries have had the option of choosing to receive their health benefits through the traditional Medicare "fee-for-service" program or through a managed care plan certified under the Medicare Advantage program. Payments Medicare makes to a Medicare Advantage plan replace the amounts Medicare otherwise would have paid under Parts A and B.

The Medicare program was also expanded by the MMA to include a prescription drug benefit, under Part D of Title XVIII of the Social Security Act. The prescription drug benefit became available to eligible individuals on January 1, 2006, and is called Medicare Part D.

Together, the four programs are known officially as "Health Insurance for the Aged and Disabled," the name of Title XVIII of the Social Security Act, which contains the basic law governing the Medicare program.

Contents of this Book

Medicare Part A, the hospital insurance program, is discussed in Chapter 2, and Medicare Part B, supplementary medical insurance, is discussed in Chapter 3. Medicare Part C, the Medicare Advantage program, is discussed in Chapter 4, and Medicare Part D, the prescription drug benefit, is discussed in Chapter 5. Certain items that are specifically excluded from coverage by Medicare are discussed in Chapter 6. Miscellaneous administrative features of the Medicare program are discussed in Chapter 7, including quality improvement organizations, recovery audit contractors, electronic health data privacy, "Medigap" insurance, and initiatives used to curb health care fraud and abuse. Payment to providers, physicians, and suppliers by Medicare is discussed in Chapter 8. Claims filing procedures and appeals of adverse determinations are discussed in Chapter 9.

Rules concerning eligibility and applications for Medicare are discussed at the beginning of Chapter 2 in the case of Part A, and at the beginning of Chapter 3 in the case of Part B. Election and enrollment in Medicare Part C are discussed in Chapter 4 (¶ 401). Eligibility and enrollment in Medicare Part D are discussed in Chapter 5 (¶ 503).

Chapter 2– MEDICARE PART A—HOSPITAL INSURANCE

Eligibility and Enrollment

[¶ 200] Entitlement to Part A Hospital Insurance Benefits

There are several ways to become entitled to hospital insurance benefits under Part A of the Medicare program. Most individuals automatically become entitled when they reach age 65 if they are eligible for monthly Social Security retirement or survivor benefits or railroad retirement benefits as "qualified railroad retirement beneficiaries." [Soc. Sec. Act § 226; 42 C.F.R. §§ 406.5, 406.10.]

Entitlement to Medicare for the above individuals begins in the month in which they become 65 years old, regardless of whether they have elected to receive Social Security (or other) retirement benefits. [42 C.F.R. § 406.10(b)(1).] Persons electing to receive Social Security benefits earlier than age 65 do not need not file an application for Medicare when they become 65; they will automatically receive an application. Persons electing not to receive Social Security, however, will need to file an application for Medicare (see below under "Application Requirements"). [42 C.F.R. § 406.6.]

Individuals under age 65 also are entitled to benefits under Part A if they are entitled to: (1) Social Security or railroad retirement disability benefits for at least the previous 24 months (see ¶ 204), or (2) end-stage renal disease (ESRD) benefits (see ¶ 205). [Soc. Sec. Act §§ 226(a), 226A(a); 42 C.F.R. §§ 406.5(a), 406.12, 406.13.]

Individuals age 65 or over who are not entitled to Part A benefits on one of the bases outlined above can enroll voluntarily in the Part A program by paying a monthly premium (see ¶ 203). [Soc. Sec. Act § 1818(a); 42 C.F.R. §§ 406.5(b), 406.20(b).]

Individuals entitled to benefits under Part A (except persons with ESRD) and enrolled in the supplementary medical insurance program (Medicare Part B—see ¶ 300–¶ 320) may choose to receive benefits under the traditional fee-for-service programs, or they may choose to enroll in a Medicare Advantage managed care plan, which offers additional benefits. [Soc. Sec. Act § 1851(a)(3).] The Medicare Advantage program, also called Medicare Part C, is discussed in detail in ¶ 400–¶ 412.

In addition, individuals entitled to benefits under Part A (except persons with ESRD) and enrolled in Part B may choose to enroll in Part D, which provides coverage for prescription drugs (see ¶ 500–¶ 535). [Soc. Sec. Act § 1860D-1 *et seq.*]

Coverage Period

Medicare entitlement usually begins on the first day of the month when an individual reaches age 65. Thus, an individual whose 65th birthday is on January 6, 2016, would be eligible for benefits on January 1, 2016. [Soc. Sec. Act § 226(c)(1); 42 C.F.R. § 406.10(b)(1).]

The Social Security and Medicare programs follow the rule that a person reaches a given age on the day before the anniversary of birth. Thus, a person born on April 1, 1951, for example, will be considered to have reached age 65 on March 31, 2016, and Medicare hospital benefits could begin March 1, 2016. [*Medicare General Information, Eligibility, and Entitlement Manual*, Pub. 100-01, Ch. 2, § 10.2.]

A Social Security applicant who applies for monthly benefits after reaching age 65 can be entitled to Part A benefits retroactively beginning with the first day of the first month in which all the requirements for benefits otherwise are met, but not more than six months (12

¶200

months for disabled widow's or widower's benefits) before the month in which the application is filed. [42 C.F.R. § 406.6(d)(2), (4).]

Suspended Benefits of Aliens

An individual whose cash Social Security benefits have been suspended under section 202(t)(1) of the Social Security Act (relating to suspension of the benefits of certain aliens who are outside the United States for more than six months) is not entitled to Part A benefits furnished in any month for which such a suspension is applicable. [Soc. Sec. Act § 202(t)(9); 42 C.F.R § 406.50.]

Conviction for Subversive Activities

If a person is convicted of certain subversive activities, the court may impose, in addition to other penalties, a penalty that affects entitlement to hospital insurance, i.e., that the individual's income (or the income of the insured individual on whose earnings record he or she became or seeks to become entitled) for the year of conviction and any previous year may not be counted in determining the insured status necessary for entitlement to hospital insurance. [Soc. Sec. Act § 202(u); 42 C.F.R § 406.52.]

Application Requirements

A person age 65 or over who has filed an application and established entitlement to monthly Social Security benefits or who is a qualified railroad retirement beneficiary ordinarily does not need to file any additional application for Part A. It comes automatically with these other benefits. [42 C.F.R. § 406.6(a).]

An application for Medicare benefits is required, however, for such an individual who has not applied for Social Security benefits. An application also is required for an individual who seeks entitlement on the basis of: (1) ESRD (¶ 205), (2) "Medicare-qualified government employment" (¶ 206), (3) deemed entitlement to disabled widow's or widower's benefits under certain circumstances, or (4) voluntary Part A enrollment (¶ 203). [42 C.F.R. § 406.6(c), (e).]

The form most people use to apply for Part A entitlement, which also may be used for enrollment in the Part B program (¶ 310), is Form CMS-18-F-5, "Application for Hospital Insurance Entitlement." ESRD applicants use Form CMS-43, "Application for Health Insurance Benefits Under Medicare for Individuals with End-Stage Renal Disease." [42 C.F.R. § 406.7.]

Except in the case of individuals seeking entitlement on the basis of ESRD, an application for Part A must be filed by an individual before death—a relative or legal representative may not file for retroactive entitlement after the individual has died. [42 C.F.R. §§ 406.10(b)(2), 406.13(d)(3).]

Filing claims for Medicare benefits by Medicare patients is discussed at ¶ 900 *et seq.*

Health Insurance Card

As evidence of entitlement to Medicare benefits, CMS issues each beneficiary a "Health Insurance Card," Form CMS-40 (in the case of railroad retirement beneficiaries, the Railroad Retirement Board issues the health insurance card). This card gives the name of the beneficiary, the Health Insurance Claim number, sex of the beneficiary, and the effective date of entitlement. The cardholder should show the card to the health care provider whenever covered services are required. [Pub. 100-01, Ch. 2, § 50.]

Social Security numbers. The HHS Secretary is required to ensure that Social Security numbers (or any derivative thereof) are not displayed, coded, or embedded on

Medicare cards issued to an individual who is entitled to Part A benefits or enrolled under Part B. HHS must also ensure that any other identifier displayed on the card is not identifiable as a Social Security account number or derivative thereof. [Soc. Sec. Act 205(c)(2)(C)(xiii), as added by Medicare Access and CHIP Reauthorization Act of 2015 (MACRA) (P.L. 114-10) § 501.]

[¶ 203] Voluntary Enrollment in the Hospital Insurance Program

Hospital insurance (Part A) coverage is available on a voluntary basis to individuals 65 or over who are not entitled to Social Security or other Medicare-qualifying benefits (see ¶ 200). This is called premium hospital insurance.

Eligibility. An individual is eligible to enroll voluntarily in Part A if he or she:

(1) has attained age 65;

(2) is enrolled in the Medicare Part B;

(3) is a resident of the United States and is either:

a. a citizen of the United States; or

b. an alien lawfully admitted for permanent residence who has continuously resided in the United States for the five years immediately before the month in which application for enrollment is made; and

(4) is not otherwise entitled to Part A benefits.

[Soc. Sec. Act § 1818(a); 42 C.F.R. §§ 406.5(b), 406.20.]

For purposes of determining U.S. residency, the term "United States" includes the District of Columbia, Commonwealth of Puerto Rico, the Virgin Islands, Guam, American Samoa, and the Northern Mariana Islands. [Soc. Sec. Act §§ 210(i), 1861(x); Northern Mariana Islands Covenant Implementation Act (P.L. 94-241).]

Enrollment. An individual may accomplish voluntary enrollment in Part A only during an "enrollment period." [Soc. Sec. Act § 1818(b).] For individuals 65 years of age or older, the initial enrollment period extends for three months before and three months after the first month the individual would be eligible for Part A. Following this initial enrollment period, an individual is able to enroll for Part A benefits from January 1 to March 31 of each subsequent year. If the individual enrolls during one of the annual enrollment periods following his or her initial enrollment, the benefits are effective on July 1 of the year in which the individual enrolls. [42 C.F.R. § 406.21.] Note that these enrollment periods do not apply to the majority of individuals who are automatically enrolled upon reaching the age 65 and enrolling for Social Security benefits.

In general, the provisions governing enrollment (see ¶ 310–¶ 312), coverage periods (see ¶ 313), and premiums (see ¶ 320) under Part B—excluding premium increases for late enrollment (see below)—also are applicable to voluntary enrollment in Part A. [Soc. Sec. Act § 1818(c).]

An individual meeting the conditions for voluntary enrollment and paying the appropriate premium may elect coverage under a Medicare Advantage managed care plan under Part C (see ¶ 401). [Soc. Sec. Act § 1851(a)(3).]

Payment of Premiums

Voluntary enrollees must pay a monthly premium based on the total cost of Part A protection for the enrolled group. The premium is updated annually according to a formula set out in the law. [Soc. Sec. Act § 1818(d)(2).] For 2016, the monthly Part A premium is $411.00. [*Notice*, 80 FR 70805, Nov. 16, 2015.]

The following table shows the monthly premium rates in effect during the past few years:

Year	$ Amount
2016	411
2015	407
2014	426
2013	441

There is a reduced Part A premium for certain individuals with 30 or more quarters of Social Security coverage. An individual who has had at least 30 months of such coverage—or who was married to, widowed from, or divorced from such an individual for certain periods of time—is entitled to a 45 percent reduction in the Part A premium. [Soc. Sec. Act § 1818(d)(4)(A).] The reduced premium for eligible individuals in 2016 is $226; the reduced premium in 2015 was $224. [*Notice*, 80 FR 70805, Nov. 16, 2015; *Notice*, 79 FR 61312, Oct. 10, 2014.]

Since January 1, 1998, the Part A premium has been reduced to zero for certain public retirees. [Soc. Sec. Act § 1818(d)(5).] Government employees are discussed in detail at ¶ 206.

Late Enrollment and Reenrollment Penalties

There is a 10 percent late enrollment penalty for individuals who enroll voluntarily in Part A 12 months or more after the expiration of the initial enrollment period. The penalty is based on the date when an individual first meets the eligibility requirements for enrollment. The penalty continues for twice the number of years (i.e., full 12-month periods) that the enrollment was delayed. [Soc. Sec. Act § 1818(c)(6); 42 C.F.R. §§ 406.32(d), 406.33.]

If an individual drops out of the program and then reenrolls, the months during which the individual was out of the program are counted in determining the re-enrollment penalty. [42 C.F.R. § 406.34.]

Example • • • _____

Agnes Williams was eligible to enroll during an initial enrollment period that ended May 31, 2013. She actually enrolled in the general enrollment period, January 1, 2016—March 31, 2016. There are 34 months elapsing after the close of her initial enrollment period and before March 31, 2016, the close of the period in which she actually enrolled. (Delinquent enrollment is counted from the end of the initial enrollment period to the end of the enrollment period in which the individual actually enrolls—see ¶ 320.) Thus, there are two 12-month periods during which she could have been, but was not, enrolled. She is assessed a 10 percent premium penalty, and that penalty expires after she has paid it for 48 months.

_____

State and local government retirees who retired before January 1, 2002, can be exempt from the Part A delayed enrollment penalties. Their exemption depends on the total amount of payroll taxes they or their employers paid. [Soc. Sec. Act § 1818(d)(6).]

Group Premium Payments

A state or any other public or private organization can pay monthly premiums on a group basis for its retired or active employees age 65 and over. If group coverage is purchased, group premium payments are made under a contract or other arrangement entered into between the agency or organization and the HHS Secretary. The Secretary may refuse to enter into a group premium payment contract if it is determined that payment of

¶203

premiums under this type of contract is not administratively feasible. [Soc. Sec. Act § 1818(e).]

Termination

An individual's entitlement to the voluntary Part A program terminates if the individual: (1) files a request for termination; (2) becomes entitled to regular Part A benefits in one of the ways described at ¶ 200; (3) is no longer entitled to Part B; (4) fails to pay voluntary Part A premiums; or (5) dies. [Soc. Sec. Act § 1818(c)(4), (5); 42 C.F.R. § 406.28.]

If the voluntary enrollee stops paying the premium, entitlement will end on the last day of the third month after the billing month. Entitlement will be reinstated, however, if the individual can show good cause for failing to pay the premiums on time, as long as all overdue premiums are paid within three calendar months after the date entitlement would have been terminated. [42 C.F.R. § 406.28(d).]

[¶ 204] Disability Beneficiaries

An individual under age 65 is entitled to hospital insurance benefits if, for 24 months, he or she has been: (1) entitled or deemed entitled to Social Security disability benefits as an insured individual, child, widow, or widower who is "under a disablity;" or (2) a disabled qualified beneficiary certified under section 7(d) of the Railroad Retirement Act. [Soc. Sec. Act § 226(b); 42 C.F.R. § 406.12(a).]

"Medicare-qualified government employment" is treated as Social Security qualifying employment for the purpose of the provision of Medicare disability benefits (see ¶ 206). [Soc. Sec. Act § 226(a)(2)(C).]

Disabled beneficiaries who are not yet 65 and continue to be disabled, and who no longer are entitled to benefits solely because their earnings are in excess of the amount permitted, may purchase Part A coverage. Enrollment can occur during special enrollment periods, as provided by law. Premiums will be similar to the premiums required for voluntary enrollees (see ¶ 203). [Soc. Sec. Act § 1818A.]

Upon reaching the age of 65, beneficiaries who are disabled can become eligible for Medicare as Social Security retirees if they satisfy the requirements for that status (see ¶ 200).

Waiting Period

Disabled individuals may not receive Part A benefits until they have satisfied a 24-month "waiting period" during which they have continuously been disabled. An exception to this rule is made for individuals with amyotrophic lateral sclerosis (ALS), who have no waiting period. [Soc. Sec. Act § 226(b), (h).]

Months of a previous period of entitlement or deemed entitlement to disability benefits count toward the 24-month requirement if any of the following conditions is met:

(1) entitlement was an insured individual or a disabled qualified railroad retirement beneficiary, and the previous period ended within the 60 months preceding the month in which the current disability began;

(2) entitlement was as a disabled child, widow, or widower, and the previous period ended within the 84 months preceding the month in which the current disability began; or

(3) the previous period ended on or after March 1, 1988, and the current impairment is the same as, or directly related to, the impairment on which the previous period of entitlement was based.

[Soc. Sec. Act § 226(f); 42 C.F.R. § 406.12(b).]

Termination of Coverage

Generally, entitlement to Part A ends with the earliest of the following:

- the last day of the last month in which he or she was entitled or deemed entitled to disability benefits or was qualified as a disabled railroad retirement beneficiary, if he or she was notified of the termination of entitlement before that month;

- the last day of the month following the month in which he or she is mailed a notice that his or her entitlement or deemed entitlement to disability benefits, or his or her status as a qualified disabled railroad retirement beneficiary, has ended;

- the last day of the month before the month he or she attains age 65; or

- the day of death.

[Soc. Sec. Act § 226(b); 42 C.F.R. § 406.12(d)(2).]

Returning to work. If an individual's entitlement to disability benefits or status as a qualified disabled railroad retirement beneficiary ends because he or she engaged in, or demonstrated the ability to engage in, substantial gainful activity after the 36 months following the nine-month trial work period provided for by Soc. Sec. Act § 222(c)(4), Medicare entitlement continues until the earlier of the following: (1) the last day of the 78th month following the first month of substantial gainful activity occurring after the 15th month of the individual's reentitlement period or, if later, the end of the month following the month the individual's disability benefit entitlement ends; or (2) the last day of the month following the month in which notice is mailed to the individual indicating that he or she is no longer entitled to hospital insurance because of an event or circumstance (for example, there has been medical improvement, or the disabled widow has remarried) that would terminate disability benefit entitlement if it had not already been terminated because of substantial gainful activity. [Soc. Sec. Act § 226(b); 42 C.F.R. § 406.12(e).]

Employer Group Health Plan Coverage

Medicare is the secondary payer for disability beneficiaries who are covered by a large group health plan (an employer with 100 or more employees) as a current employee (or as a family member of a current employee). Thus, when an employee (or a member of the employee's family) becomes disabled, the large employer's group health plan has primary coverage responsibility and Medicare has secondary coverage responsibility. The law provides that either the federal government or the individual has a cause of action against a plan that does not meet its coverage responsibilities and that double damages may be recovered. [Soc. Sec. Act § 1862(b)(1)(B), (b)(2)(B)(iii).]

Employer group health plans are discussed in more detail at ¶ 636.

[¶ 205] End-Stage Renal Disease Beneficiaries

Medicare covers individuals who have not reached age 65 and are suffering from end-stage renal (kidney) disease (ESRD) if they are: (1) fully or currently insured for Social Security or railroad retirement benefits (see ¶ 200); (2) entitled either to monthly Social Security or railroad retirement benefits; or (3) spouses or dependent children of eligible individuals. ESRD benefits are available only after an application for Medicare benefits is filed, and the application may be filed after the individual's death. [Soc. Sec. Act § 226A(a); 42 C.F.R. §§ 406.6(c), 406.13(c) and (d).]

"End-stage renal disease" is defined by regulation as "that stage of kidney impairment that appears irreversible and permanent and requires a regular course of dialysis or kidney transplantation to maintain life." [42 C.F.R. § 406.13(b).] Payment for ESRD benefits is discussed at ¶ 845.

Waiting period. Coverage for dialysis patients normally begins the third month after the month in which a course of renal dialysis is initiated. However, entitlement begins on the first day of the month in which a regular course of renal dialysis began if, before the end of the waiting period, the beneficiary participates in a self-dialysis training program offered by a participating Medicare facility. For kidney transplant candidates, coverage can begin as early as the month in which the candidate is hospitalized for transplantation, provided the surgery takes place in that month or in the following two months. [Soc. Sec. Act § 226A(b); 42 C.F.R. § 406.13(e).]

Termination of coverage. Coverage ends at the end of the 12th month after the month in which a course of dialysis ends, unless the individual receives a kidney transplant during that period or begins another regular course of dialysis. For a kidney transplant recipient, coverage ends with the end of the 36th month after the month in which the individual has received a kidney transplant, unless he or she receives another kidney transplant or begins a regular course of dialysis during that period. [Soc. Sec. Act § 226(A)(b)(2); 42 C.F.R. § 406.13(f).]

Covered ESRD Services

Dialysis treatments are covered in various settings, including hospital outpatient ESRD facilities, independent renal dialysis facilities, or the patient's home. Items and services furnished at ESRD facilities differ according to the types of patients being treated, the types of equipment and supplies used, the preferences of the treating physician, and the capability and makeup of the staff. [*Medicare Benefit Policy Manual*, Pub. 100-02, Ch. 11, § 20.]

Medicare covers the rental or purchase of home dialysis equipment for home use, all necessary supplies, and a wide range of home support services. This coverage includes delivery and installation service charges and maintenance expenses for the equipment. [Soc. Sec. Act § 1881(b)(8).]

The home dialysis support services covered by Medicare include periodic monitoring of the patient's home adaptation, visits by qualified provider or facility personnel in accordance with a plan prepared and periodically reviewed by a professional team (including the individual's physician), installation and maintenance of dialysis equipment, and testing and treatment of the water used in treatment. [Soc. Sec. Act § 1881(b)(9).]

Education services. Medicare covers kidney disease education services that are: (1) furnished to an individual with stage IV chronic kidney disease who will require dialysis or a kidney transplant; and (2) designed to provide comprehensive information about the management of comorbidities, the prevention of uremic complications, and each option for renal replacement therapy (including hemodialysis and peritoneal dialysis at home and in-center as well as vascular access options and transplantation). Medicare Part B makes payment for up to six sessions of kidney disease education services. A session is one hour long and may be provided individually or in group settings of two to 20 individuals who need not all be Medicare beneficiaries. [Soc. Sec. Act § 1861(s)(2)(EE), (ggg); 42 C.F.R. § 410.48.]

Transplantation services. Medicare covers the cost of kidney transplantation surgery only if the surgery is performed in a renal transplantation center. [42 C.F.R. § 482.72.] Medicare also covers the costs of care for actual or potential kidney donors, including all reasonable preparatory, operation, and post-operation recovery expenses associated with the donation, without regard to the usual Medicare deductible, coinsurances, and premium payments. Payments for post-operation recovery expenses are limited, however, to the actual period of recovery. [Soc. Sec. Act § 1881(d); Pub. 100-02, Ch. 11, § 140.]

[¶ 206] Government Employees

An individual who has worked in Medicare-qualified government employment (or any related individual who would be entitled to Social Security cash benefits on the employee's record if Medicare-qualified government employment qualified for those benefits) is entitled to hospital insurance benefits if he or she: (1) would meet the requirements of 42 C.F.R. §§406.10 (see ¶ 200), 406.12 (see ¶ 204), or 406.13 (see ¶ 205) if Medicare-qualified government employment were Social Security covered employment; and (2) has filed an application for hospital insurance. [Soc. Sec. Act §226(a)(2)(C); 42 C.F.R. §406.15(e).]

"Medicare-qualified government employment" means federal, state, or local government employment that is subject only to the hospital insurance portion of the tax imposed by the Federal Insurance Contributions Act (FICA), including (1) wages paid for federal employment after December 1982, (2) wages paid to state and local government employees hired after March 31, 1986, and (3) wages paid to state and local government employees hired before April 1, 1986 but whose employment after March 31, 1986 is covered, for Medicare purposes only, under an agreement under Soc. Sec. Act §218. [Soc. Sec. Act §210(p); 42 C.F.R. §406.15(a).]

Individuals entitled to Medicare by virtue of their Medicare-qualified government employment also are entitled to Medicare disability benefits (¶ 204) and end-stage renal disease benefits (¶ 205). [Soc. Sec. Act §§226(b)(2)(C), 226A(a)(1).]

Government Employment Not Considered "Medicare-Qualified"

Federal employees who are not considered "Medicare-qualified" include:

(1)　inmates in federal penal institutions;

(2)　certain interns (other than medical or dental interns or medical or dental residents in training) and student nurses employed by the federal government; and

(3)　employees serving on a temporary basis in case of fire, storm, earthquake, flood, or other similar emergency.

[Soc. Sec. Act §210(a)(6).]

State and local government employees who are not "Medicare-qualified" include:

(1)　individuals employed to relieve them from unemployment;

(2)　patients or inmates in a hospital, home, or other institution;

(3)　employees serving on a temporary basis in case of fire, storm, snow, earthquake, flood, or other similar emergency;

(4)　interns (other than medical or dental interns or medical or dental residents in training), student nurses, and other student employees of hospitals of the District of Columbia; and

(5)　an election official or election worker if the remuneration paid for services performed in a calendar year is less than $1,000.

[Soc. Sec. Act §210(p)(2).]

As noted above, state and local government employees hired before April 1, 1986, are exempt from the hospital portion of the FICA tax, so their employment is not considered to be "Medicare-qualified." A state, however, may ask the Commissioner of Social Security to enter into an agreement whereby these employees also would have their employment treated as "Medicare-qualified." In such cases, only employment occurring after March 31, 1986, is considered "Medicare-qualified." [Soc. Sec. Act §218(n).]

¶206

Payment of Premiums

Government employees who have retired but are unable to qualify for Medicare benefits in the manner described above are entitled to enroll voluntarily in the Part A program and pay the appropriate premium (see ¶ 203). [42 C.F.R. § 406.11.]

Additionally, public retirees meeting certain statutory conditions are entitled to avoid the payment of the monthly premium. The methodology for determining whether a public retiree is exempt from Part A premium payment is similar in many respects to determining the reduced premium required of individuals having 30 or more quarters of Social Security coverage (see "Payment of Premiums" at ¶ 203). Specifically, the premium will be zero for any individual receiving cash benefits under a qualified state or local government retirement system on the basis of the individual's employment for at least 40 calendar quarters (or a combination of such quarters and Social Security-covered quarters totalling 40). As is the case with reduced premiums, individuals who have been married to, widowed from, or divorced from such an individual for certain periods of time also are entitled to a zero premium. [Soc. Sec. Act § 1818(d)(5)(B).]

To be covered under this provision, certain conditions must be met: (1) the individual's Part A premium may not be payable in whole or part by a state (including a state Medicaid program) or a political subdivision of a state; and (2) in the preceding 84 months, the individual was enrolled in Part A and did not have had the Part A premium paid in whole or part by any governmental entity described above. [Soc. Sec. Act § 1818(d)(5)(A).]

The law defines a "qualified state or local government retirement system" as a system established or maintained by a state or political subdivision (or agency thereof) that covers positions of some or all employees of the governmental entity and that does not adjust cash benefits based on eligibility for the premium relief described above. [Soc. Sec. Act § 1818(d)(5)(C).]

Inpatient Hospital Services

[¶ 210] Inpatient Hospital Services: Coverage in General

Medicare Part A covers services provided to beneficiaries who are patients in qualified hospitals participating in the Medicare program for up to 90 days in any one "spell of illness." These services are defined as "inpatient" hospital services. In addition, each beneficiary has a lifetime reserve of 60 days that can be used after the 90 days have been exhausted (see ¶ 224). [Soc. Sec. Act § 1812(a)(1).]

Ordinarily, for hospital services to be covered under Part A, the hospital that provides the services must be *participating* in Medicare (to "participate" a hospital must have signed a Medicare participation agreement—see ¶ 730). In emergency situations, however, the services provided by a nonparticipating hospital also will be covered by Medicare (see ¶ 227). Nonemergency inpatient services furnished in a hospital located outside the United States also will be paid for under Part A if the beneficiary resides in the United States and the foreign hospital is closer to, or more accessible from, the beneficiary's home than the nearest adequately equipped hospital in the United States (see ¶ 610). [*Medicare Benefit Policy Manual*, Pub. 100-02, Ch. 16, § 60.]

Covered Inpatient Hospital Services

The following services or supplies provided while the beneficiary is an inpatient in the hospital are covered:

(1) bed and board;

(2) nursing services (other than the services of a private-duty nurse or attendant) and other related services that ordinarily are furnished by the hospital for the care and treatment of inpatients;

(3) use of hospital facilities;

(4) medical social services;

(5) drugs, biologicals, supplies, appliances, and equipment for use in the hospital that ordinarily are furnished by the hospital for the care and treatment of inpatients;

(6) certain other diagnostic and therapeutic items and services that ordinarily are furnished to inpatients; and

(7) transportation services, including transport by ambulance.

[Soc. Sec. Act § 1861(b); 42 C.F.R. § 409.10.]

To be covered, these services must be provided directly by the hospital or under an arrangement made by the hospital with an outside contractor. Further, when payment can be made for an inpatient hospital stay under Part A, all Medicare-covered services furnished during that stay are paid under Part A.

Limitations and exclusions related to inpatient hospital services. Covered services do not include: (1) the services of physicians and certain other health care practitioners, which are covered under Part B see ¶ 350); (2) services of private-duty nurses (see ¶ 217); and (3) pneumococcal, influenza, and hepatitis B vaccine and their administration, which are covered under Part B even when provided to an inpatient during a hospital stay covered under Part A. [Soc. Sec. Act § 1861(b)(4), (5); 42 C.F.R. § 409.10; Pub. 100-02, Ch. 1, §§ 1–60; *Medicare Claims Processing Manual*, Pub. 100-04, Ch. 18, § 10.1.]

General exclusions from Medicare coverage can be found in Chapter 6, explanations of deductible and coinsurance limitations are at ¶ 220, coverage of services in a hospital after exhaustion of Part A benefits is discussed at ¶ 361, and the lifetime limit on inpatient psychiatric hospital services is explained at ¶ 225.

"Inpatient" Defined

An "inpatient" is a person who has been admitted to a hospital for bed occupancy for purposes of receiving inpatient hospital services. A person is considered an inpatient if formally admitted as a patient with the expectation of remaining at least overnight and occupying a bed, even if it later develops that discharge or transfer to another hospital is possible and a hospital bed actually is not used overnight. [Pub. 100-02, Ch. 1, § 10.]

When a patient with a known diagnosis enters a hospital for a specific minor surgical procedure that is expected to keep him or her in the hospital for only a few hours (fewer than 24) and this expectation is realized, the individual will be considered an outpatient regardless of the hour of admission, whether a bed is used, or the hospital stay extends past midnight. [Pub. 100-02, Ch. 1, § 10.]

Special rules apply when a patient needs only extended care services but actually is placed in a hospital bed, including a "swing bed" (see ¶ 229).

"Spell of Illness" Defined

The duration of inpatient hospital services and post-hospital services in a skilled nursing facility (SNF) is limited according to the beginning and ending of a "spell of illness"—also commonly called a "benefit period."

Beginning a "spell." A "spell of illness" is a period of consecutive days that begins with the first day (that is not included in a previous spell of illness) on which a patient is furnished inpatient hospital or SNF services by a "qualified" provider during a period in which the patient is entitled to Part A benefits. [Soc. Sec. Act § 1861(a)(1); 42 C.F.R. § 409.60(a).]

A "qualified" provider is a hospital (including a psychiatric hospital) or SNF that has been certified as satisfying the requirements of the definition of such an institution (see ¶ 230 and ¶ 231). A hospital that meets the requirements related to emergency services, which are outlined at ¶ 227, is a qualified hospital for purposes of beginning a spell of illness when it furnishes the patient covered inpatient emergency services. [*Medicare General Information, Eligibility, and Entitlement Manual*, Pub. 100-01, Ch. 3, § 10.4.1; Ch. 5, § 20.2.]

Admission to a qualified SNF will begin a spell of illness even though payment for the services cannot be made because the prior hospitalization or transfer requirement has not been met (see ¶ 230).

Ending a "spell." The spell of illness ends with the close of a period of 60 consecutive days during which the patient was neither an inpatient of a hospital nor an inpatient of a SNF. The 60-consecutive-day period begins with the day on which the individual is discharged. [Soc. Sec. Act § 1861(a)(2); Pub. 100-01, Ch. 3, § 10.4.2.]

It is important to note that a stay in a nonparticipating hospital will result in continuing a spell of illness even if the services received are not covered. For example, a stay in a nonparticipating hospital is counted as a qualified stay for purposes of determining whether a spell of illness has ended, even if the nonparticipating hospital did not furnish covered emergency services. A stay in a SNF does not continue a spell of illness unless the stay meets Medicare skilled nursing care requirements. Thus, a beneficiary who is transferred from a hospital to a SNF, but receives only "custodial care" (see ¶ 244) at the SNF, would begin counting the 60-consecutive-day period on the day of discharge from the hospital. [42 C.F.R. § 409.60(b).]

An individual may be discharged from and readmitted to a hospital or SNF several times during a spell of illness and still be in the same spell if 60 days have not elapsed between discharge and readmission. The stay need not be for related physical or mental conditions. [Pub. 100-01, Ch. 3, § 10.4.3.2.]

Example • • • _____

(1) John White was entitled to Part A benefits and was hospitalized in a participating general hospital on June 1. He previously had not established a spell of illness. He remained in the hospital for 30 days and then was transferred to a SNF for 50 days, after which he was discharged to his home on August 18. John's spell of illness began on June 1 and ended on October 17, the end of the 60-day period beginning with the date of his last discharge.

(2) Assume the same set of facts as above, except that John was rehospitalized after 50 days in the SNF and remained in the hospital for another 60 days, after which he was discharged to his home on October 17. John's spell of illness still began on June 1, but it ended on December 16, the end of the 60-day period beginning with the date of his last discharge.

(3) Assume the same set of facts as in example (2), except that John was required to enter the hospital for a third time, *before* exhaustion of the 60-day period following his last hospital discharge. Assume further that he remained in the hospital until his death. No new spell of illness could begin regardless of how long John remained in the hospital during his terminal illness. The crossing from one calendar year to another does not end an ongoing spell of illness.

Once a spell of illness has ended, the beneficiary's next admission to a qualified hospital or SNF will constitute the beginning of a new spell of illness. [42 C.F.R. § 409.60.]

Note that when a beneficiary begins a new spell of illness as a hospital inpatient, a new inpatient hospital deductible (see ¶ 220) must be paid, even if it is within the same calendar year. [42 C.F.R. § 409.60.]

Medicare deductible and coinsurance payments. Beneficiaries who use covered Part A services may be subject to deductible and coinsurance requirements. A beneficiary is responsible for an inpatient hospital deductible amount ($1,288 in 2016), which is deducted from the amount payable by the Medicare program to the hospital, for inpatient hospital services furnished during each spell of illness. When a beneficiary receives such services for more than 60 days during a spell of illness, he or she is responsible for a coinsurance amount equal to one-fourth of the inpatient hospital deductible per day for the 61st through 90th day spent in the hospital ($322 in 2016). An individual has 60 lifetime reserve days of coverage, which he or she may elect to use after the 90th day in a spell of illness. The coinsurance amount for these days is equal to one-half of the inpatient hospital deductible ($644 in 2016). A beneficiary is responsible for a coinsurance amount equal to one-eighth of the inpatient hospital deductible per day for the 21st through the 100th day of SNF services furnished during a spell of illness ($161 in 2016). [*Notice*, 80 FR 70808, Nov. 16, 2015; Pub. 100-01, Ch. 3, § § 10.1, 10.3.]

"Inpatient Day of Care" Defined

The number of days of care charged to a beneficiary for inpatient hospital services is always in units of full days. A day begins at midnight and ends 24 hours later. A part of a day, including the day of admission, counts as a full day, but the day of discharge or death, or a day on which a patient begins a leave of absence, is not counted as a day. If admission and discharge occur on the same day, the day is considered a day of admission and counts as one day. As noted, the day on which a patient begins a leave of absence is treated as a day of discharge and not counted (unless the patient returns to the hospital by midnight of the same day), each day during the leave is not counted as an inpatient day, and the day the patient returns to the hospital from the leave is treated as a day of admission and counted if the patient is present at midnight of that day. [Pub. 100-02, Ch. 3, § § 20.1, 20.1.2.]

Notice of Rights and Coverage

Hospitals must issue the "Important Message from Medicare" (IM) notice within two days of admission of a Medicare beneficiary and must obtain the signature of the beneficiary or his or her representative on the notice. The IM is the notice required for all hospital inpatients with Medicare to explain their rights as hospital patients, including their appeal rights at discharge. Hospitals also must deliver a copy of the signed notice prior to discharge, but not more than two days before the discharge. For beneficiaries who request an appeal, the hospital will deliver a more detailed notice. Notice is required both for original Medicare beneficiaries and for beneficiaries enrolled in Medicare Advantage (MA) plans and other Medicare health plans subject to the MA regulations. [42 C.F.R. § § 405.1205, 422.620.]

Advance Beneficiary Notices

If a hospital determines that services will no longer be covered by Medicare, the hospital is to issue the beneficiary an Advance Beneficiary Notice (ABN). The purpose of the ABN is to inform a Medicare beneficiary, before he or she receives specified items or services, that Medicare certainly or probably will not pay for the items or services on that particular occasion. The ABN permits the beneficiary to make an informed decision whether to receive the items or services for which he or she may be financially liable requiring out-of-pocket payment or payment through other insurance. [42 C.F.R. § 411.408(f)(1); Pub. 100-04, Ch. 30, §§ 10, 50.1.] ABNs are discussed at ¶ 900.

An ABN must: (1) be in writing, in the CMS-approved format and using approved notice language, (2) cite the particular service or services for which payment is likely to be denied, and (3) cite the notifier's reasons for believing Medicare payment will be denied. Providers, practitioners, or suppliers must issue an ABN as soon as they make an assessment that Medicare payment certainly or probably will not be made. [; Pub. 100-04, Ch. 30, §§ 40.3, 40.3.8.]

Discharge Planning

Hospitals must have in effect a discharge planning process that applies to all patients and is specified in writing. A discharge planning evaluation must be administered by a registered nurse, social worker, or other appropriately qualified personnel and include an evaluation of the likelihood of a patient needing post-hospital services and the availability of the services, as well as the likelihood of a patient's capacity for self-care and the patient's pre-hospitalization environment. Patient and family members must be counseled for post-hospital care if needed. [42 C.F.R. § 482.43.]

In addition, the evaluation must be completed on a timely basis and be included in the patient's medical record. If the hospital finds that the patient does not need a discharge plan, one may be requested by the patient's physician. If factors exist that may affect the continuing care needs or the appropriateness of the discharge plan, the hospital must reassess the patient's discharge plan. Finally, a list of home health agencies or SNFs participating in Medicare must be included for the patient to refer to in the discharge plan. [42 C.F.R. § 482.43.]

Late Discharge

A stay beyond the checkout time for the comfort or convenience of the patient is not covered under the program, and the hospital's agreement to participate in the program does not preclude it from charging the patient. Medicare expects that hospitals will not impose late charges on a beneficiary unless the beneficiary has been given reasonable notice (for example, 24 hours) of impending discharge. When the patient's medical condition is the cause of the stay past the checkout time (for example, the patient needs further services, is bedridden and awaiting transportation to his or her home or a SNF, or dies in the hospital), the stay beyond the discharge hour is covered under the program and the hospital may not charge the patient. [Pub. 100-02, Ch. 3, § 20.1.1.]

[¶ 211] Accommodations

Part A generally will pay only for *semi-private* accommodations (rooms of two to four beds) or ward accommodations (five or more beds) in connection with inpatient hospital care or nursing care in a skilled nursing facility (see ¶ 232). [42 C.F.R. § 409.11(a); *Medicare Benefit Policy Manual*, Pub. 100-02, Ch. 1, § 10.1.1.]

Private Rooms

Medicare will make extra payment for a private room or other accommodations more expensive than semi-private only when such accommodations are medically necessary. Private rooms will be considered medically necessary in the following circumstances:

(1) the patient's condition requires isolation for the patient's health or that of others;

(2) the facility has no semi-private or less expensive accommodations; or

(3) all such accommodations are occupied, *and* the patient needs hospitalization immediately—that is, inpatient treatment cannot be deferred until less expensive accommodations become available.

In the situations specified in (1) and (3), Medicare pays for a private room until the patient's condition no longer requires isolation or until semi-private or ward accommodations are available. [42 C.F.R. § 409.11(b)(1), (b)(2).]

The hospital may charge the beneficiary the difference between its customary charge for the private room and its most prevalent charge for a semi-private room if (1) none of the conditions described above is met; and (2) the private room was requested by the patient or a member of the family, who, at the time of the request, was informed what the hospital's charge would be. [42 C.F.R. § 409.11(b)(3).]

Payment also will be made for intensive care facilities when medically indicated.

Example • • • _____

At the time Mary Green is admitted to the hospital, she requests a private room. It is not medically necessary that she be in a private room, and she is told by the hospital that she will be charged the difference between its "customary charge" (see below) for a private room ($2,000 per day) and the customary charge for a semi-private room at the hospital's "most prevalent rate" (see below) at the time of admission ($1,300 per day). The hospital may charge Mary $700 per day for the private room, and the rest of her bill for bed and board— less any required deductible or coinsurance amount—is covered by Part A.

_____

"Customary charges" are the current amounts that the institution uniformly charges patients for specific services and accommodations. The "most prevalent rate" for semi-private accommodations is the rate that applies to the greatest number of semi-private beds. [Pub. 100-02, Ch. 1, § 10.1.7.]

Deluxe Private Rooms

A beneficiary in need of a private room (either because isolation is needed for medical reasons or because immediate admission is needed when no other accommodations are available) may be assigned to any private room in the hospital. Part A does not pay for personal comfort items (see ¶ 616), nor does it pay for deluxe accommodations or services, such as a suite or a room that is substantially more spacious than required for treatment, specially equipped or decorated, or serviced for the comfort and convenience of persons willing to pay a differential. If a beneficiary (or the beneficiary's representative) requests deluxe accommodations, the hospital should advise that there will be a charge, not covered by Medicare, of a specified amount for each day the beneficiary occupies the deluxe accommodations. The maximum amount the beneficiary may be charged is the differential between the most prevalent private room rate at the time of admission and the customary charge for the room occupied. [Pub. 100-02, Ch. 1, § 10.1.4.]

The beneficiary may not be charged a differential in private room rates if that differential is based on factors other than personal comfort items. These factors might include, but are not limited to: differences between older and newer wings, proximity to a lounge, elevators or nursing stations, or a desirable view. [Pub. 100-02, Ch. 1, § 10.1.4.]

All-Private Room Hospitals

If the patient is admitted to a hospital that has only private rooms and no semi-private or ward accommodations, medical necessity will be deemed to exist for the accommodations furnished. Beneficiaries may not be subjected to an extra charge for a private room in an all-private room hospital. [Pub. 100-02, Ch. 1, § 10.1.5.]

[¶ 212] Drugs and Biologicals

Drugs and biologicals furnished to an inpatient are covered under Part A if they: (1) represent a cost to the institution in rendering services to the beneficiary; (2) are ordinarily furnished by the hospital for the care and treatment of inpatients; and (3) are furnished to an inpatient for use in the hospital. Medicare will, however, pay for a limited supply of drugs for use outside the hospital if it is medically necessary to facilitate the beneficiary's departure from the hospital and required until he or she can obtain a continuing supply. [Soc. Sec. Act. § 1861(b)(2); 42 C.F.R. § 409.13.]

For a drug or biological furnished by a hospital to be a covered hospital service, it must be included or approved for inclusion in the latest official edition or revision of certain drug compendia (including the *United States Pharmacopeia -National Formulary*, the *United States Pharmacopeia-Drug Information*, or the *American Dental Association Guide to Dental Therapeutics*), except for any drugs or biologicals unfavorably evaluated in the *American Dental Association Guide to Dental Therapeutics*, or expressly approved by the pharmacy and drug therapeutics committee (or equivalent committee) of the medical staff of the hospital for use in the hospital. [*Medicare Benefit Policy Manual*, Pub. 100-02, Ch. 1, § 30.]

Combination drugs are covered if the combination itself or all of the active ingredients are listed or approved for listing in any of the compendia named. Similarly, any combination drugs approved by the pharmacy and therapeutics committee for use in the hospital are covered. [Pub. 100-02, Ch. 1, § 30.3.]

Coverage is not limited to drugs and biologicals routinely stocked by the hospital. A drug or biological not stocked by the hospital that the hospital obtains for the patient from an outside source, such as a community pharmacy, also is covered if the facility rather than the patient is responsible for making payment to the supplier. [Pub. 100-02, Ch. 1, § 30.4.]

An investigational drug is not considered to meet the "reasonable and necessary" test that applies to all services (see ¶ 601) because its efficacy has not yet been established. Even if approved by an appropriate hospital committee, an investigational drug or biological cannot be reimbursed. [Pub. 100-02, Ch. 1, § 30.2.]

Part D. The Medicare prescription drug benefit (Medicare Part D) permits eligible individuals to choose from at least two prescription drug plans (PDPs) in their region, with a standard coverage plan or an alternative coverage plan with actuarial-equivalent benefits (see ¶ 510).

See Chapter 5 for a complete description of the prescription drug coverage provided under Medicare Part D. Drugs and biologicals covered under Medicare Part B are discussed at ¶ 362.

[¶ 213] Supplies, Appliances, and Equipment

Supplies, appliances, and equipment ordinarily furnished by the hospital for the care and treatment of the beneficiary during an inpatient stay in the hospital are covered inpatient hospital services. [Soc. Sec. Act. § 1861(b)(2).]

Under certain circumstances, supplies, appliances, and equipment used during the beneficiary's stay are covered even when the items leave the hospital with the patient at the time of discharge. Medicare pays for items to be used beyond the hospital stay if: (1) the item is one that the beneficiary must continue to use after he or she leaves the hospital (for example, heart valves or a heart pacemaker); or (2) the item is medically necessary to permit or facilitate the beneficiary's departure from the hospital and is required until he or she can obtain a continuing supply (for example, tracheostomy or draining tubes). [42 C.F.R. § 409.14; *Medicare Benefit Policy Manual*, Pub. 100-02, Ch. 1, § 40.]

Routine Personal Hygiene Items and Services

Hospital "admission packs," containing primarily toilet articles (such as soap, tooth-brushes, toothpaste, and combs), are covered if routinely furnished by the hospital to all of its inpatients. If not routinely furnished, the packs are not covered and the hospital may charge the beneficiary. The beneficiary may not be charged, however, unless the beneficiary requests the pack with the knowledge of what is requested and what will be charged. [Pub. 100-02, Ch. 1, § 40.]

[¶ 214] Diagnostic and Therapeutic Items and Services

Medicare covers "other diagnostic or therapeutic items or services" that ordinarily are furnished to inpatients by the hospital. [Soc. Sec. Act § 1861(b)(3).] The services must be furnished by the hospital or by others under arrangements made by the hospital. Billing for the services must be through the hospital. Included in this benefit are diagnostic and therapeutic techniques too numerous to list (for example, blood tests, x-rays, etc.). [42 C.F.R. § 409.16; *Medicare Benefit Policy Manual*, Pub. 100-02, Ch. 1, § § 50, 50.1.]

Many diagnostic and therapeutic items and services also are covered when furnished as outpatient hospital services (see ¶ 352).

Therapeutic Items

Therapeutic items are covered when ordinarily furnished by the hospital to its inpatients or when furnished to hospital inpatients by others under agreements made with the hospital. These items include, but are not limited to:

- surgical dressings, splints, casts, and other devices used for the reduction of fractures and dislocations;

- prosthetic devices (non-dental) that replace all or part of an internal body organ, including continuous tissue, or replace all or part of the function of a permanently inoperative or malfunctioning internal body organ; and

- leg, arm, back, and neck braces, trusses, and artificial legs, arms, and eyes.

Therapeutic items that leave the hospital with the patient upon discharge, such as splints or casts, are covered if they are not furnished for use only outside the hospital. Temporary or disposable items medically necessary to permit or facilitate the patient's departure from the hospital and required until the patient can obtain a continuing supply are covered. [Pub. 100-02, Ch. 1, § 50.1.]

Psychologists and Physical Therapists

When a psychologist, clinical psychologist, or physical therapist is a salaried member of the staff of a hospital, that person's diagnostic or therapeutic services to inpatients of the hospital are covered in the same manner as the services of other nonphysician hospital employees. [Pub. 100-02, Ch. 1, § 50.2.]

Rehabilitative Care

A patient may be eligible for Medicare inpatient hospital coverage solely on the basis of the need for rehabilitative services. For admissions on or after January 1, 2010, for an inpatient rehabilitative facility (IRF) claim to be considered reasonable and necessary there must be a reasonable expectation that the patient meets the following requirements at the time of admission:

- requires the active and ongoing therapeutic intervention of multiple therapy disciplines (including physical therapy, occupational therapy, speech-language pathology, or prosthetics/orthotics therapy), one of which must be physical or occupational therapy;

- generally requires and can reasonably be expected to actively participate in, and benefit from, an intensive therapy program;

- is sufficiently stable at the time of admission to actively participate in the intensive rehabilitation therapy program; and

- requires physician supervision by a rehabilitation physician.

[42 C.F.R. § 412.622(a)(3).]

A patient can be expected to benefit significantly from the intensive rehabilitation therapy program only if his or her condition and functional status are such that he or she can reasonably be expected to make measurable improvement as a result of the rehabilitation treatment and if such improvement can be expected to be made within a prescribed period of time. To meet this standard, however, the patient need not be expected to achieve complete independence in the domain of self-care or be expected to return to his or her prior level of functioning. [Pub. 100-02, Ch. 1, § 110.2.]

Documentation. The patient's medical record must include documentation of a pre-admission screening performed by qualified clinicians within the 48 hours immediately preceding the admission. The record should include a detailed and comprehensive review of the patient's condition and medical history; it serves as a basis for the initial determination of whether the patient meets the requirements of admission. A rehabilitation physician must document his or her concurrence with the findings and results of the pre-admission screening. The record must also document that a rehabilitation physician performed a post-admission evaluation within 24 hours of admission. [42 C.F.R. § 412.622(a)(4); Pub. 100-02, Ch. 1, §§ 110.1.1, 110.1.2.]

The patient's medical record must contain an individualized overall plan of care that was developed by a rehabilitation physician with input from the interdisciplinary team within four days of the patient's admission to the IRF. It must also include documentation of weekly interdisciplinary team meetings led by a rehabilitation physician and attended by a registered nurse with training or experience in rehabilitation, a social worker or case manager, and a therapist from each therapy discipline. [42 C.F.R. § 412.622(a)(4), (5); Pub. 100-02, Ch. 1, § 110.1.3.]

Rehabilitation services are also discussed at ¶ 244.

Independent Clinical Laboratory Services

Diagnostic services furnished to an inpatient by an independent clinical laboratory under arrangements with the hospital also are covered under Part A, provided the lab is certified under the Clinical Laboratory Improvement Amendments of 1988 (CLIA) (P.L. 100-578) to perform the services. An "independent laboratory" is independent of the attending or consulting physician's office and the hospital. [Pub. 100-02, Ch. 1, § 50.3.]

A "clinical laboratory" is where microbiological, serological, chemical, hematological, radiobioassay, cytological, immunohematological, or pathological examinations are performed on materials derived from the human body to provide information for the diagnosis, prevention, or treatment of a disease or assessment of a medical condition. [Pub. 100-02, Ch. 1, § 50.3.]

Alcoholism and Drug Abuse (Chemical Dependency) Treatments

Alcohol detoxification and rehabilitation services are covered by Medicare when furnished as inpatient hospital services under Part A and as physician services under Part B. [*Medicare National Coverage Determinations Manual*, Pub. 100-03, Ch. 1, § § 130.1, 130.2.]

Inpatient hospital stays for alcohol detoxification. Inpatient hospital stays for alcohol detoxification are covered during the more acute stages of alcoholism or alcohol withdrawal when medical complications occur or are highly probable. Detoxification generally can be accomplished within two to three days, but the five-day limit may be extended if required by the patient's condition. Following detoxification, a patient may be transferred to an inpatient rehabilitation unit or discharged to a residential treatment program or outpatient treatment setting. [Pub. 100-03, Ch. 1, § § 130.1, 130.2.]

Inpatient hospital stays for alcohol rehabilitation. Inpatient hospital stays for alcohol rehabilitation are covered for treatment of chronic alcoholism. Because alcohol rehabilitation can be provided in a variety of settings, an inpatient hospital stay for alcohol rehabilitation will not be covered unless it is medically necessary that care be provided in an inpatient hospital setting and not in a less costly setting or on an outpatient basis. Further, because alcoholism is classifiable as a psychiatric condition, the beneficiary must be receiving "active treatment." Generally, 16 to 19 days of rehabilitation services are considered sufficient prior to continuing care on a basis other than an inpatient hospital setting. [Pub. 100-03, Ch. 1, § § 130.1, 130.2.]

Outpatient hospital coverage. Outpatient hospital coverage is provided for both diagnostic and therapeutic services furnished for the treatment of alcoholism. The same rules that apply to outpatient hospital services in general (see ¶ 352) also apply here. All services must be reasonable and necessary for diagnosis or treatment of the patient's condition. In addition, alcoholism treatment services such as drug therapy, psychotherapy, and patient education that are provided incident to a physician's services in a freestanding clinic are covered under the same rules as clinic services (see ¶ 351). The psychiatric services limitation discussed at ¶ 387 also applies to these services. [Pub. 100-03, Ch. 1, § § 130.2, 130.5.]

Chemical aversion therapy for the treatment of alcoholism is a covered service. Electrical aversion therapy is not covered, however, because it has not been shown to be safe and effective. [Pub. 100-03, Ch. 1, § § 130.3, 130.4.]

Treatment for drug abuse or other chemical dependency, when medically necessary, is covered by Medicare in all of the settings described above as long as the services provided are reasonable and necessary for the treatment of the patient's condition. [Pub. 100-03, Ch. 1, § § 130.5, 130.6, 130.7.]

Mental Health Benefits

Inpatient psychiatric hospital benefits are covered by Medicare, subject to some important limitations (see ¶ 225). Partial hospitalization services, which are mental health services for outpatients, are covered under Part B when they would prevent the need for inpatient psychiatric care (see ¶ 387).

[¶ 215] Services of Interns, Residents-in-Training, and Teaching Physicians

The services of physicians furnished to inpatients generally are excluded under Part A (see ¶ 226); rather, they are covered under Part B. Medicare Part A covers the services of interns and residents-in-training who participate in teaching programs approved by the appropriate accrediting associations. If the intern or resident is not providing services as part of an approved teaching program, those services are covered under Part B (see further ¶ 340). [Soc. Sec. Act § 1861(b)(4), (6).]

The administrative and teaching services of teaching physicians are also covered under Part A. [42 C.F.R. § 415.55.] The services of teaching physicians to individual patients are covered under Part B (see ¶ 340 and ¶ 855).

[¶ 217] Nursing and Related Services; Private-Duty Exclusion

Nursing and other related services are covered as inpatient hospital services if ordinarily furnished by the hospital for the care and treatment of inpatients. However, the services of a private-duty nurse or other private-duty attendant are expressly excluded. [Soc. Sec. Act § 1861(b)(2), (5); 42 C.F.R. § 409.12.]

Private-duty nurses or private-duty attendants are registered professional nurses, licensed practical nurses, or any other trained attendants whose services ordinarily are rendered to, and restricted to, a particular patient by arrangement between the patient and the private-duty nurse or attendant. Private-duty services are engaged or paid by an individual patient or by someone acting on the patient's behalf, including a hospital that initially incurs the cost and looks to the patient for reimbursement of the noncovered services. When the hospital acts on behalf of a patient, the services of the private-duty nurse or other attendant are not inpatient hospital services regardless of the control the hospital may exercise over the services rendered by the private-duty nurse or attendant. [*Medicare Benefit Policy Manual*, Pub. 100-02, Ch. 1, § 20.]

[¶ 218] Inpatient Services Connected with Dental Services

Although the law contains a general exclusion of services performed in connection with the care, treatment, filling, removal, or replacement of teeth or structures directly supporting teeth (see ¶ 634), it permits payment for inpatient hospital services for dental procedures when the beneficiary, due to his or her underlying medical condition and clinical status or the severity of the dental procedure, requires hospitalization in connection with the provision of these services. [Soc. Sec. Act § 1862(a)(12).]

Thus, if a beneficiary is hospitalized for a noncovered dental procedure but the hospitalization is required due to the severity of the procedure or to assure proper medical management, control, or treatment of a nondental impairment, the inpatient hospital services are covered. Similarly, when the beneficiary is hospitalized because of a non-dental impairment and the need for the noncovered dental procedure is determined after admission (for example, a beneficiary requires hospitalization because of diabetes and after admission a decision is made to extract teeth), the inpatient hospital services also are covered. [Soc. Sec. Act § 1862(a)(12).]

When the hospital services are covered, then all ancillary services furnished by the hospital (such as x-rays, administration of anesthesia, use of the operating room) also are covered. [*Medicare Benefit Policy Manual*, Pub. 100-02, Ch. 1, § 70.]

When a beneficiary is hospitalized for a covered dental procedure and the dentist's services are covered under Part B (see ¶ 340), the inpatient hospital services furnished during the stay are covered under Part A. Both the professional services of the dentist and the inpatient hospital expenses are covered when, for example, the dentist reduces a jaw fracture of a beneficiary who is an inpatient of a participating hospital. [Pub. 100-02, Ch. 1, § 70.]

A qualified dentist may certify, for purposes of inpatient hospital coverage in connection with a dental procedure, that the beneficiary suffers from impairments of such severity as to require hospitalization (see ¶ 340).

[¶ 220] Inpatient Hospital Deductible and Coinsurance

Beneficiaries with hospital insurance coverage under Medicare Part A are entitled to have payment made on their behalf for up to 90 or more days of covered inpatient hospital services in each "spell of illness" (see ¶ 210). In addition, a beneficiary is entitled to a lifetime total of 60 days of inpatient hospital coverage after exhaustion of the 90 days of entitlement during a spell of illness—commonly called "lifetime reserve days." [Soc. Sec. Act § 1812(a)(1).] See ¶ 224 for a detailed discussion of lifetime reserve days.

The amount payable by Part A is reduced by the deductible and coinsurances described below.

Inpatient Hospital Deductible

For inpatient hospital services furnished in each "spell of illness" (defined at ¶ 210), the patient is responsible for an inpatient hospital deductible. The amount of the deductible is determined by the year in which the patient's spell of illness begins. In 2016, the deductible is $1,288 per spell of illness. There can be more than one spell of illness and, thus, more than one required deductible, in a calendar year. [*Notice*, 80 FR 70808, Nov. 16, 2015.]

The inpatient hospital deductible for each successive year is calculated by modifying the previous year's deductible by the same percentage used to determine Medicare payments to prospective payment system (PPS) hospitals. The amount calculated is rounded to the nearest multiple of $4 (an amount midway between two multiples is rounded up). The various coinsurance amounts listed above are fractions of the deductible. Once the deductible is determined, the coinsurance amounts are adjusted accordingly. [Soc. Sec. Act § 1813(b)(1), (2).]

If the hospital stay spans two calendar years, the deductible in effect on the first day of the hospitalization is applicable. The coinsurance, however, is based on the coinsurance in effect for the year in which the cost-sharing days are incurred. [Soc. Sec. Act § 1813(b)(3).]

The deductible is satisfied only by charges for *covered* services. Expenses for covered services count toward the deductible on an incurred, rather than a paid, basis, and expenses incurred during one spell of illness cannot be applied toward the deductible in a later spell of illness. The inpatient hospital deductible is imposed only once during a "spell of illness," even though the beneficiary may have been hospitalized more than once during that spell of illness (see the examples at ¶ 210). Neither expenses incurred in meeting the blood deductible nor the monthly premiums paid by those voluntarily enrolled for hospital insurance coverage (see ¶ 203) count toward the inpatient hospital deductible. [Soc. Sec. Act § 1813(a)(2).]

A reduction in benefit days resulting from the application of the psychiatric hospital carryover restriction, on and immediately preceding the date of entitlement, does not affect the amount of the deductible for which the patient is responsible. [*Medicare General Information, Eligibility, and Entitlement Manual*, Pub. 100-01, Ch. 3, § 10.1.] For a discussion of the psychiatric hospital carryover restriction, see ¶ 225.

Inpatient Hospital Coinsurance

When inpatient hospital services are received for more than 60 days during a spell of illness, the patient is responsible for a coinsurance amount for each day after the 60th and through the 90th day on which these services are furnished. There also is a coinsurance amount for each day, after the 90th and through the 150th in any spell of illness, that is chargeable against the individual's 60-day lifetime reserve (see ¶ 224). [Soc. Sec. Act § 1813(a)(1).]

The coinsurance amount for the 61st through 90th days is equal to one-fourth of the inpatient hospital deductible, as annually adjusted ($322 in 2016), and one-half of such deductible for lifetime reserve days ($644 in 2016). [Soc. Sec. Act § 1813(a)(1); *Notice*, 80 FR 70808, Nov. 16, 2015.] When a patient's hospitalization spans two calendar years, the coinsurance in effect for the year in which the cost-sharing days are incurred applies. [Soc. Sec. Act. § 1813(b)(3); 42 C.F.R. § 409.83(a).]

In determining the amount of the coinsurance met, the coinsurance charge for a day of inpatient hospital services may not exceed the charges imposed for that day with respect to the individual beneficiary. Customary charges are considered actual charges if they are greater than the charges imposed. [Soc. Sec. Act § 1813(a)(1).] In connection with the lifetime reserve days provision, however, when the actual charge is equal to or less than the coinsurance amount, the beneficiary is deemed to have elected not to use one of the lifetime reserve days. Thus, the day is treated as a noncovered day and no coinsurance amount is chargeable to the patient (see ¶ 224). [42 C.F.R. § 409.83(c)(2).]

Whole Blood and Packed Red Blood Cells

In addition to the inpatient hospital deductible, there is another deductible, equal to the cost of the first three pints of whole blood (or packed red blood cells) received by a beneficiary in a calendar year. This deductible can be satisfied under either Part A or Part B (see ¶ 335), or a combination of the two. [Soc. Sec. Act § 1813(a)(2).]

"Whole blood" is human blood from which none of the liquid or cellular components have been removed. Components of whole blood such as plasma and gamma globulin are not subject to the blood deductible because they are covered as biologicals (see ¶ 212). [Pub. 100-01, Ch. 3, § 20.5.3.]

The difference, if any, between the cost of the whole blood (or equivalent quantities of packed red blood cells) to the provider and the charge to the beneficiary will be deducted from the payments that otherwise would be made to the provider under Part A. Thus, a hospital cannot make a profit on the blood or packed red blood cells for which it charges a beneficiary. No charge may be imposed on the patient for the cost of administering, storing, and processing the blood. [Soc. Sec. Act § 1866(a)(2)(C); Pub. 100-01, Ch. 3, § 20.5.]

Replacement. The patient may not be charged for the first three pints of whole blood or equivalent quantities of packed red blood cells if he or she arranges for their replacement on a pint-for-pint basis. [Soc. Sec. Act § 1866(a)(2)(C); Pub. 100-01, Ch. 3, § 20.5.4.1.]

When a beneficiary elects to replace deductible pints or units, they are considered replaced if the beneficiary, another individual, or a group or organization acting on the beneficiary's behalf (e.g., a blood assurance plan) offers replacement pints or units, whether or not the provider actually accepts the offer. Thus, a provider may not charge a beneficiary merely because its policy is not to accept blood from a particular organization that has offered to replace blood on behalf of the beneficiary. A provider is not barred from charging a beneficiary for deductible blood, however, if there is a reasonable basis for believing replacement blood offered by or on behalf of the beneficiary would endanger the health of either the donor or a recipient. [Pub. 100-01, Ch. 3, § § 20.5.4, 20.5.4.1.]

When a provider accepts blood donated in advance for or by a beneficiary in anticipation of need, such donations are considered as replacement for any deductible pints or units subsequently furnished the beneficiary. [Pub. 100-01, Ch. 3, § 20.5.4.1.]

[¶ 224] Use of Lifetime Reserve Days

Beneficiaries who are covered under Part A are entitled to have payment made on their behalf for up to 150 days of inpatient hospital services during a single "spell of illness" (see

¶ 210). These 150 days of entitlement are calculated as follows: the first 60 days of coverage are fully paid, subject only to the initial deductible amount; the next 30 days of coverage are subject to a coinsurance amount; and the last 60 days of coverage are subject to a coinsurance amount double the coinsurance amount for days 61 through 90 (see ¶ 220 for the current amount of deductible and coinsurance). The last 60 days are "lifetime reserve" days, which may be used only once in an individual's lifetime. Therefore, if a beneficiary is hospitalized for 150 days during the first covered spell of illness, all lifetime reserve days will be expended. If a beneficiary is hospitalized for only 100 days during the first spell of illness, 50 lifetime reserve days would be left for use during a subsequent spell of illness that requires hospitalization for more than 90 days. Medicare will pay for lifetime reserve days used on the basis of the beneficiary's request for payment unless the individual elects in writing not to have the program pay for the additional days, thereby saving reserve days for a later time. [Soc. Sec. Act § 1812(a)(1), (b)(1); *Medicare Benefit Policy Manual*, Pub. 100-02, Ch. 5, § § 20, 30.1.]

The rules for lifetime reserve days described above may not apply in certain situations when a hospital is paid under the prospective payment system (see the discussion under "Period Covered by Election" below).

There is an additional lifetime limitation of 190 days on inpatient psychiatric hospital services (see ¶ 225). [Soc. Sec. Act § 1812(b)(3).]

For coverage under Part B of inpatient "ancillary" services furnished after a beneficiary's days of entitlement under Part A are exhausted, see ¶ 361.

Election by Beneficiary Not to Use Reserve Days

An election not to use lifetime reserve days may be made by the beneficiary (or by someone acting on the beneficiary's behalf) at the time of admission to a hospital or at any time thereafter, subject to the limitations on retroactive elections described below.

Election made prospectively. Ordinarily, an election *not* to use reserve days will apply prospectively. If the election is filed at the time of admission to a hospital, it may be made effective on the first day of hospitalization or on any day thereafter. If the election is filed later, it may be made effective on any day after the day it is filed. [42 C.F.R. § 409.65; Pub. 100-02, Ch. 5, § § 30.2, 30.3.]

Retroactive election. A beneficiary, while still in the hospital or within 90 days following discharge, may elect retroactively not to use reserve days, provided: (1) the beneficiary (or some other source) offers to pay the hospital for any of the services not payable under Part B, or (2) the hospital agrees to accept the retroactive election. [42 C.F.R. § 409.65; Pub. 100-02, Ch. 5, § § 30.2, 30.3.]

A beneficiary may file an election not to use the lifetime reserve days later than 90 days following discharge only if benefits are available from a third-party payer and the hospital agrees to the retroactive election. [42 C.F.R. § 409.65; Pub. 100-02, Ch. 5, § § 30.2, 30.3.]

Examples • • • _____

Before July 1, Henry Wong had used 90 days of inpatient hospital services in a spell of illness. Beginning July 1, he was hospitalized for 10 more days during the same spell of illness. On July 1, at the time of his admission, Henry indicated that he wanted to use his reserve days for that stay. One month after being discharged from the hospital, Henry informed the hospital that he now wished to save his reserve days for a future stay. Henry agreed to pay the hospital for the services he received during the 10 days of hospitalization and was permitted to file a retroactive election not to use his reserve days for those 10 days.

¶224

On July 1, Walter Brown was discharged from a hospital after being hospitalized for 105 days. The hospital billed Medicare for 90 regular days plus 15 lifetime reserve days. On October 20 (more than 90 days following discharge), Walter learned that a private insurer could pay for the last 15 days of the stay. Walter informed the hospital that he wished to file a retroactive election not to use lifetime reserve days for the last 15 days of the stay. The hospital agreed to the request, and Walter filed an election form. The hospital refunded the Medicare payment and billed the private carrier instead.

Period Covered by Election

A beneficiary election *not* to use reserve days for a particular hospital stay may apply to the entire stay or to a single period of consecutive days in the stay but cannot apply to selected days in a stay. If an election (whether made prospectively or retroactively) not to use reserve days is made effective with the first day for which reserve days are available, it may be terminated at any time. After termination of the election, all hospital days would be covered to the extent that reserve days are available. (Thus, an individual who has private insurance that covers hospitalization beginning with the first day after 90 days of benefits have been exhausted may terminate the election as of the first day not covered by the insurance plan). If an election not to use reserve days is made effective beginning with any day after the first day for which reserve days are available, it must remain in effect until the end of that stay unless the entire election is revoked. [42 C.F.R. § 409.65]

A beneficiary is deemed to have elected not to use lifetime reserve days if the charges for those days are less than the beneficiary's coinsurance obligation. [42 C.F.R. § 409.65]

Exception for hospitals reimbursed under the prospective payment system. For hospitals reimbursed under the prospective payment system (PPS), the rules stated above apply with the following exceptions:

One or more regular benefit days available at time of admission. If the beneficiary has one or more regular benefit (non-lifetime reserve) days remaining in the benefit period upon entering the hospital, Medicare will pay the entire prospective payment amount for non-outlier days (see ¶ 810 for an explanation of the term "outlier days"). Thus, there will be no advantage to a beneficiary in using any lifetime reserve days for non-outlier days if at least one day of the regular 90 days of coverage remains when the beneficiary enters the hospital. In this situation, the beneficiary will be deemed to have elected *not* to use any lifetime reserve days for the non-outlier part of the stay. The beneficiary also may elect not to use lifetime reserve days for outlier days, but such an election must apply to all outlier days. [42 C.F.R. § 409.65; Pub. 100-02, Ch. 5, § § 30.1, 30.4.1, 30.4.2.1.]

Example • • • _____

Olivia Gonzalez was admitted to a hospital on April 1 and discharged on June 29, utilizing 89 regular days of inpatient care. On August 1, Olivia entered the hospital again. For this Medicare severity diagnosis-related group (MS-DRG), outlier days would have begun August 26, but Olivia was discharged on August 23, before the commencement of outlier days. Because the first two days of the second stay were regular coverage days, Medicare will reimburse the hospital the prospective payment amount for the entire stay. Because no outlier days are involved, there is no advantage to the beneficiary in using lifetime reserve days. Therefore, Olivia will be deemed to have elected *not* to use any lifetime reserve days for that stay.

Although lifetime reserve days are not used for non-outlier days when the beneficiary has at least one regular day available at the time of admission, payment will be made for outlier days occurring after regular coverage days have been exhausted unless: (1) the beneficiary elects not to use lifetime reserve days for the outlier days or (2) the beneficiary is deemed to have elected not to use lifetime reserve days for the outlier days. A beneficiary is deemed to have elected not to use lifetime reserve days for outlier days if the average daily charge for the outlier days for which lifetime reserve days otherwise would be available is equal to or less than the daily coinsurance amount for the lifetime reserve days. In that situation, the beneficiary would be required to pay for all of the hospital's charges for such outlier days regardless of election and, therefore, would not benefit from the use of lifetime reserve days. If the beneficiary elects *not* to use lifetime reserve days for outlier days, such an election must apply to all outlier days. If the beneficiary elects not to use lifetime reserve days for outlier days, Medicare will pay for the non-outlier portion of the stay and will make no payment for the outlier days. [42 C.F.R. § 409.65; Pub. 100-02, Ch. 5, § 30.1.]

Example • • • _____

Stuart Desmond, who had never used any of his lifetime reserve days, was admitted to the hospital on April 1, 2015, and discharged on June 29, utilizing 89 regular days of covered inpatient care. On August 1, Stuart entered the hospital again; he was discharged on September 5. For this MS-DRG, outlier days began on August 26. Medicare must reimburse the hospital the prospective payment amount for the non-outlier portion of the stay. The average daily charges were $800 for the outlier portion of the stay. The lifetime reserve day coinsurance amount was $630 in 2015. Because the average daily charge for the outlier days was more than the daily coinsurance amount for lifetime reserve days, there was no deemed election not to use lifetime reserve days for the outlier portion of the stay. For outlier days Stuart had the option: (1) to make no election and, therefore, use his lifetime reserve days, in which case Medicare pays for the non-outlier portion of the stay and for the 10 outlier days, August 26 through September 4, with Stuart utilizing 10 lifetime reserve days; or (2) to elect *not* to use his lifetime reserve days for the 10 outlier days, in which case Medicare pays only for the non-outlier portion of the stay, and Stuart would not use any lifetime reserve days.

Exhaustion of regular benefit days. An election by a beneficiary not to use lifetime reserve days must apply to the entire hospital stay when no regular benefit days are available. If the beneficiary elects not to use lifetime reserve days, Medicare will not pay for any portion of the stay. A beneficiary whose 90 days of benefits are exhausted before cost outlier status is reached must elect to use lifetime reserve days for the hospital to be paid cost outlier payments. Cost outlier status is reached the day that charges reach the cost outlier status for the applicable MS-DRG under the inpatient prospective payment system (IPPS) (see ¶ 810). Use of reserve days must begin on the day following that day, to permit payment for outlier charges. If the beneficiary elects not to use lifetime reserve days when benefits are exhausted, the hospital may charge the beneficiary for the charges that would have been paid as cost outlier. [42 C.F.R. § 409.65(e)(2); Pub. 100-02, Ch. 5, § 30.4.2.]

Example • • • _____

Frances McDonald was admitted to a hospital on March 10, 2015, and discharged on June 8, utilizing 90 regular days of coverage. On August 1, Frances entered the hospital again; she was discharged on September 10. For this MS-DRG, outlier days began on August 26. At the time of the second admission, Frances still had 60 lifetime reserve days available. The hospital charges for this stay were $35,000. The sum of the coinsurance amounts for the lifetime reserve days needed to pay for this stay was $25,200 ($630 per day × 40 days).

Because the charges for the stay were greater than the sum of lifetime reserve days coinsurance amounts, there was no deemed election not to use lifetime reserve days. Frances had the option: (1) of making no lifetime reserve election, in which case Medicare pays for the entire stay, including the outlier days, and she would use 40 lifetime reserve days; or (2) of electing *not* to use lifetime reserve days, in which case Medicare does not pay for any portion of the stay.

[¶ 225] Psychiatric Hospital Restrictions

If an individual is an inpatient of a participating psychiatric hospital on the first day for which he or she is entitled to hospital insurance benefits (see ¶ 200–¶ 206), the days (not necessarily consecutive) on which the individual was an inpatient of a psychiatric hospital in the 150-day period immediately before this first day are deducted from the 150 days of inpatient hospital services for which the individual otherwise is entitled to have payment made during the first spell of illness. [Soc. Sec. Act § 1812(c); 42 C.F.R. § 409.63; *Medicare Benefit Policy Manual*, Pub. 100-02, Ch. 4, § 10.]

When an individual subject to a reduction in days is an inpatient in a general hospital, the contractor will apply the reduction only if it has determined that the individual was an inpatient primarily for the diagnosis or treatment of mental illness. The term "mental illness" means the specific psychiatric conditions described in the American Psychiatric Association's "Diagnostic and Statistical Manual—Mental Disorders." [Pub. 100-02, Ch. 4, § 30.]

In determining the number of days to be deducted, the days of admission and the days on which the patient returned from leave of absence are included. Days of discharge, days on which the patient began a leave of absence, and the days of leave during all of which the individual is absent from the hospital are not counted. [Pub. 100-02, Ch. 3, § 20.1.]

Payment may not be made for more than a total of 190 days of inpatient psychiatric hospital services during the patient's lifetime. The period spent in a psychiatric hospital before entitlement does not count against the patient's 190-day lifetime limitation, however, even though pre-entitlement days may have been counted against the 150 days in the first spell of illness. [Pub. 100-02, Ch. 4, § 50.]

Example • • • _____

Mark DeSoto was an inpatient of a participating psychiatric hospital on his first day of entitlement on February 1. He had been in such a hospital in the pre-entitlement period for 20 days. Therefore, Medicare payment can be made for 130 days during the patient's first spell of illness. Payment will be made in the following order: 60 full benefit days, 30 coinsurance days, 40 coinsurance (lifetime reserve) days.

Outpatient "partial hospitalization" services are covered under Part B when these services would prevent the need for inpatient psychiatric care (see ¶ 387). Payment for inpatient psychiatric services under the inpatient psychiatric hospital prospective payment system is discussed at ¶ 840.

[¶ 226] Physicians' Professional Services

The medical and surgical services provided to inpatients by physicians and other health care professionals (e.g., physician assistants, nurse practitioners, psychologists, clinical social workers) normally are covered under Part B and are, therefore, excluded from coverage under Part A. [Soc. Sec. Act § 1861(b)(4).]

The exclusion of physicians' professional services under Part A also applies to the services rendered to individual patients by such hospital-based physicians as radiologists, anesthesiologists, pathologists, and psychiatrists; however, the services of non-physician technicians (e.g., an x-ray technician) aiding hospital-based physicians in these services generally are covered under Part A. [*Medicare Benefit Policy Manual*, Pub. 100-02, Ch. 15, §§ 30.1, 30.2.]

The services of hospital-based physicians that are not related to the care of an individual patient—e.g., research, administration, supervision of professional or technical personnel, service on hospital committees, etc.—are covered under Part A and no charge can be made to the patient for these services. [Pub. 100-02, Ch. 15, §§ 30.1, 30.2.]

As discussed at ¶ 215, the services of interns and residents in an approved teaching program also are covered under Part A.

Coverage and payment for the services of hospital-based physicians are further discussed at ¶ 350 and ¶ 855, respectively.

[¶ 227] Emergency Services

There are emergency situations in which an individual who is eligible for Medicare goes or is taken to a hospital that does not participate in the program. For example, an accident victim might have to be taken immediately to the nearest hospital, either for outpatient diagnosis and treatment or for admission as an inpatient. The law permits the payment of benefits for emergency outpatient services or inpatient care in the United States in such cases until it is no longer necessary from a medical standpoint to care for the patient in the nonparticipating institution. Payment will be made only when, taking into account the availability of any nearby participating hospitals, the nonparticipating facility was the most accessible hospital able to furnish necessary emergency care. [Soc. Sec. Act § 1814(d)(1).]

The following discussion applies *only* to emergency services in a hospital *not participating* in Medicare. Emergency services in a participating hospital are covered under Medicare in the same manner as nonemergency services. The special requirements applicable to participating hospitals with respect to the treatment of emergency room cases are discussed at ¶ 730.

Payment for Emergency Services in Nonparticipating Hospitals

There are two possible methods of payment to a nonparticipating hospital for emergency services. Payment can be made to the hospital if it so elects and meets the conditions described below. Otherwise, payment is made to the individual on the basis of an itemized bill. For payment to be made to the hospital:

(1) the services must be emergency services;

(2) the services must be covered inpatient hospital services under Part A or covered outpatient services;

(3) the hospital must meet the definition of "emergency services hospital" (see below);

(4) the hospital must agree to not charge the patient or any other individual for covered items or services (except to the extent that a participating hospital would be permitted to charge for these services (see ¶ 730)), and must agree to return any money incorrectly collected; and

(5) the hospital must have signed a statement of election to claim payment for all inpatient and outpatient services furnished during the year.

[Soc. Sec. Act §§ 1814(d)(1), 1835(b)(1), 1866(a); 42 C.F.R. §§ 424.104, 424.108; *Medicare General Information, Eligibility, and Entitlement Manual*, Pub. 100-01, Ch. 5, § 20.1.]

If the hospital does not elect to claim payment as discussed above, payment may be made to the beneficiary on the basis of an itemized bill, subject to applicable deductible and coinsurance amounts. [Soc. Sec. Act §§ 1814(d)(2), 1835(b)(2).]

Definition of "Emergency Services Hospital"

A facility qualifies as an "emergency services hospital" if it is licensed as a hospital under applicable state or local laws, has a full-time nursing service, is engaged primarily in furnishing medical care under the supervision of a physician, and is not engaged primarily in providing skilled nursing care and related services for inpatients who require medical or nursing care. Psychiatric hospitals that meet these requirements also can qualify as emergency services hospitals. A federal hospital need not be licensed under state or local licensing laws to meet the definition of an emergency services hospital. [Soc. Sec. Act § 1861(e); 42 C.F.R. § 424.101; Pub. 100-01, Ch. 5, § 20.2.]

Definition of "Emergency Services"

"Emergency services" are inpatient or outpatient hospital services that are necessary to prevent the death or serious impairment of the health of an individual and that, because of the threat to the life or health of the individual, necessitate the use of the most accessible hospital available and equipped to furnish the services. [42 C.F.R. § 424.101.]

The following situations do not in themselves indicate a need for emergency services, unless there also is an immediate threat to the life or health of the patient: (1) the death of the patient during hospitalization, (2) a lack of adequate care at home, or (3) a lack of transportation to a participating hospital. [42 C.F.R. § 424.102.]

Termination of Emergency Services

Payment to a nonparticipating hospital for emergency services under Part A ceases when the emergency has ended. Payment under Part B may be made, however, for certain ancillary services furnished during nonemergency inpatient stays (see ¶ 361). An emergency no longer exists when it becomes safe from a medical standpoint to move the patient to a participating institution or to discharge the patient, whichever occurs first. The determination that an emergency has ended ordinarily will be based on the physician's supporting statement. [42 C.F.R. § 424.103(b)(3).]

Emergency Services Outside the United States

Under certain circumstances, Medicare will pay for emergency inpatient hospital services furnished to a beneficiary outside the United States by a foreign hospital. See ¶ 610.

[¶ 228] Religious Nonmedical Health Care Institutions

Providers qualifying as religious nonmedical health care institutions are included as hospitals and skilled nursing facilities for Medicare purposes. [Soc. Sec. Act § 1861(e), (y), (ss).] To qualify, an institution must:

(1) be a tax-exempt organization under section 501(c)(3) of the Internal Revenue Code;

(2) be lawfully operated under all applicable federal, state, and local laws and regulations;

(3) provide only nonmedical nursing items and services exclusively to individuals who choose to rely solely upon a religious method of healing, through experienced nonmedical personnel, and on a 24-hour basis;

(4) not provide medical items or services (including screening, examination, diagnosis, or administration of drugs) to its patients, or be affiliated by common ownership or otherwise with an institution that provides such services; and

(5) have in effect a specialized utilization review plan and provide the Secretary with information required to monitor quality of care and to provide for coverage determinations.

[Soc. Sec. Act § 1861 (ss); 42 C.F.R. § 403.720.]

Patients being treated in a religious nonmedical health care institution must make an election to receive such benefits. Additionally, Medicare reimbursement in these institutions is available only to individuals with a condition that would require them to be inpatients in a hospital or skilled nursing facility were it not for their religious beliefs. [Soc. Sec. Act § 1821 (a), (b).]

Payment is on a reasonable cost basis and may be made only for items and services normally furnished in such institutions (i.e., nonmedical nursing services and related items). [Soc. Sec. Act § 1861 (e), (y); 42 C.F.R. § 403.752.]

Medicare will cover specified durable medical equipment and intermittent religious nonmedical health care institution nursing visits provided in the home to beneficiaries. However, payment for nonmedical care is subject to the requirements for reasonableness and necessity. [Soc. Sec. Act § 1862 (a) (1) (A).] Religious nonmedical nursing personnel may not engage in any activities that are medical in nature. The remainder of the services covered under the Medicare home health benefit are medical in nature and must be provided under the order of a physician. The specified durable medical equipment items include canes, crutches, walkers, commodes, a standard wheelchair, hospital beds, bedpans, and urinals. [*Medicare Benefit Policy Manual*, Pub. 100-02, Ch. 1, § 130.4.]

[¶ 229] "Hospital" Defined—Qualified Hospitals

As a general rule, a beneficiary's stay in a hospital will not be covered by Medicare unless the hospital is "participating" in the Medicare program, that is, the hospital has been approved for Medicare participation by the government and has signed a participation agreement (see ¶ 730). Services provided in a nonparticipating hospital, however, may be covered by Medicare in emergency situations (see ¶ 227).

To participate as a hospital in the Medicare program, an institution must be a "hospital" within the meaning of section 1861 (e) of the Social Security Act. The section lists several requirements hospitals must meet, the most important of which is that the hospital is primarily engaged in providing, by or under the supervision of physicians, to inpatients: (1) diagnostic services and therapeutic services for medical diagnosis, treatment, and care of injured, disabled, or sick persons; or (2) rehabilitation services for the rehabilitation of injured, disabled, or sick persons. [Soc. Sec. Act § 1861 (e) (1).] In addition, section 1861 (e) requires hospitals to provide 24-hour nursing care, have in effect a utilization review plan, and meet certain health and safety requirements.

Psychiatric hospitals also must participate in Medicare for the services they furnish to be covered. The requirements for these hospitals are similar to the requirements for other hospitals, although they differ in some respects due to their different purpose. Section 1861 (f) of the Social Security Act lists the requirements psychiatric hospitals must meet, the most important of which is that the hospital be primarily engaged in providing, by or under the supervision of a physician, psychiatric services for the diagnosis and treatment of mentally ill persons. [Soc. Sec. Act § 1861 (f) (1).]

Medicare regulations describing the conditions of participation for hospitals are found at 42 C.F.R. Part 482.

Hospital Providers of Extended Care Services ("Swing-Bed" Facilities)

Because of the shortage of rural skilled nursing facility (SNF) beds for Medicare patients, rural hospitals with fewer than 100 beds may be paid under Part A for furnishing covered nursing home services to Medicare beneficiaries. Such a hospital, known as a swing-bed facility, can "swing" its beds between hospital and SNF levels of care on an as-needed basis if it has obtained a swing-bed approval from CMS. [Soc. Sec. Act § 1883; *Medicare General Information, Eligibility, and Entitlement Manual*, Pub. 100-01, Ch. 5, § 30.3.]

A hospital providing extended care services will be treated as a SNF for purposes of applying coverage rules. This means that those services are subject to all of the Part A coverage, physician certification, deductible, and coinsurance provisions that are applicable to SNF extended care services. For example:

(1) SNF level of care days in a swing-bed facility are counted against total SNF benefit days available to Medicare beneficiaries;

(2) Medicare beneficiaries receiving a SNF level of care in a swing-bed facility must first meet the three-day prior hospital stay requirement; and

(3) services needed and provided must be of the type and at the level to constitute extended care or SNF level services.

[Soc. Sec. Act § 1883(d); 42 C.F.R. § 409.30; *Medicare Benefit Policy Manual*, Pub. 100-02, Ch. 8, § § 10.3, 20.1, 30.]

Nursing Home Services

[¶ 230] Extended Care Services

Medicare Part A covers extended care services furnished to inpatients of a skilled nursing facility (SNF). A SNF is an institution or a distinct part of an institution, such as a skilled nursing home or rehabilitation center, that has a transfer agreement in effect with one or more participating hospitals and that is primarily engaged in providing skilled nursing care and related services for residents who require medical or nursing care, or rehabilitation services for the rehabilitation of injured, disabled, or sick persons. [Soc. Sec. Act § 1819(a); 42 C.F.R. § 483.5(a); *Medicare General Information, Eligibility, and Entitlement Manual*, Pub. 100-01, Ch. 5, § 30.] Conditions of participation for SNFs are discussed at ¶ 249.

Part A covers care in a SNF if the following requirements are met:

(1) the beneficiary requires skilled nursing services or skilled rehabilitation services, which are ordered by a physician and rendered for a condition for which the patient received inpatient hospital services or for a condition that arose while receiving care in a SNF for a condition for which he or she received inpatient hospital services;

(2) the beneficiary requires these skilled services on a daily basis;

(3) as a practical matter, considering economy and efficiency, the daily skilled services can be provided only on an inpatient basis in a SNF; and

(4) the services delivered are reasonable and necessary for the treatment of a patient's illness or injury.

[Soc. Sec. Act § 1814(a)(2)(B); 42 C.F.R. § 409.31(b).]

A physician, nurse practitioner, clinical nurse specialist, or physician assistant must certify that these requirements are met. [Soc. Sec. Act § 1814(a)(2).]

Documentation. Claims for skilled care coverage must include sufficient documentation to enable a reviewer to determine whether (1) skilled involvement is required for the services in question to be furnished safely and effectively; and (2) the services themselves are, in fact, reasonable and necessary for the treatment of a patient's illness or injury. [*Medicare Benefit Policy Manual*, Pub. 100-02, Ch. 8, § 30.2.2.1.]

Covered Services

Extended care services include the following:

• nursing care provided by or under the supervision of a registered professional nurse, but excluding the services of a private duty nurse or attendant (see 42 C.F.R. § 409.21);

• bed and board in connection with furnishing of such nursing care (see ¶ 232);

• physical or occupational therapy and/or speech-language pathology services furnished by the SNF or by others under arrangements with them made by the facility (see ¶ 233);

• medical social services (see 42 C.F.R. § 409.24);

• drugs, biologicals, supplies, appliances, and equipment furnished for use in the SNF, as are ordinarily furnished by such facility for the care and treatment of inpatients (see ¶ 235 and ¶ 236);

• medical services provided by an intern or resident-in-training of a hospital with which the facility has in effect a transfer agreement under an approved teaching program of the hospital, and other diagnostic or therapeutic services provided by a hospital with which the facility has such an agreement in effect (see ¶ 237); and

• other services necessary to the health of the patients as are generally provided by SNFs, or by others under arrangements, including respiratory therapy services and medically necessary ambulance transportation (see 42 C.F.R. § 409.27).

[Soc. Sec. Act § 1861(h).]

Services furnished to an inpatient of a SNF for which payment cannot be made under Part A (usually because the beneficiary has exhausted his entitlement to benefits) are reimbursable under Part B if they constitute "medical and other health services" and the beneficiary is otherwise entitled to Part B benefits. [Pub. 100-02, Ch. 8, § 70.]

Prior Hospitalization Requirement

An individual must be an inpatient of a hospital for at least three consecutive calendar days and then transfer to a participating SNF usually within 30 days after discharge from the hospital to qualify for Medicare reimbursement of post-hospital extended care services. [Soc. Sec. Act § 1861(i); 42 C.F.R. § 409.30; Pub. 100-02, Ch. 8, § 10.]

Three-day prior hospitalization. Generally, for a beneficiary to receive Medicare coverage for post-hospital SNF care, he or she must have been an inpatient in a qualifying hospital for at least three consecutive calendar days. [Soc. Sec. Act § 1861(i); 42 C.F.R. § 409.30(a).]

In the determination of whether the individual's prior hospital stay meets the required minimum of three consecutive calendar days, the day of admission is counted as a hospital inpatient day, but the day of discharge is not. The hospital discharge must have occurred on or after the first day of the month in which an individual attains age 65 or becomes entitled to Medicare benefits under the disability or end-stage renal disease provisions. [42 C.F.R. § 409.30(a)(2); Pub. 100-02, Ch. 8, § 20.1.]

A three-day stay in a psychiatric hospital satisfies the prior hospital stay requirement. A three-day stay in a foreign hospital also satisfies the prior hospital stay requirement if the foreign hospital meets the requirements of an emergency hospital. However, stays in religious nonmedical health care institutions and time spent in observation status or in the emergency room prior to (or in lieu of) an inpatient admission to the hospital do not count toward the three-day qualifying inpatient hospital stay. [Pub. 100-02, Ch. 8, §§ 20.1, 20.1.1.]

A patient who is transferred directly from an acute care hospital to a SNF and is correctly assigned a resource utilization group (RUG) will be presumed to require the SNF level of care. This presumption continues through the five-day period allowed for patient assessment under 42 C.F.R. § 413.343(b) if the assessment is completed timely. [42 C.F.R. § 409.30; Pub. 100-02, Ch. 8, § 30.1.]

To be covered, the post-hospital extended care services must have been for the treatment of a condition for which the beneficiary was receiving inpatient hospital services, or by a condition that arose while in the facility for treatment of a condition for which the patient was previously hospitalized. The condition need not have been the principal diagnosis that precipitated the beneficiary's admission to the hospital; it could be any one of the conditions present during the qualifying hospital stay. In addition, the qualifying hospital stay must have been medically necessary. [Soc. Sec. Act § 1814(a)(2)(B); 42 C.F.R. § 409.31(b)(2); Pub. 100-02, Ch. 8, § 20.1.]

CMS will cover SNF care for beneficiaries involuntarily unenrolled from Medicare Advantage (MA) plans as a result of a MA plan termination when they do not have a three-day hospital stay before SNF admission, if the beneficiary was admitted to the SNF before the effective date of disenrollment. [Pub. 100-02, Ch. 8, § 10.]

Thirty-day transfer requirement. Post-hospital extended care services represent an extension of care for a condition for which the individual received inpatient hospital services. Extended care services are "post-hospital" if initiated within 30 days after the date of discharge from a hospital. [Soc. Sec. Act § 1861(i); 42 C.F.R. § 409.30(b).]

The day of discharge from the hospital is not counted in the determination of the 30-day transfer period. For example, a patient discharged from a hospital on August 1 and admitted to a SNF on August 31 was admitted within 30 days. [Pub. 100-02, Ch. 8, § 20.2.1.]

An individual who is admitted to a SNF within 30 days after discharge from a hospital but does not require a covered level of care until more than 30 days after such discharge does not meet the 30-day requirement. [Pub. 100-02, Ch. 8, § 20.2.1.]

If an individual whose SNF stay was covered upon admission is later determined not to require a covered level of care for a period that continues for more than 30 days, payment will not be resumed for any extended care services he or she may subsequently require, even though the individual has remained in the facility, until the occurrence of a new qualifying hospital stay. In the absence of a new qualifying hospital stay, such services are not deemed to be "post-hospital" extended care services. [Pub. 100-02, Ch. 8, § 20.2.1.]

The period of extended care services may be interrupted briefly and then resumed, if necessary, without hospitalization preceding the readmission to the facility. The 30-day transfer requirement is satisfied if, for example, the beneficiary: (1) leaves the SNF and is readmitted to the same or any other participating SNF within 30 days, or (2) remains in the SNF to receive custodial care following a covered stay and subsequently develops a renewed need for covered care there within 30 consecutive days. [Pub. 100-02, Ch. 8, § 20.2.3.]

The law provides an exception to the 30-day transfer requirement. If a patient is not admitted to a SNF within 30 days after discharge from a hospital because to admit him or her within that time would not be medically appropriate, the admission to the SNF will be covered if it is within such time as would be medically appropriate to begin an active course of treatment. [Soc. Sec. Act § 1861(i); 42 C.F.R. § 409.30(b)(2)(i); Pub. 100-02, Ch. 8, § 20.2.2.]

[¶ 232] Accommodations

The coverage of ward, semi-private, and private accommodations in a skilled nursing facility (SNF) is treated in the same way as the coverage of hospital accommodations (see ¶ 211). [Soc. Sec. Act § 1861(h)(2); 42 C.F.R. § 409.22.]

Medicare covers a private room if:

(1) the patient's condition requires him or her to be isolated;

(2) the SNF has no semiprivate or ward accommodations; or

(3) the SNF semiprivate and ward accommodations are fully occupied by other patients, were so occupied at the time the patient was admitted to the SNF for treatment of a condition that required immediate inpatient SNF care, and have been so occupied during the interval.

The beneficiary is responsible for the difference between the SNF's charge for the private room and its most prevalent charge for a semi-private room if none of these conditions is met and the private room was requested by the patient or a member of the family who, at the time of request, was informed what the charge would be. [42 C.F.R. § 409.22(b).]

Unlike the Medicaid program, Medicare does not make payments to a nursing facility to hold a bed for a patient who takes a temporary leave of absence from the facility. [42 C.F.R. § 489.22(d).]

Patients in inappropriate beds. When patients requiring inpatient hospital services occupy beds in a SNF or in the hospital's distinct part SNF, they are considered inpatients of the SNF. In such cases, the services furnished in the SNF may not be considered inpatient hospital services, and payment may not be made under the program for those services. Such a situation may arise where the SNF is a distinct part of an institution, the remainder of which is a hospital, and either there is no bed available in the hospital, or for any other reason the institution fails to place the patient in the appropriate bed. The same rule applies where the SNF is a separate institution. [*Medicare Benefit Policy Manual*, Pub. 100-02, Ch. 8, § 50.]

In the special case of patients who require extended care services but occupy beds in a hospital, the general rule is that no payment will be made on their behalf for the hospital services furnished to them. However, when such patients occupy hospital beds because there are no SNF beds available to them, the general rule may not apply. A physician or a utilization review committee may certify to the need for continued hospitalization in these situations. [42 C.F.R. § 424.13(c).]

Similarly, under Soc. Sec. Act § 1861(v)(1)(G), a quality improvement organization or the HHS Secretary may also require continued coverage for the extended care services at a special nursing home rate of payment. Rural hospitals entering into "swing-bed" agreements, as well as other hospitals without such agreements, are eligible for special rates of reimbursement for patients inappropriately occupying hospital beds because there are no SNF beds available. [Pub. 100-02, Ch. 8, § 10.3.]

Patients who are denied coverage because they have been placed in the wrong bed may nevertheless be entitled to Medicare coverage under the "waiver of liability" provision (see ¶ 915). The law recognizes that the patient is not in a position to make a choice or influence an incorrect action taken by hospital or SNF. [Soc. Sec. Act § 1879; Pub. 100-02, Ch. 8, § 50.]

[¶ 233] Physical and Occupational Therapy and Speech-Language Pathology Services

Physical and occupational therapy and speech-language pathology furnished by a skilled nursing facility (SNF) or by others under arrangements made by the facility are covered when provided in accordance with a physician's orders, by or under the supervision of a qualified therapist, and in accordance with a plan satisfying the requirements of 42 C.F.R. § 409.17. [Soc. Sec. Act § § 1832(a)(2)(C), 1833(a)(8), 1861(h)(3); 42 C.F.R. § 409.23.]

Coverage for skilled therapy services turns on the beneficiary's need for skilled care, not on the presence or absence of a beneficiary's potential for improvement from therapy services. Therapy services are considered skilled when they are so inherently complex that they can be safely and effectively performed only by, or under the supervision of, a qualified therapist. These skilled services may be necessary to improve the patient's current condition, to maintain the patient's current condition, or to prevent or slow further deterioration of the patient's condition. [*Medicare Benefit Policy Manual*, Pub. 100-02, Ch. 8, § 30.4.]

Limits on the amount Medicare will pay for outpatient rehabilitation therapy services, generally called therapy caps, apply to outpatient physical therapy, speech-language pathology services, and occupational therapy services under Medicare Part B (see ¶ 860). [Soc. Sec. Act § 1833(g).] Since the limitations apply to outpatient services, they do not apply to SNF residents in a covered Part A stay, including patients occupying swing beds. Rehabilitation services are included within the global Part A per diem payment that the SNF receives under the prospective payment system for the covered stay. [*Medicare Claims Processing Manual*, Pub. 100-04, Ch. 5, § 10.2.]

[¶ 235] Drugs and Biologicals

Medicare covers drugs and biologicals as posthospital SNF care if they: (1) represent a cost to the facility; (2) are ordinarily furnished by the facility for the care and treatment of inpatients; and (3) are furnished to an inpatient for use in the facility. Medicare will, however, pay for a limited supply of drugs for use outside the facility if it is medically necessary to facilitate the beneficiary's departure from the facility and required until he or she can obtain a continuing supply. [Soc. Sec. Act § 1861(h)(3); 42 C.F.R. § 409.25(a), (b).]

Because the provision of drugs and biologicals is considered an essential part of skilled nursing care, a facility must ensure their availability to inpatients. When a facility secures drugs and biologicals from an outside source, their availability is ensured only if the facility assumes financial responsibility for the necessary drugs and biologicals, i.e., the supplier looks to the facility, not the patient, for payment. [*Medicare Benefit Policy Manual*, Pub. 100-02, Ch. 8, § 50.5.]

Payment may not be made for particular uses of drugs that the Food and Drug Administration (FDA) has expressly disapproved or that do not meet the coverage requirements specified in Pub. 100-02, Ch. 1, section 30. If the Medicare administrative contractor has reason to question whether the FDA has approved a drug or biological for marketing, it must obtain satisfactory evidence of the FDA's approval. [Pub. 100-02, Ch. 8, § 50.5.]

A drug that is not approved by Medicare can still be covered in a SNF if the drug:

    (1) was furnished to the patient during his or her prior hospitalization;

    (2) was approved for use in the hospital by the hospital's pharmacy and drug therapeutics committee;

    (3) is required for the continuing treatment of the patient in the SNF; and

    (4) is reasonable and necessary.

Under these limited circumstances, a combination drug approved by a hospital pharmacy and drug therapeutics committee also may be covered as an extended care service. [Pub. 100-02, Ch. 8, § 50.5.]

Rules for drugs and biologicals applicable to hospital inpatients and inpatients of SNFs are found in the *Medicare Benefit Policy Manual*, Pub. 100-02, Ch. 1, sections 30 through 30.4. [Pub. 100-02, Ch. 8, § 50.5.]

With respect to drugs or biologicals furnished to an *inpatient* for use *outside* a SNF, see the comparable provisions pertaining to hospital inpatients at ¶ 212. Special limitations on payment for certain "less than effective" drugs applicable under the Part B program are described at ¶ 644.

[¶ 236] Supplies, Appliances, and Equipment

Supplies, appliances, and equipment are covered as extended care services only if they: (1) are ordinarily furnished by the skilled nursing facility (SNF) for the care and treatment of inpatients; and (2) are furnished to an inpatient for use in the SNF. Examples of covered SNF supplies include oxygen, surgical dressings, splints, casts, and personal hygiene items and services. [Soc. Sec. Act § 1861(h)(5); 42 C.F.R. § 409.25(c); *Medicare Benefit Policy Manual*, Pub. 100-02, Ch. 1, § 40; Ch. 8, § 50.6.]

Under certain circumstances, supplies, appliances, and equipment used during the beneficiary's stay are covered even though they leave the facility with the patient when discharged. Medicare pays for items to be used after the individual leaves the facility if the item: (1) is one that the beneficiary must continue to use after leaving, such as a leg brace; or (2) is necessary to permit or facilitate the beneficiary's departure from the facility and is required until he or she can obtain a continuing supply. [42 C.F.R. § 409.25(d); Pub. 100-02, Ch. 1, § 40.]

A temporary or disposable item, such as a sterile dressing, that is medically necessary to permit or facilitate a patient's departure from the facility and is required until such time as the patient can obtain a continuing supply, is covered as an extended care service. [Pub. 100-02, Ch. 1, § 40; Ch. 8, § 50.6.]

[¶ 237] Interns and Residents-in-Training

Medicare pays for medical services that are furnished by an intern or a resident-in-training under a hospital teaching program as post-hospital skilled nursing facility (SNF) care if the intern or resident is in: (1) a participating hospital with which the SNF has in effect a transfer agreement; or (2) a hospital that has swing-bed approval and is furnishing services to a SNF-level inpatient of that hospital. [Soc. Sec. Act § 1861(h)(6); 42 C.F.R. § 409.26(a).]

The medical and surgical services furnished to the facility's patients by interns and residents-in-training of a hospital with which the facility has a transfer agreement are covered under Part B if the services are not covered under Part A. [*Medicare Benefit Policy Manual*, Pub. 100-02, Ch. 8, § 50.7.]

[¶ 238] Whole Blood and Packed Red Blood Cells

Medicare coverage includes the cost of unreplaced blood (after satisfaction of the three-pint blood deductible discussed at ¶ 220) and the cost of administering the blood to inpatients of participating skilled nursing facilities. [Soc. Sec. Act § 1866(a)(2)(C); *Medicare General Information, Eligibility, and Entitlement Manual*, Pub. 100-01, Ch. 3, § 20.5.]

[¶ 239] Services Payable Under Part B

The medical and other health services listed below are covered under Part B when furnished by a participating skilled nursing facility (SNF), either directly or under arrangements to inpatients who are not entitled to have payment made under Part A, or to outpatients:

- diagnostic x-ray tests, diagnostic laboratory tests, and other diagnostic tests;

- x-ray, radium, and radioactive isotope therapy, including materials and services of technicians;

- surgical dressings, and splints, casts, and other devices used for reduction of fractures and dislocations;

- prosthetic devices (other than dental) that replace all or part of an internal body organ (including contiguous tissue), or all or part of the function of a permanently inoperative or malfunctioning internal body organ, including replacement or repairs of such devices;

- leg, arm, back, and neck braces, trusses, and artificial legs, arms, and eyes, including adjustments, repairs, and replacements required because of breakage, wear, loss, or a change in the patient's physical condition;

- outpatient physical therapy, outpatient speech-language pathology services, and outpatient occupational therapy;

- screening mammography services;

- screening pap smears and pelvic exams;

- influenza, pneumococcal pneumonia, and hepatitis B vaccines;

- some colorectal screening;

- diabetes self-management;

- prostate screening;

- ambulance services;

- hemophilia clotting factors; and

- Epoetin Alfa (EPO) for end-stage renal disease beneficiaries when given in conjunction with dialysis.

[42 C.F.R. § § 409.27(a), 410.60(b); *Medicare Benefit Policy Manual*, Pub. 100-02, Ch. 8, § 70.]

[¶ 242] Skilled Nursing Facility Coinsurance

The beneficiary is required to pay a coinsurance amount equal to one-eighth of the inpatient hospital deductible for each day after the 20th and before the 101st day of skilled nursing facility (SNF) services furnished during a spell of illness (see ¶ 210). [Soc. Sec. Act § 1813(a)(3).]

This coinsurance amount, like the inpatient hospital deductible on which it is dependent, is subject to annual change. Daily coinsurance for the 21st through 100th day in a SNF is $161.00 in 2016, up from $157.50 in 2015. [*Medicare General Information, Eligibility and Entitlement Manual*, Pub. 100-01, Ch. 3, § 10.3; *Notices*, 80 FR 70808, Nov. 16, 2015; 79 FR 61309, Oct. 10, 2014.]

[¶ 243] Duration of Covered SNF Services

A patient who has Part A coverage is entitled to have payment made on his or her behalf for up to 100 days of covered inpatient extended care services in each spell of illness subject to the coinsurance requirement discussed at ¶ 242. [Soc. Sec. Act § 1812(a)(2), (b)(2).]

The number of days of care charged to a beneficiary for inpatient skilled nursing facility (SNF) services is counted in units of full days. A day begins at midnight and ends 24 hours later. A part of a day, including the day of admission, counts as a full day. [*Medicare Benefit Policy Manual*, Pub. 100-02, Ch. 3, § 20.1.]

However, the day of discharge or death or a day on which a patient begins a leave of absence is not counted as a day. Charges for ancillary services on the day of discharge or death or the day on which a patient begins a leave of absence are covered. If admission and discharge or death occur on the same day, the day is considered a day of admission and counts as one inpatient day. [Pub. 100-02, Ch. 3, §§ 20.1, 20.1.3.]

Late discharge. When a patient chooses to occupy accommodations in a SNF beyond the normal check-out time for personal reasons, the facility may charge the patient for a continued stay. The SNF, however, must provide the beneficiary with an Advance Beneficiary Notice (ABN) before the non-covered services are provided (see ¶ 210). When the patient's medical condition is the cause of the stay past the checkout time (e.g., the patient needs further services, is bedridden and awaiting transportation to his or her home, or dies in the SNF), the stay beyond the discharge hour is covered under the program and the SNF may not charge the patient. [Pub. 100-02, Ch. 3, § 20.1.1.]

The imposition of a late checkout charge by a hospital or SNF does not affect the counting of days for: (1) ending a benefit period; (2) the number of days of inpatient care available to the individual in a SNF; and (3) the three-day prior hospitalization requirement for coverage of post-hospital extended care services and Part A home health services. A late charge by a hospital does not affect counting of days for meeting the prior inpatient stay requirement for coverage of extended care services. [Pub. 100-02, Ch. 3, § 20.1.1.]

Leaves of absence. The day on which the patient begins a leave of absence is treated as a day of discharge and is not counted as an inpatient day unless the patient returns to the facility by midnight of the same day. The day the patient returns to the facility from a leave of absence is treated as a day of admission and is counted as an inpatient day if he or she is present at midnight of that day. [Pub. 100-02, Ch. 3, § 20.1.2.]

Charges to the beneficiary for admission or readmission are not allowable. However, when temporarily leaving a SNF, a resident may choose to make bed-hold payments to the SNF. Under Soc. Sec. Act § 1819(c)(1)(B)(iii) and 42 C.F.R. § 483.10(b)(5)–(6), the SNF must inform residents in advance of their option to make bed-hold payments, as well as the amount of the facility's charge. [*Medicare Claims Processing Manual*, Pub. 100-04, Ch. 1, § 30.1.1.1.]

Days counting toward maximum. Post-hospital extended care services count toward the maximum number of benefit days payable per benefit period only if: (1) payment for the services is made; or (2) payment for the services would be made if a request for payment were properly filed, the physician certified that the services were medically necessary, if that is a requirement, and the provider submitted all necessary evidence. When payment cannot be made because of the extended care coinsurance requirement, the days used nevertheless count toward the beneficiary's maximum days of extended care. [Pub. 100-02, Ch. 3, § 30.]

[¶ 244] Levels of Care

Medicare covers post-hospital extended care only if a physician, nurse practitioner, clinical nurse specialist, or physician assistant certifies—and recertifies when required—that the services are or were necessary because the individual needs or needed on a daily basis skilled nursing care or other skilled rehabilitation services, which as a practical matter can be provided only in a skilled nursing facility (SNF) on an inpatient basis for any of the conditions with respect to which he or she was receiving inpatient hospital services. [Soc. Sec. Act § 1814(a)(2)(B).]

Thus, for a patient to be eligible for post-hospital extended care as an inpatient of a SNF, he or she must require the type and level of care that is defined as "post-hospital extended care," a level of care often distinguished from "custodial care," which is excluded (see ¶ 625). [42 C.F.R. § 411.15(g).]

Three criteria must be met to satisfy the level-of-care requirement under the extended care benefit: (1) the beneficiary must require skilled nursing services or skilled rehabilitation services on a daily basis; (2) the services must be furnished for a condition: (a) for which the beneficiary received inpatient hospital or inpatient critical access hospital (CAH) care, or (b) that arose while the beneficiary was receiving care in a SNF for a condition for which the beneficiary had received inpatient hospital or inpatient CAH services; and (3) as a practical matter, the service can be provided only in a SNF on an inpatient basis. [42 C.F.R. § 409.31(b).]

See ¶ 915 for a discussion of waiver of liability when a beneficiary is improperly transferred to a lower level of care.

"Skilled Nursing/Rehabilitation Services" Defined

Skilled nursing and skilled rehabilitation services are services that: (1) are ordered by a physician; (2) require the skills of technical or professional personnel, for example, a registered nurse, licensed practical (vocational) nurse, physical therapist, occupational therapist, speech-language pathologist, or audiologist; and (3) are provided either directly by or under the supervision of such personnel. [42 C.F.R. § 409.31(a).]

In the determination of whether a service is skilled, the inherent complexity of the service and special medical complications are considered. The restoration potential of a patient is not the deciding factor in determining whether skilled services are needed. Even when full recovery or medical improvement is not possible, skilled care may be needed to prevent, to the extent possible, deterioration of the patient's condition or to sustain current capacities. [42 C.F.R. § 409.32.]

Inherent complexity. If the inherent complexity of a service prescribed for a patient is such that it can be performed safely and effectively only by or under the supervision of technical or professional personnel, the service constitutes a skilled service. For example, certain intravenous or intramuscular injections, types of aspiration, insertion of catheters, and other inherently complex services qualify as SNF services. [42 C.F.R. §§ 409.32, 409.33.]

Special medical complications. A service that is usually nonskilled may be considered skilled when, because of special medical complications, its performance or supervision, or the observation of the patient, requires the use of skilled nursing or skilled rehabilitation personnel. For example, while heat treatments are usually unskilled, they may be considered skilled when specifically ordered by a physician as part of active treatment that requires a nurse's observation to adequately evaluate the patient's progress. [42 C.F.R. §§ 409.32, 409.33.]

Personal care services. Personal care services that do not require the skills of qualified technical or professional personnel are not skilled services and, therefore, not covered, except when special medical complications are involved. Personal care services include administration of routine medications, changes of dressings for noninfected conditions, and other general or routine care services. [42 C.F.R. §§ 409.32(b), 409.33(d).]

"Daily Basis" Requirement

Skilled nursing services or skilled rehabilitation services must be required and provided on a "daily basis." To meet the daily basis requirement, the following frequency is required: (1) skilled nursing services or skilled rehabilitation services must be needed and provided seven days a week; or (2) as an exception, if skilled rehabilitation services are not available seven days a week, those services must be needed and provided at least five days a week. A break of one or two days in the furnishing of rehabilitation services will not preclude coverage if discharge would not be practical for the one or two days during which, for instance, the physician has suspended the therapy sessions because the patient exhibited extreme fatigue. [42 C.F.R. § 409.34.]

[¶ 248] Rights of SNF Residents

A skilled nursing facility (SNF) must promote and protect the rights of each resident, including a resident's:

(1) free choice with respect to medical care and treatment;

(2) freedom from restraints;

(3) privacy;

(4) confidentiality;

(5) accommodation of needs;

(6) grievance procedures;

(7) participation in resident and family groups;

(8) participation in social, religious, and community activities;

(9) access of his or her medical records;

(10) refusal of treatment, including formulation of advance directives;

(11) receipt of information regarding significant changes in his or her treatment;

(12) management of his or her financial affairs;

(13) refusal or choice to perform work services for the SNF;

(14) examination of state certification survey results; and

(15) refusal of a transfer to a nonskilled nursing part of the facility.

[Soc. Sec. Act § 1819(c)(1)(A); 42 C.F.R. § 483.10.]

Notice of rights. The facility is required to: (1) give notice, orally and in writing at the time of admission to the facility, of the resident's legal rights during the stay at the facility; (2) make available to each resident, upon reasonable request, a written statement of such rights; and (3) inform each resident, in writing before or at the time of admission and periodically during the resident's stay, of services available in the facility and of related charges for such services, including any charges for services not covered under Medicare or by the facility's basic per diem charge. [Soc. Sec. Act § 1819(c)(1)(B); 42 C.F.R. § 483.10(b).]

The written description of legal rights must include a description of the SNF's protection of personal funds (see Soc. Sec. Act § 1819(c)(6)) and a statement that a resident may file a complaint with a state survey and certification agency regarding resident abuse and neglect or misappropriation of resident property in the facility. [Soc. Sec. Act § 1819(c)(1)(B).]

Payment Issues

If a beneficiary requests a noncovered service or a service that is more expensive than the amount of Medicare payment, the provider must inform the beneficiary that there will be a specific charge for that service. [42 C.F.R. § 489.32.] However, providers, including a SNF, may not impose any of the following prepayment requirements:

(1) require an individual entitled to hospital insurance benefits to prepay in part or in whole for inpatient services as a condition of admittance as an inpatient, except where it is clear upon admission that payment under Medicare Part A cannot be made;

(2) deny covered inpatient services to an individual entitled to have payment made for those services on the ground of inability or failure to pay a requested amount at or before admission;

(3) evict, or threaten to evict, an individual for inability to pay a deductible or a coinsurance amount required under Medicare;

(4) charge an individual for an agreement to admit or readmit the individual on some specified future date for covered inpatient services; or

(5) charge a resident for failure to remain an inpatient for any agreed-upon length of time or for failure to give advance notice of departure from the provider's facilities.

[42 C.F.R. § 489.22.]

Privacy Issues

HHS regulations protect the privacy of individually identifiable information in accordance with the Health Insurance Portability and Accountability Act (HIPAA) (P.L. 104-191). Under these regulations, a facility must provide notice to a patient on the first service visit regarding the facility's use of the beneficiary's medical data and the beneficiary's right to access that data. [45 C.F.R. § 164.520.] See ¶ 715 for a full description of HIPAA protections.

SNF residents have the right to personal privacy and confidentiality of their personal and clinical records, including information about accommodations, medical treatment, written and telephone communications, personal care, visits, and meetings of family and resident groups. A resident may refuse the release of personal and clinical records to any individual outside the facility, unless the resident is transferred to another health care institution or release is required by law. [42 C.F.R. § 489.10(e).]

Discharge or Transfer from a SNF

A SNF cannot discharge or transfer a resident from the facility unless: (1) the transfer or discharge is necessary to meet the resident's welfare, (2) the resident's health has improved to the extent that the resident no longer needs the SNF's services, (3) the safety or health of other residents is endangered, (4) the resident has failed, after reasonable and appropriate notice, to pay for a stay at the facility, or (5) the facility ceases to operate. If a transfer or discharge is warranted, the reason must be documented in the resident's clinical record. [Soc. Sec. Act § 1819(c)(2)(A); 45 C.F.R. § 483.12(a)(2).]

Before the discharge or transfer occurs, the SNF must notify the resident (or family member or legal representative) about the transfer and discharge, as well as the reasons for it, generally 30 days in advance. [Soc. Sec. Act § 1819(c)(2)(B)(ii); 45 C.F.R. § 483.12(a)(4)–(6).]

[¶ 249] "Skilled Nursing Facility"—Conditions of Participation

As a general rule, a beneficiary's stay in a skilled nursing facility (SNF) will not be covered by Medicare unless the SNF is "participating" in the Medicare program, that is, the SNF has been approved for Medicare participation by the government and has signed a participation agreement (see ¶ 730).

To participate as a SNF in the Medicare program, an institution must fit the statutory definition at Soc. Sec. Act § 1819(a). The law defines "skilled nursing facility" as an institution or a distinct part (see below) of an institution that:

(1) is primarily engaged in providing skilled nursing care and related services for residents who require medical or nursing care, or rehabilitation services for the rehabilitation of injured, disabled, or sick residents;

(2) has in effect a transfer agreement with one or more participating hospitals ("transfer agreement" is further explained below); and

(3) meets detailed requirements relating to services provided, residents' rights, professional standards, health and safety standards, and notification to the state of changes in ownership or control.

Facilities that primarily treat mental illness are specifically excluded from the SNF definition. [Soc. Sec. Act § 1819(a); 42 C.F.R. § 483.5(a).]

The term "skilled nursing facility" includes institutions operated or listed as religious nonmedical health care institutions. A Medicare beneficiary may choose to have services in these facilities covered as post-hospital extended care services. [Soc. Sec. Act § 1861(y).] See ¶ 228 for a discussion of religious nonmedical health care institutions.

As part of the Nursing Home Quality Initiative, SNFs are required to post facility census information, as well as nurse staffing data for both licensed and unlicensed staff directly responsible for the care at the facility on a daily basis and for each shift. The goal of this program is to provide beneficiaries, their families, and the general public with access to information that can assist them in making nursing home care decisions. SNFs must retain this posted census data for 18 months. [42 C.F.R. § 483.30(e).]

A state may require higher health and safety standards of SNFs than those mandated by accrediting bodies or by the federal government; a state's higher Medicaid standards then become Medicare standards. [42 C.F.R. § 488.3(b).]

A SNF of the Indian Health Service (IHS), whether operated by the IHS or a tribal organization, is eligible for Medicare payments if it meets all of the Medicare requirements for SNFs. [Soc. Sec. Act § 1880(a).]

A single set of requirements is applicable to SNFs under both Medicare and Medicaid. Thus, a SNF eligible to participate under one program is eligible to participate under the other, provided it agrees to the contract terms. The identical definition also permits a single consolidated survey to determine a facility's qualifications to participate in either program. [Soc. Sec. Act § 1919(a); 42 C.F.R. § 483.1(b).]

Skilled Nursing Beds in Hospitals

It is possible to treat part of an institution as a SNF. This may be done either by having a "distinct part" of the institution certified as a SNF or by having an agreement with the HHS Secretary under which inpatient hospital beds may be used for skilled nursing care on a "swing" basis (see ¶ 229). [Soc. Sec. Act § 1819(a); 42 C.F.R. § 483.5(a); *Medicare Claims Processing Manual*, Pub. 100-04, Ch. 6, § 100.]

To qualify for participation in the program as a "distinct part" SNF, the "distinct part" must be physically separated from the rest of the institution, that is, it must represent an entire, physically identifiable unit consisting of all the beds within that unit, such as a separate building, floor, wing, or ward. A distinct part must include all of the beds within the designated area and cannot consist of a random collection of individual rooms or beds that are scattered throughout the physical plant. [42 C.F.R. § 483.5(b)(1); *Medicare General Information, Eligibility, and Entitlement Manual*, Pub. 100-01, Ch. 5, § 30.1.]

Transfer Agreements

To participate in Medicare, a SNF must have a written transfer agreement with one or more participating hospitals providing for the transfer of patients between the hospital and the facility and for the interchange of medical and other information. If an otherwise qualified SNF has attempted in good faith, but without success, to enter into a transfer agreement, this requirement may be waived. [Soc. Sec. Act §§ 1819(a)(2), 1861(l); 42 C.F.R. § 483.75(n); Pub. 100-01, Ch. 5, § 30.2.]

Home Health Services

[¶ 250] Home Health Services: Qualifying Conditions for Coverage

Home health services are covered only if furnished by a home health agency (HHA) participating in the Medicare program and acting on a physician's certification that the individual: (1) is confined to the home; (2) needs intermittent skilled nursing care or physical or occupational therapy or speech-language pathology services; and (3) is under the care of a physician who has established a plan of care. [Soc. Sec. Act § 1814(a)(3)(C); 42 C.F.R. §§ 409.42, 424.22.]

Coverage of skilled nursing care or therapy to perform a maintenance program is based on the patient's need for skilled care and does not require the patient to have the potential for improvement as a result of the nursing care or therapy. Skilled care may be necessary to improve or maintain a patient's current condition or to prevent or slow further deterioration of the patient's condition. [*Medicare Benefit Policy Manual*, Pub. 100-02, Ch. 7, § 20.1.2.]

Part A finances up to 100 visits during one home health spell of illness if the following criteria are met: (1) the beneficiary is enrolled in Part A and B and qualifies for home health benefits; (2) the beneficiary meets the three-consecutive-day-stay requirement; and (3) the home health services are initiated and the first covered home health visit is rendered within 14 days of discharge from a three-consecutive-day stay in a hospital or rural primary care hospital or within 14 days of discharge from a skilled nursing facility (SNF) in which the individual was provided post-hospital extended care services. If the first home health visit is not initiated within 14 days of discharge or if the three-consecutive-day stay requirement is not met, then the services are covered under Part B. See ¶ 383 for a discussion of coverage of home health services under Part B. [Soc. Sec. Act § 1812(a)(3); Pub. 100-02, Ch. 7, § 60.1.]

If a beneficiary is enrolled only in Part A and qualifies for the Medicare home health benefit, then all of the home health services are financed under Part A. The 100-visit limit does not apply to beneficiaries who are only enrolled in Part A. If a beneficiary is enrolled only in Part B and qualifies for the Medicare home health benefit, then all of the home health services are financed under Part B. There is no 100-visit limit under Part B. [Soc. Sec. Act § 1812(a)(3); Pub. 100-02, Ch. 7, § 60.3.]

Definitions

"Post-institutional home health services" are defined as the services furnished to a beneficiary: (1) after discharge from a hospital in which the individual was an inpatient for at least three consecutive days before discharge if the services are initiated within 14 days of

¶250

discharge; or (2) after discharge from a SNF in which the beneficiary was provided post-hospital extended care services if the services were initiated within 14 days after discharge. [Soc. Sec. Act § 1861(tt)(1).]

"Home health spell of illness" refers to a period of consecutive days beginning with the first day that an individual is furnished post-institutional home health services during a month in which the individual is entitled to benefits under Part A. It ends when the beneficiary has not received hospital, critical access hospital, SNF, or home health services for 60 days. [Soc. Sec. Act § 1861(tt)(2).]

A "home health episode of care" is a 60-day period starting on the day that the first billable services are provided to a beneficiary under a plan of care and ending 60 days later. On the 61st day that services are provided, a new home health episode of care begins, regardless of whether a service was delivered on that day. A beneficiary may have an unlimited number of non-overlapping episodes of care, and an episode can be shorter than 60 days. The 60-day episode of care is used to determine the amount of payment made on behalf of a beneficiary (see payment rates at ¶ 830). [*Medicare Claims Processing Manual*, Pub. 100-04, Ch. 10, § 10.1.5.]

"Home health services" are defined as the following items and services, provided on a visiting basis in a place of residence used as the individual's home, except as noted in item (7), below:

(1) part-time or intermittent nursing care provided by or under the supervision of a registered professional nurse;

(2) physical or occupational therapy or speech-language pathology services;

(3) medical social services under the direction of a physician;

(4) part-time or intermittent services of a home health aide who has completed an approved training program successfully;

(5) medical supplies (other than drugs and biologicals), durable medical equipment, and, effective January 1, 2017, applicable disposable devices while under the plan of care;

(6) medical services of interns and residents-in-training under an approved teaching program of a hospital with which the HHA is affiliated; and

(7) any of the items and services that: (a) are provided on an outpatient basis under arrangements made by the HHA at a hospital or SNF, or at a rehabilitation center meeting standards prescribed in regulations, and (b) involve the use of equipment that cannot be made readily available to the individual in the place of residence, or that are furnished at the facility while the individual is there to receive any item or service involving the use of such equipment. Transportation of the individual is not covered (see ¶ 257).

[Soc. Sec. Act § 1861(m); 42 C.F.R. § § 409.44, 409.45.]

[¶ 251] Skilled Nursing Care

If a patient qualifies for home health services, Medicare covers either part-time or intermittent skilled nursing services. For purposes of receiving home health care, the term "part-time or intermittent care" means skilled nursing and home health aide services furnished for up to 28 hours per week combined over any number of days per week so long as they are furnished for fewer than eight hours per day. Medicare may approve additional time of up to 35 hours per week, but for fewer than eight hours per day, on a case-by-case basis. For purposes of an individual qualifying for home health benefits and for purposes of payment for provider claims, when the individual needs intermittent skilled nursing care, the term "intermittent" means skilled nursing care that is either provided or needed fewer than seven days each week, or fewer than eight hours of each day for periods up to and including 21 days, with extensions in exceptional circumstances. [Soc. Sec. Act § 1861(m); *Medicare Benefit Policy Manual*, Pub. 100-02, Ch. 7, § 50.7.1.]

Skilled nursing care in excess of the amounts of care that meet the definitions of "part-time" or "intermittent" may be provided to a home care patient or purchased by other payers without bearing on whether the care is covered to the extent allowed by Medicare. The HHA may bill the home care patient or other payer for care that exceeds the hours of care that Medicare allows as reasonable and necessary. [Pub. 100-02, Ch. 7, § 50.7.1.]

Skilled nursing services are services that:

(1) require the skills of a registered nurse or a licensed practical nurse (or licensed vocational nurse) under the supervision of a registered nurse;

(2) are reasonable and necessary to the treatment of the patient's illness or injury; and

(3) are needed on an intermittent basis.

Coverage of skilled nursing care does not turn on the presence or absence of a patient's potential for improvement from the nursing care but, rather, on the patient's need for skilled care. [Pub. 100-02, Ch. 7, § 40.1.] Skilled nursing services are covered when they are necessary to maintain the patient's current condition or prevent or slow further deterioration, as long as the beneficiary requires skilled care for the services to be safely and effectively provided. [Pub. 100-02, Ch. 7, § 40.1.1.]

In general, the third requirement is met if a patient needs skilled nursing care at least once every 60 days. A one-time nursing service, such as giving a gamma globulin injection following exposure to hepatitis, for example, is not considered a need for intermittent skilled nursing care because a recurrence of the problem every 60 days is not medically predictable. If the need for a skilled nursing visit at least once every 60 days is medically predictable, but a situation arises after the first visit making additional visits unnecessary—for example, the patient is institutionalized or dies—the one visit made is covered. [Pub. 100-02, Ch. 7, § 40.1.3.]

Home health records for every visit should reflect the need for the skilled medical care provided, including objective measurements of physical outcomes of treatment. [Pub. 100-02, Ch. 7, § 40.1.1.]

[¶ 252] Physical and Occupational Therapy and Speech-Language Pathology Services

Physical and occupational skilled therapy and speech-language pathology services furnished by a home health agency (HHA) or by others under arrangements made by the HHA are covered when provided in accordance with a physician's orders and by, or under the supervision of, a qualified therapist. To be covered as skilled therapy, the services must require the skills of a qualified therapist and must be reasonable and necessary for the treatment of the beneficiary's illness or injury or for the restoration or maintenance of the function affected by the illness or injury. Coverage depends on the beneficiary's need for skilled care, not on the presence or absence of the beneficiary's potential for improvement. [42 C.F.R. § 409.44(c); *Medicare Benefit Policy Manual*, Pub. 100-02, Ch. 7, §§ 40.2, 40.2.1.]

For therapy services to be covered in the home health setting, they must relate directly to the patient's plan of care, and they must be reasonable and necessary to the treatment of the patient's illness or injury or to the restoration or maintenance of function affected by the patient's illness or injury. Also, one of the following three criteria must be met:

(1) there is an expectation that the beneficiary's condition will improve materially in a reasonable (and generally predictable) period of time based on the physician's assessment of the beneficiary's restoration potential and unique medical condition;

(2) the unique clinical condition of a patient may require the specialized skills, knowledge, and judgment of a qualified therapist to design or establish a safe and effective maintenance program required in connection with the patient's specific illness or injury; or

(3) the unique clinical condition of a patient may require the specialized skills of a qualified therapist to perform a safe and effective maintenance program required in connection with the patient's specific illness or injury.

[42 C.F.R. § 409.44(c)(2)(iii); Pub. 100-02, Ch. 7, § 40.2.1.]

For each therapy discipline, a qualified therapist (not an assistant) must assess and reassess the patient's function at least once every 30 calendar days. [42 C.F.R. § 409.44(c)(2)(i); Pub. 100-02, Ch. 7, § 40.2.1.]

Payment for therapy services is included in the home health prospective payment amount received by the HHA for the episode of care. The Part B outpatient limitations on the total amount of therapy services that can be claimed in a year do not apply to therapy furnished by HHAs. See ¶ 830 for a discussion on the home health prospective payment system. [Pub. 100-02, Ch. 7, § 30.4; *Medicare Claims Processing Manual*, Pub. 100-04, Ch. 5, § 10.2.]

[¶ 253] Medical Social Services

Medical social services are covered as home health services if ordered by a physician and included in the plan of care. The frequency and nature of the services must be reasonable and necessary for the treatment of the Medicare beneficiary's condition. Medical social services are "dependent" services that are covered only if the beneficiary needs: (1) skilled nursing care on an intermittent basis, (2) physical therapy or speech-language pathology services, or (3) occupational therapy services on a continuing basis. [42 C.F.R. § 409.45(a), (c)(1).]

Medical social services are covered under Part A only if: (1) the services are necessary to resolve social or emotional problems that are, or are expected to become, an impediment to the effective treatment of the patient's medical condition or rate of recovery; (2) the frequency and nature of the services are reasonable and necessary to the treatment of the patient's conditions; (3) the medical social services are furnished by a qualified social worker or qualified social work assistant under the supervision of a social worker; and (4) the services needed to resolve the problems that are impeding the beneficiary's recovery require the skills of a qualified social worker or social worker assistant under the supervision of a qualified medical social worker. [42 C.F.R. § 409.45(c).]

Covered services include, but are not limited to, the following:

(1) assessment of the social and emotional factors related to the patient's illness, need for care, response to treatment, and adjustment to care;

(2) appropriate action to obtain community services to assist in resolving problems in these areas;

(3) assessment of the relationship of the patient's medical and nursing requirements to the home situation, financial resources, and availability of community resources; and

(4) counseling services required by the patient.

[*Medicare Benefit Policy Manual*, Pub. 100-02, Ch. 7, § 50.3.]

Counseling services furnished to the patient's family are covered only when the home health agency (HHA) can demonstrate that a brief intervention (that is, two or three visits) by a medical social worker is necessary to remove a clear and direct impediment to the effective treatment of the patient's medical condition or to his or her rate of recovery. To be considered clear and direct, the behavior or actions of the family member or caregiver must plainly obstruct, contravene, or prevent the patient's medical treatment or rate of recovery. Medical social services to address general problems that do not clearly and directly impede treatment or recovery, as well as long-term social services furnished to family members, such as ongoing alcohol counseling, are not covered. [42 C.F.R. § 409.45(c)(2)(ii); *Medicare Benefit Policy Manual*, Pub. 100-02, Ch. 7, § 50.3.]

[¶ 254] Home Health Aides

Medicare covers part-time or intermittent services of a home health aide who has successfully completed a training program approved by the HHS Secretary. To be covered, these services must be ordered by a physician in the plan of care for a beneficiary who qualifies for home health services. The reason for the visits by the home health aide must be to provide hands-on personal care to the beneficiary or services that are needed to maintain the beneficiary's health or to facilitate treatment of the beneficiary's illness or injury. Services provided by the home health aide must be reasonable and necessary. The physician's order should indicate the frequency of the home health aide services required. [Soc. Sec. Act § § 1861(m)(4), 1891(a)(3); 42 C.F.R. § 409.45(b)(2) and (3).]

To be considered reasonable and necessary, the services must meet the requirements above and must be: (1) the type of services that the patient cannot perform himself or herself; and (2) services that no able or willing caregiver can provide, or if there is a potential caregiver, the patient must be unwilling to receive care from that caregiver. [42 C.F.R. § 409.45(b)(3).]

Covered home health aide services include the following: (1) personal care of a patient; (2) simple dressing changes that do not require the skills of a licensed nurse; (3) assistance with medications that ordinarily are self-administered and do not require the skills of a licensed nurse; (4) assistance with activities that are directly supportive of skilled therapy, such as routine exercises and the practice of functional communication skills; and (5) routine care of prosthetic and orthotic devices. [42 C.F.R. § 409.45(b)(1); *Medicare Benefit Policy Manual*, Pub. 100-02, Ch. 7, § 50.2.]

The discussion on intermittent services at ¶ 251 is applicable also to home health aides.

[¶ 255] Medical Supplies and Durable Medical Equipment

Covered medical supplies are items that, due to their therapeutic or diagnostic characteristics, are essential to enable the home health agency (HHA) to effectively carry out the plan of care that the physician ordered for the treatment or diagnosis of the patient's illness or injury. They include such items as: catheters and catheter supplies; ostomy bags and ostomy care supplies; dressings and wound care supplies, such as sterile gloves, gauze, and applicators; and intravenous supplies. [Soc. Sec. Act § 1861(m)(5); 42 C.F.R. § 409.45(f); *Medicare Benefit Policy Manual*, Pub. 100-02, Ch. 7, § § 50.4.1.1 and 50.4.2.]

Effective January 1, 2017, also included are applicable disposable devices, defined as disposable devices that are: (1) disposable negative pressure wound therapy devices that are integrated systems composed of a nonmanual vacuum pump, a receptacle for collecting exudate, and dressings for the purposes of wound therapy; and (2) substitutes for, and used in lieu of, negative pressure wound therapy durable medical equipment items that are an integrated systems of a negative pressure vacuum pump, a separate exudate collection canister, and dressings that would otherwise be covered for individuals for such wound therapy. [Soc. Sec. Act §§ 1834(s)(2), 1861(m)(5).]

Limited amounts of medical supplies may be left in the home between visits when repeated applications are required and rendered by the patient or by caregivers. These items must be part of the plan of care in which the home health staff is actively involved. For example, if the patient is independent in giving himself or herself insulin injections but the nurse visits once a day to change wound dressings, the wound dressings/irrigation solution may be left in the home between visits. Supplies that require administration by a nurse, such as needles, syringes, and catheters, should not be left in the home between visits. [Pub. 100-02, Ch. 7, § 50.4.1.3.]

HHAs must offer to furnish catheters, catheter supplies, ostomy bags, and supplies related to ostomy care to any individual who needs them as part of the provision of health services. [Soc. Sec. Act § 1866(a)(1)(P); 42 C.F.R. § 489.20(k).]

Durable medical equipment (DME) furnished by the HHA is reimbursed under Medicare Part B (see ¶ 356). DME is not included in the home health prospective payment rate and has been eliminated from the consolidated billing requirement. [Soc. Sec. Act §§ 1814(k), 1834(a)(1), 1861(m)(5); 42 C.F.R. § 484.205(b); *Medicare General Information, Eligibility, and Entitlement Manual*, Pub. 100-01, Ch. 3, § 20.4; Pub. 100-02, Ch. 7, § 50.4.2.]

Exclusion of Drugs and Biologicals

Drugs and biologicals are generally excluded from coverage as home health benefits. [Soc. Sec. Act § 1861(m)(5); 42 C.F.R. § 409.49(a).] In certain cases they may be covered under Part B, such as when they are administered by a physician as a part of his or her professional services (see ¶ 351 and ¶ 362). The administration of medication also may be covered if the services of a licensed nurse are required to administer the medications safely and effectively for the reasonable and necessary treatment of the illness or injury. [Pub. 100-02, Ch. 7, § 40.1.2.4.]

Osteoporosis drugs. Injections of osteoporosis drugs are covered as non-routine medical supplies for homebound female beneficiaries in certain circumstances (the nursing visit to perform the injection may be the individual's qualifying service for home health coverage) if:

(1) the individual's physician certifies that the individual sustained a bone fracture that a physician certifies was related to post-menopausal osteoporosis and she is unable to learn the skills needed to self-administer the drug, and that her family or caregivers are unable or unwilling to administer the drug, or she is otherwise physically or mentally incapable of administering the drug; and

(2) the individual is confined to the home.

[Soc. Sec. Act § 1861(kk); Pub. 100-02, Ch. 7, § 50.4.3; *Medicare Claims Processing Manual*, Pub. 100-04, Ch. 10, § 90.1.]

[¶ 256] Interns and Residents-in-Training

Home health services include the medical services of interns and residents-in-training under an approved hospital teaching program if the services are ordered by the physician who is responsible for the plan of care and the home health agency (HHA) is affiliated with, or under common control of, a hospital providing the medical services. "Approved" means:

(1) approved by the Accreditation Council for Graduate Medical Education;

(2) in the case of an osteopathic hospital, approved by the Committee on Hospitals of the Bureau of Professional Education of the American Osteopathic Association;

(3) in the case of an intern or resident-in-training in the field of dentistry, approved by the Council on Dental Education of the American Dental Association; or

(4) in the case of an intern or resident-in-training in the field of podiatry, approved by the Council on Podiatric Education of the American Podiatric Association.

[42 C.F.R. § 409.45(g); *Medicare Benefit Policy Manual*, Pub. 100-02, Ch. 7, § 50.5.]

[¶ 257] Outpatient Services

In certain instances, the services described in ¶ 251–¶ 256, provided on an outpatient basis, can be included as home health services (see ¶ 250, item (7)). While the beneficiary ordinarily must be homebound to be eligible for home health services, such services are covered if furnished under arrangements at a hospital, skilled nursing facility (SNF), or rehabilitation center, and if the services: (1) require the use of equipment (for example, hydrotherapy) that cannot be made available at the beneficiary's home, or (2) are furnished while the beneficiary is at the facility to receive services requiring the use of such equipment. The hospital, SNF, or outpatient department affiliated with a medical school must be a qualified provider of services. [42 C.F.R. § 409.47(b); *Medicare Benefit Policy Manual*, Pub. 100-02, Ch. 7, § 50.6.]

In some cases, special transportation arrangements may have to be made to bring the homebound patient to the institution providing these special services. The cost of transporting an individual to a facility cannot be reimbursed as a home health service. [42 C.F.R. § 409.49(b); Pub. 100-02, Ch. 7, § 50.6.]

[¶ 260] Care of a Physician

The home health patient must be under the care of a physician who established the plan of care (POC). [42 C.F.R. § 424.22(a)(1)(iv).] The physician must be qualified to sign the physician certification and the POC (see ¶ 262). Such a physician may be a doctor of medicine, osteopathy, or podiatric medicine. A podiatrist may establish a POC only if consistent with the functions authorized for that specialty by state law. [42 C.F.R. § 409.42(b).]

Certification and Recertification

As a condition for payment of home health services under Medicare Part A or Medicare Part B, a physician must certify the following:

(1) the individual needs or needed intermittent skilled nursing care, or physical therapy speech-language pathology services;

(2) home health services were required because the individual was confined to the home except when receiving outpatient services;

(3) a plan for furnishing the services has been established and is periodically reviewed by a physician who is a doctor of medicine, osteopathy, or podiatric medicine;

(4) the services were furnished while the individual was under the care of a physician who is a doctor of medicine, osteopathy, or podiatric medicine; and

(5) a face-to-face patient encounter (described below) occurred.

[42 C.F.R. § 424.22(a).]

The certification of need for home health services must be obtained at the time the POC is established or as soon thereafter as possible and must be signed and dated by the physician who establishes the plan. Documentation in the certifying physician's medical records and/or the acute/post-acute care facility's medical records must used as the basis for certification of home health eligibility. [42 C.F.R. § 424.22(a), (c).]

Recertification. Recertification is required when there is a need for continuous home health care after an initial 60-day episode. Recertification should occur at the time the plan of care is reviewed, and must be signed and dated by the physician who reviews the plan of care. Recertification is required every 60 days unless there is a: (1) beneficiary-elected transfer; or (2) discharge with goals being met and/or no expectation of a return to home health care. [42 C.F.R. § 424.22(b).]

The recertification statement must indicate the continuing need for services and estimate how much longer the services will be required. The need for occupational therapy may be the basis for continuing services that were initiated because the individual needed skilled nursing care or physical therapy or speech therapy. [42 C.F.R. § 424.22(b)(2).]

Face-to-Face Encounter

The physician responsible for performing the initial certification must document that a face-to-face patient encounter, which is related to the primary reason the patient requires home health services, has occurred no more than 90 days prior to the home health start of care date or within 30 days of the start of the home health care. The physician must include the date of the encounter and an explanation of why the clinical findings support that the patient is homebound and in need of either intermittent skilled nursing services or therapy services. [Soc. Sec. Act § 1814(a)(2)(C); 42 C.F.R. § 424.22(a)(1)(v).]

The face-to-face encounter may be performed by one of the following:

- the certifying physician himself or herself;
- a physician with privileges who cared for the patient in an acute or post-acute care facility from which the patient was directly admitted to home health;
- a nurse practitioner or a clinical nurse specialist working in collaboration with either of the above physicians;
- a certified nurse-midwife working under the supervision of either of the above physicians; or
- a physician assistant working under the supervision of either of the above physicians.

[Soc. Sec. Act § 1814(a)(2)(C); 42 C.F.R. § 424.22(a)(1)(v)(A).]

The face-to-face patient encounter may occur through telehealth. [Soc. Sec. Act § 1814(a)(2)(C); 42 C.F.R. § 424.22(a)(1)(v)(B).]

[¶ 262] Establishment of a Plan of Care

Items and services must be furnished under a plan of care (POC) established and periodically reviewed by a physician. [Soc. Sec. Act § 1861(m); 42 C.F.R. §§ 409.42(d), 409.43.] The same physician must certify the medical necessity of the home health services, signing the certification at the time the POC is established (see ¶ 260). [42 C.F.R. § 424.22(a).]

Home health services may not be certified or recertified, and a POC may not be established and reviewed, by a physician who has a financial relationship with the home health agency (HHA) furnishing the service. [42 C.F.R. § 424.22(d).] See ¶ 720 on fraud and abuse.

Content of the Plan of Care

The POC must contain the following:

(1) all pertinent diagnoses, including the beneficiary's mental status;

(2) types of services, supplies, and equipment required;

(3) frequency of visits, prognosis, rehabilitation potential;

(4) functional limitations;

(5) activities permitted;

(6) nutritional requirements;

(7) all medications and treatments;

(8) safety measures to protect against injury;

(9) instructions for timely discharge or referral; and

(10) any additional items the HHA or physician choose to include.

[42 C.F.R. §§ 409.43(a), 484.18(a); *Medicare Benefit Policy Manual*, Pub. 100-02, Ch. 7, § 30.2.1.]

If the POC includes a course of treatment for therapy services, it must be established by the physician after any needed consultation with the qualified therapist. The course of treatment for therapy services in a POC must: (1) include measurable therapy treatment goals pertaining directly to the patient's illness or injury and the patient's resultant impairments; (2) include the expected duration of therapy services; and (3) describe a course of treatment consistent with the qualified therapist's assessment of the patient's function. [42 C.F.R. § 484.18(a); Pub. 100-02, Ch. 7, § 30.2.1.]

The physician's orders in the POC must indicate the type of services to be provided to the beneficiary, both with respect to the professional who will provide them and with respect to the nature and frequency of the individual services. Orders that are described as "as needed" or PRN should be accompanied by a description of the patient's medical signs and symptoms that would occasion the visit. These provisions in a POC also must include a specific number of such visits to be made under the order until an additional physician order must be obtained. [42 C.F.R. § 409.43(b); Pub. 100-02, Ch. 7, § 30.2.2.]

The physician must sign the POC before a claim for payment is submitted. Services may be provided before the POC is signed because a claim is not submitted until the end of a 60-day episode of care. Any changes to the POC must also be signed and dated by the physician. [42 C.F.R. § 409.43(c); Pub. 100-02, Ch. 7, § 30.2.3.]

If any services are provided based on a physician's oral orders, the orders must be put in writing and be signed and dated with the date of receipt by the registered nurse or qualified therapist responsible for furnishing or supervising the ordered services. The oral orders must also be countersigned and dated by the physician before the HHA bills for the care. [42 C.F.R. § 409.43(d); Pub. 100-02, Ch. 7, § 30.2.4A.]

Review of Plan of Care

The POC must be reviewed and signed by a physician in consultation with the HHA professional personnel at least every 60 days. [42 C.F.R. § 409.43(e); Pub. 100-02, Ch. 7, § 30.2.6.]

[¶ 264] Patient Confined to Home

For a beneficiary to be eligible to receive covered home health services, he or she must be confined to home, except as discussed at ¶ 257. The law requires a physician to certify this confinement to home in all cases. [Soc. Sec. Act § 1814(a)(2)(C); , 42 C.F.R. §§ 409.42(a), 409.47.]

An individual is considered "confined to home" if both of the following criteria are met:

    (1) The patient must either:

- need the aid of supportive devices such as crutches, canes, wheelchairs, and walkers; the use of special transportation; or the assistance of another person in order to leave his or her place of residence because of illness or injury; or

- have a condition such that leaving his or her home is medically contraindicated.

    (2) The patient must also:

- have a normal inability to leave home; and

- require a considerable and taxing effort to leave home.

[*Medicare Benefit Policy Manual*, Pub. 100-02, Ch. 7, § 30.1.1.]

Beneficiaries are considered homebound even if they take an occasional absence from the home for nonmedical purposes. The absences must be infrequent, relatively short in duration, and not indicate that the patient has the ability to obtain health care outside of the home. In determining whether a beneficiary has the general inability to leave home and leaves the home only infrequently or for periods of short duration, it is necessary to look at the patient's condition over a period of time, rather than for short periods. [Pub. 100-02, Ch. 7, § 30.1.1.]

Attendance at a religious service is considered an absence of infrequent or short duration. Beneficiaries can be considered homebound while receiving therapeutic, psychosocial, or medical treatment in a state-licensed adult day-care program on a regular basis. [Soc. Sec. Act § § 1814(a), 1835(a).]

Patient's Place of Residence

Home health services must be furnished on a visiting basis in a place used as the patient's residence. This may be his or her own dwelling, an apartment, a relative's home, a home for the aged, or some other type of institution. However, an institution may not be considered a patient's place of residence if it meets at least the most important requirement in the definition of "hospital" (see ¶ 229) or in the definition of "skilled nursing facility" (see ¶ 249). [42 C.F.R. § 409.47(a); Pub. 100-02, Ch. 7, § 30.1.2.]

[¶ 266] Visits

A visit is an episode of personal contact in the patient's residence made for the purpose of providing a covered service by a health worker on the staff of the home health agency (HHA) or by others under contract or arrangement with the HHA. A visit can also be made by a patient on an outpatient basis to a hospital, skilled nursing facility, or rehabilitation center, or an outpatient department affiliated with a medical school when arrangements have been made by the HHA for one or more covered services (see ¶ 257). [42 C.F.R. § 409.48(c); *Medicare Benefit Policy Manual*, Pub. 100-02, Ch. 7, § 70.2.]

There is nothing to preclude an HHA from adopting telemedicine or other technologies that they believe promote efficiencies; however, those technologies will not be specifically recognized or reimbursed by Medicare under the home health benefit. [Soc. Sec. Act § 1895(e)(1)(B); Pub. 100-02, Ch. 7, § 110.]

Evaluation Visits

When personnel of the HHA make an initial evaluation visit, the cost of this visit is considered an administrative expense of the HHA because at this point the patient has not been accepted for care. If during the course of this initial evaluation visit the HHA determines that the patient is suitable for home health care, and provides the first skilled service as ordered under the physician's plan of treatment, the visit would become the first billable visit. An observation and evaluation, or reevaluation visit made by a nurse or other appropriate personnel, ordered by the physician for the purpose of evaluating the patient's condition and his or her continuing need for skilled services is covered as a skilled visit. [Pub. 100-02, Ch. 7, § 70.2C.]

A supervisory visit made by a nurse or other personnel to evaluate the specific personal care needs of the patient or to review the manner in which the personal care needs of the patient are being met by the aide is considered an administrative function and is not chargeable to the patient as a skilled visit. [Pub. 100-02, Ch. 7, § 70.2C.]

Patient-Specific Comprehensive Assessments

HHAs participating in Medicare are required to conduct patient-specific comprehensive assessments on certain patients using a standard core assessment data set, the "Outcomes and Assessment Information Set" (OASIS). OASIS is a fundamental component of CMS's efforts to achieve broad-based and measurable improvements in the quality of health care and patient satisfaction in the Medicare and Medicaid home health benefit. HHAs are required to incorporate OASIS data items into the HHA's own assessment instrument. The items include information regarding demographics and patient history, living arrangements, supportive assistance, sensory status, integumentary status, elimination status, neuro/emotional/behavioral status, activities of daily living, medications, equipment management, emergent care, and discharge. [42 C.F.R. § 484.55(e).]

Initial assessment. Within 48 hours of the patient's referral or return home, or on the start-of-care date ordered by the physician, a registered nurse or an appropriate therapist, if therapy is the only component of a plan of care, must complete an initial assessment. Eligibility for the Medicare home health benefit must be evaluated during the initial assessment. [42 C.F.R. § 484.55(a).]

Comprehensive assessments. Except for a patient whose physician orders only physical, occupational, or speech therapy, the comprehensive assessment must be completed by a registered nurse no later than five calendar days after the start of care. A speech-language pathologist, physical therapist, or occupational therapist may conduct the assessment if the physician ordered only these types of therapy. [42 C.F.R. § 484.55(b).]

The comprehensive assessment should reflect the patient's current health status accurately and include information that demonstrates the patient's progress toward achievement of desired outcomes. Comprehensive assessments must be updated within the last five days of every 60 days beginning with the start-of-care date unless there is a:

(1) significant change in condition;

(2) transfer to another HHA elected by the beneficiary; or

(3) discharge and then a return to the same HHA during a 60-day episode.

[42 C.F.R. § 484.55(d).]

Comprehensive assessments also must be updated at discharge and within 48 hours of a beneficiary's return home from a hospital stay longer than 24 hours for any reason other than diagnostic testing. [42 C.F.R. § 484.55(d).]

Drug regimen review. Part of the comprehensive assessment of the patient is a drug regimen review of all medications the patient is using at the time of the assessment. The purpose of the review is to identify any potential adverse effects and drug reactions, including ineffective drug therapy, duplicate drug therapy, significant side effects, significant drug interactions, and noncompliance with drug therapy. [42 C.F.R. § 484.55(c).]

Confidentiality. The HHA must ensure the confidentiality of all patient-identifiable information contained in the clinical record, including OASIS data, and may not release patient-identifiable OASIS information to the public. [42 C.F.R. § 484.11.] Under the conditions of participation for HHAs, patients whose data will be collected and used by the federal government must receive a notice of their privacy rights, including the right to refuse to answer questions. Standard statements notifying patients of their privacy rights have been prepared by CMS and are available on the CMS website at http://www.cms.gov/Center/ Provider-Type/Home-Health-Agency-HHA-Center.html. The statements, which are available in English and Spanish in versions for Medicare/Medicaid beneficiaries and for non-Medicare/non-Medicaid patients, must be incorporated into HHAs' admission processes. [42 C.F.R. § 484.10.]

See ¶ 715 for more discussion on the privacy of beneficiaries' medical data and the requirements for providers, including the need to obtain authorizations from beneficiaries prior to the release of individually identifiable health information in certain circumstances.

Prospective payment system. The weighted answers to several OASIS items, including the need for therapy, provide a key element of Medicare reimbursement under the home health prospective payment system (HH PPS) (see ¶ 830).

Advance Directives

Advance medical directives are written instructions, such as a living will or durable power of attorney for health care, recognized under state law relating to the provision of care when the individual is incapacitated. Beneficiaries must be informed about advance directives and their choices must be documented in their medical records. HHAs must provide the information to the beneficiary before care is provided during the initial visit. [Soc. Sec. Act § 1866(f)(3); 42 C.F.R. § 489.102(a).]

Beneficiaries are not *required* to make advance directives, and the amount and type of care may not be conditioned upon the completion or noncompletion of an advance directive. HHAs must provide written information to beneficiaries about their rights under state law to make decisions concerning their medical care, including the right to accept or refuse medical care and the right to formulate medical directives before care is started. [Soc. Sec. Act § 1866(f)(1); 42 C.F.R. § 489.102(a).]

[¶ 267] Specific Exclusions from Coverage

Any service that would not be covered if furnished to an inpatient of a hospital, such as private-duty nurse services, is excluded from coverage as a home health service (see ¶ 217). [Soc. Sec. Act § 1861(b), (m); 42 C.F.R. § 409.49(c).]

In addition to the general exclusions applicable to both parts of the Medicare program, which are discussed in Chapter 6, the following are excluded from home health services:

(1) domestic or housekeeping services unrelated to patient care;

(2) transportation services from place of residence to a facility to receive home health services on an outpatient basis (see ¶ 257);

(3) drugs and biologicals, except for osteoporosis drugs (see ¶ 255);

(4) end-stage renal disease (ESRD) services covered under the ESRD program;

(5) prosthetic devices covered under Part B (catheters, ostomy bags, and supplies are not considered prosthetic devices if furnished under a home health plan of care and are not subject to this exclusion);

(6) medical social services provided to members of the beneficiary's family that are not incidental to covered social services being provided to the beneficiary;

(7) respiratory care furnished by a respiratory therapist in a beneficiary's home;

(8) in-home visits by dietitians or nutritionists; and

(9) services that would not be covered as inpatient services.

[42 C.F.R. § 409.49; *Medicare Benefit Policy Manual*, Pub. 100-02, Ch. 7, § 80.]

[¶ 268] "Home Health Agency" Defined—Qualified Home Health Agencies

As a general rule, services furnished by a home health agency (HHA) will not be covered by Medicare unless the HHA is participating in the Medicare program; that is, the HHA has been approved for Medicare participation by the government and has signed a participation agreement (see ¶ 730). [42 C.F.R. § 409.41.]

To participate in Medicare as a "home health agency," an organization must:

(1) be a public agency or private organization or a subdivision of such an agency or organization;

(2) be primarily engaged in providing skilled nursing and other therapeutic services;

(3) have policies established by a group of professional personnel (including at least one physician and one registered nurse) associated with the agency;

(4) maintain clinical records on all patients;

(5) provide for supervision of services by a physician or nurse;

(6) be licensed by the state licensing agency where required;

(7) have in effect an overall plan and budget that meets certain requirements;

(8) meet certain conditions of participation (COPs) and health and safety and financial stability requirements;

(9) provide the Secretary with a surety bond in the form specified by the HHS Secretary (in an amount of at least $50,000), which the Secretary determines is commensurate with the volume of payments made to the HHA; and

(10) meet an any additional requirements that the Secretary finds necessary for the effective and efficient implementation of the program.

[Soc. Sec. Act § 1861(o), as amended by Medicare Access and CHIP Reauthorization Act of 2015 (MACRA) (P.L. 114-10) § 513; *Medicare General Information, Eligibility, and Entitlement Manual*, Pub. 100-01, Ch. 5, § 50.]

For Part A, but not for Part B, the definition of an HHA does not include any agency or organization that is primarily for the care and treatment of mental diseases. [Soc. Sec. Act § 1861(o).]

Arrangements may be made by an HHA with other HHAs to furnish items or services under certain circumstances. Whether the services and items are furnished by the HHA itself or by another HHA under arrangements made by the HHA, both must agree not to charge the patient for covered services or items and must agree to return money incorrectly collected (see ¶ 830). [Pub. 100-01, Ch. 5, § 50.2.]

Conditions of Participation

The requirements for participating HHAs and the additional health and safety requirements prescribed by the HHS Secretary are incorporated into COPs for HHAs. These conditions are included in the regulations governing the Medicare program. [42 C.F.R. Part 484.]

HHAs that are out of compliance with COPs may correct their performance and achieve prompt compliance through new methods, such as directed plans of correction or directed in-service training. CMS may impose sanctions on and terminate HHAs that are out of compliance with COPs. [42 C.F.R. §§488.810, 488.850, 488.855.]

Hospice Care

[¶ 270] Hospice Care: Coverage in General

Hospice care is an interdisciplinary approach to caring for terminally ill individuals by treating pain and providing comfort rather than seeking a cure for the terminal disease. The patient and family (or other caregivers in the home) are considered a unit receiving care. Pain control, counseling—including bereavement counseling for caregivers and family—and social services are required aspects of hospice care. A hospice program must be a public agency or private organization that meets Medicare conditions of participation in order to qualify as a Medicare provider. [Soc. Sec. Act § 1861(dd).]

A Medicare beneficiary becomes eligible for hospice care upon a physician's certification that he or she has a terminal illness, i.e., is expected to live six months or less if the illness proceeds at its normal course. The prognosis is based on the physician's clinical judgment regarding the normal course of the individual's illness. [Soc. Sec. Act §§1814(a)(7)(A), 1861(dd)(3)(A); 42 C.F.R. §418.20.]

Covered Services

"Hospice care" includes the following services and supplies:

(1) nursing care provided by or under the supervision of a registered professional nurse;

(2) physical or occupational therapy or speech-language pathology services;

(3) medical social services under the direction of a physician;

(4) homemaker services and the services of a home health aide (also known as a hospice aide) who has successfully completed an approved training program;

(5) medical supplies (including drugs and biologicals) and the use of medical appliances;

(6) physicians' and nurse practitioners' services;

(7) short-term inpatient care, including both procedures necessary for pain control and symptom management and occasional respite care for periods up to five days;

(8) counseling (including dietary counseling) with respect to care of the terminally ill beneficiary and the family's and caregivers' adjustment to the beneficiary's death; and

(9) any other item or service that is specified in the plan of care and otherwise covered by Medicare.

[Soc. Sec. Act § 1861(dd)(1), (3)(B); 42 C.F.R. §418.202.]

Nursing, home health aide, and homemaker services may be provided on a 24-hour, continuous basis during periods of crisis as necessary to maintain the terminally ill individual at home. Respite care is short-term inpatient care provided to the individual only when necessary to relieve family members or other persons caring for the individual. Bereavement counseling is a required hospice service but is not separately reimbursable. [Soc. Sec. Act

§ 1861(dd)(1); 42 C.F.R. § 418.204; *Medicare Benefit Policy Manual*, Pub. 100-02, Ch. 9, § 40.2.3.]

Custodial care and personal comfort items, while generally excluded by Medicare, are covered when the beneficiary is under the care of a hospice. [Soc. Sec. Act § 1862(a)(1)(C); 42 C.F.R. § 411.15(g), (j).] Palliative care is defined as patient- and family-centered care that optimizes quality of life by anticipating, preventing, and treating suffering. Palliative care addresses physical, intellectual, emotional, social, and spiritual needs and facilitates patient autonomy, access to information, and choice. [42 C.F.R. § 418.3.]

A beneficiary who is denied coverage for hospice care because services received were determined not to be reasonable or necessary may nevertheless be entitled to Medicare coverage under the waiver-of-liability rules discussed at ¶ 915. Personal comfort items and custodial care are described at ¶ 616 and ¶ 625.

[¶ 272] Benefit Periods

A Medicare beneficiary may elect to receive hospice care for up to two periods of 90 days each and an unlimited number of subsequent periods up to 60 days each. [Soc. Sec. Act § 1812(a)(4); 42 C.F.R. § 418.21(a).] A beneficiary electing to receive hospice care must choose to receive it through a particular hospice program. [Soc. Sec. Act § 1812(d)(1); 42 C.F.R. § 418.24(a)(1).]

Election of Hospice Benefits

In order to receive hospice care, a Medicare beneficiary (or, in the event of physical or mental incapacitation, his or her representative) must file an election statement with a particular hospice. Election statements must include all of the following:

(1) Identification of the particular hospice and of the attending physician that will provide care to the individual. The individual or representative must acknowledge that the identified attending physician was his or her choice.

(2) The individual's or representative's acknowledgment that he or she has been given a full understanding of the palliative rather than curative nature of hospice care, as it relates to the individual's terminal illness.

(3) Acknowledgment that certain Medicare services (see below) are waived by the election.

(4) The effective date of the election, which may be the first day of hospice care or a later date, but cannot be earlier than the date of the election statement.

(5) The signature of the individual or representative.

[42 C.F.R. § 418.24(b).]

The election to receive hospice care continues through the initial election period and through subsequent election periods without a break in care as long as the individual remains in the care of a hospice, does not revoke the election, and is not discharged from the hospice. [42 C.F.R. § 418.24(c).]

Revocation of election. The Medicare beneficiary or his or her representative may revoke the election of hospice care at any time during an election period. To revoke the election of hospice care, the beneficiary or representative must file a signed statement with the hospice that the election is revoked, as well as the revocation's effective date. Upon revocation, the individual is no longer covered under Medicare for hospice care and resumes Medicare coverage of the benefits waived by election. If he or she remains (or later becomes) eligible for hospice coverage, the individual may file an election statement to receive hospice coverage at any time. [Soc. Sec. Act § 1812(d)(2)(B); 42 C.F.R. §§ 418.24(e), 418.28.]

Attending physician. An individual receiving hospice benefits may change the designated attending physician by filing a signed statement with the hospice stating that he or she is changing his or her attending physician. The statement must identify the new attending physician and include both the effective date of the change and the date signed. The effective date cannot be before the date the statement is signed. The statement must also acknowledge that the change in the attending physician is due to the beneficiary's choice. [42 C.F.R. § 418.24(f).]

Beneficiary Rights During A Hospice Benefit Period

When an individual elects hospice care, he or she waives all rights to Medicare payments for certain services. The individual cannot receive payment for hospice care provided by a different hospice than the one designated by the individual (unless provided under arrangements made by the designated hospice). He or she also waives the right to payment for any Medicare services that are related to the treatment of the individual's terminal condition or a related condition, as well as to services that are equivalent to hospice care, unless the services are provided by the designated hospice, provided by another hospice under arrangements made by the designated hospice, or provided by the individual's attending physician if that physician is not an employee of the designated hospice or receiving compensation from the hospice for those services. [Soc. Sec. Act § 1812(d)(2)(A); 42 C.F.R. § 418.24(d).]

Medicare will pay for any item or service that is specified in the hospice plan of care as reasonable and necessary for the palliation and management of the patient's terminal illness and related conditions and for which Medicare payment would otherwise be made. [Soc. Sec. Act § 1861(dd)(1)(I); 42 C.F.R. § 418.202(i).]

A beneficiary also is entitled to change from one hospice program to another hospice program once per period. Such a change is not considered to be a revocation of an election if the individual is otherwise entitled to hospice care benefits within that period. [Soc. Sec. Act § 1812(d)(2)(C); 42 C.F.R. § 418.30.]

Example

Sam Green has elected to receive hospice care for a 90-day period at Hospice A. He now wants to move to Hospice B. During the 90-day period, he may elect to change programs to Hospice B, or Hospice A can make arrangements for services to be provided by Hospice B. If Sam changes to Hospice B, he cannot change to Hospice C within that 90-day period, but Hospice B can make arrangements for Hospice C to provide services for the remainder of the period. At the end of the period, Sam may change to Hospice C for the next period.

[¶ 274] Certification and Care Requirements

The hospice must obtain written certification of the beneficiary's terminal illness for each election period. In addition, the hospice medical director must recommend the patient for admission to the hospice in consultation with, or with input from, the patient's attending physician, if any. The recommendation must be signed by the physician and included in the patient's medical records. [42 C.F.R. §§ 418.22, 418.25.]

Certification and Recertification of Terminal Illness

At the beginning of the initial 90-day hospice benefit period, both the individual's attending physician, if any, and the medical director or physician member of the hospice interdisciplinary group must certify in writing that the individual is terminally ill. At the beginning of each subsequent period, only the hospice physician or the physician member of the hospice interdisciplinary group must recertify that the individual is terminally ill. [Soc. Sec. Act § 1814(a)(7)(A); 42 C.F.R. § 418.22(a)(1), (c).]

The initial certification of terminal illness must be made within two days of admission to the hospice. If the hospice cannot obtain a written certification within two days, it must obtain an oral certification, and the written certification must be obtained before submission of a claim for payment. Subsequent certifications may be made orally, but the written certification must be made before the claim is submitted for payment, and documentation must support the certification. [42 C.F.R. § 418.22(a)(3).]

Face-to-face encounter. If a beneficiary elects to continue to receive hospice care, a hospice physician or nurse practitioner must have a face-to-face encounter with the individual to determine continued eligibility of the individual for hospice care, before the 180th-day recertification and then each subsequent recertification. [Soc. Sec. Act § 1814(a)(7)(D); 42 C.F.R. § 418.22(a)(4).]

Content of certification. Certification of terminal illness must be based on the physician's or medical director's clinical judgment regarding the normal course of the individual's illness. The certification must:

(1) specify that the individual's prognosis is for a life expectancy of six months or less if the terminal illness runs its normal course;

(2) contain clinical information and other documentation that supports the medical prognosis;

(3) include a brief narrative explanation of the clinical findings that supports a life expectancy of six months or less;

(4) include a written attestation by the physician or nurse practitioner who performed the face-to-face encounter; and

(5) be signed and dated by the physicians, and include the benefit period dates to which the certification or recertification applies.

[42 C.F.R. § § 418.22(b), 418.25.]

Although nurse practitioners may serve as the attending physician, they may not certify or recertify the beneficiary's terminal illness or prognosis. [Soc. Sec. Act § 1814(a)(7)(A)(i)(I).]

Mandatory medical review. There is a mandatory medical review of hospice care provided to an individual receiving care for more than 180 days if a certain percentage, determined by the HHS Secretary, of all hospice patients receive care for more than 180 days. [Soc. Sec. Act § 1814(a)(7)(E).]

Written Plan of Care

All hospice care must be provided according to a written plan of care (POC), established by the hospice medical director in conjunction with the hospice's interdisciplinary staff, before hospice care begins. The POC must be reviewed periodically by both the beneficiary's attending physician and the hospice medical director and interdisciplinary staff. [Soc. Sec. Act § 1814(a)(7)(B), (C); 42 C.F.R. § § 418.56, 418.200.]

The hospice must develop an individualized POC reflecting patient and family goals and interventions based on the problems identified in initial, comprehensive, and updated comprehensive assessments. The plan must include all services necessary for the palliation and management of the terminal illness and related conditions, including: (1) interventions to manage pain and symptoms; (2) a detailed statement of the scope and frequency of services necessary to meet the specific patient and family needs; (3) measurable outcomes anticipated from implementing and coordinating the POC; (4) drugs and treatment necessary to meet the needs of the patient; (5) medical supplies and appliances necessary to meet the needs of the patient; and (6) the interdisciplinary group's documentation of the patient's or representative's level of understanding, involvement, and agreement with the POC. [42 C.F.R. § 418.56(c).]

The hospice interdisciplinary group (in collaboration with the individual's attending physician, if any) must review, revise, and document the individualized POC as frequently as the patient's condition requires, but no less frequently than every 15 calendar days. A revised POC must include information from the patient's updated comprehensive assessment and must note the patient's progress toward outcomes and goals specified in the plan. [42 C.F.R. § 418.56(d).]

Coordination of Services

The hospice must develop and maintain a system of communication and integration that: (1) ensures that the interdisciplinary group maintains responsibility for directing, coordinating, and supervising the care and services provided; (2) ensures that the care and services are provided in accordance with the POC; (3) ensures that the care and services provided are based on all assessments of the patient and family needs; (4) provides for and ensures the ongoing sharing of information between all disciplines providing care and services in all settings; and (5) provides for an ongoing sharing of information with other non-hospice health care providers furnishing services unrelated to the terminal illness and related conditions. [42 C.F.R. § 418.56(e).]

[¶ 276] Discharge from Hospice Care

A patient may be discharged from a hospice program in three situations:

(1) the hospice determines that the patient is no longer terminally ill;

(2) the patient moves out of the hospice service area or transfers to another hospice; or

(3) for cause, because the behavior of the patient (or another individual in the patient's home) is disruptive, abusive, or uncooperative to the extent that delivery of care to the patient or the ability of the hospice to operate effectively is seriously impaired.

[42 C.F.R. § 418.26(a).]

Before discharging a patient for any of these reasons, the hospice must obtain a written physician's discharge order from the hospice medical director. If a patient has an attending physician involved in his or her care, this physician should be consulted before discharge and his or her review and decision included in the discharge note. [42 C.F.R. § 418.26(b).]

Before discharging a patient for cause, the hospice must:

(1) advise the patient that discharge is being considered;

(2) ascertain that the patient's proposed discharge is not due to the patient's use of necessary hospice services;

(3) make a serious effort to resolve the problem(s) presented by the patient or family; and

(4) document in the patient's records both the problems and the efforts made to resolve them.

[42 C.F.R. § 418.26(a)(3).]

Discharge planning. Hospices must have a process for discharge planning and must begin planning when the staff begins to consider discharge. The discharge planning process must include planning for any necessary family counseling, patient education, or other services before the patient is discharged because he or she is no longer terminally ill. [42 C.F.R. § 418.26(d).]

Effect of discharge. A patient who has been discharged from hospice care no longer has an election of hospice care in effect. A patient whose condition remains terminal or becomes terminal again may make a new election of hospice care. Until a new election is made, the patient is not eligible for hospice care but is eligible for all of the care that is covered by Medicare. [42 C.F.R. § 418.26(c).]

[¶ 278] Deductibles and Coinsurance

During the period of an election by an individual for hospice care, no copayments or deductibles other than those for drugs, biologicals, and respite care apply with respect to hospice care services furnished to the individual, regardless of the setting in which such services are furnished. [Soc. Sec. Act § 1813(a)(4).]

Drugs and biologicals. An individual is liable for a coinsurance payment for each palliative drug and biological prescription furnished by the hospice except when the individual is an inpatient. The amount of coinsurance for each prescription must approximate 5 percent of the cost of the drug or biological to the hospice, up to $5, in accordance with the hospice's established drug copayment schedule approved by the Medicare contractor. The cost of the drug or biological may not exceed what a prudent buyer would pay in similar circumstances. [Soc. Sec. Act § 1813(a)(4)(A)(i); 42 C.F.R. § 418.400(a).]

Respite care. The amount of coinsurance for each respite care day is 5 percent of the Medicare payment for a respite care day. The amount of the individual's coinsurance liability for respite care during a hospice coinsurance period may not exceed the inpatient hospital deductible applicable for the year that the hospice coinsurance period began (see ¶ 220). The term "hospice coinsurance period" means a period of consecutive days beginning with the first day for which a hospice program election is in effect for the individual and ending after 14 consecutive days on which a hospice election is not in effect for the individual. [Soc. Sec. Act § 1813(a)(4)(A)(ii); 42 C.F.R. § 418.400(b).]

[¶ 280] Hospice Program Requirements

To qualify as a Medicare provider, a hospice program must be a public agency or a private organization that is primarily engaged in providing the care and services described above and that makes these services available as needed, on a 24-hour basis. The hospice program must provide care and services in individuals' homes, on an outpatient basis, and on a short-term inpatient basis. The total number of days of inpatient care in any 12-month period to individuals who have an election in effect may be no more than 20 percent of the days during that period for which hospice care has been elected. [Soc. Sec. Act § 1861(dd)(2)(A).]

Hospices must have an interdisciplinary group of staff that includes at least a physician medical director, a registered nurse, a social worker, and a pastoral or other counselor. All must be hospice employees except the physician, who can be under contract with the hospice, and the pastoral counselor. The functions of the group are to:

- establish and review the plan of care for each patient;
- maintain central records on each patient;

- provide or supervise the provision of hospice care and services;

- govern and set policy for the hospice;

- continue providing service even if the patient is no longer able to pay;

- use volunteers in accordance with standards set by the HHS Secretary;

- maintain records on the use of volunteers and the costs savings and expanded services achieved; and

- ensure that the hospice complies with state licensing laws and state and federal regulations.

[Soc. Sec. Act § 1861(dd)(2)(B)–(G); 42 C.F.R. §§ 418.56, 418.58.]

In addition, a hospice program is required to make reasonable efforts to arrange for volunteer clergy or other members of religious organizations to visit patients who desire such visits and to advise patients of this opportunity. Hospice programs are also required to provide counseling services. [42 C.F.R. § 418.64(d)(3).]

Generally, hospice services must be provided directly by hospice employees and volunteer staff. The nursing, counseling, and medical social service obligations are considered "core services," which must be provided directly by hospice employees, except that the hospice may use contracted physicians. Hospices may contract with other hospices to provide nursing or medical social services in exigent circumstances, such as an unanticipated period of high patient load, staffing shortages due to illness or other events, or temporary travel of a patient outside a hospice program's service area, and to provide highly specialized services that are not frequently required. [42 C.F.R. § 418.64.]

A hospice in non-urban areas may apply for a waiver to contract for nursing services if it: (1) was operating before January 1, 1983; and (2) demonstrates that it has made a good-faith effort to hire a sufficient number of nurses to directly provide nursing care. [Soc. Sec. Act § 1861(dd)(5).]

A hospice that contracts for services remains responsible for providing and supervising those services professionally, administratively, and financially. All authorizations and all services provided by the contractor must be documented as necessary. [42 C.F.R. § 418.310.] If a hospice makes arrangements with another hospice to provide services under exigent circumstances, the hospice that the beneficiary elected is reimbursed. [Soc. Sec. Act § 1861(dd)(5)(D); 42 C.F.R. § 418.302(d)(2).]

A provider that is certified for Medicare participation as a hospital, skilled nursing facility, or home health agency may also be certified as a hospice. If so, the provider must have separate provider agreements and must file separate cost reports. [Soc. Sec. Act § 1861(dd)(4).]

A certified hospice program is surveyed by its state or local survey agency (see ¶ 703) at least once every three years. [Soc. Sec. Act § 1861(dd)(4)(C).]

Chapter 3– MEDICARE PART B—SUPPLEMENTAL MEDICAL INSURANCE

Eligibility and Enrollment

[¶ 300] Eligibility for Part B Benefits

Unlike the inpatient hospital insurance benefits program (Part A of Title XVIII of the Social Security Act), which is largely financed by Federal Insurance Contributions Act (FICA) taxes, the Supplementary Medical Insurance (SMI) Benefits for the Aged and Disabled (Part B) program is financed by monthly premium payments by enrollees and federal contributions to the SMI Trust Fund from the federal government. Medicare Part B covers physician services, medical supplies, and other outpatient services, which are not paid by Medicare Part A. [Soc. Sec. Act § 1844; 42 C.F.R. § 407.2.]

For most individuals who are entitled to Part A benefits, enrollment in Part B occurs automatically, unless they elect to decline enrollment (see ¶ 312).

Enrollment for Part B benefits is open to all persons who are entitled to Part A benefits (see ¶ 200). An individual also may enroll in Part B even if he or she is not entitled to Part A benefits if the individual is: (1) age 65 or over; (2) a resident of the United States; and (3) either (a) a citizen of the United States, or (b) an alien lawfully admitted to the United States for permanent residence who has resided in the United States continuously during the five years immediately preceding the month in which application for enrollment was made. [Soc. Sec. Act § 1836; 42 C.F.R. § 407.10(a).] The term "United States" includes the Commonwealth of Puerto Rico, the Virgin Islands, Guam, American Samoa, and the Northern Mariana Islands. [Soc. Sec. Act § § 210(i), 1861(x).]

For the disabled under age 65 (see ¶ 204), neither Part A nor Part B coverage can begin before the 25th month of the individual's entitlement to disability benefits, except for Amyotrophic Lateral Sclerosis (ALS) patients (see ¶ 204) and individuals exposed to public health hazards (see below). [Soc. Sec. Act § § 226(b) and (h), 1881A.]

The Medicare coverage period for persons diagnosed with end-stage renal disease (ESRD) generally begins in the third month after the month when dialysis begins. Specific coverage rules for ESRD patients are described at ¶ 205.

Exposure to Health Hazards

Individuals diagnosed with a medical condition caused by exposure to a public health hazard to which an emergency declaration applies are deemed immediately eligible for Medicare benefits, regardless of the individual's age. Deemed individuals are eligible to enroll in Medicare Part B beginning with the month in which they are deemed to be eligible. [Soc. Sec. Act § 1881A(a).]

An "environmental exposure affected individual" means an individual who:

(1) is diagnosed with one or more medical conditions such as asbestosis, pleural thickening, or pleural plaques;

(2) has been present for an aggregate total of six months in a geographic area subject to an emergency declaration during a period not less than 10 years prior to such diagnosis and prior to the implementation of all remedial and removal actions; and

(3) has filed an application for benefits.

[Soc. Sec. Act § 1881A(e).]

Suspended Benefits for Aliens Outside of the U.S.

Part B benefits are suspended in the same manner they are suspended under Part A in the case of certain aliens who are or were outside the United States (see ¶ 200). [Soc. Sec. Act § 202(t)(9).]

Conviction for Subversive Activities

An individual convicted of any of the offenses stipulated in section 202(u)(1) of the Social Security Act, relating to subversive activities, cannot enroll in the Part B plan. [Soc. Sec. Act § 202(u); 42 C.F.R. § 407.10(b).]

[¶ 310] Enrollment in Part B

Persons entitled to Medicare benefits under Part A are enrolled automatically and covered for Medicare benefits under Part B, unless they indicate they do not want to be enrolled in the Part B plan (see ¶ 312). [Soc. Sec. Act § 1837(f); 42 C.F.R. § 407.17.]

In the case of individuals who are not enrolled automatically, the eligible individual must file a written request for enrollment, signed by or on behalf of the individual, during the initial enrollment period, a general enrollment period, or a special enrollment period to receive benefits (see ¶ 311). [42 C.F.R. § 407.22.]

To request enrollment, an individual may complete one of the following CMS forms (which may be obtained by mail from CMS or at any local Social Security office): (1) Application for Enrollment in the Supplementary Medical Insurance Program (CMS-4040 or CMS 40-D); (2) Application for Medical Insurance (CMS-40-B or CMS 40-F); or (3) Application for Hospital Insurance Entitlement (CMS-18-F-5). Alternatively, an individual may request enrollment by either answering the Part B enrollment questions on an application for monthly Social Security benefits or signing a simple statement of request. [42 C.F.R. § 407.11.]

Note that the coverage period—the period during which premiums are due and during which an individual is entitled to benefits under Part B—is not the same as the enrollment period (see ¶ 313).

Health Insurance Card

As evidence of eligibility, each beneficiary entitled to Part A or Part B benefits is issued a Health Insurance Card. This card gives the beneficiary's name, claim number, sex, extent of entitlement, and effective date(s) of entitlement—the beginning dates of the beneficiary's Part A and Part B coverage. [*Medicare General Information, Eligibility and Entitlement Manual*, Pub. 100-01, Ch. 2, § 50.]

Beneficiaries may order a replacement for a lost or damaged Medicare card by visiting the Medicare Card Replacement section of the Social Security Administration's (SSA) website at https://faq.ssa.gov/link/portal/34011/34019/Article/3708/How-do-I-get-a-re-placement-Medicare-card. The new card will be mailed within 30 days to the address the SSA has on record. An individual needing immediate proof of Medicare coverage can call 1-800-772-1213 or contact a local SSA office.

Social Security numbers. The HHS Secretary is required to ensure that Social Security numbers (or any derivative thereof) are not displayed, coded, or embedded on Medicare cards issued to an individual who is entitled to Part A benefits or enrolled under Part B. HHS must also ensure that any other identifier displayed on the card is not identifiable as a Social Security account number or derivative thereof. [Soc. Sec. Act § 205(c)(2)(C)(xiii), as added by Medicare Access and CHIP Reauthorization Act of 2015 (MACRA) (P.L. 114-10) § 501.]

[¶ 311] Enrollment Periods

An individual ordinarily may enroll in the Part B program, either by a positive act or through automatic enrollment (see ¶ 312), only during an "enrollment period." There are three kinds of enrollment periods:

(1) the "initial enrollment period," which is based on the date when an individual first meets the eligibility requirements for enrollment (see ¶ 300);

(2) the "general enrollment period," during which individuals may enroll if they have missed their initial enrollment period; and

(3) certain special enrollment periods (see below).

[Soc. Sec. Act § 1837; 42 C.F.R. § 407.12.]

Initial enrollment period. The "initial enrollment period" is seven months long. It begins three months before the month in which an individual first meets the eligibility requirements (see ¶ 300) and ends three months after the first month of eligibility. For example, an individual first meeting the eligibility requirements in July 2016 would have a seven-month enrollment period beginning April 1, 2016, and ending October 31, 2016. An individual age 65 qualifying solely on the basis of hospital insurance entitlement is deemed to meet the eligibility requirements on the first day on which he or she becomes entitled to hospital insurance benefits. [Soc. Sec. Act § 1837(d); 42 C.F.R. § 407.14(a).]

The Social Security Administration (SSA) or CMS will establish a deemed initial enrollment period for an individual who fails to enroll during the initial enrollment period because of a belief, based on erroneous documentary evidence, that he or she had not yet attained age 65. The period will be established as though the individual had attained age 65 on the date indicated by the incorrect information. [Soc. Sec. Act § 1837(d); 42 C.F.R. § 407.14(b).]

In most cases, individuals who do not enroll in the supplementary medical insurance program within a year of the close of their initial enrollment period will be required to pay a permanently increased premium. Individuals who drop out of the program and re-enroll later also will have to pay an increased premium in most cases. [Soc. Sec. Act § 1839(b).] Increased premiums are discussed at ¶ 320.

General enrollment period. The law also provides a "general enrollment period" for those who failed to enroll in their initial enrollment period, or for those who terminated their enrollment but want to re-enroll. The "general enrollment period" is from January 1 through March 31 of each year. [Soc. Sec. Act § 1837(e); 42 C.F.R. § 407.15(a).]

An individual who fails to enroll during the initial enrollment period, or whose enrollment has been terminated, may enroll thereafter only during a general enrollment period or, if he or she meets the specified conditions, during a special enrollment period. There is no limit on how many times an individual can unenroll and re-enroll. [42 C.F.R. §§ 407.12(a)(2), 407.30(b).]

Example • • • _____

Roger Green became a Social Security beneficiary when he reached age 65 in May 2015. His initial enrollment period was February 1, 2015, through August 31, 2015. Because he failed to enroll during this period, his next chance to enroll will be during the next general enrollment period, January 1, 2016, through March 31, 2016. Assuming that he also fails to enroll in 2016, he may now enroll during any subsequent general enrollment period (January 1 to March 31 of each year), but he will be required to pay an increased premium due to his late enrollment (see ¶ 320).

Special Enrollment Periods

Individuals who fail to enroll during their initial enrollment period or whose enrollment has been terminated may enroll or reenroll during a special enrollment period if they meet the required conditions.

Employer group health plans. Elderly or disabled employees and their spouses who receive primary health coverage under an employer group health plan, as discussed at ¶ 636, are not required to enroll in the same enrollment period applicable to other individuals. They may wish to delay enrollment because Part B benefits may duplicate the employer plan's benefits. A special enrollment period applicable to these individuals is available for eight full months after they terminate participation in the employer plan (or six months in the case of disabled individuals whose group plan is involuntarily terminated). [Soc. Sec. Act § 1837(i); 42 C.F.R. § 407.20(b).]

The coverage period for an individual enrolling during this type of special enrollment period begins on the first day of the month of enrollment, if the individual enrolls in the first month of the special enrollment period, or the first day of the month following the month in which the individual enrolls, if the enrollment occurs in a month after the first month of the special enrollment period. [Soc. Sec. Act § 1838(e).]

Volunteers. Beneficiaries who volunteer outside of the United States for at least 12 months through a program sponsored by a tax-exempt organization also may enroll during a special enrollment period, provided they can demonstrate health coverage while serving in the program. This also includes individuals who terminated enrollment while in a volunteer program. The special enrollment period is the six-month period beginning on the first day of the month that includes the date that the individual no longer satisfies these requirements. [Soc. Sec. Act § 1837(k); 42 C.F.R. § 407.21.] Coverage for an individual enrolling during this type of special enrollment period begins on the first day of the month following the month in which he or she enrolls. [Soc. Sec. Act § 1838(f); 42 C.F.R. § 407.21(c).]

TRICARE beneficiaries. TRICARE is a managed health care program for active duty and retired members of the uniformed services and their families and survivors. Section 3110(a) of the Patient Protection and Affordable Care Act (ACA) (P.L. 111-148) established a special Part B enrollment period for military retirees, their spouses (including widows/widowers), and their dependent children, who are otherwise eligible for TRICARE and entitled to Medicare Part A based on disability or end-stage renal disease (ESRD), but who have declined Part B by not enrolling during their initial enrollment period for Medicare. These individuals may elect to enroll in Medicare Part B during the 12-month period beginning on the day after the last day of the initial enrollment period of the individual or, if later, the 12-month period beginning with the month the individual is notified of deemed enrollment in Medicare Part A. This special enrollment period may be used only once during an individual's lifetime. [Soc. Sec. Act § 1837(l).]

[¶ 312] Automatic Enrollment

As individuals become entitled to Medicare Part A, they also become entitled to Part B. They are automatically enrolled in Part B by the Social Security Administration, unless they elect to decline coverage. [42 C.F.R. § 407.17.]

To be automatically enrolled in Part B, the enrollee must reside in the United States, excluding Puerto Rico. [Soc. Sec. Act § 1837(f).] Persons eligible for automatic enrollment are, to the extent possible, fully informed of the automatic enrollment provisions and given at least two months to decline coverage. Those who do not decline coverage before it is scheduled to begin are deemed to have enrolled automatically. [42 C.F.R. § 407.17.]

An individual who:

(1) is receiving Social Security retirement or disability benefits or otherwise is entitled to Medicare benefits on the first day of the initial enrollment period (see ¶ 311); or

(2) becomes entitled to Social Security retirement benefits during any one of the first three months of the initial enrollment period

is *deemed* to have enrolled in the third month of the initial enrollment period, and coverage begins with the first day of the following month. [Soc. Sec. Act § 1837(f), (g).]

An individual who first becomes entitled to Social Security retirement or survivors benefits during the last four months of the seven-month initial enrollment period will be deemed to have enrolled automatically in the month in which he or she files the application establishing entitlement to Medicare. A person who defers establishing entitlement to Medicare until after the end of the initial enrollment period will be deemed to have enrolled in Part B on the first day of the general enrollment period in effect at the time, or immediately following the time, at which the individual establishes entitlement to Part A. [Soc. Sec. Act § 1837(g)(2)(B), (g)(3).]

Disability beneficiaries. In the case of disability beneficiaries, the initial enrollment period cannot be determined on the basis of attainment of age 65. The law provides that the initial enrollment period for an individual eligible for Part B by reason of entitlement to disability benefits for a period of 24 months will begin on the first day of the third month before the 25th month of entitlement to disability benefits. Enrollment periods will recur with each continuous period of eligibility and upon attainment of age 65. [Soc. Sec. Act § 1837(g)(1).]

Examples • • • _____

(1) Bill Miller, a Social Security retirement beneficiary who elected to receive Social Security benefits at age 62, reached age 65 and became automatically entitled to Medicare Part A in May 2016. His initial enrollment period under Part B (see ¶ 311) began February 1, 2016, and extends through August 31, 2016. Bill automatically is deemed to have enrolled in the Part B program in the third month (April) of his enrollment period, and coverage begins May 1, 2016.

(2) Jennifer Green became age 65 and potentially entitled to Social Security benefits in August 2015. She did not file an application for Social Security benefits, however, until January 2016. Because her application for Medicare benefits, which was made automatically when she filed for Social Security benefits (see ¶ 200), did not occur until after the end of her first enrollment period (November 30, 2015, see ¶ 311), her enrollment in Part B is deemed to have occurred on January 1, 2016, the first day of the general enrollment period. Her coverage period begins on July 1, 2016 (see ¶ 313).

_____

[¶ 313] Coverage Period

The "coverage period" of an individual enrolled in the Part B program is the period during which the individual is entitled to Part B benefits. Except in the case of an individual who is enrolled automatically (see ¶ 312), the earliest possible coverage can be obtained if an individual enrolls during the three months of the initial enrollment period that are *before* the month in which the individual reaches age 65. [Soc. Sec. Act § 1838(a).]

An individual's coverage period begins on whichever of the following dates is the *latest*:

(1) For an individual who enrolls in the initial enrollment period: (a) if the individual enrolls during the first three months, coverage begins with the first month of eligibility; (b) if the individual enrolls during the fourth month, coverage begins with the following month; (c) if the individual enrolls during the fifth month, coverage begins with the second month after the month of enrollment; and (d) if the individual enrolls in either the sixth or seventh month, coverage begins with the third month after the month of enrollment;

(2) For an individual who enrolls in a general enrollment period, coverage becomes effective the July 1 following the month of enrollment;

(3) For an individual deemed to have enrolled automatically in the first three months of the enrollment period (see ¶ 312), Part B coverage begins on the first day of the month in which the individual meets the eligibility requirements (see ¶ 300). If an individual is automatically enrolled but is deemed to have enrolled after the first three months of his enrollment period, then his or her coverage period will begin as described in (1) and (2), above.

[Soc. Sec. Act § 1838(a); 42 C.F.R. § § 407.18, 407.25.]

Example • • • _____

An individual first meets the eligibility requirements for enrollment in April. Therefore, the initial enrollment period runs from January through July of that year. Depending upon the month of enrollment, the coverage period will begin as follows:

Enrolls in—	*Coverage period begins on—*
Initial enrollment period:	
January	April 1 (month eligibility requirements first met)
February	April 1
March	April 1
April	May 1 (month following month of enrollment)
May	July 1 (second month after month of enrollment)
June	September 1 (third month after month of enrollment)
July	October 1 (third month after month of enrollment)

The beginning of coverage for end-stage renal disease (ESRD) beneficiaries is described at ¶ 205. For details on the coverage period for elderly and disabled employees and their spouses who receive primary health coverage under an employer group health plan, see ¶ 311.

Termination or Cancellation of Coverage

An individual's coverage period continues until enrollment is terminated or the individual's death. An individual's enrollment may be terminated: (1) by the filing of notice that the individual no longer wishes to participate in the program; or (2) for nonpayment of premiums. If an enrollment is terminated by the filing of a notice, the termination will take effect at the close of the month following the month in which the notice is filed. A termination for nonpayment of premiums will take effect with the end of the grace period (see ¶ 320) during which overdue premiums may be paid and coverage continued. [Soc. Sec. Act § 1838(b); 42 C.F.R. § § 407.27, 408.8.]

Automatically enrolled beneficiaries. A termination request filed by an individual deemed to have enrolled automatically (see ¶ 312) before the month in which Part B

¶313

coverage becomes effective will cancel the coverage. A termination request filed by an automatically enrolled individual on or after the first day coverage will cancel the coverage as of the close of the month following the month in which the notice is filed. [Soc. Sec. Act § 1838(b).]

Disability beneficiaries. In the case of an individual entitled to Medicare on the basis of 24 or more months of disability, rather than on the basis of having reached age 65, coverage and enrollment under Part B ends with the close of the last month for which the individual is entitled to hospital insurance benefits. [Soc. Sec. Act § 1838(c).]

Reenrollment. An individual whose enrollment has terminated may reenroll only during a general enrollment period or a special enrollment period, if the requirements are met (see ¶ 311). [Soc. Sec. Act § 1837.]

[¶ 320] Premiums

The following table shows the standard monthly premium rates in effect under the Part B program during the past several years:

Year	Premium	Year	Premium
2016	121.80	2014	104.90
2015	104.90	2013	104.90

Part B premiums are set by actuaries to cover 50 percent of the monthly actuarial rate. [Soc. Sec. Act § 1839(a)(3); 42 C.F.R. § 408.20.] The federal government is required by statute to supplement the remainder of Part B costs out of general revenues. [Soc. Sec. Act § 1844(a).]

Income-related monthly adjustment. Beneficiaries with modified adjusted gross incomes (MAGI) above a specified threshold must pay a higher percentage of the cost of Medicare Part B medical coverage than those with MAGIs below the threshold. This beneficiary premium adjustment is called an income-related monthly adjustment amount (IRMAA). Premiums are based on MAGI for the second year before the year for which the premium is being determined; accordingly, 2016 premiums are based on 2014 MAGI. [Soc. Sec. Act § 1839(i); 42 C.F.R. § 408.28.]

For 2016, beneficiaries who filed an individual tax return with income—

- less than or equal to $85,000, there is no IRMAA and the monthly premium is $121.80;

- greater than $85,000 and less than or equal to $107,000, the monthly premium is $170.50;

- greater than $107,000 and less than or equal to $160,000, the monthly premium is $243.60;

- greater than $160,000 and less than or equal to $214,000, the monthly premium is $316.70;

- greater than $214,000, the monthly premium is $398.80.

For beneficiaries who file a joint tax return with income—

- less than or equal to $170,000, there is no IRMAA and the monthly premium is $121.80 per beneficiary;

- greater than $170,000 and less than or equal to $214,000, the monthly premium is $170.50 per beneficiary;

- greater than $214,000 and less than or equal to $320,000, the monthly premium is $243.60 per beneficiary;

- greater than $320,000 and less than or equal to $428,000, the monthly premium is $316.70 per beneficiary;

- greater than $428,000, the monthly premium is $398.80 per beneficiary.

Other rates apply to beneficiaries who are married and lived with their spouse at any time during the taxable year but file a separate tax return. [*Notice*, 80 FR 70811, Nov. 16, 2015.]

Income thresholds used in determining Part B premiums are frozen at 2010 amounts from January 1, 2011, through December 31, 2017. [Soc. Sec. Act § 1839(i)(3)(C), (i)(6).]

Beneficiaries "held harmless." Most people with Medicare Part B will be "held harmless" from any increase in premiums in 2016 and will pay the same monthly premium as 2015, which is $104.90. This provision protects individuals from an increase that would result in a reduction in monthly Social Security benefits when the Social Security cost-of-living increase is insufficient to cover the amount of the premium increase. [Soc. Sec. Act 1839(f); *Notice*, 80 FR 70811, Nov. 16, 2015.]

Increased Premium for Late Enrollment

If an individual who enrolls after the "initial enrollment period" (see ¶ 311) or re-enrolls after terminating enrollment, the monthly premium otherwise applicable will be increased by 10 percent for each full 12 months (in the same "continuous period of eligibility") in which the individual could have been, but was not, enrolled. For these purposes, the length of the period of delay is computed by totalling:

(1) the months that elapsed between the close of the initial enrollment period and the close of the enrollment period in which enrollment occurred, plus

(2) in the case of an individual who re-enrolls, the months that elapsed between the date of the termination of the previous coverage period and the close of the enrollment period in which reenrollment occurred. Any premium that is not a multiple of 10 cents is rounded to the nearest multiple of 10 cents.

[Soc. Sec. Act § 1839(b)–(c); 42 C.F.R. § § 408.22, 408.27.]

The beginning of a disabled individual's "continuous period of eligibility" serves as the beginning of an initial enrollment period for purposes of determining whether the premium increase applicable to late enrollees should apply. In general, a "continuous period of eligibility" is:

(1) the period beginning with the first day a person is eligible to enroll in Part B (see ¶ 300) and ending with the person's death; or

(2) a period during all of which an individual is entitled to disability benefits and that ended in or before the month preceding the month in which the individual became 65 years of age.

[Soc. Sec. Act § 1839(d).]

Examples• • _____

(1) Paul Jones was eligible to enroll in an initial enrollment period that ended May 31, 2013. He actually enrolled in the general enrollment period January 1, 2015, through March 31, 2015. There were 22 months between the close of his initial enrollment period (May 31, 2013) and the close of the period in which he actually enrolled (March 31, 2015). Because there was only one full 12-month period during which he could have been, but was not, enrolled, his premium was (permanently) increased 10 percent.

(2) Marlene Blum became age 65 in July 2008 and first enrolled in March 2010. She paid premiums increased by 10 percent above the regular rate because there was one 12-month

¶320

period (17 total months) between the end of her initial enrollment period, October 2008 (see ¶ 311), and the end of the general enrollment period, March 2010, in which she actually enrolled. A few years later, she failed to pay the premiums and her coverage was terminated (after the end of her grace period) on June 30, 2013. She enrolled for a second time in January 2014.

Added to her previous 17 months of delinquency is the period of nine months between July 2013 through March 2014 (the end of the general enrollment period in which she reenrolled), for a total of 26 months. Because this amounts to two full 12-month periods, her monthly premium is (permanently) increased 20 percent.

(3) John Foley was late in enrolling by 38 months. Accordingly, his Part B premium was permanently increased by 30 percent. Thus, in 2016, when the standard premium is $121.80 per month, he is required to pay $158.34 per month ($121.80 × 130 percent = $158.34). Monthly premiums are rounded to the nearest multiple of 10 cents, which in this case is $158.30.

Elderly and disabled employees and their spouses who delay enrollment in the Part B program because they elect primary health coverage under an employer group plan, as discussed at ¶ 636, have been accorded a special enrollment period (see ¶ 311). Therefore, the months in which they are enrolled in such a plan are not counted in determining the penalty for delinquent enrollment. Beneficiaries who volunteer outside of the United States for at least 12 months through a program sponsored by a tax-exempt organization also have a special enrollment period and will not incur a delayed enrollment penalty. [Soc. Sec. Act § 1839(b).]

Collection of Premiums

Premiums are payable for the period beginning with the first month of the individual's coverage and ending with the month in which the individual dies or, if earlier, in which the individual's coverage ends. [Soc. Sec. Act § 1840(g); 42 C.F.R. § 408.4.]

Social Security and railroad retirement beneficiaries, and civil service annuitants— except those enrolled by a state as public assistance recipients—have their premiums deducted, when possible, from their monthly benefit, annuity, or pension checks paid in the preceding month. [Soc. Sec. Act § 1840(a)–(d); 42 C.F.R. § 408.40.] In the case of beneficiaries who have premiums deducted from their Social Security checks, if there is a Social Security cost-of-living adjustment that is less than the amount of the increased premium, the premium increase otherwise applicable will be reduced to avoid a reduction in the beneficiaries' Social Security checks. [Soc. Sec. Act § 1839(f); 42 C.F.R. § 408.6(a)(2)(ii).]

The premiums of public assistance recipients enrolled under a state "buy-in" agreement are paid by the state that enrolled them. [Soc. Sec. Act §§ 1840(h), 1843; 42 C.F.R. § 408.6(c).]

Premiums are paid by direct remittance in certain circumstances. Direct payment must be made by individuals who are: (1) not entitled to a monthly cash Social Security benefit, a railroad retirement annuity or pension, or a federal civil service annuity; or (2) entitled to one of these benefits, but for some reason the benefit cannot be paid during the period in question. These individuals are sent premium notices, together with a card and envelope for use in sending payment to the proper servicing center. [42 C.F.R. § 408.60 *et seq.*]

Refund of Excess Premiums

CMS refunds premiums received for any month after the month in which a Part B enrollee dies. Refunds are paid to: (1) the person or persons who paid the premiums; (2) the legal representative of the estate, if the enrollee paid the premiums before death; or (3) the person or persons in the priorities specified in the law, if there is no person meeting the requirements in (1) or (2). [Soc. Sec. Act § 1870(g); 42 C.F.R. § 408.112.]

Failure to Pay Premiums

CMS terminates a beneficiary's enrollment for nonpayment of premiums. However, a grace period extending from the date payment is due through the last day of the third month following the month in which such payment is due applies for beneficiaries who are billed directly. For example, if an enrollee's premium payment became due on March 1 of any given year, the grace period would extend to June 30 of that year. If the beneficiary does not make payment on or before the end of the grace period, coverage and enrollment terminate. [Soc. Sec. Act § 1838(b); 42 C.F.R. § § 408.8(a), (c), 408.100.]

The initial grace period may be extended for up to an additional three months if there is a finding that the enrollee had good cause for not paying the overdue premiums during the initial grace period. Good cause will be found if the enrollee establishes that the failure to pay within the initial grace period was due to conditions over which he or she had no control or reasonably could not have been expected to foresee. [Soc. Sec. Act § 1838(b); 42 C.F.R. § 408.8(d).] For example, good cause may be found if the enrollee was mentally or physically incapable of paying premiums on a timely basis or had some reasonable basis to believe that payment had been made, or if the failure to pay was due to administrative error. [*Medicare General Information, Eligibility, and Entitlement Manual*, Pub. 100-01, Ch. 2, § 40.7.4.]

Reinstatement. Coverage may be reinstated without interruption of benefits if the enrollee: (1) appeals the termination of benefits by the end of the month following the month in which the notice of termination was sent; (2) the enrolles alleges and it is found to be true that the enrollee did not receive timely and adequate notice that the payments were overdue; and (3) within 30 days of a subsequent request for payment, pays all premiums due through the month in which the enrollee appealed the termination. If the evidence establishes that the enrollee acted diligently to pay the premiums and the delay in payment was not the fault of the enrollee or if the enrollee reasonably believed that the premiums were being paid by deduction from benefits or by some other means, coverage may be reinstated. Coverage may not be reinstated if it is found that the enrollee failed to make payment within the grace period due to insufficient income or or the termination was appealed more than one month after the termination notice was sent. [42 C.F.R. § § 408.102, 408.104.]

Benefits

[¶ 330] Part B Benefits: In General

Medicare medical insurance benefits (Part B) supplement the coverage provided by Medicare hospital insurance benefits (Part A). Part A covers inpatient institutional services at hospitals, skilled nursing facilities, hospices, and home health services after hospitalization. Part B covers the services of physicians and other health practitioners as well as a variety of "medical and other health services" not covered under Part A. The kinds of "medical and other health services" included in Part B are described beginning at ¶ 340.

Method of Payment

In general, there are two methods of payment for items or services covered by the Medicare program:

(1) Medicare pays the provider or facility on the patient's behalf for services including hospital and skilled nursing care, home health services, medical and other health services, outpatient physical therapy services, and rural health clinic services, among others. [Soc. Sec. Act § 1832(a)(2); 42 C.F.R. § 410.150.] The provider or facility files the claim for payment, and the patient's obligation is fully satisfied once he or she has paid any required deductible or coinsurance amounts (see ¶ 335). The Medicare payment amount is based on prospective payment rates, reasonable costs, fee schedules, and in some cases, competitive bidding by providers (see ¶ 800 *et seq.*).

(2) In the case of all other Part B services, Medicare may pay the provider or the patient. If assignment is accepted, Medicare pays the supplier or practitioner, and the patient's obligation is fully satisfied once he or she has paid any required deductible or coinsurance amounts (see ¶ 868). If the supplier or practitioner does not accept assignment, Medicare pays the patient, and the patient is responsible for paying the supplier or practitioner.

[Soc. Sec. Act § 1832(a)(1); 42 C.F.R. § 424.53(e).]

Medicare payment and assignment rules are discussed in Chapter 8.

Limitations

Benefits provided under the Part B program have limitations. Financial limitations include an annual deductible and 20 percent coinsurance payments applicable to most services covered under Part B, as well as a deductible for the cost of outpatient blood transfusions (see ¶ 335).

Benefits are limited to named items and services listed as covered by the Medicare program. Coverage is often limited to certain kinds of services or frequencies and must be reasonable and necessary for the diagnosis or symptoms presented by the beneficiary. In addition, a number of items and services are listed as excluded from Medicare coverage. Exclusions are discussed in Chapter 6.

Payment also may not be made under Part B for services furnished to an individual if he or she is entitled to have payment made for those services under Part A. [Soc. Sec. Act § 1833(d).] In general, all services provided to an inpatient of a hospital will be paid for by Part A if they are covered Medicare services, with the exception of certain services that are only covered under Part B, such as physician services, the influenza vaccine, and screening mammography, among others. [*Medicare Benefit Policy Manual*, Pub. 100-02, Ch. 6, § 10.]

[¶ 335] Deductible and Coinsurance

In addition to the monthly premium charged to individuals enrolled in Part B (see ¶ 320), an annual deductible and a 20 percent "coinsurance" or "copayment" normally are required. For 2016, the Part B deductible is $166; for 2014 and 2015, it was $147. The law requires the deductible to be indexed to the growth in Part B expenditures. [Soc. Sec. Act § 1833(b); *Notice*, 80 FR 70811, Nov. 16, 2015; *Notice*, 79 FR 61314, Oct. 10, 2014.]

Application of the Deductible and Coinsurance

The Part B annual deductible applies only to services covered by Medicare. If the deductible is not applied because the service is not covered or because the service is included in the list under "Exceptions" below, the deductible for that year remains unsatisfied. [42 C.F.R. § 410.160.]

The deductible is satisfied by the initial expenses incurred in each calendar year. Even in cases in which an individual is not eligible for the entire calendar year (for example, when coverage begins after the first month of the year), the individual is subject to the full deductible. The date of service generally determines when expenses were incurred, but expenses are allocated to the deductible in the order in which the bills are received by the Medicare administrative contractor administering the Part B program. [*Medicare General Information, Eligibility, and Entitlement Manual*, Pub. 100-01, Ch. 3, § 20.2.]

Medicare patients normally are required to pay 20 percent of the cost of each Medicare covered service, their coinsurance amount. Medicare pays the other 80 percent. For Medicare purposes, the cost of a Medicare service is the "Medicare-approved charge" for that service. The coinsurance percentage applies to the Medicare-approved charge. [Soc. Sec. Act § 1833(a), (b).]

Examples• • • _____

(1) Robert White visited his doctor in January 2016 for his annual routine checkup, which is covered as his annual "wellness visit." No deductible or copayment applies. In February, a dental checkup, which indicated that Mr. White's teeth were in good condition, cost $150. Later in the year, it was discovered that he had high blood pressure. Successive visits to the doctor during the remainder of the year in connection with the treatment for this condition resulted in a total of $600 in Medicare-approved charges for the doctor's services. The $150 for the dental checkup cannot be counted toward Mr. White's Part B deductible because it is not a covered expense. Services in connection with the care and treatment of teeth or structures directly supporting the teeth are generally not covered, with some exceptions such as treatment of an oral infection (see ¶ 634). Of the remaining $600 in covered expenses, $166 satisfies the deductible for the year and 80 percent of the remaining $434 ($347) is paid by Medicare. Mr. White's charges total $402 ($150 (noncovered dental checkup) + $166 deductible + $86 coinsurance).

Note the exception to deductible and copayments for prevention services described below.

(2) Sarah visits her doctor in 2016 and has various clinical diagnostic laboratory tests performed in the doctor's office lab. Because the doctor accepts assignment for these tests and is paid under the fee schedule applicable to these services, no deductible (or coinsurance) is required (see "Exceptions" below) for the lab tests. Later, Sarah visits the doctor on another matter, incurring $250 in Medicare-approved charges for the doctor's services. She then has to pay the $166 deductible and an additional $17 as coinsurance ([$250 – $166] × 20 percent = $17). Medicare pays $67.

(3) Mary needs emergency surgery in 2016. She is taken to a participating hospital in an ambulance. She has no previous medical expenses of any kind for the year, and she has no previous "spell of illness" (see ¶ 210). Her hospital stay lasts 16 days. Her expenses are as follows:

Hospital costs (including room and board, nursing services, drugs, and use of the operating room)	$9,000
Fees for services to her of personal physician, surgeon, and anesthesiologist	$2,500
Emergency ambulance services	$300
Follow-up visits to personal physician following hospital discharge	$300
	$12,100

After payment of the $1,288 inpatient hospital deductible (¶ 220), the remainder of Mary's hospital costs are paid for under Part A (see ¶ 210 *et seq.*). The nonhospital portion of her expenses ($3,100) is covered under Part B, except that Mary is required to pay the $166

Part B deductible, plus 20 percent of the remaining $2934 in expenses, or $587. Mary pays a total of $2,041 ($1,288 + $166 + $587). The rest is paid for by Medicare.

Note that if Mary has Medicare supplement (or "Medigap") insurance (see ¶ 740), some or all of what she is required to pay in the above example will be paid by her Medigap insurance.

Exceptions

Several exceptions apply to the deductible and coinsurance requirements.

Noncovered services. No deductible or coinsurance is required for items or services that are not reasonable and medically necessary. If the provider knew, or should have known, that Medicare considered such services medically unnecessary, but failed to inform the beneficiary before furnishing them, the provider is held liable for their cost. If the beneficiary made payment for such items or services, he or she can be indemnified for them. [Pub. 100-01, Ch. 3, § 20.4.1.]

Clinical diagnostic laboratory tests. Medicare payment for clinical diagnostic laboratory tests (other than tests performed by a hospital or other provider for its inpatients) is made according to fee schedules established by the HHS Secretary (see ¶ 875 for details). In the case of tests provided on an assignment basis (see ¶ 868), Medicare pays for 100 percent of the fee schedule rate, and the deductible and coinsurance are waived. [Soc. Sec. Act § 1833(a)(1)(D), (a)(2)(D), (b)(3), (h)(1).]

In the case of a diagnostic laboratory test that is paid on the basis of a negotiated rate instead of a fee schedule, the amount paid under the negotiated rate is considered the full charge for the test, and the deductible and coinsurance do not apply. Otherwise, the payment is equal to 80 percent of the lesser of:

(1) the amount determined under such fee schedule;

(2) the determined limitation amount for a clinical diagnostic laboratory test performed; or

(3) the amount of charges billed for the tests.

[Soc. Sec. Act §§ 1833(a)(1)(D), (a)(2)(D), (b)(3), (h)(4)(B), (h)(6).]

Note that the Protecting Access to Medicare Act of 2014 (PAMA) (P.L. 113-93) requires CMS to implement a new Medicare payment system for clinical diagnostic laboratory tests based on private payer rates beginning January 1, 2017. [Soc. Sec. Act § 1834A, as added by PAMA § 216.]

Home health services. No deductible or coinsurance generally is applied to home health services. When a home health agency furnishes services that are not included in the definition of "home health services," however, the deductible and coinsurance do apply. Also, the coinsurance applies to supplies, drugs, durable medical equipment, and prosthetics/orthotics furnished by home health agencies. [Soc. Sec. Act § 1833(a)(1), (a)(2)(A), (b)(2); Pub. 100-01, Ch. 3, § 20.4.]

Donation of kidney for transplant surgery. There are no deductible or coinsurance requirements with respect to services furnished to an individual who donates a kidney for transplant surgery. [42 C.F.R. § 410.163.]

Federally qualified health center services. No deductible is required for federally qualified health center services (see ¶ 382). [Soc. Sec. Act § 1833(b)(4); *Medicare Claims Processing Manual*, Pub. 100-04, Ch. 9, § 150.]

Blood Deductibles

Part B requires a deductible for the expenses incurred during any calendar year for the first three pints of whole blood (or equivalent quantities of packed red blood cells) furnished to outpatients. As in the case of the similar deductible for inpatients under Part A, this deductible is reduced to the extent that the blood (or equivalent quantities of packed red blood cells) has been appropriately replaced. [42 C.F.R. § 410.161.] Satisfaction of the deductible through replacement is discussed in greater detail at ¶ 220.

The blood deductible under Part B is not required to the extent it has been satisfied under Part A. [Soc. Sec. Act § § 1813(a)(2), 1833(b).]

"Welcome to Medicare" Exam and Preventive Services

No deductible applies to an initial preventive physical exam (IPPE), also called the "Welcome to Medicare" exam (see ¶ 369), including IPPE services rendered in rural health clinics. Similarly, no deductible is required for screening mammography services, screening pap smears, screening pelvic exams, ultrasound screening for abdominal aortic aneurysm, or colorectal cancer screening tests. [Soc. Sec. Act § 1833(b); 42 C.F.R. § § 410.152(l)(12), 410.160(b)(9).]

Coinsurance amounts are waived for most preventive services, including medical nutrition therapy, IPPEs, and personalized preventive plan services in connection with an annual wellness visit. [Soc. Sec. Act § 1833(a)(1)(B), (W), (X), (Y), (b)(1).]

Pneumococcal and influenza vaccines. Pneumococcal and influenza vaccines and their administration are covered without imposition of deductible or coinsurance requirements. [Soc. Sec. Act § § 1833(a)(1)(B), (b)(1), 1861(s)(10)(A).]

[¶ 340] Medical and Other Health Services

The law divides the kinds of services covered under Part B into various categories, one of which is "medical and other health services" (see ¶ 330). [Soc. Sec. Act § 1832(a).]

"Medical and other health services" includes the following items or services identified at Soc. Sec. Act § 1861(s):

- physicians' services (see ¶ 350);

- services and supplies furnished incident to a physician's professional services, of kinds that commonly are furnished in physicians' offices and that commonly either are rendered without charge or are included in the physician's bills (see ¶ 351);

- outpatient hospital services furnished incident to physicians' services (see ¶ 352) and partial hospitalization (mental health) services incident to such services (see ¶ 387);

- outpatient diagnostic services furnished by a hospital (see ¶ 352);

- outpatient physical and occupational therapy and speech-language pathology services (see ¶ 381);

- rural health clinic and federally qualified health center services (see ¶ 382);

- home dialysis supplies and equipment, self-care home dialysis support services, institutional dialysis services and supplies, renal dialysis services, and kidney disease education services (see ¶ 845);

- services of nonphysician health care practitioners, including physician assistants, nurse practitioners and clinical nurse specialists, certified registered nurse anesthetists (CRNAs) and anesthesia assistants, nurse-midwives, clinical psychologists, and clinical social workers (see ¶ 351 and ¶ 366);

- diagnostic x-ray tests, laboratory tests, and other diagnostic tests (see ¶ 353);

- x-ray, radium, and radioactive isotope therapy, including materials and services of technicians (see ¶ 354);

- surgical dressings, splints, casts, and other devices used for reduction of fractures and dislocations (see ¶ 359);

- durable medical equipment (see ¶ 356);

- prosthetic devices (other than dental) that replace all or part of an internal body organ (including colostomy bags and supplies directly related to colostomy care), and replacement of such devices (see ¶ 357);

- leg, arm, back, and neck braces, and artificial legs, arms, and eyes (including required adjustments, repairs, and replacements) (see ¶ 357);

- certain drugs and biologicals, including pneumococcal pneumonia, influenza, and hepatitis B vaccines, antigens, blood clotting factors for hemophilia patients, immunosuppressant therapy drugs furnished to an individual who receives an organ transplant, erythropoietin (EPO) for dialysis patients, oral anti-cancer drugs, anti-emetic drugs used in conjunction with chemotherapy treatments, and intravenous immune globulin administered in the home for the treatment of primary immune deficiency diseases (see ¶ 362);

- ambulance services, if the use of other methods of transportation is contraindicated by the individual's condition (see ¶ 355);

- certain preventive and screening services (if specifically exempted from the exclusion for routine checkups), including an initial preventive physical exam (IPPE), personalized prevention plan services, cardiovascular screening blood tests, pap smears, pelvic exams, mammograms, bone mass measurement tests, and screening tests and services for diabetes, colorectal cancer, prostate cancer, and glaucoma, (see ¶ 369);

- diabetes outpatient self-management training services or medical nutrition therapy services for beneficiaries who have not received diabetes self-management training (see ¶ 369);

- therapeutic shoes for individuals with severe diabetic conditions (see ¶ 370 and ¶ 619);

- ultrasound screening for abdominal aortic aneurysm (see ¶ 369); and

- items and services furnished under a cardiac or pulmonary rehabilitation program, or an intensive cardiac rehabilitation program.

All "medical and other health services" provided to an inpatient of a qualified hospital (except for the services of physicians and other practitioners and pneumococcal and hepatitis B vaccine) are paid for by Part A if Part A coverage is available. Payment may not be made under Part B for services furnished to an inpatient if the inpatient is entitled to have payment made for services under Part A. [*Medicare Benefit Policy Manual*, Pub. 100-02, Ch. 15, § 10.]

[¶ 350] Physicians' Services

Part B covers reasonable and medically necessary physicians' services. [Soc. Sec. Act § § 1832(a)(2)(B), 1861(s)(1).] Physicians' services are the professional services performed by physicians for a patient, including diagnosis, therapy, surgery, consultation, and care plan oversight. A service may be considered to be a physician's service when the physician either examines the patient in person or is able to visualize (e.g., by means of x-rays, electrocardiogram and electroencephalogram tapes, and tissue samples) some aspect of the patient's condition without the interposition of a third person's judgment. [42 C.F.R. § 410.20(a), (b); *Medicare Benefit Policy Manual*, Pub. 100-02, Ch. 15, § 30.]

Services by means of a telephone call between a physician and a beneficiary or between a physician and a member of a beneficiary's family are covered under Part B; however, because the physician work resulting from telephone calls is considered to be an integral part of the prework and postwork of other physician services, the fee schedule amount for these services includes payment for the telephone calls. [Pub. 100-02, Ch. 15, § 30B.]

"Concurrent care" refers to services more extensive than consultative services and rendered by more than one physician during a period of time. The reasonable and necessary services of each physician rendering concurrent care may be covered when each physician is required to play an active role in the patient's treatment, for example, because of the existence of more than one medical condition requiring diverse specialized medical services. [Pub. 100-02, Ch. 15, § 30.]

Part B covers patient-initiated "second opinions" related to the medical need for surgery or for major nonsurgical diagnostic and therapeutic procedures. [Pub. 100-02, Ch. 15, § 30D.]

Physicians' services furnished to a patient are ordinarily paid by Medicare according to the physician fee schedule discussed at ¶ 855.

"Physician" Defined

The term "physician" means a licensed doctor of medicine, osteopathy (including an osteopathic practitioner), dental surgery or dental medicine, podiatric medicine, chiropractic services, or optometry. [Soc. Sec. Act § 1861(q), (r); 42 C.F.R. § 410.20(b).] Only certain services of dentists, podiatrists, chiropractors, and optometrists, however, are covered. These are discussed below. The term "physician" does not include a Christian Science practitioner or naturopath. [*Medicare General Information, Eligibility, and Entitlement Manual*, Pub. 100-01, Ch. 5, § 70.]

For services to be covered as services of a "physician," the doctor performing them must have "legal authorization"; that is, the doctor must be licensed to practice by the state. Coverage will not extend to services that the practitioner is not legally authorized to perform. For example, if state licensing law limits the scope of practice of osteopaths and osteopathic practitioners to the manipulation of bones and muscles, only these authorized osteopathic services are covered. [Pub. 100-01, Ch. 5, § 70.1.]

Dentists

A dentist qualifies as a physician if he or she is a doctor of dental surgery or dental medicine who is legally authorized to practice dentistry by the state in which he or she performs such functions and who is acting within the scope of his or her license when performing such functions. Such services include any otherwise covered service that may legally and alternatively be performed by doctors of medicine, osteopathy, and dentistry, e.g., dental examinations to detect infections prior to certain surgical procedures, treatment of oral infections, and interpretations of diagnostic x-ray examinations in connection with covered services. [Soc. Sec. Act § 1861(r)(2); Pub. 100-01, Ch. 5, § 70.2.]

Because of the general exclusion of payment for dental services (see ¶ 634), payment for the services of dentists is limited to those procedures that are not primarily provided for the care, treatment, removal, or replacement of teeth or structures directly supporting teeth. The coverage or exclusion of any given dental service is not affected by the professional designation of the physician rendering the services; i.e., an excluded dental service remains excluded, and a covered dental service is covered whether furnished by a dentist or a doctor of medicine or osteopathy. [Pub. 100-01, Ch. 5, § 70.2.]

¶350

A dentist also qualifies as a physician for purposes of (1) providing the physician's certification required for inpatient hospital services connected with a dental procedure when the patient requires hospitalization, and (2) performing outpatient ambulatory surgical procedures that can be safely performed on an ambulatory basis in the dentist's office. [42 C.F.R. § 424.13(d)(2).]

A description of inpatient hospital services connected with dental procedures is at ¶ 218.

Dental care in rural facilities. In an effort to increase access to dental care in rural and other underserved communities, section 5304 of the Patient Protection and Affordable Care Act (ACA) (P.L. 111-148) required HHS to establish a demonstration program to award grants to eligible entities to create training programs to train or employ alternative dental health care providers beginning March 23, 2012, and ending by March 23, 2017. [Public Health Service Act § 340G-1.]

Optometrists

A doctor of optometry is considered a physician for all the covered vision care services he or she is legally authorized to perform in the state in which he or she performs them. To be covered under Medicare, the services must be medically reasonable and necessary for the diagnosis or treatment of illness or injury and must meet all applicable coverage requirements. [Soc. Sec. Act § 1861(r)(4); 42 C.F.R. § 410.22; Pub. 100-01, Ch. 5, § 70.5.]Note, however, that many vision care services are excluded from Medicare coverage (see ¶ 619).

Podiatrists

A doctor of podiatric medicine is included within the definition of "physician," but only with respect to functions he or she is legally authorized to perform by the state in which he or she performs them. [Soc. Sec. Act § 1861(r)(3); 42 C.F.R. § 410.25; Pub. 100-01, Ch. 5, § 70.3.]Certain types of foot treatment or foot care, however, are excluded from Medicare coverage (see ¶ 619), whether performed by a doctor of medicine or a doctor of podiatric medicine.

A doctor of podiatric medicine also is considered a "physician" with respect to satisfying the physician certification and recertification requirements, for establishing and reviewing a home health plan of treatment, and utilization review. A podiatrist, however, is not considered a "physician" for purposes of the physician activities required to qualify an institution or organization as a skilled nursing facility. [Pub. 100-01, Ch. 5, § 70.3.]

Chiropractors

A chiropractor licensed by the state—or, if the state does not license chiropractors, a chiropractor legally authorized to practice in the jurisdiction in which he or she performs services—is included in the definition of physician, but only with respect to the coverage of his or her own professional services, services and supplies "incident" to the services, and treatment by means of manual manipulation of the spine. In addition, a chiropractor's services are covered only if the treatment is to correct a subluxation demonstrated to exist by x-ray. No reimbursement may be made, however, for x-rays or other diagnostic or therapeutic services furnished or ordered by a chiropractor. [Soc. Sec. Act § 1861(r)(5); 42 C.F.R. § 410.21; Pub. 100-01, Ch. 5, § 70.6.]

Provider-Based Physician Services

The services of hospital- and other provider-based physicians (e.g., radiologists, anesthesiologists, and pathologists) include two distinct elements: the professional component and the provider component.

The *professional component* of provider-based physicians' services includes those services directly related to the medical care of the individual patient. Payment for those services is made according to the Medicare physician fee schedule (see ¶ 855) by the Part B Medicare administrative contractor. The *provider component* of provider-based physicians' services includes those services not directly related to the medical care of individual patients (e.g., teaching, administrative, and autopsy services, and other services that benefit the provider's patients as a group). Those services are reimbursed to the provider as provider services under Part A. [Pub. 100-02, Ch. 15, § 30.1.]

Physicians in federal hospitals. Physicians' services performed in hospitals operated by the federal government—military hospitals, Veterans Administration hospitals, and Public Health Service hospitals—are normally reimbursable only when that hospital provides services to the public generally as a community institution. A physician working in the scope of his or her federal employment may be considered as coming within the statutory definition of "physician" even though the physician may not have a license to practice in the state in which he or she is employed. [Pub. 100-01, Ch. 5, § 70.4.]

Interns and residents. The services of interns and residents-in-training provided in the hospital setting as part of an approved training program are normally paid under Part A as hospital services and not under Part B as physicians' services. Services not part of the training program or provided outside the hospital or in the hospital's outpatient department or emergency room are covered under Part B. [42 C.F.R. §§ 415.200–415.208; Pub. 100-01, Ch. 5, § 70.7.]

Teaching physician services. Physicians teaching or supervising in an approved teaching program are normally regarded as providing Part A provider services, reimbursable to the hospital. If the teaching or supervising physician is the patient's attending physician, however, his or her services usually will be covered under Part B as physicians' services. [Pub. 100-02, Ch. 15, § 30.2.]

Payment for the services of provider-based physicians is discussed in greater detail at ¶ 855.

Psychiatrists and Psychologists

Psychiatrists are medical doctors and their services are covered by Medicare to the same extent as other physicians' services. Note, however, that there are special limits on Medicare coverage of psychiatric services (see ¶ 225 and ¶ 387). Psychiatric services also may be covered as incident to physicians' services as an outpatient hospital benefit (see ¶ 352).

Clinical psychologists generally are not considered physicians. Their services can be covered as incident to physicians' services (see ¶ 351), and their diagnostic services can be covered additionally as "other diagnostic tests" see ¶ 353). The services of a "qualified psychologist" are covered as a separate Part B benefit (see ¶ 366).

Care Management Services

Beginning in calendar year 2015, CMS will make a separate payment for non-face-to-face chronic care management services furnished to patients with multiple chronic conditions that are expected to last at least 12 months or until the death of the patient, and that place the patient at significant risk of death, acute exacerbation/decompensation, or functional decline. [Soc. Sec. Act § 1848(b)(8); *Final rule*, 79 FR 67548, Nov. 13, 2014; *Final rule*, 78 FR 74230, Dec. 10, 2013.]

Part B also covers transitional care management services for a patient whose medical and/or psychosocial problems require moderate or high complexity medical decision making during transitions in care from an inpatient hospital setting (including acute hospital, rehabilitation hospital, long-term acute care hospital), partial hospital, observation status in a hospital, or skilled nursing facility/nursing facility, to the patient's community setting (home, domiciliary, rest home, or assisted living). Transitional care management starts on the date of discharge and continues for the next 29 days. [*Final rule*, 77 FR 68892, Nov. 16, 2012.]

[¶ 351] Services and Supplies Furnished Incident to Physicians' Services

Medicare Part B covers services and supplies furnished incident to a physician's professional services, of kinds that are commonly furnished in physicians' offices and are commonly either furnished without charge or are included in the physicians' bills. [Soc. Sec. Act § 1861(s)(2)(A); 42 C.F.R. §§ 410.10(b), 410.26(b).]

"Incident to a physician's professional services" means that the services or supplies are furnished as an integral, although incidental, part of the physician's or nonphysician practitioner's personal professional services in the course of diagnosis or treatment of an injury or illness. To be covered incident to the services of a physician, services and supplies (including drugs and biologicals not usually self-administered by the patient) must be:

(1) furnished in a noninstitutional setting to noninstitutional patients;

(2) integral, although incidental, parts of the physician's professional services;

(3) rendered without charge or included in the physician's bill;

(4) of a type that are commonly furnished in physician's offices or clinics;

(5) furnished by the physician, practitioner with an incident-to benefit, or auxiliary personnel; and

(6) furnished in accordance with applicable state law.

[Soc. Sec. Act § 1861(s)(2)(A); 42 C.F.R. § 410.26(b).]

Auxiliary personnel performing incident-to services must meet state licensing requirements. [42 C.F.R. § 410.26(a)(1).]

This provision does not apply when supplies are clearly of a type a physician would not be expected to have on hand in the office or the services are of a type not considered medically appropriate to provide in the office setting. Supplies usually furnished by the physician in the course of diagnosis and treatment, such as gauze, ointments, bandages (including ace bandages), and oxygen, are covered, but charges for the supplies must be included in the physician's bills. To be covered, supplies must represent an expense to the physician. [*Medicare Benefit Policy Manual*, Pub. 100-02, Ch. 15, § 60.1.]

See ¶ 810 for a discussion of services furnished in a prospective payment system (PPS) hospital to hospital inpatients that are incident to a physician's services.

Incident-to Drugs and Biologicals

To meet all the general requirements for coverage under the incident-to provision, a Food and Drug Administration-approved drug or biological must be:

• be of a form that is not usually self-administered;

• furnished by a physician; and

• administered by the physician, or by auxiliary personnel employed by the physician and under the physician's personal supervision.

[Pub. 100-02, Ch. 15, § 50.3.]

While Medicare Part B does generally not cover drugs that can be self-administered, such as those in pill form or used for self-injection, some self-administered drugs are covered under Part B. Examples of self-administered drugs that are covered include blood-clotting factors, drugs used in immunosuppressive therapy, erythropoietin for dialysis patients, osteoporosis drugs for certain homebound patients, and certain oral cancer drugs. [42 C.F.R. §§ 410.26(c)(1), 410.29(a); Pub. 100-02, Ch. 15, § 50.]

Furthermore, the administration of a drug, regardless of the source, is a service that represents an expense to the physician. Therefore, administration of the drug is payable if the drug would have been covered if the physician purchased it. [Pub. 100-02, Ch. 15, § 60.1.]

Claims for drugs payable administered by a physician to refill an implanted item of durable medical equipment (DME) may only be paid under Part B to the physician as a drug incident to a physician's service and are not payable to a pharmacy/supplier as DME under Soc. Sec. Act § 1861(s)(6). [42 C.F.R. § 410.26(b)(9).]

Drugs and biologicals are also subject to the limitations specified in 42 C.F.R. § 410.29. [42 C.F.R. § 410.26(c)(1).]

Direct Supervision Requirement

To be covered, incident-to services and supplies must generally be furnished under the direct supervision of the physician or other practitioner. The supervising physician/practitioner supervising the auxiliary personnel need not be the same physician/practitioner upon whose professional service the incident-to service is based; however, only the supervising physician (or other practitioner) may bill Medicare for incident-to services. [42 C.F.R. § 410.26(b)(5); *Final rule*, 80 FR 70886, Nov. 16, 2015.]

"Auxiliary personnel" includes any individual who is acting under the supervision of a physician (or other practitioner), regardless of whether the individual is an employee, leased employee, or independent contractor of the physician (or other practitioner) or of the same entity that employs or contracts with the physician (or other practitioner). Auxiliary personnel who have been excluded from Medicare, Medicaid, and all other federally funded health care programs or who have had their enrollment revoked for any reason are prohibited from providing incident-to services. [42 C.F.R. § 410.26(a)(1); *Final rule*, 80 FR 70886, Nov. 16, 2015.]

"Direct supervision" in the office setting means the physician is present in the office suite and immediately available to furnish assistance and direction throughout the performance of the procedure. It does not mean that the physician must be present in the room when the procedure is performed. [42 C.F.R. §§ 410.26(a)(1) and (a)(2), 410.32(b)(3)(ii); Pub. 100-02, Ch. 15, § 60.1.]

If auxiliary personnel perform services outside the office setting, their services are covered as incident to the physician's services only if there is direct supervision by the physician. For example, if a nurse accompanies the physician on house calls and administers an injection, the nurse's services are covered; if the same nurse makes the calls alone and administers the injection, the services are not covered (even when billed by the physician) because the physician is not providing direct personal supervision. [Pub. 100-02, Ch. 15, § 60.1.]

Homebound patients. There are exceptions to the direct supervision requirement for homebound patients when home health services are not readily available. Homebound patients may receive services such as injections, venipuncture, and EKGs furnished by qualified personnel who are not under a physician's direct supervision. (See Pub. 100-02, Ch. 15, § 60.4, for the complete list of such services.)

Transitional care management and chronic care management services. While incident-to services and supplies must, in general, be furnished under the supervision of a physician or other practitioner, effective January 1, 2015, services and supplies furnished incident to transitional care management and chronic care management services can be furnished under general supervision when provided by clinical staff. [42 C.F.R. § 410.26(b)(5).]

Nonphysician Practitioners

Medicare Part B covers services and supplies incident to the services of clinical psychologists (CPs), physicians assistants (PAs), nurse practitioners (NPs), clinical nurse specialists (CNSs), and certified nurse-midwives (CNMs) if the requirements of 42 C.F.R. § 410.26 are met. [Soc. Sec. Act § 1861(gg)(1), (ii); 42 C.F.R. §§ 410.71(a)(2), 410.74(b), 410.75(d), 410.76(d), 410.77(c).] See ¶ 366 for a discussion of coverage of nonphysician practitioners' services.

Further, Part B covers the services of certain nonphysician practitioners, including CNMs, CPs, clinical social workers, PAs, NPs, and CNSs, as services incident to a physician's professional services. For services of a nonphysician practitioner to be covered as incident to the services of a physician, they must meet all of the requirements for coverage, as described in 42 C.F.R. § 410.26 and Pub. 100-02, Ch. 15, § 60. [Pub. 100-02, Ch. 15, § 60.2.]

The amount of separate Medicare payment for the services of nonphysician practitioners is discussed at ¶ 860.

Incident-to Services in Outpatient and Clinic Settings

Services furnished in a prospective payment system hospital to hospital inpatients that are "incident to" a physician's services are included within the hospital's prospective payment rate and are paid under Part A.

All hospital outpatient services that are not diagnostic are services that aid the physician or practitioner in the treatment of the patient. Such therapeutic services include clinic services, emergency room services, and observation services. Coverage of outpatient *therapeutic* services incident to a physician's service furnished on or after January 1, 2010, is described at 42 C.F.R. § 410.27 and Pub. 100-02, Ch. 6, § 20.5.2.

Except in the case of rural health clinics, to which special rules apply (see ¶ 382), the guidelines for coverage of services and supplies incident to a physician's service in a "physician-directed clinic" or group association are generally the same as the general rules described above. A "physician-directed clinic" is one in which (a) a physician (or a number of physicians) is present to perform medical (rather than administrative) services at all times the clinic is open; (b) each patient is under the care of a clinic physician; and (c) the nonphysician services are under medical supervision. [Pub. 100-02, Ch. 15, § 60.3.]

In highly organized clinics, however, "direct personal physician supervision" may be the responsibility of several physicians as opposed to an individual attending physician. The physician ordering a particular service need not be the physician who is supervising the service. Therefore, services performed by therapists and other aides are covered even though they are performed in another department of the clinic. [Pub. 100-02, Ch. 15, § 60.3.]

Supplies provided by the clinic during the course of treatment also are covered. When auxiliary personnel perform services outside the clinic premises, the services are covered as "incident to" the professional services of a physician only if performed under the direct personal supervision of a clinic physician. If the clinic refers a patient for auxiliary services performed by personnel who are not employed by the clinic, such services are not "incident to" a physician's service. [Pub. 100-02, Ch. 15, § 60.3.]

Outpatient hospital services are discussed at ¶ 352. The special rules concerning ambulatory surgical centers are discussed at ¶ 386.

[¶ 352] Outpatient Hospital Services

Hospitals and critical access hospitals (CAHs) provide two distinct types of services to outpatients: (1) *therapeutic* services that aid the physician in the treatment of the patient, and (2) *diagnostic* services such as diagnostic x-rays or diagnostic laboratory services. Both kinds of services furnished by hospitals to outpatients are covered under Part B. The following rules pertaining to the coverage of outpatient hospital services are not applicable to physical therapy, speech-language pathology, occupational therapy, or end-stage renal disease (ESRD) services furnished by hospitals to outpatients. [Soc. Sec. Act § 1861(s)(2)(B) and (C); 42 C.F.R. §§ 410.27, 410.28; *Medicare Benefit Policy Manual*, Pub. 100-02, Ch. 6, § 20.] See ¶ 381 for a description of coverage for therapy services.

"Outpatient services" defined. A "hospital outpatient" is a person who has not been admitted by the hospital as an inpatient, is registered on the hospital records as an outpatient, and receives services (rather than supplies alone) from hospital personnel. If a hospital uses the category "day patient," that is, an individual who receives hospital services during the day and is not expected to be lodged in the hospital at midnight, the individual is classified as an outpatient. An inpatient of a participating hospital may not be considered an outpatient of that or any other hospital. An inpatient of a skilled nursing facility (SNF), however, may be considered an outpatient of a participating hospital. [Pub. 100-02, Ch. 6, § 20.2.]

When a tissue sample, blood sample, or specimen is taken by personnel that are neither employed nor arranged for by the hospital and is sent to the hospital for the performance of tests, the test is not an outpatient hospital service because the patient does not receive services directly from the hospital. Similarly, supplies provided by a hospital supply room for use by physicians in the treatment of private patients are not covered as an outpatient service because the patients receiving the supplies are not outpatients of the hospital. [Pub. 100-02, Ch. 6, § 20.2.]

Outpatient observation services. Outpatient observation services are covered only when provided by the order of a physician or another individual authorized by state licensure law and hospital staff bylaws to admit patients to the hospital or order outpatient tests. In the majority of cases, the decision whether to discharge a patient from the hospital following resolution of the reason for the observation care or admit the patient as an inpatient can be made in less than 48 hours, usually in less than 24 hours. In only rare and exceptional cases do reasonable and necessary outpatient observation services span more than 48 hours. [Pub. 100-02, Ch. 6, § 20.6.]

Beginning August 6, 2016, a hospital or CAH must provide each individual who receives observation services as an outpatient at such hospital or CAH for more than 24 hours an oral and written notification that explains the status of the individual as an outpatient receiving observation services and the implications of such status (such as implications for cost-sharing requirements and subsequent eligibility for coverage for services furnished by a SNF). The notification must occur within 36 hours of the time the individual begins receiving observation services (or, if sooner, upon release), and the written notification must be signed by the beneficiary. [Soc. Sec. Act § 1861(a)(1)(Y), as added by Notice of Observation Treatment and Implication for Care (NOTICE) Act (P.L. 114-42) § 2.]

Outpatient Hospital Therapeutic Services

Medicare Part B pays for therapeutic hospital services and supplies furnished incident to a physician's or nonphysician practitioner's service, which are defined as all services and supplies furnished to hospital outpatients that are not diagnostic services and that aid the physician or nonphysician practitioner in the treatment of the patient, including drugs and biologicals that are not usually self-administered. [Soc. Sec. Act §1861(s)(2)(B); 42 C.F.R. §410.27(a).] These services include clinic services, emergency room services, and observation services. [Pub. 100-02, Ch. 6, §20.5.2.]

To be covered, the services must be furnished (1) by or under arrangements made by the participating hospital or CAH, except in the case of a SNF resident (see 42 C.F.R. §411.15(p)); (2) as an integral although incidental part of a physician's or nonphysician practitioner's services; and (3) in the hospital or CAH or in a department of the hospital or CAH. [42 C.F.R. §410.27(a)(1).]

Physician supervision. Therapeutic hospital services must be furnished under the direct supervision (or other level of supervision as specified by CMS for the particular service) of a physician or a nonphysician practitioner. For services furnished in the hospital or CAH, or in an outpatient department of the hospital or CAH, both on- and off-campus, "direct supervision" means that the physician or nonphysician practitioner must be immediately available to furnish assistance and direction throughout the performance of the procedure (see ¶ 351). It does not mean that the physician or nonphysician practitioner must be present in the room when the procedure is performed. [42 C.F.R. §410.28(a)(1)(iv)(A).]

Pulmonary rehabilitation, cardiac rehabilitation, and intensive cardiac rehabilitation services must be performed under the direct supervision of a doctor of medicine or a doctor of osteopathy. [42 C.F.R. §410.28(a)(1)(iv)(D).]

For nonsurgical extended duration therapeutic services, which are hospital or CAH outpatient therapeutic services that can last a significant period of time, have a substantial monitoring component that is typically performed by auxiliary personnel, have a low risk of requiring the physician's or appropriate nonphysician practitioner's immediate availability after the initiation of the service, and are not primarily surgical in nature, Medicare requires a minimum of direct supervision during the initiation of the service, which may be followed by general supervision at the discretion of the supervising physician or the appropriate nonphysician practitioner. [42 C.F.R. §410.28(a)(1)(iv)(E).]

CMS has delayed enforcement of the direct supervision requirement for CAHs and small and rural hospitals with fewer than 100 beds. Most recently, Congress extended the enforcement delay through calendar year 2015. [P.L. 114-112, amending P.L. 113-198.]

Outpatient Hospital Diagnostic Services

Medicare Part B covers hospital or CAH diagnostic services furnished to outpatients, including drugs and biologicals required in the performance of the services (even if those drugs or biologicals are self-administered), if the services: (1) are furnished by or under arrangements made by a participating hospital or participating CAH, except in the case of a SNF resident as provided in 42 C.F.R. §411.15(p); (2) are ordinarily furnished by, or under arrangements made by, the hospital or CAH to its outpatients for the purpose of diagnostic study; and (3) would be covered as inpatient hospital services if furnished to an inpatient. The services must also be provided under the appropriate level of supervision. [Soc. Sec. Act §1861(s)(2)(C); 42 C.F.R. §410.28(a), (e).]

A service is "diagnostic" if it is an examination or procedure to which the patient is subjected, or that is performed on materials derived from the patient, to obtain information to aid in the assessment of a medical condition or the identification of a disease. Among these examinations and tests are diagnostic laboratory services such as hematology and chemistry, diagnostic x-rays, isotope studies, electrocardiograms (EKGs), pulmonary function studies, thyroid function tests, psychological tests, and other tests given to determine the nature and severity of an ailment or injury. [Pub. 100-02, Ch. 6, § 20.4.1.]

Covered diagnostic services to outpatients include: the services of nurses, psychologists, and technicians; drugs and biologicals necessary for diagnostic study; and the use of supplies and equipment. When a hospital sends hospital personnel and hospital equipment to a patient's home to furnish a diagnostic service, the service is covered as if the patient had received the service in the hospital outpatient department. [Pub. 100-02, Ch. 6, § 20.4.4.]

Under arrangements. When the hospital makes arrangements with another facility for diagnostic services furnished on an outpatient basis, the services may be covered whether furnished in the hospital or in the other facility. Independent laboratory services furnished to an outpatient under an arrangement with the hospital are covered under the diagnostic laboratory tests provision of Part B. Laboratory services also may be furnished to a hospital outpatient under arrangements by the laboratory of another participating hospital or by the laboratory of an emergency hospital or participating SNF that meets the hospital conditions of participation relating to laboratory services. [Pub. 100-02, Ch. 6, § 20.4.5.]

Outpatient Surgery

The rules on coverage of outpatient surgery in hospital outpatient departments, free-standing ambulatory surgical centers, and hospital-affiliated ambulatory surgical centers are described at ¶ 386.

Psychiatric Services

For a discussion of services and programs that a hospital may provide to its outpatients who need psychiatric care, see ¶ 387.

Payment Rules

For a discussion of payment methods for outpatient hospital items and services, see ¶ 820.

[¶ 353] Diagnostic X-Ray, Laboratory, and Other Diagnostic Tests

Diagnostic x-ray, laboratory, and other diagnostic tests are covered under Part B. [Soc. Sec. Act § 1861(s)(3); 42 C.F.R. § 410.10(e).]

Ordering diagnostic tests. In most cases, the services must be furnished by a physician or must be incident to a physician's services. As a general rule, diagnostic tests must be ordered by the physician who is treating the beneficiary—that is, the physician furnishes a consultation or treats the beneficiary for a specific medical problem and uses the test results in the management of the beneficiary's medical problem. Nonphysician practitioners licensed to provide physician services under state law also are subject to the physician ordering requirement. [42 C.F.R. § 410.32(a).]

An order from a physician may be delivered via the following forms of communication: (1) a written document signed by the physician, which is hand-delivered, mailed, or faxed to the testing facility; (2) a telephone call from the physician's office to the testing facility documented in their respective copies of the beneficiary's medical records; or (3) an electronic mail from the physician's office to the testing facility. No signature is required, however, on orders for clinical diagnostic tests paid under the clinical laboratory fee schedule or the physician fee schedule. [*Medicare Benefit Policy Manual*, Pub. 100-02, Ch. 15, § 80.6.1.]

There is an exception to the treating physician requirement: a physician who meets the qualification requirements for an interpreting physician may order a diagnostic mammogram based on the findings of a screening mammogram, even though the physician does not treat the patient. [42 C.F.R. § 410.32(a).]

Physician supervision. Generally, to be considered reasonable and necessary, all diagnostic x-ray and other diagnostic tests covered under Soc. Sec. Act § 1861(s)(3) and payable under the physician fee schedule must be furnished under the appropriate level of supervision by a physician. The degree of physician supervision (general supervision, direct supervision, or personal supervision) required at the time the test is conducted depends on the difficulty and risk of the test. [42 C.F.R. § 410.32(b)(1), (3).]

Exceptions to the basic rule include the following diagnostic tests:

(1) mammography procedures;

(2) audiology tests personally furnished by a qualified audiologist;

(3) psychological testing services when personally furnished by a clinical psychologist or an independently practicing psychologist or furnished under the general supervision of a physician or a clinical psychologist;

(4) tests personally performed by a physical therapist certified by the American Board of Physical Therapy Specialties as a qualified electrophysiologic clinical specialist and permitted to provide the service under state law;

(5) diagnostic tests performed by a nurse practitioner or clinical nurse specialist authorized to perform the tests under applicable state laws;

(6) certain pathology and laboratory procedures; and

(7) diagnostic tests performed by a certified nurse-midwife authorized to perform the tests under applicable state laws.

[42 C.F.R. § 410.32(b)(2).]

Nurse practitioners, clinical nurse specialists, and physician assistants may not function as supervisory physicians under the diagnostic tests benefit. When these practitioners personally perform diagnostic tests, however, they may perform diagnostic tests pursuant to state scope of practice laws and under the applicable state requirements for physician supervision or collaboration. [Pub. 100-02, Ch. 15, § 80.]

Appropriate use criteria. Section 218(b) of the Protecting Access to Medicare Act of 2014 (PAMA) (P.L. 113-93) requires the HHS Secretary to establish a program to promote the use of appropriate use criteria for certain diagnostic imaging services to assist ordering and furnishing professionals in making the most appropriate treatment decision for a specific clinical condition for an individual. Beginning in 2020, outlier ordering professionals must begin applying for prior authorization to order imaging services. [Soc. Sec. Act § 1834(q); 42 C.F.R. § 414.94.]

Portable X-ray Suppliers

Diagnostic x-ray services furnished by a portable x-ray supplier are covered when furnished in a place of residence used as the patient's home or in nonparticipating institutions. Diagnostic x-ray services also are covered under Part B when provided in participating skilled nursing facilities (SNFs) and hospitals under circumstances in which they cannot be covered under Part A. [Soc. Sec. Act § 1861(s)(3); 42 C.F.R. § 410.32(c); Pub. 100-02, Ch. 15, § 80.4.1.]

Portable x-ray services must be ordered by a physician licensed to practice in the state or a nonphysician practitioner (including a nurse practitioner, clinical nurse specialist, physician assistant, certified nurse-midwife, or clinical psychologist) acting within the scope of the law. They must be performed under the general supervision of a physician or nonphysician practitioner by a supplier that meets the conditions of participation described to 42 C.F.R. Part 486, Subpart C. [42 C.F.R. § 410.32(c).]

Coverage for portable x-ray services is limited to: (1) skeletal films involving the extremities, pelvis, vertebral column, and skull; (2) chest and abdominal films that do not involve the use of contrast media; and (3) diagnostic mammograms if the supplier is approved for this service. [42 C.F.R. § 410.32(c)(4); Pub. 100-02, Ch. 15, § 80.4.3.]

A physician or nonphysician practitioner's written, signed order must specify the reason a portable x-ray test is required, the area of the body to be exposed, the number of radiographs to be obtained, the views needed, and a statement concerning the condition of the patient that indicates why portable x-ray services are necessary. For each patient, the supplier must make a record of the date of the portable x-ray examination, the name of the patient, a description of the procedures ordered and performed, the referring physician or nonphysician practitioner, the operator of the portable x-ray equipment who performed the examination, the physician to whom the radiograph was sent, and the date it was sent. [42 C.F.R. § 486.106.]

Diagnostic Laboratory Tests

Part B covers diagnostic laboratory tests when furnished by a qualified hospital, physician's office laboratory, rural health clinic, federally qualified health center, a SNF to its residents, or a laboratory that meets the applicable requirements for laboratories of 42 C.F.R. Part 493. [Soc. Sec. Act § 1861(s)(3); 42 C.F.R. §§ 410.10(e), 410.32(d).]

Clinical laboratory services involve the biological, microbiological, serological, chemical, immunohematological, hematological, biophysical, cytological, pathological, or other examination of materials derived from the human body for the diagnosis, prevention, or treatment of a disease or assessment of a medical condition. These examinations also include procedures to determine, measure, or otherwise describe the presence or absence of various substances or organisms in the body. Facilities only collecting or preparing specimens (or both) or only serving as a mailing service and not performing testing are not considered laboratories. [42 C.F.R. § 493.2; 100-02, Ch. 15, § 80.1.]

Prohibited referrals. The law prohibits Medicare payment to a laboratory that has a financial relationship with the referring physician. Violators are subject to civil money penalties and exclusion from the program. Laboratories are required to include information on referring physicians when submitting claims for payment (see "Stark Law" at ¶ 720). [Soc. Sec. Act §§ 1833(q), 1877.]

Licensing requirements. Diagnostic laboratory services furnished by laboratories in physician offices or independent laboratories are covered under Part B only if the laboratories are licensed pursuant to state or local law or are approved as meeting the requirements for licensing by the state or local agency responsible for licensing laboratories. These laboratories also must meet the standards prescribed in the Medicare regulations (42 C.F.R. Part 493) pursuant to the Clinical Laboratory Improvement Amendments of 1988 (CLIA) (P.L. 100-578).

Payment for clinical diagnostic laboratory tests is discussed at ¶ 875.

Other Diagnostic Tests

"Other diagnostic tests" are covered under Part B if the services are furnished by physicians or nonphysician practitioners operating within the scope of their authority under state law. [Soc. Sec. Act § 1861(s)(3); 42 C.F.R. § 410.10(e).] Some examples of "other diagnostic tests" are psychological and neuropsychological tests and hearing and balance assessment services performed by a qualified audiologist. [Pub. 100-02, Ch. 15, §§80.2, 80.3.]

Psychological tests. Part B covers diagnostic testing services when performed by a qualified psychologist (who is not a clinical psychologist) practicing independently of an institution, agency, or physician's office, if a physician orders such testing. Examples of psychologists whose services are covered under this provision include educational psychologists and counseling psychologists. [Pub. 100-02, Ch. 15, §80.2.]

Hearing evaluations. Diagnostic testing performed by a qualified audiologist (or a nurse practitioner or clinical nurse specialist authorized to perform the tests under applicable state laws) is covered when a physician orders such testing to evaluate the need for, or appropriate type of, treatment of a hearing deficit or related medical problem. Diagnostic services performed only to determine the need for, or the appropriate type of, a hearing aid are not covered. If a physician refers a beneficiary to an audiologist for evaluation of signs or symptoms associated with hearing loss or ear injury, however, the audiologist's diagnostic services are covered even if the only outcome is the prescription of a hearing aid. [Pub. 100-02, Ch. 15, §80.3.]

Audiologists may not bill Medicare for nonaudiology services such as nonauditory evoked potentials or cerumen removal; however, the labor of certain other diagnostic tests or treatment services may qualify to be billed when furnished by audiologists under physician supervision when all the appropriate policies are followed. [Pub. 100-02, Ch. 15, §80.3.]

Screening for HIV infection. CMS has determined that screening for HIV infection, which is recommended with a grade of A by the U.S. Preventive Services Task Force (USPSTF) for certain individuals, is reasonable and necessary for early detection of HIV and is appropriate for individuals entitled to benefits under Part A or enrolled under Part B. CMS, therefore, covers both standard Food and Drug Administration-approved HIV rapid screening tests for:

(1) annual voluntary HIV screening of Medicare beneficiaries at increased risk for HIV infection per USPSTF guidelines; and

(2) a maximum of three voluntary HIV screening of pregnant Medicare beneficiaries: (a) when the diagnosis of pregnancy is known, (b) during the third trimester, and (c) at labor.

[*Medicare National Determinations Manual*, Pub. 100-03, Ch. 1, §210.7.]

Independent Diagnostic Testing Facilities

Diagnostic tests provided by an independent diagnostic testing facility (IDTF) are covered and paid under the physician fee schedule. An IDTF may be a fixed location, a mobile entity, or an individual nonphysician practitioner. An IDTF is independent of a physician's office or hospital, but it may furnish diagnostic procedures in a physician's office. In most cases, an IDTF must have one or more supervising physicians who are responsible for direct and ongoing oversight of the quality of the testing performed, proper operation and calibration of testing equipment, and the qualification of nonphysician personnel who use the equipment. [42 C.F.R. §410.33(a), (b).]

All procedures performed by the IDTF must be ordered in writing by the physician who is treating the beneficiary, although nonphysician practitioners may order tests in accordance with the scope of their licenses. The supervising physician for the IDTF may not order tests to be performed by the IDTF unless the IDTF's supervising physician is the beneficiary's treating physician. [42 C.F.R. §410.33(d).]

With the exception of hospital-based and mobile IDTFs, a fixed-base IDTF may not share a practice location with another Medicare-enrolled individual or organization, lease or sublease its operations or its practice location to another Medicare-enrolled individual or organization, or share diagnostic testing equipment used in the initial diagnostic test with another Medicare-enrolled individual or organization. [42 C.F.R. § 410.33(g)(15).]

[¶ 354] X-Ray, Radium, and Radioactive Isotope Therapy

X-ray, radium, and radioactive isotope therapy are covered under the Part B program. These services also include materials and the services of technicians. [Soc. Sec. Act § 1861(s)(4); 42 C.F.R. § 410.35.]

X-ray, radium, and radioactive isotope therapy furnished in a nonprovider facility require direct personal supervision of a physician. The physician need not be in the same room, but must be in the area and immediately available to provide assistance and direction throughout the time the procedure is being performed. This level of physician involvement does not represent a physician's service and cannot be billed as a Part B service. Radiologists' weekly treatment management services, however, are covered. [*Medicare Benefit Policy Manual*, Pub. 100-02, Ch. 15, § 90.]

A separate charge for the services of a physicist is not recognized unless such services are covered under the "incident to" provision (see Pub. 100-02, Ch. 15, § 60.1) or the services are included as part of a technical component service billed by a freestanding radiation therapy center. The "incident to" provision also may be extended to include all necessary and appropriate services supplied by a radiation physicist assisting a radiologist when the physicist is in the physician's employ and working under his or her direct supervision. [Pub. 100-02, Ch. 15, § 90.]

[¶ 355] Ambulance Services

Medicare Part B covers ambulance services when the use of other methods of transportation is contraindicated by the individual's condition. [Soc. Sec. Act § 1861(s)(7); 42 C.F.R. § 410.10(i).] For Part B to cover ambulance services, the following conditions must be met: (1) the supplier meets the requirements of 42 C.F.R. § 410.41; (2) the services meet the medical necessity and origin and destination requirements of 42 C.F.R. § 410.40; and (2) Medicare Part A payment is not made directly or indirectly for the services. [42 C.F.R. § 410.40(a).] See ¶ 880 for information on payment for ambulance services.

Medical Necessity Requirements

Medicare covers ambulance services only if they are furnished to a beneficiary whose medical condition is such that other means of transportation are contraindicated. To satisfy the medical necessity requirement, the beneficiary's condition must require both the ambulance transportation itself and the level of service provided. [42 C.F.R. § 410.40(d); *Medicare Benefit Policy Manual*, Pub. 100-02, Ch. 10, § 10.2.]

Nonemergency transportation. For nonemergency ambulance transportation, medical necessity is satisfied if either:

(1) the beneficiary is bed-confined and it is documented that other methods of transportation are contraindicated, or

(2) the beneficiary's medical condition, regardless of bed confinement, is such that ambulance transportation is medically required.

For a beneficiary to be considered bed-confined, the beneficiary must be unable to: (1) get up from bed without assistance; (2) ambulate; or (3) sit in a chair or wheelchair. [42 C.F.R. § 410.40(d).]

Medicare covers nonemergency, scheduled, repetitive ambulance services if the ambulance provider or supplier, before furnishing the service, obtains a written order from the beneficiary's attending physician certifying that the medical necessity requirements discussed above are met. The physician's order must be dated no earlier than 60 days before the date the service is furnished. Under certain circumstances, Medicare also covers medically necessary nonemergency ambulance services that are either unscheduled or that are scheduled on a nonrepetitive basis. [42 C.F.R. § 410.40(d)(2).]

Effect of beneficiary death. In general, if the beneficiary dies before being transported in a ground ambulance, no Medicare payment may be made. Medicare does, however, allow payment for an air ambulance service when the ambulance is dispatched to pick up a beneficiary but he or she is pronounced dead before being loaded onto the ambulance. The allowed amount is the appropriate base rate, but no allowance is made for mileage or for rural adjustment. If the beneficiary dies after pickup, before or upon arrival at the receiving facility, the entire ambulance service is covered. [Pub. 100-02, Ch. 10, §§ 10.2.6, 10.4.9.]

Covered Levels of Ambulance Transportation

Ambulance services are divided into different levels of ground (including water) and air ambulance services based on the medically necessary treatment provided during transport. These services include several different levels of service for ground and air transport of patients.

Medicare covers the following levels of ambulance service:

- basic life support (BLS) (emergency and nonemergency);
- advanced life support, level 1 (ALS1) (emergency and nonemergency);
- advanced life support, level 2 (ALS2);
- paramedic ALS intercept (PI);
- specialty care transport (SCT);
- fixed wing air ambulance (FW); and
- rotary wing air ambulance (RW) (helicopter).

[42 C.F.R. § 410.40(b).]

Paramedic ALS intercept services are covered under specific conditions in small towns and rural areas. Intercept services are ALS services furnished by a paramedic in connection with the services of a volunteer BLS ambulance supplier. The coverage applies only if there is a state law prohibiting the volunteer ambulance supplier from billing for any services. [42 C.F.R. § 410.40(c).]

Air ambulance services. There are two categories of air ambulance services: fixed wing (airplane) and rotary wing (helicopter) aircraft. Medicare covers medically appropriate air ambulance transportation only if the beneficiary's medical condition is such that transportation by basic or advanced life support ground ambulance is not appropriate, and either (1) the point of pickup is inaccessible by ground vehicle (e.g., in Hawaii, Alaska, and remote or sparsely populated areas of the continental United States); or (2) great distances or other obstacles are involved in getting the patient to the nearest hospital with appropriate facilities. [42 C.F.R. § 410.40(b)(6), (7); Pub. 100-02, Ch. 10, § 10.4.]

A "rural air ambulance service" means fixed wing and rotary wing air ambulance service in which the point of pick up occurs in a rural area or in a rural census tract of a metropolitan statistical area. To be covered, the service must be reasonable and necessary based on the health condition of the individual being transported at or immediately before the time of transport and must comply with equipment and crew requirements established by the Secretary. [Soc. Sec. Act. § 1834(l)(14).]

Origin and Destination Requirements

Medicare covers the following ambulance transportation:

(1) from any point of origin to the nearest hospital, critical access hospital (CAH), or skilled nursing facility (SNF) that is capable of furnishing the required level and type of care for the beneficiary's illness or injury;

(2) from a hospital, CAH, or SNF to the beneficiary's home;

(3) from a SNF to the nearest supplier of medically necessary services not available at the SNF where the beneficiary is a resident, including the return trip; and

(4) for a beneficiary who is receiving renal dialysis for treatment of end-stage renal disease (ESRD), from the beneficiary's home to the nearest facility that furnishes renal dialysis, including the return trip.

[42 C.F.R. § 410.40(e).]

The reference in 42 C.F.R. § 410.40(e) to the "nearest" facility continues a long-standing policy that the Medicare beneficiary must be taken to the "nearest appropriate facility." This means that the patient must be transported to a Medicare-participating institution that is generally equipped to provide the needed hospital or skilled nursing care for the illness or injury involved. That a more distant institution is better equipped to care for the patient does not warrant a finding that a closer institution does not have "appropriate facilities." Such a finding is warranted, however, if the beneficiary's condition requires a higher level of trauma care or other specialized service available only at the more distant hospital. [Pub. 100-02, Ch. 10, § 10.3.6.]

If two or more facilities that meet the destination requirements can treat the patient appropriately and the locality of each facility encompasses the place where the ambulance transportation of the patient began, then the full mileage to any one of the facilities to which the beneficiary is taken is covered. [Pub. 100-02, Ch. 10, § 10.3.]

Requests by a home health agency. When a home health agency finds it necessary to have a beneficiary transported by ambulance to a hospital or SNF to obtain services not otherwise available, the trip is covered as a Part B service only if all the usual coverage requirements are met for ambulance transportation from wherever the patient is located. Such transportation is not covered as a home health service. [Pub. 100-02, Ch. 10, § 10.3.9.]

Ambulance Services Outside the United States

If services are furnished outside the United States, Medicare Part B covers ambulance transportation to a foreign hospital only as part of the beneficiary's admission for medically necessary inpatient services, as specified in 42 C.F.R. §§ 424.120–424.127. [42 C.F.R. § 410.40(f).] See ¶ 610.

[¶ 356] Durable Medical Equipment

Medicare Part B pays for the rental or purchase of durable medical equipment (DME) if the equipment is used in the patient's home or in an institution that is used as a home. [Soc. Sec. Act § 1861(s)(6); 42 C.F.R. §§ 410.10(h), 410.38(a).]

For a list of DME and the coverage status of each item, see § 280.1 in the *Medicare National Coverage Determinations Manual*, Pub. 100-03.

"Durable Medical Equipment" Defined

DME is equipment that: (1) can withstand repeated use; (2) is primarily and customarily used to serve a medical purpose; (3) generally is not useful to a person in the absence of illness or injury; and (4) is appropriate for use in the home. [*Medicare Benefit Policy Manual*, Pub. 100-02, Ch. 15, § 110.1.]

The term "durable medical equipment" includes iron lungs, oxygen tents, hospital beds, and wheelchairs used in the patient's home (including an institution used as his or her home), whether furnished on a rental basis or purchased. It also includes blood-testing strips and blood glucose monitors for individuals with diabetes regardless of whether the beneficiary has Type I or Type II diabetes or his or her use of insulin. With respect to a seat-lift chair, only the seat-lift mechanism (and not the chair) is considered DME. [Soc. Sec. Act § 1861(n); 42 C.F.R. § 410.38(a).]

Medical supplies of an expendable nature, such as incontinence pads, catheters, bandages, and elastic stockings, are not considered durable (although they may fall into other coverage categories). There are other items that, although durable in nature, may fall into other Medicare coverage categories such as prosthetic devices, braces, or artificial arms, legs, and eyes. Implantable items for which payment may be made under Soc. Sec. Act § 1833(t), such as intraocular lenses, are not considered DME. [Soc. Sec. Act § 1834(a)(13).]

Equipment presumptively nonmedical. Equipment that is used primarily and customarily for a nonmedical purpose may not be considered "medical" equipment for which payment may be made under Medicare, even though the item has some remote medically related use. For example, devices and equipment used for environmental control or to enhance the environmental setting in which the beneficiary is placed are not considered covered DME. [Pub. 100-02, Ch. 15, § 110.1.]

Special exception items. Specified items of equipment may be covered under certain conditions even though they do not meet the definition of DME because they are not used primarily and customarily to serve a medical purpose and/or are generally useful in the absence of illness or injury. These items are covered if it is clearly established that they serve a therapeutic purpose in an individual case. Examples include heat lamps for a medical rather than a soothing or cosmetic purpose, and gel pads and pressure and water mattresses when prescribed for a patient who has bed sores or if there is medical evidence indicating the patient is highly susceptible to ulceration. [Pub. 100-02, Ch. 15, § 110.1.]

Supplies and accessories. Medicare covers supplies such as oxygen that are necessary for the effective use of DME. Such supplies include those drugs and biologicals that must be put directly into the equipment to achieve the therapeutic benefit of the DME or to ensure the proper functioning of the equipment, e.g., tumor chemotherapy agents used with an infusion pump or heparin used with a home dialysis system. The coverage of such drugs or biologicals, however, does not preclude the need for a determination that the drug or biological itself is reasonable and necessary for treatment of the illness or injury or to improve the functioning of a malformed body member. [Pub. 100-02, Ch. 15, § 110.3.]

Definition of Beneficiary's Home

To be covered as DME the item must be used in the patient's home. For purposes of rental or purchase of DME, a patient's home may be his or her own dwelling, an apartment, a relative's home, a home for the aged, or some other type of institution. An institution may not be considered a beneficiary's home, however, if it is a hospital, critical access hospital, or skilled nursing facility. [Pub. 100-02, Ch. 15, § 110.1.]

Medical Necessity for DME

To be covered, the DME must be necessary and reasonable for treatment of an illness or injury, or to improve the functioning of a malformed body member. In most cases the physician's prescription for the equipment and other medical information available to the durable medical equipment Medicare administrative contractor (DME MAC) will be sufficient to establish that the equipment meets this requirement. [Pub. 100-02, Ch. 15, § 110.1.]

Reasonableness. Even though an item of DME may serve a useful medical purpose, the DME MAC also will consider to what extent, if any, it would be reasonable for the Medicare program to pay for the item prescribed. In determining reasonableness, the MAC will consider the following:

(1) Would the expense of the item to the program be clearly disproportionate to the therapeutic benefits that could ordinarily be derived from use of the equipment?

(2) Is the item substantially more costly than a medically appropriate and realistically feasible alternative pattern of care?

(3) Does the item serve essentially the same purpose as equipment already available to the beneficiary?

[Pub. 100-02, Ch. 15, § 110.1.]

Certificate of medical necessity. For items or services billed to a DME MAC, the supplier must receive a signed certificate of medical necessity (CMN) from the treating physician. A supplier must have a signed original, faxed, photocopied, or electronic CMN in its records before it can submit a claim for payment to Medicare. [*Medicare Program Integrity Manual,* Pub. 100-08, Ch. 5, § 5.3.]

Advance Beneficiary Notice. Suppliers must provide Advance Beneficiary Notices (ABNs) that advise beneficiaries, before items or services such as DME are furnished, when Medicare is likely to deny payment for them due to lack of medical necessity. [*Medicare Claims Processing Manual*, Pub. 100-04, Ch. 1, § 60.]

Written Order Requirements for DME

In addition to the CMN requirement and in an effort to to prevent fraud, waste, and abuse, CMS has designated a list of certain covered DME items, referred to as Specified Covered Items, that require a written order. Specified Covered Items include:

- transcutaneous electrical nerve stimulation units, rollabout chairs, oxygen and respiratory equipment, hospital beds and accessories, and traction-cervical;

- any item of DME that appears on the Durable Medical Equipment, Prosthetics, Orthotics, and Supplies Fee Schedule with a price ceiling at or greater than $1,000; and

- any other item of DME that CMS adds to the list of Specified Covered Items through the notice and comment rulemaking process to reduce the risk of fraud, waste, and abuse.

[Soc. Sec. Act § 1834(a)(11)(B)(i); 42 C.F.R. § 410.38(g)(1), (2); *Program Integrity Manual*, Pub. 100-08, Ch. 5, § 5.2.]

Written orders issued for Specified Covered Items must include all of the following:

(1) beneficiary's name,

(2) item of DME ordered,

(3) signature of the prescribing practitioner,

(4) prescribing practitioner's National Provider Identifier, and

(5) the date of the order.

[42 C.F.R. § 410.38(g)(4).]

A supplier must maintain the written order and the supporting documentation provided by the physician, physician assistant, nurse practitioner, or clinical nurse specialist and make them available to CMS upon request for seven years from the date of service. [42 C.F.R. §§ 410.38(g)(5), 424.516(f).]

Face-to-face encounter requirement. For orders issued for Specified Covered Items pursuant to 42 C.F.R. § 410.38(g)(1) and (2), the physician must document and communicate to the DME supplier that the physician or a physician assistant, a nurse practitioner, or a clinical nurse specialist has had a face-to-face encounter with the beneficiary within six months before the written order. During the face-to-face encounter the physician or practitioner must conduct a needs assessment and evaluate and/or treat the beneficiary for the medical condition that supports the need for each covered item of DME ordered. [Soc. Sec. Act § 1834(a)(11)(B)(ii); 42 C.F.R. § 410.38(g)(3).]

Repairs, Maintenance, Replacement, and Delivery

Under certain circumstances, payment may be made for repair, maintenance, and replacement of medically required DME, including equipment that had been in use before the beneficiary enrolled in the Part B program. [Pub. 100-02, Ch. 15, § 110.2.]

Repairs. Repairs to equipment that a beneficiary owns are covered when necessary to make the equipment serviceable. If the expense for repairs exceeds the estimated expense of purchasing or renting another item of equipment for the remaining period of medical need, no payment can be made for the amount of the excess. Because renters of equipment recover from the rental charge the expenses they incur in maintaining the equipment they rent out, separately itemized charges for repair of rented equipment are not covered. [Pub. 100-02, Ch. 15, § 110.2.]

Maintenance. Routine periodic servicing, such as testing, cleaning, regulating, and checking of the beneficiary's equipment, is not covered. The owner is expected to perform such routine maintenance rather than a retailer or some other person who charges the beneficiary. More extensive maintenance, which, based on the manufacturers' recommendations, is to be performed by authorized technicians, is covered as repairs. This might include, for example, breaking down sealed components and performing tests that require specialized testing equipment not available to the beneficiary. Because renters of equipment recover from the rental charge the expenses they incur in maintaining in working order the equipment they rent out, separately itemized charges for maintenance of rented equipment are generally not covered. [Pub. 100-02, Ch. 15, § 110.2.]

Replacement. Equipment that the beneficiary owns or that is a capped rental item may be replaced in cases of loss or irreparable damage, i.e., as a result of a specific accident or a natural disaster. Replacement of equipment due to irreparable wear takes into consideration the reasonable useful lifetime of the equipment. [Pub. 100-02, Ch. 15, § 110.2.]

If equipment or a device is replaced free of charge by the warrantor, no program payment may be made because there was no charge involved. If the warrantor supplied the replaced equipment or device, but some charge or a pro rata payment was imposed, program payment may be made for the partial payment imposed for the device furnished by the warrantor. [Pub. 100-02, Ch. 16, § 40.4.]

Cases suggesting malicious damage, culpable neglect, or wrongful disposition of equipment will be investigated and denied when the MAC determines that it would be unreasonable to make program payment under the circumstances. [Pub. 100-02, Ch. 15, § 110.2.]

Delivery. Payment for delivery of DME whether rented or purchased generally is included in the fee schedule allowance for the item. [Pub. 100-02, Ch. 15, § 110.2.]

Coverage Rules for Power Mobility Devices

Special rules apply to coverage of power mobility devices (PMDs), DME that is in a class of wheelchairs that includes a power wheelchair (a four-wheeled motorized vehicle whose steering is operated by an electronic device or a joystick to control direction and turning) or a power-operated vehicle (a three- or four-wheeled motorized scooter that is operated by a tiller) that a beneficiary uses in the home. [42 C.F.R. § 410.38(c)(1).]

For Medicare Part B to cover PMDs, the physician or treating practitioner must:

(1) conduct a face-to-face examination of the beneficiary to determine the medical necessity for the PMD as part of an appropriate overall treatment plan;

(2) write a prescription, which is received by the supplier within 45 days after the face-to-face examination;

(3) provide supporting documentation, including pertinent parts of the benefici-ary's medical record, that supports the medical necessity for the device, which is received by the supplier within 45 days after the face-to-face examination.

Beneficiaries discharged from a hospital do not need to receive a separate face-to-face examination as long as the physician or treating practitioner who performed the face-to-face examination in the hospital issues a PMD prescription and supporting documentation that is received by the supplier within 45 days after the date of discharge. In addition, the physician or treating practitioner may order accessories for PMDs without conducting a face-to-face examination. [42 C.F.R. § 410.38(c)(2), (3).]

Oxygen Services in the Home

Oxygen and oxygen equipment provided in the home are covered by Medicare under the DME benefit. Oxygen is considered reasonable and necessary only for patients with significant hypoxemia if requirements for medical documentation, laboratory evidence, and health conditions are met. [*Medicare National Coverage Determinations Manual*, Pub. 100-03, Ch. 1, § 240.2.]

A patient may qualify for coverage of a portable oxygen system either by itself or to use in addition to a stationary oxygen system. Portable oxygen is not covered when it is provided only as a backup to a stationary oxygen system. A portable oxygen system is covered for a particular patient if medical documentation indicates that the patient is mobile in the home and would benefit from the use of a portable oxygen system in the home. [Pub. 100-03, Ch. 1, § 240.2.]

A new physician certification is required every 90 days for certain patients receiving home oxygen therapy. The recertification must be made if, at the time the home oxygen therapy is initiated, the patient has an initial arterial blood gas value at or above a partial pressure of 56 or an arterial oxygen saturation at or above 89 percent. The recertification must be based on a follow-up test of these indications within the final 30 days of the 90-day period. [Soc. Sec. Act § 1834(a)(5)(E).]

Payments for maintenance and servicing (for parts and labor not covered by the supplier's or manufacturer's warranty) will be made if the Secretary determines them to be reasonable and necessary. [Soc. Sec. Act § 1834(a)(5)(F)(III).]

After the 36th continuous month during which payment is made for oxygen equipment, the supplier must continue to furnish the equipment during any period of medical need for the remainder of the reasonable useful lifetime of the equipment. [Soc. Sec. Act § 1834(a)(5)(F)(ii).]

Change in the Patient's Condition

A beneficiary may sell or otherwise dispose of equipment purchased under the program and for which there is no further use, for example, because of recovery from the illness or injury that gave rise to the need for the equipment. There is no authority for the program to repossess the equipment. If, after disposal, there is again medical need for similar equipment, payment can be made for the rental or purchase of that equipment. When, however, an arrangement is motivated solely by a desire to profit from artificial expenses to be met by the program and realize a profit thereby, such expenses are not covered. [Pub. 100-02, Ch. 15, § 110.4.]

When payments stop because the beneficiary's condition has changed and the equipment is no longer medically necessary or because the beneficiary dies, the individual or his or her estate is responsible for the remaining noncovered charges. [Pub. 100-02, Ch. 15, § 110.4.]

[¶ 357] Prosthetic Devices and Prosthetics/Orthotics

Medicare Part B covers prosthetic devices, other than dental, that replace all or part of an internal body organ, including colostomy bags and supplies directly related to colostomy care. Coverage includes replacement of prosthetic devices and one pair of conventional eyeglasses or conventional contact lenses furnished after each cataract surgery during which an intraocular lens is inserted. A written physician order is required. [Soc. Sec. Act § 1861(s)(8); 42 C.F.R. § 410.36(a)(2), (b).]

Examples of prosthetic devices include parenteral and enteral nutrition (PEN), cardiac pacemakers, prosthetic lenses, breast prostheses, maxillofacial devices, and devices that replace all or part of the ear or nose as well as urinary collection and retention systems with or without a tube and a Foley catheter that replace bladder function in cases of permanent urinary incontinence. Medicare does not cover a prosthetic device dispensed before the beneficiary undergoes the procedure that makes the use of the device necessary. [*Medicare Benefit Policy Manual,* Pub. 100-02, Ch. 15, § 120; *Medicare Coverage Determinations Manual,* Pub. 100-03, Ch. 1, § 20.8.]

No payment may be made for prosthetics and certain custom-fabricated orthotics unless they are furnished by a qualified practitioner and fabricated by a qualified practitioner or a qualified supplier at an approved facility. Affected custom-fabricated orthotics are items requiring education, training, and experience to custom fabricate. [Soc. Sec. Act § 1834(h)(1)(F).]

Vacuum erection systems. Effective for claims with dates of service on or after July 1, 2015, Medicare Part B no longer covers vacuum erection system prosthetic devices and related accessories, in the same manner that erectile dysfunction drugs are excluded under Part D. [Soc. Sec. Act § 1834(a)(1)(I).]

Dentures. Dentures are excluded from coverage; however, when a denture or a portion thereof is an integral part (built-in) of a covered prosthesis (e.g., an obturator to fill an opening in the palate), it is covered as part of that prosthesis. [Pub. 100-02, Ch. 15, § 120.]

Prosthetic lenses. Prostheses replacing the lens of an eye include post-surgical lenses customarily used during convalescence from eye surgery in which the lens of the eye was removed. In addition, permanent lenses are also covered when required by an individual lacking the organic lens of the eye because of surgical removal or congenital absence. Prosthetic lenses obtained on or after the beneficiary's date of entitlement to supplementary medical insurance benefits may be covered even though the surgical removal of the crystalline lens occurred before entitlement. [42 C.F.R. § 411.15(b); Pub. 100-02, Ch. 15, § 120.]

The general exclusion applicable to refractive services regardless of the reason for them, however, means that refractive services for the purpose of prescribing or providing prosthetic lenses are not covered. [42 C.F.R. § 411.15(c).]

Repair and replacement. Replacements of prosthetic devices that are artificial limbs or the replacement of any parts of artificial limbs are covered when there is a change in the condition of the patient or a change in the condition of the device. The physician's determination in these situations is controlling, except that confirmation may be required for devices or parts that are less than three years old. [Soc. Sec. Act § 1834(h)(1)(G).] Necessary supplies, adjustments, repairs, and replacements are covered even when the device had been in use before the user enrolled in Part B of the program, so long as the device continues to be medically required. [Pub. 100-02, Ch. 15, § 120.]

Enteral and Parenteral Nutrition Therapy

For PEN nutrition to be covered under Part B, the beneficiary must have a permanently inoperative internal body organ or function thereof. Coverage of such therapy, however, does not require a medical judgment that the impairment giving rise to the therapy will persist throughout the patient's remaining years. If the medical record, including the judgment of the attending physician, indicates that the impairment will be of long and indefinite duration, the test of permanence is considered met. [Pub. 100-03, Ch. 1, § 180.2.]

For PEN therapy to be covered under Part B, the claim must contain a physician's written order or prescription and sufficient medical documentation to permit an independent conclusion that the requirements of the prosthetic device benefit are met and that PEN therapy is medically necessary. If the coverage requirements for enteral or parenteral nutritional therapy are met, related supplies, equipment and nutrients are also covered. [Pub. 100-02, Ch. 15, § 120; Pub. 100-03, Ch. 1, § 180.2.]

Braces, Trusses, and Artificial Limbs

Part B covers leg, arm, back, and neck braces, trusses, and artificial legs, arms, and eyes when furnished incident to physicians' services or on a physician's order. [Soc. Sec. Act § 1861(s)(9); 42 C.F.R. § 410.36(a)(3); Pub. 100-02, Ch. 15, § 130.]

Braces include rigid and semi-rigid devices that support weak or deformed body member or restrict or eliminate motion in diseased or injured parts of the body. Back braces include, but are not limited to, special corsets, including sacroiliac, sacrolumbar and dorsolumbar corsets, and belts. Elastic stockings, garter belts, and similar devices do not come within the scope of the definition of a brace. [Pub. 100-02, Ch. 15, § 130.]

Although orthopedic shoes or other supportive devices for the feet generally are excluded from coverage, the exclusion does not apply to such a shoe if it is an integral part of a leg brace. [42 C.F.R. § 411.15(f); Pub. 100-02, Ch. 15, § 290.]

A terminal device (e.g., hand or hook) is covered under this provision regardless of whether an artificial limb is required by the patient. Stump stockings and harnesses (including replacements) also are covered when these appliances are essential to the effective use of the artificial limb. [Pub. 100-02, Ch. 15, § 130.]

Adjustments to an artificial limb or other appliance required by wear or a change in the patient's condition are covered when ordered by a physician. Adjustments, repairs, and replacements are covered even when the item had been in use before the user enrolled in

Part B of the program as long as the device continues to be medically required. [Soc. Sec. Act § 1861(s)(9); 42 C.F.R. § 410.36(a)(3); Pub. 100-02, Ch. 15, § 130.]

[¶ 359] Surgical Dressings, Splints, and Casts

Surgical dressings, splints, casts, and other devices used for the reduction of fractures and dislocations are covered under the Part A program for inpatients (see ¶ 214) and under the Part B program for other patients. [Soc. Sec. Act § 1861(s)(5); 42 C.F.R. § § 410.10(g), 410.36(a).]

The coverage of splints and casts includes dental splints. [*Medicare Benefit Policy Manual*, Pub. 100-02, Ch. 15, § 100.]

Surgical dressings are limited to primary and secondary dressings required for the treatment of a wound caused by, or treated by, a surgical procedure performed by a physician or other health care professional. In addition, surgical dressings required after debridement of a wound are covered. [Pub. 100-02, Ch. 15, § 100.]

"Primary dressings" are therapeutic or protective coverings applied directly to wounds or lesions either on the skin or caused by an opening to the skin. Secondary dressing materials that serve a therapeutic or protective function and are needed to secure a primary dressing are also covered. Secondary dressings include adhesive tape, roll gauze, bandages, and disposable compression material. [Pub. 100-02, Ch. 15, § 100.]

Examples of items *not* ordinarily covered as surgical dressings include elastic stockings, support hose, foot coverings, leotards, knee supports, surgical leggings, gauntlets, and pressure garments for the arms and hands. Some items, such as transparent film, may be used as a primary or secondary dressing. [Pub. 100-02, Ch. 15, § 100.]

If a physician, certified nurse-midwife, physician assistant, nurse practitioner, or clinical nurse specialist applies surgical dressings as part of a professional service that is billed to Medicare, the surgical dressings are considered incident to the practitioner's professional services. When surgical dressings are not covered incident to the services of a health care practitioner and are obtained by a patient from a supplier pursuant to an order from a physician or other health care professional, the dressings are covered separately under Part B. [Pub. 100-02, Ch. 15, § 100.]

[¶ 361] Inpatient Ancillary Services

No payment may be made under Part B with respect to any services furnished to an individual to the extent that the individual is entitled (or would be entitled, except for the deductible and coinsurances) to have payment made for these services under Part A. [Soc. Sec. Act § 1833(d).] This precludes payment under Part B and Part A for the same services. When such payment is not precluded, however—for example, when an inpatient has exhausted his or her 90 days of entitlement in a "spell of illness"— payment may be made for certain "medical and other health services" under Part B, even though they are furnished to an inpatient of a skilled nursing facility (SNF). These services are usually referred to as "Part B ancillary services."

The following medical and other health services are covered under Part B when furnished by a participating SNF either directly or under arrangements to inpatients who are not entitled to have payment made under Part A (e.g., benefits exhausted or three-day prior-stay requirement not met):

- diagnostic x-ray tests, diagnostic laboratory tests, and other diagnostic tests;
- x-ray, radium, and radioactive isotope therapy, including materials and services of technicians;

- surgical dressings and splints, casts, and other devices used for reduction of fractures and dislocations;

- prosthetic devices (other than dental) that replace all or part of an internal body organ (including contiguous tissue), or all or part of the function of a permanently inoperative or malfunctioning internal body organ, including replacement or repair of such devices;

- leg, arm, back, and neck braces; trusses; and artificial legs, arms, and eyes, including adjustments, repairs, and replacements required because of breakage, wear, loss, or a change in the patient's physical condition;

- outpatient physical and occupational therapy and outpatient speech-language pathology services;

- screening mammography services;

- screening pap smears and pelvic exams;

- influenza, pneumococcal pneumonia, and hepatitis B vaccines;

- some colorectal screening;

- prostate screening;

- ambulance services;

- hemophilia clotting factors; and

- Epoetin Alfa (EPO) for end-stage renal disease beneficiaries when given in conjunction with dialysis.

[42 C.F.R. §§ 409.27(a), 410.60(b); *Medicare Benefit Policy Manual*, Pub. 100-02, Ch. 8, § 70.]

Medical and Other Services Furnished to Hospital Inpatients

If a Medicare Part A claim for inpatient hospital services is denied because the inpatient admission was not reasonable and necessary, or if a hospital determines after a beneficiary is discharged that the inpatient admission was not reasonable and necessary, and if waiver of liability payment is not made, the hospital may be paid for the following Part B inpatient services that would have been reasonable and necessary if the beneficiary had been treated as a hospital outpatient:

(1) Part B services paid under the outpatient prospective payment system (OPPS), excluding observation services and hospital outpatient visits that require an outpatient status; and

(2) the following services excluded from OPPS payment that are instead paid under the respective Part B fee schedules or prospectively determined rates for which payment is made when provided to hospital outpatients:

(a) physical therapy services, speech-language pathology services, and occupational therapy services;

(b) ambulance services;

(c) prosthetic devices, prosthetic supplies, and orthotic devices paid under the durable medical equipment, prosthetics/orthotics, & supplies (DMEPOS) fee schedule (excludes implantable prosthetic devices (other than dental) that replace all or part of an internal body organ (including colostomy bags and supplies directly related to colostomy care) and replacement of such devices);

(d) durable medical equipment (DME) supplied by the hospital for the patient to take home, except DME that is implantable;

(e) certain clinical diagnostic laboratory services;

    (f) screening and diagnostic mammography services; and

    (g) annual wellness visit providing personalized prevention plan services.

[42 C.F.R. § 414.5(a); Pub. 100-02, Ch. 15, § 10.1.]

Hospitals also may be paid under Part B for services included in the payment window before the point of inpatient admission for outpatient services treated as inpatient services, including services requiring an outpatient status. [42 C.F.R. § 414.5(b); Pub. 100-02, Ch. 15, § 10.1.]

Other circumstances. Part B payment can be made to a hospital for certain medical and other services for inpatients enrolled in Part B if: (1) no Part A prospective payment is made at all for the hospital stay because of patient exhaustion of benefit days before or during the admission; or (2) the patient was not otherwise eligible for or entitled to coverage under Part A. For hospitals paid under the OPPS, certain Part B inpatient services (including diagnostic tests; x-ray, radium, and radioactive isotope therapy; certain screening tests; acute dialysis of a hospital inpatient; and immunosuppressive and oral anti-cancer drugs) are separately payable under Part B and are excluded from OPPS packaging if the primary service with which the service would otherwise be bundled is not a payable Part B inpatient service. [Pub. 100-02, Ch. 6, § 10.2.]

The following inpatient services are payable under the non-OPPS Part B fee schedules or prospectively determined rates:

    (1) surgical dressings and splints, casts, and other devices used for reduction of fractures and dislocations;

    (2) prosthetic devices (other than dental) that replace all or part of an internal body organ (including contiguous tissue) or all or part of the function of a permanently inoperative or malfunctioning internal body organ, including replacement of such devices;

    (3) leg, arm, back, and neck braces; trusses; and artificial legs, arms, and eyes, including replacements required because of a change in the patient's physical condition;

    (4) physical and occupational therapy services and outpatient speech-language pathology services;

    (5) screening mammography services; and

    (6) ambulance services.

[Pub. 100-02, Ch. 6, § 10.2.]

The services listed below, when provided to a hospital inpatient, may be covered under Part B even if the patient has Part A coverage for the hospital stay, because these services are covered under Part B and not covered under Part A:

    • physicians' services (including the services of residents and interns in unapproved teaching programs) and the services of physician assistants, certified nurse-midwives, and qualified clinical psychologists;

    • influenza, pneumococcal pneumonia, and hepatitis B vaccines and their administration;

    • screening mammography services, screening pap smears and pelvic exams, glaucoma screening, colorectal screening, and prostate screening;

    • bone mass measurements; and

    • diabetes self-management training services.

¶361

[Pub. 100-02, Ch. 6, § 10.3; Ch. 15, § 250.]

To have any Medicare coverage at all (Part A or Part B), any nonphysician service rendered to a hospital inpatient must be provided directly or arranged for by the hospital. [Pub. 100-02, Ch. 6, § 10.]

[¶ 362] Drugs and Biologicals

Drugs and biologicals must meet the same Medicare criteria for coverage under Part B as under Part A. These requirements are discussed at ¶ 212.

There are, however, significant limitations on Part B coverage of drugs and biologicals that do not apply under Part A. Drugs and biologicals generally are covered under Part B only if they: (1) meet the specific definition of drugs and biologicals; (2) are of the type that are not usually self-administered by the patient; (3) are reasonable and necessary to diagnose or treat an existing illness or condition; (4) are administered by a physician or other health professional as an "incident to" service (see ¶ 351); (5) are not excluded as noncovered immunizations; and (6) are not found by the Food and Drug Administration (FDA) to be "less than effective" (see ¶ 644). [Soc. Sec. Act § 1861(s)(2); 42 C.F.R. § 410.29; *Medicare Benefit Policy Manual*, Pub. 100-02, Ch. 15, § 50.]

A drug or biological may be covered only where it is included, or approved for inclusion, in the latest official edition of the United States Pharmacopoeia National Formulary, the United States Pharmacopoeia-Drug Information, or the American Dental Association Guide to Dental Therapeutics. The term "drugs" also includes any drugs or biologicals used in an anticancer chemotherapeutic regimen for a medically accepted indication. Combination drugs are also included in the definition of drugs if the combination itself or all of the therapeutic ingredients of the combination are included, or approved for inclusion, in any of these drug compendia. [Soc. Sec. Act § 1861(t)(1); Pub. 100-02, Ch. 15, § 50.1.]

Prescription drugs are covered under Medicare Part D. A description of Medicare coverage of prescription drugs begins at ¶ 500.

See ¶ 885 for a discussion of payment rules for drugs and biologicals.

Determining Self-Administration

Whether a drug or biological is a type not usually self-administered by the patient is based on the usual method of administration of the form of that drug or biological as furnished by the physician. Injectable drugs, including intravenously administered drugs, are typically covered; with limited exceptions, other routes of administration including oral drugs, suppositories, and topical medications are considered to be usually self-administered by the patient. [Pub. 100-02, Ch. 15, § 50.2.]

The *Medicare Benefit Policy Manual* defines "usually administered" as meaning a route of administration used more than 50 percent of the time. Thus, if a drug is self-administered by more than 50 percent of Medicare beneficiaries, the drug is excluded from Medicare coverage. [Pub. 100-02, Ch. 15, § 50.2.]

Reliable statistical information on the extent of self-administration by patients may not always be available. In the absence of reliable statistical information on the extent of self-administration by patients, contractors are to consider the following presumptions:

- Drugs delivered intravenously are not usually self-administered.

- Drugs delivered by intramuscular injection are not usually self-administered. The contractor may consider the depth and nature of the particular intramuscular injection in applying this presumption. However, contractors should examine use of the particular drug and consider: (1) whether the drug is used for an acute condition (if so, it is less likely that a patient would self-administer the drug); and (2) how often the injection is given (for example, if the drug is administered once or more per week, it is likely to be self-administered by the patient).

- Drugs delivered by subcutaneous injection are self-administered; however, contractors should examine use of the particular drug and consider whether it is used for an acute condition and the frequency of administration, as described above.

[Pub. 100-02, Ch. 15, § 50.2.]

Drugs as supplies. Some drugs that usually are self-administered by the patient may, nevertheless, be covered by Medicare Part B when they function as supplies, such as when they are provided as an integral component of a procedure or when they facilitate the performance of or recovery from a particular procedure. Except for the applicable copayment, hospitals may not bill beneficiaries for these types of drugs because their costs, as supplies, are packaged into the prospective payment system payment for the procedure with which they are used. [Pub. 100-02, Ch. 15, § 50.2.]

Exclusion of Immunizations

Vaccinations and inoculations are excluded as "immunizations" unless they are directly related to the treatment of an injury or direct exposure to a disease or condition, such as antirabies treatment, tetanus antitoxin or booster vaccine, botulin antitoxin, antivenin sera, or immune globulin. In the absence of injury or direct exposure, preventive immunizations (vaccinations or inoculations) against such diseases as smallpox, polio, and diphtheria are not covered. Pneumococcal pneumonia, hepatitis B, and influenza virus vaccines are exceptions to this rule and are covered (see below). [Pub. 100-02, Ch. 15, § 50.4.4.2.]

Statutory Exceptions to Above Rules

There are a number of exceptions to the rule against self-administered drugs and preventive immunizations:

Antigens. Payment may be made for a reasonable supply of antigens that have been prepared for a particular patient if: (1) the antigens are prepared by a physician who is a doctor of medicine or osteopathy; and (2) the physician who prepared the antigens has examined the patient and has determined a plan of treatment and a dosage regimen. Antigens must be administered in accordance with the plan of treatment and by a physician or by a properly instructed person (who could be the patient) under the supervision of the physician. A reasonable supply of antigens is considered to be not more than a 12-month supply of antigens that has been prepared for a particular patient at any one time. [Soc. Sec. Act § 1861(s)(2)(G); 42 C.F.R. § 410.68.]

Pneumococcal pneumonia vaccine. To protect the elderly from pneumococcal pneumonia, a disease to which they are particularly susceptible, pneumococcal pneumonia vaccine and its administration are covered without deductible or coinsurance. Coverage includes revaccination of patients at highest risk of pneumococcal infection. The vaccine may be requested by the patient; neither a physician's order nor physician supervision is required. [Soc. Sec. Act § 1861(s)(10)(A); 42 C.F.R. § 410.57; Pub. 100-02, Ch. 15, § 50.4.4.2.]

Hepatitis B vaccine. Hepatitis B vaccine and its administration are covered when furnished to an individual who is at high or intermediate risk of contracting Hepatitis B. [Soc. Sec. Act § 1861(s)(10)(B).]

High-risk groups include: (1) end-stage renal disease (ESRD) patients; (2) hemophiliacs who receive Factor VIII or IX concentrates; (3) clients of institutions for individuals with intellectual disabilities; (4) persons who live in the same household as a hepatitis B carrier; (5) homosexual men; (6) illicit injectable drug abusers; (7) Pacific Islanders; and (8) persons diagnosed with diabetes mellitus. Intermediate risk groups include: (1) staff in institutions for individuals with intellectual disabilities and classroom employees who work with individuals with intellectual disabilities; (2) health care workers who have frequent contact with blood or blood-derived body fluids during their routine work; and (3) heterosexually active persons with multiple sexual partners (which means those Medicare beneficiaries who have had at least two documented episodes of sexually transmitted diseases within the past five years). Persons in these groups, however, are not considered at high or intermediate risk of contracting Hepatitis B if they have undergone a prevaccination screening and been found to be currently positive for antibodies to hepatitis B. [42 C.F.R. § 410.63; Pub. 100-02, Ch. 15, § 50.4.4.2.]

Payment for hepatitis B vaccine and its administration for ESRD beneficiaries is made on a reasonable-charge basis and is not included in the prospective payment amount paid to ESRD facilities or in the comprehensive fee amount paid to physicians for treating ESRD patients. [Soc. Sec. Act § 1881(b)(11)(A).]

Influenza virus vaccine. Influenza virus vaccine and its administration are covered without deductible or coinsurance when furnished in compliance with applicable state law by any provider of services or any entity or individual with a supplier number. Typically, these vaccines are administered once a year in the fall or winter. Medicare does not require for coverage purposes that the vaccine be ordered by a physician. Therefore, the beneficiary may receive the vaccine upon request without a physician's order and without physician supervision. [Soc. Sec. Act § 1861(s)(10)(A); 42 C.F.R. § 410.57(b); Pub. 100-02, Ch. 15, § 50.4.4.2.]

Blood clotting factors. Medicare covers blood clotting factors for hemophilia patients competent to use such factors to control bleeding without medical or other supervision. Items related to the administration of the factors also are covered. This coverage is subject to utilization controls deemed necessary by the Medicare program for the efficient use of the factors. [Soc. Sec. Act § 1861(s)(2)(I); Pub. 100-02, Ch. 15, § 50.5.5.] Medicare will make a separate payment for administration of clotting factors. The separate payment may take into account the mixing and delivery of clotting factors to a beneficiary, including special inventory management and storage requirements, as well as ancillary supplies and patient training necessary for self-administration. [Soc. Sec. Act § 1842(o)(5).]

Immunosuppressive drugs. Medicare covers prescription drugs used in immunosuppressive therapy when furnished to an individual who receives a covered organ transplant. [Soc. Sec. Act § 1861(s)(2)(J).] There is no time limit on Medicare coverage for immunosuppressive drugs. [Pub. 100-02, Ch. 15, § 50.5.1.]

Coverage is limited to those immunosuppressive drugs that specifically are labeled as such and approved for marketing by the FDA. Also included are prescription drugs, such as prednisone, that are used in conjunction with immunosuppressive drugs as part of a therapeutic regimen reflected in FDA-approved labeling for immunosuppressive drugs. Antibiotics, hypertensives, and other drugs not directly related to preventing organ rejection are not covered. [Pub. 100-02, Ch. 15, § 50.5.1.]

Erythropoietin. Erythropoietin (EPO) is covered, even when self-administered, for the treatment of anemia for patients with chronic renal failure who are on dialysis. It is covered for self-administration by a home dialysis patient if the patient (or an appropriate caregiver) is trained to inject EPO. The patient's doctor or the renal dialysis facility also must develop a protocol for follow-up review and reevaluation of the patient's condition and the patient's ability to use the drug safely and effectively. [Soc. Sec. Act § 1861(s)(2)(O); Pub. 100-02, Ch. 15, § 50.5.2.]

¶362

Osteoporosis drugs. Medicare covers injectable drugs approved for the treatment of a bone fracture related to post-menopausal osteoporosis if: (1) the drugs are administered by a home health agency, (2) the patient's attending physician certifies that the patient has suffered a bone fracture related to post-menopausal osteoporosis and the patient is incapable of self-administering the drugs, and (3) the patient is confined to her home. [Soc. Sec. Act § 1861(m)(5), (kk).]

Oral anti-cancer and anti-emetic drugs. Oral anti-cancer chemotherapeutic drugs are covered, even when self-administered, if they contain the same active ingredients as intravenously administered anti-cancer drugs. [Soc. Sec. Act § 1861(s)(2)(Q), (t)(2); Pub. 100-02, Ch. 15, § 50.5.3.] Off-label uses of FDA-approved drugs and biologicals for anti-cancer chemotherapeutic regimens are covered by Medicare when they are clinically recognized for the treatment of a specific type of cancer and are listed by CMS in its benefits manual under one or more compendia or under peer-reviewed medical literature. [Pub. 100-02, Ch. 15, § 50.4.5.]

Coverage is provided also for self-administered anti-emetic drugs when prescribed by a physician for use with a covered anti-cancer drug when necessary for the administration and absorption of the oral anti-cancer drug (for example, when a high likelihood of vomiting exists). The anti-emetic must be used during the period that begins immediately before and ends within 48 hours after the time of the administration of the anti-cancer drug and it must be used as a full replacement for the anti-emetic therapy that otherwise would be administered intravenously. [Soc. Sec. Act § 1861(s)(2)(T); Pub. 100-02, Ch. 15, § 50.5.4.]

IVIG for immune deficiency diseases. Medicare covers intravenous immune globulin (IVIG), a pooled plasma derivative, for the treatment of primary immune deficiency diseases in a patient's home. The benefit does not include coverage for items or services related to the administration of the derivative. For coverage of IVIG under this benefit, it is not necessary for the derivative to be administered through a piece of durable medical equipment. [Soc. Sec. Act § 1861(s)(2)(Z), (zz); 42 C.F.R. § 410.10(y); Pub. 100-02, Ch. 15, § 50.6.]

[¶ 366] Other Health Care Practitioners

Over the years Medicare has expanded coverage for the services of nonphysician health care practitioners. Included in this group are physician assistants (PAs), nurse practitioners (NPs) and clinical nurse specialists (CNSs), certified registered nurse anesthetists (CRNAs) and anesthesia assistants (AAs), certified nurse-midwives, clinical psychologists, and clinical social workers (CSWs). (See ¶ 860 for the details of payment rules for these practitioners.)

Physician Assistants, Nurse Practitioners, and Clinical Nurse Specialists

Medicare Part B covers the services of PAs, NPs, and CNSs if the services would be covered as physicians' services if furnished by a physician. Such services are covered if the PA, NP, or CNS is legally authorized to perform them in the state in which they are performed and does not perform services that are otherwise excluded from coverage because of one of the statutory exclusions. Medicare covers these services in all settings in both rural and urban areas. [Soc. Sec. Act § 1861(s)(2)(K); 42 C.F.R. §§ 410.74(a), 410.75(c), 410.76(c).]

Examples of the types of services that PAs, NPs, and CNSs may furnish include services that traditionally have been reserved to physicians, such as physical examinations, minor surgery, setting casts for simple fractures, interpreting x-rays, and other activities that involve an independent evaluation or treatment of the patient's condition. Also included are PAs', NPs', and CNSs' performance of the initial preventive physical examination and the annual wellness visit. [Soc. Sec. Act § 1861(s)(2)(K); *Medicare Benefit Policy Manual*, Pub. 100-02, Ch. 15, §§ 190, 200, 210.]

Personal performance. PA, NP, and CNS professional services are covered only when they have been personally performed by the PA, NP, or CNS. Supervision of other nonphysician staff does not constitute personal performance of a professional service. [42 C.F.R. §§ 410.74(d)(1), 410.75(e)(1), 410.76(e)(1).]

Physician assistants. To be covered, PA services must be performed under the general supervision of a physician. The supervising physician need not be physically present when the physician assistant is performing the services unless required by state law; however, the supervising physician must be immediately available to the PA for consultation. [Soc. Sec. Act § 1861(s)(2)(K)(i); 42 C.F.R. § 410.74(a)(2)(iv).]

CNSs and NPs. Both NPs and CNSs must perform services while working in collaboration with a physician. Collaboration is a process in which the practitioner works with one or more physicians to deliver health care services within the scope of the practitioner's expertise, with medical direction and appropriate supervision as provided for in jointly developed guidelines or other mechanisms as provided by the law of the state in which the services are performed. The collaborating physician does not need to be present with the NP when the services are furnished or to make an independent evaluation of each patient who is seen by the NP. [Soc. Sec. Act § 1861(s)(2)(K)(ii), (aa)(6); 42 C.F.R. §§ 410.75(c)(3), 410.76(c)(3).]

CRNAs and Anesthesia Assistants

Medicare Part B covers anesthesia services and related care furnished by a CRNA or an anesthesiologist's assistant who is legally authorized to perform the services by the state in which the services are furnished. [Soc. Sec. Act § 1861(s)(11), (bb); 42 C.F.R. § 410.69(a).]

Nurse-Midwife Services

Medicare Part B covers certified nurse-midwife services. The term "certified nurse-midwife services" means such services furnished by a certified nurse-midwife and such services and supplies furnished as an incident to the nurse midwife's service that the certified nurse-midwife is legally authorized to perform under state law as would otherwise be covered if furnished by a physician or as an incident to a physicians' service. [Soc. Sec. Act § 1861(s)(2)(L), (gg); 42 C.F.R. § 410.77.]

Covered services are those furnished by a certified nurse-midwife that are within the scope of practice authorized by the law of the state in which they are furnished and would otherwise be covered if furnished by a physician, including obstetrical and gynecological services. Coverage of service to the newborn continues only to the point that the newborn is or would normally be treated medically as a separate individual. [42 C.F.R. § 410.77(b)(1); Pub. 100-02, Ch. 15, § 180.]

Incident-to services. Part B covers services and supplies incident to the services of a certified nurse-midwife if the requirements of 42 C.F.R. § 410.26 are met. [42 C.F.R. § 410.77(b), (c).]

Personal performance. A nurse-midwife can be paid for professional services only when the services have been performed personally by the nurse-midwife. Supervision of other nonphysician staff by a nurse-midwife does not constitute personal performance of a professional service by the nurse-midwife. [42 C.F.R. § 410.77(d); Pub. 100-02, Ch. 15, § 180.]

Place of service. There is no restriction on place of service. Nurse-midwife services are covered if provided in the nurse-midwife's office, the patient's home, or a hospital or other facility, such as a clinic or birthing center owned or operated by a nurse-midwife. [Pub. 100-02, Ch. 15, § 180.]

¶366

Relationship with physician. Unless required by state law, nurse-midwife services are covered regardless of whether he or she is under the supervision of, or associated with, a physician or other health care provider. [42 C.F.R. § 410.77(b)(2); Pub. 100-02, Ch. 15, § 180.]

Clinical Psychologists

Medicare Part B covers services furnished by a clinical psychologist that are within the scope of his or her state license, if the services would be covered if furnished by a physician or as an incident to a physician's services. [Soc. Sec. Act § 1861(s)(2)(M), (ii).]

Incident-to services and supplies. Part B also covers services and supplies furnished "incident to" a CP's services if the requirements of 42 C.F.R. § 410.26 are met. [42 C.F.R. § 410.71(a)(2).]

Requirement for consultation. A CP must agree that, upon the beneficiary's consent, the CP will attempt to consult with the beneficiary's attending or primary care physician within a reasonable time to consider any conditions contributing to the beneficiary's symptoms. If the CP's attempts to consult directly with the physician are not successful, the CP must notify the physician within a reasonable time that he or she is furnishing services to the patient. Neither the CP nor the attending or primary care physician may bill Medicare or the beneficiary for this consultation. [42 C.F.R. § 410.71(c), (e); Pub. 100-02, Ch. 15, § 160.]

Noncovered services. The services of CPs are not covered if they are otherwise excluded from Medicare coverage even though a clinical psychologist is authorized by state law to perform them. In addition, any therapeutic services that are billed by CPs under Current Procedural Terminology® (CPT®) psychotherapy codes that include medical evaluation and management services are not covered. [Pub. 100-02, Ch. 15, § 160.]

Clinical Social Workers

Part B coverage of clinical social worker services includes the diagnosis and treatment of mental illnesses that the CSW is legally authorized to perform under state law and would otherwise be covered if performed by a physician or as incident to a physician's services. [Soc. Sec. Act § 1861(s)(2)(N), 1861(hh)(2); 42 C.F.R. § 410.73(b)(1).]

Noncovered services. Part B does not cover services furnished to an inpatient of a hospital or skilled nursing facility that the facility is required to provide, or to a patient in a Medicare-participating dialysis facility if the services are those required by the conditions for coverage for end-stage renal disease facilities. CSW services are not covered if they are otherwise excluded from Medicare coverage even though a CSW is authorized by state law to perform them. [42 C.F.R. § 410.73(b)(2); Pub. 100-02, Ch. 15, § 170.]

Requirement for consultation. A CSW must agree that, upon the patient's consent, the CSW will attempt to consult with the patient's attending or primary care physician. Neither the CSW nor the attending or primary care physician may bill Medicare or the beneficiary for this consultation. [42 C.F.R. § 410.73(c), (d)(2).]

Registered Dietitians and Nutrition Professionals

Medicare covers medical nutrition therapy (MNT) services for certain beneficiaries who have diabetes or a renal disease when furnished by registered dietitians or nutritional professionals. [Soc. Sec. Act § 1861(s)(2)(V); 42 C.F.R. §§ 410.130–410.134; *Medicare National Coverage Determinations Manual*, Pub. 100-03, Ch. 1, § 180.1.] MNT services are included in the physician fee schedule. The definition of "practitioner" in the regulations includes registered dietitians and nutrition professionals. [Soc. Sec. Act § 1842(b)(18)(C); 42 C.F.R. § 405.400.]

[¶ 369] Prevention Services

Medicare Part B covers specific preventive screening services and tests. The initial preventive physical exam (IPPE), performed within the first year of Part B enrollment, begins the process. Medicare beneficiaries are eligible to receive personalized prevention plan services every year after their IPPEs as long as they have not received either an IPPE or personalized prevention plan services within the preceding 12-month period.

The Patient Protection and Affordable Care Act (ACA) (P.L. 111-148), enacted on March 23, 2010, expanded coverage of preventive services. The ACA added a definition of "preventive services" and removed barriers to Medicare beneficiaries' use of such services by waiving coinsurance and deductibles for most preventive services. Under § 4104(a) of the ACA, "preventive services" are defined as: (1) the screening and preventive services currently listed in Soc. Sec. Act § 1861(ww)(2); (2) an initial preventive physical examination; and (3) personalized preventive plan services. [Soc. Sec. Act § 1861(ddd)(3).]

Sections 4103(c)(1), 4104(b) and 10406 of the ACA waive coinsurance amounts for most preventive services; thus, Medicare will be responsible for 100 percent of the costs. [Soc. Sec. Act § 1833(a)(1)(B).] Preventive services for which no coinsurance amount will be charged to beneficiaries are those services given a grade of "A" or "B" by the United States Preventive Services Task Force (USPSTF). [Soc. Sec. Act § 1833(b)(1).]

"Welcome to Medicare" Exams

Medicare pays for one IPPE, also called the "Welcome to Medicare Physical," within the first year after the effective date of the beneficiary's first Part B coverage period, if the coverage began on or after January 1, 2009. [Soc. Sec. Act §§ 1861(s)(2)(W) and (ww), 1862(a)(1)(K); 42 C.F.R. §§ 410.16, 411.15(a)(1) and (k)(11).]

The IPPE includes: (1) a physical examination, including measurement of height, weight, body mass index, and blood pressure, with the goal of health promotion and disease detection; (2) end-of-life planning; and (3) education, counseling, and referral for screening and other covered preventive benefits separately authorized under Part B. The statutory screening and other preventive services authorized under Part B include:

- pneumococcal, influenza, and hepatitis B vaccine and their administration;
- screening mammography;
- screening pap smear and screening pelvic exam services;
- prostate cancer screening services;
- colorectal cancer screening tests;
- diabetes outpatient self-management training services;
- bone mass measurements;
- screening for glaucoma;
- medical nutrition therapy services for individuals with diabetes or renal disease;
- cardiovascular screening tests;
- diabetes screening tests;
- ultrasound screening for abdominal aortic aneurysm;
- an electrocardiogram; and
- additional preventive services, as defined by Soc. Sec. Act § 1861(ddd)(1).

[Soc. Sec. Act § 1861(ww).] The IPPE also includes screening for depression and a review of the beneficiary's medical and social history and functional abilities. A physician or qualified nonphysician practitioner must perform the IPPE as a condition for coverage. [42 C.F.R. § 410.16; *Medicare Claims Processing Manual,* Pub. 100-04, Ch. 12, § 30.6.1.1.]

The deductible and coinsurance for the IPPE are waived. [Soc. Sec. Act § 1833(b)(9); 42 C.F.R. §§ 410.152(l)(12), 410.160(b)(9); Pub. 100-04, Ch. 12, § 30.6.1.1.]

Excluded coverage. Excluded routine physical checkups include: (1) examinations performed for a purpose other than the treatment or diagnosis of a specific illness, symptom, complaint, or injury (such as routine chest x-rays), and (2) examinations required by third parties such as insurance companies, business establishments, or government agencies. [42 C.F.R. § 411.15(a); *Medicare Benefit Policy Manual*, Pub. 100-02, Ch. 16, § 90.]

The routine services exclusion does not apply to services furnished in a federally qualified health center. [Soc. Sec. Act § 1862(a).]

Annual Wellness Exams

Medicare beneficiaries are eligible to receive an annual wellness visit (AWV) providing personalized prevention plan services. [Soc. Sec. Act § 1861(s)(2)(FF) and (hhh)(1); 42 C.F.R. § 410.15(c).]

"Personalized prevention plan services" means the creation of a plan for an individual that includes a health risk assessment. A plan must take into account the results of the assessment and may include elements such as:

(1) the individual's medical and family history;

(2) a list of his or her current providers or suppliers;

(3) the individual's height, weight, body mass index, blood pressure, and other measurements;

(4) detection of any cognitive impairments;

(5) establishment of a screening schedule for the next five years based on recommendations of the USPSTF and a list of risk factors and conditions for which preventive measures or treatment are recommended;

(6) personalized health advice and a referral, as necessary, to address risk factors; and

(7) any other element identified by the HHS Secretary.

Beginning January 1, 2016, at the discretion of the beneficiary, AWVs include advance care planning services, including discussions about future care decisions that might need to be made, how the beneficiary can let others know about care preferences, and an explanation of advance directives that may involve the completion of standard forms. [Soc. Sec. Act § 1861(hhh); 42 C.F.R. § 410.15(a); *Final rule*, 80 FR 70886, Nov. 16, 2015.]

The health risk assessment must be performed by a health professional, which includes a physician, physician assistant, nurse practitioner, clinical nurse specialist, or other medical professionals or teams of professionals. [42 C.F.R. § 410.15(b).]

Medicare pays for an AWV for a beneficiary who is no longer within 12 months after the effective date of his or her first Medicare Part B coverage period and who has not received either an IPPE or an AWV providing personalized prevention plan services within the past 12 months. The deductible and coinsurance for personalized prevention plan services, including those performed in the outpatient department of a hospital, are waived. [Soc. Sec. Act § 1833(a)(1)(X) and (b)(10), (t)(1)(B)(iv); 42 C.F.R. §§ 410.152(l)(13), 410.160(b)(12); Pub. 100-04, Ch. 12, § 30.6.1.1.]

Mammograms

Medicare Part B covers screening mammography, which includes the radiological procedure itself as well as a physician's interpretation of the results of the procedure. [Soc. Sec. Act § 1861(s)(13) and (jj); 42 C.F.R. §§ 410.10(r), 410.34.]

Women between the ages of 35 and 39 are covered for one screening mammogram during that five-year age period. Women age 40 and over are covered for one screening mammogram per 12-month period. [Soc. Sec. Act § 1834(c)(2)(A); 42 C.F.R. § 410.34(d).] Division H Title II section 229 of the Consolidated Appropriations Act, 2016 requires the HHS Secretary, from November 1, 2015, through January 1, 2018, to cover annual screening mammograms starting at age 40, despite federal recommendations that screenings start at 50.

The usual Part B deductible is waived for screening mammograms. [Soc. Sec. Act § 1833(b)(5); 42 C.F.R. §§ 410.152(l)(2), 410.160(b)(5).]

Pap Smears and Pelvic Exams

Medicare covers screening pap smears and screening pelvic examinations. Screening pap smear coverage includes routine exfoliative cytology tests and the physician's interpretation of the results of the tests. Screening pelvic exam coverage includes testing for the early detection of cervical or vaginal cancer and includes clinical breast examinations. [Soc. Sec. Act § 1861(s)(14), (nn); 42 C.F.R. § 410.56; Pub. 100-02, Ch. 15, § 280.4.]

Pap smears and pelvic exams are covered at two-year intervals. Annual exams, however, are covered for women identified as being at high risk for developing cervical or vaginal cancer and for women of childbearing age who have had an abnormality detected during any of the three preceding years. [Soc. Sec. Act §§ 1861(nn), 1862(a)(1)(F); 42 C.F.R. § 410.56(b).]

The usual Part B deductible is waived for these exams. [Soc. Sec. Act § 1833(b)(6); 42 C.F.R. §§ 410.152(l)(3), 410.160(b)(6); Pub. 100-04, Ch. 18, § 30.3.]

Colorectal Cancer Screening Tests

Part B covers colorectal cancer screening tests. [Soc. Sec. Act § 1861(s)(2)(R), (pp); Pub. 100-02, Ch. 15, § 280.2.2.]Covered screening procedures include: (1) one annual fecal-occult blood test every 12 months for individuals age 50 and older; (2) flexible sigmoidoscopy every four years for individuals age 50 and older; (3) colonoscopy for high-risk individuals every two years and for other individuals every 10 years, including, effective January 1, 2015, anesthesia furnished in conjunction with the service; and (4) screening barium enemas every four years for individuals age 50 and older who are not at high risk of developing colorectal cancer or every two years for individuals who are at high risk. [Soc. Sec. Act §§ 1834(d), 1861(pp); 42 C.F.R. § 410.37.]

An individual is at high risk for developing colorectal cancer if he or she has one or more of the following characteristics: (1) a close relative (sibling, parent, or child) who has had colorectal cancer or an adenomatous polyp; (2) a family history of familial adenomatous polyposis; (3) a family history of hereditary nonpolyposis colorectal cancer; (4) a personal history of colorectal cancer; (5) a personal history of adenomatous polyps; or (6) inflammatory bowel disease, including Crohn's Disease and ulcerative colitis. [42 C.F.R. § 410.37(a)(3); Pub. 100-02, Ch. 15, § 280.2.3.]

Effective January 27, 2014, physician assistants, nurse practitioners, and clinical nurse specialists, in addition to the beneficiary's attending physician, are allowed to order screening fecal-occult blood tests. [42 C.F.R. § 410.37(b).]

¶369

Deductibles are waived for colorectal cancer screening tests. The deductible is also waived for surgical and anesthesia services furnished in connection with, as a result of, and in the same clinical encounter (i.e., furnished on the same date) as a planned colorectal cancer screening test. [Soc. Sec. Act § 1833(b)(8); 42 C.F.R. §§ 410.152(l)(5), 410.160(b)(7); Pub. 100-04, Ch. 18, § 60.1.1.]

Diabetes Self-Management Services

Medicare covers diabetes outpatient self-management educational and training services furnished by a certified provider who meets certain quality standards. This program is intended to educate beneficiaries in the successful self-management of diabetes. [Soc. Sec. Act § 1861(qq).] The program includes instructions in self-monitoring of blood glucose, education about diet and exercise, an insulin treatment plan developed specifically for the patient who is insulin-dependent, and motivation for patients to use these skills for self-management. [42 C.F.R. § 410.141(c); Pub. 100-02, Ch. 15, § 300.]

The doctor or qualified nonphysician practitioner who is managing the beneficiary's diabetic condition must certify that these services are needed. The services must be provided under a comprehensive plan of care to ensure therapy compliance or provide the patient with the necessary skills and knowledge (including the skill to self-administer injectable drugs) to participate in the management of his or her own condition. Up to 10 hours of initial training and two hours of annual additional training are authorized. [Pub. 100-02, Ch. 15, §§ 300, 300.1, 300.3.]

Diabetes screening. Part B covers also diabetes screening tests after a referral from a physician or qualified nonphysician practitioner to an individual at risk for diabetes for the purpose of early detection of diabetes. Medicare covers diabetes screening once every 12 months for a beneficiary who is not pre-diabetic and once every six months for a beneficiary who is pre-diabetic. [Soc. Sec. Act § 1861(s)(2)(Y), (yy); 42 C.F.R. § 410.18.]

Bone Mass Measurement Tests

Medicare covers biannual bone mass measurement tests ordered by physicians or qualified nonphysician practitioners to identify bone mass, detect bone loss, or determine bone quality for: (1) estrogen-deficient women at clinical risk for osteoporosis; (2) individuals with vertebral abnormalities; (3) individuals receiving long-term glucocorticoid steroid therapy; (4) individuals with primary hyperparathyroidism; and (5) individuals being monitored to assess the response to or efficacy of an approved osteoporosis drug therapy. A physician must interpret these test results. [Soc. Sec. Act § 1861(s)(15), (rr); 42 C.F.R. § 410.31.]

Prostate Cancer Screening Tests

Medicare covers annual prostate cancer screening tests, including digital rectal examinations and prostate-specific antigen (PSA) blood tests, for men over age 50. The tests must be performed (or in the case of the PSA blood test, ordered) by the patient's physician, physician assistant, nurse practitioner, clinical nurse specialist, or certified nurse-midwife. [Soc. Sec. Act § 1861(s)(2)(P), (oo); 42 C.F.R. § 410.39.]

The screening PSA test is not subject to the Part B deductible and coinsurance requirements. The deductible and coinsurance requirements apply to screening rectal examinations. [Pub. 100-04, Ch. 18, § 50.2.]

Screening Glaucoma Tests

Medicare covers annual screening glaucoma tests for individuals determined to be at high risk for glaucoma, including: (1) individuals with diabetes mellitus; (2) individuals with a family history of glaucoma; (3) African-Americans age 50 and over; and (4) Hispanic-

Americans age 65 and over. [Soc. Sec. Act § 1861(s)(2)(U), (uu); 42 C.F.R. § 410.23; Pub. 100-02, Ch. 15, § 280.1.]

Covered screening tests include: (1) a dilated eye exam with an intraocular pressure measurement, and (2) a direct ophthalmoscopy exam or a slit-lamp biomicroscopic exam. Glaucoma screening examinations must be furnished by, or under the direct supervision of, an optometrist or opthalmologist. "Direct supervision" means the optometrist or opthalmologist must be present in the office suite and be immediately available to furnish assistance and direction throughout the performance of the procedure. [42 C.F.R. § 410.23; Pub. 100-02, Ch. 15, § 280.1.]

Abdominal Aortic Ultrasound

Medicare covers a one-time ultrasound screening for abdominal aortic aneurysm for an individual who, after a referral from a physician or a qualified nonphysician practitioner: (1) has not been previously furnished such an ultrasound screening; and (2) is included in at least one of the following risk categories: (a) has a family history of abdominal aortic aneurysm, (b) is a man age 65 to 75 who has smoked at least 100 cigarettes in his lifetime, or (c) is a beneficiary with other factors specified in national coverage determinations. The test must be performed by a supplier or supplier who is authorized to provide covered diagnostic services. [Soc. Sec. Act § 1861(s)(2)(AA), (bbb); 42 C.F.R. § 410.19; Pub. 100-04, Ch. 18, § 110.2.]

Effective January 27, 2014, CMS eliminated the requirement that an eligible beneficiary must receive a referral for aortic aneurism screening as a result of an IPPE. [*Final rule*, 78 FR 74230, Dec. 10, 2013.]

Medical Nutrition Therapy Services

Medicare covers medical nutrition therapy (MNT) services for beneficiaries with diabetes or a renal disease who: (1) have not received diabetes outpatient maintenance self-management training services within a specified time period; and (2) are not receiving maintenance dialysis benefits. Services covered include nutritional diagnostic, therapy, and counseling services for the purpose of disease management. The services must be provided by a registered dietitian or nutritional professional pursuant to a referral by the beneficiary's treating physician. [Soc. Sec. Act § 1861(s)(2)(V), (vv); 42 C.F.R. §§ 410.130–410.134.]

Basic coverage of MNT for the first year a beneficiary receives MNT is three hours, and basic coverage for subsequent years is two hours. If the beneficiary's treating physician determines that both MNT and diabetes self-management training are medically necessary in the same episode of care, Medicare will cover both services without decreasing either benefit as long as MNT and diabetes self-management training are not provided on the same date of service. Additional hours are covered if the treating physician determines that there is a change in medical condition, diagnosis, or treatment regimen that requires a change in MNT and orders additional hours during that episode of care. [Pub. 100-03, Ch. 1, § 180.1.]

The Part B deductible is waived for this test. [42 C.F.R. § 410.160(b)(11).]

Cardiovascular Screening

Medicare covers cardiovascular screening tests once every five years for an asymptomatic individual. These blood tests measure cholesterol levels and other lipid or triglyceride levels. [Soc. Sec. Act § 1861(s)(2)(X), (xx); 42 C.F.R. § 410.17.]

[¶ 370] Therapeutic Shoes

Therapeutic shoes and inserts are covered for beneficiaries with severe diabetic foot disease. The beneficiary's treating physician, either a doctor of medicine or a doctor of osteopathy who is responsible for diagnosing and treating the patient's diabetic condition, must certify the need for diabetic shoes. [Soc. Sec. Act § 1861(s)(12); *Medicare Benefit Policy Manual*, Pub. 100-02, Ch. 15, § 140.]

The treating physician must:

(1) document in the medical record that the beneficiary has diabetes;

(2) certify that the beneficiary is being treated under a comprehensive plan of care for diabetes and needs diabetic shoes; and

(3) document in the patient's record that the patient has one or more of the following conditions: peripheral neuropathy with evidence of callus formation, a history of pre-ulcerative calluses, a history of previous ulceration, foot deformity, previous amputation, or poor circulation.

[Soc. Sec. Act § 1861(s)(12)(A); Pub. 100-02, Ch. 15, § 140.]

After the physician managing the beneficiary's systemic diabetic condition certifies the need for therapeutic shoes, a podiatrist or other qualified physician who is knowledgeable in the fitting of diabetic shoes and inserts may prescribe the particular type of footwear necessary. A podiatrist or other qualified individual must fit and furnish the footwear. The certifying physician may not furnish the therapeutic shoes unless he or she is the only qualified individual in the area. [Soc. Sec. Act § 1861(s)(12)(B), (C); Pub. 100-02, Ch. 15, § 140.]

Limitations. Coverage is limited to one of the following within a calendar year: (1) one pair of custom-molded shoes (including inserts provided with such shoes) and two additional pairs of inserts, or (2) one pair of depth shoes and three pairs of inserts (not including the noncustomized inserts provided with such shoes). [Pub. 100-02, Ch. 15, § 140.]

[¶ 381] Physical Therapy, Occupational Therapy, and Speech-Language Pathology Services

The Part B program covers physical therapy, occupational therapy, and speech-language pathology services. [Soc. Sec. Act § 1861(s)(2)(D).] The following discussion refers to physical therapy, occupational therapy, and speech-language pathology services, collectively, as "therapy" services.

Providers of Outpatient Therapy Services

Outpatient physical and occupational therapy and speech-language pathology services (including audiology services) must be furnished by a provider of services, a clinic, rehabilitation agency, or public health agency, or by others under an "arrangement" with, and under the supervision of, such provider, clinic, or agency. The services must be furnished to an individual: (1) who is under the care of a physician, and (2) with respect to whom a plan describing the type, amount, and duration of therapy services that are to be furnished has been established by a physician or the therapist providing the services, and is periodically reviewed by the physician. Excluded, however, are: (a) any item or service if it would not be included if furnished to an inpatient of a hospital; and (b) any such service furnished by a clinic, rehabilitation agency, or by others under arrangements with a clinic or agency, unless the clinic or agency meets Medicare standards and requirements. [Soc. Sec. Act § 1861(g), (p), (ll).]

Therapy services are payable under the physician fee schedule when furnished by—

(1) a provider to its outpatients in the patient's home;

(2) a provider to patients who come to the facility's outpatient department;

(3) a provider to inpatients of other institutions; or

(4) a supplier to patients in the office or in the patient's home.

[*Medicare Benefit Policy Manual,* Pub. 100-02, Ch. 15, § 220.1.4.]

Part B coverage includes therapy services furnished by participating hospitals and skilled nursing facilities (SNFs) to inpatients who have exhausted their Part A inpatient benefits or who are otherwise not eligible for Part A benefits. Providers of outpatient therapy services that have inpatient facilities but are not participating hospitals and SNFs may not furnish covered outpatient therapy services to their own inpatients. Providers of therapy services that have inpatient facilities, other than participating hospitals and SNFs, may not furnish covered therapy services to their own inpatients. However, since the inpatients of one institution may be considered the outpatients of another institution, all providers of therapy services may furnish such services to inpatients of another health facility. [42 C.F.R. §§ 410.59(b), 410.60(b), 410.62; Pub. 100-02, Ch. 15, § 220.1.4.]

Comprehensive outpatient rehabilitation facilities. Comprehensive outpatient rehabilitation facilities (CORFs) may provide these outpatient therapy services in the home as long as the patient also does not receive home health benefits. The CORF plan of treatment must be reviewed every 60 days for respiratory therapy and every 90 days for physical therapy, occupational therapy, and speech-language pathology. [42 C.F.R. § 410.105(b)(3)(i), (c)(2); Pub. 100-02, Ch. 12, §§ 10, 30.]

Rehabilitation agencies. Rehabilitation agencies that are Medicare Part B providers must have a physician's signature in the clinical record of a rehabilitation plan within 30 days of an initial therapy visit and within each 90-day recertification period thereafter, or as often as the patient's condition changes. [42 C.F.R. §§ 424.24(c)(2), 485.711(b)(3).]

Private practice therapists. The Part B program covers the services of a "qualified" physical therapist, speech-language pathologist, or occupational therapist in "private practice" if the therapist or speech-language pathologist: (1) is legally authorized to engage in private practice by the state in which he or she practices and practices only within the scope of his or her license; (2) engages in private practice on a regular basis as an individual in a solo practice, partnership, or group practice, or as an employee of one of these; (3) bills Medicare only for services furnished in his or her private practice office space or in the patient's home (excluding any institution that is a hospital, a critical access hospital (CAH), or a SNF); and (4) treats individuals who are patients of the practice and for whom the practice collects fees for the services furnished. [Soc. Sec. Act § 1861(p); 42 C.F.R. §§ 410.59(c), 410.60(c), 410.62(c).]

The services must be provided either by or under the direct personal supervision of the therapist in private practice, and the supporting personnel, including other therapists, must be employees of the therapist in private practice. Services furnished by a therapist in the therapist's office under arrangements with hospitals in rural communities and public health agencies, or services provided in the beneficiary's home under arrangements with a provider of therapy services, are not covered under this provision. [Pub. 100-02, Ch. 15, § 230.4.]

Reasonableness and Necessity of Outpatient Therapy Services

To be considered reasonable and necessary to treat an illness or an injury, therapy services must meet all of the following conditions:

(1) the services must be considered under accepted standards of medical practice to be a specific and effective treatment for the patient's condition;

(2) the services must be of such a level of complexity and sophistication, or the condition of the patient must be such, that the services required can be safely and effectively performed only by a qualified therapist or under a therapist's supervision;

(3) while a beneficiary's particular medical condition is a valid factor in deciding if skilled therapy services are needed, a beneficiary's diagnosis or prognosis cannot be the sole factor in deciding that a service is or is not skilled; the key issue is whether the skills of a therapist are needed to treat the illness or injury, or whether the services can be carried out by nonskilled personnel; and

(4) the amount, frequency, and duration of services must be reasonable.

Services related to activities for the general good and welfare of patients, e.g., general exercises to promote overall fitness and flexibility and activities to provide diversion or general motivation, do not constitute therapy services for Medicare purposes. [Pub. 100-02, Ch. 15, § 220.2.]

Medicare coverage does not turn on the presence or absence of a beneficiary's potential for improvement from the therapy but, rather, on the beneficiary's need for skilled care. Skilled therapy services may be necessary to improve a patient's current condition, to maintain the patient's current condition, or to prevent or slow further deterioration of the patient's condition. [Pub. 100-02, Ch. 15, § 220.2.]

Maintenance therapy. If the specialized skill, knowledge, and judgment of a qualified therapist are required to establish or design a maintenance program to maintain the patient's current condition or to prevent or slow further deterioration, the establishment or design of a maintenance program by a qualified therapist is covered. Once a maintenance program is established, coverage of therapy services to carry out a maintenance program turns on the beneficiary's need for skilled care. [Pub. 100-02, Ch. 15, § 220.2.]

Types of Covered Outpatient Therapy Services

Part B covers the following types of therapy services:

Occupational therapy. Occupational therapy may involve:

(1) evaluation of a patient's level of function by administering diagnostic and prognostic tests;

(2) teaching task-oriented therapeutic activities designed to restore physical function, such as woodworking activities on an inclined table to restore shoulder, elbow, and wrist range of motion lost as a result of burns;

(3) individualized therapeutic activity programs for patients with a diagnosed psychiatric illness, such as sewing activities following a pattern to reduce confusion and restore reality orientation in a schizophrenic patient;

(4) activities to increase sensory input and improve response for stroke patients with functional loss resulting in a distorted body image; and

(5) teaching compensatory technique to improve the level of independence in daily activities or adapt to an evolving deterioration in health and function.

[42 C.F.R. § 410.59; Pub. 100-02, Ch. 15, § 230.2.]

Physical therapy. Covered physical therapy services are not limited to services typically provided in clinics. They may include services such as aquatic therapy in a community center pool or functional electrical stimulation to enhance walking in spinal cord injury patients. The *Medicare Benefit Policy Manual* discusses types of covered physical therapy services in chapter 15, § § 220 and 230. [42 C.F.R. § 410.60; Pub. 100-02, Ch. 15, § 230.1.]

Speech-language pathology. Speech-language pathology services are those services necessary for the diagnosis and treatment of speech and language disorders, which result in communication disabilities and for the diagnosis and treatment of swallowing disorders (dysphagia), regardless of the presence of a communication disability. [42 C.F.R. § 410.62; Pub. 100-02, Ch. 15, § 230.3.]

Conditions for Coverage of Outpatient Therapy

Outpatient rehabilitation services must be furnished under a written plan of treatment established and certified by a physician or qualified nonphysician practitioner (NPP). Services must also be furnished while the beneficiary is under the care of a physician. An order, while not required by Medicare, provides evidence that the patient both needs therapy services and is under the care of a physician. [Pub. 100-02, Ch. 15, § 220.1.1; 42 C.F.R. § § 410.60–410.62.]

Plan of treatment. Outpatient physical, occupational, and speech therapy must be furnished under a plan of care established by a physician, nurse practitioner, clinical nurse specialist, or physician assistant, or the therapist providing the services. The plan must be established before treatment is begun. It must prescribe the type, amount, frequency, and duration of the physical therapy, occupational therapy, or speech-language pathology services to be furnished to the individual and indicate the diagnosis and anticipated goals that are consistent with the patient function reporting on claims for services. [42 C.F.R. § § 410.59(a)(2), 410.60(a)(2), 410.61, 410.62(a)(2).]

Physician certification. As soon as possible after the plan of care is established, the physician/NPP or therapist/pathologist that established the plan must by sign the plan, certifying that: (1) the beneficiary needs therapy or speech-language pathology services; (2) the services were furnished while the beneficiary was under the care of a physician, nurse practitioner, clinical nurse specialist, or physician assistant; and (3) the services were furnished under a plan of treatment that meets the requirements of 42 C.F.R. § 410.61. Recertification is required at least every 90 days. [42 C.F.R. § 424.24(c); Pub. 100-02, Ch. 15, § 220.1.3.]

Outpatient Therapy Provided Under Arrangements

A provider may make arrangements with other providers to furnish covered outpatient physical, occupational, or speech therapy. [Soc. Sec. Act § 1861(p).] Services under "arrangements" are services for which receipt of payment by the provider for the arranged services must (as with services provided directly) relieve the beneficiary or any other person of further liability to pay for the services.

The provider must assume professional responsibility for the services and put into place many of the same controls applied to services furnished by salaried employees. The provider must:

(1) accept the patient for treatment in accordance with its admission policies;

(2) maintain a complete and timely clinical record on the patient that includes diagnosis, medical history, orders, and progress notes relating to all services received;

(3) maintain liaison with the attending physician or NPP with regard to the progress of the patient and to assure that the required plan of treatment is periodically reviewed by the physician;

(4) secure from the physician/NPP the required certifications and recertifications; and

(5) ensure that the medical necessity of such service is reviewed on a sample basis by the agency's staff or an outside review group.

¶381

[Pub. 100-02, Ch. 15, § 230.6.]

Providers "under an arrangement" must furnish services in accordance with the terms of a written contract specifying that the provider retains responsibility for and control and supervision of such services. The contract also must:

(1) provide that the therapy services be furnished in accordance with a plan of care;

(2) specify the geographic areas in which the services are to be furnished;

(3) provide that personnel and services meet the same requirements as if furnished directly by the provider;

(4) provide that the therapist will participate in conferences required to coordinate patient care;

(5) provide for the preparation of treatment records that will be incorporated into clinical records;

(6) specify the financial arrangements, i.e., the contracting organization or individual may not bill the patient or the health insurance program; and

(7) specify the contract's time period and manner of termination or renewal.

[Pub. 100-02, Ch. 15, § 230.6.]

Hospital billing "under arrangements." A hospital may bill Medicare for outpatient therapy (physical therapy, occupational therapy, or speech-language pathology) services that it furnishes to its outpatients, either directly or under arrangements in the hospital's outpatient department. Services provided to residents of a Medicare-certified SNF may not be billed by the hospital as services to its outpatients; these services are covered under a SNF's global prospective payment system payment for the covered Part A stay. [Pub. 100-02, Ch. 15, § 230.6.]

Payment Methodology

Except for outpatient therapy services furnished by critical access hospitals, payment for therapy services furnished to outpatients, hospital, or SNF patients not in a covered Part A stay, or individuals provided therapy services by a home health agency who are not homebound or under a home health plan of care (see ¶ 860), is made under the Medicare physician fee schedule. Reimbursement for therapy provided to Part A inpatients of hospitals or SNFs is included in the prospective payment system (PPS) rate (see ¶ 810). Reimbursement for therapy provided by home health agencies under a home health plan of care is included in the home health PPS rate. Outpatient therapy services furnished by CAHs are paid on a reasonable cost basis. [Soc. Sec. Act § 1832(a)(2)(C).]

[¶ 382] Rural Health Clinics and Federally Qualified Health Centers

Part B covers rural health clinic (RHC) and federally qualified health center (FQHC) services in medically underserved localities. [Soc. Sec. Act §§ 1832(a)(2)(D), 1861(aa); 42 C.F.R. § 410.10(j), (s).]

RHCs are clinics located in areas designated by the Bureau of the Census as rural and the Secretary of HHS as medically underserved or having an insufficient number of physicians. FQHCs are defined similarly but are usually in urban areas. [Soc. Sec. Act § 1861(aa); 42 C.F.R. § 491.2.]

RHC and FQHC services reimbursable under Part B include:

(1) physicians' services, and services and supplies incident to a physician's services;

(2) similar services furnished by a physician assistant, nurse practitioner, certified nurse-midwife, clinical psychologist, or clinical social worker, and services and supplies incident to their services;

(3) visiting nurse services furnished to homebound patients in areas where there is a shortage of home health agencies; and

(4) otherwise covered drugs furnished by, and incident to, services of physicians and nonphysician practitioners.

[42 C.F.R. §§ 405.2411, 405.2446, 410.45(a); *Medicare Benefit Policy Manual*, Pub. 100-02, Ch. 13, § 40.]

Medical nutrition therapy services and diabetes outpatient self-management training services also are included FQHC services. [42 C.F.R. § 405.2446(b)(9).]

In addition, Medicare covers certain preventive primary services furnished by FQHCs, including physical examinations targeted to risk, visual acuity screening, hearing screening, cholesterol screening, blood pressure measurement, and nutritional assessment and referral. Preventive primary services furnished by FQHCs do *not* include group or mass information programs, health education classes, group education activities, eyeglasses, hearing aids, or preventive dental services. Screening mammography is not considered an FQHC service but may be provided at an FQHC if the center meets the applicable regulatory requirements. [Soc. Sec. Act § 1861(aa)(3)(A); 42 C.F.R. § 405.2448; Pub. 100-02, Ch. 13, §§ 50.1, 50.2.]

In the case of a RHC located in an area in which there exists a shortage of home health agencies, the term "rural health service" includes part-time or intermittent nursing care and related medical supplies (other than drugs and biologicals) furnished by a registered professional nurse or licensed practical nurse to a homebound individual under a written plan of treatment. [Soc. Sec. Act § 1861(aa)(1)(C).]

RHC and FQHC services are reimbursable when furnished to a patient at the clinic other outpatient setting, including a patient's place of residence, or the scene of an accident. RHC and FQHC services are not covered in a hospital. [42 C.F.R. §§ 405.2411(b), 405.2446(c) and (d); Pub. 100-02, Ch. 13, § 40.1.]

A clinic certified as an RHC or FQHC may furnish services beyond the scope of the services covered under the RHC or FQHC benefit. If the services are authorized to be furnished by a RHC or FQHC and covered under another separate Medicare benefit category, they must be separately billed to the Medicare administrative contractor under the payment rules that apply to the service. Items and services that are *not* RHC or FQHC services include: certain laboratory services; durable medical equipment; prosthetic devices; leg, arm, back, and neck braces; ambulance services; and the technical component of certain services. [Pub. 100-02, Ch. 13, §§ 60, 60.1.]

Except for preventive services, which Medicare pays 100 percent, FQHC and RHC services are subject to the Part B coinsurance requirements. The deductible applies to RHC services but not to FQHC services. [42 C.F.R. §§ 405.2410, 405.2462(d).]

As discussed at ¶ 607, services paid for directly or indirectly by a governmental entity usually are excluded from coverage under the Medicare program. The law, however, makes a specific exception to this exclusion in the case of RHC and FQHC services. [Soc. Sec. Act § 1862(a)(3).]

See ¶ 847 for a discussion of payment for RHC services and ¶ 850 for a discussion of payment for FQHC services.

¶382

[¶ 383] Home Health Services

For Medicare beneficiaries that are enrolled in both Medicare Part A and Part B, Part A pays home health services for the first 100 visits following a "spell of illness" that required a hospital or skilled nursing home (SNF) stay, referred to as a "post institutional" stay. Part A finances up to 100 visits during one home health spell of illness if the following criteria are met:

(1) the beneficiary is enrolled in Part A and Part B and qualifies for home health benefits;

(2) the beneficiary meets the three-consecutive-day stay requirement; and

(3) the home health services are initiated and the first covered home health visit is rendered within 14 days of discharge from a three-consecutive-day stay in a hospital or rural primary care hospital or within 14 days of discharge from a skilled nursing facility in which the individual was provided post-hospital extended care services.

If the first home health visit is not initiated within 14 days of discharge or if the three-consecutive-day stay requirement is not met, then services are covered under Part B. [Soc. Sec. Act § 1812(a)(3); *Medicare Benefit Policy Manual*, Pub. 100-02, Ch. 7, § § 60.1, 60.2, 60.3.]

After a beneficiary exhausts 100 visits of Part A post-institutional home health services, Part B finances the balance of the home health spell of illness. [Pub. 100-02, Ch. 7, § 60.1.]

Post-institutional defined. Home health services are considered "post-institutional" if they were furnished to a beneficiary after discharge from: (1) a hospital in which the individual was an inpatient for not less than three consecutive days before discharge and the home health services are initiated within 14 days of discharge; or (2) a SNF in which the beneficiary was provided post-hospital extended care services and services are initiated within 14 days after discharge. [Soc. Sec. Act § 1861(tt)(1); Pub. 100-02, Ch. 7, § 60.3.]

Spell of illness defined. A "spell of illness" in the case of home health services means a period of consecutive days beginning with the first day that the individual is furnished post-institutional home health services and that occurs in a month for which the individual is entitled to benefits under Part A. The home health spell of illness ends when the individual has not received inpatient hospital, SNF, or home health services for 60 consecutive days. [Soc. Sec. Act § 1861(tt)(2); Pub. 100-02, Ch. 7, § 60.1.]

Requirements for home health benefits. To qualify for home health benefits, a beneficiary must: (1) be confined to the home, (2) be under a physician's care, (3) be receiving services under a plan of care established and periodically reviewed by a physician, (4) be in need of skilled nursing care on an intermittent basis, or physical therapy or speech-language pathology services, or (5) have a continued need for occupational therapy. [Soc. Sec. Act § 1835(a)(2)(A); Pub. 100-02, Ch. 7, § 30.]

Face-to-face encounter. A physician, nurse practitioner, clinical nurse specialist, certified nurse-midwife, or physician assistant must have a face-to-face encounter with the beneficiary related to the reason for the beneficary's admission into home health no more than 90 days before the home health start of care or within 30 days of the start of the home health care. The encounter must be documented by the certifying physician. Documentation must include:

(1) the date of the encounter;

(2) an explanation of why the clinical findings of the encounter, which was was related to the primary reason for home care, support that the patient is homebound and in need of Medicare covered home health services; and

(3) a physician signature.

[Soc. Sec. Act § 1814(a)(2)(C); 42 C.F.R. § 424.22(a)(1)(v).]

Part A home health benefits are discussed beginning at ¶ 250. The home health prospective payment system is discussed at ¶ 830.

[¶ 385] Comprehensive Outpatient Rehabilitation Facility Services

Medicare Part B covers comprehensive outpatient rehabilitation facility (CORF) services. [Soc. Sec. Act § 1832(a)(2)(E).] A CORF is a public or private institution that is capable of providing a broad array of rehabilitation services on an outpatient basis at a central location in a coordinated fashion. Outpatient therapy services furnished by a CORF may be provided in a patient's home (absent any home health benefits) and other off-site locations. CORFs cover items and services such as:

(1) physicians' services;

(2) physical, occupational, and respiratory therapy and speech-language pathology services;

(3) prosthetic and orthotic devices, including testing, fitting, or training in the use of such devices;

(4) social and psychological services;

(5) nursing care provided by or under the supervision of a registered professional nurse;

(6) drugs and biologicals that are administered by or under the supervision of a physician or registered nurse, and are not usually self-administered by the patient;

(7) supplies and durable medical equipment; and

(8) home environment evaluation visits.

[Soc. Sec. Act § 1861(cc)(1); 42 C.F.R. § 410.100.]

Except for a home environment evaluation and physical, occupational, and speech-language pathology services, all CORF services must be provided on the premises of the CORF. [42 C.F.R. § 410.105(b).]

None of the services listed above is covered as a CORF service if it: (1) would not be covered as an inpatient hospital service if furnished to a hospital inpatient, or (2) is not reasonable and necessary for the diagnosis or treatment of illness or injury or to improve the functioning of a malformed body member. [Soc. Sec. Act § 1861(cc)(1); 42 C.F.R. § 410.102.]

There must be potential for restoration or improvement of lost or impaired functions for CORF services to be covered. For example, treatments involving repetitive exercises (i.e., maintenance programs, general conditioning, or ambulation) that do not require the skilled services of therapists or other professional rehabilitation practitioners are not covered because nonmedical personnel such as family members or exercise instructors could perform these services in the patient's residence. [*Medicare Benefit Policy Manual*, Pub. 100-02, Ch. 12, § 10.]

Written plan of treatment. CORF services must be furnished under a written plan of treatment that (1) is established and signed by a physician before treatment is begun; and (2) prescribes the type, amount, frequency, and duration of the services to be furnished and indicates the diagnosis and anticipated rehabilitation goals that are consistent with the patient function reporting on the claims for services. A facility physician or the referring physician must review the CORF plan of treatment every 60 days for respiratory therapy and every 90 days for physical therapy, occupational therapy, and speech-language pathology services. [42 C.F.R. § 410.105(c).]

Functional reporting. Pursuant to section 3005(g) of the Middle Class Tax Relief and Jobs Creation Act of 2012, at the beginning of treatment, specified reporting intervals consistent with progress reporting, and discharge from therapy, claims for CORF physical therapy, occupational therapy, and speech-language pathology services must include nonpayable G-codes and severity modifiers, which report the functional status of CORF patients. [42 C.F.R. § 410.105(d); Pub. 100-02, Ch. 12, § 30.]

Administrative services. Certain administrative services provided by physicians associated with a CORF are considered CORF physician services, which are not billable by the CORF. These services include consultation with and medical supervision of nonphysician staff, team conferences, case reviews, and other facility medical and administration activities relating to the comprehensive coordinated skilled rehabilitation service. [Pub. 100-02, Ch. 12, § 40.1.]

Diagnostic and therapeutic services. Physicians' diagnostic and therapeutic services furnished to an individual patient are not CORF physicians' services. The physician must bill the Medicare administrative contractor for these services, and payment is based on the Medicare physician fee schedule. [Pub. 100-02, Ch. 12, § 40.1.]

Payment. CORF services are paid under a special prospective payment system and are subject to the same annual payment limitation rules applicable to other therapy and rehabilitation services. The Medicare physician fee schedule constitutes the prospective payment system for these services. [Soc. Sec. Act § 1834(k); *Medicare Claims Processing Manual*, Pub. 100-04, Ch. 5, § 10.2.]

The conditions of participation applicable to CORFs are contained in 42 C.F.R. Chapter IV (Subchapter G, Part 485, Subpart B) of the regulations.

[¶ 386] Ambulatory Surgical Services

There are a number of surgical procedures covered by Medicare, usually performed on an inpatient basis, that may, consistent with sound medical practice, be performed on an outpatient basis. Surgical procedures that do not have a significant safety risk when performed in an outpatient ambulatory surgical center (ASC) and do not require an overnight stay are covered by Medicare. [42 C.F.R. § 416.166.]

ASC Definition

An ASC is a distinct entity that operates exclusively for the purpose of furnishing outpatient surgical services to patients not requiring hospitalization and in which the expected duration of services would not exceed 24 hours following admission. It must enter into an agreement with CMS to participate in Medicare as an ASC and meet the conditions of participation set forth in 42 C.F.R. §§ 416.40–416.49. [42 C.F.R. § 416.2.]

An ASC is either independent (that is, not part of a provider of services or any other facility), or operated by a hospital. To be considered an ASC operated by a hospital, a facility must:

(1) elect to be covered as an ASC;

(2) constitute a separately identifiable entity that is physically, administratively, and financially independent and distinct from the hospital's other operations, with costs for the ASC treated as a nonreimbursable cost center on the hospital's cost report;

(3) meet all health and safety requirements and agree to the assignment, coverage, and payment rules that apply to independent ASCs; and

(4) be surveyed and approved as complying with the ASC conditions of coverage.

[*Medicare Benefit Policy Manual*, Pub. 100-02, Ch. 15, §260.1; *Medicare Claims Processing Manual*, Pub. 100-04, Ch. 14, §10.1.]

An ASC must meet several conditions for coverage to be reimbursed by Medicare for services provided. The ASC conditions for coverage are comparable to the conditions of participation for other providers, including compliance with state licensure requirements. [42 C.F.R. §§416.40–416.52.]

Admissions and discharge planning. Not more than 30 days before a scheduled surgery, each patient must have a complete medical history and physical assessment by a physician or other qualified practitioner, and upon admission each patient must have a pre-surgical assessment. The patient's post-surgical condition must be assessed and documented in the patient's medical record. Each patient must have a discharge order signed by the physician who performed the surgery along with instructions about follow-up care and must be discharged into the company of a responsible adult unless exempted by the attending physician. [42 C.F.R. §416.52.]

Surgical services. The ASC must have an effective procedure for the immediate transfer to a qualified hospital of a patient requiring emergency medical care beyond the capabilities of the ASC. The ASC must have a written transfer agreement with such a hospital, or all physicians performing surgery in the ASC must have admitting privileges with such a hospital. [42 C.F.R. §416.41(b).]

Surgical procedures must be performed in a safe manner by qualified physicians who have been granted clinical privileges by the governing body of the ASC. The center must ensure that a physician will evaluate a patient's anesthetic risk and anesthetic recovery, anesthesia is administered only by qualified personnel, and proper discharge procedures are followed. [42 C.F.R. §416.42.]

Evaluation of quality. The center must conduct an ongoing self-assessment of the quality, medical necessity, and appropriateness of care provided and use these findings to revise policies if necessary. The ASC must measure, analyze, and track quality indicators, adverse patient events, infection control, and other aspects of performance. Performance improvement priorities must focus on high risk, high volume, and problem-prone areas. Performance improvement projects must be implemented and documented. [42 C.F.R. §416.43.]

Patients' rights. ASCs must provide patients and the patient's representative with both verbal and written notice of the patient's rights in advance of the date of the procedure and in a language that the patient and the patient's representative understand. A notice of patients' rights must be posted in the facility. Patients have a right to personal privacy, receive care in a safe setting, and be free from all forms of abuse or harassment. [42 C.F.R. §416.50(a), (f).]

Grievance procedure. The ASC must establish a grievance procedure that has time frames for review and response. All allegations, including, but not limited to, mistreatment; neglect; and verbal, mental, sexual, or physical abuse must be immediately reported, documented, investigated, and disposed of in an appropriate manner. Only substantial allegations must be reported to the state or local authority. [42 C.F.R. §416.50(d).]

Advance directives. The ASC must provide the patient or the patient's representative with information concerning its policies on advance directives before the date of admission. The ASC must document in the patient's record whether he or she has executed an advance directive. [42 C.F.R. §416.50(c).] The fees of physicians and other health care practitioners for surgery and anesthesia are paid under the physician fee schedule (see ¶ 855); reimbursement for ASC or hospital outpatient facility costs is described at ¶ 825.

Covered ASC Services

Subject to specified exclusions, covered surgical procedures are surgical procedures specified by the HHS Secretary and published in the *Federal Register* and/or on the CMS website that are separately paid under the hospital outpatient prospective payment system (OPPS), that would not be expected to pose a significant safety risk to a Medicare beneficiary when performed in an ASC, and for which standard medical practice dictates that the beneficiary would not typically be expected to require active medical monitoring and care at midnight following the procedure. [42 C.F.R. § 416.166(b).]

Covered procedures do not include procedures that:

    (1) generally result in extensive blood loss;

    (2) require major or prolonged invasion of body cavities;

    (3) directly involve major blood vessels;

    (4) are generally emergent or life-threatening in nature;

    (5) commonly require systemic thrombolytic therapy;

    (6) are designated as requiring inpatient care under 42 C.F.R. § 419.22(n);

    (7) can only be reported using a CPT® unlisted surgical procedure code; or

    (8) are otherwise excluded under 42 C.F.R. § 411.15.

[42 C.F.R. § 416.166(c).]

Included facility services. The regulations list the services for which payment is packaged into the ASC payment for a covered surgical procedure under 42 C.F.R. § 416.166. Examples include nursing, technician, and related services; use of the facility where the surgical procedures are performed; equipment; and surgical dressings. [42 C.F.R. § 416.164(a).]

Ancillary services. Medicare makes separate payments to ASCs for certain covered ancillary services that are provided integral to a covered ASC surgical procedure. Covered ancillary services include the following:

    (1) brachytherapy sources;

    (2) certain implantable items with pass-through status under the OPPS;

    (3) certain items and services that CMS designates as contractor-priced, including, but not limited to, the acquisition or procurement of corneal tissue for corneal transplant procedures;

    (4) certain drugs and biologicals for which separate payment is allowed under the OPPS; and

    (5) certain radiology services for which separate payment is allowed under the OPPS.

[42 C.F.R. § 416.164(b).]

Excluded services. ASC services do not include items and services outside the scope of ASC services for which payment may be made under 42 C.F.R. Part 414 in accordance with 42 C.F.R. § 410.152, including, but not limited to (1) physicians' services (including surgical procedures and all preoperative and postoperative services that are performed by a physician); (2) anesthetists' services; (3) radiology services (other than those integral to performance of a covered surgical procedure); (4) diagnostic procedures (other than those directly related to performance of a covered surgical procedure); (5) ambulance services; (6) leg, arm, back, and neck braces other than those that serve the function of a cast or splint; (7) artificial limbs; and (8) nonimplantable prosthetic devices and durable medical equipment. [42 C.F.R. § 416.164(c).]

[¶ 387] Mental Health Services

Services generally covered by Medicare Part B for the treatment of psychiatric patients include:

- individual and group therapy with physicians, psychologists, or other mental health professionals authorized by the state;

- occupational therapy services, if the patient requires the skills of a qualified occupational therapist and the services are performed by or under the supervision of a qualified occupational therapist or by an occupational therapy assistant;

- services of social workers, trained psychiatric nurses, and other staff trained to work with psychiatric patients;

- drugs and biologicals furnished to outpatients for therapeutic purposes, but only if they are of a type that cannot be self-administered;

- activity therapies, but only those that are individualized and essential for the treatment of the patient's condition; the treatment plan must clearly justify the need for each particular therapy utilized and explain how it fits into the patient's treatment;

- family counseling services (counseling services with members of the household are covered only when the primary purpose of such counseling is the treatment of the patient's condition);

- patient education programs, but only when the educational activities are closely related to the care and treatment of the patient; and

- diagnostic services for the purpose of diagnosing those individuals for whom an extended or direct observation is necessary to determine functioning and interactions, identify problem areas, and formulate a treatment plan.

[*Medicare Benefit Policy Manual*, Pub. 100-02, Ch. 6, § 70.1.]

The following are generally not covered: (1) meals and transportation; (2) activity therapies, group activities, or other services and programs that are primarily recreational or diversional in nature; (3) psychosocial programs; and (4) vocational training. [Pub. 100-02, Ch. 6, § 70.1.]

There are no specific limits on the length of time that services may be covered. There are many factors that affect the outcome of treatment, including the nature of the illness, prior history, goals of treatment, and a patient's response. As long as a patient continues to show improvement in accordance with his or her individualized treatment plan and the frequency of services is within accepted norms of medical practice, coverage may be continued, but if a patient reaches a point in treatment when further improvement does not appear to be indicated, mental health treatment must be reevaluated. [Pub. 100-02, Ch. 6, § 70.1.]

Partial Hospitalization Coverage

Medicare covers partial hospitalization services connected with the treatment of mental illness. Outpatient partial hospitalization services are covered only if the individual otherwise would require inpatient psychiatric care. The treatment offered by partial hospitalization programs closely resembles that of a highly structured, short-term hospital inpatient program. [Soc. Sec. Act §§ 1835(a)(2)(F), 1861(s)(2)(B).]

¶387

Under this benefit, Medicare covers:

(1) individual and group therapy with physicians or psychologists (or other authorized mental health professionals);

(2) occupational therapy;

(3) services of social workers, trained psychiatric nurses, and other staff trained to work with psychiatric patients;

(4) drugs and biologicals furnished for therapeutic purposes that cannot be self-administered;

(5) individualized activity therapies that are not primarily recreational or diversionary;

(6) family counseling (for treatment of the patient's condition);

(7) patient training and education; and

(8) diagnostic services.

[Soc. Sec. Act § 1861(ff)(2); 42 C.F.R. § 410.43(a)(4).]

Meals and transportation are specifically excluded from coverage. Programs involving primarily social, recreational, or diversionary activities are not considered partial hospitalization. [Pub. 100-02, Ch. 6, § 70.3.]

The services must be reasonable and necessary for the diagnosis or active treatment of the individual's condition. They also must be reasonably expected to improve or maintain the individual's condition and functional level and prevent relapse or hospitalization. The course of treatment must be prescribed, supervised, and reviewed by a physician. Patients must require a minimum of 20 hours per week of therapeutic services, as evidenced by their plan of care. The program must be hospital-based or hospital-affiliated and must be a distinct and organized intensive ambulatory treatment service offering less than 24-hour daily care. The program also is covered when provided in a community health center (see ¶ 382). [Soc. Sec. Act § 1861(ff); 42 C.F.R. § 410.43; Pub. 100-02, Ch. 6, § 70.3.]

[¶ 388] Telehealth Services

Medicare covers consultations furnished by means of interactive telecommunications systems if the consultation services are provided for a Medicare patient located in certain rural areas. These services are also known as "telehealth services." [Soc. Sec. Act § 1834(m); 42 C.F.R. § 410.78.]

The teleconsultation must be referred and performed by a physician, physician assistant, nurse practitioner, clinical nurse specialist, nurse-midwife, clinical psychologist, clinical social worker, registered dietitian or nutrition professional, or, effective January 1, 2016, a certified registered nurse anesthetist. The medical examination of the patient must be under the control of the consulting practitioner. [Soc. Sec. Act § 1834(m); 42 C.F.R. § 410.78(b).]

Telecommunication system. An "interactive telecommunications system" means multimedia communications equipment that includes, at a minimum, audio and video equipment permitting two-way, real-time interactive communication between the patient and the distant site physician or practitioner. Telephones, fax machines, and e-mail systems do not meet this definition. [42 C.F.R. § 410.78(a)(3); *Medicare Benefit Policy Manual*, Pub. 100-02, Ch. 15, § 270.3.]

For any federal telemedicine demonstration program conducted in Alaska or Hawaii, the use of store-and-forward technologies that provide for the asynchronous transmission of health care information in single or multimedia formats is permitted. [Soc. Sec. Act § 1834(m)(1); 42 C.F.R. § 410.78(a).]

Originating site. Facilities that may act as the originating site (the location of the beneficiary at the time the telehealth service is furnished) include the office of a physician or practitioner, a critical access hospital (CAH), a rural health clinic, a federally qualified health center, a hospital, a hospital-based or CAH-based renal dialysis center (including satellites), a skilled nursing facility, or a community mental health center. [Soc. Sec. Act § 1834(m)(4)(C)(ii); 42 C.F.R. § 410.78(b)(3).]

The originating site must be: (1) located in a rural Health Professional Shortage Area (HPSA) that is either outside of an Metropolitan Statistical Area (MSA) as of December 31st of the preceding calendar year or within rural census tracts as determined by the Office of Rural Health Policy as of December 31st of the preceding calendar year; (2) in a county that is not included in an MSA as of December 31st of the preceding year; or (3) participating in a federal telemedicine demonstration project that was approved by HHS as of December 31, 2000. [Soc. Sec. Act § 1834(m)(4)(C)(i); 42 C.F.R. § 410.78(b)(4).]

List of covered telehealth services. Changes to the list of covered Medicare telehealth services are made through the annual physician fee schedule rulemaking process. [Soc. Sec. Act § 1834(m)(4)(F)(ii); 42 C.F.R. § 410.78(f).] A list of covered telehealth services is available on the CMS website at http://www.cms.gov/Medicare/Medicare-General-Information/Telehealth/Telehealth-Codes.html. For example, the physician fee schedule final rule for calendar year 2016 added certain codes for prolonged services in the inpatient or observation setting (Current Procedure Terminology® (CPT®) codes 99356 and 99357) and end-stage renal disease-related services for home dialysis (CPT® codes 90963 through 90966) to the list of telehealth services. The 2015 final rule added psychotherapy services (CPT® codes 90845, 90846, and 90847), prolonged service office (CPT® codes 99354 and 99355), and annual wellness visits (CPT® codes G0438 and G0429) to the list of telehealth services. [*Final rule*, 80 FR 70886, Nov. 16, 2015; *Final rule*, 79 FR 67548, Nov. 13, 2014; *Medicare Claims Processing Manual*, Pub. 100-04, Ch. 12, § 190.3.]

[¶ 390] National and Local Coverage Determinations

To the extent a specific item or service is not mentioned in the law, the Secretary of HHS has authority to make coverage decisions within a broad range of categories. Items and services that are not specifically excluded from coverage must be determined by the Secretary to be reasonable and necessary for the diagnosis and treatment of illnesses and injuries, or to improve the functioning of a malformed body member. HHS decisions as to whether Medicare will cover new services are issued as national coverage determinations (NCDs). [Soc. Sec. Act § 1862(l).]

NCDs are developed by CMS to describe the circumstances for Medicare coverage nationwide for an item or service. NCDs generally outline the conditions for which an item or service is considered to be covered (or not covered) under Soc. Sec. Act § 1862(a)(1) or other applicable provisions of the Social Security Act. NCDs are usually issued as a program instruction. Once published in a CMS program instruction, an NCD is binding on all Medicare contractors and Medicare Advantage organizations. NCDs are binding on administrative law judges (ALJs) during the claim appeal process. [*Medicare Program Integrity Manual*, Pub. 100-08, Ch. 13, § 13.1.1.]

The NCD development process includes:

(1) the internal and external processes for requesting an NCD or an NCD reconsideration;

(2) a tracking system that provides public notice of acceptance of a complete, formal request and subsequent actions in a web-based format;

(3) a process to allow notice and opportunity to comment before implementation of an NCD;

(4) standardization of the information required to complete a formal request; and

(5) publication of a decision memorandum explaining the purpose and basis of the decision.

CMS considers coverage of additional services with the help of the Medicare Evidence Development & Coverage Advisory Committee, which is composed of members of the health care industry and consumer groups, or other consultants. [*Notice*, 78 FR 48164, Aug. 7, 2013.]

Local coverage determinations. Medicare administrative contractors that process claims can issue local coverage determinations (LCDs). LCDs are made only on the reasonableness and necessity of an item or service, not addressing statutory and other exclusions. Providers may ask the contractor to review an LCD or consider a new item or service. [Pub. 100-08, Ch. 13, § 13.1.3.]

Reconsiderations and reviews of NCDs and LCDs. For a discussion of LCD and NCD reconsiderations and reviews, see ¶ 928.

Recent announcements of coverage decisions. In 2015, CMS announced new or expanded coverage of the following services as a result of the NCD process:

- Effective February 5, 2015, Medicare covers lung cancer screening with low dose computed tomography if all eligibility requirements are met. [*Medicare National Coverage Determinations Manual*, Pub. 100-03, Ch. 1, § 210.14; Transmittal No. 185, Aug. 21, 2015.]

- Effective October 9, 2014, CMS covers Cologuard ™, a multitarget stool DNA test, as a colorectal cancer screening test for asymptomatic, average risk beneficiaries aged 50 to 85 years. [Pub. 100-03, Ch. 1, § 210.3; Transmittal No. 183, Aug. 6, 2015.]

- Effective August 13, 2013, CMS covers implanted permanent cardiac pacemakers, single chamber or dual chamber, for the treatment of non-reversible symptomatic bradycardia due to sinus node dysfunction and second and/or third degree atrioventricular block. [Pub. 100-03, Ch. 1, § 20.8.3; Transmittal No. 179, Feb. 20, 2015.]

Chapter 4– MEDICARE PART C—MEDICARE ADVANTAGE

[¶ 400] Overview

The Medicare Advantage (MA) program—also known as Medicare Part C—offers beneficiaries the option of receiving all of their Medicare benefits from health plans run by private companies. The MA program succeeded the Medicare+Choice program, in which enrollment had declined steadily from 1999 to 2003. According to Kaiser Family Foundation data, since 2010, enrollment in MA plans has grown by 50 percent, and 16.8 million Medicare beneficiaries were enrolled in private MA plans in March 2014, up almost 10 percent since March 2013. About 30 percent of Medicare beneficiaries were enrolled in MA plans in 2015, with enrollment in these plans increased in almost every state. [*Medicare Advantage 2015 Spotlight: Enrollment Market Update*, Kaiser Family Foundation, June 2015.]

The MA program is administered according to federal regulations found at 42 C.F.R. Part 422. CMS also publishes updates to information regarding the administration of the MA program in the *Medicare Managed Care Manual,* CMS Pub. 100-16.

MA Regional Plans

CMS established 26 regions for MA plans. [*Medicare Managed Care Manual*, Pub. 100-16, Ch. 1, § 30.2.3.] The purpose of the regions is to maximize the availability of MA regional plans to all MA-eligible individuals without regard to health status or geographic location, especially to individuals in rural areas. CMS may periodically review and revise the regions if it determines it is appropriate. By regulation, there must be no fewer than 10 regions and no more than 50 regions. [Soc. Sec. Act § 1858(a); 42 C.F.R. § 422.455.]

Types of Plans

MA organizations can offer three types of plans to beneficiaries: (1) a coordinated care plan (which includes special needs plans); (2) a combination of a medical savings account (MSA) plan and a contribution into a MSA; and (3) a private fee-for-service (PFFS) plan. [Soc. Sec. Act § 1859(a)(2); 42 C.F.R. § 422.4(a).] **WK Note:** "Medicare cost plans," which are available in some areas of the country and have some of the same rules as MA plans, are not MA plans and are not covered in detail in this chapter.

Coordinated care plans. Coordinated care plans include a network of providers that are under contract or arrangement with the MA organization to deliver a benefit package approved by CMS. The plans may include health maintenance organizations (HMOs), provider-sponsored organizations (PSOs), regional or local preferred provider organizations (PPOs), and other network plans (other than PFFS plans). [42 C.F.R. § 422.4(a)(1), (a)(1)(iii).] In 2015, 64 percent of MA plan beneficiaries were in HMOs. [*Medicare Advantage 2015 Spotlight: Enrollment Market Update*, Kaiser Family Foundation, June 2015.]

Special needs plans (SNPs), mostly HMOs, are an option for three groups of beneficiaries with significant or relatively specialized care needs, including those: (1) who are dually eligible for Medicare and Medicaid; (2) who require a nursing home or institutional level of care; or (3) with severe chronic or disabling conditions. SNPs offer the same benefits as traditional Medicare, but they also must provide the Part D prescription drug benefit as well as additional services tailored to the special needs population. Section 206 of the Medicare Access and CHIP Reauthorization Act of 2015 (P.L. 114-10) extended the SNP program through December 31, 2018. [Soc. Sec. Act § 1859(b)(6), (f)(1); 42 C.F.R. § § 422.2, 422.4(a)(1)(iv).] See ¶ 402 for more information about SNPs.

Private fee-for-service plans. Similar to fee-for-service Medicare, PFFS plans reimburse providers at a rate determined by the plan on a fee-for-service basis, without putting the provider at risk. These plans do not vary reimbursement based on utilization, and they do not limit the selection of providers. [42 C.F.R. § 422.4(a)(3).]

Medical savings accounts. MSA plans have two parts: (1) an MA medical savings account health insurance plan that pays for a basic set of health benefits approved by CMS and includes a uniform premium and a uniform level of cost-sharing for beneficiaries in the plan's service area, and (2) an MSA, which is a trust or custodial account into which CMS will make deposits. [42 C.F.R. § 422.4(a)(2).]

Part D coverage. An organization that offers an MA coordinated plan in a specific area must offer qualified Part D prescription drug coverage in that plan or in another MA plan in the same area. MA organizations offering MSA plans generally are not permitted to offer prescription drug coverage. MA organizations offering PFFS plans can choose whether to offer Part D coverage. [42 C.F.R. §§ 422.4(c), 422.114.]

Medical Loss Ratio Requirements

The Patient Protection and Affordable Care Act (ACA) (P.L. 111-148) made a number of changes to Medicare Part C, including that for contracts beginning in 2014 or later, MA plans must have a medical loss ratio (MLR) of at least 85 percent. [Soc. Sec. Act § 1857(e)(4).]

The minimum MLR requirement is intended to create incentives for MA organizations to reduce administrative costs such as for marketing costs, profits, and other uses of the funds earned by MA organizations and to help ensure that taxpayers and enrolled beneficiaries receive value from Medicare health plans. A MLR is determined based on the percentage of Medicare contract revenue spent on clinical services, prescription drugs, quality improving activities, and direct benefits to beneficiaries in the form of reduced Part B premiums. MA organizations and Part D sponsors remit payment to CMS when their spending on clinical services, prescription drugs, quality improving activities, and Part B premium rebates, in relation to their total revenue, is less than the 85 percent MLR requirement. If an MA organization fails to meet MLR requirements for more than three consecutive years, it will be subject to enrollment sanctions and, after five consecutive years, to contract termination. [Soc. Sec. Act § 1857(e)(4); 42 C.F.R. § 422.2410.]

[¶ 401] Eligibility, Election, Enrollment, and Disenrollment

An individual's eligibility for a Medicare Advantage (MA) plan is determined, in part, by his or her eligibility for Medicare Part A and Part B. [42 C.F.R. § 422.50.] CMS has issued guidance for MA eligibility and enrollment on its website at: http://www.cms.hhs.gov/home/medicare.asp under the "Eligibility and Enrollment" heading.

Eligibility to Elect an MA Plan

In general, an individual is eligible to elect an MA plan if he or she is a U.S. citizen and: (1) is entitled to Medicare Part A and enrolled under Part B; (2) either resides in the service area of the MA plan or resides outside this service area but is enrolled in a health plan offered by the MA organization during the month immediately preceding the month in which the individual is entitled to both Medicare Part A and Part B; and (3) has not been medically determined to have end-stage renal disease (ESRD). [42 C.F.R. § 422.50.]

Special rules for ESRD. An individual who develops ESRD while enrolled in an MA plan or in a health plan offered by an MA organization is nonetheless eligible to elect an MA plan offered by that organization. An individual with ESRD whose enrollment in an MA plan was terminated or discontinued after December 31, 1998, because CMS or the MA organization terminated the MA organization's contract for the plan or discontinued the plan in the area in which the individual resides, is eligible to elect another MA plan. If the plan so elected is later terminated or discontinued in the area in which the individual resides, he or she may elect another MA plan. An individual with ESRD also may elect an MA special needs plan (SNP) as long as that plan has chosen to enroll ESRD individuals. [Soc. Sec. Act § 1851(a)(3)(B); 42 C.F.R. § 422.50(a)(2).]

An individual who receives a kidney transplant and who no longer requires a regular course of dialysis to maintain life is not considered to have ESRD for purposes of MA eligibility. In addition, an individual who initiated dialysis treatments for ESRD but subsequently recovered native kidney function and no longer requires a regular course of dialysis to maintain life is not considered to have ESRD for purposes of MA eligibility. Such individuals may elect to enroll in an MA plan if they meet other applicable eligibility requirements. [*Medicare Managed Care Manual*, Pub. 100-16, Ch. 2, § 20.2.]

SNP eligibility. To elect a special needs plan for a special needs individual, an individual must: (1) meet the definition of a special needs individual, i.e., an individual who is institutionalized, is entitled to assistance under a state Medicaid plan, or has a severe or disabling condition and would benefit from enrollment in a specialized MA plan; (2) meet the eligibility requirements for that specific SNP; and (3) be eligible to elect an MA plan. If a SNP determines that an enrollee no longer meets the eligibility criteria but can reasonably be expected to again meet the criteria within a six-month period, the enrollee is deemed to continue to be eligible for the MA plan for a period of not less than 30 days but not to exceed six months. [42 C.F.R. §§ 422.2, 422.52.]

Hospice patients. MA organizations do not provide hospice care but must inform each Medicare enrollee eligible to select hospice care about the availability of hospice care under certain circumstances. [42 C.F.R. §§ 422.320, 422.100(c)(1).]

Continuation of enrollment. An MA organization may offer a continuation of enrollment option to enrollees when they no longer reside in the service area of a plan and permanently move into the area designated as the MA organization's "continuation area." The beneficiary may choose whether to continue enrollment in the plan after the move or to disenroll. [Soc. Sec. Act § 1851(b)(1); 42 C.F.R. § 422.54.]

Election and Enrollment

Generally, each MA organization must accept without restriction individuals who are eligible to elect an MA plan that the MA organization offers and who elect the plan during initial coverage election periods and annual election periods. If CMS determines that a plan has a capacity limit, the MA organization may limit enrollment in the plan under certain circumstances. [42 C.F.R. §§ 422.60, 422.62.]

Beneficiaries may make elections during three different types of election periods:

- the initial coverage election period (ICEP);
- the annual election period (AEP); or
- a special election period (SEP).

[Soc. Sec. Act § 1851(e); 42 C.F.R. § 422.62.]

Initial coverage election period. The ICEP is the period during which a newly MA-eligible individual may make an initial election. The ICEP begins three months before the month an individual is first entitled to Medicare Part A and Part B and ends the last day of the individual's Part B initial enrollment period. [Soc. Sec. Act § 1851(e)(1); 42 C.F.R. § 422.62(a)(1).] An individual who fails to make an election during the initial coverage election period is deemed to have elected original fee-for-service Medicare. [Soc. Sec. Act § 1851(c)(3)(A); 42 C.F.R. § 422.66(c).]

Annual election period. The AEP for MA and Part D prescription drug plans (PDPs) runs from October 15 through December 7. During the AEP, individuals may switch to a different MA plan, or from original Medicare to an MA plan. [Soc. Sec. Act § 1851(e)(3)(B)(v); 42 C.F.R. § 422.62(a)(2).]

Special election period. SEPs constitute periods outside of the usual enrollment periods when an individual may elect a plan or change his or her current plan election. SEPs include situations when:

(1) CMS or the MA organization has terminated the organization's contract for the plan or discontinued the plan in the area in which the individual resides, or the organization has notified the individual of the impending termination of the plan or the impending discontinuation of the plan in the area in which he or she resides;

(2) an individual has made a change in residence outside of the service area or continuation area or has experienced another change in circumstances as determined by CMS (other than termination for non-payment of premiums or disruptive behavior) that causes the individual to no longer be eligible to elect the MA plan;

(3) the individual demonstrates that the MA organization offering the plan substantially violated a material provision of its contract under MA in relation to the individual, including, but not limited to, failure to provide medical services in accordance with quality standards or failure to provide medically necessary services in a timely fashion;

(4) the individual demonstrates that the MA organization materially misrepresented the plan's contract provision in marketing the plan to the individual; or

(5) the individual meets other exceptional conditions as CMS may provide.

[Soc. Sec. Act § 1851(e)(4); 42 C.F.R. § 422.62(b).]

Open enrollment for institutionalized individuals. An individual who is eligible to elect an MA plan and who is institutionalized is not limited in the number of elections or changes he or she may make. An MA-eligible institutionalized individual may at any time elect an MA plan or change his or her election from an MA plan to original Medicare, to a different MA plan, or from original Medicare to an MA plan. [Soc. Sec. Act § 1851(e)(2)(D); 42 C.F.R. § 422.62(a)(6).]

Annual 45-day period for disenrollment from MA plans to original Medicare. During the first 45 days of each calendar year (January 1 to February 14), MA beneficiaries may choose to disenroll from an MA plan and return to traditional fee-for-service Medicare coverage, and they also may choose Part D prescription drug coverage. [Soc. Sec. Act § 1851(e)(2)(C); 42 C.F.R. § § 422.62(a)(7), 423.38(d).]

Forms. An individual who wishes to elect an MA plan may make or change his or her election during the election periods specified above by filing the appropriate election forms with the MA organization or through other mechanisms approved by CMS. An individual who wishes to disenroll from an MA plan may change his or her election during the election periods by either filing a new election form or by filing the appropriate disenrollment form with the MA organization or through other mechanisms determined by CMS. [42 C.F.R. § 422.66(a), (b).]

Alternate employer or union election mechanism. MA organizations that offer MA plans to employers or unions may choose to accept voluntary elections directly from that group without obtaining an MA election form from each individual. Choices of coverage made by individual enrollees using their employer's or union's selection processes are reported to the MA organization. MA organizations may specify the employers or unions, if any, from which they will accept this election format and may choose to accept enrollment and/or voluntary disenrollment elections. [Pub. 100-16, Ch. 2, § 20.4.1.]

Conversion of enrollment. An MA plan must accept any individual (even if the individual has ESRD) who is enrolled in a health plan offered by the MA organization during the month immediately preceding the month in which he or she is eligible for Medicare. [42 C.F.R. § 422.66(d).]

Plan closure. An MA organization has the option to voluntarily close one or more of its MA plans to open enrollment period (OEP) enrollment elections. However, if an MA organization has an MA plan that is open during an OEP and decides to change this process, it must notify CMS and the general public 30 calendar days in advance of the new limitations on the open enrollment process. When an MA plan is voluntarily closed for the OEP, it is closed to all OEP requests, but it must still accept elections made during the ICEP and SEP and be open for the AEP, unless an approved capacity limit applies and has been reached. [Pub. 100-16, Ch. 2, § 30.9.1.]

Passive enrollment. When MA plans immediately terminate or when CMS determines that continued enrollment in an MA plan poses potential harm to the members, CMS may implement passive enrollment procedures. Under passive enrollment procedures, individuals are considered to have elected a plan selected by CMS unless they: (1) decline the plan selected by CMS, or (2) request enrollment in another plan. The MA organization that receives the passive enrollment must provide notice to the potential enrollee that describes the costs and benefits of the plan and the process for accessing care under the plan and clearly explains the beneficiary's ability to decline the enrollment or choose another plan. The notification must be provided to all potential enrollees prior to the enrollment effective date. [42 C.F.R. § 422.60(g).]

Effective dates of elections.

(1) An election made during an ICEP is effective as of the first day of the month of entitlement to both Part A and Part B.

(2) Elections or changes of election made during the AEP are effective the first day of the following calendar year.

(3) Elections made during an OEP are effective the first day of the first month following the month in which the election is made (note: OEPs are available only to institutionalized individuals).

(4) The effective date of elections made during SEPs depend on the circumstances and are made by CMS in a manner consistent with protecting the continuity of health benefits coverage.

(5) The effective date for an election of coverage under original Medicare made during a SEP for an individual age 65 is the first day of the first calendar month following the month in which the election is made.

(6) The effective date for an election made from January 1 through February 14 to disenroll from an MA plan to original Medicare is effective the first day of the first month following the month in which the election is made.

[Soc. Sec. Act § 1851(f); 42 C.F.R. § 422.68.]

Disenrollment

An individual may disenroll from an MA plan only during one of the election periods noted above. The individual may disenroll by: (1) enrolling in another plan during a valid enrollment period; (2) giving or faxing a signed written notice to the MA organization, or through his or her employer or union where applicable; (3) submitting a request via the Internet to the MA organization, if the MA organization offers such an option; or (4) calling 1-800-MEDICARE. If a verbal request is made, the MA organization must instruct the individual to make the request in one of the ways described above. [42 C.F.R. § 422.66(b); Pub. 100-16, Ch. 2, § 50.1.]

Disenrollment by the MA organization. Generally, an MA organization may not disenroll an individual from any MA plan it offers or request or encourage disenrollment. The organization may, however, disenroll an individual if he or she: (1) does not pay any monthly basic or supplementary premium in a timely manner; (2) engages in disruptive behavior; or (3) provides fraudulent information on an election form or permits the fraudulent use of an enrollment card. [42 C.F.R. § 422.74(a), (b)(1).]

The MA organization *must* disenroll an individual under the following circumstances:

(1) the individual no longer resides in the MA plan's service area (including when the individual is incarcerated and does not reside in the service area of the MA plan);

(2) the individual loses entitlement to Part A or Part B benefits;

(3) the individual dies;

(4) for special needs individuals enrolled in a specialized MA plan, the individual no longer meets the special needs status of that plan; or

(5) the individual is not lawfully present in the United States.

[42 C.F.R. § 422.74(b)(2), (d).]

The MA organization also *must* disenroll enrollees: if the organization has its contract with CMS terminated; if it terminates the MA plan; or if it discontinues the plan in an area where it had previously been available. However, when an MA organization discontinues offering an MA plan in a portion of its service area, it may elect to offer enrollees residing in all or portions of the affected area the option to continue enrollment in an MA plan offered by the organization, provided that there is no other MA plan offered in the affected area at the time of the organization's election. The organization may require an enrollee who chooses to continue enrollment to agree to receive the full range of basic benefits (excluding emergency and urgently needed care) exclusively through facilities designated by the organization within the plan service area. [42 C.F.R. § 422.74(b)(3).]

Notice of disenrollment. If the disenrollment is for any of the reasons other than death or loss of entitlement to Medicare Part A or Part B benefits, the MA organization must give the individual a written notice of the disenrollment with an explanation of why the MA organization is planning to disenroll the individual. Notices of disenrollment must be provided to the individual before submission of the disenrollment to CMS, and they must include an explanation of the individual's right to a hearing under the MA organization's grievance procedures. [42 C.F.R. § 422.74(c).]

Consequences of disenrollment. An individual who is disenrolled for nonpayment of premiums, disruptive behavior, fraud and abuse, or loss of Part A or B benefits is deemed to have elected original Medicare. If the individual is disenrolled because the plan was terminated, the area covered by the plan was reduced, or the individual no longer resides in the MA plan's service area, he or she will have a SEP to make a new choice. If the individual fails to make an election during the SEP, he or she will be enrolled in original Medicare. [42

C.F.R. §422.74(e).] MA organizations are required to notify members of their Medigap-guaranteed issue rights when members disenroll to original Medicare during a special election period. [Pub. 100-16, Ch. 2, §50.1.7.]

[¶ 402] Benefits and Beneficiary Protections

A Medicare Advantage (MA) organization offering an MA plan must provide enrollees, at a minimum, with all basic Medicare-covered services (except hospice benefits) by furnishing the benefits directly or through arrangements, or by paying for the benefits. MA organizations also may provide supplemental benefits through their plans. [42 C.F.R. §422.100.] MA organizations must comply with CMS national coverage decisions (NCDs), general coverage guidelines included in original Medicare manuals and instructions (unless superseded by regulations), and written coverage decisions of local Medicare contractors. If an MA organization covers geographic areas encompassing more than one local coverage policy area, it may elect to uniformly apply to plan enrollees in all areas the coverage policy that is the most beneficial to MA enrollees. [42 C.F.R. §422.101(b)(1)–(3).]

Medicare as secondary payer. CMS does not pay for services to the extent that Medicare is not the primary payer (see ¶ 636). An MA organization must, for each MA plan: (1) identify payers that are primary to Medicare; (2) identify the amounts payable by those payers; and (3) coordinate its benefits to Medicare enrollees with the benefits of the primary payers. [42 C.F.R. §422.108.]

Benefits Provided by MA Plans

An MA plan must include basic benefits and also may include supplemental benefits. Basic benefits are all Medicare-covered services, except hospice services; they must be provided through providers meeting the requirements of the Medicare conditions of participation. Supplemental benefits consist of: (1) mandatory supplemental benefits not covered by Medicare that an MA enrollee must purchase as part of an MA plan that are paid for in full, directly by Medicare enrollees, in the form of premiums or cost-sharing; and (2) optional supplemental benefits not covered by Medicare that are purchased at the option of the MA enrollee and paid for in full, directly by the Medicare enrollee, in the form of premiums or cost-sharing. [Soc. Sec. Act §1852(a)(3); 42 C.F.R. §§422.100(a), (c), (h), 422.101–422.104.]

Noncontracting providers and suppliers. An MA organization must make timely and reasonable payment to or on behalf of the plan enrollee for the following services obtained from a provider or supplier that does not contract with the MA organization to provide services covered by the MA plan:

(1) ambulance services dispatched through 911 or its local equivalent;

(2) emergency and urgently needed services;

(3) maintenance and post-stabilization care services;

(4) renal dialysis services provided while the enrollee was temporarily outside the plan's service area; and

(5) services for which coverage has been denied by the MA organization and found upon appeal to be services the enrollee was entitled to have furnished, or paid for, by the MA organization.

[42 C.F.R. §422.100(b)(1).]

An MA plan and an MA medical savings account (MSA) plan offered by an MA organization, after the annual deductible has been met, satisfy the basic requirements with respect to benefits for services furnished by a noncontracting provider if that MA plan provides payment in an amount the provider would have received under original Medicare, including balance billing permitted under Medicare Part A and Part B. [42 C.F.R. § 422.100(b)(2).]

Availability of plans. An MA organization must offer an MA plan to all Medicare beneficiaries residing in the service area of the MA plan. The organization must offer the plan at a uniform premium, with uniform benefits and level of cost-sharing throughout the plan's service area or segment of service area. [42 C.F.R. § 422.100(d).]

Review and approval of benefits and cost-sharing. CMS reviews and approves MA benefits and associated cost-sharing using written policy guidelines and requirements and other CMS instructions to ensure:

- Medicare-covered services meet CMS fee-for-service guidelines.

- MA organizations are not designing benefits to discriminate against beneficiaries, promote discrimination, discourage enrollment or encourage disenrollment, steer subsets of Medicare beneficiaries to particular MA plans, or inhibit access to services.

- Benefit design meets other MA program requirements.

- MA local plans have an out-of-pocket maximum for Medicare Parts A and B services that is no greater than the annual limit set by CMS.

- With respect to a local preferred provider organization (PPO) plan, the annual out-of-pocket limit applies only to use of network providers. Such local PPO plans must include a total catastrophic limit on beneficiary out-of-pocket expenditures for both in-network and out-of-network Parts A and B services that is: (1) consistent with the requirements applicable to MA regional plans; and (2) not greater than the annual limit set by CMS.

- Cost-sharing for Medicare Part A and B services specified by CMS does not exceed levels annually determined by CMS to be discriminatory for such services.

[42 C.F.R. § 422.100(f).]

Mammography, influenza, and pneumococcal benefits. Enrollees of MA organizations may directly access (through self-referral) mammography screening and influenza and pneumococcal vaccines. Cost-sharing for influenza vaccine and pneumococcal vaccine may not be imposed. [42 C.F.R. § 422.100(g).]

Coverage of durable medical equipment. An MA organization must cover and ensure enrollee access to all categories of durable medical equipment (DME) covered under Medicare Part B. However, an MA organization may, within specific categories of DME, limit coverage to certain brands, items, and supplies of preferred manufacturers, provided that:

(1) its contracts with DME suppliers ensure that enrollees have access to all DME brands, items, and supplies of preferred manufacturers;

(2) its enrollees have access to all medically necessary DME brands, items, and supplies of non-preferred manufacturers;

(3) at the request of new enrollees, it provides for a 90-day transition period during which the MA organization will ensure a supply of DME brands, items, and supplies of non-preferred manufacturers, and provide for the repair of same;

(4) it makes no negative changes to its DME brands, items, and supplies of preferred manufacturers during the plan year;

(5) it treats denials of DME brands, items, and supplies of non-preferred manufacturers as organization determinations subject to appeal;

(6) it discloses, as part of its description of benefits, DME coverage limitations and beneficiary appeal rights in the case of a denial of a DME brand, item, or supply of a non-preferred manufacturer; and

(7) it provides full coverage, without limitation on brand and manufacturer, to all DME categories or subcategories annually determined by CMS to require full coverage.

[42 C.F.R. § 422.100(l).]

Special rules for ambulance, emergency, and urgently needed services. The MA organization is financially responsible for ambulance services, including ambulance services dispatched through 911 or its local equivalent, where other means of transportation would endanger the beneficiary's health. The MA organization is also financially responsible for emergency and urgently needed services regardless of whether the services are obtained within or outside the MA organization, and regardless of whether there is prior authorization for the services. [42 C.F.R. § 422.113(a), (b).]

Special rules for maintenance and post-stabilization care services. In addition, the MA organization is financially responsible for post-stabilization care services obtained within or outside the MA organization that: (1) are pre-approved by a plan provider or other MA organization representative; (2) are not pre-approved by a plan provider or other MA organization representative, but are administered to maintain the enrollee's stabilized condition within one hour of a request to the MA organization for pre-approval of further post-stabilization care services; and (3) are not pre-approved by a plan provider or other MA organization representative, but are administered to maintain, improve, or resolve the enrollee's stabilized condition under certain conditions. [42 C.F.R. § 422.113(c)(2).]

Requirements during a disaster or emergency. When a state of disaster is declared, an MA organization must ensure access to benefits by covering Part A, Part B, and supplemental Part B benefits furnished at non-contracted facilities, waive requirements for gatekeeper referrals where applicable, provide the same cost-sharing for enrollees as if the service or benefit had been furnished at a plan-contracted facility, and make changes that benefit the enrollee effective immediately without the 30-day notification requirement. [42 C.F.R. § 422.100(m).]

Return to home skilled nursing facility services. MA plans must provide coverage of post-hospital extended care services to Medicare enrollees through a home skilled nursing facility (SNF) if the enrollee elects to receive the coverage through the home SNF, and if the home SNF either has a contract with the MA organization or agrees to accept substantially similar payment under the same terms and conditions that apply to similar SNFs that contract with the MA organization. A home SNF is: (1) the SNF in which the enrollee resided at the time of admission to the hospital preceding the receipt of post-hospital extended care services, (2) a SNF that is providing post-hospital extended care services through a continuing care retirement community in which the MA plan enrollee was a resident at the time of admission to the hospital, or (3) the SNF in which the spouse of the enrollee is residing at the time of discharge from the hospital. [42 C.F.R. § 422.133.]

Effect of NCDs and legislative changes in benefits. If CMS determines and announces that an individual NCD or legislative change in benefits meets the criteria for "significant cost," an MA organization is not required to assume risk for the costs of that service or benefit until the contract year for which payments are appropriately adjusted to take into account the cost of the NCD service or legislative change in benefits. If CMS determines that an NCD or legislative change in benefits does not meet the "significant cost" threshold, the MA organization is required to provide coverage for the NCD or legislative change in benefits and assume risk for the costs of that service or benefit as of the effective date stated in the NCD or specified in the legislation. [42 C.F.R. § 422.109(b).]

"Significant cost" is defined as either: (1) the average cost of furnishing a single service that exceeds a cost threshold of the preceding year's dollar threshold adjusted to reflect the national per capita growth percentage; or (2) the estimated cost of all Medicare services furnished as a result of a particular NCD or legislative change in benefits representing at least 0.1 percent of the national average per capita costs. [42 C.F.R. § 422.109(a).]

Special Rules for Self-Referral and Point-of-Service Option

If an MA plan member receives an item or service of the plan that is covered upon referral or pre-authorization from a contracted provider of that plan, the member cannot be financially liable for more than the normal in-plan cost-sharing if he or she correctly identifies himself or herself as a member of that plan to the contracted provider before receiving the covered item or service. However, if the contracted provider can show that the enrollee was notified before receiving the item or service that the item or service is covered only if further action is taken by the enrollee, then this requirement does not apply. [42 C.F.R. § 422.105(a).]

Point-of-service option. As a general rule, a point-of-service (POS) benefit is an option that an MA organization may offer in a health maintenance organization (HMO) plan to provide enrollees with additional choice in obtaining specified health care services. The organization may offer a POS option under a coordinated care plan as an additional benefit under an HMO plan as a mandatory or optional supplemental benefit. [42 C.F.R. § 422.105(b).]

Access to Services

An MA organization offering a coordinated care plan may specify the networks of providers that enrollees can use, as long as the organization ensures that all covered services, including supplemental services contracted for the Medicare enrollee, are available and accessible under the plan. [42 C.F.R. § 422.112(a).]

To accomplish this, the MA organization must do the following:

(1) maintain and monitor a network of appropriate providers supported by written agreements that is sufficient to provide necessary access to meet the needs of enrollees (except that MA regional plans can use methods other than written agreements with CMS approval);

(2) establish a panel of primary care providers (PCPs) from which an enrollee may choose a PCP;

(3) provide or arrange for necessary specialty care and, in particular, give women enrollees the option of direct access to a women's health specialist;

(4) demonstrate, if seeking to expand the service area of an MA plan, that the number and type of providers available to the plan are sufficient to meet the needs of the population;

(5) demonstrate to CMS that its providers in a plan are credentialed;

(6) establish written standards for timely access to care, medical necessity determinations, and provider consideration of enrollee input for treatment plans;

(7) establish convenient and non-discriminatory hours of operation and make plan services available 24 hours per day, seven days per week, when medically necessary;

(8) ensure that services are provided in a culturally competent manner to all enrollees;

(9) provide coverage for ambulance services, emergency and urgently needed services, and post-stabilization care services; and

(10) ensure that coordinated care and private fee-for-service (PFFS) MA plans that meet Medicare access and availability requirements through direct contracting network providers are consistent with the prevailing community pattern of health care delivery in the areas where the network is being offered.

[42 C.F.R. § 422.112(a).]

MA organizations also must ensure continuity of care and integration of services through arrangements with contracted providers. [42 C.F.R. § 422.112(b).]

Access to services under private fee-for-service plans. An MA organization that offers a PFFS plan must demonstrate to CMS that it has a sufficient number and range of providers willing to furnish services under the plan. An MA organization meets this requirement if it has: (1) payment rates that are not less than the rates that apply under original Medicare for the provider in question; and (2) contracts or agreements with a sufficient number and range of providers to furnish the services covered under the plan or meet the required access standards. [42 C.F.R. § 422.114(a)(1), (2).]

Reward and Incentive Programs

MA organizations may create reward and incentive programs that focus on promoting improved health, preventing illness and injuries, and encouraging the efficient use of health care resources. These rewards or incentives must: (1) be offered in connection with an entire service or activity; (2) be offered without discrimination; (3) have a monetary cap that is determined by CMS and that is expected to affect enrollee behavior but not exceed the value of the activity or service; and (4) be compliant with all relevant fraud and abuse laws. [42 C.F.R. § 422.134.]

To be considered nondiscriminatory, a reward or incentive program must be designed so that all enrollees may earn rewards and must not discriminate based on race, national origin (including limited English proficiency), gender, disability, chronic disease, whether a person resides in an institutional setting, frailty, health status, or any other prohibited basis. Moreover, reward and incentive programs within MA organizations may not offer items in the form of cash or other monetary rebates and may not be used to target potential enrollees. [42 C.F.R. § 422.134.]

Special Needs Plans

MA organizations seeking to offer a special needs plan (SNP) serving beneficiaries eligible for both Medicare and Medicaid (dual eligibles) must have a contract with the state Medicaid agency. The MA organization retains responsibility under the contract for providing benefits for individuals entitled to receive medical assistance. Such benefits may include long-term care services. At a minimum, the contract must document:

- the MA organization's responsibility, including financial obligations, to provide or arrange for Medicaid benefits;

- the category (or categories) of eligibility for dual-eligible beneficiaries to be enrolled under the SNP;

- the Medicaid benefits covered under the SNP;

- the cost-sharing protections covered under the SNP;

- the identification and sharing of information on Medicaid provider participation;

- the verification of enrollees' eligibility for both Medicare and Medicaid;

- the service area covered by the SNP; and
- the contract period for the SNP.

[42 C.F.R. § 422.107.]

SNPs that meet a high standard of integration and minimum performance and quality-based standards may offer additional supplemental benefits when CMS finds that such benefits could better integrate care for the dual-eligible population. To offer these additional benefits, the special needs plan must: (1) have operated in the MA contract year prior to the MA contract year for which it is submitting its bid; and (2) offer its enrollees such benefits without cost-sharing or additional premium charges. [42 C.F.R. § 422.102(e).]

Model of care for SNPs. MA organizations offering SNPs must implement an evidence-based model of care (MOC) with appropriate networks of providers and specialists. The organization must: (1) conduct a comprehensive initial health risk assessment of each enrollee's physical, psychosocial, and functional needs as well as an annual health risk reassessment, using a comprehensive risk assessment tool that CMS will review during oversight activities; (2) develop and implement a comprehensive individualized plan of care through an interdisciplinary care team in consultation with the beneficiary, identifying goals and objectives, including measurable outcomes as well as specific services and benefits to be provided; and (3) use an interdisciplinary team in the management of care. [42 C.F.R. § 422.101(f)(1).]

MA organizations offering SNPs must also ensure an effective management structure by developing and implementing the following MOC components: (1) target one of the three SNP populations; (2) have appropriate staff trained on the SNP plan MOC to coordinate and deliver all services and benefits; (3) coordinate the delivery of care across health care settings, providers, and services to ensure continuity of care; (4) coordinate the delivery of specialized benefits and services that meet the needs of the most vulnerable beneficiaries among the three target special needs populations, including frail or disabled beneficiaries and beneficiaries near the end of life; and (5) coordinate communication among plan personnel, providers, and beneficiaries. All MA organizations wishing to offer or continue to offer an SNP are required to be approved by the National Committee for Quality Assurance. [42 C.F.R. § 422.101(f)(2).]

Coordination of Benefits

If an MA organization contracts with an employer group health plan (EGHP) or labor union that covers enrollees in an MA plan, or with a state Medicaid agency to provide Medicaid benefits to enrollees who are eligible for both Medicare and Medicaid and who are enrolled in an MA plan, the enrollees must be provided the same benefits as all other enrollees in the MA plan, with the EGHP, labor union, or Medicaid benefits supplementing the MA plan benefits. [42 C.F.R. § 422.106(a).]

Permissible employer, labor organization, or Medicaid plan benefits include: (1) payment of a portion or all of the MA basic and supplemental premiums; (2) payment of a portion or all of other cost-sharing amounts approved for the MA plan; or (3) other employer-sponsored benefits that may require additional premium and cost-sharing, or other benefits provided by the organization under a contract with the state Medicaid agency. [42 C.F.R. § 422.106(b).]

MA organizations may request a CMS waiver or modification of those requirements that hinder the design of, the offering of, or the enrollment in MA plans under contracts between MA organizations and employers, labor organizations, or the trustees of funds established by one or more employers or labor organizations to furnish benefits to the entity's employees,

¶402

former employees, or members or former members of the labor organizations. [42 C.F.R. § 422.106(c).]

Beneficiary Protections

An MA organization may not deny, limit, or condition coverage or benefits to beneficiaries on the basis of health status, including medical condition, claims experience, receipt of health care, medical history, genetic information, evidence of insurability (including conditions arising out of acts of domestic violence), or disability. An MA organization may not enroll an individual who has been medically determined to have end-stage renal disease (ESRD). However, if an individual is diagnosed with ESRD while enrolled in an MA plan, he or she may not be disenrolled for that reason. [42 C.F.R. § 422.110.]

Advance directives. An MA organization must maintain written policies and procedures concerning advance directives with respect to all adults receiving medical care by or through the MA organization. [42 C.F.R. § 422.128.]

Disclosure requirements. An MA organization must disclose to each beneficiary enrolling in one of its plans a plan description, including the plan's service area, benefits, access (including out-of-area coverage), emergency coverage, supplemental benefits, prior authorization and review rules, grievance and appeals procedures, quality improvement program, disenrollment rights and responsibilities, catastrophic caps and single deductible, and claims information. This information must be provided at the time of enrollment and at least annually thereafter, 15 days before the annual coordinated election period, in a clear, accurate, and standardized form. [42 C.F.R. § 422.111.]

The plan description for a SNP for dual-eligible individuals must include a comprehensive written statement describing cost-sharing protections and benefits that the individual is entitled to under Medicare and Medicaid. [42 C.F.R. § 422.111(b)(2)(iii).]

Confidentiality of enrollee records. For any medical records or enrollment information it maintains, an MA organization must abide by all federal and state laws regarding confidentiality and disclosure of medical records; ensure that medical information is released only in accordance with federal or state laws or under court orders or subpoenas; maintain the records in an accurate manner; and ensure timely access by enrollees to their own records. [42 C.F.R. § 422.118.]

[¶ 403] Beneficiary Grievances, Organizational Determinations, and Appeals

Medicare Advantage (MA) plans must provide meaningful procedures for hearing and resolving grievances between the plan and enrolled beneficiaries and for organization determinations and appeals. [Soc. Sec. Act § 1852(f), (g); 42 C.F.R. § 422.560.]

Grievance procedures are separate and distinct from appeal procedures, which address organization determinations. For the purposes of these procedures:

- An *"appeal"* is a procedure that deals with the review of an adverse organization determination on the health care services an enrollee believes he or she is entitled to receive. The basis of this process includes delay in providing, arranging for, or approving health care services (such that a delay would adversely affect the health of the enrollee), or disputes of any amounts the enrollee must pay for a service. These procedures include reconsiderations by the MA organization and, if necessary, an independent review entity (IRE), hearings before administrative law judges (ALJs), review by the Medicare Appeals Council, and judicial review. Disputes involving optional supplemental benefits offered by cost plans and health care prepayment plans (HCPPs) are treated as appeals.

- A *"grievance"* is any complaint or dispute, other than one involving an organization determination, expressing dissatisfaction with any aspect of an MA organization's or provider's operation, activities, or behavior, regardless of whether remedial action is requested. Grievances may include complaints regarding access to or the timeliness, appropriateness, or setting of a provided health service, procedure, or item. Grievance issues also may include complaints that a covered health service procedure or item during a course of treatment did not meet accepted standards for delivery of health care.

[42 C.F.R. § § 422.561, 422.564(b); *Medicare Managed Care Manual,* Pub. 100-16, Ch. 13, § 10.1.]

Grievance Procedures

Each MA organization must provide meaningful procedures for timely hearing and resolving grievances between enrollees and the organization or any other entity or individual through which the organization provides health care services under any MA plan it offers. Upon receiving a complaint, an MA organization must promptly determine and inform the enrollee whether the complaint is subject to its grievance or appeal procedures. [Soc. Sec. Act § 1852(f); 42 C.F.R. § 422.564(a).]

Grievance disposition. An MA organization must notify the enrollee of its decision as expeditiously as the case requires, based on the enrollee's health status, but no later than 30 days after the date the organization receives the oral or written grievance. The notification time frame may be extended by up to 14 days if the enrollee requests the extension or if the organization justifies a need for additional information and documents how the delay is in the interest of the enrollee. If the organization extends the deadline, it must immediately notify the enrollee in writing of the reasons for the delay. [42 C.F.R. § 422.564(e).]

The MA organization must notify the enrollee of the disposition of the grievance as follows: (1) it must respond in writing to all grievances submitted in writing; (2) it may respond either orally or in writing to grievances submitted orally, unless the enrollee requests a written response; and (3) it must respond in writing to all grievances related to quality of care, regardless of how the grievance is filed. The response must also include a description of the enrollee's right to file a written complaint with the quality improvement organization (QIO). [42 C.F.R. § 422.564(e).]

Expedited grievances. An MA organization must respond to an enrollee's grievance within 24 hours if the complaint involves an MA organization's: (1) decision to invoke an extension relating to an organization determination or reconsideration, or (2) refusal to grant an enrollee's request for an expedited organization determination or reconsideration. [42 C.F.R. § 422.564(f).]

Organization Determinations

Each MA organization must have a procedure for making timely organization determinations regarding the benefits an enrollee is entitled to receive under an MA plan, including basic benefits and mandatory and optional supplemental benefits, and the amount, if any, that the enrollee is required to pay for a health service. The MA organization must have a standard procedure for making determinations and an expedited procedure for situations in which applying the standard procedure could seriously jeopardize the enrollee's life, health, or ability to regain maximum function. [Soc. Sec. Act § 1852(g)(1); 42 C.F.R. § 422.566(a).]

Organization determinations. An organization determination is any determination made by an MA organization regarding any of the following:

(1) payment for temporarily out-of-the-area renal dialysis services, emergency services, post-stabilization care, or urgently needed services;

(2) payment for any other health services furnished by a provider other than the MA organization that the enrollee believes are covered under Medicare or, if not covered under Medicare, should have been furnished, arranged for, or reimbursed by the MA organization;

(3) the MA organization's refusal to provide or pay for services, in whole or in part, including the type or level of services, that the enrollee believes should be furnished or arranged for by the MA organization;

(4) reduction or premature discontinuation of a previously authorized ongoing course of treatment; or

(5) failure of the MA organization to approve, furnish, arrange for, or provide payment for health care services in a timely manner, or to provide the enrollee with timely notice of an adverse determination, such that a delay would adversely affect the health of the enrollee.

[42 C.F.R. § 422.566(b).]

Individuals or entities who can request an organization determination include the enrollee or his or her representative; any provider that furnishes, or intends to furnish, services to the enrollee; or the legal representative of a deceased enrollee's estate. An enrollee or a physician (regardless of whether the physician is affiliated with the MA organization) can request an expedited determination. [42 C.F.R. § 422.566(c).]

An enrollee must ask for a standard organization determination by making a request with the MA organization or, if applicable, to the entity responsible for making the determination. Generally, the request may be made orally or in writing; however, requests for payment must be made in writing, unless the MA organization or entity responsible for making the determination has implemented a voluntary policy of accepting verbal payment requests. [42 C.F.R. § 422.568(a).]

Notice requirements. When a party makes a request for a service, the MA organization must notify the enrollee of its determination as expeditiously as the enrollee's health condition requires, but no later than 14 calendar days after the date the organization receives the request for a standard organization determination. The MA organization may extend the time frame by up to 14 calendar days if (1) the enrollee requests the extension, (2) the extension is justified and in the enrollee's interest due to the need for additional medical evidence from a noncontract provider that may change an MA organization's decision to deny an item or service; or (3) the extension is justified due to extraordinary, exigent, or other non-routine circumstances and is in the enrollee's interest. When the time frame is extended, the organization must notify the enrollee in writing of the reasons for the delay and inform the enrollee of the right to file an expedited grievance if he or she disagrees with the decision to grant an extension. The MA organization must notify the enrollee of its determination as expeditiously as the enrollee's health condition requires, but no later than upon expiration of the extension. [42 C.F.R. § 422.568(b).]

Reconsiderations

MA organizations provide reconsideration of a determination upon request by the enrollee not later than 60 days after the date of the receipt of the request for reconsideration. [Soc. Sec. Act § 1852(g); 42 C.F.R. § 422.578.]

Expedited determinations and reconsiderations. Generally, MA plans must maintain procedures for expediting determinations and reconsiderations when, on the request of an enrollee or a physician, the organization determines that the normal time frame for a determination or reconsideration could seriously jeopardize the affected enrollee's life or health. When it has received such a request, the MA organization must notify the enrollee or the physician, as appropriate, of its determination. If the MA organization denies the request for expedited reconsideration, it must make the determination within the standard 14-day time frame. If it grants the request, it must make the determination no later than 72 hours after receiving the request. [Soc. Sec. Act § 1852(g)(3); 42 C.F.R. §§ 422.570(d), 422.572(a).]

Administrative Law Judge Hearings

If the amount remaining in controversy after reconsideration meets the threshold requirement, any party to the reconsideration (except the MA organization) who is dissatisfied with the reconsidered determination has a right to a hearing before an ALJ. A request for an ALJ hearing must be in writing and filed with the entity specified in the IRE's reconsideration notice within 60 days. The parties to a hearing are the parties to the reconsideration, the MA organization, and any other person or entity whose rights with respect to the reconsideration may be affected by the hearing. [42 C.F.R. §§ 422.600, 422.602; Pub. 100-16, Ch. 13, §§ 100.1, 100.2.]

Amount in controversy. In 2016, plan enrollees who are dissatisfied, either because they have not received health care to which they believe they are entitled, or because they contest the cost of a service they have received, are entitled to a hearing before an ALJ if the amount in controversy is $150 or more, which is the same as the amount in controversy requirement in 2015. [*Notice,* 80 FR 57827, Sept. 25, 2015.]

Medicare Appeals Council Review

Any party to an ALJ hearing, including the MA organization, who is dissatisfied with the ALJ hearing decision may request that the Medicare Appeals Council review the ALJ's decision or dismissal (see ¶ 924). [42 C.F.R. § 422.608.]

Judicial Review

Any party, including the MA organization, may request judicial review of an ALJ's decision if the Medicare Appeals Council denied the party's request for review and the amount in controversy meets the threshold requirement established annually. Any party may also request judicial review of a Medicare Appeals Council decision if it is the final decision of CMS and the amount in controversy meets the threshold requirement. [Soc. Sec. Act § 1852(g)(5); 42 C.F.R. § 422.612.]

To request judicial review, a party must file a civil action in a district court of the United States. The minimum amount in controversy for judicial review of Medicare claims made on or after January 1, 2016, is $1,500, up from $1,460 in 2015. [*Notice,* 80 FR 57827, Sept. 25, 2015.]

Effectuating Reconsidered Determinations or Decisions

If, on reconsideration of a *request for service*, the MA organization completely reverses its organization determination, the organization must authorize or provide the service under dispute as expeditiously as the enrollee's health condition requires, but no later than 30 calendar days after the date the MA organization receives the request for reconsideration. [42 C.F.R. § 422.618(a)(1).]

If, on reconsideration of a *request for payment*, the MA organization completely reverses its organization determination, the organization must pay for the service no later than 60 calendar days after the date the MA organization receives the request for reconsideration. [42 C.F.R. § 422.618(a)(2).]

¶403

Reversals by the independent outside entity. If, on reconsideration of a *request for service*, the MA organization's determination is reversed in whole or in part by the independent outside entity, the MA organization must authorize the service under dispute within 72 hours from the date it receives notice reversing the determination or provide the service under dispute as expeditiously as the enrollee's health condition requires, but no later than 14 calendar days from that date. [42 C.F.R. § 422.618(b)(1).]

If, on reconsideration of a *request for payment*, the MA organization's determination is reversed in whole or in part by the independent outside entity, the MA organization must pay for the service no later than 30 calendar days from the date it receives notice reversing the organization determination. [42 C.F.R. § 422.618(b)(2).]

Other reversals. If the independent outside entity's determination is reversed in whole or in part by the ALJ or at a higher level of appeal, the MA organization must pay for, authorize, or provide the service under dispute as expeditiously as the enrollee's health condition requires, but no later than 60 calendar days from the date it receives notice reversing the determination. However, if the MA organization requests Medicare Appeals Council review, the organization may await the outcome of the review before it pays for, authorizes, or provides the service under dispute. [42 C.F.R. § 422.618(c).]

Expedited requests. If, on reconsideration of an expedited request for service, the MA organization completely reverses its organization determination, the MA organization must authorize or provide the service under dispute as expeditiously as the enrollee's health condition requires, but no later than 72 hours after the date the MA organization receives the request for reconsideration. [42 C.F.R. § 422.619(a).]

If the MA organization's determination is reversed in whole or in part by the independent outside entity, the MA organization must authorize or provide the service under dispute as expeditiously as the enrollee's health condition requires, but no later than 72 hours from the date it receives notice reversing the determination. [42 C.F.R. § 422.619(b).]

If the independent outside entity's expedited determination is reversed in whole or in part by the ALJ, or at a higher level of appeal, the MA organization must authorize or provide the service under dispute as expeditiously as the enrollee's health condition requires, but no later than 60 days from the date it receives notice reversing the determination. The MA organization must inform the independent outside entity that the organization has effectuated the decision. [42 C.F.R. § 422.619(c)(1).]

If the MA organization requests Medicare Appeals Council review consistent with 42 C.F.R. § 422.608, it may await the outcome of the review before it authorizes or provides the service under dispute. An MA organization that files an appeal with the Medicare Appeals Council must concurrently send a copy of its appeal request and any accompanying documents to the enrollee and must notify the independent outside entity that it has requested an appeal. [42 C.F.R. § 422.619(c)(2).]

Notification of Hospital Discharge Appeal Rights

Hospitals must deliver a standardized written notice of an MA enrollee's rights as a hospital inpatient, including discharge appeal rights, at or near admission, but no later than two calendar days following the enrollee's admission to the hospital. The notice of rights must include: (1) the enrollee's rights as a hospital inpatient, including the right to benefits for inpatient services and for post-hospital services; (2) the enrollee's right to request an immediate review, including a description of the process and the availability of other appeals processes if the enrollee fails to meet the deadline for an immediate review; (3) the circumstances under which an enrollee will or will not be liable for charges for continued stay in the hospital; (4) the enrollee's right to receive additional information; and (5) any other information required by CMS. [42 C.F.R. § 422.620(b)(1), (2).]

For delivery of the written notice of rights to be valid, the enrollee (or the enrollee's representative) must sign and date the notice to indicate that he or she has received the notice and can comprehend its contents. [42 C.F.R. § 422.620(b)(3).]

Follow-up notification. The hospital must present a copy of the signed notice to the enrollee (or enrollee's representative) before discharge. The notice should be given as far in advance of discharge as possible, but not more than two calendar days before discharge. Before discharging an enrollee from the inpatient hospital level of care, the MA organization must obtain concurrence from the physician who is responsible for the enrollee's inpatient care. [42 C.F.R. § 422.620(c), (d).]

QIO review of the decision to discharge. An enrollee who wishes to appeal a determination by an MA organization or hospital that inpatient care is no longer necessary must request immediate QIO review of the determination in writing or by telephone no later than the day of discharge. An enrollee who requests immediate QIO review may remain in the hospital with no additional financial liability for inpatient services received before noon of the day after the QIO notifies the enrollee of its review determination. [42 C.F.R. § 422.622.]

Termination of Provider Services

Before any termination of service, the provider of the service must deliver valid written notice to the enrollee of the MA organization's decision to terminate services. "Termination of service" is defined as the discharge of an enrollee from covered provider services, or discontinuation of covered provider services, when the enrollee has been authorized by the MA organization to receive an ongoing course of treatment from that provider (including home health agencies, skilled nursing facilities, and comprehensive outpatient rehabilitation facilities). Termination includes cessation of coverage at the end of a course of treatment pre-authorized in a discrete increment, regardless of whether the enrollee agrees that such services should end. [42 C.F.R. § 422.624(a).]

The provider must notify the enrollee of the MA organization's decision to terminate covered services no later than two days before the proposed end of the services and must use a standardized notice. The standardized termination notice must include: (1) the date that coverage of services ends; (2) the date that the enrollee's financial liability for continued services begins; (3) a description of the enrollee's right to a fast-track appeal, including information on how to contact an IRE, an enrollee's right to submit evidence showing that services should continue, and the availability of other MA appeal procedures if the enrollee fails to meet the deadline for a fast-track IRE appeal; (4) the enrollee's right to receive detailed information about the termination notice and all documents sent by the provider to the IRE; and (5) any other information required by the Secretary. [42 C.F.R. § 422.624(b).]

Enrollees have a right to a fast-track appeal of an MA organization's decision to terminate provider services. Enrollees must submit a request for appeal to an IRE under contract with CMS, in writing or by telephone, by noon of the first day after the day the termination notice was delivered. [42 C.F.R. § 422.626(a).]

[¶ 405] Contracts with Medicare Advantage Organizations

Entities seeking a contract as a Medicare organization offering a Medicare Advantage (MA) plan must fulfill certain application requirements. MA organizations offering prescription drug plans must, in addition to these requirements, follow the requirements in Chapter 5 related to the prescription drug benefit. [42 C.F.R. § 422.500.]

Minimum enrollment requirements. CMS will not enter into a contract with a managed care organization unless the organization enrolls: (1) at least 5,000 individuals (or 1,500 individuals if the organization is a provider-sponsored organization (PSO)) for the purpose of receiving health benefits from the organization; (2) or at least 1,500 individuals (or 500 individuals if the organization is a PSO) for the purpose of receiving health benefits from the organization and this organization primarily serves patients in non-urbanized (rural) areas. CMS may waive the minimum enrollment requirement at the time of application or during the first three years of the contract if the organization demonstrates that it is capable of administering and managing an MA contract and is able to manage the level of risk required under the contract. [42 C.F.R. § 422.514.]

Application Requirements and CMS's Evaluation

An organization submitting an application for a particular contract year must first submit a completed Notice of Intent to Apply by the date established by CMS. Submitting a Notice of Intent to Apply does not bind that organization to submit an application for the applicable contract year, and failure to submit a Notice will not form the basis of any CMS action against the organization. [42 C.F.R. § 422.501(b).]

Content of application. To become an MA organization and be qualified to provide a particular type of MA plan, the applicant must fully complete all parts of a certified application, in the form and manner required by CMS, including: (1) documentation of appropriate state licensure or certification that the applicant is able to offer health insurance or health benefits coverage that meets state-specified standards applicable to MA plans, and is authorized by the state to accept prepaid capitation for providing, arranging, or paying for the comprehensive health care services to be offered under the MA contract; (2) for regional plans, documentation of application for state licensure in any state in the region that the organization is not already licensed; and (3) for specialized MA plans for special needs individuals (SNPs), documentation that the entity meets the SNP requirements of 42 C.F.R. Part 422. [42 C.F.R. § 422.501(c).]

CMS use of information from a current or prior contract. If, during the 14 months preceding the application deadline, an MA organization fails to comply with the requirements of the MA program under any current or prior contract with CMS, or if it fails to complete a corrective action plan during the 14 months preceding the application deadline, CMS may deny an application even if the applicant currently meets all of the requirements. In the absence of 14 months of performance history, CMS may deny an application based on a lack of information available to determine an applicant's capacity to comply with the requirements of the MA program. [42 C.F.R. § 422.502(b).]

Notice. CMS must notify each applicant that applies for an MA contract or to be designated a SNP of its determination and the basis for the determination. CMS gives written notice to the applicant in the event of an approval or a denial. If CMS finds that the applicant does not appear to meet the requirements for an MA organization and has not provided enough information to evaluate the application, it must give the applicant notice of intent to deny the application and allow the applicant 10 days to respond in writing. [42 C.F.R. § 422.502(c).]

Contract period and effectiveness. CMS contracts with MA plans are for a term of at least 12 months. Contracts are renewed annually only if the MA organization has not notified CMS of its intention not to renew and CMS has not provided the MA organization with a notice of its intention not to renew. Renewal of a contract is contingent on the parties reaching an agreement on the bid. [42 C.F.R. § 422.505.]

¶405

Contract provisions. The MA organization agrees to apply with all applicable requirements and conditions, including to accept new enrollments, make enrollments effective, process voluntary disenrollments, and limit involuntary disenrollments. Other requirements include the prohibition on discrimination in beneficiary enrollment, the provision of basic and supplemental benefits, and the operation of a quality assurance and performance improvement program. [42 C.F.R. § 422.504(a).]

Contract Nonrenewal, Modification, and Termination

An MA organization may elect not to renew its contract with CMS as of the end of the term of the contract for any reason, provided it meets the following time frames. If an MA organization does not intend to renew its contract, it must notify: (1) CMS in writing, by the first Monday in June of the year in which the contract would end; and (2) each Medicare enrollee by mail at least 90 calendar days before the date on which the nonrenewal is effective.

If an MA organization does not renew its contract, CMS may deny an application for a new contract or a service area expansion for two years unless there are special circumstances that warrant special consideration. During this two-year period, CMS will not contract with an organization whose covered persons also served as covered persons for the non-renewing sponsor. [42 C.F.R. § 422.506(a).]

CMS decision not authorize renewal. CMS may decide not to authorize renewal of an MA contract: (1) if the MA organization has not fully implemented or shown discernible progress in implementing quality improvement projects; (2) for any of the reasons that would also permit CMS to terminate the contract; and (3) if the MA organization has committed acts that would support the imposition of intermediate sanctions or civil money penalties. The contract must be nonrenewed as to an individual MA plan if that plan does not have a sufficient number of enrollees to establish that it is a viable independent plan option. CMS must provide notice of its decision not to authorize renewal of a contract to the MA organization by August 1 of the contract year, and to each of the MA organization's Medicare enrollees by mail at least 90 calendar days before the date on which the nonrenewal is effective, or at the conclusion of the appeals process, if applicable. [42 C.F.R. § 422.506(b).]

Modification or termination by mutual consent. A contract may be modified or terminated at any time by written mutual consent. If the contract is terminated by mutual consent, the MA organization must provide notice to its Medicare enrollees and the general public. However, if the contract terminated by mutual consent is replaced the following day by a new MA contract, the MA organization is not required to provide the notice. If the contract is modified by mutual consent, the MA organization must notify its Medicare enrollees of any changes that CMS determines are appropriate for notification. [42 C.F.R. § 422.508(a), (b).]

As a condition of a consent to a mutual termination, CMS will prohibit the MA organization from applying for new contracts or service area expansions for a period of two years, absent circumstances warranting special consideration. During the same two-year period, CMS will not contract with an organization whose covered persons (as defined above) also served as covered persons for the mutually terminating sponsor. [42 C.F.R. § 422.508(c), (d).]

Termination of contract by CMS. The HHS Secretary may cancel a contract at any time if an MA plan: (1) substantially fails to carry out the terms of its contract with CMS; (2) carries out the terms of the contract in a manner that is inconsistent with the efficient, effective administration of the MA program; or (3) no longer substantially meets applicable requirements of a contracting organization under the MA program. CMS may find that one of these three preceding events has occurred upon a finding that the MA organization did any of the following:

- based on credible evidence, has committed or participated in false, fraudulent, or abusive activities affecting the Medicare, Medicaid, or other state or federal health care programs, including submission of false or fraudulent data;

- substantially fails to comply with the requirements relating to grievances and appeals;

- fails to provide CMS with valid data;

- fails to implement an acceptable quality assessment and performance improvement program;

- substantially fails to comply with the prompt payment requirements;

- substantially fails to comply with the service access requirements;

- fails to comply with the requirements regarding physician incentive plans;

- substantially fails to comply with marketing requirements;

- fails to comply with the regulatory requirements contained in Part C or Part D;

- fails to meet CMS performance requirements in carrying out the regulatory requirements contained in Part C or Part D or both;

- achieves a Part C summary plan rating of less than three stars for three consecutive contract years (plan ratings issued by CMS before September 1, 2012, are not included in the calculation of the three-year period); or

- fails to report medical loss ratio data in a timely and accurate manner.

[42 C.F.R. § 422.510(a).]

Termination of contract by the MA organization. The MA organization may terminate the contract if CMS fails to substantially carry out the terms of the contract. The MA organization must give advance notice to CMS at least 90 days before the intended date of termination and to its Medicare enrollees and the general public at least 60 days before the termination effective date. The notice to beneficiaries must include a written description of alternatives available for obtaining Medicare services within the services area, including alternative MA plans, Medigap options, and original Medicare, and it must receive CMS approval. [42 C.F.R. § 422.512(a), (b).]

CMS's liability for payment to the MA organization ends as of the first day of the month after the last month for which the contract is in effect. CMS may deny an application for a new contract or a service area expansion from an MA organization that has terminated its contract within the preceding two years unless there are circumstances that warrant special consideration. During the same two-year period, CMS will not contract with an organization whose covered persons also served as covered persons for the terminating sponsor. [42 C.F.R. § 422.512(d), (e).]

Contract Determinations

CMS can make four types of contract determinations:

(1) a determination that an entity is not qualified to enter into a contract with CMS;

(2) a determination to terminate a contract with an MA organization;

(3) a determination not to authorize a renewal of a contract with an MA organization; and

(4) a determination that an entity is not qualified to offer a specialized MA plan for special needs individuals.

[42 C.F.R. § 422.641.]

Notice of contract determination. When CMS makes a contract determination, it gives the MA organization written notice specifying the reasons for the determination and the MA organization's right to request a hearing. Generally, for CMS-initiated terminations, CMS mails a notice 45 calendar days before the anticipated effective date of the termination. When CMS determines that it will not authorize a contract renewal, CMS mails the notice to the MA organization by August 1 of the current contract year. [42 C.F.R. § 422.644.]

Effect of contract determination. A contract determination is final and binding unless a timely request for a hearing is filed with a CMS office within 15 calendar days from the date CMS notifies the MA organization of its determination. [42 C.F.R. § § 422.646, 422.662(b).]

Right to a hearing. Parties entitled to a hearing include: (1) a contract applicant that has been determined to be unqualified to enter into a contract with CMS; (2) an MA organization whose contract has been terminated or not renewed or has had an intermediate sanction imposed; or (3) an applicant that has been determined to be unqualified to offer a specialized MA plan for special needs individuals. [42 C.F.R. § 422.660.]

Notice and effect of hearing decision. The hearing officer's decision must be based upon the evidence of record and must contain separately numbered findings of fact and conclusions of law. A copy of the hearing decision is provided to each party. The decision is final and binding unless it is reversed or modified by the Administrator following review or it is reopened and revised. [42 C.F.R. § 422.690.]

Review by Administrator. CMS or an MA organization that has received a hearing decision regarding a contract determination may request review by the Administrator within 15 calendar days of receiving the hearing decision. Both CMS and the MA organization may provide written arguments to the Administrator. The Administrator has the discretion to elect to review the hearing decision or to decline review and must notify both parties of his or her determination regarding review within 30 calendar days of receiving the request. [42 C.F.R. § 422.692.]

Reopenings. CMS may reopen and revise an initial contract determination upon its own motion. A decision of a hearing officer that is unfavorable to any party, but is otherwise final, may be reopened and revised by the hearing officer upon the officer's own motion within one year of the notice of the hearing decision. Another hearing officer designated by CMS may reopen and revise the decision if the hearing officer who issued the decision is unavailable. A decision by the Administrator that is otherwise final may be reopened and revised by the Administrator upon the Administrator's own motion within one year of the notice of the Administrator's decision. The notice of reopening and of any revisions following the reopening must be mailed to the parties and specify the reasons for revisions. [42 C.F.R. § 422.696.]

[¶ 407] Bids, Benchmarks, Premiums, and Cost-Sharing

This section discusses the requirements for Medicare Advantage (MA) bidding payment methodology, including the submission of plan bids by MA organizations, the negotiation and approval of bids by CMS, the calculation of benchmarks by CMS, the establishment of beneficiary premiums and rebates, and beneficiary cost-sharing. [42 C.F.R. § 422.250.]

Submission of Bids

Not later than the first Monday in June, each MA organization must submit to CMS an aggregate monthly bid amount for each MA plan (other than a medical savings account

(MSA) plan) the organization intends to offer in the upcoming year in a given service area. An MA organization's bid submissions must reflect differences in benefit packages or plan costs that CMS determines represent substantial differences in relation to the sponsor's other bid submissions. [42 C.F.R. § 422.254(a).]

Bid requirements. The monthly aggregate bid amount submitted by an MA organization for each plan is the organization's estimate of the revenue required for the following categories for providing coverage to an MA-eligible beneficiary with a national average risk profile:

- the unadjusted MA statutory non-drug monthly bid amount, which is the MA plan's estimated average monthly required revenue for providing benefits under the original Medicare fee-for-service program option;

- the amount to provide basic prescription drug coverage, if any; and

- the amount to provide supplemental health care benefits, if any.

Each bid is for a uniform benefit package for the service area. Each bid submission must contain all estimated revenue required by the plan, including administrative costs and return on investment. [42 C.F.R. § 422.254(b).] Bids for coordinated care plans, including regional MA plans and specialized MA plans for special needs beneficiaries, and for MA private fee-for-service plans must include specific information, including the plan type and the actuarial basis for determining the bid amount. [42 C.F.R. § 422.254(c).]

Beneficiary rebate information. In the case of a plan required to provide a monthly rebate for a year, the MA organization offering the plan must inform CMS how the plan will distribute the beneficiary rebate. [42 C.F.R. § 422.254(d).]

Medical savings account plan information. MA organizations intending to offer MA MSA plans must submit: (1) the enrollment capacity (if any) for the plan; (2) the amount of the MSA monthly premium for basic benefits under the original Medicare fee-for-service program option; (3) the amount of the plan deductible; and (4) the amount of the beneficiary supplemental premium, if any. [42 C.F.R. § 422.254(e).]

Separate bids must be submitted for Part A and Part B enrollees and Part B-only enrollees for each MA plan offered. [42 C.F.R. § 422.254(f).]

Review, Negotiation, and Approval of Bids

CMS has the authority to review the aggregate bid amounts submitted by MA organizations and conduct negotiations regarding the bids (including the supplemental benefits) and the proportions of the aggregate bid attributable to basic benefits, supplemental benefits, and prescription drug benefits. CMS may deny a bid if the plan sponsor proposes significant increases in cost-sharing or decreases in benefits offered under the plan. [42 C.F.R. § 422.256(a).]

Standards of bid review. CMS can accept bid amounts or proportions only if it determines that the bid amount and proportions are supported by actuarial bases and that the bid amount and proportions reasonably and equitably reflect the plan's estimated revenue requirements for providing the benefits under that plan. For coordinated care plans (including regional MA plans and specialized MA plans) and private fee-for-service plans, the actuarial value of plan basic cost-sharing, reduced by any supplemental benefits, may not exceed the actuarial value of deductibles, coinsurance, and copayments that would be applicable for the benefits to individuals entitled to benefits under Part A and enrolled under Part B in the plan's service area if they were not members of an MA organization for the year. [42 C.F.R. § 422.256(b).]

Substantial differences between bids. CMS will approve a bid only if it finds that the benefit package and plan costs represented by that bid are substantially different from the MA organization's other bid submissions, i.e., significantly different from other plans of its plan type with respect to premiums, benefits, or cost-sharing structure. [42 C.F.R. § 422.256(b)(4).]

Negotiation process. The negotiation process may include the resubmission of information to allow MA organizations to modify their initial bid submissions to account for the outcome of CMS's regional benchmark calculations and CMS's calculation of the national average monthly bid amount. [42 C.F.R. § 422.256(c).]

Exceptions. For private fee-for-service plans, CMS will not review, negotiate, or approve the bid amount, proportions of the bid, or the amounts of the basic beneficiary premium and supplemental premium. In addition, CMS does not review, negotiate, or approve amounts submitted with regard to MA MSA plans, except to determine that the deductible does not exceed the statutory maximum. [42 C.F.R. § 422.256(d), (e).]

Calculation of Benchmarks

CMS uses MA plan bid information to arrive at an amount to pay MA plans in each region, the monthly "benchmark" amount.

Area plans. The term "MA area-specific non-drug monthly benchmark amount" means, for a month in a year:

- for MA local plans with service areas entirely within a single MA local area, $\frac{1}{12}$ of the blended benchmark amount, adjusted as appropriate for the purpose of risk adjustment; or

- for MA local plans with service areas including more than one MA local area, an amount equal to the weighted average of the amount described above for the year for each local area (county) in the plan's service area, using as weights the projected number of enrollees in each MA local area that the plan used to calculate the bid amount, and adjusted as appropriate for the purpose of risk adjustment.

[42 C.F.R. § 422.258(a).]

Regional plans. For MA regional plans, the term "MA region-specific non-drug monthly benchmark amount" is the sum of two components: (1) the statutory component (based on a weighted average of local benchmarks in the region), and (2) the plan bid component (based on a weighted average of regional plan bids in the region). [42 C.F.R. § 422.258(b).] CMS calculates the monthly regional non-drug benchmark amount for each MA region using the components of described in 42 C.F.R. § 422.258(c).

"Blended benchmark" calculation. Beginning in 2012, a "blended benchmark" is used to determine payments for all MA plans except for MA plans under the Program of All-inclusive Care of the Elderly (PACE). [Soc. Sec. Act § 1853(n)(1); 42 C.F.R. § 422.258(d).]

The use of the "blended benchmark" was to be phased in over a four-year period if the benchmark amount was at least $30 and less than $50. If the benchmark amount is greater than $50, then the new blended benchmark will be phased in over six years. In no case will the blended benchmark for an MA area for the year be greater than the applicable amount for an MA area for the year. [Soc. Sec. Act § 1853(n)(3) and (4).]

Applicable amount. The "applicable amount" is equal to the amount for the area for the previous year increased by the national per capita MA growth percentage, for that succeeding year. [42 C.F.R. § 422.258(d)(2).]

¶407

Specified amount. The specified amount is the product of the base payment amount for an area for a year (adjusted as required) multiplied by the applicable percentage for an area for a year. [Soc. Sec. Act § 1853(n)(2); 42 C.F.R. § 422.258(d)(3).]

Base payment amount. The "base payment amount" is calculated by taking the previous year's base payment amount and increasing it by the national per capita MA growth percentage taking into account the phase-out in indirect cost of medical education from capitation rates. [Soc. Sec. Act § 1853(n)(2)(E); 42 C.F.R. § 422.258(d)(4).]

Applicable percentage. The "applicable percentage" is as follows:

- for MA plans in the highest quartile ranking of payments for the previous year, the applicable percentage will be 95 percent;

- for MA plans in the second highest quartile ranking of payments for the previous year, the applicable percentage will be 100 percent;

- for MA plans in the third highest quartile ranking of payments for the previous year, the applicable percentage will be 107.5 percent; and

- for MA plans in the fourth highest quartile ranking of payments for the previous year, the applicable percentage will be 115 percent.

[Soc. Sec. Act § 1853(n)(2)(B); 42 C.F.R. § 422.258(d)(5).]

Increases to the applicable percentage for quality of care. Plans rated at least four stars based on a five-star system stemming from the data collected under Soc. Sec. Act § 1852(e) receive bonus payments. Plans that fail to report data receive a rating of fewer than 3.5 stars.

For 2014 and later, MA plans that have a quality rating of four stars or higher will have their applicable percentage increased by 5.0 percent. A new plan (i.e., an organization that has not had a contract as a MA provider in the previous three years) that meets the criteria to be considered a qualifying plan will have its applicable percentage increased by 3.5 percent. [Soc. Sec. Act § 1853(o); 42 C.F.R. § 422.258(d)(7).]

Beneficiary Cost-Sharing

There are three forms of beneficiary cost-sharing under the MA program: copayments, coinsurance, and deductibles. A copayment is a fixed amount that can be charged for a service; coinsurance is a fixed percentage of the total cost of a service that can be charged. [42 C.F.R. § 422.2.]

Balance billing. "Balance billing" is the amount billed by a provider that is the difference between the amount the provider charges an individual for a service, and the sum of the amount the individual's health insurer will pay, plus any cost-sharing by the individual. [42 C.F.R. § 422.2.]

An MA organization that offers a private fee-for-service plan must furnish enrolled beneficiaries with an appropriate explanation of benefits, including a clear statement of the beneficiary's liability. The organization also must require that hospitals provide notice to beneficiaries, before they receive inpatient hospital or other services, when the amount of balance billing could be $500 or more. This notice must include a good faith estimate of the balance billing. [42 C.F.R. § 422.216(d).]

Services of noncontracting providers. An MA organization must make timely and reasonable payment to, or on behalf of, the plan enrollee for certain services obtained from a provider or supplier that does not contract with the MA organization to provide services covered by the MA plan. These services are outlined in ¶ 402. An MA plan (and an MA MSA plan, after the annual deductible has been met) offered by an MA organization satisfies the timely and reasonable payment requirements with respect to benefits for services furnished by a noncontracting provider if that MA plan provides payment in an amount the provider would have received under original Medicare, including balance billing permitted under Medicare Part A and Part B. [42 C.F.R. § 422.100(b).] An MA plan may charge a higher copayment if a beneficiary chooses to receive covered health care services from providers who do not have contracts or agreements with the MA plan. [Soc. Sec. Act § 1852(d)(4)(b).]

Cost-sharing for certain benefits. MA beneficiaries who need: (1) chemotherapy administration services, (2) renal dialysis services, (3) skilled nursing care, and (4) other services that the HHS Secretary determines appropriate, generally will not be subjected to higher cost-sharing for these services than traditional fee-for-service Medicare (Medicare Parts A and B) beneficiaries pay. [Soc. Sec. Act § 1852(a)(1)(B)(iii).]

In the case of an individual who is a full-benefit dual eligible or a qualified Medicare beneficiary enrolled in an MA special needs plan (SNP), the plan may not impose cost-sharing that exceeds the amount of cost-sharing that would be permitted under Medicaid. [Soc. Sec. Act § 1852(a)(7).]

Deductibles. MA regional and local preferred provider organization (PPO) plans, to the extent they apply a deductible: (1) must have a single deductible related to all in-network and out-of-network Medicare Part A and Part B services; (2) may specify separate deductible amounts for specific in-network Medicare Part A and Part B services, to the extent these deductible amounts apply to that single deductible amount; (3) may waive other plan-covered items and services from the single deductible; and (4) must waive all Medicare-covered preventive services from the single deductible. [42 C.F.R. § 422.101(d)(1).]

Refunds. An MA organization must agree to refund all amounts incorrectly collected from its Medicare enrollees, or from others on behalf of the enrollees, and to pay any other amounts due the enrollees or others on their behalf. The MA organization must use lump-sum payments for: (1) amounts incorrectly collected that were not collected as premiums, (2) other amounts due, and (3) all amounts due if the MA organization is going out of business or terminating its MA contract for an MA plan. If the amounts incorrectly collected were in the form of premiums or included premiums as well as other charges, the MA organization may refund by adjustment of future premiums or by a combination of premium adjustment and lump-sum payments. If an enrollee has died or cannot be located after reasonable effort, the MA organization must make the refund in accordance with state law. [42 C.F.R. § 422.270(b), (c).]

If the MA organization does not make the required refund by the end of the contract period following the contract period during which an amount was determined to be due to an enrollee, CMS will reduce the premium the MA organization is allowed to charge an MA plan enrollee by the amounts incorrectly collected or otherwise due. In addition, the MA organization is subject to sanction for failure to refund amounts incorrectly collected from MA plan enrollees. [42 C.F.R. § 422.270(d).]

Beneficiary Premiums

If an MA plan has an unadjusted statutory non-drug bid amount that is less than the relevant unadjusted CMS non-drug benchmark amount, the monthly basic beneficiary premium is zero. If the plan's bid amount is equal to or greater than the relevant unadjusted non-drug benchmark amount, the basic beneficiary premium is the amount by which the bid amount exceeds the benchmark amount. The benchmark is a bidding target used by CMS and based on rates paid to MA plans before 2006. [42 C.F.R § 422.262(a).]

Consolidated monthly premium. MA organizations must charge enrollees a consolidated monthly MA premium, which is equal to the sum of the MA monthly basic beneficiary premium (if any), the MA monthly supplementary beneficiary premium (if any), and the MA monthly prescription drug beneficiary premium (if any). For MSA plans offered by an MA organization, the monthly beneficiary premium is the supplemental premium. [42 C.F.R § 422.262(b).]

Uniformity of premiums. Except as permitted for supplemental premiums for MA contracts with employers and labor organizations, the MA monthly bid amount, the MA monthly basic beneficiary premium, the MA monthly supplemental beneficiary premium, the MA monthly prescription drug premium, and the monthly MSA premium of an MA organization may not vary among individuals enrolled in an MA plan. In addition, the MA organization cannot vary the level of cost-sharing charged for basic benefits or supplemental benefits among individuals enrolled in an MA plan. An MA organization may apply these uniformity requirements to segments of an MA local plan service area (rather than to the entire service area) as long as such a segment is composed of one or more MA payment areas. The bid information required by 42 C.F.R. § 422.254 (as discussed above) is submitted separately for each segment. This rule does not apply to MA regional plans. [42 C.F.R § 422.262(c).]

Monetary inducement prohibited. An MA organization may not provide cash or other monetary rebates as an inducement for enrollment or for any other reason or purpose. [42 C.F.R § 422.262(d).]

Timing of payments. The MA organization must permit payments of MA monthly basic and supplemental beneficiary premiums and monthly prescription drug beneficiary premiums on a monthly basis. [42 C.F.R § 422.262(e).]

Method of payment. An MA organization must permit each enrollee, at the enrollee's option, to make payment of premiums to the organization through: (1) withholding from the enrollee's Social Security benefit payments, or benefit payments by the Railroad Retirement Board or the Office of Personnel Management, in the manner that the Part B premium is withheld (a charge may not be imposed on beneficiaries for the election of this withholding option); (2) an electronic funds transfer mechanism; or (3) by other means that CMS may specify, including payment by an employer or under employment-based retiree health coverage on behalf of an employee, former employee, or by other third parties such as a state. An enrollee may opt to make a direct payment of premium to the plan. [42 C.F.R § 422.262(f).]

Retroactive premium collection. In circumstances where retroactive collection of premium amounts is necessary and the enrollee is without fault in creating the premium arrearage, the MA organization must offer the enrollee the option of payment either by lump sum, by equal monthly installment spread out over at least the same period for which the premiums were due, or through other arrangements mutually acceptable to the enrollee and the MA organization. For example, for monthly installments, if seven months of premiums are due, the member would have at least seven months to repay. [42 C.F.R § 422.262(h).]

Calculation of Savings

MA local plan computation. The average per capita monthly savings for an MA local plan is 100 percent of the difference between the plan's risk-adjusted statutory non-drug monthly bid amount and the plan's risk-adjusted area-specific non-drug monthly benchmark amount. Plans with bids equal to or greater than plan benchmarks will have zero savings. [42 C.F.R. § 422.264(b).]

The risk-adjusted MA statutory non-drug monthly bid amount is the unadjusted plan bid amount for coverage of original Medicare benefits adjusted using the factors for local and regional plans. [42 C.F.R. § 422.264(a)(1).]

¶407

The risk-adjusted MA *area-specific* and *region-specific* non-drug monthly benchmark amounts are the unadjusted benchmark amount for coverage of original Medicare benefits by a local MA plan. [42 C.F.R. § 422.264(a)(2).]

For MA local plans, CMS has the authority to apply risk adjustment factors that are plan-specific average risk adjustment factors or statewide average risk adjustment factors or to use other factors. If CMS applies statewide average risk adjustment factors, the statewide factor for each state is the average of the risk factors based on all enrollees in MA local plans in that state in the previous year. [42 C.F.R. § 422.264(c).]

MA regional plan computation. The average per capita monthly savings for an MA regional plan and year is 100 percent of the difference between the plan's risk-adjusted statutory non-drug monthly bid amount and the plan's risk-adjusted region-specific non-drug monthly benchmark amount, using the risk adjustment factors described below. Plans with bids equal to or greater than plan benchmarks will have zero savings. [42 C.F.R. § 422.264(d).]

Risk adjustment factors for regional plan savings. For regional plans, CMS has the authority to apply risk adjustment factors that are plan-specific average risk adjustment factors, region-wide average risk adjustment factors, or factors determined on a basis other than MA regions. In the event that CMS applies region-wide average risk adjustment factors, the region-wide factor for each MA region is the average of all risk factors, based on all enrollees in MA regional plans in that region in the previous year. [42 C.F.R. § 422.264(e).]

Beneficiary Rebates

An MA organization must provide to the enrollee a monthly rebate equal to a specified percentage of the average per capita savings for MA local plans and regional plans. For 2014 and later, this percentage is determined based only on the final rebate percentage. For 2014 and subsequent years, the final applicable rebate percentage is as follows:

- for plans with at least 4.5 stars, 70 percent of the average per capita savings;
- for plans with at least 3.5 stars and fewer than 4.5 stars, 65 percent of the average per capita savings; and
- for plans with fewer than 3.5 stars, 50 percent of the average per capita savings.

[Soc. Sec. Act § 1854(b)(1)(C); 42 C.F.R. § 422.266(a).]

New MA plans. A new MA plan is treated as having a rating of 3.5 stars for purposes of determining the beneficiary rebate amount. [Soc. Sec. Act § 1854(b)(1)(C)(vi); 42 C.F.R. § 422.266(a)(2)(iv).]

Form of rebate. The rebate must be provided by crediting the amount to supplemental health care benefits, payment of the premium for prescription drug coverage, or payment toward the Part B premium. [42 C.F.R. § 422.266(b).]

Disclosure of rebate. MA organizations must disclose to CMS information on the amount of the rebate provided. MA organizations must also distinguish, for each MA plan, the amount of rebate applied to enhance original Medicare benefits from the amount of rebate applied to enhance Part D benefits. [Soc. Sec. Act § 1854(b)(1)(C)(vii); 42 C.F.R. § 422.266(c).]

[¶ 408] Payments to Medicare Advantage Organizations

CMS makes advance monthly payments to Medicare Advantage (MA) plans for coverage of original fee-for-service (FFS) benefits for an individual in an MA payment area for a month. [Soc. Sec. Act § 1853(a)(1); 42 C.F.R. § 422.304(a)(1).]

For MA plans that have average per capita monthly savings, i.e., bids below the benchmark (see ¶ 407), CMS pays:

- the unadjusted MA statutory non-drug monthly bid amount risk-adjusted and adjusted (if applicable) for variations in rates within the plan's service area and for the effects of risk adjustment on beneficiary premiums; and

- the amount (if any) of any rebate.

[Soc. Sec. Act § 1853(a)(1)(B)(i); 42 C.F.R. § 422.304(a).]

For MA plans that do not have average per capita monthly savings, i.e., plans with bids at or above benchmark, CMS pays the unadjusted MA area-specific non-drug monthly benchmark amount, risk-adjusted and adjusted (if applicable) for variations in rates within the plan's service area and for the effects of risk adjustment on beneficiary premiums. [Soc. Sec. Act § 1853(a)(1)(B)(ii); 42 C.F.R. § 422.304(a).]

Federal drug subsidies. In the case of an MA prescription drug (MA-PD) plan, the MA organization offering such a plan also receives: (1) direct and reinsurance subsidy payments for qualified prescription drug coverage, and (2) reimbursement for premium and cost-sharing reductions for low-income individuals. [Soc. Sec. Act § 1853(a)(1)(D); 42 C.F.R. § 422.304(b).]

Enrollees with ESRD. For enrollees with end-stage renal disease (ESRD), CMS establishes special rates that are actuarially equivalent to rates in effect before the enactment of the Medicare Modernization Act of 2003 (MMA) (P.L. 108-173). CMS publishes annual changes in these capitation rates no later than the first Monday in April each year. [Soc. Sec. Act § 1853(a)(1)(H); 42 C.F.R. § 422.304(c)(1).]

Medical savings account enrollees. For medical savings account (MSA) plans, CMS pays the unadjusted MA area-specific non-drug monthly benchmark amount for the service area, subject to risk adjustment at 42 C.F.R. § 422.308(c), less $\frac{1}{12}$ of the annual lump sum amount (if any) CMS deposits to the enrollee's MA MSA. [Soc. Sec. Act § 1853(e); 42 C.F.R. § 422.304(c)(2).]

Religious fraternal benefit plan enrollees. For enrollees in religious fraternal benefit (RFB) plans, CMS adjusts the capitation payments to ensure that the payment level is appropriate for the actuarial characteristics and experience of these enrollees. This adjustment can be made on an individual or organization basis. [42 C.F.R. § 422.304(c)(3).]

Annual Capitation Rates

Except for years when CMS rebases the FFS rates, the annual capitation rate for each MA local area is equal to the minimum percentage increase rate, which is the annual capitation rate for the area for the preceding year increased by the national per capita MA growth percentage for the year. [42 C.F.R. § 422.306(a); *Medicare Managed Care Manual*, Pub. 100-16, Ch. 8, § 20.2.]

In rebasing years, the annual capitation rate for each MA local area is the greater of: (1) the minimum percentage increase rate; or (2) the amount determined, no less frequently than every three years, to be the adjusted average per capita cost for the MA local area, based on 100 percent of FFS costs for individuals who are not enrolled in an MA plan for the year, adjusted: (a) as appropriate for the purpose of risk adjustment; (b) to exclude costs attributable to payments for the costs of direct graduate medical education; (c) to include CMS's estimate of the amount of additional per capita payments that would have been made in the MA local area if individuals entitled to benefits under this title had not received services from facilities of the Department of Defense or the Department of Veterans Affairs;

and (d) to exclude costs attributable to Medicare FFS incentive payments for meaningful use of electronic health records. [42 C.F.R. § 422.306(b).]

Phase-out of the indirect cost of medical education as an MA capitation rate component. After CMS determines the annual capitation rate for each MA local area, it adjusts the amount to exclude the phase-in percentage for the year of the estimated costs for payments of indirect medical education costs in the area for the year. [42 C.F.R. § 422.306(c).]

Announcement of annual capitation rate. All payment rates are annual rates, determined and promulgated by HHS. The HHS Secretary will determine and announce, not later than the first Monday in April before the calendar year concerned, the annual capitation rate, payment area, and risk adjustment factors. Proposed changes to the payment methodology must be published no later than 45 days (or, beginning in 2017, at least 60 days) before annual announcement of rates. Beginning in 2017, MA organizations will have at least 30 days to comment on the proposed changes. [Soc. Sec. Act § 1853(b)(2); 42 C.F.R. § 422.312.]

2016 capitation rates. In accordance with section 1853(b)(1) of the Social Security Act, CMS notified MA organizations of the annual MA capitation rate for each MA payment area for calendar year 2016 and the risk and other factors to be used in adjusting such rates. The capitation rate tables for 2016 are posted on the CMS website at http://www.cms.gov/Medicare/Health-Plans/MedicareAdvtgSpecRateStats/index.html under Ratebooks and Supporting Data. The statutory component of the regional benchmarks, transitional phase-in periods for the rates from the Patient Protection and Affordable Care Act (ACA) (P.L. 111-148), qualifying counties, and each county's applicable percentage are also posted at this website. CMS issued final capitation rates on April 6, 2015, which are found at the website noted above.

Special Rules for Payments to MA Organizations

Services for beneficiaries enrolled in MA plans that are subject to a plan's moral or religious exception approved by CMS (see ¶ 411) are billable as fee-for-service to Medicare contractors for coverage and payment determinations. The lists of services may vary between MA plans. Beneficiaries enrolled in such plans are responsible for applicable coinsurance for the excepted services, but the deductible will be deemed met. [42 C.F.R. § 422.206(b); *Medicare Claims Processing Manual*, Pub. 100-04, Ch. 1, § 91.]

Rules for MSA plans. A beneficiary who elects coverage under an MA MSA plan must establish an MA MSA with a trustee that meets certain requirements and, if he or she has more than one MA MSA, designate the particular account to which payments under the MA MSA plan are to be made. [42 C.F.R. § 422.314.]

Payments to the MA MSA are calculated by comparing the monthly MA MSA premium with 1/12 of the annual capitation rate for the area. If the monthly MA MSA premium is less than 1/12 of the annual capitation rate applied for the area, the difference is the amount to be deposited in the MA MSA for each month for which the beneficiary is enrolled in the MSA plan. CMS deposits the full amount to which a beneficiary is entitled for the calendar year, beginning with the month in which MA MSA coverage begins. If the beneficiary's coverage under the MA MSA plan ends before the end of the calendar year, CMS recovers the amount that corresponds to the remaining months of that year. [42 C.F.R. § 422.314.]

Special rules for payments to federally qualified health centers. If an enrollee in an MA plan receives a service from a federally qualified health center (FQHC) that has a written agreement with the MA organization offering services to the plan, CMS will pay the FQHC directly for the services at a minimum on a quarterly basis, less the amount the FQHC would receive for the MA enrollee from the MA organization and taking into account the cost-sharing amount paid by the enrollee. [42 C.F.R. § 422.316.]

Special rules for coverage that begins or ends during an inpatient hospital stay. If coverage under an MA plan begins while the beneficiary is an inpatient, the previous MA organization or original Medicare, as appropriate, makes payment for inpatient services until the date of the beneficiary's discharge. The MA organization offering the newly elected MA plan is not responsible for the inpatient services until the date after the beneficiary's discharge. The MA organization offering the newly elected MA plan is paid the full amount otherwise payable. [42 C.F.R. § 422.318(b).]

If coverage under an MA plan ends while the beneficiary is an inpatient, the MA organization is responsible for the inpatient services until the date of the beneficiary's discharge. Neither original Medicare nor any succeeding MA organization offering a newly elected MA plan will make payment for those services during the remainder of the stay. The MA organization that no longer provides coverage receives no payment for the beneficiary for the period after coverage ends. [42 C.F.R. § 422.318(c).]

Special rules for hospice care. MA organizations do not provide hospice care. An MA organization must inform each Medicare enrollee eligible to elect hospice care about the availability of hospice care if a Medicare hospice program is located within the plan's service area or it is common practice to refer patients to hospice programs outside that area. Unless the enrollee disenrolls from the MA plan, a beneficiary electing hospice continues his or her enrollment in the MA plan and is entitled to receive, through the MA plan, any benefits other than those that are the responsibility of the Medicare hospice. No payment is made to an MA organization on behalf of a Medicare enrollee who has elected hospice care, except for the portion of the payment attributable to the beneficiary rebate for the MA plan plus the amount of the monthly prescription drug payment, if any. This no-payment rule is effective from the first day of the month following the month of election to receive hospice care until the first day of the month following the month in which the election is terminated. [42 C.F.R. § 422.320.]

[¶ 409] Marketing Requirements

A Medicare Advantage (MA) organization may not distribute any marketing materials or election forms or make such materials or forms available to individuals eligible to elect an MA organization unless it submits the material or form to CMS for review and CMS did not disapprove the distribution. [Soc. Sec. Act § 1851(h); 42 C.F.R. § 422.2262(a).]

Marketing Materials

Marketing materials include any informational materials targeted to Medicare beneficiaries that: (1) promote the MA organization or MA plan; (2) inform beneficiaries that they may enroll, or remain enrolled, in a plan; (3) explain the benefits of enrollment or the rules that apply to enrollees; and (4) explain how Medicare services are covered under an MA plan, including coverage conditions. These marketing materials may include:

(1) general audience materials in such mediums as general circulation brochures, newspapers, magazines, television, radio, billboards, yellow pages, or the Internet;

(2) marketing representative materials such as scripts or outlines for telemarketing or other presentations;

(3) presentation materials such as slides and charts;

(4) promotional materials such as brochures or leaflets, including materials for circulation by third parties such as physicians or other providers;

(5) membership communication materials such as membership rules, subscriber agreements, member handbooks, and wallet card instructions;

(6) letters to members about contractual changes, changes in providers, premiums, benefits, and plan procedures; and

(7) membership activities, such as materials on rules involving non-payment of premiums, confirmation of enrollment or disenrollment, or non-claim specific notification information.

[42 C.F.R. 422.2260.]

Ad hoc materials excluded. Marketing materials exclude ad hoc enrollee communications materials, meaning materials: (1) targeted to current enrollees, (2) customized or limited to a subset of enrollees or that apply to a specific situation, (3) that do not include information about the plan's benefit structure, and (4) that apply to a specific situation or cover claims processing or other operational issues. [42 C.F.R. 422.2260(6).] CMS may review such ad hoc enrollee communication materials and determine whether they must be modified or may no longer be used. [42 C.F.R. § 422.2262(d).]

CMS Review of Marketing Materials

An MA organization may not distribute any marketing materials or election forms or make such materials or forms available to individuals eligible to elect an MA organization unless, at least 45 days before the date of distribution, the organization submitted the material or form to CMS for review and CMS did not disapprove the distribution. The time period may be reduced to 10 days if the materials use CMS proposed model language and format. [Soc. Sec. Act § 1851(h)(1), (3), (5); 42 C.F.R. § 422.2262(a).]

File and use. The MA organization may distribute certain CMS-designated marketing materials five days following their submission to CMS if the organization certifies that it followed all applicable marketing guidelines and, when applicable, used CMS-specified model language without modification. When specified by CMS, organizations must use standardized formats and language in model materials. [42 C.F.R. § 422.2262(b), (c).]

Review guidelines. In reviewing marketing material or election forms, CMS determines whether the materials provide: (1) adequate written description of rules, procedures, basic benefits and services, and fees and other charges; (2) adequate written description of any supplemental benefits and services; (3) adequate written explanation of the grievance and appeals process (including differences between the two, and when it is appropriate to use each); and (4) any other information necessary to enable beneficiaries to make an informed enrollment decision. [42 C.F.R. § 422.2264(a).]

CMS must also make sure that the materials: (1) notify the general public of its enrollment period in an appropriate manner, through appropriate media, throughout its service area and, if applicable, continuation areas; (2) include a written notice that the MA organization is authorized by law to refuse to renew its contract with CMS, that CMS also may refuse to renew the contract, and that termination or non-renewal may result in termination of the beneficiary's enrollment in the plan; (3) are not materially inaccurate or misleading or otherwise make material misrepresentations; and (4) for markets with a significant non-English-speaking population, are provided in the language of these individuals. [42 C.F.R. § 422.2264(b)–(e).]

Marketing Prohibitions

When conducting marketing activities, an MA plan or organization may not:

- provide cash or other monetary rebates as an inducement for enrollment or otherwise;

- offer gifts to potential enrollees, unless the gifts are of nominal value, are offered to all potential enrollees without regard to whether they enroll, and are not in the form of cash or other monetary rebates;

- engage in any discriminatory activity, such as attempts to recruit Medicare beneficiaries from higher income areas without making comparable efforts to enroll Medicare beneficiaries from lower income areas;

- solicit door-to-door for Medicare beneficiaries or through other unsolicited means of direct contact, including calling a beneficiary when the beneficiary did not initiate the contact;

- engage in activities that could mislead or confuse Medicare beneficiaries or misrepresent the MA organization, such as claiming it is recommended or endorsed by CMS or Medicare or that CMS or Medicare recommends that the beneficiary enroll in the MA plan;

- market non-health care-related products to prospective enrollees during any MA or Part D sales activity or presentation;

- market any health care-related product during a marketing appointment beyond the scope agreed upon by the beneficiary, and documented by the plan, before the appointment (48 hours in advance, when practicable);

- market additional health-related lines of plan business not identified before an individual appointment without a separate appointment identifying the additional lines of business to be discussed;

- distribute marketing materials for which, before expiration of the 45-day period, the MA organization receives from CMS written notice of disapproval because it is inaccurate or misleading or misrepresents the MA organization, its marketing representatives, or CMS;

- use providers or provider groups to distribute printed information comparing the benefits of different health plans unless the providers, provider groups, or pharmacies accept and display materials from all health plans with which the providers, provider groups, or pharmacies contract;

- conduct sales presentations or distribute and accept MA plan enrollment forms in provider offices or other areas where health care is delivered to individuals, except in the case where such activities are conducted in common areas in health care settings;

- conduct sales presentations or distribute and accept plan applications at educational events;

- employ MA plan names that suggest that a plan is not available to all Medicare beneficiaries (this prohibition does not apply to MA plan names in effect on July 31, 2000);

- display the names and/or logos of co-branded network providers on the organization's member identification card, unless the provider names and/or logos are related to the member selection of specific provider organizations (other marketing materials that include names and/or logos of provider co-branding partners must clearly indicate that other providers are available in the network);

- engage in any other marketing activity prohibited by CMS in its marketing guidance;

- provide meals for potential enrollees, regardless of value; and

¶409

- use a plan name that does not include the name of the plan type at the end of the plan name.

[Soc. Sec. Act § 1851(h)(4), (j); 42 C.F.R. § 422.2268.]

Confirmation of Marketing Resources

The MA organization must demonstrate to CMS that its marketing resources are allocated to marketing to the disabled Medicare population as well as to beneficiaries age 65 and over. MA organizations must also establish and maintain a system for confirming that enrolled beneficiaries have, in fact, enrolled in the MA plan and understand the rules applicable under the plan. [42 C.F.R. § 422.2272(a), (b).]

Licensing of Marketing Representatives

MA organizations must employ as marketing representatives only individuals who are licensed by the state to conduct marketing activities in that state. The organization must inform the state that it has appointed these individuals as marketing representatives as required by the appointment process provided for under state law. [Soc. Sec. Act § 1851(h)(7); 42 C.F.R. § 422.2272(c).]

The MA organization must also report the termination of any such agent or broker to the state, including the reasons for such termination if the state requires that the reasons for the termination be reported. Finally, an MA organization must terminate any unlicensed agent or broker employed as a marketing representative and notify any beneficiaries who have been enrolled by an unqualified agent or broker of the agent's or broker's termination and, if requested, of their options to confirm enrollment or make a plan change, including a special election period. [Soc. Sec. Act § 1851(h)(7); 42 C.F.R. § 422.2272(d), (e).]

Broker and Agent Requirements

If an MA organization uses agents and brokers to sell its plans, it must: (1) follow compensation rules established by CMS; (2) ensure agents selling Medicare products are trained annually on Medicare rules and regulations and details specific to the plan products they intend to sell; and (3) ensure agents selling Medicare products are tested annually to ensure appropriate knowledge and understanding of Medicare rules and regulations and details specific to the plan products they intend to sell. [Soc. Sec. Act § 1851(j)(2); 42 C.F.R. § 422.2274(b)–(f).]

"Compensation" defined. Compensation includes monetary or nonmonetary remuneration of any kind relating to the sale or renewal of the policy, including commissions, bonuses, gifts, prizes, awards, and referral or finder fees. Compensation does *not* include: (1) the payment of fees to comply with state appointment laws, training, certification, and testing costs; (2) reimbursement for mileage to and from appointments with beneficiaries; or (3) reimbursement for actual costs associated with beneficiary sales appointments such as venue rent, snacks, and materials. [42 C.F.R. § 422.2274(a).]

Compensation amounts. If an MA organization pays compensation, it must compensate independent brokers and agents as follows. For an initial year enrollment of a Medicare beneficiary into an MA plan, the compensation must be at or below the fair market value of such services, published annually as a cut-off amount by CMS. For renewal years, compensation may be up to 50 percent of the current fair market value cut-off amounts published annually by CMS. [Soc. Sec. Act § 1851(j)(2)(D); 42 C.F.R. § 422.2274(b)(1).]

If the MA organization contracts with a third-party entity such as a field management organization or similar type entity to sell its insurance products or perform services: (1) the amount paid to the third party and its agents for enrollment of a beneficiary into a plan must be the same as paid to non-third-party agents and brokers; and (2) the amount paid to the third party for services other than selling insurance products, if any, must be fair market value and must not exceed an amount that is commensurate with the amounts paid by the MA organization to a third party for similar services during each of the previous two years. [42 C.F.R. § 422.2274(b)(1).]

Aggregate compensation. An entity must not provide aggregate compensation to its agents or brokers greater than the renewal compensation payable by the replacing plan on renewal policies if an existing policy is replaced with a "like plan type" at any time. The initial compensation is paid for replacements between unlike plan types. [42 C.F.R. § 422.2274(b)(2).]

Plan year compensation. Compensation may be paid only for the beneficiary's months of enrollment during a plan year. Compensation payments may be made up front for the entire current plan year or in installments throughout the year. When a beneficiary disenrolls from an MA plan, the MA organization must recover compensation paid to agents and brokers for those months of the plan year for which the beneficiary is not enrolled. For disenrollments occurring within the first three months, the entire compensation must be recovered unless CMS determines that recoupment is not in the best interests of the Medicare program. [42 C.F.R. § 422.2274(b)(3).]

Finder's fees. Finder's (referral) fees paid to all agents and brokers (1) may not exceed an amount that CMS determines could reasonably be expected to provide financial incentive for an agent or broker to recommend or enroll a beneficiary into a plan that is not the most appropriate to meet his or her needs; and (2) must be included in the total compensation not to exceed the fair market value for that calendar year. [42 C.F.R. § 422.2274(h).]

Compensation structure. MA organizations must establish a compensation structure for new and replacement enrollments and renewals effective in a given plan year. Compensation structures must be in place by the beginning of the plan marketing period, October 1. [42 C.F.R. § 422.2274(b)(4).]

Employer Group Retirees

MA organizations may develop marketing materials designed for members of an employer group who are eligible for employer-sponsored benefits through the MA organization and furnish these materials only to the group members. These materials are not subject to CMS prior review and approval. [42 C.F.R. § 422.2276.]

[¶ 410] Quality Improvement Programs

Each Medicare Advantage (MA) organization that offers one or more MA plans must have, for each of those plans, an ongoing quality improvement program for services it provides to enrollees. An MA plan must: (1) create a quality improvement program plan that sufficiently outlines the elements of the plan's quality improvement program; (2) have a chronic care improvement program; (3) conduct quality improvement projects that can be expected to have a favorable effect on health outcomes and enrollee satisfaction; and (4) encourage its providers to participate in CMS and HHS quality improvement initiatives. [Soc. Sec. Act § 1852(e); 42 C.F.R. § 422.152(a), (c), (d); *Medicare Managed Care Manual*, Pub. 100-16, Ch. 5, § 20.1.]

Requirements for all plans. For all types of plans that it offers, an organization must: (1) maintain a health information system that collects, analyzes, and integrates the data necessary to implement its quality improvement program; (2) ensure that the information it receives from providers of services is reliable and complete; and (3) make all collected information available to CMS. For each plan, there must be in effect a process for formal evaluation, at least annually, of the impact and effectiveness of its quality improvement program. In addition, the organization must correct all problems that come to its attention through internal surveillance, complaints, or other mechanisms. [42 C.F.R. §422.152(f); Pub. 100-16, Ch. 5, §§20, 20.1.]

Requirements for MA coordinated care plans. An MA coordinated care plan (except for local and regional preferred provider organization (PPO) plans) must have a quality improvement program that: (1) in processing requests for initial or continued authorization of services, follows written policies and procedures that reflect current standards of medical practice; (2) has in effect mechanisms to detect both under-utilization and over-utilization of service; and (3) measures and reports performance. These requirements also apply to MA local PPO-type plans that are offered by an organization that is licensed or organized under state law as a health maintenance organization. [42 C.F.R. §422.152(b).]

All coordinated care contracts (including local and regional PPOs, contracts with exclusively special needs plan (SNP) benefit packages, private fee-for-service (PFFS) contracts, and medical savings account (MSA) contracts) and all cost contracts under §1876 of the Social Security Act with 600 or more enrollees in July of the prior year must contract with approved Medicare Consumer Assessment of Healthcare Providers and Systems (CAHPS) survey vendors to conduct the Medicare CAHPS satisfaction survey of plan enrollees and submit the survey data to CMS. [42 C.F.R. §422.152(b)(5).]

Requirements for MA regional plans and MA local plans. MA organizations offering an MA regional plan or local PPO plan must: (1) measure performance under the plan using standard measures required by CMS and report its performance to CMS; (2) collect, analyze, and report the data; and (3) evaluate the continuity and coordination of care furnished to enrollees. If the organization uses written protocols for utilization review, the organization must: (1) base those protocols on current standards of medical practice; and (2) have mechanisms to evaluate utilization of services and to inform enrollees and providers of services of the results of the evaluation. [42 C.F.R. §422.152(e).]

Requirements for MA PSSF plans and Medicare MSA plans. MA PFFS and MSA plans are subject to the requirement that may not exceed the requirement specified for MA regional plans and MA local plans. [42 C.F.R. §422.152(h).]

Specialized MA plans for special needs individuals. All SNPs for special needs individuals must be approved by the National Committee for Quality Assurance (NCQA) and must submit their model of care to CMS for NCQA evaluation and approval. A SNP, in addition to the requirements of 42 C.F.R. §422.152(a) and (f), must conduct a quality improvement program that: (1) provides for the collection, analysis, and reporting of data that measures health outcomes and indices of quality pertaining to its targeted special needs population (i.e., dual eligible, institutionalized, or chronic condition) at the plan level; (2) makes available information on quality and outcomes measures that will enable beneficiaries to compare health coverage options and CMS to monitor the plan's model of care performance; and (3) measures the effectiveness of its model of care through the collection, aggregation, analysis, and reporting of data that demonstrate the following:

- access to care as evidenced by measures from the care coordination domain (e.g., service and benefit utilization rates);

- improvement in beneficiary health status as evidenced by measures from functional, psychosocial, or clinical domains (e.g., quality of life indicators, depression scales, or chronic disease outcomes);

- staff implementation of the SNP model of care as evidenced by measures of care structure and process from the continuity of care domain (e.g., NCQA accreditation measures or medication reconciliation associated with care setting transitions indicators);

• comprehensive health risk assessment as evidenced by measures from the care coordination domain (e.g., accuracy of acuity stratification, safety indicators, or timeliness of initial assessments or annual reassessments);

• implementation of an individualized plan of care as evidenced by measures from functional, psychosocial, or clinical domains;

• a provider network that has targeted clinical expertise as evidenced by measures from medication management, disease management, or behavioral health domains;

• delivery of services across the continuum of care;

• delivery of extra services and benefits that meet the specialized needs of the most vulnerable beneficiaries as evidenced by measures from the psychosocial, functional, and end-of-life domains;

• use of evidence-based practices and nationally recognized clinical protocols; and

• use of integrated systems of communication as evidenced by measures from the care coordination domain (e.g., call center utilization rates, rates of beneficiary involvement in care plan development, etc.).

[Soc. Sec. Act § 1852(e)(3)(A)(ii); 42 C.F.R. § 422.152(g).]

Compliance Deemed on the Basis of Accreditation

CMS has the authority to deem MA organizations compliant with Medicare requirements. An MA organization is deemed to meet any of the following seven requirements if it is fully accredited, and periodically reaccredited, for the standards by a private, national accreditation organization approved by CMS and the accreditation organization used the standards approved by CMS for the purposes of assessing the MA organization's compliance with Medicare requirements:

(1) quality improvement;

(2) antidiscrimination;

(3) access to services;

(4) confidentiality and accuracy of enrollee records;

(5) information on advance directives;

(6) provider participation rules; and

(7) certain requirements for Part D prescription drug benefit programs offered by MA programs, including access to covered drugs, drug utilization management programs, quality assurance measures and methods, medication therapy management programs, and privacy, confidentiality, and accuracy of enrollee records.

[Soc. Sec. Act § 1852(e)(4); 42 C.F.R. §§ 422.156(a) and (b), 423.165(b).]

[¶ 411] Relationships with Providers

CMS has established requirements and standards for the Medicare Advantage (MA) organization's relationships with providers, including physicians, other health care professionals, and institutional providers and suppliers, under contracts or arrangements or deemed contracts under MA private fee-for-service (PFFS) plans. [Soc. Sec. Act § 1852(j)(1); 42 C.F.R. § 422.200.]

The term "providers" means individuals who are licensed or certified by a state to deliver health care services, such as doctors, nurse practitioners, and clinical social workers.

The term also refers to the entities that deliver those services, including hospitals, nursing homes, and home health agencies. [42 C.F.R. § 422.2.]

Antidiscrimination rules. In selecting practitioners, an MA organization may not discriminate, in terms of participation, reimbursement, or indemnification, against any health care professional who is acting within the scope of his or her license or certification under state law solely on the basis of the license or certification. If an organization declines to include a given provider or group of providers in its network, it must furnish written notice to the affected providers of the reason for the decision. This antidiscrimination prohibition does not preclude the MA organization from: (1) refusing to grant participation to health care professionals in excess of the number necessary to meet the needs of the plan's enrollees (except for MA PFFS plans, which may not refuse to contract on this basis); (2) using different reimbursement amounts for different specialties or for different practitioners in the same specialty; or (3) implementing measures designed to maintain quality and control costs. [Soc. Sec. Act § 1852(b)(2); 42 C.F.R. § 422.205.]

Physician incentive plans. Any physician incentive plan operated by an MA organization must meet the following basic requirements:

(1) The MA organization may not make any specific payment, directly or indirectly, to a physician or physician group as an inducement to reduce or limit medically necessary services furnished to any particular enrollee. Indirect payments may include offerings of monetary value measured in the present or future.

(2) If the physician incentive plan places a physician or physician group at substantial financial risk for services that the physician or physician group does not furnish itself, the MA organization must ensure that all physicians and physician groups at substantial financial risk have either aggregate or per-patient stop-loss protection.

[Soc. Sec. Act § 1852(j)(4); 42 C.F.R. § 422.208(c).]

An MA organization may not operate a physician incentive plan unless it provides information the HHS Secretary requires on the plan. [42 C.F.R. §§ 422.208(c)(3), 422.210.]

Limits on provider indemnification. An MA organization is prohibited from having a provider or a provider group indemnify the organization against civil liability for damage arising from the organization's denial of medically necessary care. [Soc. Sec. Act § 1852(j)(5); 42 C.F.R. § 422.212.]

Special rules for noncontract providers. A provider that does not have a contract establishing the amount of payment for services furnished to a Medicare beneficiary enrolled in an MA plan must accept the amount that would have been paid under the original Medicare program as payment in full. [Soc. Sec. Act § 1852(k); 42 C.F.R. § 422.214(a)(1).]

Special rules for MA PFFS plans. For MA PFFS plans, the MA organization: (1) must establish payment rates for plan-covered items and services that apply to deemed providers; (2) may vary payment rates for providers; (3) must reimburse providers on a fee-for-service basis; and (4) must make information on its payment rates available to providers that furnish services that may be covered under the MA PFFS plan. Any provider of services that does not have in effect a contract establishing payment amounts for services furnished to a beneficiary enrolled in an MA PFFS plan must receive, and accept as payment in full, at least the amount that it could collect if the beneficiary were enrolled in original Medicare. [Soc. Sec. Act § 1852(j)(6); 42 C.F.R. § 422.216(a).]

Private contracting. An MA organization may not pay a physician or other practitioner for services (other than emergency or urgently needed services) furnished to a Medicare enrollee by a health care professional who has filed with the Medicare administrative

contractor an affidavit promising to furnish Medicare-covered services to Medicare beneficiaries only through private contracts (see ¶ 872). An MA organization must pay for
emergency or urgently needed services furnished by a physician or practitioner who has not
signed a private contract with the beneficiary. [Soc. Sec. Act § 1852(k); 42 C.F.R. § 422.220.]

Provider Participation Requirements

An MA organization that operates a coordinated care plan or network medical savings
account (MSA) plan must provide for the participation of individual physicians, and the
management and members of groups of physicians, through reasonable procedures that
include:

- written notice of rules of participation, including terms of payment, credentialing,
and other rules directly related to participation decisions;

- written notice of material changes in participation rules before the changes are
put in effect;

- written notice of participation decisions that are adverse to physicians; and

- a process for appealing adverse participation decisions, including the right of
physicians to present information and their views on the decision.

[42 C.F.R. § 422.202(a).]

Formal consultation with physicians. An MA organization must establish a formal
mechanism to consult with the physicians who have agreed to provide services under the
MA plan, regarding the organization's medical policy, quality improvement programs, and
medical management procedures. The organization must ensure that practice guidelines and
utilization management guidelines are communicated to providers and enrollees: (1) are
based on reasonable medical evidence or a consensus of health care professionals in the
particular field; (2) consider the needs of the enrolled population; (3) are developed in
consultation with contracting health care professionals; and (4) are reviewed and updated
periodically. [42 C.F.R. § 422.202(b).]

Subcontracted groups. These provider participation procedures extend not only to
direct contracting health care professionals, but also to those with subcontracted agreements. [42 C.F.R. § 422.202(c).]

Provider Selection and Credentialing

An MA organization must have written policies and procedures for the selection and
evaluation of providers. The organization must follow a documented process with respect to
providers and suppliers who have signed contracts or participation agreements.

- For providers (other than physicians and other health care professionals), the
documented process requires determination, and redetermination at specified intervals,
that each provider: (1) is licensed to operate in the state and is in compliance with any
other applicable state or federal requirements; and (2) has been reviewed and approved
by an accrediting body or meets the standards established by the organization itself. [42
C.F.R. § 422.204(b)(1).]

- For physicians and other health care professionals, including members of physician groups, the process must include: (1) initial credentialing that includes written
application, verification of licensure or certification from primary sources, disciplinary
status, eligibility for payment under Medicare, and site visits; (2) recredentialing at
least every three years that updates information obtained during initial credentialing,
considers performance indicators such as those collected through quality improvement
programs, utilization management systems, handling of grievances and appeals, en-

rollee satisfaction surveys, and other plan activities, and includes an attestation of the correctness and completeness of the new information; and (3) a process for consulting with contracting health care professionals with respect to criteria for credentialing and recredentialing. [42 C.F.R. § 422.204(b)(2).]

The documented process must also require that basic benefits be provided through, or payments be made to, providers and suppliers that meet applicable Medicare requirements. [42 C.F.R. § 422.204(b)(3).]

An MA organization may not employ or contract with a provider excluded from participation in the Medicare program. [42 C.F.R. §§ 422.204(b)(4), 422.752(a)(8).] HHS's investigatory arm, the Office of Inspector General, maintains a list of excluded providers on its website at https://exclusions.oig.hhs.gov/.

Interference with Health Care Professional Advice Prohibited

An MA organization may not prohibit or restrict a health care professional from advising, or advocating on behalf of, a patient enrolled under an MA plan regarding: (1) health status, medical care, or treatment options, including the provision of sufficient information to the patient to provide an opportunity to decide among all relevant treatment options; (2) the risks, benefits, and consequences of treatment or non-treatment; or (3) the opportunity for the patient to refuse treatment and to express preferences about future treatment. Health care professionals must provide information regarding treatment options, including the option of no treatment, in a culturally competent manner, and must ensure that individuals with disabilities have effective communications with participants throughout the health system in making decisions regarding treatment options. [Soc. Sec. Act § 1852(j)(3); 42 C.F.R. § 422.206(a).]

However, an MA plan is not required to cover, furnish, or pay for a particular counseling or referral service if the MA organization that offers the plan: (1) objects to that service on moral or religious grounds; and (2) through appropriate written means, makes information available regarding those policies available to CMS (through its Medicare application) and current and prospective enrollees. [42 C.F.R. § 422.206(b).]

[¶ 412] Intermediate Sanctions and Civil Money Penalties

The following sanctions may be imposed on Medicare Advantage (MA) organizations for certain deficiencies: (1) suspension of enrollment of Medicare beneficiaries; (2) suspension of payment to the MA organization for Medicare beneficiaries who are enrolled in the plan after the notice of the intermediate sanction; and (3) suspension of all marketing activities to Medicare beneficiaries by the MA organization for specified MA plans. CMS may also terminate an MA organization's contract or impose civil money penalties (CMPs). [Soc. Sec. Act § 1857(g)(2), (3); 42 C.F.R. §§ 422.750, 422.752(d).]

Intermediate sanctions. CMS may impose one or more of the intermediate sanctions listed in 42 C.F.R. § 422.750(a) on an MA organization for the following violations:

- failing to provide a beneficiary with medically necessary services and the beneficiary is adversely affected;

- imposing premiums that exceed the MA monthly basic and supplemental beneficiary premiums;

- expelling or refusing to re-enroll a beneficiary in violation of MA requirements;

- engaging in any practice that would have the effect of denying or discouraging the enrollment of eligible individuals whose medical condition or history indicates a need for substantial future medical services;

- misrepresenting or falsifying information to CMS, an individual, or any other entity;

- interfering with practitioners' advice to enrollees;

- failing to enforce the limit on balance billing under a private fee-for service plan;

- employing or contracting with providers who are excluded from Medicare participation for the provision of health care, utilization review, medical social work, or administrative services;

- enrolling an individual in an MA plan without his or her prior consent;

- transferring an individual enrolled in an MA plan to another plan without his or her prior consent or solely for the purposes of making a commission;

- failing to comply with applicable marketing requirements or implementing guidance; or

- employing or contracting with any individual, agent, provider, supplier, or entity that engages in any of the conduct described above.

[Soc. Sec. Act § 1857(g)(1); 42 C.F.R. § 422.752(a).]

Procedures for imposing intermediate sanctions. Before imposing intermediate sanctions, CMS must send a written notice to the MA organization stating the nature and basis of the proposed intermediate sanction and the organization's right to a hearing and send the HHS Office of Inspector General (OIG) a copy of the notice. CMS allows the MA organization 10 calendar days from receipt of the notice to provide a written rebuttal. A request for a hearing must be received within 15 calendar days of the MA organization's receipt of the intent to impose an intermediate sanction. [42 C.F.R. § 422.756(a), (b).]

Effective date and duration of sanction. The effective date of the sanction is the date specified by CMS in the notice. If, however, CMS determines that the MA organization's conduct poses a serious threat to an enrollee's health and safety, CMS may make the sanction effective on an earlier date. The sanction remains in effect until CMS is satisfied that the deficiencies that are the basis for the sanction determination have been corrected and are not likely to recur. If an immediate sanction has been imposed, CMS may require the MA organization to market and/or accept enrollments for a certain period of time in order to assess whether the deficiencies have been cured and are not like to reoccur. In addition to or as an alternative to these sanctions, CMS may decline to authorize the renewal of an organization's contract or terminate the contract. [42 C.F.R. § 422.756(c), (d).]

Civil Money Penalties

In addition to, or in place of, any intermediate sanctions, CMS may impose CMPs for any of the reasons for contract terminations contained in 42 C.F.R. § 422.510(a), except by reason of the existence of credible evidence that the MA organization committed or participated in false, fraudulent, or abusive activities affecting the Medicare program under 42 C.F.R. § 422.510(a)(4)(i). [42 C.F.R. § 422.752(c)(1).]

In addition to, or in place of any intermediate sanctions imposed by CMS, the OIG may impose CMPs for any of the 12 bases for intermediate sanctions listed above (see 42 C.F.R. § 422.752(a)) or determinations made based on the existence of credible evidence that the MA organization committed or participated in false, fraudulent, or abusive activities affecting the Medicare program under 42 C.F.R. § 422.510(a)(4)(i). [42 C.F.R. § 422.752(c)(2); *Final rule*, 79 FR 29844, May 23, 2014.]

If CMS makes a determination to impose a CMP, it must send a written notice of the decision containing a description of the basis for the determination, the basis for the penalty, the amount of the penalty, the date the penalty is due, the MA organization's right to a hearing, and information about where to file the hearing request. [42 C.F.R. §§ 422.752(c), 422.756(e).]

Collection of CMPs. When an MA organization does not request an administrative law judge (ALJ) hearing, CMS initiates collection of the CMP following the expiration of the time frame for requesting the ALJ hearing. If an MA organization requests a hearing and CMS's decision to impose a CMP is upheld, CMS may initiate collection of the CMP once the administrative decision is final. [42 C.F.R. § 422.758.]

Determining the amount of CMPs. In determining the amount of the CMP, CMS will consider the nature of the conduct, the degree of culpability, the harm that resulted or could have resulted from the conduct, the financial condition of the organization, the history of prior offenses by the organization or its principals, and such other matters as justice may require. If the deficiency on which the determination is based has directly adversely affected one or more MA enrollees, CMS may assess CMPs of up to $25,000 for each determination. For each week that a deficiency remains uncorrected after the week in which the MA organization receives notice of the determination, CMS may assess up to $10,000. If CMS makes a determination that an MA organization has failed to substantially carry out the terms of its contract, CMS may assess $250 per Medicare enrollee from the terminated MA plan or plans at the time the MA organization terminated its contract, or $100,000, whichever is greater. [42 C.F.R. § 422.760.]

Chapter 5– MEDICARE PART D—PRESCRIPTION DRUG BENEFIT

[¶ 500] Overview

Beneficiaries entitled to Part A and enrolled in Part B, enrollees in Medicare Advantage (MA) private fee-for-service plans, and enrollees in Part C medical savings account plans are eligible for the Part D prescription drug benefit. Under the prescription drug benefit, eligible individuals have access to at least two prescription drug plans (PDPs) in their region. In regions where eligible individuals do not have access to at least two PDPs, limited risk or fallback prescription drug plans must be offered. [Soc. Sec. Act §§ 1860D-1(a), 1860D-3(a).] As a practical matter, however, fallback plans have not been necessary since the Part D program started in 2006 as at least two qualified PDPs have been offered in each region.

An individual eligible for the prescription drug benefit may enroll in a private plan during specified enrollment periods by filing the appropriate enrollment form with the PDP. Full benefit dual-eligible individuals (those eligible for both Medicare and Medicaid) who fail to enroll in a plan will be automatically enrolled by CMS (see ¶ 503).

Under the PDP program, eligible individuals have the choice of either a standard coverage plan or an alternative coverage plan with actuarially equivalent benefits. In addition to the standard coverage plan, participating plans may offer a supplemental benefit (see ¶ 510). Coinsurance and deductibles for 2016 are discussed at ¶ 507, and premium and cost-sharing subsidies for low-income individuals are discussed at ¶ 508.

Establishment of Prescription Drug Service Areas

CMS established 26 MA regions and 34 PDP regions consisting of the 50 states and the District of Columbia, as well as five separate PDP regions for the territories. PDP regions were established in a manner that was consistent, to the extent practicable, with MA regions, usually on a state-by-state basis. [Soc. Sec. Act § 1860D-11(a); 42 C.F.R. § 423.112; *Final rule,* 70 FR 4194, 4246, Jan. 28, 2005.]

Covered Part D Drugs

To be covered, a Part D drug must be approved by the U.S. Food and Drug Administration (FDA) for use and sale in the U.S. and be prescribed and used for a medically accepted reason. Part D drugs include biological products, insulin, medical supplies associated with the injection of insulin (including syringes, needles, alcohol swabs, and gauze), vaccines and their administration, supplies directly associated with delivering insulin into the body (such as an inhalation chamber used to deliver the insulin through inhalation), and a combination product approved and regulated by the FDA as a drug, vaccine, or biologic. [Soc. Sec. Act § 1860D-2(e)(1); 42 C.F.R. § 423.100.]

Excluded drugs. Part D cannot pay for drugs when they would be covered under Medicare Part A or Part B. In addition, the following drugs cannot be included in standard coverage: (1) drugs or classes of drugs, or their medical uses, that may be excluded from coverage or otherwise restricted under Medicaid under Soc. Sec. Act § 1927(d)(2) or (d)(3), except for smoking cessation agents; (2) medical foods, defined as foods that are formulated to be consumed or administered enterally under the supervision of a physician and are intended for the specific dietary management of a disease or condition for which distinctive nutritional requirements, are established by medical evaluation, and are not regulated as drugs under section 505 of the Federal Food, Drug, and Cosmetic Act; (3) drugs for erectile dysfunction; (4) drugs for relief of cough and colds; (5) non-prescription drugs; (6) drugs used for cosmetic purposes or hair growth; (7) drugs used to promote fertility; and (8) prescription vitamins and minerals, except prenatal vitamins and fluoride preparation products. [Soc. Sec. Act § 1860D-2(e)(2); 42 C.F.R. § 423.100; *Medicare Prescription Drug Manual*, Pub. 100-18, Ch. 6, § 20.1.]

[¶ 503] Eligibility and Enrollment

To be eligible for prescription drug benefits under Part D, an individual must (1) be entitled to Medicare benefits under Part A or enrolled in Medicare Part B, (2) live in the service area of a Part D plan, and (3) be a U.S. citizen or be lawfully present in the U.S. Except for those enrolled in a Medicare Advantage prescription drug plan (MA-PD), a Program of All-inclusive Care for the Elderly (PACE) plan, or a cost-based health maintenance organization (HMO) or competitive medical plan (CMP), individuals may enroll in prescription drug plans (PDPs) if they are eligible for Part D, live in the PDP service area, and are not enrolled in another Part D plan. [42 C.F.R. § 423.30(a).]

Medicare Advantage plan enrollees. A Part D eligible individual enrolled in an MA-PD plan must obtain qualified prescription drug coverage from that plan. Medicare Advantage enrollees may not enroll in a PDP unless they are enrolled in a MA private fee-for-services plan that does not provide qualified prescription drug coverage or they are enrolled in a medical savings account plan. [42 C.F.R. § 423.30(b).]

PACE plan enrollees. A Part D eligible individual enrolled in a PACE plan offering qualified prescription drug coverage must obtain coverage through that PACE plan. [42 C.F.R. § 423.30(c).]

Cost-based HMO or CMP enrollees. A Part D eligible individual enrolled in a cost-based HMO or CMP that provides qualified prescription drug coverage is eligible to enroll in a PDP only if the individual does not elect prescription drug coverage under the cost-based HMO or CMP and otherwise meets general PDP eligibility requirements. [42 C.F.R. § 423.30(d).]

Incarcerated individuals. Individuals incarcerated in correctional facilities are not eligible to enroll in PDPs, even when they are located within a PDP service area. [*Medicare Prescription Drug Benefit Manual*, Pub. 100-18, Ch. 3, § 20.2.]

State mental institution patients. Unlike incarcerated individuals, individuals who are residing in state mental institutions are not considered by CMS to be out of service areas. Medicare beneficiaries residing in such institutions have access to Medicare benefits under Part A and Part B and are entitled to enroll in Part D plans. CMS, however, recognizes that individuals in state mental institutions may be limited to enrolling in the pharmacy network that contracts with their institution. As a result, CMS provides a special enrollment period to enable them to join the appropriate Part D plan based upon their situation. [Pub. 100-18, Ch. 3, §§ 20.2, 30.3.8.]

The Enrollment Process

An individual eligible for a Part D benefit may enroll in a private PDP during the specified regulatory enrollment periods by filing the appropriate enrollment form with the PDP or through other CMS-approved enrollment mechanisms. [42 C.F.R. § 423.32(a).]

Enrollment forms. The enrollment must be completed by the beneficiary and must include an acknowledgment of the disclosure and exchange of necessary information between CMS and the PDP sponsor. Individuals who assist in the completion of an enrollment, including authorized representatives of the beneficiary, must indicate that they provided assistance and disclose their relationship to the beneficiary. Part D eligible individuals must provide information regarding reimbursement through other insurance, group health plans, other third-party payment arrangements, or other sources, and consent to the release of such information. [42 C.F.R. § 423.32(b).]

Timely processing and prompt notice. A PDP sponsor must timely process an enrollment request in accordance with CMS enrollment guidelines and enroll a Part D eligible individual who elects to enroll or is enrolled in the plan during the specified enrollment periods. A sponsor also must provide an individual with prompt notice of acceptance or denial of an enrollment request. [42 C.F.R. § 423.32(c), (d).]

Maintenance of enrollment. An enrolled individual remains enrolled in a PDP until: (1) the individual successfully enrolls in another PDP or MA-PD, (2) the individual voluntarily disenrolls from the PDP, (3) the individual is involuntarily disenrolled from the PDP, (4) the PDP is discontinued within the individual's area of residence, or (5) the individual is enrolled after the initial enrollment. [42 C.F.R. § 423.32(e).]

Cost-based HMOs, CMPs, and PACE plans. Individuals enrolled in cost-based HMOs, CMPs, and PACE plans that offered prescription drug coverage as of December 31, 2005, were permitted to remain enrolled in those plans and receive Part D benefits offered by the plans until one of the five conditions for disenrollment is met (see above). [42 C.F.R. § 423.32(f).]

Passive enrollment by CMS. In situations involving either immediate termination based on serious financial difficulties or other situations in which CMS determines that remaining enrolled in a plan poses potential harm to plan members, CMS may implement passive enrollment procedures. Under passive enrollment procedures, individuals will be considered to have enrolled in the plan selected by CMS unless they decline the plan or request enrollment in another plan. The organization that receives the passive enrollment beneficiaries must provide them with notification that describes the costs and benefits of the new plan, the process for accessing care under the plan, and the beneficiary's ability to decline the enrollment or choose another plan. The notification must be provided to all potential enrollees prior to the enrollment effective date (or as soon as possible after the effective date if prior notice is not practicable). [42 C.F.R. § 423.32(g).]

Enrollment of Low-Income Subsidy Eligible Individuals

CMS must ensure the enrollment into Part D plans of low-income subsidy eligible individuals who fail to enroll in a Part D plan. A low-income subsidy eligible individual is an individual who meets the definition of full-subsidy eligible, including those eligible for both Medicare and Medicaid, or other subsidy-eligible individual. [42 C.F.R. § 423.34(a), (b).]

Automatic enrollment. Except for low-income subsidy eligible individuals who are qualifying covered retirees with a group health plan sponsor, CMS automatically enrolls individuals who fail to enroll in a Part D plan into a PDP offering basic prescription drug coverage in the area where the beneficiary resides. The PDP must have a monthly beneficiary premium amount that does not exceed the low-income subsidy amount. If there is more than one PDP in an area with a monthly beneficiary premium at or below the low-income premium subsidy amount, individuals are enrolled on a random basis. Low-income subsidy eligible individuals enrolled in an MA private fee-for-service plan, a cost-based HMO or CMP that does not offer qualified prescription drug coverage, or a medical savings account plan, and who fail to enroll in a Part D plan, also will be enrolled automatically. [Soc. Sec. Act § 1860D-1(b)(1)(C); 42 C.F.R. § 423.34(d).]

Exception for employer group health plans. Full-benefit dual-eligible individuals who are qualifying covered retirees, and for whom CMS has approved the group health plan sponsor to receive the retiree drug subsidy (see ¶ 530), also are automatically enrolled in a Part D plan, unless they elect to decline that enrollment. Before effectuating the enrollment, however, CMS will provide notice to such individuals of their choices and advise them to discuss the potential impact of Medicare Part D coverage on their group health plan coverage. The notice informs such individuals that they will be deemed to have declined to enroll in Part D unless they affirmatively enroll in a Part D plan or contact CMS and confirm that they wish to be auto-enrolled in a PDP. Individuals who elect not to be auto-enrolled may enroll in Medicare Part D at a later time if they choose to do so. All other low-income subsidy eligible beneficiaries who are qualified covered retirees are not automatically enrolled into PDPs. [42 C.F.R. § 423.34(d)(3).]

PDP plans that voluntarily waive a de minimis premium amount. CMS may include in the automatic enrollment process PDPs that voluntarily waive a *de minimis* premium amount if CMS determines that such inclusion is warranted. [Soc. Sec. Act § 1860D-1(b)(1)(D); 42 C.F.R. § 423.34(d)(4).]

Declining enrollment or disenrollment by dual-eligible individuals. A low-income subsidy eligible individual may decline enrollment in Part D or disenroll from a Part D plan and elect to enroll in another Part D plan during the special enrollment period. [42 C.F.R. § 423.34(e).]

Full-benefit dual eligibles' effective date of enrollment. Enrollment for full-benefit dual-eligible individuals must be effective: (1) for Part D for individuals who are Medicaid eligible and subsequently become newly eligible for Part D, the first day of the month the individual is eligible for Part D; and (2) for individuals who are eligible for Part D and subsequently become newly eligible for Medicaid, the first day of the month when the individual becomes eligible for both Medicaid and Part D. [42 C.F.R. § 423.34(f).]

Effective date of enrollment for non-full-benefit dual eligibles who are low-income subsidy eligible. The effective date for non-full-benefit dual-eligible individuals who are low-income subsidy eligible is no later than the first day of the second month after CMS determines that they meet the criteria for enrollment. [42 C.F.R. § 423.34(g).]

Reassigning low-income subsidy eligible individuals. During the annual coordinated election period, CMS may reassign certain low-income subsidy eligible individuals to another PDP if CMS determines that the further enrollment is warranted. However, if a PDP offering basic prescription drug coverage in the area where the beneficiary resides has a monthly beneficiary premium amount that exceeds the low-income subsidy amount by a *de minimis* amount and the PDP volunteers to waive the *de minimis* amount, then CMS will not reassign low-income subsidy individuals who would otherwise be enrolled on the basis that the monthly beneficiary premium exceeds the low-income subsidy by a *de minimis* amount. [Soc. Sec. Act § 1860D-14(a)(5); 42 C.F.R. § 423.34(c).]

Formulary and coverage information. Subsidy-eligible individuals enrolled in a PDP who subsequently are reassigned to a new PDP by the HHS Secretary must be provided, within 30 days of the reassignment, with: (1) information on formulary differences between the individual's former plan and the plan to which the individual is reassigned with respect to the individual's drug regimen; and (2) a description of the individual's right to request a coverage determination, exception, or reconsideration; bring an appeal; or resolve a grievance. [Soc. Sec. Act § 1860D-14(d).]

Voluntary Disenrollment

An individual may disenroll from a PDP during the specified enrollment periods by enrolling in a different PDP, submitting a disenrollment request to a PDP, or filing an appropriate disenrollment request through other mechanisms approved by CMS. The PDP sponsor must submit a disenrollment notice to CMS within the time frames CMS specifies, provide the enrollee with a CMS notice of disenrollment, and file and retain disenrollment requests for the period specified by CMS. CMS may grant retroactive disenrollment to an individual if there never was a legally valid enrollment or if a valid request for disenrollment was properly made but not processed or acted upon. [42 C.F.R. § 423.36.]

Enrollment Periods

Law and regulations provide for an initial enrollment period (IEP), an annual coordinated election period (AEP), and special enrollment periods (SEPs) for PDPs.

Initial enrollment period. The IEP is the period during which an individual is first eligible to enroll in a Part D plan. [42 C.F.R. § 423.38(a).]

The IEP for an individual who is first eligible to enroll on or after March 2006 is the same as the IEP for Medicare Part B, i.e., a seven-month period beginning with the third month before the month in which an individual first meets the eligibility requirements and ending seven months later (see ¶ 311). An exception is made for individuals not eligible to enroll in Part D at any time during their IEP for Part B. Their IEP runs from three months before becoming eligible for Part D to three months following eligibility. In addition, for individuals who become entitled to Medicare Part A or enrolled in Part B for a retroactive effective date, their IEP under Part D starts with the month in which notification of Medicare determination is received and ends on the last day of the third month following the month in which the notification was received. [42 C.F.R. § 423.38(a)(3).]

Annual coordinated election period. The Part D AEP for a calendar year runs from October 15 through December 7 of the preceding year. [42 C.F.R. § 423.38(b)(3).]

Special enrollment periods. SEPs allow an individual to enroll in a PDP or disenroll from a PDP and enroll in another PDP or MA-PD plan at any time under any of the following circumstances:

(1) creditable prescription drug coverage is lost or involuntarily reduced so that it is no longer creditable coverage (loss of coverage due to failure to pay premiums is not considered involuntary);

(2) the individual is not adequately informed that he or she has lost creditable prescription drug coverage, that he or she never had credible prescription drug coverage, or that the coverage is involuntarily reduced so that the coverage is no longer creditable;

(3) the individual's enrollment or non-enrollment in a PDP is unintentional, inadvertent, or erroneous because of error, misrepresentation, or inaction of a federal employee or any person authorized to act on behalf of the federal government;

(4) the individual is a full-subsidy eligible or other subsidy eligible under 42 C.F.R. § 423.772;

(5) the individual elects to disenroll from an MA-PD plan and elects coverage under Medicare Part A and Part B;

(6) the PDP's contract is terminated by the PDP or CMS or the PDP plan no longer is offered in the area where the individual resides;

(7) the individual is no longer eligible for the PDP because of a change of residence; or

(8) the individual demonstrates in accordance with CMS guidelines that the PDP sponsor substantially violated a material provision of its contract, including: failure to provide benefits on a timely basis, failure to provide benefits in accordance with applicable quality standards, or material misrepresentation of the plan's provisions

during marketing; or the individual meets other exceptional circumstances as determined by CMS.

[42 C.F.R. § 423.38(c).] CMS also reserves the right to establish SEPs on a case-by-case basis, when warranted by an immediate exceptional circumstance, such as when an individual has a life-threatening condition or illness. [Pub. 100-18, Ch. 3, § 30.3.8.]

Coordination with MA annual 45-day disenrollment period. An individual enrolled in an MA plan who switches to original Medicare between January 1 through February 14 also may elect a PDP during this time. [42 C.F.R. § 423.38(d).]

Effective Dates of Coverage and Change of Coverage

CMS must apply the effective date requirements provided under the MA program to Part D enrollments.

(1) **Initial enrollment period.** An enrollment made before the month of entitlement to Medicare Part A or enrollment in Part B is effective the first day of the month the individual is entitled to or enrolled in Part A or enrolled in Part B. Except as indicated for full-benefit dual-eligible individuals, an enrollment made during or after the month of entitlement to Part A or enrollment in Part B is effective the first day of the calendar month following the month in which the enrollment in Part D is made. If the individual, however, is not eligible to enroll in Part D on the first day of the calendar month following the month in which the election to enroll is made, the enrollment is effective the first day of the month the individual is eligible for Part D. [42 C.F.R. § 423.40(a).]

(2) **Annual coordinated election period.** For an enrollment or change of enrollment in Part D made during an AEP, the coverage or change in coverage is effective as of the first day of the following calendar year. [42 C.F.R. § 423.40(b).]

(3) **Special enrollment periods.** For an enrollment or change of enrollment in Part D made during a SEP, the effective date is determined by CMS in a manner consistent with protecting the continuity of health benefits coverage. [42 C.F.R. § 423.40(c).]

45-day MA annual disenrollment period. If an individual who has disenrolled from an MA plan enrolls in a PDP plan from January 1 through February 14, enrollment is effective the first day of the month following the month in which the enrollment in the PDP is made. [42 C.F.R. § 423.40(d).]

Involuntary Disenrollment

Generally, a PDP sponsor is prohibited from involuntarily disenrolling an individual from a PDP it offers or requesting or encouraging an individual to disenroll, either through verbal or written communication or through action or inaction. The PDP sponsor is, however, required to disenroll an individual under various conditions (see below) and may disenroll an individual for failing to timely pay monthly premiums or for disruptive behavior. [42 C.F.R. § 423.44(a), (b).]

Notice requirements. If the disenrollment is for any reason other than death or loss of Part D eligibility, the PDP sponsor must give the individual timely notice of the disenrollment with an explanation of why the PDP is planning to disenroll the individual. This notice must be provided to the individual before submission of the disenrollment notice to CMS and must explain the individual's right to file a grievance under the PDP's grievance procedures. [42 C.F.R. § 423.44(c).]

Mandatory disenrollment. A PDP sponsor must disenroll an individual from a PDP it offers if:

    (1) the individual no longer resides in the PDP's service area;

    (2) the individual loses eligibility for Part D;

    (3) the individual dies;

    (4) the PDP's contract is terminated by CMS, by the PDP, or through mutual consent;

    (5) the individual materially misrepresents information to the PDP sponsor as to whether his or her costs are expected to be reimbursed through insurance or other third-party means; or

    (6) the individual is not lawfully present in the United States.

[42 C.F.R. § 423.44(b)(2).]

Optional involuntary disenrollment for unpaid premiums. A PDP sponsor may disenroll an individual from a PDP it offers for failure to pay any monthly premium if the sponsor demonstrates to CMS that it made reasonable efforts to collect the unpaid premium and the PDP gives the enrollee proper notice of disenrollment. The PDP sponsor must give the enrollee a two-month grace period to pay the past due premiums, beginning on the first day of the month the premium is unpaid or the first day of the month following the date on which the premium is requested, whichever is later. When disenrollment occurs for failure to pay monthly premiums, the PDP may refuse reenrollment of the individual until all past premiums have been paid. A PDP sponsor must not disenroll an individual who has premiums withheld from his or her Social Security, Railroad Retirement Board, or Office of Personnel Management check, or who is in "premium withhold" as defined by CMS. [42 C.F.R. § 423.44(b)(1)(i), (d)(1)(i)–(v).]

Extension of grace period for good cause. When an individual is disenrolled for failure to pay the plan premium, CMS (or a third party to which CMS has assigned this responsibility, such as a Part D sponsor) may reinstate enrollment in the PDP without interruption of coverage if he or she shows good cause for failure to pay within the initial grace period and pays all overdue premiums within three calendar months after the disenrollment date. The individual must establish by a credible statement that failure to pay premiums within the initial grace period was due to circumstances for which the individual had no control or the individual could not reasonably have been expected to foresee. However, enrollment in the PDP cannot be reinstated if the only basis for the reinstatement is a change in the individual's circumstances after the involuntary disenrollment for nonpayment of premiums. [42 C.F.R. § 423.44(d)(1)(vi), (vii).]

Optional involuntary disenrollment for disruptive behavior. A PDP may disenroll an individual whose behavior is disruptive only after: (1) the PDP sponsor makes an effort to resolve the problem, (2) the PDP sponsor documents the enrollee's behavior, and (3) CMS has reviewed and approved the proposed disenrollment. A PDP enrollee is considered disruptive if his or her behavior substantially impairs the PDP's ability to arrange or provide for services to the individual or other plan members. An individual cannot be considered disruptive if the behavior is related to the use of medical services or compliance (or noncompliance) with medical advice or treatment. The PDP sponsor must make a serious effort to resolve the problems presented by the individual, including providing reasonable accommodations for individuals with mental or cognitive conditions. [42 C.F.R. § 423.44(d)(2).]

Involuntary disenrollment for failure to pay IRMAA. CMS will disenroll individuals who fail to pay the Part D income-related monthly adjustment amount (IRMAA). For all Part D IRMAA amounts directly billed to an enrollee, the initial grace period ends with the last day of the third month after the billing month. When an individual is disenrolled for failing to pay the IRMAA within the initial grace period, CMS (or an entity acting for CMS) may reinstate enrollment, without interruption of coverage, if the individual shows good cause and pays all IRMAA arrearages and any overdue premiums due the Part D plan sponsor within three calendar months after the disenrollment date. When CMS has disenrolled an individual for failure to pay the IRMAA, the PDP sponsor must provide notice of termination in a form and manner determined by CMS. The effective date of disenrollment is the first day following the last day of the initial grace period. [42 C.F.R. § 423.44(e).]

Late Enrollment Penalty

A Part D eligible individual must pay a late enrollment penalty (LEP) if there is a continuous period of 63 days or longer at any time after the end of the individual's IEP during which the individual was eligible to enroll in a PDP, was not covered under any creditable prescription drug coverage, and was not enrolled in a Part D plan. [42 C.F.R. § 423.46(a).]

Part D plan sponsors are responsible for determining, at the time of enrollment, whether a member was previously enrolled in Part D or had other creditable coverage prior to applying to enroll in his or her plan and whether there were any lapses in coverage of 63 days or more. [42 C.F.R. § 423.46(b).]

Reconsideration. Individuals determined to be subject to a LEP may request reconsideration, which will be conducted by CMS or an independent review entity contracted by CMS. Decisions made through this review are not subject to appeal but may be reviewed and revised at the discretion of CMS. [42 C.F.R. § 423.46(c).]

Calculation of the late enrollment penalty. The LEP is equal to 1 percent of the base beneficiary premium or another amount specified by CMS based on available analysis or other information. [42 C.F.R. § 423.286(d)(3); Pub. 100-18, Ch. 4, § 40.1.]

Determining Creditable Status of Prescription Drug Coverage

A Part D enrollee who otherwise would be subject to a late enrollment penalty may avoid the penalty if his or her previous coverage meets the standards of "creditable prescription drug coverage." Previous coverage will meet those standards only if it is determined (in a manner specified by CMS) to provide coverage of the cost of prescription drugs the actuarial value of which (as defined by CMS) to the individual equals or exceeds the actuarial value of standard prescription drug coverage. [42 C.F.R. § 423.56(a).]

The following coverage is considered creditable:

    (1) coverage under a PDP or a MA-PD;

    (2) Medicaid;

    (3) a group health plan (including coverage provided by a federal or a nonfederal government plan and by a church plan for its employees);

    (4) a State Pharmaceutical Assistance Program;

    (5) veterans' coverage (including survivors and dependents) of prescription drugs;

    (6) prescription drug coverage under a Medigap policy;

    (7) military coverage (including TRICARE);

(8) individual health insurance coverage that includes coverage for outpatient prescription drugs and that does not meet the definition of an excepted benefit;

(9) coverage provided by the medical care program of the Indian Health Service, tribe, or tribal organization, or Urban Indian organization;

(10) coverage provided by a PACE organization;

(11) coverage provided by a cost-based HMO or CMP;

(12) coverage provided through a state high-risk pool; and

(13) other coverage as CMS may determine appropriate.

[42 C.F.R. § 423.56(b).]

Calculation of actuarial equivalence standard. The basic actuarial equivalence value test for the determination of creditable coverage or alternative coverage is determined by calculating whether the expected plan payout on average will be at least equal to the expected plan payout under defined prescription drug coverage, not taking into account the value of any discount or coverage provided during the coverage gap ("donut hole"). [Soc. Sec. Act § 1860D-22(a)(2)(A); 42 C.F.R. § 423.884(d).]

Disclosure of creditable or non-creditable coverage status. With the exception of PDPs and MA-PD plans and PACE or cost-based HMO or CMP plans that provide qualified prescription drug coverage under Part D, each entity that offers prescription drug coverage must disclose to all enrolled or eligible individuals whether the coverage offered is creditable prescription drug coverage. If the coverage is not creditable, the entity also must disclose to eligible individuals that there are limitations on the periods in a year in which the individual may enroll in Part D plans and that the individual may be subject to a late enrollment penalty. [42 C.F.R. §§ 423.56(c), (d), 423.884(e).]

Clarifying notice of creditable coverage. An individual who is not adequately informed that his or her prescription drug coverage was not creditable may apply for CMS review. If CMS determines that the individual did not receive adequate notice or received incorrect information, CMS may deem the individual to have had creditable coverage, regardless of whether it was actually creditable, so that the LEP will not be imposed. [42 C.F.R. § 423.56(g).]

[¶ 505] Payment of Premiums

Generally, the monthly beneficiary premium for a prescription drug plan (PDP) must be the same for all Part D eligible individuals enrolled in a plan. The monthly beneficiary premium is the base beneficiary premium adjusted to reflect the difference between the bid and the national average monthly bid amount, any supplemental benefits, and any late enrollment penalties. [Soc. Sec. Act § 1860D-13(a); 42 C.F.R. § 423.286(a).]

2016 national average monthly bid amount. For each coverage year, CMS computes the national average monthly bid amount from the applicable Part D plan bid submissions to calculate the base beneficiary premium. The national average monthly bid amount for 2016 is $64.66, which is down from the 2015 national average monthly bid amount of $70.18. [42 C.F.R. § 423.279; *CMS Notice to Medicare Advantage Organizations and Medicare Prescription Drug Plan Sponsors,* July 29, 2015.]

Calculation of the beneficiary premium. The beneficiary premium percentage for any year is a fraction, the numerator of which is 25.5 percent. The denominator is 100 percent minus a percentage equalling (1) the total estimated reinsurance payments for the coverage year, divided by (2) the total estimated reinsurance payments plus total estimated payments to Part D plans attributable to the standardized bid amount during the coverage year. [Soc. Sec. Act § 1860D-13(a)(3); 42 C.F.R. § 423.286(b).]

Base beneficiary premium. The base beneficiary premium for a month is equal to the product of the beneficiary premium percentage and the national average monthly bid amount. If the amount of the standardized bid amount exceeds the adjusted national average monthly bid amount, the monthly base beneficiary premium is increased by the amount of the excess. If the amount of the adjusted national average monthly bid amount exceeds the standardized bid amount, the monthly base beneficiary premium is decreased by the amount of the excess. [Soc. Sec. Act § 1860D-13(a)(2); 42 C.F.R. § 423.286(c)–(e).] The Part D base beneficiary premium for 2016 is $34.10, which is up from $33.13 in 2015. [*CMS Notice to Medicare Advantage Organizations and Medicare Prescription Drug Plan Sponsors*, July 29, 2015.]

Monthly beneficiary premium. Part D beneficiary premiums are calculated as the base beneficiary premium adjusted by the following factors: (1) the difference between the plan's standardized bid amount and the national average monthly bid amount; (2) an increase for any supplemental premium; (3) an increase for any late enrollment penalty; (4) an increase for income-related monthly adjustment amount (IRMAA) (see below); and (5) elimination or decrease with the application of the low-income premium subsidy. [Soc. Sec. Act § 1860D-13(a); 42 C.F.R. § 423.286(d), (e).]

Increase in individual monthly premium based on income. The monthly amount of the beneficiary premium applicable for each month after December 2010 is increased by an IRMAA for individuals whose modified adjusted gross income (MAGI) exceeds the threshold amount applicable under Soc. Sec. Act § 1839(i) for the calendar year. This IRMAA for an individual for a month in a year is equal to the product of: (1) the quotient obtained by dividing (a) the applicable percentage described below for the individual for the calendar year reduced by 25.5 percent, by (b) 25.5 percent; and (2) the base beneficiary premium. [Soc. Sec. Act § 1860D-13(a)(7)(A), (B); 42 C.F.R. § 423.286(d)(4).]

For 2016, the MAGI amounts, percentage increases, and monthly adjustment amounts are as follows for beneficiaries who filed an individual tax return in 2015:

- if the MAGI is less than or equal to $85,000, there is no monthly adjustment amount;

- if the MAGI is more than $85,000 but not more than $107,000, the applicable percentage is 35 percent, with a monthly adjustment of $12.70;

- if the MAGI is more than $107,000 but not more than $160,000, the applicable percentage is 50 percent, with a monthly adjustment of $32.80;

- if the MAGI is more than $160,000 but not more than $214,000, the applicable percentage is 65 percent, with a monthly adjustment of $52.80; and

- if the MAGI is more than $214,000, the applicable percentage is 80 percent, with a monthly adjustment of $72.90.

[Soc. Sec. Act § 1839(i)(3)(C); *CMS Notice to Medicare Advantage Organizations and Medicare Prescription Drug Plan Sponsors*, July 29, 2015.] The MAGI levels subject to the IRMAA will increase beginning in 2018. [Soc. Sec. Act § 1838(i)(3)(C)(i)(II), as added by Medicare Access and CHIP Reauthorization Act of 2015 (MACRA) (P.L. 114-10) § 402.]

In the case of a joint return, the MAGI dollar amount is twice the dollar amounts otherwise applicable for the calendar year. [Soc. Sec. Act § 1839(i)(3)(C)(ii).]

Also, in 2016, for beneficiaries who are married but file separate tax returns from their spouses, with income: less than or equal to $85,000, there is no monthly adjustment amount;

¶505

greater than $85,000 and less than or equal to $129,000, the monthly adjustment is $52.80; or, greater than $129,000, the monthly adjustment is $72.90. [*CMS Notice to Medicare Advantage Organizations and Medicare Prescription Drug Plan Sponsors*, July 29, 2015.]

Premium collection. Plan enrollees have the option to make premium payments to PDP sponsors using any of the methods available to enrollees in MA plans listed in 42 C.F.R. § 422.262(f), including withholding from Social Security payments, electronic funds transfers, or through employers or third parties specified by CMS. Medicare will pay a plan sponsor only the portion of a late enrollment penalty attributable to increased PDP actuarial costs not taken into account through risk adjustment. [42 C.F.R. § 423.293.]

Collection of the IRMAA. The IRMAA must be paid through withholding from the enrollee's Social Security benefit payments, or benefit payments by the Railroad Retirement Board or the Office of Personnel Management, in the same manner that the Part B premium is withheld. If an enrollee's benefit payment from one of the three sources above is insufficient to have the IRMAA withheld, or if an enrollee is not receiving any such benefits, the beneficiary must be billed directly. The beneficiary may pay the amount through an electronic funds transfer mechanism or by other means specified by CMS. CMS must terminate Part D coverage for any individual who fails to pay the IRMAA. [42 C.F.R. § 423.293(d).]

[¶ 507] Deductible and Coinsurance Requirements

"Standard prescription drug coverage" consists of coverage of covered Part D drugs subject to an annual deductible, 25 percent coinsurance (or an actuarially equivalent structure) up to an initial coverage limit, and catastrophic coverage after an individual incurs out-of-pocket expenses above a certain annual threshold. [Soc. Sec. Act § 1860D-2(b); 42 C.F.R. § 423.104(d).]

Deductible. The annual deductible is increased over the previous year's amount by the annual percentage increase in average per capita aggregate expenditures for Part D drugs for the 12-month period ending in July of the previous year, rounded to the nearest multiple of $5. [Soc. Sec. Act § 1860D-2(b)(1); 42 C.F.R. § 423.104(d)(1)(ii).] For 2016, the annual deductible is $360, which is up from $320 in 2015. [*Announcement of Calendar Year 2016 Medicare Advantage Capitation Rates and Medicare Advantage and Part D Payment Policies and Final Call Letter*, April 6, 2015.]

Cost-sharing under the initial coverage limit. Coinsurance for actual costs for covered Part D drugs covered under the Part D plan above the annual deductible and up to the initial coverage limit is (1) 25 percent of the actual cost, or (2) actuarially equivalent to an average expected coinsurance of no more than 25 percent of actual cost. A Part D plan providing actuarially equivalent standard coverage may apply tiered copayments if certain requirements are met. [Soc. Sec. Act § 1860D-2(b)(2)(A) and (B); 42 C.F.R. § 423.104(d)(2).]

Initial coverage limit. The initial coverage limit is increased over the previous year's amount by the annual percentage increase in average per capita aggregate expenditures for Part D drugs for the 12-month period ending in July of the previous year, rounded to the nearest multiple of $10. [Soc. Sec. Act § 1860D-2(b)(3); 42 C.F.R. § 423.104(d)(3).] For 2016, the initial coverage limit is $3,310, up from $2,960 in 2015. [*Announcement of Calendar Year 2016 Medicare Advantage Capitation Rates and Medicare Advantage and Part D Payment Policies and Final Call Letter*, April 6, 2015.]

Before the enactment of the Patient Protection and Affordable Care Act (ACA) (P.L. 111-148), as amended by the Health Care and Education Reconciliation Act of 2010 (HCERA) (P.L. 111-152), beneficiaries paid 100 percent of all costs in the coverage gap, also known as the "donut hole," which occurs between the initial coverage limit and the out-of-pocket threshold. [42 C.F.R. § 423.100.]

The ACA reduced the effect of the "donut hole" through:

(1) a rebate of $250 in 2010 only;

(2) a 50 percent discount for brand-name drugs;

(3) gradually increasing generic drug discounts; and

(4) increased Medicare coverage of brand-name drugs.

[Soc. Sec. Act § 1860D-2.]

See below for a discussion of the ACA's changes to close the coverage gap.

Annual out-of-pocket threshold. The annual out-of-pocket threshold for 2016 through 2019 is increased over the previous year's amount by: (1) the annual percentage increase in average per capita aggregate expenditures for Part D drugs for the 12-month period ending in July of the previous year, or (2) the annual percentage increase in the consumer price index for all urban consumers (U.S. city average) for the 12-month period ending in July of the previous year. [Soc. Sec. Act § 1860D-2(b)(4)(B); 42 C.F.R. § 423.104(d)(5)(iii).] For 2016, the annual out-of-pocket threshold is $4,850. [*Announcement of Calendar Year 2016 Medicare Advantage Capitation Rates and Medicare Advantage and Part D Payment Policies and Final Call Letter*, April 6, 2015.]

Once a beneficiary's "incurred costs" reach the annual out-of-pocket threshold, the beneficiary's cost-sharing equals the greater of (1) coinsurance of 5 percent of the actual cost, or (2) copayment amounts from the previous year increased by the annual percentage increase in average per capita aggregate expenditures for Part D drugs for the 12-month period ending in July of the previous year, rounded to the nearest multiple of $.05. [Soc. Sec. Act § 1860D-2(b)(4)(A); 42 C.F.R. § 423.104(d)(5)(i), (ii).]

In 2016, once the PDP enrollee reaches the annual out-of-pocket threshold, his or her nominal cost-sharing is equal to the greater of 5 percent coinsurance or a copayment of $2.95 for a generic drug or a preferred multiple source drug and $7.40 for any other drug. [*Announcement of Calendar Year 2016 Medicare Advantage Capitation Rates and Medicare Advantage and Part D Payment Policies and Final Call Letter*, April 6, 2015.]

For purposes of calculating the annual out-of-pocket threshold, costs are considered "incurred" if they are paid with respect to covered Part D drugs for the annual deductible, cost-sharing, and for amounts for which benefits were not provided due to the coverage gap (excluding costs for covered Part D drugs that are not included in the plan's formulary). Generally, costs are treated as incurred only if they are paid by the Part D eligible individual (or another person on behalf of the individual) and he or she is not reimbursed through insurance, a group health plan, or other third-party arrangement. Costs are considered incurred if they are paid (1) under Soc. Sec. Act § 1860D-14, (2) under a State Pharmaceutical Assistance Program, (3) by the Indian Health Service (IHS), an Indian tribe or tribal organization, or an urban Indian organization; or (4) by an AIDS Drug Assistance Program under Part B of Title XXVI of the Public Health Service Act. [Soc. Sec. Act § 1860D-2(b)(4)(C).]

Drug Costs in the Coverage Gap

The HHS Secretary provided a one-time rebate of $250 for certain beneficiaries whose incurred costs for covered Part D drugs exceeded the initial coverage limit in 2010. [Soc. Sec. Act § 1860D-42(c).]

¶507

Coverage gap discount program. For drugs to be covered under Part D, a manufacturer must participate in a coverage gap discount program that provides a 50 percent discount on applicable brand-name drugs provided to applicable beneficiaries while in the coverage gap. To participate, the manufacturer must enter into an agreement with the Secretary of HHS and with a third-party contractor designated by the Secretary to administer the program. [Soc. Sec. Act § 1860D-43(a), (b); 42 C.F.R. §§ 423.2315, 423.2325.]

Generic drugs in the coverage gap. The ACA provided for increased generic drug plan coverage starting in 2011. The coverage for an applicable beneficiary who has coinsurance for costs within the coverage gap for covered generic Part D drugs is equal to the generic-gap coinsurance percentage or actuarially equivalent to an average expected payment of such percentage of costs for covered Part D drugs that are not applicable drugs. [Soc. Sec. Act § 1860D-2(b)(2)(C)(i); 42 C.F.R. § 423.104(d)(4)(i).]

For 2012 through 2019, the generic-gap coinsurance percentage is the generic-gap coinsurance percentage for the previous year decreased by 7 percentage points. For 2020 and later, it is 25 percent. [Soc. Sec. Act § 1860D-2(b)(2)(C)(ii); 42 C.F.R. § 423.104(d)(4)(iii).]

Increased Part D coverage for applicable name-brand drugs in the coverage gap. In 2013 and later years, the Part D coverage for a beneficiary in the coverage gap also increases due to the ACA. The coinsurance is (1) the difference between the applicable gap percentage and the discount percentage for applicable drugs, or (2) actuarially equivalent to an average expected payment of such percentage of such costs, for covered Part D drugs that are applicable drugs. [Soc. Sec. Act § 1860D-2(b)(2)(D)(i); 42 C.F.R. § 423.104(d)(4)(ii).]

The applicable gap percentage for applicable drugs in the coverage gap is:

- in 2013 and 2014, 97.5 percent;
- in 2015 and 2016, 95 percent;
- in 2017, 90 percent;
- in 2018, 85 percent;
- in 2019, 80 percent; and
- in 2020 and each subsequent year, 75 percent.

[Soc. Sec. Act § 1860D-2(b)(2)(D)(ii); 42 C.F.R. § 423.104(d)(4)(iv).]

[¶ 508] Premium and Cost-Sharing Subsidies for Low-Income Individuals

CMS subsidizes the monthly beneficiary premium and cost-sharing amounts incurred by Part D eligible individuals with low income and resources. [Soc. Sec. Act § 1860D-14.]

For purposes of low-income subsidy eligibility, "income" includes the income of the applicant and spouse who is living in the same household, if any, regardless of whether the spouse is also an applicant. Support and maintenance is exempted from income. "Resources" include the liquid resources of the applicant (and, if married, his or her spouse who is living in the same household), such as checking and savings accounts, stocks, bonds, and other resources that can be readily converted to cash within 20 days, and real estate that is not the applicant's primary residence or the land on which the primary residence is located. The value of any life insurance policy is exempted from the definition of resources. [42 C.F.R. § 423.772.]

Requirements for Eligibility

The primary goal under the low-income subsidy program is to have nationally uniform standards and rules for determining eligibility for a subsidy. CMS has not permitted states to use the more liberal methodologies that they use to determine eligibility for Medicare savings programs under Medicaid to determine Medicare Part D low-income subsidy eligibility because CMS does not have the authority to extend more liberal methodologies to the Social Security Administration. [*Final rule*, 70 FR 4194, 4374, Jan. 28, 2005.]

Determinations for the low-income subsidy can be made in advance of a person enrolling in a Part D plan. A subsidy-eligible individual is not entitled to the subsidy, however, until such time as the person's enrollment in the plan is effective. [*Final rule*, 70 FR 4194, 4374, Jan. 28, 2005.]

Subsidy-eligible individual. A subsidy-eligible individual is a Part D eligible individual residing in a state who: (1) is enrolled in, or seeking to enroll in a Part D plan; (2) has an income below 150 percent of the federal poverty level (FPL) applicable to the individual's family size; and (3) has resources that are at or below the resource thresholds described below. [42 C.F.R. § 423.773(a).]

Full-subsidy-eligible individual. A full-subsidy-eligible individual is a subsidy-eligible individual who: (1) has income below 135 percent of the FPL applicable to the individual's family size; and (2) has resources that do not exceed the amount of resources allowable for the previous year increased by the annual percentage increase in the consumer price index (all items, U.S. city average) as of September of that previous year, rounded to the nearest multiple of $10. [42 C.F.R. § 423.773(b).]

An individual must be treated as meeting the eligibility requirements for full-subsidy-eligible individuals described above if the individual is a: (1) full-benefit dual-eligible individual; (2) recipient of Social Security Income (SSI) benefits under Title XVI of the Social Security Act; or (3) eligible for Medicaid as a qualified Medicare beneficiary (QMB), specified low-income Medicare beneficiary (SLMB), or a qualifying individual (QI) under a state's plan. [42 C.F.R. § 423.773(c)(1).]

CMS will notify all individuals treated as full-subsidy eligible that they do not need to apply for the subsidies and they are deemed eligible. For an individual deemed eligible between January 1 and June 30 of a calendar year, the individual will be deemed eligible for a full subsidy for the rest of the calendar year. If deemed eligible between July 1 and December 1 of the calendar year, the individual will be deemed eligible for the rest of the calendar year and the following calendar year. [42 C.F.R. § 423.773(c)(2).]

Other low-income subsidy individuals. Other low-income subsidy individuals are subsidy-eligible individuals who: (1) have income less than 150 percent of the FPL applicable to the individual's family size; and (2) have resources that do not exceed the resource amount allowable for the previous year, increased by the annual percentage increase in the consumer price index (all items, U.S. city average) as of September of the previous year, rounded to the nearest multiple of $10. [42 C.F.R. § 423.773(d).]

Low-income Part D eligible individuals must reside in the 50 states or the District of Columbia to receive premium and cost-sharing subsidies. [42 C.F.R. §§ 423.773(a), 423.907.]

Eligibility Determinations, Redeterminations, and Applications

An application for subsidy assistance may be filed with a state's Medicaid program office or with the Social Security Administration (SSA). Part D plans are to refer individual inquiries concerning application or eligibility for the low-income subsidy to state agencies or SSA. [42 C.F.R. § 423.774(d); *Medicare Prescription Drug Benefit Manual*, Pub. 100-18, Ch. 13, § 40.1.]

Eligibility determinations. If an individual applies with the state Medicaid agency, the determination of eligibility for subsidies is made by the state under its state plan under Title

XIX of the Social Security Act. If an individual applies with the SSA, the Commissioner of Social Security will make the determination. [42 C.F.R. § 423.774(a).]

Effective date of initial eligibility determinations. Initial eligibility determinations are effective beginning with the first day of the month in which the individual applies, and they remain in effect for no more than one year. [42 C.F.R. § 423.774(b).]

Redeterminations and appeals of low-income subsidy eligibility. Redeterminations and appeals of low-income subsidy eligibility determinations by states must be made in the same manner and frequency as the redeterminations and appeals are made under the state's Medicaid plan, which must be conducted at least annually. Redeterminations and appeals of eligibility determinations made by the Commissioner will be made in the manner specified by the Commissioner of Social Security. [42 C.F.R. § 423.774(c).]

Application requirements. For subsidy applications to be considered complete, applicants or personal representatives applying on the applicants' behalf must: (1) complete all required elements of the application; (2) provide any statements from financial institutions, as requested, to support information in the application; and (3) certify, under penalty of perjury or similar sanction for false statements, as to the accuracy of the information provided on the application form. [42 C.F.R. § 423.774(d).]

Special eligibility rule for widows and widowers. Section 3304(a) of the Patient Protection and Affordable Care Act (ACA) (P.L. 111-148) created a special rule for widows and widowers regarding eligibility for the low-income subsidy. If the spouse dies during the effective period for a favorable determination or redetermination that has been made related to an individual's eligibility for a low-income subsidy, the effective period will be extended for one year after the date on which the determination or redetermination would otherwise cease to be effective. [Soc. Sec. Act § 1860D-14(a)(3)(B)(vi); Pub. 100-18, Ch. 13, § 40.1.]

Premium Subsidy

The Part D premium subsidy amounts available to subsidy-eligible individuals vary depending upon the individual's income and resources/asset levels. [Soc. Sec. Act § 1860D-14(b); 42 C.F.R. § 423.780.]

Full-subsidy-eligible individuals are entitled to a premium subsidy equal to 100 percent of the premium subsidy amount. The premium subsidy amount is the lesser of:

- under the Part D plan selected by the beneficiary, the portion of the monthly beneficiary premium attributable to basic coverage for enrollees in prescription drug plans (PDPs) or the portion of the Medicare Advantage (MA) monthly beneficiary premium attributable to basic prescription drug coverage for enrollees in MA-PD plans; or

- the greater of the low-income benchmark premium amount for a PDP region or the lowest monthly beneficiary premium for a PDP that offers basic prescription drug coverage in the PDP region.

[42 C.F.R. § 423.780(a), (b)(1).]

The low-income benchmark premium amount for a PDP region is a weighted average of the monthly beneficiary premium amounts (see below) for the Part D plans, with the weight for each PDP and MA-PD plan equal to a percentage. The numerator of the percentage is the number of Part D eligible individuals enrolled in the plan in the reference month, and the denominator is the total number of Part D eligible individuals enrolled in all PDP and MA-PD plans in a PDP region in the reference month. [42 C.F.R. § 423.780(b)(2).]

The regional low-income premium subsidy amounts are provided in a file on the CMS website at https://www.cms.gov/Medicare/Health-Plans/MedicareAdvtgSpecRateStats/Downloads/RegionalRatesBenchmarks2016.pdf.

Premium amounts. The premium amounts used to calculate the low-income benchmark premium amount are as follows: (1) the monthly beneficiary premium for a PDP that is basic prescription drug coverage; (2) the portion of the monthly beneficiary premium attributable to basic prescription drug coverage for a PDP that is enhanced alternative coverage; or (3) the MA monthly prescription drug beneficiary premium for a MA-PD plan determined before application of the monthly rebate. [42 C.F.R. § 423.780(b)(2)(ii).]

Other low-income subsidy-eligible individuals—sliding scale premium. Other low-income subsidy-eligible individuals are entitled to a premium subsidy based on a linear sliding scale, as follows:

(1) a full premium subsidy amount (100 percent) for individuals with income at or below 135 percent of the FPL applicable to their family size;

(2) a premium subsidy equal to 75 percent of the premium subsidy amount for individuals with income greater than 135 percent but at or below 140 percent of the FPL applicable to the family size;

(3) a premium subsidy equal to 50 percent of the premium subsidy amount for individuals with income greater than 140 percent but at or below 145 percent of the FPL applicable to the family size; or

(4) a premium subsidy equal to 25 percent of the premium subsidy amount for individuals with income greater than 145 percent but below 150 percent of FPL applicable to the family size.

[42 C.F.R. § 423.780(d).]

Waiver of late enrollment penalty for subsidy-eligible individuals. Subsidy-eligible individuals are not subject to a late enrollment penalty. [42 C.F.R. § 423.780(e).]

Waiver of minimal monthly premiums. The Secretary of HHS will allow a PDP or MA-PD plan to waive the monthly beneficiary premium for a subsidy-eligible individual if the amount of the premium is minimal. If the premium is waived, the Secretary will not reassign subsidy-eligible individuals enrolled in the plan to other plans based on the fact that the monthly beneficiary premium under the plan was greater than the low-income benchmark premium amount. [Soc. Sec. Act § 1860D-14(a)(5); 42 C.F.R. § 423.780(f).]

Cost-Sharing Subsidy

Full-subsidy-eligible individuals have no annual deductible, and there is no coverage gap for full-subsidy individuals. In addition, they are entitled to a reduction in cost-sharing for all covered Part D drugs covered under the PDP or MA-PD plan below the out-of-pocket limit, including Part D drugs covered under the PDP or MA-PD plan obtained after the initial coverage limit. Finally, all cost-sharing for covered Part D drugs covered under the PDP or MA-PD plan above the out-of-pocket limit is eliminated for full-subsidy-eligible individuals. In other words, Medicare pays the full benefit once the catastrophic level is reached. [42 C.F.R. § 423.782(a).]

Elimination of cost-sharing for noninstitutionalized full-benefit dual eligibles. Full-benefit dual-eligible individuals who are institutionalized or who are receiving home- and community-based services have no cost-sharing for Part D drugs covered under their PDP or MA-PD plans. [Soc. Sec. Act § 1860D-14(a)(1)(D)(i); 42 C.F.R. § 423.782(a)(2)(ii).]

2016 reductions in cost-sharing. Reductions in copayments are applied as follows:

(1) For full-benefit dual-eligible individuals who are not institutionalized and who have income above 100 percent of the FPL applicable to the individual's family size and for individuals who have income under 135 percent of the FPL applicable to the individual's family size who meet the resources test for costs up to the out-of-pocket threshold, copayment amounts must not exceed the copayment amounts specified for standard prescription drug coverage. For 2016, copayment amounts will not exceed $2.95 for a generic or preferred multiple source drug and $7.40 for any other drug (but see (2) below because such individuals who are receiving home- and community-based services have no cost-sharing as of January 1, 2012).

(2) Full-benefit dual-eligible individuals who are institutionalized or who are receiving home and community-based services have no cost-sharing for covered Part D drugs covered under their PDP or MA-PD plans.

(3) Full-benefit dual-eligible individuals with incomes that do not exceed 100 percent of the FPL applicable to the individual's family size are subject to cost-sharing for covered Part D drugs equal to the lesser of: (1) the amount specified for the percentage increase in the consumer price index, rounded to the nearest multiple of 5 cents or 10 cents, respectively; or (2) the copayment amount charged to other individuals described in (1). For 2016, the costs for these individuals must be capped at $1.20 for a generic drug or preferred multiple source drug and $3.60 for any other drug (but see (2) above because such individuals who are receiving home and community-based services have no cost-sharing as of January 1, 2012).

[42 C.F.R. § 423.782(a); *Announcement of CY 2016 MA Capitation Rates and MA and Part D Payment Policies and Final Call Letter*, April 6, 2015.]

Other low-income subsidy-eligible individuals. In addition to continuation of coverage (no coverage gap), other low-income subsidy-eligible individuals are entitled to the following:

(1) For 2016, the annual deductible for these individuals is $74;

(2) 15 percent coinsurance for all covered Part D drugs obtained after the annual deductible under the plan up to the out-of-pocket limit; and

(3) For 2016, copayments may not exceed $2.95 for a generic drug and $7.40 for any other drug.

[42 C.F.R. § 423.782(b); *Announcement of CY 2016 MA Capitation Rates and MA and Part D Payment Policies and Final Call Letter*, April 6, 2015.]

Administration of Subsidy Program

CMS notifies the Part D sponsor offering the Part D plan in which a subsidy-eligible individual is enrolled of the individual's eligibility for a subsidy and the amount of the subsidy. [Soc. Sec. Act § 1860D-14(c); 42 C.F.R. § 423.800(a).]

Reduction of premium or cost-sharing by PDP sponsor or organization. The Part D sponsor offering the Part D plan in which a subsidy-eligible individual is enrolled must reduce the individual's premiums and cost-sharing as applicable and provide information to CMS on the amount of those reductions. The Part D sponsor must track the application of the subsidies to be applied to the out-of-pocket threshold. [42 C.F.R. § 423.800(b).]

Reimbursement for cost-sharing paid before notification of eligibility for low-income subsidy. The Part D sponsor must reimburse subsidy-eligible individuals and organizations that pay cost-sharing on behalf of such individuals after the effective date of the individual's eligibility for a subsidy. [42 C.F.R. § 423.800(c).]

Best available evidence. Part D sponsors must accept the best available evidence received from beneficiaries and respond to requests for assistance in securing acceptable evidence of subsidy eligibility from beneficiaries according to processes established by CMS and within the reasonable time frames as determined by CMS. [42 C.F.R. 423.800(d).]

Retroactive adjustment time frame. Sponsors must process retroactive adjustments to cost-sharing for low-income subsidy-eligible individuals and any resulting refunds and recoveries within 45 days of the sponsor's receipt of complete information. [42 C.F.R. 423.800(e).]

[¶ 510] Benefits and Beneficiary Protections

Requirements regarding standards for access to covered Part D drugs; Part D sponsor formularies; information dissemination by Part D sponsors; disclosure to beneficiaries of pricing information for generic versions of covered Part D drugs; and the privacy, confidentiality, and accuracy of prescription drug plan (PDP) sponsors beneficiary records are implemented in Subpart C, Part 423 of the Part D regulations.

Requirements Related to Qualified Prescription Drug Coverage

CMS may approve as Part D sponsors only those entities proposing to offer qualified prescription drug coverage. Qualified prescription drug coverage may consist of either standard prescription drug coverage or alternative prescription drug coverage, both of which provide access to Part D drugs at negotiated prices. A sponsor offering a prescription drug plan (PDP) must offer that plan to all Part D eligible beneficiaries residing in the plan's service area with the same premium, benefits, and level of cost-sharing throughout the service area. [42 C.F.R. § 423.104(b), (d).]

Alternative prescription drug coverage. Alternative prescription drug coverage provides coverage for Part D drugs and includes access to negotiated prices. Alternative prescription drug coverage also must:

(1) have an annual deductible that does not exceed the annual deductible for standard prescription drug coverage;

(2) impose cost-sharing no greater than that specified for standard prescription drug coverage once the annual out-of-pocket threshold is met;

(3) have a total or gross value that is at least equal to the total or gross value of defined standard coverage;

(4) have an unsubsidized value that is at least equal to the unsubsidized value of standard prescription drug coverage (*Note:* The unsubsidized value of coverage is the amount by which the actuarial value of the coverage exceeds the actuarial value of the subsidy payments for the coverage); and

(5) provide coverage that is designed, based upon an actuarially representative pattern of utilization, to provide for the payment of costs that are equal to the initial coverage limit, in an amount at least equal to the product of: (a) the amount by which the initial coverage limit for the year exceeds the deductible and (b) 100 percent minus the coinsurance percentage specified for standard prescription drug coverage.

[42 C.F.R. § 423.104(e).]

Negotiated prices. A PDP sponsor is required to provide enrollees with access to negotiated prices for covered Part D drugs included in its formulary. [42 C.F.R. § 423.104(g).]

Access to Covered Part D Drugs

PDPs must secure the participation of a pharmacy network consisting of retail pharmacies sufficient to ensure that all beneficiaries residing in each state in a PDP's service area, each state in a regional Medicare Advantage (MA) organization's service area, the entire service area of a local MA organization, or the entire geographic area of a cost contract have convenient access to covered drugs. As a result, PDPs must establish pharmacy networks in which:

> (1) in urban areas, at least 90 percent of Medicare beneficiaries in the PDP service area live, on average, within two miles of the retail pharmacy participating in the plan's network;

> (2) in suburban areas, at least 90 percent of Medicare beneficiaries in the PDP service area live, on average, within five miles of a retail pharmacy participating in the plan's network; and

> (3) in rural areas, at least 70 percent of Medicare beneficiaries in the PDP service area live, on average, within 15 miles of a retail pharmacy participating in the plan's network.

[Soc. Sec. Act § 1860D-4(b); 42 C.F.R. § 423.120(a)(1).]

Part D plans may count Indian tribes and tribal organizations, urban Indian organizations (I/T/U) pharmacies, and pharmacies operated by federally qualified health centers and rural health centers toward the required percentages for urban, suburban, and rural areas. [42 C.F.R. § 423.120(a)(2).]

A PDP's contracted pharmacy network must provide adequate access to home infusion pharmacies and convenient access and standard contracting terms and conditions to all long-term care and I/T/U pharmacies in its service area. [42 C.F.R. § 423.120(a)(4), (5), (6).]

Part D sponsors are required to permit the participation in their pharmacy networks of any pharmacy willing to accept the plan's standard terms and conditions, and they may not require a pharmacy to accept insurance risk as a condition of participation in the network. [Soc. Sec. Act § 1860D-4(b)(1)(A), (E); 42 C.F.R. § 423.120(a)(8).]

A PDP sponsor offering a plan that provides coverage other than defined standard coverage may reduce copayments or coinsurance for covered drugs obtained through a preferred pharmacy relative to the copayments or coinsurance applicable for such drugs when obtained through a non-preferred pharmacy. [Soc. Sec. Act § 1860D-4(b)(1)(B); 42 C.F.R. § 423.120(a)(9).]

A PDP sponsor must permit its enrollees to receive benefits, which may include an extended (90-day) supply of covered drugs, at any of its network pharmacies that are retail pharmacies. A Part D plan, however, may require an enrollee obtaining a covered drug at a retail network pharmacy to pay any higher cost-sharing applicable to that pharmacy instead of the cost-sharing applicable to the drug at the mail-order network pharmacy. [Soc. Sec. Act § 1860D-4(b)(1)(D); 42 C.F.R. § 423.120(a)(10).]

Formulary Requirements

A Part D sponsor that uses a formulary under its qualified prescription drug coverage must meet the following requirements:

> (1) development and revision by a pharmacy and therapeutic committee;

> (2) provision of an adequate formulary;

> (3) a drug transition process for enrollees prescribed Part D drugs that are not on its Part D plan's formulary;

(4) a limitation on changes in therapeutic classification;

(5) the provision of notice regarding formulary changes;

(6) a limitation on formulary changes before the beginning of a contract year; and

(7) policies and procedures to educate and inform health care providers and enrollees concerning its formulary.

[Soc. Sec. Act § 1860D-4(b)(3); 42 C.F.R. § 423.120(b).]

A Part D plan's formulary must:

(1) include within each therapeutic category and class of Part D drugs at least two Part D drugs that are not therapeutically equivalent and bioequivalent, with different strengths and dosage forms available for each of those drugs, except that only one Part D drug must be included in a particular category or class of covered Part D drugs if the category or class includes only one Part D drug;

(2) include at least one Part D drug within a particular category or class of Part D drugs to the extent the Part D plan demonstrates, and CMS approves, that only two drugs are available in that category or class of Part D drugs, and that one drug is clinically superior to the other drug in that category or class of Part D drugs;

(3) include adequate coverage of the types of drugs most commonly needed by Part D enrollees, as recognized in national treatment guidelines; and

(4) be approved by CMS consistent with 42 C.F.R. § 423.272(b)(2).

[42 C.F.R. § 423.120(b)(2).]

Until the Secretary determines, through rulemaking, criteria to identify, as appropriate, categories and classes of clinical concern, the following six classes must be included in PDP formularies:

(1) anticonvulsants;

(2) antidepressants;

(3) antineoplastics;

(4) antipsychotics

(5) antiretrovirals; and

(6) immunosuppressants for the treatment of transplant rejection.

[Soc. Sec. Act § 1860D-4(b)(3)(G); 42 C.F.R. § 423.120(b)(2)(v).]

Exceptions to the requirements related to the categories and classes of clinical concern are:

(1) drug products that are rated as therapeutically equivalent (under the FDA's most recent publication of "Approved Drug Products with Therapeutic Equivalence Evaluations," also known as the Orange Book);

(2) utilization management processes that limit the quantity of drugs due to safety; and

(3) other drugs that CMS specifies through a process that is based upon scientific evidence and medical standards of practice (and, in the case of antiretroviral medications, is consistent with HHS Guidelines for the Use of Antiretroviral Agents in HIV-1-Infected Adults and Adolescents) and that permits public notice and comment.

[42 C.F.R. § 423.120(b)(2)(vi).]

¶510

Transition process. A Part D sponsor must provide for an appropriate transition process for enrollees prescribed Part D drugs that are not on its Part D plan's formulary (including Part D drugs that are on a sponsor's formulary but require prior authorization or step therapy under a plan's utilization management rules). The transition process must:

(1) be applicable to new enrollees into Part D plans following the annual coordinated election period, newly eligible Medicare enrollees from other coverage, individuals who switch from one plan to another after the start of the contract year, and current enrollees remaining in the plan affected by formulary changes;

(2) ensure access to a temporary supply of drugs within the first 90 days of coverage under a new plan for retail, home infusion, long-term care, and mail-order pharmacies;

(3) ensure the provision of a temporary fill when an enrollee requests a fill of a non-formulary drug (including Part D drugs that are on a plan's formulary but require prior authorization or step therapy under a plan's utilization management rules);

(4) ensure written notice is provided to each affected enrollee within three business days after adjudication of the temporary fill;

(5) ensure that reasonable efforts are made to notify prescribers of affected enrollees who receive a transition notice; and

(6) charge cost-sharing for a temporary supply of drugs provided under its transition process such that the following conditions are met: (a) for low-income subsidy (LIS) enrollees, a sponsor must not charge higher cost-sharing for transition supplies than the statutory maximum copayment amounts; and (b) for non-LIS enrollees, a sponsor must charge the same cost-sharing for non-formulary Part D drugs provided during the transition that would apply for non-formulary drugs approved through a formulary exception; and the same cost-sharing for formulary drugs subject to utilization management edits provided during the transition that would apply once the utilization management criteria are met.

[42 C.F.R. § 423.120(b)(3).]

Limitation on changes in therapeutic classification. Except as CMS may permit to account for new therapeutic uses and newly approved Part D drugs, a Part D sponsor may not change the therapeutic categories and classes in a formulary other than at the beginning of each plan year. [42 C.F.R. § 423.120(b)(4).]

Provision of notice regarding formulary changes. Before removing a covered Part D drug from its Part D plan's formulary or making any change in the preferred or tiered cost-sharing status of a covered Part D drug, a Part D sponsor must provide at least 60 days' notice to CMS, State Pharmaceutical Assistance Programs, entities providing other prescription drug coverage, authorized prescribers, network pharmacies, and pharmacists. The sponsor must also either provide direct written notice to affected enrollees at least 60 days before the date the change becomes effective or, at the time an affected enrollee requests a refill of the Part D drug, provide such enrollee with a 60-day supply of the Part D drug under the same terms as previously allowed and written notice of the formulary change. [42 C.F.R. § 423.120(b)(5)(i).]

The written notice to the affected enrollee must contain:

(1) the name of the affected covered Part D drug;

(2) whether the plan is removing the covered Part D drug from the formulary or changing its preferred or tiered cost-sharing status;

(3) the reason why the plan is removing such covered Part D drug from the formulary or changing its preferred or tiered cost-sharing status;

(4) alternative drugs in the same therapeutic category or class or cost-sharing tier and expected cost-sharing for those drugs; and

(5) the means by which enrollees may obtain a coverage determination or exception.

[42 C.F.R. § 423.120(b)(5)(ii).]

Part D sponsors may immediately remove from their Part D plan formularies covered Part D drugs deemed unsafe by the Food and Drug Administration (FDA) or removed from the market by their manufacturer. Part D sponsors must provide retrospective notice of any such formulary changes to affected enrollees, CMS, State Pharmaceutical Assistance Programs, entities providing other prescription drug coverage, authorized prescribers, network pharmacies, and pharmacists consistent with the above requirements. [42 C.F.R. § 423.120(b)(5)(iii).]

Limitation on formulary changes before the beginning of a contract year. A Part D sponsor may not remove a covered Part D drug from its Part D plan's formulary, or make any change in the preferred or tiered cost-sharing status of a covered Part D drug on its plan's formulary, between the beginning of the annual coordinated election period and 60 days after the beginning of the contract year associated with that annual coordinated election period. [42 C.F.R. § 423.120(b)(6).]

Provider and patient education. A Part D sponsor must establish policies and procedures to educate and inform health care providers and enrollees concerning its formulary. [42 C.F.R. § 423.120(b)(7).]

Use of standardized technology. A Part D sponsor must issue and reissue, as necessary, a card or other type of technology that its enrollees may use to access negotiated prices for covered Part D drugs. When processing Part D claims, a sponsor or its intermediary must comply with the electronic transaction standards established by 45 C.F.R. § 162.1102. A sponsor must require its network pharmacies to submit claims to the sponsor or its intermediary whenever the card is presented or is on file at the pharmacy unless the enrollee expressly requests that a particular claim not be submitted to the sponsor or its intermediary. [42 C.F.R. § 423.120(c)(1)–(3).]

A Part D sponsor must assign and exclusively use a unique: (1) Part D bank identification number (BIN) or RxBIN and Part D processor control number (RxPCN) combination in its Medicare line of business; and (2) Part D cardholder identification number (RxID) to clearly identify its Medicare Part D beneficiaries. [42 C.F.R. § 423.120(c)(4).]

Beginning in plan year 2016, a claim for a covered Part D drug under a Part D PDP or a Medicare Advantage prescription drug plan (MA-PD) must include a valid prescriber national provider identifier (NPI). The physician or eligible professional who prescribed the drug must be enrolled in the Medicare program in an approved status or have a valid opt-out affidavit on file with a Medicare administrative contractor. However, pharmacy claims for Part D drugs prescribed by an "other authorized prescriber" (defined as an individual other than a physician or eligible professional who is authorized under state law to write prescriptions) are not subject to this requirement. [Soc. Sec. Act § 1860D-4(c)(4), as added by Medicare Access and CHIP Reauthorization Act of 2015 (MACRA) (P.L. 114-10) § 502; 42 C.F.R. § § 423.120(c)(6), 423.160(a)(4).]

Upon receipt of a pharmacy claim or beneficiary request for reimbursement for a drug that a Part D sponsor would otherwise be required to reject or deny for the reasons described in 42 C.F.R. § 423.120(c)(6)(ii) or (iii), the sponsor must provide the beneficiary with a three-month provisional supply of the drug (as prescribed by the prescriber and if allowed by applicable law) and written notice within three business days after adjudication of the claim or request in a form and manner specified by CMS. [42 C.F.R. § 423.120(c)(6)(v)(B).]

Compounded drug products. For multi-ingredient compounds, a Part D sponsor must determine whether the compound is covered under Part D. A compound that contains at least one ingredient covered under Part B is considered a Part B compound, regardless of whether other ingredients in the compound are covered under Part B. Only compounds that contain at least one ingredient that independently meets the definition of a Part D drug and do not contain any Part B ingredients may be considered Part D compounds and covered under Part D. For a Part D compound to be considered on-formulary, all ingredients that independently meet the definition of a Part D drug must be considered on-formulary. For a Part D compound to be considered off-formulary, transition rules apply such that all ingredients in the Part D compound that independently meet the definition of a Part D drug must become payable in the event of a transition fill and all ingredients that independently meet the definition of a Part D drug must be covered if an exception is approved for coverage of the compound. [42 C.F.R. § 423.120(d)(1).]

Compound payment liabilities. A Part D sponsor must establish consistent rules for beneficiary payment liabilities for both ingredients of the Part D compound that independently meet the definition of a Part D drug and non-Part D ingredients. For low-income subsidy beneficiaries, the copayment amount is based on whether the most expensive ingredient that independently meets the definition of a Part D drug in the Part D compound is a generic or brand name drug. For any non-Part D ingredient of the Part D compound, the Part D sponsor's contract with the pharmacy must prohibit balance billing the beneficiary for the cost of any such ingredients. [42 C.F.R. § 423.120(d)(2).]

Out-of-Network Access to Covered Part D Drugs

PDPs are required to ensure that their enrollees have adequate access to drugs dispensed at out-of-network pharmacies when enrollees cannot reasonably be expected to obtain covered drugs at a network pharmacy and do not access covered Part D drugs at an out-of-network pharmacy on a routine basis. [42 C.F.R. § 423.124(a)(1).] Provided the enrollees do not routinely access out-of-network pharmacies, CMS expects PDPs to guarantee out-of-network access if an enrollee:

(1) is traveling outside the plan's service area, runs out of or loses covered drugs or becomes ill and needs a covered drug, and cannot access a network pharmacy;

(2) cannot obtain a covered drug in a timely manner within a service area because, for example, there is no network pharmacy within a reasonable driving distance that provides 24 hour/7 day per week service;

(3) must fill a prescription for a covered drug and that particular drug is not regularly stocked at accessible network retail or mail-order pharmacies;

(4) is provided covered drugs dispensed by an out-of-network institution-based pharmacy while a patient in an emergency department, provider-based clinic, outpatient surgery, or other outpatient setting and, as a result, cannot get the medications filled at a network pharmacy; or

(5) experiences a declared federal disaster or other declared public health emergency in which Part D enrollees are evacuated or otherwise displaced from their place of residence and cannot reasonably be expected to obtain covered Part D drugs at a

network pharmacy and, in addition, in circumstances in which normal distribution channels are unavailable.

[*Medicare Prescription Drug Benefit Manual*, Pub. 100-18, Ch. 5, § 60.1.]

In addition, plans must provide coverage for vaccines and other covered Part D drugs that are appropriately dispensed and administered in a physician's office. [42 C.F.R. § 423.124(a)(2).]

Limits on out-of-network access. CMS requires PDPs to establish reasonable rules to ensure that enrollees use out-of-network pharmacies in an appropriate manner, provided that the plans also ensure adequate access to out-of-network pharmacies on a non-routine basis when enrollees cannot reasonably access network pharmacies. For example, PDPs may wish to limit the amount of covered drugs dispensed at an out-of-network pharmacy and require that a beneficiary purchase maintenance medications via mail order for extended out-of-area travel or require a plan notification or authorization process for individuals who fill their prescriptions at out-of-network pharmacies. [42 C.F.R. § 423.124(a), (c); Pub. 100-18, Ch. 5, § 60.1.]

Financial responsibility for out-of-network access. Enrollees obtaining covered Part D drugs at out-of-network pharmacies must assume financial responsibility for any differential between the out-of-network pharmacy's (or provider's) usual and customary price and the Part D sponsor's plan allowance. [42 C.F.R. § 423.124(b).]

Dissemination of Part D Plan Information

To ensure that eligible or enrolled individuals in PDPs receive the information they need to make informed choices about their coverage options, sponsors must disclose a detailed description of each qualified PDP. The description must be provided in a clear, accurate, and standardized form at the time of enrollment and annually thereafter, 15 days before the annual coordinated election period. The information required is similar to the information MA plans must disclose to their enrollees. [Soc. Sec. Act § 1860D-4(a); 42 C.F.R. § 423.128(a).]

The description must include information regarding:

(1) service area;

(2) benefits, including applicable conditions and limitations, premiums, cost-sharing, cost-sharing for subsidy-eligible individuals, and other benefit-associated conditions;

(3) how to obtain more information on cost-sharing requirements, including tiered or other copayment levels applicable to each drug;

(4) the plan's formulary, including a list of included drugs, the manner in which the formulary functions, the process for obtaining an exception to the plan's formulary or tiered cost-sharing structure, and a description of how an eligible individual may obtain additional information on the formulary;

(5) the number, mix, and addresses of network pharmacies from which enrollees may reasonably be expected to obtain covered drugs and how the sponsor meets the access requirements;

(6) provisions for access to covered drugs at out-of-network pharmacies;

(7) all grievance, coverage determination, and appeal rights and procedures;

(8) policies and procedures for quality assurance and the medication therapy management program;

(9) disenrollment rights and responsibilities; and

¶510

(10) the fact that a sponsor may terminate or refuse to renew its contract, or reduce the service area, and the effect that this may have on plan enrollees.

[42 C.F.R. § 423.128(b).]

Information available on request of the eligible individual. Upon request of a Part D eligible individual, a Part D sponsor must provide: general coverage information; the procedures the sponsor uses to control utilization of services and expenditures; the number of grievances, appeals, and exceptions, and their disposition in the aggregate; and the financial condition of the Part D sponsor, including the most recently audited information regarding the sponsor offering the plan. "General coverage information" includes information on: (1) how to exercise election options, (2) procedural rights, (3) benefits, (4) premiums, (5) the plan's formulary, (6) the plan's service area, and (7) quality and performance indicators for benefits under the plan. [42 C.F.R. § 423.128(c).]

Mechanisms for providing specific information to enrollees. Part D sponsors must have mechanisms in place to provide specific information requested by current and prospective enrollees. The mechanisms must include: a toll-free customer call center, an Internet website, and responses in writing upon beneficiary request. The plans' customer call centers must:

(1) be open during usual business hours;

(2) provide telephone service to customers, including pharmacists, pursuant to standard business practices;

(3) provide interpreters for non-English speaking and limited-English-speaking individuals; and

(4) provide immediate access to the coverage determination and redetermination process.

[42 C.F.R. § 423.128(d).]

Explanation of benefits. Part D sponsors must furnish an explanation of benefits (EOB) to enrollees who receive covered Part D drugs. EOBs must be written in a form easily understandable to beneficiaries and must be provided at least monthly for those enrollees utilizing their prescription drug benefits in a given month. EOBs for Part D plans also must:

(1) include a listing of the item or service for which payment was made, as well as the amount of such payment for each item or service;

(2) include a notice of the individual's right to request an itemized statement;

(3) include information regarding the cumulative, year-to-date amount of benefits provided relative to the deductible, the initial coverage limit, and the annual out-of-pocket threshold for that year, and a beneficiary's cumulative, year-to-date total of incurred costs;

(4) include information regarding any applicable formulary changes; and

(5) be provided no later than the end of the month following any month when prescription drug benefits are provided, including for covered Part D spending between the initial coverage limit and the out-of-pocket threshold.

[42 C.F.R. § 423.128(e).]

Disclosure of deficiencies. CMS may require a Part D plan sponsor to disclose to its enrollees or potential enrollees the Part D plan sponsor's performance and contract compliance deficiencies in a manner specified by CMS. [42 C.F.R. § 423.128(f).]

¶510

Changes in rules. If a Part D sponsor intends to change its rules for a Part D plan, it must do all of the following: (1) submit the changes for CMS review; (2) for changes that take effect on January 1, notify all enrollees at least 15 days before the beginning of the annual coordinated election period; and (3) provide notice of all other changes in accordance with Part D notice requirements. [42 C.F.R. § 423.128(g).]

Disclosure of formulary and coverage information for auto-assigned subsidy eligibles. Subsidy-eligible individuals enrolled in a PDP who subsequently are reassigned to a new PDP by the HHS Secretary must be provided, within 30 days of the reassignment, with: (1) information on formulary differences between the individual's former plan and the plan to which the individual is reassigned with respect to the individual's drug regimen; and (2) a description of the individual's right to request a coverage determination, exception, or reconsideration, bring an appeal, or resolve a grievance. [Soc. Sec. Act § 1860D-14(d).]

Disclosure of Prices for Equivalent Drugs (Generic Differential Notice)

Part D sponsors must ensure that pharmacies inform enrollees of any differential between the price of a covered Part D drug and the price of the lowest-priced generic version available under the plan at that pharmacy. This generic price differential information must be provided at the time the plan enrollee purchases the drug or, in the case of drugs purchased by mail order, at the time of delivery. Disclosure of this information, however, is not necessary if the particular covered drug purchased by an enrollee is the lowest-priced generic version of that drug available at a particular pharmacy. [Soc. Sec. Act § 1860D-4(k); 42 C.F.R. § 423.132(a), (b).]

CMS is permitted to waive the generic differential notice requirement in the following cases:

(1) whenever a private fee-for-service MA plan offers qualified prescription drug coverage and provides plan enrollees with access to covered Part D drugs dispensed at all pharmacies, without regard to whether they are contracted network pharmacies, and does not charge additional cost-sharing for access to covered drugs dispensed at all pharmacies;

(2) at out-of-network pharmacies;

(3) at pharmacies of Indian tribes and tribal organizations, and urban Indian organizations' network pharmacies;

(4) at network pharmacies located in any of the U.S. territories (American Samoa, the Commonwealth of the Northern Mariana Islands, Guam, Puerto Rico, and the Virgin Islands);

(5) at long-term care network pharmacies; and

(6) at any other place, when CMS deems compliance is impossible or impracticable.

[Soc. Sec. Act § 1860D-4(k); 42 C.F.R. § 423.132(c).]

Privacy, Confidentiality, and Accuracy of Enrollee Records

To the extent that a PDP sponsor maintains medical records or other health information regarding Part D enrollees, the sponsor must meet the same requirements regarding confidentiality and accuracy of enrollee records as MA organizations offering MA plans. [Soc. Sec. Act § 1860D-4(i).]

PDP sponsors must:

(1) abide by all federal and state laws regarding confidentiality and disclosure of medical records or other health and enrollment information, including the Health

Insurance Portability and Accountability Act of 1996 (HIPAA) and the privacy rule promulgated under HIPAA;

(2) ensure that medical information is released only in accordance with applicable federal or state law or under court orders or subpoenas;

(3) maintain the records and information in an accurate and timely manner; and

(4) ensure timely access by enrollees to records and information pertaining to them.

[42 C.F.R. § 423.136.]

PDPs are covered entities under the HIPAA privacy rule because they meet the definition of "health plan." Any violations by a PDP sponsor of its obligations under the privacy rule are subject to enforcement by the HHS Office for Civil Rights. [*Final rule*, 70 FR 4194, 4277, Jan. 28, 2005.]

[¶ 515] Grievances, Coverage Determinations, Redeterminations, and Reconsiderations

The law and regulations concerning grievances, coverage determinations, redeterminations, and reconsiderations under the Part D prescription drug benefit establish a process that largely mirrors the procedures required under the Medicare Advantage (MA) program (see ¶ 403). Definitions for these terms, as used in Part D, follow.

Grievance. A grievance is any complaint or dispute expressing dissatisfaction with a Part D plan sponsor's operations or behavior. Grievances do not include coverage determinations. [42 C.F.R. § 423.560.]

Coverage determination. A coverage determination is a decision by a Part D sponsor regarding the benefits an enrollee is entitled to receive for drug coverage. [42 C.F.R. § 423.566.]

Reconsideration. A reconsideration is a review of an adverse coverage determination by an independent review entity (IRE) and includes review of the evidence upon which the determination was based and any additional evidence the enrollee submits or the IRE obtains. [42 C.F.R. § 423.560.]

Redetermination. A redetermination is a review of an adverse coverage determination by a Part D plan sponsor and includes the review of evidence upon which the determination was based and any other evidence the enrollee submits or the plan obtains. [42 C.F.R. § 423.560.]

This section sets forth the requirements related to: (1) Part D plan sponsors with respect to grievances, coverage determinations, and redeterminations; (2) Part D IREs with respect to reconsiderations; and (3) Part D enrollees' rights with respect to grievances, coverage determinations, redeterminations, and reconsiderations. The requirements regarding reopenings, administrative law judge (ALJ) hearings, Medicare Appeals Council review, and judicial review are discussed in ¶ 516. [42 C.F.R. § 423.558.]

Responsibilities of Part D Plan Sponsors and Rights of Enrollees

For each prescription drug plan (PDP) that it offers, a Part D plan sponsor must establish and maintain:

(1) a grievance procedure addressing issues unrelated to coverage determinations;

(2) a single, uniform exceptions and appeals process that includes procedures for accepting oral and written requests for coverage determinations and redeterminations;

(3) a procedure for making timely coverage determinations, including determinations on requests for exceptions to a tiered cost-sharing formulary structure or exceptions to a formulary; and

(4) appeal procedures for issues related to coverage determinations that meet the requirements of the Part D regulations.

[Soc. Sec. Act § 1860D-4(b)(3)(H), (g), (h); 42 C.F.R. § 423.562(a)(1).]

A PDP must ensure that enrollees receive written information related to grievance and appeal procedures available to them through the plan and the complaint process available to them under the quality improvement organization process. In addition, a PDP must arrange with its network pharmacies to post or distribute notices instructing enrollees to contact their plans to obtain a coverage determination or request an exception. [42 C.F.R. § 423.562(a)(2), (3).]

Delegated responsibilities. If the Part D plan sponsor delegates any of its responsibilities to another entity or individual through which the sponsor provides covered benefits, the sponsor is ultimately responsible for ensuring that the entity or individual satisfies these requirements. [42 C.F.R. § 423.562(a)(4).]

Medical director requirement. A Part D plan sponsor must employ a medical director who is responsible for ensuring the clinical accuracy of all coverage determinations and redeterminations involving medical necessity. The medical director must be a physician with a current and unrestricted license to practice medicine in a state, territory, Puerto Rico, or the District of Columbia. [42 C.F.R. § 423.562(a)(5).]

Rights of enrollees. Enrollees have the right to: (1) have grievances between the enrollee and the Part D plan sponsor heard and resolved by the plan; (2) have the plan make a timely coverage determination, including a request for an exception to the plan's tiered cost-sharing structure or formulary; and (3) request an expedited coverage determination from the plan.

If an enrollee is dissatisfied with any part of a coverage determination, he or she has the right to:

(1) a redetermination of the adverse coverage determination by the PDP sponsor;

(2) request an expedited redetermination;

(3) a reconsideration or expedited reconsideration by an IRE contracted by CMS if, as a result of a redetermination, a plan affirms, in whole or in part, its adverse coverage determination;

(4) an ALJ hearing if the IRE affirms the plan's adverse coverage determination, in whole or in part, and the amount in controversy requirement is met;

(5) request a Medicare Appeals Council review of the ALJ hearing decision if the ALJ affirms the IRE's adverse coverage determination, in whole or in part; and

(6) judicial review of the Medicare Appeals Council hearing decision if it affirms the ALJ's adverse coverage determination, in whole or in part, and the amount in controversy requirement is met.

[42 C.F.R. § 423.562(b)(4).]

Grievance Procedure

PDPs must have meaningful procedures for timely hearing and resolution of grievances from enrollees against PDP sponsors or any other entity or individual providing covered benefits under the such plans. The grievance procedures must be separate and distinct from appeals procedures. When the plan receives a complaint, it must promptly determine and inform the enrollee whether the complaint is subject to its grievance or appeal procedures. [42 C.F.R. § 423.564(a), (b).]

Method for filing a grievance. An enrollee must file any grievance with a plan either orally or in writing no later than 60 calendar days after the event or incident that precipitated the grievance. [42 C.F.R. § 423.564(d).]

Disposition and notification. The plan must notify the enrollee of its decision as expeditiously as the case requires based on the enrollee's health status, but no later than 30 calendar days after the date the plan receives the oral or written grievance. The 30-calendar-day time frame may be extended by up to 14 calendar days if the enrollee requests the extension or if the plan justifies a need for additional information and documents how the delay is in the interest of the enrollee. [42 C.F.R. § 423.564(e).]

Expedited grievances. A PDP is required to respond to an enrollee's grievance within 24 hours if the complaint involves a refusal by the plan to grant an enrollee's request for an expedited coverage determination or an expedited redetermination and the enrollee has not yet purchased or received the drug that is in dispute. [42 C.F.R. § 423.564(f).]

Recordkeeping. The PDP must maintain records on grievances received orally and in writing. Records minimally must include the date of receipt, final disposition of the grievance, and the date that the plan notified the enrollee of the disposition. [42 C.F.R. § 423.564(g).]

Complaint system. As part of its contract with CMS, the Part D plan sponsor must agree to address complaints received by CMS against the sponsor by (1) addressing and resolving complaints in the CMS complaint tracking system; and (2) displaying a link to the electronic complaint form on the Medicare.gov website on the Part D plan's main website. [42 C.F.R. § 423.505(b)(22).]

Coverage Determinations

Each PDP must have a procedure for making timely coverage determinations regarding the prescription drug benefits an enrollee is entitled to receive under the plan, including basic coverage and supplemental benefits, and the amount, including cost-sharing, that the enrollee is required to pay. The plan must have a standard procedure and an expedited procedure when use of the standard procedure may seriously jeopardize the enrollee's life, health, or ability to regain maximum function. [Soc. Sec. Act § 1860D-4(g); 42 C.F.R. § 423.566(a).]

Only adverse coverage determinations are subject to the appeals process. Plan actions that constitute coverage decisions include:

(1) a decision not to provide or pay for a Part D drug that the enrollee believes may be covered by the plan, including a decision not to pay because: (a) the drug is not on the plan's formulary, (b) the drug is determined not to be medically necessary, (c) the drug is furnished by an out-of-network pharmacy, or (d) the PDP determines that the drug is otherwise excludable from coverage if applied to Medicare Part D;

(2) failure to provide a coverage determination in a timely manner when a delay would adversely affect the health of the enrollee;

(3) a decision concerning an exceptions request to the plan's tiered cost-sharing structure;

(4) a decision concerning an exceptions request involving a non-formulary Part D drug; or

(5) a decision on the amount of cost-sharing for a drug.

[42 C.F.R. § 423.566(b).]

The enrollee or the enrollee's appointed representative, on behalf of the enrollee, or the prescribing physician, on behalf of the enrollee, may request a standard or expedited coverage determination. [42 C.F.R. § 423.566(c).]

Medical review of coverage determinations. If a Part D plan sponsor expects to issue a partially or fully adverse medical necessity decision based on the initial review of a request, the coverage determination must be reviewed by a physician or other appropriate health care professional with sufficient medical and other expertise, including knowledge of Medicare coverage criteria, before the sponsor issues the coverage determination decision. The physician or other health care professional must have a current and unrestricted license to practice within the scope of his or her profession in a state, territory, Puerto Rico, or the District of Columbia. [42 C.F.R. § 423.566(d).]

Standard coverage determination requests. An enrollee must ask for a standard coverage determination by making a request with the Part D sponsor orally or in writing, except that requests for payment must be in writing unless the sponsor has implemented a policy of accepting oral requests. The sponsor must establish and maintain a method of documenting all oral request and retain documentation in the case file. [42 C.F.R. § 423.568(a).]

Time frames for notification. When a party makes a request for a drug benefit, the plan sponsor must notify the enrollee and the prescribing physician involved, if appropriate, of its determination as expeditiously as the enrollee's health condition requires, but no later than 72 hours after receipt of the request or, for an exceptions request, no later than 72 hours after receipt of the physician's or other prescriber's supporting statement. [42 C.F.R. § 423.568(b).]

When a party makes a request for payment, the Part D plan sponsor must notify the enrollee of its determination and make payment (when applicable) no later than 14 calendar days after receipt of the request. [42 C.F.R. § 423.568(c).]

If the plan fails to notify the enrollee of its determination in the appropriate time frame, the failure constitutes an adverse coverage determination, and the plan must forward the enrollee's request to the IRE within 24 hours of the expiration of the adjudication time frame. [42 C.F.R. § 423.568(h).]

Written notice. If a Part D plan sponsor makes a completely favorable decision regarding a request for drug benefits, it must give the enrollee written notice of the determination. The initial notice may be provided orally as long as a written follow-up notice is sent within three calendar days. The notice must explain the conditions of the approval in a readable and understandable form. [42 C.F.R. § 423.568(d) and (e).]

If a Part D plan sponsor decides to deny a drug benefit in whole or in part, it must give the enrollee written notice of the determination. The initial notice may be oral as long as a written follow-up notice is mailed within three calendar days of the oral notice. The notice of denial must:

(1) use approved notice language in a readable and understandable form;

(2) state the specific reasons for the denial;

(3) inform the enrollee of his or her right to a redetermination; and

(4) comply with any other notice requirements specified by CMS.

For drug coverage denials, the denial notice must describe both the standard and expedited redetermination processes, including the enrollee's right to obtain and conditions for obtaining an expedited redetermination, and the rest of the appeals process. For payment denials, the denial notice must describe the standard redetermination process and the rest of the appeals process. [42 C.F.R. § 423.568(f) and (g).]

Effect of a coverage determination. A coverage determination is binding on the Part D plan and the enrollee unless it is reviewed and revised by a redetermination or it is reopened and revised. [42 C.F.R. § 423.576.]

Requirements for an Expedited Coverage Determination

An enrollee or an enrollee's prescribing physician or other prescriber may request that a PDP expedite a coverage determination. An expedited review is not available for requests for payment of Part D drugs that have been furnished. An enrollee or an enrollee's prescribing physician or other prescriber on behalf of the enrollee must submit an oral or written request directly to the plan or, if applicable, to the entity responsible for making the determination, as directed by the plan. The prescribing physician or other prescriber may provide oral or written support for an enrollee's request for an expedited determination. [Soc. Sec. Act § 1860D-4(g); 42 C.F.R. § 423.570(a), (b).]

Processing the request. When a request for an expedited review is received, the PDP must provide for an expedited determination in the following situations:

- when the request has been made by an enrollee if the plan determines that applying the standard time frame for making a determination may seriously jeopardize the life or health of the enrollee or the enrollee's ability to regain maximum function; and

- when the request has been made or is supported by an enrollee's prescribing physician or other prescriber if the physician or other prescriber indicates that applying the standard time frame for making a determination may seriously jeopardize the life or health of the enrollee or the enrollee's ability to regain maximum function.

[42 C.F.R. § 423.570(c).]

Time frame and notice for denied requests. If a plan denies a request for expedited determination, it must make the determination within the 72-hour time frame established for a standard determination. The 72-hour period begins on the day the plan receives the request for expedited determination or, for an exceptions request, the day the plan receives the physician's or other prescriber's supporting statement. [42 C.F.R. § 423.570(d)(1).]

The PDP also must give the enrollee and prescribing physician or other prescriber prompt oral notice of the denial that explains that the plan must process the request using the 72-hour time frame for standard determinations and informs the enrollee of the right to file an expedited grievance if he or she disagrees with the plan's decision not to expedite. In addition, the PDP must inform the enrollee of the right to resubmit a request for an expedited determination with the prescribing physician's or other prescriber's support and provide instructions about the plan's grievance process and its time frames. Within three calendar days of the oral notice, the plan must deliver an equivalent written notice. [42 C.F.R. § 423.570(d)(2), (3).]

Time frame and notice requirements for expedited determinations. A plan that approves a request for expedited determination must make its determination and notify the enrollee and the prescribing physician or other prescriber involved, when appropriate, of its decision whether adverse or favorable, as expeditiously as the enrollee's health condition requires, but no later than 24 hours after receiving the request or, for an exceptions request, after the physician's or other prescriber's supporting statement. If the plan fails to notify the enrollee of its determination within the 24-hour time frame, the failure constitutes an adverse coverage determination and the plan must forward the enrollee's request to the IRE within 24 hours of the expiration of the adjudication time frame. [42 C.F.R. § 423.572(a), (d).]

If the Part D plan sponsor first notifies an enrollee of an adverse or favorable expedited determination orally, it must mail written confirmation to the enrollee within three calendar days of the oral notification. If the determination is completely favorable, the notice must explain the conditions of the approval in a readable and understandable form. If the determination is not completely favorable, the notice must:

(1) use approved language in a readable and understandable form;

(2) state the specific reasons for the denial;

(3) inform the enrollee of his or her right to a redetermination; and

(4) describe the standard and expedited redetermination processes, including the enrollee's right to request an expedited redetermination; conditions for obtaining an expedited redetermination; and other aspects of the appeal process.

[42 C.F.R. § 423.572(b), (c).]

Formulary Exception Procedures General Rules

A decision by a PDP concerning an exceptions request constitutes a coverage determination. If the plan fails to make a decision on an exceptions request and provide notice of the decision within the time frame required for a standard determination or an expedited determination, as applicable, the failure constitutes an adverse coverage determination and the plan must forward the enrollee's request to the IRE within 24 hours of the expiration of the adjudication time frame. [42 C.F.R. § 423.578(c)(1), (c)(2).]

An enrollee may not use the exceptions process to request or be granted coverage for a prescription drug that does not meet the definition of a Part D drug. In addition, a physician's or other prescriber's supporting statement required for an exceptions request will not result in an automatic favorable determination. [42 C.F.R. § 423.578(e), (f).]

Exceptions Processes

PDP sponsors must establish exceptions processes to a plan's tiered cost-sharing structure and for receipt of an off-formulary drug. [Soc. Sec. Act § 1860D-4(g)(2); 42 C.F.R. § 423.578(a), (b).]

Exception process to tiered cost-sharing structure. Under a tiered cost-sharing structure, drugs are assigned to different copayment tiers based on cost-sharing, clinical considerations, or both. An enrollee's level of cost-sharing is based on the tier into which the prescribed drug falls. Typically, drugs fall into one of three tiers—generic drugs, preferred brand-name drugs, or non-preferred brand-name drugs. All of a plan's cost-sharing tiers make up its formulary. [42 C.F.R. § 423.4.]

A PDP's exception procedures must encompass all types of tiering exceptions requests. The plan must grant an exception to its tiered cost-sharing structure whenever it determines that the non-preferred drug for treatment of the enrollee's condition is medically necessary, consistent with the physician's statement. [Soc. Sec. Act § 1860D-4(g)(2); 42 C.F.R. § 423.578(a).]

The PDP's exceptions criteria must include, but are not limited to: (1) a description of the criteria the plan uses to evaluate a determination made by the enrollee's prescribing physician or other prescriber; (2) consideration of whether the requested Part D drug that is the subject of the exceptions request is the therapeutic equivalent of any other drug on the plan's formulary; and (3) consideration of the number of drugs on the plan's formulary that are in the same class and category as the requested prescription drug that is the subject of the exceptions request. [42 C.F.R. § 423.578(a)(2).]

An enrollee or the enrollee's prescribing physician or other prescriber may file a request for an exception. The prescribing physician or other prescriber must provide an oral or written supporting statement that the preferred drug for the treatment of the enrollee's condition:

(1) would not be as effective for the enrollee as the requested drug; and/or

(2) would have adverse effects for the enrollee.

If the physician or other prescriber provides an oral supporting statement, the plan subsequently may require the physician or other prescriber to provide a written supporting statement to demonstrate the medical necessity of the drug as well as provide additional supporting medical documentation. [42 C.F.R. § 423.578(a)(3)–(5).]

Request for exceptions involving a non-formulary Part D drug. Part D plan sponsors that offer PDPs with formularies must establish and maintain exceptions procedures subject to CMS's approval for PDP enrollees who require non-formulary drugs. A non-formulary drug is a drug that is not on a plan's formulary. Formulary use includes the application of cost utilization tools such as: (1) a dose restriction, including the dosage form, that causes a particular Part D drug not to be covered for the number of doses prescribed; or (2) a step therapy requirement that causes a particular Part D drug not to be covered until the requirements of the plan's coverage policy are met; or (3) a therapeutic substitution requirement. [42 C.F.R. § 423.578(b).]

The PDP must grant an exception whenever it determines that the drug is medically necessary, consistent with the physician's statement, and the drug would be covered but for the fact that it is an off-formulary drug. The plan's formulary exceptions process must address:

(1) situations in which a formulary changes during the year and situations in which an enrollee is already using a given drug;

(2) continued coverage of a particular Part D prescription drug that the PDP is discontinuing on the formulary for reasons other than safety or because the Part D prescription drug cannot be supplied by or was withdrawn from the market by the drug's manufacturer; and

(3) an exception to a plan's coverage policy that causes a Part D prescription drug not to be covered because of cost utilization tools, such as a requirement for step therapy, dosage limitations, or therapeutic substitution.

[42 C.F.R. § 423.578(b)(1).]

An enrollee, the enrollee's appointed representative, or the prescribing physician or other prescriber on behalf of the enrollee may file a request for an exception. The prescribing physician or other prescriber must provide an oral or written supporting statement that the requested prescription drug is medically necessary to treat the enrollee's disease or medical condition. [42 C.F.R. § 423.578(b)(4), (5).]

If the plan covers a non-formulary drug, the costs incurred by the enrollee for that drug are treated as being included for purposes of calculating and meeting the annual out-of-pocket threshold. [42 C.F.R. § 423.578(b)(3).]

When a non-formulary exceptions request is approved, the plan may not require the enrollee to request approval for a refill, or a new prescription to continue using the Part D prescription drug after the refills for the initial prescription are exhausted, as long as: (1) the enrollee's prescribing physician or other prescriber continues to prescribe the drug; (2) the drug continues to be considered safe for treating the enrollee's disease or medical condition; and (3) the enrollment period has not expired. [42 C.F.R. § 423.578(c)(4).]

Coverage determination. A decision by a PDP concerning an exceptions request constitutes a coverage determination. If the plan fails to make a decision on an exceptions request and provide notice of the decision within the time frame required for a standard determination or an expedited determination, as applicable, the failure constitutes an adverse coverage determination and the plan must forward the enrollee's request to the IRE within 24 hours of the expiration of the adjudication time frame. [42 C.F.R. § 423.578(c)(1), (c)(2).]

Rules for Redeterminations

To appeal a coverage determination, an enrollee or an enrollee's prescribing physician or other prescriber must file a written request for redetermination with the plan that made the coverage determination within 60 calendar days from the date of the notice of the coverage determination. The plan may adopt a policy for accepting oral requests and may extend the time frame for filing the request if the enrollee can show good cause for late filing. [Soc. Sec. Act § 1860D-4(g); 42 C.F.R. §§ 423.580, 423.582.]

Who must conduct the review of an adverse coverage determination. A person who was not involved in making the coverage determination must conduct the redetermination. When the issue is the denial of coverage based on a lack of medical necessity, the redetermination must be made by a physician with expertise in the field of medicine that is appropriate for the services at issue. The physician making the redetermination need not, in all cases, be of the same specialty or subspecialty as the prescribing physician. [42 C.F.R. § 423.590(f).]

Time frames for standard redetermination requests. If the Part D plan sponsor makes a redetermination of a request for coverage that is completely favorable to the enrollee or a redetermination that affirms, in whole or in part, its adverse coverage determination, the sponsor must notify the enrollee in writing of its redetermination as expeditiously as the enrollee's health condition requires, but no later than seven calendar days from the date it receives the request for a standard redetermination. If the Part D plan sponsor makes a redetermination of a request for payment that is completely favorable to the enrollee or affirms, in whole or in part, its adverse coverage determination, the sponsor must issue its redetermination and effectuate it no later than seven calendar days from the date it receives the request for redetermination. [42 C.F.R. § 423.590(a), (b).]

If the PDP fails to provide the enrollee with a redetermination within these time frames, the failure constitutes an adverse redetermination decision and the plan must forward the enrollee's request to the IRE within 24 hours of the expiration of the adjudication time frame. [42 C.F.R. § 423.590(c).]

Notice of adverse redetermination. The notice of any adverse determination must use approved notice language in a readable and understandable form, state the specific reasons for the denial, and inform the enrollee of his or her right to a reconsideration. For adverse drug coverage redeterminations, the notice must describe the standard and expedited reconsideration processes, including the enrollee's right to, and conditions for, obtaining an expedited reconsideration, and the remainder of the appeals process. For adverse payment redeterminations, the notice must describe the standard reconsideration process and the remainder of the appeals process. [42 C.F.R. § 423.590(g).]

¶515

Notice of completely favorable redeterminations. The notice of any completely favorable determination must explain the conditions of the approval in a readable and understandable form. [42 C.F.R. § 423.590(h).]

Expedited Redeterminations

An enrollee or an enrollee's prescribing physician or other prescriber acting on behalf of an enrollee may request that a Part D plan sponsor expedite a redetermination of a coverage determination. Requests for redetermination on payment of drugs already received, however, may not be expedited because a medical emergency does not exist for an enrollee who has obtained the medication in dispute. [Soc. Sec. Act § 1860D-4(g); 42 C.F.R. § 423.584(a).]

The enrollee or prescribing physician or other prescriber must submit an oral or written request directly to the PDP or, if applicable, to the entity responsible for making the redetermination, as directed by the plan. A prescribing physician or other prescriber may provide oral or written support for an enrollee's request for an expedited redetermination. [42 C.F.R. § 423.584(b).]

Processing expedited redetermination requests. The PDP must: (1) establish an efficient and convenient means for individuals to submit oral or written expedited redetermination requests, (2) document all oral requests in writing, and (3) maintain the documentation in the case file. In addition, the PDP must decide promptly whether to expedite the redetermination or follow the time frame for standard redetermination based on the following requirements:

• for a request made by an enrollee, the plan must provide an expedited redetermination if it determines that applying the standard time frame for making a redetermination may seriously jeopardize the life or health of the enrollee or the enrollee's ability to regain maximum function; and

• for a request made or supported by a prescribing physician or other prescriber, the plan must provide an expedited redetermination if the physician indicates that applying the standard time frame for conducting a redetermination may seriously jeopardize the life or health of the enrollee or the enrollee's ability to regain maximum function.

[42 C.F.R. § 423.584(c).]

Denial of an expedited redetermination request. If a PDP denies a request for expedited redetermination, it must make the determination within the seven-calendar-day time frame that begins the day the plan receives the request for expedited redetermination. The plan must give the enrollee prompt oral notice of the denial that:

(1) explains that the plan processes the enrollee's request using the seven-calendar-day time frame for standard redetermination;

(2) informs the enrollee of the right to file an expedited grievance if he or she disagrees with the decision by the plan not to expedite;

(3) informs the enrollee of the right to resubmit a request for an expedited redetermination with the prescribing physician's or other prescriber's support; and

(4) provides instructions about the expedited grievance process and its time frames.

Within three calendar days of the oral notice to the enrollee, the PDP must deliver an equivalent written notice that contains the required information. [42 C.F.R. § 423.584(d).]

Time frame for expedited redeterminations. A Part D plan sponsor that approves a request for expedited redetermination must complete its redetermination and give the enrollee and the prescribing physician or other prescriber involved, when appropriate, notice of its decision as expeditiously as the enrollee's health condition requires, but no later than 72 hours after receiving the request. If notice of an adverse or favorable expedited redetermination is given orally, the sponsor must mail written confirmation within three calendar days of the oral notice. [42 C.F.R. § 423.590(d).]

Failure to meet time frame for expedited redetermination. If the PDP fails to provide the enrollee or the prescribing physician or other prescriber, when appropriate, with the results of its expedited redetermination within the 72-hour time frame, the failure constitutes an adverse redetermination decision and the plan must forward the enrollee's request to the IRE within 24 hours of the expiration of the adjudication time frame. [42 C.F.R. § 423.590(e).]

Reconsideration by an Independent Review Entity

An enrollee (or the prescribing physician or other prescriber, acting on behalf of the enrollee) who is dissatisfied with the redetermination of a PDP has a right to a reconsideration by an IRE that contracts with CMS. [Soc. Sec. Act § 1860D-4(h); 42 C.F.R. § 423.600(a).]

The enrollee, or the enrollee's prescribing physician or other prescriber, must file a written request for reconsideration with the IRE within 60 calendar days of the date of the redetermination by the plan. When an enrollee or an enrollee's prescribing physician or other prescriber files an appeal, the IRE is required to solicit the views of the prescribing physician or other prescriber, either orally or in writing. The IRE must maintain a written account of the prescribing physician's views, prepared by the prescribing physician, other prescriber, or IRE. [42 C.F.R. § 423.600(a), (b).]

Requirements for reconsideration for non-formulary drugs. For an enrollee to request an IRE reconsideration of a determination by a plan not to provide for a Part D drug that is not on the formulary, the prescribing physician or other prescriber must determine that all covered Part D drugs on any tier of the formulary for treatment of the same condition would not be as effective for the individual as the non-formulary drug, would have adverse effects for the individual, or both. [42 C.F.R. § 423.600(c).]

Time frame for reconsideration. The IRE must conduct the reconsideration as expeditiously as the enrollee's health condition requires but no later than seven calendar days from the date of a request for a reconsideration. When a request for an expedited reconsideration is received and granted, the IRE must conduct the reconsideration as expeditiously as the enrollee's health condition requires, but no later than 72 hours after receiving the request. [42 C.F.R. § 423.600(d).]

Medical necessity issues. When the issue is the denial of coverage based on a lack of medical necessity (or any substantively equivalent term used to describe the concept of medical necessity), the reconsideration must be made by a physician with expertise in the field of medicine that is appropriate for the services at issue. The physician making the reconsideration need not, in all cases, be of the same specialty or subspecialty as the prescribing physician or other prescriber. [42 C.F.R. § 423.600(e).]

Notice of reconsideration determination. The IRE is responsible for mailing a notice of its reconsideration determination to the enrollee and the PDP and sending a copy to CMS. When the prescribing physician or other prescriber requests the reconsideration on behalf of the enrollee, the IRE is also responsible for notifying the prescribing physician or other prescriber of its decision. The notice must state the specific reasons for the IRE's decision in understandable language. If the reconsideration determination is adverse, the notice must inform the enrollee of his or her right to an ALJ hearing if the amount in controversy meets the threshold requirement and describe the procedures that the enrollee must follow to obtain an ALJ hearing. [42 C.F.R. § 423.602.]

Effect of a reconsideration determination. A reconsideration determination is final and binding on the enrollee and the plan, unless the enrollee files a request for an ALJ hearing. [42 C.F.R. § 423.604.]

Effectuation of Standard and Expedited Determinations, Reconsiderations, and Decisions

If a PDP reverses its coverage determination in a redetermination of a request for benefits, the plan must authorize or provide the benefit under dispute as expeditiously as the enrollee's health condition requires, but no later than seven calendar days from the date it receives the request for redetermination. [42 C.F.R. § 423.636(a)(1).]

If the PDP reverses its coverage determination on a redetermination of a request for payment, the Part D plan sponsor must authorize payment for the benefit within seven calendar days from the date it receives the request for redetermination and make payment no later than 30 calendar days after the date the plan sponsor receives the request for redetermination. [42 C.F.R. § 423.636(a)(2).]

On an expedited redetermination of a request for benefits, if the plan reverses its coverage determination, the plan must authorize or provide the benefit under dispute as expeditiously as the enrollee's health condition requires, but no later than 72 hours after the date the Part D plan sponsor receives the request for redetermination. [42 C.F.R. § 423.638(a).]

Reversals other than by the Part D plan sponsor. On appeal of a request for benefit, if the plan's determination is reversed in whole or in part by the IRE or at a higher level of appeal, the PDP must authorize or provide the benefit under dispute within 72 hours from the date it receives notice reversing the determination. On appeal of a request for payment, if the plan's determination is reversed in whole or in part by the IRE or at a higher level of appeal, the Part D plan sponsor must authorize payment for the benefit within 72 hours and make payment no later than 30 calendar days from the date it receives notice reversing the coverage determination. [42 C.F.R. § 423.636(b).]

If the expedited determination or expedited redetermination for benefits by the plan is reversed in whole or in part by the IRE or at a higher level of appeal, the plan must authorize or provide the benefit under dispute as expeditiously as the enrollee's health condition requires, but no later than 24 hours from the date it receives notice reversing the determination. [42 C.F.R. § 423.638(b).]

In all cases, when a plan's determination is reversed in whole or in part by the IRE or at any higher level of appeal, the plan must inform the IRE that it has effectuated the decision. [42 C.F.R. §§ 423.636(b), 423.638(b).]

[¶ 516] Reopenings, ALJ Hearings, Medicare Appeals Council Review, and Judicial Review

The regulations at 42 C.F.R. Part 423 Subpart U set forth the regulatory requirements for: (1) Part D sponsors, the Part D independent review entity (IRE), administrative law judges (ALJs), and the Medicare Appeals Council with respect to reopenings; (2) ALJs with respect to hearings; (3) the Medicare Appeals Council with respect to review of Part D appeals; and (4) Part D enrollees' rights with respect to reopenings, ALJ hearings, Medicare Appeals Council reviews, and judicial review by a federal district court. [42 C.F.R. § 423.1968.] The requirements for Part D plan sponsors with respect to grievances, coverage determinations, redeterminations, and reconsiderations are covered in ¶ 515.

Reopenings

A reopening is a remedy designed to change a binding determination or decision, even though the determination or decision may have been correct at the time it was made. A reopening may be taken by:

(1) a Part D plan sponsor to revise the coverage determination or redetermination;

(2) an IRE to revise the reconsideration;

(3) an ALJ to revise the hearing decision; or

(4) the Medicare Appeals Council to revise the hearing or review decision.

[42 C.F.R. §§ 423.1978(a), 423.1980(a).]

When an enrollee has filed a valid request for an appeal of a coverage determination, redetermination, reconsideration, hearing, or Medicare Appeals Council review, no adjudicator has jurisdiction to reopen an issue that is under appeal until all appeal rights for that issue are exhausted. The Part D plan sponsor's, IRE's, ALJ's, or Medicare Appeals Council's decision on whether to reopen is binding and not subject to appeal. [42 C.F.R. §§ 423.1978(d), 423.1980(a)(2).]

Reopening coverage determinations and redeterminations. A Part D plan sponsor may reopen its coverage determination or redetermination on its own motion: (1) within one year from the date of the coverage determination or redetermination for any reason; (2) within four years from the date of the coverage determination or redetermination for good cause; or (3) at any time if there exists reliable evidence that the coverage determination was procured by fraud or similar fault. [42 C.F.R. § 423.1980(b).]

"Good cause" for reopening may be established when: (1) there is new and material evidence that was unavailable or unknown at the time of the determination or decision and may result in a different conclusion; or (2) the evidence that was considered clearly shows on its face that an obvious error was made. Generally, a change of legal interpretation or policy by CMS in a regulation, CMS ruling, or CMS general instruction, whether made in response to judicial precedent or otherwise, is not a basis for reopening a determination or hearing decision. [42 C.F.R. § 423.1986.]

An enrollee may request that a Part D plan sponsor reopen its coverage determination or redetermination: (1) within one year from the date of the coverage determination or redetermination for any reason; or (2) within four years from the date of the coverage determination or redetermination for good cause. [42 C.F.R. § 423.1980(c).]

IRE, ALJ, and Medicare Appeals Council reopening of reconsiderations, hearings, and reviews. Reopenings of IRE reconsiderations, ALJ hearing decisions, and Medicare Appeals Council reviews may be requested by an IRE, ALJ, or the Medicare Appeals Council on its own motion within 180 calendar days from the date of the reconsideration, decision, or review for good cause, but if the action was procured by fraud or similar fault, the reopening may be made at any time. [42 C.F.R. § 423.1980(d).]

Enrollee or sponsor request for reopening of reconsiderations, hearings, and reviews. A Part D plan sponsor or an enrollee who received an IRE reconsideration, ALJ hearing decision, or Medicare Appeals Council review may request a reopening within 180 calendar days from the date of its reconsideration, hearing decision, or review for good cause. [42 C.F.R. § 423.1980(e).]

Notice requirement. Regardless of whether a reopening is initiated by an adjudicator, an enrollee, or the Part D plan sponsor, when any determination or decision is reopened and revised, the Part D plan sponsor, IRE, ALJ, or Medicare Appeals Council must mail its revised determination or decision to the enrollee at his or her last known address, and the IRE, ALJ, or Medicare Appeals Council must mail its revised determination or decision to the Part D plan sponsor. An adverse revised determination or decision must state the rationale and basis for the reopening and revision and any right to appeal. [42 C.F.R. § 423.1982.]

Effect of revised determination or decision. A revised determination or decision is binding unless it is appealed or otherwise reopened. [42 C.F.R. § 423.1978(c).] The methods of appeal are as follows:

- **Coverage determinations.** The revision of a coverage determination is binding unless an enrollee submits a request for a redetermination that is accepted and processed.

- **Redeterminations.** The revision of a redetermination is binding unless an enrollee submits a request for an IRE reconsideration that is accepted and processed.

- **Reconsiderations.** The revision of a reconsideration is binding unless an enrollee submits a request for an ALJ hearing that is accepted and processed.

- **ALJ hearing decisions.** The revision of an ALJ hearing decision is binding unless an enrollee submits a request for a Medicare Appeals Council review that is accepted and processed.

- **Medicare Appeals Council review.** The revision of a Medicare Appeals Council determination or decision is binding unless an enrollee files a civil action in a federal district court that accepts jurisdiction and issues a decision.

[42 C.F.R. § 423.1984.]

Administrative Law Judge Hearings

If the amount remaining in controversy after the IRE reconsideration meets the threshold requirement established annually by the HHS Secretary, an enrollee who is dissatisfied with the IRE reconsideration determination has a right to a hearing before an ALJ. The threshold amount for 2016, which is $150, is the same as it was for 2015. If the basis for the appeal is the refusal by the Part D plan sponsor to provide drug benefits, CMS uses the projected value of those benefits to compute the amount remaining in controversy. The projected value of a drug must include any costs the enrollee could incur based on the number of refills prescribed for the drug in dispute during the plan year. [42 C.F.R. § 423.1970(a), (b); *Notice*, 80 FR 57827, Sept. 25, 2015.]

Two or more appeals may be aggregated by a single enrollee or multiple enrollees to meet the amount in controversy for an ALJ hearing if: (1) the appeals have previously been reconsidered by an IRE; (2) the request for ALJ hearing lists all of the appeals to be aggregated and each aggregated appeal meets the specified filing requirement; and (3) the ALJ determines that the appeals the enrollee seeks to aggregate involve the delivery of prescription drugs to a single enrollee or, in the case of multiple enrollees, the ALJ determines that the appeals the enrollees seek to aggregate involve the same prescription drug. [42 C.F.R. § 423.1970(c).]

Filing a request for an ALJ hearing. The enrollee must file a written request for an ALJ hearing with the entity specified in the IRE's reconsideration notice within 60 calendar days of the date of the notice of an IRE reconsideration determination. If a request for a hearing clearly shows that the amount in controversy is less than that required, the ALJ must dismiss the request. If, after the hearing starts, the ALJ finds that the amount in controversy is less than the amount required, the ALJ must discontinue the hearing and must not rule on the substantive issues raised in the appeal. [42 C.F.R. § 423.1972.]

Expedited hearing request. An enrollee also may request that the hearing before an ALJ be expedited. An expedited hearing must involve an issue specified in 42 C.F.R. § 423.566(b), but must not include solely a request for payment of Part D drugs already furnished. The enrollee must submit a written or oral request for an expedited ALJ hearing within 60 calendar days of the date of the written notice of an IRE reconsideration determination. The request for an expedited ALJ hearing should also explain why the standard time frame may seriously jeopardize the life or health of the enrollee. [42 C.F.R. § 423.2002(b).]

Review of IRE dismissal. An enrollee has a right to have an IRE's dismissal of a request for reconsideration reviewed by an ALJ if the enrollee files a request within 60 calendar days after receipt of the written notice of the IRE's dismissal and meets the amount-in-controversy requirements. If the ALJ determines that the IRE's dismissal was in error, he or she must vacate the dismissal and remand the case to the IRE for reconsideration. An ALJ's decision regarding an IRE's dismissal of a reconsideration request is binding and not subject to further review. The dismissal of a request for ALJ review of an IRE's dismissal of a reconsideration request is also binding and not subject to further review, unless vacated by the Medicare Appeals Council. [42 C.F.R. § 423.2004.]

Time frames for ALJ decision. When a request for an ALJ hearing is filed after an IRE has issued a written reconsideration, the ALJ must issue a decision, dismissal order, or remand, as appropriate, no later than the end of the 90-calendar-day period beginning on the date the request for hearing is received by the entity specified in the IRE's notice of reconsideration, unless the 90-calendar-day period has been extended. The ALJ must provide an expedited hearing decision if the appeal involves an issue specified in 42 C.F.R. § 423.566(b), but not solely a request for payment of Part D drugs already furnished, and the enrollee's prescribing physician or other prescriber indicates, or the ALJ determines, that applying the standard time frame for making a decision may seriously jeopardize the enrollee's life, health, or ability to regain maximum function. [42 C.F.R. § 423.2016.]

Submission of evidence. An enrollee may submit any written evidence that he or she wishes to have considered at the ALJ hearing. An ALJ must not consider any evidence submitted regarding a change in condition of an enrollee after the appealed coverage determination was made. An ALJ will remand a case to the IRE when an enrollee wishes evidence on his or her change in condition after the coverage determination to be considered. A represented enrollee must submit all written evidence he or she wishes to have considered at the hearing with the request for hearing or within 10 calendar days of receiving the notice of hearing. For an expedited ALJ hearing, an enrollee must submit all written evidence with the request for hearing or within two calendar days of receiving the notice of hearing. [42 C.F.R. § 423.2018.]

Hearing notice. The ALJ must send a notice of hearing to the enrollee, the Part D plan sponsor that issued the coverage determination, and the IRE that issued the reconsideration, advising them of the proposed time and place of the hearing. The notice of the hearing must be mailed or otherwise transmitted to the enrollee and other potential participants at their last known addresses or given by personal service. The ALJ must mail or serve the notice at least 20 calendar days before the hearing, except for expedited hearings, when written notice is mailed or served at least three calendar days before the hearing. [42 C.F.R. § 423.2022.]

Permissible issues. The issues before the ALJ include all the issues brought out in the coverage determination, redetermination, or reconsideration that were not decided entirely in an enrollee's favor. If evidence presented before the hearing causes the ALJ to question a favorable portion of the determination, he or she may consider a new issue at the hearing as long at the enrollee was notified before the hearing. The ALJ, however, may consider a new issue, whether raised by the ALJ or the enrollee, only if its resolution: (1) could have a material impact on the issues that are the subject of the hearing; and (2) is permissible under the rules governing reopening of determinations and decisions. An ALJ may not add any issue to a pending appeal unless it has been adjudicated at the lower appeals levels and the enrollee is notified of the new issues before the start of the hearing. [42 C.F.R. § 423.2032.]

Hearing process. An enrollee has the right to appear at the hearing before the ALJ to present evidence and state his or her position by video-teleconferencing or telephone or in person. An enrollee may waive his or her right to appear by sending the ALJ a written statement indicating that he or she does not wish to appear at the hearing. An enrollee (or an enrollee's appointed representative) may appear before the ALJ to state the enrollee's case, present a written summary of the case, or enter written statements about the facts and law material to the case in the record. The ALJ may receive evidence at the hearing even though the evidence is not admissible in court under the rules of evidence used by the court. The ALJ, however, may not consider evidence on any change in condition of an enrollee after a coverage determination. [42 C.F.R. § § 423.2000, 423.2036.]

ALJ subpoenas. An ALJ may, on his or her own initiative, issue subpoenas for the appearance and testimony of witnesses and for the enrollee or the Part D plan sponsor to make books, records, correspondence, papers, or other documents that are material to an issue at the hearing available for inspection and copying. An ALJ may not issue a subpoena to CMS or the IRE to compel an appearance, testimony, or the production of evidence, or to the Part D plan sponsor to compel an appearance or testimony. To the extent that a subpoena compels disclosure of a matter for which an objection based on privilege, or other protection from disclosure such as case preparation, confidentiality, or undue burden, was made before an ALJ, the Medicare Appeals Council may review immediately the ruling of the ALJ on the objections to the subpoena or that portion of the subpoena, as applicable. [42 C.F.R. § 423.2036(f).]

Notice and effect of ALJ decisions. Unless the ALJ dismisses the hearing, the ALJ must issue a written decision that gives the findings of fact, conclusions of law, and the reasons for the decision. For expedited hearings, the ALJ must issue a written decision within 10 calendar days of the hearing. For nonexpedited hearings, the ALJ must issue a decision no later than the end of the 90-calendar-day period beginning on the date the request for hearing is received by the entity specified in the IRE's reconsideration, unless the 90-calendar-day period is extended. [42 C.F.R. § 423.2046.]

The decision of the ALJ is binding unless:

(1) an enrollee requests a review of the decision by the Medicare Appeals Council within the stated time period or the Medicare Appeals Council reviews the ALJ decision and issues a final decision or remand order;

(2) the decision is reopened and revised by an ALJ or the Medicare Appeals Council;

(3) the expedited access to judicial review process is used;

(4) the ALJ's decision is a recommended decision directed to the Medicare Appeals Council and the Medicare Appeals Council issues a decision; or

(5) in a case remanded by a federal district court, the Medicare Appeals Council assumes jurisdiction and issues a decision.

[42 C.F.R. § 423.2048.]

Removal by the Medicare Appeals Council. If a request for hearing is pending before an ALJ, the Medicare Appeals Council may assume responsibility for the hearing by requesting that the ALJ forward the hearing request. If the Medicare Appeals Council holds a hearing, however, it must conduct the hearing according to the rules for ALJ hearings. [42 C.F.R. § 423.2050.]

Medicare Appeals Council Reviews

An enrollee who is dissatisfied with an ALJ hearing decision or dismissal may request Medicare Appeals Council review. The Medicare Appeals Council's review of an ALJ's written decision is a new review (conducted as though no review has yet taken place). After review, the Medicare Appeals Council must issue a final decision or dismissal order or remand the case. One of these actions must be issued no later than the end of the 90-calendar-day period beginning on the date the request for review is received by the entity specified in the ALJ's written notice of decision, unless the 90-calendar-day time frame is extended or the enrollee requests expedited Medicare Appeals Council review. If an enrollee requests expedited Medicare Appeals Council review, the Medicare Appeals Council must issue a final decision, dismissal order, or remand as expeditiously as the enrollee's health condition requires, but no later than the end of the 10-calendar-day period beginning on the date the request for review is received by the entity specified in the ALJ's written notice of decision, unless the 10-calendar-day period is extended. [42 C.F.R. §§ 423.1974, 423.2100.]

Filing the Medicare Appeals Council review request. An enrollee requests a Medicare Appeals Council review by submitting a written request for review within 60 calendar days after receipt of the ALJ's written decision or dismissal to the entity specified in the notice of the ALJ's action. An enrollee may request that Medicare Appeals Council review be expedited if the appeal involves an issue specified in 42 C.F.R. § 423.566(b) but does not include solely a request for payment of Part D drugs already furnished. If an enrollee is requesting that the Medicare Appeals Council review be expedited, the enrollee must submit an oral or written request within 60 calendar days after the receipt of the ALJ's written decision or dismissal. [42 C.F.R. §§ 423.2102, 423.2106.]

Reviews on Medicare Appeals Council's own motion. The Medicare Appeals Council may decide on its own motion to review a decision or dismissal issued by an ALJ. CMS or the IRE may refer a case to the Medicare Appeals Council to consider reviewing on its own motion any time within 60 calendar days after the ALJ's written decision or dismissal is issued if the decision or dismissal contains an error of law material to the outcome of the claim or presents a broad policy or procedural issue that may affect the public interest. CMS or the IRE also may request that the Medicare Appeals Council take own-motion review of a case if: (1) CMS or the IRE participated or requested to participate in the appeal at the ALJ level, and (2) the ALJ's decision or dismissal is not supported by the preponderance of evidence in the record or the ALJ abused his or her discretion. [42 C.F.R. § 423.2110.]

Dismissing review requests. The Medicare Appeals Council must dismiss a request for review if the enrollee did not file the request within the stated period of time and the time for filing has not been extended. The Medicare Appeals Council also must dismiss the request for review if: (1) the enrollee asks to withdraw the request for review; (2) the individual or entity does not have a right to request review; or (3) the enrollee dies while the request for review is pending and the enrollee's estate or representative either has no remaining financial interest in the case or does not want to continue the appeal. [42 C.F.R. § 423.2114.]

Briefs and evidence. Upon request, the Medicare Appeals Council must give the enrollee a reasonable opportunity to file a brief or other written statement. The Medicare Appeals Council also may request, but not require, CMS, the IRE, and/or the Part D plan sponsor to file a brief if it determines that it is necessary. [42 C.F.R. § 423.2120.] When the Medicare Appeals Council reviews an ALJ decision, it must consider the evidence contained in the record of the proceedings before the ALJ and any new evidence that relates to the period before the coverage determination. If the hearing decision decides a new issue that the enrollee was not afforded an opportunity to address at the ALJ level, the Medicare Appeals Council must consider any evidence related to that new issue. The Medicare Appeals Council must not consider any new evidence submitted regarding a change in condition of an enrollee after a coverage determination is made. [42 C.F.R. § 423.2122(a).]

Oral argument. An enrollee may request oral argument or the Medicare Appeals Council may decide on its own that oral argument is necessary to decide the case. The Medicare Appeals Council will grant oral argument if it decides that the case raises an important question of law, policy, or fact that cannot be decided based on written submissions alone. If it decides on its own to hear oral argument, it must inform the enrollee of the time and place of the oral argument at least 10 calendar days before the scheduled date or, in the case of an expedited review, at least two calendar days before the scheduled date. [42 C.F.R. § 423.2124.]

Medicare Appeals Council remand. The Medicare Appeals Council may remand a case when additional evidence is needed or additional action by the ALJ is required. The Medicare Appeals Council will designate in its remand order whether the ALJ will issue a decision or a recommended decision on remand. The case must be remanded to the appropriate Part D IRE if it determines that the enrollee wishes evidence on his or her change in condition after the coverage determination to be considered in the appeal. [42 C.F.R. § 423.2126.]

Final Medicare Appeals Council action. After it has reviewed the evidence in the administrative record and any additional evidence, the Medicare Appeals Council must make a decision or remand the case to an ALJ. The Medicare Appeals Council has the authority to adopt, modify, or reverse the ALJ hearing decision or recommended decision. A copy of the decision is mailed to the enrollee at his or her last known address, CMS, the IRE, and the Part D plan sponsor. The decision of the Medicare Appeals Council is final and binding unless a federal district court modifies it or it is revised as the result of a reopening. [42 C.F.R. §§ 423.2128, 423.2130.]

Judicial Review

An enrollee may obtain court review of a Medicare Appeals Council decision if the amount in controversy meets the threshold requirement estimated annually by the HHS Secretary. The enrollee may request judicial review of an ALJ's decision if the Medicare Appeals Council denied the enrollee's request for review and the amount in controversy meets the threshold requirements. The threshold amount for filing for judicial review on or after January 1, 2016, is $1,500, up from $1,460 in 2015. [*Notice*, 80 FR 57827, Sept. 25, 2015.] A civil action for judicial review must be filed in the District Court of the United States for the judicial district in which the enrollee resides. If the enrollee does not reside within any judicial district, the civil action must be filed in the District Court of the United States for the District of Columbia. [42 C.F.R. §§ 423.1976, 423.2136(a), (b).]

In any civil action for judicial review, the proper party defendant is the Secretary of HHS, in his or her official capacity. Upon judicial review, the findings of the Secretary as to any fact, if supported by substantial evidence, are to be considered conclusive by the federal district court. [42 C.F.R. § 423.2136(d), (e).]

Filing requirements. Any civil action for judicial review must be filed with the appropriate federal district court within 60 calendar days after the date the enrollee receives written notice of the Medicare Appeals Council's decision. The date of receipt of the notice of the Medicare Appeals Council's decision is presumed to be five calendar days after the date of the notice, unless there is a reasonable showing to the contrary. Likewise, if a case is certified for judicial review in accordance with the expedited access to judicial review process, the civil action must be filed within 60 calendar days after receipt of the review entity's certification, unless the time for filing is extended by the ALJ or Medicare Appeals Council upon a showing of good cause. [42 C.F.R. § 423.2136(c).]

Remand of the case by the court. When a federal district court remands a case to the HHS Secretary for further consideration, the Medicare Appeals Council may (1) make a decision, or (2) remand the case to an ALJ with instructions to take action and either issue a decision, take other action, or return the case to the Medicare Appeals Council with a recommended decision. [42 C.F.R. § 423.2138.] When a federal district court remands a case for further consideration and the Medicare Appeals Council further remands the case to an ALJ, a decision subsequently issued by the ALJ becomes the final decision of the Secretary unless the Medicare Appeals Council assumes jurisdiction. [42 C.F.R. § 423.2140(a).]

Written exceptions to ALJ remand decision. If an enrollee disagrees with an ALJ decision (after remand of the case from the district court and further remand from the Medicare Appeals Council), he or she may file exceptions to the decision with the Medicare Appeals Council. The enrollee must submit a written statement setting forth the reasons for disagreeing with the ALJ decision within 30 calendar days of receiving the decision (and the Medicare Appeals Council will grant a timely request for a 30-day extension). [42 C.F.R. § 423.2140(b).]

If the Medicare Appeals Council concludes that there is no reason to change the ALJ's decision, it must issue a notice addressing the exceptions and explaining why no change is necessary. When this occurs, the decision of the ALJ is considered a final decision of the HHS Secretary. When an enrollee files written exceptions to the decision of the ALJ, the Medicare Appeals Council may decide to assume jurisdiction. If it assumes jurisdiction, it makes a new, independent decision based on its consideration of the entire record adopting, modifying, or reversing the decision of the ALJ or remanding the case to an ALJ for further proceedings, including a new decision. This new decision of the Medicare Appeals Council is the final decision of the Secretary. [42 C.F.R. § 423.2140(b).]

Medicare Appeals Council jurisdiction without written exceptions. Any time within 60 calendar days after the date of the written decision of the ALJ, the Medicare Appeals Council may decide to assume jurisdiction of the case even though no written exceptions have been filed by the enrollee. After giving notice to the enrollee and providing the opportunity to file a brief regarding the relevant facts and law in the case (usually 30 calendar days), the Medicare Appeals Council will either issue a final decision of the HHS Secretary affirming, modifying, or reversing the decision of the ALJ, or remand the case to an ALJ for further proceedings, including a new decision. [42 C.F.R. § 423.2140(c).]

Expedited Access to Judicial Review

To obtain expedited access to judicial review (EAJR), a "review entity" must certify that the Medicare Appeals Council does not have the authority to decide the question of law or regulation relevant to the matters in dispute and there is no material issue of fact in dispute. For purposes of EAJR, a "review entity" is defined as an entity of up to three reviewers who are ALJs or members of the Departmental Appeals Board. [42 C.F.R. § 423.1990(a).]

An enrollee may request EAJR in place of an ALJ hearing or Medicare Appeals Council review if:

     (1) an IRE has made a reconsideration determination and the enrollee has filed a request for an ALJ hearing and a final decision, dismissal order, or remand order of the ALJ has not been issued; or an ALJ has made a decision and the enrollee has filed a

request for Medicare Appeals Council review and a final decision, dismissal order, or remand order of the Medicare Appeals Council has not been issued;

    (2) the requestor is an enrollee;

    (3) the amount remaining in controversy meets the threshold requirements;

    (4) when there is more than one enrollee to the ALJ hearing or Medicare Appeals Council review, each enrollee concurs, in writing, with the request for the EAJR; and

    (5) there are no material issues of fact in dispute.

[42 C.F.R. § 423.1990(b).]

Method of filing. An enrollee may include an EAJR request in his or her request for an ALJ hearing or Medicare Appeals Council review or, if an appeal is already pending, the enrollee may file a written EAJR request with the ALJ hearing office or Medicare Appeals Council where the appeal is being considered. The ALJ hearing office or Medicare Appeals Council must forward the EAJR request to the review entity within five calendar days of receipt. The enrollee must file a request for EAJR: (1) any time before receipt of the notice of the ALJ's decision, if the enrollee has requested an ALJ hearing; or (2) any time before receipt of notice of the Medicare Appeals Council's decision, if the enrollee has requested Medicare Appeals Council review. [42 C.F.R. § 423.1990(d).]

Review entity's action on EAJR request. Within 60 calendar days after the date the review entity receives a EAJR request and the accompanying documents and materials, the review entity will issue either a certification or a denial of the request. The certification or denial by the review entity is binding and not subject to review by the HHS Secretary. If the review entity fails to certify or deny the EAJR request within the 60-calendar-day time frame, the enrollee may bring a civil action in federal district court within 60 calendar days. [42 C.F.R. § 423.1990(e).]

If the review entity certifies the EAJR request, the enrollee automatically waives any right to completion of the remaining steps in the administrative appeals process and has 60 calendar days, beginning on the date of the certification, to bring a civil action in federal district court. If a request for EAJR does not meet the conditions set forth above or if the review entity does not certify the request, the review entity must advise the enrollee in writing that the request has been denied and return the request to the ALJ hearing office or the Medicare Appeals Council. The ALJ or Medicare Appeals Council will treat the rejection as a request for an ALJ hearing or for Medicare Appeals Council review. [42 C.F.R. § 423.1990(g), (h).]

[¶ 525] Cost Control and Quality Improvement Requirements

Part D sponsors must implement certain cost control and quality improvement requirements, includitng the establishment ofa drug utilization management program, quality assurance measures and systems, and a medication therapy management program (MTMP). Part 423 Subpart D of the Medicare Part D regulations and chapter 7 of the *Medicare Prescription Drug Benefits Manual*, Pub. 100-18, implement these administrative provisions.

Drug Utilization Management, QA, and MTMPs

Each Part D sponsor must establish a drug utilization management program, QA measures and systems, and an MTMP. Each of these requirements affects the quality and cost of care provided to beneficiaries. [Soc. Sec. Act § 1860D-4(c); 42 C.F.R. § 423.153(a).] The drug utilization management and MTMP requirements, however, do not apply to private fee-for-service Medicare Advantage plans offering qualified prescription drug coverage. [Soc. Sec. Act § 1860D-21(d)(3); 42 C.F.R. § 423.153(e).]

Drug utilization management program. The Part D regulations provide minimum requirements and give considerable flexibility to sponsors in the design of their drug utilization management programs. The minimum requirements are that a plan must:

(1) maintain a program that includes incentives to reduce costs where medically appropriate;

(2) maintain policies and systems to assist in preventing over-utilization and under-utilization of prescribed medications;

(3) provide CMS with information concerning the procedures and performance of its drug utilization management program, according to guidelines specified by CMS; and

(4) establish a daily cost-sharing rate for drugs dispensed for a supply less than the approved month's supply, if the drug is in the form of a solid oral dose (except for solid oral doses of antibiotics and solid oral doses that are dispensed in their original container) and may be dispensed for less than the approved month's supply under applicable law; the co-payment is calculated by multiplying the applicable daily cost-sharing rate by the days' supply actually dispensed.

[42 C.F.R. § 423.153(b).]

Quality assurance measures and systems. A Part D sponsor must have established QA measures and systems to reduce medication errors and adverse drug interactions and improve medication use. The QA measures and systems must include:

(1) representation that network providers are required to comply with minimum standards for pharmacy practice as established by the states;

(2) concurrent drug utilization review systems, policies, and procedures designed to ensure that a review of the prescribed drug therapy is performed before each prescription is dispensed (the review must include, but not be limited to: screening for potential drug therapy problems due to therapeutic duplication; age/gender-related contraindications; over-utilization and under-utilization; drug-drug interactions; incorrect drug dosage or duration of drug therapy; drug-allergy contraindications; and clinical abuse/misuse);

(3) retrospective drug utilization review systems, policies, and procedures designed to ensure ongoing periodic examination of claims data and other records, through computerized drug claims processing and information retrieval systems, to identify patterns of inappropriate or medically unnecessary care among enrollees or patterns associated with specific drugs;

(4) internal medication error identification and reduction systems; and

(5) provision of information to CMS regarding quality assurance measures and systems.

[42 C.F.R. § 423.153(c).]

Medication therapy management programs. A Part D sponsor must establish a MTMP that is designed to:

(1) optimize therapeutic outcomes for targeted beneficiaries (described below) by improving medication use,

(2) reduce adverse drug events (including adverse drug interactions) for targeted beneficiaries,

(3) be furnished by a pharmacist or other qualified provider,

(4) distinguish between services in ambulatory and institutional settings,

(5) target beneficiaries using an opt-out method of enrollment only,

(6) target enrollees for enrollment in the MTMP at least quarterly, and

(7) offer a minimum level of MTMP services to each beneficiary.

[Soc. Sec. Act § 1860D-4(c); 42 C.F.R. § 423.153(d)(1); Pub. 100-18, Ch. 7, § 30.1.]

The minimum level of MTMP services include:

(1) interventions for both beneficiaries and prescribers;

(2) annual comprehensive medication review with written summaries, which must include an interactive, person-to-person, or telehealth consultation performed by a pharmacist or other qualified provider (unless the beneficiary is in a long-term care setting) and may result in a recommended medication action plan;

(3) quarterly targeted medication reviews with follow-up interventions when necessary; and

(4) standardized action plans and summaries that comply with requirements for the standardized format.

[Soc. Sec. Act § 1860D-4(c)(2)(C); 42 C.F.R. § 423.153(d)(1)(vii).]

Targeted beneficiaries. Targeted beneficiaries for the MTMP are enrollees in the sponsor's Part D plan who:

(1) have multiple chronic diseases, with three chronic diseases being the maximum number a Part D plan sponsor may require (sponsors must target at least four of the following seven core chronic conditions: hypertension; heart failure; diabetes; dyslipidemia; respiratory disease such as asthma, chronic obstructive pulmonary disease, or chronic lung disorders; bone disease-arthritis such as osteoporosis, osteoarthritis, or rheumatoid arthritis; and mental health such as depression, schizophrenia, bipolar disorder, or chronic and disabling disorders);

(2) are taking multiple Part D drugs, with eight Part D drugs being the maximum number of drugs a plan sponsor may require; and

(3) are likely to incur annual Part D drug costs in an amount greater than or equal to $3000 increased by the annual percentage specified in 42 C.F.R. 423.104(d)(5)(iv).

[Soc. Sec. Act § 1860D-4(c)(2)(A)(ii); 42 C.F.R. § 423.153(d)(2); Pub. 100-18, Ch. 7, § 30.2.]

Cooperation with pharmacists and physicians. The MTMP must be developed in cooperation with licensed and practicing pharmacists and physicians and coordinated with any care management plan established for a targeted individual under a chronic care improvement program (CCIP). A sponsor must provide drug claims data to CCIPs for those beneficiaries who are enrolled in CCIPs. [Soc. Sec. Act § 1860D-4(c)(2)(E), (F); 42 C.F.R. § 423.153(d)(3), (4); Pub. 100-18, Ch. 7, § 30.4.]

To become a Part D sponsor, an applicant must describe how it takes into account the resources used and time required to implement the MTMP it chooses to adopt in establishing fees for pharmacists or others providing MTMP services, and disclose to CMS upon request the amount of the management and dispensing fees and the portion paid for MTMP services to pharmacists. Reports of these amounts are protected. [Soc. Sec. Act § 1860D-4(c)(2)(G); 42 C.F.R. § 423.153(d)(5).]

Dispensing Drugs in Long-Term Care Facilities

Generally, when dispensing covered Part D drugs to enrollees who reside in long-term care (LTC) facilities, a Part D sponsor must:

(1) require all pharmacies servicing LTC facilities to dispense solid oral doses of brand-name drugs in no greater than 14-day increments at a time and permit the use of uniform dispensing techniques as defined by the LTC facilities in which the enrollees reside;

(2) not penalize LTCs' choice of more efficient uniform dispensing techniques by prorating dispensing fees based on days' supply or quantity dispensed;

(3) ensure that any difference in payment methodology among LTC pharmacies incentivizes more efficient dispensing techniques; and

(4) collect and report information on the dispensing methodology used for each dispensing event described in (1).

[Soc. Sec. Act § 1860D-4(c)(3); 42 C.F.R. § 423.154(a).]

Excluded from the above LTC dispensing requirements are: (1) solid oral doses of antibiotics; and (2) solid oral doses that are dispensed in their original container as indicated in the Food and Drug Administration Prescribing Information or are customarily dispensed in their original packaging to assist patients with compliance (for example, oral contraceptives). [42 C.F.R. § 423.154(b).]

CMS waives these dispensing requirements, except for (2) and (3), for pharmacies when they service intermediate care facilities for the mentally retarded, institutes for mental disease, and Indian Tribe and Tribal Organization, and Urban Indian Organization (I/T/U) pharmacies. [42 C.F.R. § 423.154(c).]

The terms and conditions offered by a Part D sponsor must be in accordance with federal and state law and address the disposal of drugs that have been dispensed to an enrollee in a LTC facility, but not used, and that have been returned to the pharmacy. The terms for return for credit and reuse must also be permitted under state law. [42 C.F.R. § 423.154(d).]

Customer Satisfaction Surveys

Part D plans with 600 or more enrollees as of July of the prior year must contract with approved Medicare Consumer Assessment of Healthcare Providers and Systems (CAHPS) survey vendors to conduct the Medicare CAHPS satisfaction survey of Part D plan enrollees in accordance with CMS specifications and submit the survey data to CMS. [Soc. Sec. Act § 1860D-4(d); 42 C.F.R. § 423.156.]

Electronic Prescription Drug Program

Prescribers and dispensers who electronically transmit prescription and certain other information for covered drugs prescribed for Medicare Part D eligible beneficiaries are required to comply with any electronic prescription standards that are in effect. [Soc. Sec. Act § 1860D-4(e); 42 C.F.R. § 423.159(c).]

Promotion of electronic prescribing. A Medicare Advantage (MA) organization offering an MA prescription drug plan (MA-PD) may provide for a separate or differential payment to a participating physician who prescribes covered Part D drugs in accordance with electronic prescription standards. These electronic standards may include initial standards and any final standards established by CMS. Any separate or differential payments must be in compliance with applicable federal and state laws related to fraud and abuse, including the physician self-referral prohibition and the federal anti-kickback statute. [42 C.F.R. § 423.159(d).]

Part D sponsors, prescribers, and dispensers must maintain a regulatory-compliant electronic prescription drug program when transmitting, directly or through an intermediary, prescriptions and prescription-related information using electronic media for covered Part D drugs for Part D eligible individuals. The electronic prescription drug program standards supersede any state law or regulation that is contrary to the standards or restricts the ability to carry out Part D and that pertains to the electronic transmission of medication history and of information on eligibility, benefits, and prescriptions with respect to covered Part D drugs under Part D. [42 C.F.R. § 423.160(a); Pub. 100-18, Ch. 7, §§ 50.1, 50.2.]

Quality Improvement Activities

QIOs must offer providers, practitioners, and Part D sponsors quality improvement assistance pertaining to health care services, including those related to prescription drug therapy. To accomplish this requirement, QIOs need access to data from transactions between pharmacies and Part D plans. Any such information collected by the QIOs is subject to CMS confidentiality requirements. Part D sponsors are required to provide information directly to QIOs and to CMS for distribution to QIOs. [42 C.F.R. § 423.162; Pub. 100-18, Ch. 7, § 20.8.]

Compliance Based on Accreditation

A Part D sponsor can be deemed to meet certain requirements if: (1) it is fully accredited (and periodically reaccredited) for the standards related to the applicable area by a private, national accreditation organization (AO) approved by CMS; and (2) the AO uses the standards approved by CMS for the purposes of assessing the Part D sponsor's compliance with Medicare requirements. [Soc. Sec. Act § 1860D-4(j); 42 C.F.R. § 423.165(a).]

The requirements related to the following areas are deemable:

    (1) access to covered drugs (42 C.F.R. §§ 423.120 and 423.124);

    (2) drug utilization management programs, quality assurance measures and systems, and MTMPs (42 C.F.R. §§ 423.120 and 423.124); and

    (3) privacy, confidentiality, and accuracy of enrollee records (42 C.F.R. § 423.136).

[Soc. Sec. Act § 1860D-4(j); 42 C.F.R. § 423.165(b).]

Deemed Part D sponsor obligations. A Part D sponsor that is deemed to meet Medicare requirements must submit to CMS surveys, which are intended to validate AO processes. CMS will remove part or all of a Part D sponsor's deemed status if: (1) CMS determines, on the basis of its own investigation, that the sponsor does not meet the Medicare requirements for which deemed status was granted; (2) CMS withdraws its approval of the AO that accredited the sponsor; or (3) the sponsor fails to meet the above requirements of a deemed Part D sponsor. [42 C.F.R. § 423.165(d), (e).]

Enforcement authority. CMS retains the authority to initiate enforcement action against any Part D sponsor that it determines, on the basis of a CMS survey or the results of the accreditation survey, no longer meets the Medicare requirements for which deemed status was granted. [42 C.F.R. § 423.165(f).]

Accreditation organizations. An AO may be approved by CMS for a given standard if the organization, in accrediting Part D sponsors and Part D plans, applies and enforces standards that are at least as stringent as Medicare requirements. Secondly, the AO must comply with CMS application and reapplication procedures. Finally, the AO must also ensure that: (1) any individual associated with it, or associated with an entity it accredits, does not influence the accreditation decision concerning that entity; (2) the majority of its governing body is not composed of managed care organizations, Part D sponsors, or their representatives; and (3) its governing body has a broad and balanced representation of interests and acts without bias. [42 C.F.R. §§ 423.168(a), 423.171.]

[¶ 530] Payments to Sponsors of Retiree Prescription Drug Plans

The sponsors of qualified retiree prescription drug plans (PDPs) can receive an annual subsidy equal to 28 percent of specified retiree drug costs for each qualifying covered retiree. [Soc. Sec. Act § 1860D-22(a)(3); 42 C.F.R. § 423.886.]

Requirements for Qualified Retiree Prescription Drug Plans

Employment-based retiree health coverage is considered to be a qualified retiree PDP if all of the following requirements are satisfied:

(1) an actuarial attestation is submitted;

(2) Part D eligible individuals covered under the plan are provided with creditable coverage notices; and

(3) records are maintained and made available for audit.

[Soc. Sec. Act § 1860D-22(a)(2); 42 C.F.R. § 423.884(a).]

Disclosure of information. The sponsor must have a written agreement with its health insurance issuer or group health plan regarding disclosure of information to CMS, and the issuer or plan must disclose to CMS, on behalf of the sponsor, the information necessary for the sponsor to comply with CMS requirements. [42 C.F.R. § 423.884(b).]

Submitting an Application for Subsidy

The sponsor must submit an application for the subsidy to CMS along with the following information:

(1) employer tax ID number;

(2) sponsor name and address;

(3) contact name and e-mail address;

(4) actuarial attestation (see below) and any other supporting documentation required by CMS for each qualified retiree PDP for which the sponsor seeks subsidy payments;

(5) a list of all individuals the sponsor believes are qualifying covered retirees enrolled in each PDP, including spouses and dependents, if Medicare eligible, along with the listed individual's: (a) full name, (b) Health Insurance Claim (HIC) number or Social Security number, (c) date of birth, (d) gender, and (e) relationship to the retired employee (Note: a sponsor may satisfy this requirement by entering into a voluntary data sharing agreement with CMS);

(6) a signed sponsor agreement; and

(7) any other information specified by CMS.

[42 C.F.R. § 423.884(c)(1), (2).]

An authorized representative of the requesting sponsor must sign the completed application and certify that the information contained in the application is true and accurate. [42 C.F.R. § 423.884(c)(4).]

Terms and conditions for subsidy payment. To receive a subsidy payment, the sponsor must specifically accept and agree to:

(1) comply with the terms and conditions of eligibility for a subsidy payment;

(2) acknowledge that at the same time that CMS releases Part C and Part D summary payment data, it also will release Part D retiree drug subsidy payment data for

the most recently reconciled year, including the name of the eligible sponsor, the total gross aggregate dollar amount of the CMS subsidy, and the number of eligible retirees;

(3) acknowledge that the information in the application is being provided to obtain federal funds; and

(4) require that all subcontractors, including plan administrators, acknowledge that information provided in connection with the subcontract is used for purposes of obtaining federal funds.

[42 C.F.R. § 423.884(c)(3).]

Application timing and required updates. An application for a given plan year must be submitted before the beginning of the plan year, unless an extension has been filed and approved by CMS. The sponsor must provide updates of the application's information to CMS on a monthly basis or at a frequency specified by CMS. [42 C.F.R. § 423.884(c)(5), (6).]

CMS data match. Once the full application for the subsidy payment is submitted, CMS matches the names and identifying information of the individuals submitted as qualifying covered retirees with a CMS database to determine which retirees are Part D eligible individuals who are not enrolled in a Part D plan. CMS provides information concerning the results of the search (names and identifying information) to the sponsor. [42 C.F.R. § 423.884(c)(7).]

Actuarial Attestation Requirements

The sponsor of the plan must provide to CMS an attestation (in a form and manner specified by CMS) that the actuarial value of the retiree prescription drug coverage under the plan is at least equal to the actuarial value of the defined standard prescription drug coverage, not taking into account the value of any discount or coverage provided in the coverage gap. The attestation must include the following assurances:

(1) the actuarial gross value of the retiree prescription drug coverage under the plan for the plan year is at least equal to the actuarial gross value of the defined standard prescription drug coverage under Part D for the plan year in question, not taking into account the value of any discount or coverage provided in the coverage gap;

(2) the actuarial net value of the retiree prescription drug coverage under the plan for that plan year is at least equal to the actuarial net value of the defined standard prescription drug coverage under Part D for the plan year in question, not taking into account the value of any discount or coverage provided in the coverage gap; and

(3) the actuarial values must be determined using the methodology described below.

[42 C.F.R. § 423.884(d)(1).]

Actuarial requirements. The attestation must be made and signed by a qualified actuary (member of the American Academy of Actuaries) and must state that the attestation is true and accurate. Applicants may use qualified outside actuaries, including actuaries employed by the plan administrator or an insurer providing benefits under the plan. If an applicant uses an outside actuary, the attestation can be submitted directly by the outside actuary or by the plan sponsor. The attestation must contain an acknowledgment that the information being provided in the attestation is being used to obtain federal funds. [42 C.F.R. § 423.884(d)(2)–(4).]

Methodology. The attestation must be based on generally accepted actuarial principles and any actuarial guidelines established by CMS. To the extent CMS has not provided guidance on a specific aspect of the actuarial equivalence standard, an actuary providing the attestation may rely on any reasonable interpretation of the CMS regulations and Soc. Sec. Act § 1860D-22(a) consistent with generally accepted actuarial principles in determining actuarial values. [42 C.F.R. § 423.884(d)(5).]

Timing. The attestation must be provided annually at the time the sponsor's subsidy application is submitted. If there is a material change to the drug coverage of the sponsor's retiree prescription drug plan, the attestation must be provided no later than 90 days before the implementation of the change. The term "material change" means the addition of a benefit option that does not affect the actuarial value of the retiree prescription drug coverage under the sponsor's plan. [42 C.F.R. § 423.884(d)(6).]

Notice of a failure to continue to satisfy the actuarial equivalence standard. A sponsor must notify CMS no later than 90 days before the implementation of a change to the drug coverage that affects the actuarial value of the retiree prescription drug coverage under the sponsor's plan such that it no longer meets the actuarial equivalence standards. [42 C.F.R. § 423.884(d)(7).]

Retiree Drug Subsidy Amounts

For each qualifying covered retiree enrolled with the sponsor of a qualified retiree PDP in a plan year, the sponsor receives a subsidy payment in the amount of 28 percent of the allowable retiree costs in the plan year that are attributable to gross retiree costs that exceed the cost threshold and do not exceed the cost limit (see below). The subsidy payment is calculated by first determining gross retiree costs between the cost threshold and cost limit and then determining allowable retiree costs attributable to the gross retiree costs. [Soc. Sec. Act § 1860D-22(a)(3)(A); 42 C.F.R. § 423.886(a).]

Cost threshold and cost limit. The cost threshold and cost limit for qualified retiree prescription drug plans that end in years after 2006 are adjusted in the same manner as the annual Part D deductible and out-of-pocket threshold are adjusted annually. For 2016, the cost threshold is $360 and the cost limit is $7,400. [Soc. Sec. Act § 1860D-22(a)(3)(B); 42 C.F.R. § 423.886(b)(3); *Announcement of Calendar Year 2016 Medicare Advantage Capitation Rates and Medicare Advantage and Part D Payment Policies and Final Call Letter*, April 6, 2015.]

Payment Methods and Providing Necessary Information

The provisions governing payment to Part D plan sponsors for qualified prescription drug coverage, including requirements to provide information necessary to ensure accurate subsidy payments, also govern the subsidy payment to sponsors of retiree PDPs. Payment by CMS is conditioned on provision of accurate information. The information must be submitted in a form and manner and at the times provided by CMS. CMS will make payment after the submission of the cost data by the sponsor and in a time and manner specified by CMS. [42 C.F.R. § 423.888(a), (b)(3).]

Timing and submission of cost data. Payment can be made on a monthly, quarterly, or annual basis, as elected by the plan sponsor, unless CMS determines that the options must be restricted because of operational limitations. If the plan sponsor elects for payment on a monthly or quarterly basis, it must provide cost data on the same monthly or quarterly basis, or at such time as CMS specifies. If the sponsor elects an annual payment, it must submit to CMS actual rebate and other price concession data within 15 months after the end of the plan year. [42 C.F.R. § 423.888(b).]

Special rule for insured plans. Sponsors of group health plans that provide benefits through health insurance coverage and choose monthly payments, quarterly payments, or an interim annual payment may elect to determine gross covered plan-related retiree prescription drug costs for purposes of the monthly, quarterly, or interim annual payments based on a portion of the premium costs paid by the sponsor or the qualifying covered retirees. Premium costs that are determined using generally accepted actuarial principles may be attributable to the gross prescription drug costs incurred by the health insurance issuer for the sponsor's qualifying covered retirees, except that administrative costs and risk charges must be subtracted from the premium. [42 C.F.R. § 423.888(b)(5)(i).]

Maintaining records. The sponsor of the qualified retiree PDP or a designee must maintain for a period of six years and furnish to CMS or the Office of Inspector General, upon request, the following records:

(1) reports and working documents of the actuaries who wrote the attestation;

(2) all documentation of costs incurred and other relevant information utilized for calculating the amount of the subsidy payment, including the underlying claims data; and

(3) any other records specified by CMS.

[42 C.F.R. § 423.888(d).]

Appeals

A sponsor is entitled to an informal written reconsideration of an adverse initial determination by CMS. An initial determination is a determination regarding the amount of the subsidy payment; the actuarial equivalence of the sponsor's retiree PDP; whether an enrollee in a retiree PDP is a qualifying covered retiree; or any other similar determination affecting eligibility for, or the amount of, a subsidy payment. An initial determination is final and binding unless reconsidered. [42 C.F.R. § 423.890(a)(1), (2).]

A request for reconsideration must be made in writing and filed with CMS within 15 days of the date on the notice of adverse determination. A reconsideration decision, whether delivered orally or in writing, is final and binding unless it is revised or a request for hearing is filed. [42 C.F.R. § 423.890(a).]

Informal hearing request. A sponsor dissatisfied with the CMS reconsideration decision is entitled to an informal hearing. A request for a hearing must be made in writing and filed with CMS within 15 days of the date the sponsor receives the CMS reconsideration decision. The CMS hearing officer is limited to the review of the record that was before CMS when CMS made both its initial and reconsideration determinations. [42 C.F.R. § 423.890(b)(1), (2), (3).]

The CMS hearing officer decides the case and sends a written decision to the sponsor, explaining the basis for the decision. The hearing officer decision is final and binding, unless the decision is reversed or modified by the Administrator. [42 C.F.R. § 423.890(b)(4), (5).]

Review by the Administrator. A sponsor that has received a hearing officer decision upholding a CMS initial or reconsidered determination may request review by the Administrator within 15 days of receipt of the decision. The Administrator may review the hearing officer's decision, any written documents submitted to CMS or to the hearing officer, and any other information included in the record of the hearing officer's decision and determine whether to uphold, reverse, or modify the decision. The Administrator's determination is final and binding. [42 C.F.R. § 423.890(c).]

Reopening of initial or reconsidered determination. CMS may reopen and revise an initial or reconsidered determination upon its own motion or upon the request of a sponsor within one year of the date of the notice of determination for any reason, within four years for good cause, and at any time when the underlying decision was obtained through fraud or similar fault. [42 C.F.R. § 423.890(d)(1).]

A decision by CMS not to reopen an initial or reconsidered determination is final and binding and cannot be appealed. [42 C.F.R. § 423.890(d)(6).]

Change of Ownership

Sponsors who apply for a retiree drug subsidy payment must comply with certain change of ownership requirements. A change of ownership includes:

- the removal, addition, or substitution of a partner, unless the partners expressly agree otherwise as permitted by applicable state law;

- transfer of all or substantially all of the assets of the sponsor to another party; or

- the merger of the sponsor's corporation into another corporation or the consolidation of the sponsor's organization with one or more other corporations, resulting in a new corporate body.

The transfer of corporate stock or the merger of another corporation into the sponsor's corporation with the sponsor surviving will not ordinarily constitute change of ownership. [42 C.F.R. § 423.892(a), (b).]

Notice requirement. A sponsor that has a retiree PDP in effect and is considering or negotiating a change in ownership must notify CMS at least 60 days before the anticipated effective date of the change. [42 C.F.R. § 423.892(c).]

Automatic assignment. When there is a change of ownership that results in a transfer of the liability for prescription drug costs, the existing sponsor agreement is automatically assigned to the new owner. The new owner to whom a sponsor agreement is assigned is subject to all applicable statutes and regulations and to the terms and conditions of the sponsor agreement. [42 C.F.R. § 423.892(d), (e).]

[¶ 535] Marketing Requirements

CMS has established prohibitions and limitations on the sales and marketing activities of Medicare Advantage (MA) and prescription drug plans (PDPs).

Marketing materials include any information targeted to Medicare beneficiaries that: (1) promotes a Part D plan; (2) informs beneficiaries that they may enroll or remain enrolled in a plan; (3) explains the benefits or applicable rules of enrollment; or (4) explains how Medicare services are covered under a plan, including coverage conditions. [42 C.F.R. § 423.2260.]

Marketing materials may include:

(1) general audience materials such as general circulation brochures, newspapers, magazines, television, radio, billboards, yellow pages, or the Internet;

(2) scripts or outlines for telemarketing or other presentations;

(3) slides and charts;

(4) promotional materials such as brochures or leaflets, including materials for circulation by third parties (such as physicians or other providers);

(5) membership communication materials such as membership rules, subscriber agreements, member handbooks, and wallet card instructions to enrollees;

(6) letters to members about contractual changes and changes in providers, premiums, benefits, and plan procedures; and

(7) membership activities, such as materials on rules for nonpayment of premiums, confirmation of enrollment or disenrollment, or non-claim-specific notification information.

[42 C.F.R. § 423.2260.]

Excluded information. Marketing materials do not include ad hoc enrollee communications materials, such as informational materials that: (1) are targeted to current enrollees; (2) are customized or limited to a subset of enrollees or apply to a specific situation; (3) do not include information about the plan's benefit structure; and (4) apply to a specific situation or cover member-specific claims processing or other operational issues. [42 C.F.R. § 423.2260.]

CMS Review of Marketing Materials

A Part D plan may not distribute any marketing materials or make such materials or forms available to eligible individuals unless, at least 45 days before the date of distribution, the sponsor submits the material or form to CMS for review, and CMS does not disapprove of the distribution. This time period may be reduced to 10 days if the plan's marketing materials use, without modification, CMS-specified proposed model language and format, including standardized language and formatting. [Soc. Sec. Act §§ 1851(h)(1), (5), 1860D-1(b)(1)(B)(vi); 42 C.F.R. § 423.2262(a).]

File and use. The Part D sponsor may distribute certain designated marketing materials five days following their submission to CMS if the sponsor certifies that it followed all applicable marketing guidelines and, when applicable, used CMS model language without modification. [42 C.F.R. § 423.2262(b).]

CMS review guidelines. CMS examines marketing materials and enrollment forms to see that they provide information in a format, print size, and standard terminology that may be specified by CMS. This information includes adequate written description of rules, procedures, basic benefits, services, fees, the grievance and appeals process, and any other information necessary to enable beneficiaries to make informed enrollment decisions. [Soc. Sec. Act §§ 1851(h)(2), 1860D-1(b)(1)(B)(vi); 42 C.F.R. § 423.2264(a).]

CMS also must make sure that the materials:

(1) notify the public of its enrollment period in an appropriate manner; including notice that (a) the plan may refuse to renew its contract with CMS, (b) CMS may refuse to renew the plan's contract, and (c) termination or nonrenewal may result in termination of the beneficiary's enrollment in the plan;

(2) include notice that the plan may reduce its service area and no longer be offered in the area where a beneficiary resides;

(3) are not materially inaccurate or misleading or otherwise make material misrepresentations; and

(4) in markets with a significant non-English-speaking population, are provided in the language of these individuals.

[42 C.F.R. § 423.2264.]

Materials "deemed" approved. If CMS does not disapprove marketing materials within the specified review time frame, the materials are deemed approved and the Part D sponsor may use them. [Soc. Sec. Act §§ 1851(h)(3), 1860D-1(b)(1)(B)(vi); 42 C.F.R. § 423.2262(a)(2).]

Marketing Standards

In conducting marketing activities, a Part D plan may not:

- provide cash or other remuneration as an inducement for enrollment;

- offer gifts to potential enrollees, unless the gifts are of nominal value, are offered to all potential enrollees without regard to whether the beneficiary enrolls, and are not in the form of cash or other monetary rebates;

- engage in any discriminatory activity such as attempts to recruit beneficiaries from higher income areas without making comparable efforts to enroll beneficiaries from lower income areas;

- solicit door-to-door or through other unsolicited means of direct contact, including calling a beneficiary without the beneficiary initiating the contact;

- engage in activities that could mislead or confuse Medicare beneficiaries, misrepresent the sponsor or its plan, or claim that it is recommended or endorsed by CMS or Medicare or that CMS or Medicare recommends that the beneficiary enroll in the Part D plan;

- cross-sell non-health-care-related products to prospective enrollees during any Part D sales activity or presentation;

- market any health-care-related product during a marketing appointment that is beyond the scope agreed upon by the beneficiary and documented by the plan, prior to the appointment (48 hours in advance, when practicable);

- market additional health-related lines of plan business not identified before an individual appointment without a separate appointment identifying the additional lines of business to be discussed;

- distribute marketing materials for which the sponsor receives from CMS written notice of disapproval because they are inaccurate or misleading or misrepresent the sponsor, its marketing representatives, or CMS;

- use providers, provider groups, or pharmacies to distribute printed information for beneficiaries to use when comparing the benefits of different plans unless the providers, provider groups, or pharmacies accept and display materials from all plan sponsors with which they contract;

- conduct sales presentations or distribute and accept plan enrollment forms in provider offices, pharmacies, or other areas where health care is delivered to individuals, except when such activities are conducted in common areas in health care settings;

- conduct sales presentations or distribute and accept plan applications at educational events;

- employ plan names that suggest that a plan is not available to all beneficiaries;

- display the names and logos of co-branded network providers on the organization's member identification card;

- engage in any other marketing activity prohibited by CMS in its marketing guidance;

- provide meals for potential enrollees, regardless of value; and

- use a plan name that does not include the plan type.

[Soc. Sec. Act §§ 1851(h)(4), (6), (j), 1860D-4(l); 42 C.F.R. § 423.2268.]

In its marketing, the Part D organization must demonstrate to the satisfaction of CMS that marketing resources are allocated to marketing to the disabled Medicare population (under age 65) as well as beneficiaries age 65 and over. A Part D plan also must establish and maintain a system for confirming that enrolled beneficiaries have enrolled in the PDP and understand the rules applicable under the plan. [42 C.F.R. § 423.2272(a), (b).]

Licensing of Marketing Representatives

A Part D organization must employ as marketing representatives only those individuals who are licensed by the state to conduct direct marketing activities in that state. The sponsor must inform the state that it has appointed these individuals as marketing representatives as required by the appointment process provided for under state law. [Soc. Sec. Act §§ 1851(h)(7), 1860D-4(l); 42 C.F.R. § 423.2272(c).]

The organization must also report the termination of any such agent or broker to the state, including the reasons for such termination if state law requires that the reasons for the termination be reported. Finally, an organization must terminate upon discovery any unlicensed agent or broker employed as a marketing representative and notify any beneficiaries enrolled by an unqualified agent or broker of the agent's or broker's status and, if requested, of their options to confirm enrollment or make a plan change, including a special election period. [Soc. Sec. Act §§ 1851(h)(7), 1860D-4(l); 42 C.F.R. § 423.2272(d), (e).]

Broker and Agent Requirements

A Part D sponsor must meet the following requirements if it markets Part D plan products through any broker or agent: (1) ensure agents selling Medicare products are trained and tested annually on Medicare rules and regulations and details specific to the plan products they sell; (2) at CMS's request, provide CMS the information necessary for it to conduct oversight of marketing activities; (3) comply with state requests for information about the performance of a licensed agent or broker as part of a state investigation into the individual's conduct; and (4) report to CMS annually on whether it intends to use independent agents or brokers or both in the upcoming plan year and, if applicable, the specific amount or range of amounts independent agents or brokers or both will be paid. [42 C.F.R. § 423.2274(c)–(g).]

Compensation requirements. Part D plan sponsor may provide compensation to an independent broker or agent for the sale of a Part D plan if the following compensation rules are followed:

- The compensation amount paid to an agent or broker for enrollment of a Medicare beneficiary into a PDP is: (1) for an initial enrollment, at or below the fair market value cut-off amounts published annually by CMS; and (2) for renewals, an amount equal to 50 percent of the current fair market value cut-off amounts.

- If the Part D sponsor contracts with a third-party entity such as a field marketing organization or similar type entity to sell its insurance products or perform services: (1) the amount paid to the third party, or its agents, for enrollment of a beneficiary into a plan must be the same as paid to non-third-party agents and brokers; and (2) the amount paid to the third party for services other than selling insurance products, if any, must be fair market value and must not exceed an amount that is commensurate with the amounts paid by the PDP organization to a third party for similar services during each of the previous two years.

[42 C.F.R. § 423.2274(b)(1).]

Aggregate compensation. No entity may provide, and no agent or broker shall receive, aggregate compensation greater than the renewal compensation payable by the replacing plan on renewal policies if an existing policy is replaced with a like plan type. The initial compensation is paid for replacements between unlike plan types. [42 C.F.R. § 423.2274(b)(2).]

Plan year compensation. Compensation may be paid only for the beneficiary's months of enrollment during a plan year. Compensation payments may be made up front for the entire current plan year or in installments throughout the year. When a beneficiary disenrolls from a plan, compensation paid to agents and brokers must be recovered for those months of the plan year for which the beneficiary is not enrolled. For disenrollments occurring within the first three months, the entire compensation must be recovered unless CMS determines that recoupment is not in the best interests of the Medicare program. [42 C.F.R. § 423.2274(b)(3).]

Compensation structure. A Part D sponsor must establish a compensation structure for new and replacement enrollments and renewals effective in a given plan year. They must be in place by October 1 and must be available upon CMS's request. [42 C.F.R. § 423.2274(b)(4).]

Finder's fees. Finder's (referral) fees paid to all agents and brokers may not exceed an amount that CMS determines could reasonably be expected to provide financial incentive for an agent or broker to recommend or enroll a beneficiary into a plan that is not the most appropriate to meet his or her needs. The fee must be included in the total compensation not to exceed the fair market value for that calendar year. [42 C.F.R. § 423.2274(h).]

"Compensation" defined. For the purposes of broker and agent requirements, "compensation" includes pecuniary or nonpecuniary remuneration of any kind relating to the sale or renewal of a policy including, but not limited to, commissions, bonuses, gifts, prizes, awards, and referral or finder's fees. Compensation does *not* include: (1) the payment of fees to comply with state appointment laws or training, certification, and testing costs; (2) reimbursement for mileage to and from appointments with beneficiaries; or (3) reimbursement for actual costs associated with beneficiary sales appointments such as venue rent, snacks, and materials. [42 C.F.R. § 423.2274(a).]

Employer Group Retirees

Part D sponsors may develop marketing materials for members of an employer group who are eligible for employer-sponsored benefits through the Part D sponsor. These materials may be furnished only to the employer group members. These marketing materials are exempt from prior review and approval by CMS. [42 C.F.R. § 423.2276.]

¶535

Chapter 6– EXCLUSIONS FROM COVERAGE

[¶ 600] Exclusions Under Part A and Part B

In addition to the limitations and exclusions discussed in the preceding chapters, other items or services are excluded under both Medicare Part A and Part B. Soc. Sec. Act § 1862(a) discusses the items and services for which payment may not be made under Medicare Part A and B. In general, CMS will not cover items and services that are not reasonable or necessary for the diagnosis or treatment of illness or injury or to improve the functioning of a malformed body member. Particular services and items are also excluded from payment eligibility and are discussed in the following sections. [42 C.F.R. § 411.1 *et seq.*]

[¶ 601] Services Not Reasonable and Necessary

Items and services that are not reasonable and necessary for the diagnosis or treatment of illness or injury or to improve the functioning of a malformed body part are excluded from coverage. Many items and services are considered reasonable and necessary for some conditions but not for others. [Soc. Sec. Act § 1862(l)(1); 42 C.F.R. § 411.15(k).]

Procedures to assist a patient in committing suicide or to cause the patient's death are excluded, but this exclusion does not prevent the withholding or withdrawal of medical treatment, nutrition, or hydration or the provision of a service for the purpose of alleviating pain or discomfort, even if the use may increase the risk of death, as long as the service is not furnished for the specific purpose of causing death. [Soc. Sec. Act § 1862(a)(16); 42 C.F.R. § 411.15(q).]

Medicare Coverage Determinations Manual, Pub. 100-03, discusses specific coverage decisions and exclusions.

Note that a beneficiary can be "held harmless" (not required to pay) in certain situations in which claims are disallowed under this exclusion. This "waiver of liability" provision is discussed at ¶ 915. [Soc. Sec. Act § 1879.]

Services Related to Non-Covered Services

Services related to services that are typically excluded from coverage under Medicare Parts A and B (for instance, cosmetic surgery, non-covered organ transplants, non-covered artificial organ implants), including follow-up services and those related to complications arising out of non-covered services, are also excluded. [*Medicare Benefit Policy Manual,* Pub. 100-02, Ch. 15, § 180.] For a list of examples of services that are considered "related to" non-covered services, see Pub. 100-02, Ch. 15, § 180.

Experimental and Investigational Devices and Treatments

Medicare generally does not cover experimental and investigational devices and treatments. However, Medicare does cover the routine costs of care furnished to a beneficiary in a qualifying Category A (experimental) clinical trial. [Soc. Sec. Act § 1862(m)(1).] Furthermore, Medicare covers Category B (nonexperimental/investigational) devices and routine care items and services furnished in Food and Drug Administration-approved Category B investigational device exemption studies if specified criteria are met. [42 C.F.R. §§ 405.201–405.213, 411.15(o); Pub. 100-03, Ch. 1, § 310.1.]

[¶ 604] No Legal Obligation to Pay

Payment may not be made for items or services for which neither the beneficiary nor any other person or organization has a legal obligation to pay or to provide. This exclusion does not apply, however, to services furnished in a federally qualified community health center (see ¶ 382). [Soc. Sec. Act § 1862(a)(2); 42 C.F.R. § 411.4(a).]

Items/services are furnished free of charge. This exclusion applies when items and services are furnished free of charge regardless of the beneficiary's ability to pay and without expectation of payment from any source. Examples are free x-rays or immunizations provided by health organizations. The exclusion does not apply, however, where items and services are furnished to an indigent individual without charge because of their inability to pay, if the provider, physician, or supplier bills other patients to the extent that they are able to pay. If a provider, physician, or supplier waives his or her charges for individuals of limited means but also expects to be paid when the patient has insurance, a legal obligation to pay exists and benefits are payable for services rendered to patients with medical insurance if the provider, physician, or supplier customarily bills all insured patients, even though non-insured patients are not charged. [*Medicare Benefit Policy Manual*, Pub. 100-02, Ch. 16, § 40.]

Other health coverage. Except as discussed at ¶ 636 (involving workers' compensation, automobile and liability insurance, and certain employer group health plans), payment is not precluded under Medicare even though the patient is covered by another health insurance plan or program that is obligated to provide or pay for the same services. In these cases, the other plan pays the primary benefits and if it does not pay the entire bill, secondary Medicare benefits may be payable. [Pub. 100-02, Ch. 16, § 40.3.] The amount of secondary benefits Medicare will pay is determined by rules discussed at ¶ 636.

Items covered under a warranty. When a defective medical device such as a cardiac pacemaker is replaced under a warranty, Medicare may cover hospital and physician charges despite the warrantor's liability. If the device is replaced free of charge by the warrantor, no program payment may be made because there was no charge involved. For other rules regarding circumstances in which items under warranty are replaced or substituted, see Pub. 100-02, Ch. 16, § 40.4.

Members of religious orders. A legal obligation to pay exists when a religious order either pays for or furnishes services to members of the order. Medical services furnished in such a setting ordinarily would not be expressed in terms of a legal obligation; however, the religious order has an obligation to care for its members who have rendered life-long services, so the order pays for such services whether they are furnished by the religious order itself or by independent sources that customarily charge for their services. [Pub. 100-02, Ch. 16, § 40.5.]

State or local prisoners. Medicare payment may be made for services furnished to individuals who are in the custody of the police or other penal authorities only if: (1) state or local law requires the individuals to repay the cost of medical services they receive while in custody; and (2) the state or local government entity enforces the requirement to pay by billing all such individuals and by pursuing collection of the amounts they owe in the same way and with the same vigor that it pursues the collection of other debts. [42 C.F.R. § 411.4(b).]

[¶ 607] Services Paid for by Governmental Entity

Generally, Medicare does not pay for items or services that are paid for directly or indirectly by a governmental entity, including state and local governments. [Soc. Sec. Act § 1862(a)(3); 42 C.F.R. § 411.8(a).]

Payment, however, may be made for:

    (1) services furnished under a health insurance plan established for employees of the governmental entity;

(2) services furnished under a program based on a title of the Social Security Act other than Medicare, such as Medicaid;

(3) services furnished in or by a participating general or special hospital that is operated by a state or local governmental entity and serves the general community;

(4) services furnished by a hospital or elsewhere, as a means of controlling infectious diseases or because of the individual's medical indigency;

(5) services furnished by participating hospitals and skilled nursing facilities of the Indian Health Service (IHS) (see below);

(6) services furnished by a public or private health facility (other than a federal provider or facility operated by a federal agency) that: (a) receives United States government funds under a federal program that provides support to facilities furnishing health care services, (b) customarily seeks reimbursement for items and services not covered under Medicare from all resources available for the health care of its patients—for example, private insurance and patients' cash resources, and (c) limits the amounts it collects or seeks to collect from a Part B beneficiary and others on the beneficiary's behalf;

(7) rural and community health clinic services (see ¶ 382);

(8) certain emergency services (see ¶ 227); and

(9) services furnished under arrangements made by a participating hospital.

[Soc. Sec. Act § 1862(a)(3); 42 C.F.R. § § 411.6, 411.8(b).]

Indian Health Service

The IHS is the primary health care provider to the American Indian/Alaska Native Medicare population. The IHS, consisting of tribal, urban, and federally operated IHS health programs, delivers a spectrum of clinical and preventive health services to its beneficiaries via a network of hospitals, clinics, and other entities. Although sections 1814(c) and 1835(d) of the Social Security Act generally prohibit payment to any federal agency, an exception applies to the IHS/tribally owned and operated facilities. IHS facilities may bill for Medicare Part B covered services and items, including all screening and preventive services covered by Medicare, physician services, diagnostic x-ray and other diagnostic tests, anesthesia services, practitioner services, drugs and biologicals incident to physician services, physical therapy services, occupational therapy services, speech-language pathology services, ambulance services, and telehealth services. [Soc. Sec. Act § 1880(e)(1)(A); *Medicare Claims Processing Manual*, Pub. 100-04, Ch. 19, § § 10, 70.]

Social admissions. Services rendered to American Indian/Alaska Native beneficiaries admitted to IHS/tribal facilities for social reasons are not covered by Medicare. These social admissions are for the patients' and families' convenience and include occasions when IHS/tribal hospitals elect to admit patients prior to a scheduled day of surgery, or place a patient in a room after an inpatient discharge. [Pub. 100-04, Ch. 19, § 100.3.3.]

Department of Veterans Affairs

Medicare payment may not be made for any item or service that a provider, physician, or supplier provided pursuant to an authorization issued by the Department of Veterans Affairs (VA) under which the VA agrees to pay for the services. An authorization issued by the VA binds the VA to pay in full for the items and services provided. However, when the VA does not give an authorization to the party rendering the services, Medicare payment is not precluded even though the individual might have been entitled to have payment made by the VA if the individual had requested the authorization. [*Medicare Benefit Policy Manual*, Pub. 100-02, Ch. 16, § 50.1.1.]

If a physician accepts a veteran as a patient and bills the VA, the physician must accept the VA's "usual and customary" charge determination as payment in full and neither the patient nor any other party can be charged an additional amount. Therefore, Medicare cannot make payment if the physician's bill for authorized services exceeds the amount the VA paid the physician or reimbursed the beneficiary. Medicare can, however, pay secondary benefits to the beneficiary or physician to cover the VA copayment or deductible. Medicare also may pay for services not covered by the VA. [Pub. 100-02, Ch. 16, § § 50.1.1, 50.1.4.]

Under certain circumstances, Medicare reimbursement for care provided to a nonveteran Medicare beneficiary in a VA hospital is authorized if the care was provided on the mistaken (but good faith) assumption that the beneficiary was an eligible veteran. [Soc. Sec. Act § 1814(h)(1).]

TRICARE and CHAMPVA

TRICARE is a Department of Defense health care program for all branches of the armed services. Civilian Health and Medical Program of the Veterans Administration (CHAMPVA) is a health program administered by the VA under which the VA shares the cost of covered services with eligible family members of certain veterans. If a TRICARE or CHAMPVA beneficiary also has Medicare coverage, Medicare is the primary payer. TRICARE or CHAMPVA covers the Medicare deductible and coinsurance amounts and portions of the bill not covered by Medicare. [Pub. 100-02, Ch. 16, § 50.4.]

TRICARE/CHAMPVA have established policies and procedures that provide for: (1) the identification of claimants who have coverage under both TRICARE/CHAMPVA and Medicare; and (2) the detection of duplicate payments under both programs. If TRICARE or CHAMPVA inadvertently pays amounts that duplicate Medicare payments for the same items or services, TRICARE/CHAMPVA will take steps to recover the incorrect payments. [Pub. 100-02, Ch. 16, § 50.4.]

Medicare-participating hospitals are required to participate in the programs and to accept patients from those programs. [Soc. Sec. Act § 1866(a)(1)(J).]

[¶ 610] Services Outside the United States

Generally, Medicare does not pay for services furnished outside the United States, which includes the 50 states, the District of Columbia, the Commonwealth of Puerto Rico, the Virgin Islands, Guam, the Northern Mariana Islands, American Samoa, and for purposes of services rendered on a ship, the territorial waters adjoining the land areas of the United States. For Medicare purposes, services rendered aboard a ship in an American port or within six hours of the time at which the ship arrives at, or departs from, that port will be considered to have been rendered in American waters. [Soc. Sec. Act § § 210(h) and (i), 1862(a)(4); 42 C.F.R. § 411.9; *Medicare Claims Processing Manual*, Pub. 100-04, Ch. 1, § 10.1.4.]

Payment will not be made for a medical service (or a portion of it) that is subcontracted to a provider or supplier located outside the United States. For example, if a radiologist who practices in India analyzes imaging tests that were performed on a beneficiary in the United States, Medicare will not pay the radiologist or the U.S. facility that performed the imaging test for any of the services that were performed by the radiologist in India. [*Medicare Benefit Policy Manual*, Pub. 100-02, Ch. 16, § 60.]

Qualified railroad retirement beneficiaries submit their claims for inpatient services received in Canada to the Railroad Retirement Board (RRB) for a determination of coverage.

If the RRB finds the inpatient services are covered, it forwards the claim to a Medicare administrative contractor for consideration of whether the other requirements for Part B coverage are met and for further processing. The RRB does not cover services furnished in Mexico; Medicare rules will apply to services received in Mexico. [Pub. 100-04, Ch. 1, § 10.1.4.6.]

Exceptions to Geographic Limits

There are some situations in which Medicare does pay for services rendered outside of the United States. Medicare pays for inpatient hospital services furnished to an individual entitled to hospital insurance benefits by a hospital located outside of the United States if: (1) the individual is a resident of the United States; (2) the hospital is closer to or substantially more accessible to the individual's residence than the nearest hospital within the United States; (3) the hospital is adequately equipped to deal with the individual's illness or injury; and (4) the hospital is available for the treatment of such individual's illness or injury. [Soc. Sec. Act § § 1814(f)(1), 1862(a)(4).]

Emergency inpatient hospital services also are covered when the emergency occurred while the beneficiary was in the United States or, at the time of the emergency, the beneficiary was in Canada while traveling directly between Alaska and another state without unreasonable delay and by the most direct route and the Canadian hospital was closer or more accessible with adequate facilities to care for the beneficiary's needs. An emergency occurring within the Canadian inland waterway between the states of Washington and Canada is considered to have occurred in Canada. [Soc. Sec. Act § 1814(f)(2); 42 C.F.R. § 424.122(a), (b); Pub. 100-02, Ch. 16, § 60; Pub. 100-04, Ch. 3, § 110.5.]

Medicare will pay 100 percent of the foreign hospital's charges. [42 C.F. R. § 413.74(b).]

Physicians' services in connection with foreign hospitalization. Physicians' services provided to a Medicare beneficiary outside a hospital on the day of the beneficiary admission as an inpatient are covered, provided the services were for the same condition for which the beneficiary was hospitalized. The physician must be legally licensed to practice in the country in which the services were furnished. This provision includes the services of a Canadian ship's physician who furnishes emergency treatment in Canadian waters on the day the beneficiary is admitted to a Canadian hospital for a covered emergency stay. [Soc. Sec. Act § 1862(a)(4); 42 C.F.R. § 424.124(a); Pub. 100-04, Ch. 3, § 110.7.]

Ambulance services in connection with foreign hospitalizations. Payment made be made for necessary ambulance service to a hospital in conjunction with a beneficiary's admission as an inpatient; however, return trips from a foreign hospital are not covered. [Soc. Sec. Act § 1862(a)(4); 42 C.F.R. § 424.124(a), (c); Pub. 100-04, Ch. 3, § 110.7.]

Regular deductible and coinsurance requirements apply to physicians' and ambulance services rendered outside the United States. [Pub. 100-04, Ch. 3, § 110.7.]

[¶ 613] Services Resulting from War

Items and services that are required as a result of war, or an act of war, occurring after the effective date of the patient's current coverage for hospital insurance benefits or supplemental medical insurance benefits are not covered. [Soc. Sec. Act § 1862(a)(5); 42 C.F.R. § 411.10.]

[¶ 616] Personal Comfort Items

Personal comfort items, meaning those items that do not contribute meaningfully to the treatment of an illness or injury or the functioning of a malformed body member, are not covered except when provided in the course of hospice care (see ¶ 270). Charges for radios, televisions, telephones, or air conditioners are examples of personal comfort items excluded from Medicare coverage. [Soc. Sec. Act § 1862(a)(6); 42 C.F.R. § 411.15(j); *Medicare Benefit Policy Manual*, Pub. 100-02, Ch. 16, § 80.]

Basic personal services, such as simple barber and beautician services (for example, shaves, haircuts, shampoos, and simple hair sets) that patients need and cannot perform for themselves, may be viewed as ordinary patient care when furnished by a long-stay institution. Such services are included in the flat rate charge covered under Part A and provided routinely without charge to the patient by a hospital or skilled nursing facility. [Pub. 100-02, Ch. 16, § 80.]

Providers may charge patients for excluded personal comfort items that the patient requests only if the patient has knowledge that he or she will be charged for those items. [Pub. 100-02, Ch. 16, § 80.]

Providers also are allowed to charge patients when they request services that are more expensive than those covered by Medicare (see ¶ 730 under "Allowable Charges").

[¶ 619] Eye, Ear, and Foot Care

Medicare does not cover routine eye, ear, and foot care services. [Soc. Sec. Act § 1862(a)(7), (8), (13); 42 C.F.R. § 411.15.]

Eye Care

Excluded routine eye care includes: (1) eyeglasses; (2) most contact lenses; (3) eye examinations for the purpose of prescribing, fitting, or changing eyeglasses or contact lenses for refractive error only; and (4) procedures performed in the course of any eye examination to determine the refractive state of the eyes. [Soc. Sec. Act § 1862(a)(7); 42 C.F.R. § 411.15(b), (c).]

The eye care services exclusion does not apply to: (1) physicians' services (and services incident to a physician's service) performed in conjunction with an eye disease, for example, glaucoma or cataracts; (2) post-surgical prosthetic lenses customarily used during convalescence for eye surgery in which the lens of the eye was removed (for example, cataract surgery); (3) prosthetic intraocular lenses and one pair of conventional eyeglasses or contact lenses furnished subsequent to each cataract surgery with insertion of an intraocular lens; or (4) prosthetic lenses used by beneficiaries who are lacking the natural lens of the eye and who were not furnished with an intraocular lens. [42 C.F.R. § 411.15(b)(2); *Medicare Benefit Policy Manual*, Pub. 100-02, Ch. 16, § 90.]

Note that the law specifically authorizes coverage for one pair of conventional eyeglasses or contact lenses furnished subsequent to each cataract surgery in which an intraocular lens is inserted. [Soc. Sec. Act § 1861(s)(8).]

Ear Care

Hearing aids and examinations for the purpose of prescribing, fitting, or changing hearing aids are excluded from Medicare coverage. The scope of the hearing aid exclusion encompasses all types of air conduction hearing aids that provide acoustic energy to the cochlea via stimulation of the tympanic membrane with amplified sound and bone conduction hearing aids that provide mechanical stimulation of the cochlea via stimulation of the scalp with amplified mechanical vibration or by direct contact with the tympanic membrane or middle ear ossicles. [Soc. Sec. Act § 1862(a)(7); 42 C.F.R. § 411.15(d).]

Certain devices that produce perception of sound by replacing the function of the middle ear, cochlea, or auditory nerve are payable by Medicare as prosthetic devices. These devices are indicated only when hearing aids are medically inappropriate or cannot be utilized due to congenital malformations, chronic disease, severe sensorineural hearing loss, or surgery. The following are covered as prosthetic devices: (1) osseointegrated implants in the skull bone that provide mechanical energy to the cochlea via a mechanical transducer; or (2) cochlear implants and auditory brainstem implants that replace the function of cochlear structures or auditory nerve and provide electrical energy to auditory nerve fibers and other neural tissue via implanted electrode arrays. [42 C.F.R. § 411.15(d)(2); Pub. 100-02, Ch. 16, § 100.]

Foot Care

Medicare does not cover the following foot-related services:

(1) routine foot care;

(2) the evaluation or treatment of subluxations (structural misalignments of the joints) of the feet; or

(3) the evaluation or treatment of flattened arches and the prescription of supportive devices.

[Soc. Sec. Act § 1862(a)(13); 42 C.F.R. § 411.15(l)(1).]

Routine foot care. Routine foot care includes the cutting or removal of corns or calluses, the trimming of nails (including mycotic nails), and other hygienic and preventive maintenance care in the realm of self-care, such as cleaning and soaking the feet, the use of skin creams to maintain skin tone of both ambulatory and bed-confined patients, and any services performed in the absence of localized illness, injury, or symptoms involving the foot. For example, foot care such as routine soaking and application of topical medication on a physician's order between required physician visits is not covered. [42 C.F.R. § 411.15(l)(1)(i); Pub. 100-02, Ch. 15, § 290.]

Exceptions to foot-care exclusion. Services may be covered: (1) for the treatment of warts; (2) for the treatment of mycotic toenails if furnished no more often than every 60 days or the billing physician documents the need for more frequent treatment; and (3) when they are incident to, at the same time as, or as a necessary integral part of a primary covered procedure performed on the foot, or initial diagnostic services (regardless of the resulting diagnosis) in connection with a specific symptom or complaint that might arise from a condition whose treatment would be covered. [42 C.F.R. § 411.15(l)(2); Pub. 100-02, Ch. 15, § 290.]

Orthopedic shoes. Expenses for orthopedic shoes or other supportive devices for the feet generally are not covered, except when the shoe is an integral part of a leg brace and its expense is included as part of the cost of the brace. [Soc. Sec. Act § 1861(a)(8); 42 C.F.R. § 411.15(f).] The exclusion also does not apply to therapeutic shoes and inserts for individuals with severe diabetic foot disease (see ¶ 370). [Soc. Sec. Act § 1861(s)(12).]

[¶ 625] Custodial Care

Custodial care, except in the case of hospice care (see ¶ 270), is excluded from Medicare coverage. [Soc. Sec. Act § 1862(a)(9); 42 C.F.R. § 411.15(g).]

Custodial care is personal care that does not require the continuing attention of trained medical or paramedical personnel and serves to assist the individual in meeting the activities of daily living. The following activities are considered custodial care: (1) help in walking and getting in or out of bed; (2) assistance in bathing, dressing, feeding, and using the toilet; (3) preparation of special diets; and (4) supervision over medication that usually can be self-administered. Institutional care that is below the level of care covered in a skilled nursing facility (SNF) is custodial care. [*Medicare Benefit Policy Manual*, Pub. 100-02, Ch. 16, § 110.] For a discussion of noncovered levels of care in a SNF, see ¶ 244.

Note that a beneficiary can be "held harmless" (i.e., not required to pay) in certain situations in which claims are disallowed under this exclusion. This provision is discussed at ¶ 915.

[¶ 628] Cosmetic Surgery

Cosmetic surgery and expenses incurred in connection with such surgery are not covered. This exclusion applies to any surgical procedure directed at improving appearance, except when required for the prompt (i.e., as soon as medically feasible) repair of accidental injury or for the improvement of the functioning of a malformed body member. For example, this exclusion does not apply to surgery: (1) in connection with treatment of severe burns or repair of the face following a serious automobile accident; or (2) for therapeutic purposes that coincidentally also serve some cosmetic purpose. [Soc. Sec. Act § 1862(a)(10); 42 C.F.R. § 411.15(h); *Medicare Benefit Policy Manual*, Pub. 100-02, Ch. 16, § 120.]

[¶ 631] Charges by Immediate Relatives and Household Members

Medicare does not pay for charges imposed by physicians or other persons who are immediate relatives of the patient or members of the patient's household. The intent of this exclusion is to bar payment for items and services that would ordinarily be furnished gratuitously because of the relationship of the beneficiary to the person imposing the charge. [Soc. Sec. Act § 1862(a)(11); 42 C.F.R. § 411.12(a).]

Immediate relatives and household members. "Immediate relative" means spouse; natural or adoptive parent, child, and sibling; stepparent, stepchild, stepbrother, and stepsister; parent-in-law, child-in-law, brother-in-law, and sister-in-law; grandparent and grandchild; and spouse of grandparent and grandchild. "Members of the patient's household" means those persons sharing a common abode with the patient as part of a single family unit, including domestic employees and others who live together as part of a single family unit. A roommate or boarder is not included. [42 C.F.R. § 411.12(b).]

A brother-in-law or sister-in-law relationship does not exist between a physician (or supplier) and the spouse of his wife's (her husband's) brother or sister. A father-in-law or mother-in-law relationship does not exist between a physician and the stepfather or step-mother of the physician's spouse. A step-relationship or an in-law relationship continues to exist even if the marriage upon which the relationship is based is terminated through divorce or through the death of one of the parties. For example, if a physician provides services to a stepparent after the death of (or divorce by) the natural parent, or if the physician provides services to an in-law after the death of the spouse of the physician, the services are considered to have been furnished to an immediate relative and, therefore, excluded from coverage. [*Medicare Benefit Policy Manual*, Pub. 100-02, Ch. 16, § 130.]

Physicians' services. The exclusion applies to the charges for physicians' services furnished by an immediate relative of the beneficiary or member of the beneficiary's household, even if the bill or claim is submitted by another individual or by an entity such as a partnership or a professional corporation. It also applies to charges for services furnished incident to a physician's professional services (for example, by the physician's nurse or technician) only if the physician who ordered or supervised the services has an excluded relationship to the beneficiary. [42 C.F.R. § 411.12(c)(1).]

Services other than physicians' services. In the case of services other than physicians' services, charges are excluded if they are provided by: (1) an individually owned provider or supplier, if the owner has an excluded relationship with the patient; or (2) a partnership, if any of the partners has an excluded relationship with the patient. [42 C.F.R. § 411.12(c)(2).]

Corporations. This exclusion does not apply to charges imposed by a corporation, other than a professional corporation, regardless of the patient's relationship to any of the stockholders, officers, or directors of the corporation or to the person who furnished the service. [42 C.F.R. § 411.12(d); Pub. 100-02, Ch. 16, § 130.]

[¶ 634] Dental Services

Items and services in connection with the care, treatment, filling, removal, or replacement of teeth or structures directly supporting the teeth (i.e., the periodontium, which includes the gingivae, dentogingival junction, periodontal membrane, cementum of the teeth, and alveolar process) generally are not covered. Payment may, however, be made under Part A for inpatient hospital services in connection with the provision of such dental services if the beneficiary, because of his or her underlying medical condition and clinical status or because of the severity of the dental procedure, requires hospitalization in connection with the provision of such services (see ¶ 218). [Soc. Sec. Act § 1862(a)(12); 42 C.F.R. § 411.15(i); *Medicare Benefit Policy Manual*, Pub. 100-02, Ch. 16, § 140.]

Medicare makes payment for the wiring of teeth when this is done in connection with the reduction of a jaw fracture. The extraction of teeth to prepare the jaw for radiation treatments of neoplastic disease also is covered. [Pub. 100-02, Ch. 15, § 150; Ch. 16, § 140.]

Whether such services as the administration of anesthesia, diagnostic x-rays, and other related procedures are covered depends upon whether the primary procedure being performed by the dentist is covered. An x-ray taken in connection with the reduction of a fracture of the jaw or facial bone is covered, but a single x-ray or x-ray survey taken in connection with the care or treatment of teeth or the periodontium is not covered. [Pub. 100-02, Ch. 15, § 150; Ch. 16, § 140.]

[¶ 635] Services Not Provided In-House

Any services furnished to an inpatient of a hospital or to a hospital outpatient during an encounter by an entity other than the hospital are not covered, unless the hospital has an arrangement with that entity to furnish that particular service to the hospital's patients. The Medicare program requires hospitals and skilled nursing facilities (SNFs) caring for Medicare patients to provide in-house all the services that are furnished to those patients. This requirement is satisfied if the hospital or SNF has made arrangements to have the services provided by another entity, such as an independent laboratory or physical therapy group. Services not provided in-house that are supposed to be provided in-house are excluded from coverage and will not be covered by Medicare. [Soc. Sec. Act § 1862(a)(14), (18); 42 C.F.R. § 411.15(m)(1).]

The reason for this exclusion is that under each prospective payment system (PPS), in-house services are included in the calculation of the hospital's and SNF's PPS diagnosis-related group (DRG) payment rate, and Medicare will not pay for these services twice (see ¶ 810 and ¶ 835).

This exclusion applies, but is not limited, to the following items and services: (1) clinical laboratory services; (2) pacemakers and other prostheses and prosthetic devices (other than dental) that replace all or part of an internal body organ (for example, intraocular lenses); (3) artificial limbs, knees, and hips; (4) equipment and supplies covered under the prosthetic device benefits; and (5) services furnished incident to physicians' services. [42 C.F.R. § 411.15(m)(2).]

This exclusion does *not* apply to physicians' services or to the services of the following health care practitioners: (1) physician assistants; (2) nurse practitioners and clinical nurse specialists; (3) certified nurse-midwives; (4) qualified psychologists; and (5) certified registered nurse anesthetists and anesthesiologist's assistants. [42 C.F.R. § 411.15(m)(3).]

Charges to Beneficiaries

Under the regulations governing provider agreements, hospitals are prohibited from charging beneficiaries for inpatient hospital services furnished by entities with which there is no arrangements agreement. Furthermore, because services furnished under arrangements are included in the hospital's DRG rate, if an entity other than the hospital charges the hospital inpatient for its services, that charge is treated as a charge by the hospital and is regarded as a violation of its provider agreement. [42 C.F.R. § 489.21(f).]

[¶ 636] Medicare as Secondary Payer

Medicare payment is excluded for services to the extent that payment has been made, or reasonably can be expected to be made, when the following alternate types of insurance are available:

    (1) workers' compensation;

    (2) automobile, no-fault, or liability insurance; and

    (3) employer group health plans (GHPs).

This exclusion is referred to as the Medicare Secondary Payer (MSP) rule. [Soc. Sec. Act § 1862(b)(2)(A); 42 C.F.R. § 411.20.]

To improve Medicare's identification of MSP situations, CMS mails questionnaires to individuals before they become entitled to benefits under Part A or enroll in Part B to determine possible coverage under a primary plan. Payment for otherwise covered services will not be denied, however, solely on the grounds that a beneficiary failed to complete the questionnaire properly. [Soc. Sec. Act § 1862(b)(2)(C), (b)(5)(D).]

Providers and suppliers also are required to furnish information concerning potential coverage under other plans. Payment may not be made for Part B claims if the provider or supplier fails to complete MSP questions on the claim form. Fines of up to $2,000 for each incident have been established for entities that knowingly, willfully, and repeatedly fail to complete a claim form or fail to provide accurate MSP information. [Soc. Sec. Act § 1862(b)(6).]

Coordination of benefits. There may be instances when Medicare is secondary payer to more than one primary insurer (e.g., an individual who is covered under his or her own GHP and under the GHP of an employed spouse or under no-fault insurance). In such cases, the other primary payers will customarily coordinate benefits. If a portion of the charges remains unpaid after the other insurers have paid primary benefits, a secondary Medicare payment may be made. [*Medicare Secondary Payer Manual*, Pub. 100-05, Ch. 1, § 10.9.]

Workers' Compensation

Medicare payment is excluded for any items and services to the extent that payment has been made or reasonably can be expected to be made under a workers' compensation law or plan of the United States or a state. This exclusion also applies to the workers' compensation plans of the District of Columbia, American Samoa, Guam, the Virgin Islands, Puerto Rico, and the Virgin Islands. [Soc. Sec. Act § 1862(b)(2)(A)(ii); 42 C.F.R. § 411.40; Pub. 100-05, Ch. 1, § 10.4.]

¶636

The beneficiary is responsible for taking whatever action is necessary to obtain payment under workers' compensation when payment reasonably can be expected. Failure to take proper and timely action under such circumstances will preclude Medicare payment to the extent that payment reasonably could have been expected to be made under workers' compensation had the individual exhausted benefit rights under that system. [42 C.F.R. § 411.43(a).]

If a lump-sum workers' compensation award stipulates that the amount paid is intended to compensate the individual for all future medical expenses required because of the work-related injury or disease, Medicare payments for such services are excluded until medical expenses related to the injury or disease equal the amount of the lump-sum payment. [42 C.F.R. § 411.46(a).]

No Medicare payment will be made if: (1) workers' compensation pays an amount that equals or exceeds the gross amount payable by Medicare without regard to deductible and coinsurance; (2) workers' compensation pays an amount that equals or exceeds the provider's, physician's, or supplier's charges for Medicare-covered services; or (3) the provider accepts or is required under the workers' compensation law to accept such workers' compensation payment as payment in full. If workers' compensation pays less than these amounts and the provider is not obligated to accept the amount as payment in full, secondary Medicare payments can be made. [42 C.F.R. § 411.32(b).]

Liability claims. Most state laws provide that if an employee is injured at work due to the negligent act of a third party, the employee cannot receive payments from both workers' compensation and the third party for the same injury. Generally, the workers' compensation carrier pays benefits while the third-party claim is pending. However, once a settlement of the third-party claim is reached or an award has been made, the workers' compensation carrier may recover the benefits it paid from the third-party settlement and may deny any future claims for that injury up to the amount of the liability payment made to the individual. Regardless of the liabilities of any other parties to one another, Medicare is the residual payer. [Soc. Sec. Act § 1862(b)(2)(B)(ii); Pub. 100-05, Ch. 1, § 10.9.]

Automobile and Liability Insurance Coverage

Medicare payment is excluded for any items and services to the extent that payment has been made or reasonably can be expected to be made under an automobile or liability insurance policy or plan, including a self-insured plan, or under no-fault insurance. [Soc. Sec. Act § 1862(b)(2)(A)(ii); 42 C.F.R. §§ 411.20(a)(2), 411.50(c).]

In no-fault insurance cases, the beneficiary is responsible for taking whatever action is necessary to obtain any payments from the no-fault insurer that reasonably can be expected. Medicare normally will not make any payments until the beneficiary has exhausted all remedies to obtain payments from the no-fault insurer. [42 C.F.R. § 411.51.]

It is common for insurance companies to settle claims without admitting liability. Therefore, any payment by a liability insurer constitutes a liability insurance payment regardless of whether there has been a determination of liability. Medicare is entitled to seek repayment of the amount it paid, less a proportionate share of procurement costs, from any payment a claimant receives from a liability insurer or self-insured party. [42 C.F.R. § 411.37(a).]

Generally, if settlement or other payment is greater than Medicare's claim, Medicare must be paid in full. If, however, a court or other adjudicator designates certain amounts as compensation for pain and suffering or other losses not related to medical services, Medicare will accept the designation and will not seek recovery from those portions of awards. [Pub. 100-05, Ch. 7, § 50.4.4.]

Employer Group Health Plans

Medicare payment is excluded for employees entitled to Medicare based on old age, disability, or (during a 30-month coordination-of-benefits period) end-stage renal disease (ESRD) to the extent that health care benefit payments have been made or reasonably can be expected to be made under a GHP. [Soc. Sec. Act § 1862(b)(2)(A)(i); 42 C.F.R. § 411.20(a)(1).]

Working aged. The working aged exclusion applies to Medicare-eligible individuals age 65 or over whose employer group health coverage is based on the current employment of the individual or spouse by an employer that employs 20 or more employees. Health insurance plans for retirees or spouses of retirees are not affected because retirement does not constitute "current employment." [Soc. Sec. Act § 1862(b)(1)(A); 42 C.F.R. § 411.20(a)(1)(ii); Pub. 100-05, Ch. 2, § § 10, 10.3.]

Under this exclusion, employers are required to offer their employees age 65 or over the same GHP coverage offered to younger workers. Similarly, employers are required to offer their workers with Medicare-eligible spouses age 65 or over the same spousal GHP benefits they offer to workers with spouses that are not Medicare-eligible. [Soc. Sec. Act § 1862(b)(1)(A)(i).] Employees and their spouses then have the option of choosing either the employer plan or Medicare as their primary health insurer. If the employee or spouse elects the employer plan, Medicare will assume back-up coverage. If the employee or spouse elects Medicare as the primary insurer, however, the employer plan may not offer back-up coverage. [42 C.F.R. § 411.172(c); Pub. 100-05, Ch. 2, § 10.]

Medicare may assume primary responsibility in paying for a beneficiary's health care if the services furnished are not covered under the employer plan or the beneficiaries have exhausted their benefits under the plan. Conditional Medicare payments can be made if the employer plan denies the claim or the beneficiary failed to file a claim due to physical or mental incapacity. [42 C.F.R. § 411.175.]

The working aged employee provisions do not apply to disability beneficiaries or ESRD beneficiaries. [Soc. Sec. Act § 1862(b)(1)(A)–(C).]

Disabled employees. Medicare is the secondary payer for individuals under age 65 entitled to Medicare based on disability (see ¶ 204) who are covered by a "large group health plan" (LGHP) and whose coverage is based on the current employment status of the individual or of a family member. When an employee (or a member of the employee's family) becomes disabled, the LGHP has primary coverage responsibility and Medicare has secondary coverage responsibility. [Soc. Sec. Act § 1862(b)(1)(B); 42 C.F.R. § § 411.200–411.206.]

An LGHP is defined as a group health plan of either: (1) a single employer or employee organization; or (2) at least one of two or more employers or employee organizations that employed at least 100 full-time employees or part-time employees on 50 percent or more of its regular business days during the previous calendar year. [Soc. Sec. Act § 1862(b)(1)(B)(iii); Pub. 100-05, Ch. 2, § 30.2.]

As in the case of elderly employees, there is a special enrollment period for disabled employees who do not enroll in Part B because they have chosen disability coverage under the employer's plan (see ¶ 311).

ESRD beneficiaries. Medicare benefits are secondary for a limited period of time, known as the coordination-of-benefits period, for individuals who are eligible or entitled to Medicare benefits because of ESRD (see ¶ 845) and who are entitled to primary health care coverage under an employer GHP regardless of the number of employees employed by the employer and regardless of the individual's current employment status. [42 C.F.R. § 411.162(a).]

The coordination-of-benefits period begins with the first month in which the individual becomes eligible for Medicare, or the first month in which the individual would have been eligible for Medicare if he or she had filed an application for Medicare ESRD benefits. The coordination-of-benefits period ends 30 months later. During the coordination-of-benefits period, Medicare has secondary payment responsibility. After the coordination-of-benefits period ends, Medicare has primary payment responsibility, as the patient becomes entitled to Medicare. [Soc. Sec. Act § 1862(b)(1)(C); 42 C.F.R. § 411.162.]

During the coordination-of-benefits period, Medicare will pay primary benefits for Medicare covered services that: (1) are furnished to Medicare beneficiaries who have declined to enroll in the GHP; (2) are not covered by the employer plan; (3) are covered under the GHP but not available to particular enrollees because they have exhausted their benefits; or (4) are furnished to individuals whose continuation coverage under the Consolidated Omnibus Budget Reconciliation Act of 1985 (COBRA) (P.L. 99-272) (i.e., continued health insurance coverage after leaving employment) has been terminated because of the individual's Medicare entitlement. Medicare will make secondary payments to supplement the amount paid by the employer plan if that plan pays only a portion of the charge for the service. [42 C.F.R. § 411.162(a).]

Medicare benefits are primary without a coordination-of-benefits period for ESRD-eligible individuals if the following conditions are met: (1) the beneficiary was already entitled to Medicare because of age or disability; (2) either the group health insurance was not based on current employment status, or the employer had fewer than 20 employees (in the case of the aged) or fewer than 100 employees (in the case of the disabled); and (3) the plan is paying secondary to Medicare because the plan had justifiably taken into account the age-based or disability-based entitlement. The employer health plan may continue to pay benefits secondary to Medicare but may not differentiate in the services covered and the payments made between persons who have ESRD and those who do not. [42 C.F.R. § 411.163(b)(4).]

Conditional Medicare Payments

If a primary plan has not made or cannot reasonably be expected to make payment with respect to such item or service promptly, Medicare may make a conditional payment. The conditional payment will be recovered later if it is determined that Medicare's liability is secondary. Regardless of any time limit on filing a claim under an employer group health plan, the government has three years to file a claim for recovery of conditional benefits paid by Medicare, beginning on the date the item or service was furnished. [Soc. Sec. Act § 1862(b)(2)(B); 42 C.F.R. §§ 411.45, 411.52, 411.53.]

A primary payer, and an entity that receives payment from a primary payer, must reimburse CMS for any payment if it is demonstrated that the primary payer has or had a responsibility to make payment, which is demonstrated by: (1) a judgment; (2) a payment conditioned upon the recipient's compromise, waiver, or release (whether or not there is a determination or admission of liability) of payment for items and services included in a claim against the primary plan or the primary plan's insured; or (3) by other means, including a settlement, award, or contractual obligation. [Soc. Sec. Act § 1862(b)(2)(B)(ii); 42 C.F.R. § 411.22.]

Prompt payment. In general, a payment is considered to be made promptly if it is made within 120 days after receipt of the claim. In the case of liability insurance, however, a claim is considered paid promptly if it is paid within 120 days after the earlier of: (1) the date a claim is filed; or (2) the date the services were furnished. In the case of inpatient hospital services, services are considered to be furnished, for purposes of this provision, on the date of discharge. [42 C.F.R. § § 411.21, 411.50(b).]

Government action. If conditional Medicare payments are made, Medicare can bring an action to recover the payments it made against any entity that is responsible for payment under the MSP rules. In addition, it is possible for recovery to be made from a portion of the proceeds from the settlement of a lawsuit. The law further provides for subrogation, to the extent Medicare payment has been made for an item or service, to any right to payment for the item or service from the third party having primary payer responsibility. Medicare also is entitled to collect double damages against an alternate insurer that does not pay when it is required to do so. [Soc. Sec. Act § 1862(b)(2)(A), (b)(2)(B); 42 C.F.R. § 411.26.]

The beneficiary is required to cooperate in Medicare's attempt to recover conditional payments. If the beneficiary does not, Medicare is entitled to recover the payments from him or her. If the beneficiary receives a payment from the alternate insurer, he or she must reimburse Medicare within 60 days. [42 C.F.R. § § 411.23, 411.24(g) and (h).]

ESRD beneficiaries covered under a GHP. For ESRD beneficiaries who are also covered under a GHP, as a general rule, conditional primary Medicare payments may not be made if the claim is denied for one of the following reasons: (1) the GHP asserts it is secondary to Medicare or to the liability, no-fault, or workers' compensation insurer; (2) the GHP limits its payment when the individual is entitled to Medicare; (3) the services are covered by the GHP for younger employees and spouses but not for employees and spouses age 65 or over; or (4) the claim was not filed properly (including failure to file timely), if that failure is for any reason other than physical or mental incapacity of the beneficiary. Conditional primary Medicare benefits may be paid if the beneficiary, the provider, or the supplier that has accepted assignment files a proper claim under the GHP and the plan denies the claim in whole or in part; or the beneficiary, because of physical or mental incapacity, fails to file a proper claim. [42 C.F.R. § 411.165.]

Partial Payments by Alternate Insurer

If the alternate insurer pays less than the full amount of the charge for the services rendered, Medicare may make secondary payments to supplement the alternate insurer's payments. In no case, however, will the Medicare secondary payment exceed the amount that otherwise would have been payable if there were no alternate insurance. Medicare secondary payments also can be made to pay the alternate insurer's deductible and coinsurance requirements. [Soc. Sec. Act § 1862(b)(4); 42 C.F.R. § § 411.32, 411.33.]

Some third-party payments obligate the provider, physician, or supplier to accept the payment as payment in full. No Medicare payment is payable in such a case. [42 C.F.R. § 411.32(b).]

For physicians and suppliers who are not obligated to accept the third-party payment as payment in full, the amount of the Medicare secondary benefit payable is the lowest of the following:

(1) the actual charge by the physician or supplier minus the amount paid by the third-party payer;

(2) the amount Medicare would pay if services were not covered by the third-party payer; or

(3) the higher of: (a) the Medicare fee schedule or other amount payable under Medicare (without regard to any deductible and/or coinsurance amounts), or (b) the third-party payer's allowable charge (without regard to any deductible and/or coinsur-

ance amounts imposed by the policy or plan), minus the amount actually paid by the third-party payer.

[42 C.F.R. § 411.33(a).]

For hospitals and other providers that are not obligated to accept third-party payments as payment in full, the Medicare secondary payment is the lowest of the following:

(1) the gross amount payable by Medicare minus the applicable deductible and coinsurance amount;

(2) the gross amount payable by Medicare minus the amount paid by the third-party payer for Medicare-covered services;

(3) the provider's charges (or the amount the provider is obligated to accept as payment in full) minus the amount paid by the third-party payer; or

(4) the provider's charges (or the amount the provider is obligated to accept as payment in full) minus the applicable Medicare deductible and coinsurance amount.

[42 C.F.R. § 411.33(e).]

[¶ 644] Excluded Drugs and Biologicals

Prescription drugs that were approved before the 1962 amendments to the federal Food, Drug and Cosmetic Act (FDC Act), and that the HHS Secretary subsequently determines to be "less than effective" in use, are excluded under Part B. Also, no payment can be made for drug products that are identical, related, or similar to a drug that is excluded. To exclude a drug under this provision, the Secretary must publish a notice of an opportunity for hearing in accordance with section 505(e) of the FDC Act. [Soc. Sec. Act § 1862(c); *Medicare Benefit Policy Manual*, Pub. 100-02, Ch. 15, § 50.4.6.] This provision applies only under Part B. There is no comparable provision for excluding such drugs under Part A.

Drugs and biologicals (except for covered osteoporosis drugs) also are excluded from coverage as items or services administered by home health agencies. [Soc. Sec. Act § 1861(m)(5).]

Immunizations are also excluded, except for: (1) vaccinations or inoculations directly related to the treatment of an injury or direct exposure; (2) pneumococcal vaccinations that are reasonable and necessary for the prevention of an illness; (3) Hepatitis B vaccinations that are reasonable and necessary for the prevention of an illness for those individuals at high or intermediate risk of contracting Hepatitis B; and (4) influenza vaccinations that are reasonable and necessary for the prevention of an illness. [42 C.F.R. § 411.15(e).]

For a discussion of when drugs and biologicals are covered under Medicare, see ¶ 212 and ¶ 235 with respect to Part A, and ¶ 351 and ¶ 362 with respect to Part B. The Part D prescription drug benefit is discussed in Chapter 5.

[¶ 646] Services of Excluded Individuals and Entities

No Medicare payment may be made, except in an emergency, to an entity or individual, such as a provider, supplier, physician, or other health care practitioner, who has been excluded from the Medicare program due to program abuses (see ¶ 720). Similarly, Medicare payment will not be made for items or services furnished at the medical direction or on the prescription of a physician who is excluded from program participation if the person furnishing the items or services knew or had reason to know of the exclusion. [Soc. Sec. Act § 1862(e)(1).]

If a beneficiary submits a claim for items or services received from a physician or supplier who has been excluded from program participation, Medicare will pay for the items or services if the beneficiary did not know or did not have reason to know about the exclusion. [Soc. Sec. Act § 1862(e)(2).]

[¶ 654] Certain Services of Surgery Assistants

The following assistant-at-surgery services are excluded: (1) services of an assistant at surgery in cataract operations, including subsequent insertions of intraocular lenses, unless, before the surgery is performed, the appropriate quality improvement organization (QIO) (see ¶ 710) or a Medicare administrative contractor (MAC) has approved the use of the assistant due to the existence of a complicating medical condition; and (2) services of an assistant at surgery in a surgical procedure (or class of surgical procedures) for which assistants at surgery on average are used in fewer than 5 percent of such procedures nationally. Services subject to this exclusion include, but are not limited to, clinical laboratory services, pacemakers, artificial limbs, knees, and hips, intraocular lenses, total parenteral nutrition, and services incident to physicians' services. [Soc. Sec. Act §§ 1862(a)(15), 1848(i)(2)(B); 42 C.F.R. § 411.15(n).]

The Office of Inspector General may exclude a physician that (1) knowingly and willfully presented or caused to be presented a claim, or billed an individual enrolled under Part B of the Medicare program (or his or her representative) for services of an assistant at surgery during a cataract operation, or charges that include a charge for an assistant at surgery during a cataract operation; and (2) failed to obtain prior approval for the use of such assistant from the appropriate QIO or MAC. [42 C.F.R. § 1001.1701(a).]

Chapter 7- ADMINISTRATIVE PROVISIONS

[¶ 700] HHS and CMS Organizational Structure

The Secretary of the U.S. Department of Health and Human Services (HHS) oversees the Medicare program. Within HHS, the Medicare program is administered by the Centers for Medicare and Medicaid Services (CMS). CMS is responsible for: enrolling providers; enforcing provider standards, called "conditions of participation"; evaluating and paying claims; reviewing utilization; developing and reviewing policies governing coverage of developing services; and preventing and prosecuting fraud and abuse by providers. HHS contracts with other entities to perform many of these functions, including Medicare administrative contractors (MACs) (see ¶ 705), state and local survey and Medicaid agencies (see ¶ 703), private insurance companies, and quality improvement organizations. In addition to using such agencies or organizations under the conditions described below, the HHS Secretary is authorized to purchase or contract separately for such services as auditing or cost analysis. [Soc. Sec. Act § 1874(b).]

CMS Programs

In addition to the Medicare program, CMS operates the state-federal Medicaid program and Children's Health Insurance Program, the Health Care Quality Improvement Program (see ¶ 710), and a variety of related programs designed to control program costs, ensure appropriate utilization of health services by eligible beneficiaries and recipients, and eliminate provider fraud and abuse. CMS's goal is to ensure that the best possible care is delivered in the most economical manner to eligible beneficiaries and recipients. CMS also provides national policy planning for health care financing and for delivery of health services within these operating programs.

Medicare integrity. To ensure the integrity of the Medicare program, CMS has a number of fraud control and prevention initiatives, which work in collaboration with the HHS Office of Inspector General (OIG) and the Department of Justice. The HHS Secretary is also authorized to contract with private entities known as recovery audit contractors (RACs) to perform specified review and audit functions (see ¶ 711 for a full discussion of RACs). [Soc. Sec. Act § 1893(b).] The Social Security Administration is also involved in the administration of the Medicare program, primarily in the enrollment of beneficiaries in the program and the maintenance of beneficiary rolls.

Beneficiary information programs. The Secretary must issue all beneficiaries an "Explanation of Medicare Benefits" for all medical services or items furnished, including a notice of the right to request itemized statements. Within 30 days of a beneficiary's request, providers must furnish itemized statements of items or services or face a possible civil money penalty of not more than $100 for each such failure. Beneficiaries have 90 days after receiving the statement to submit written requests identifying billing irregularities to the Secretary, who must take all appropriate measures to recover any amounts unnecessarily paid. [Soc. Sec. Act § 1806.]

The Secretary must provide an annual notice to beneficiaries, including a statement of the beneficiary's right to request itemized statements of items or services provided, as well as an instruction to check explanations of benefits and itemized statements carefully for accuracy. The notice also must contain a description of the Medicare fraud and abuse information collection program (see below) and a toll-free telephone number to report errors or questionable charges. [Soc. Sec. Act § 1804(c).]

Reports of fraud or abuse. The Secretary is required to establish a separate program to encourage individuals to report other individuals and entities who are engaging, or have engaged, in acts or omissions that qualify for the imposition of sanctions under the OIG's civil penalty, exclusion, or law enforcement authorities (see below). A portion of the amount collected as the result of this program will be paid to the reporting individual when at least $100 is collected by the Secretary or the U.S. Attorney General. [Health Insurance Portability and Accountability Act of 1996 (HIPAA) (P.L. 104-191) § 203(b); 42 C.F.R. § 420.405.]

Information on program efficiency. The Secretary established a program to encourage individuals to submit suggestions for improving the efficiency of the Medicare program. As with the fraud and abuse reporting program, the Secretary may make an appropriate payment to individuals whose suggestions result in program savings. [HIPAA § 203(c); 42 C.F.R. § 420.410.]

The Center for Medicare Management serves as the focal point for CMS's interactions with providers and MACs concerning fee-for-service policies and procedures. It is responsible for policies concerning the scope of benefits and payment methods for all services covered by Medicare. [*Notice*, 78 FR 48164, Aug. 7, 2013.]

CMS Regional Offices

In addition to a central office in Baltimore, CMS maintains 10 regional offices, which are located in Atlanta, Boston, Chicago, Dallas, Denver, Kansas City (Mo.), New York, Philadelphia, San Francisco, and Seattle. CMS regional offices are often the first point of contact for beneficiaries, health care providers, state and local governments, and the general public. The regional offices provide customer service, program management, and education and outreach programs, and they develop partnerships with state and local health and social service agencies. Additional information on the CMS regional offices can be found at http://www.cms.gov/RegionalOffices/.

Medicare Beneficiary Ombudsman

Pursuant to Soc. Sec. Act § 1808(c), the HHS Secretary appointed a Medicare Beneficiary Ombudsman within HHS who has expertise and experience in health care and in the assistance of Medicare beneficiaries. The ombudsman's responsibilities include responding to the complaints, grievances, and inquiries of Medicare beneficiaries and providing assistance to those beneficiaries. This assistance includes providing help to beneficiaries to: (1) collect relevant information needed to file appeals; (2) terminate enrollment under Medicare Part C; and (3) present information related to income-related premium adjustments. The ombudsman also must submit annual reports to Congress and the Secretary of HHS describing its activities and providing recommendations regarding the administration of the Medicare programs. [Soc. Sec. Act § 1808(c).] The ombudsman's website is located at http://www.cms.gov/Center/Special-Topic/Ombudsman-Center.html.

HHS Office of Inspector General

The OIG is an independent unit within HHS that is headed by an Inspector General and a Deputy Inspector General. The OIG is charged with: (1) conducting audits and investigations relating to HHS programs and operations; (2) promoting economy and efficiency in the administration of HHS programs and operations, as well as preventing and detecting fraud and abuse; and (3) providing a means of keeping the Secretary and Congress fully and currently informed about problems and deficiencies relating to the administration and operation of HHS programs and the necessity of corrective action. Reports on OIG activities must be submitted annually to Congress and quarterly to the Secretary and appropriate congressional committees. The OIG must report immediately on any serious problems or abuses. [Inspector General Act of 1978 (P.L. 95-452).]

The OIG has primary responsibility for detecting abuses and applying sanctions against providers, physicians, entities, and suppliers of health care items and services that commit federal health care program abuses. The Health Care Fraud and Abuse Control Program, required by HIPAA, is administered under the joint direction of the U.S. Attorney General and the Secretary of HHS, acting through the OIG (see ¶ 720).

Health Care Reform Initiatives

The Patient Protection and Affordable Care Act (ACA) (P.L. 111-148) required the HHS Secretary to oversee various programs to enhance health care quality, some of which are administered by CMS and some of which are administered by other HHS agencies and entities.

National Strategy to Improve Health Care Quality. Pursuant to section 3011 of the ACA, the HHS Secretary established a national strategy to improve the delivery of health care and patient outcomes and created a comprehensive strategic plan to achieve those priorities. [Public Health Service Act (PHSA) § 399HH(a), 399HH(a)(2)(C) and (D).] HHS's Agency for Healthcare Research and Quality submitted its first national strategy to Congress in March 2011, and updates the report annually. The national priorities for improvement of health care quality and the agency-specific strategic plans are posted on an agency website available to the public (http://www.ahrq.gov/workingforquality/).

Center for Medicare and Medicaid Innovation. Section 3021 of the ACA established the Center for Medicare and Medicaid Innovation (CMMI) within CMS. Its purpose is to test systems of provider payment and delivery of services in order to cut costs while preserving or enhancing the quality of care delivered to Medicare and Medicaid beneficiaries. The HHS Secretary selects test models, giving preference to models that have the effect of improving the coordination, quality, and efficiency of health care services available to Medicare and Medicaid beneficiaries. [Soc. Sec. Act § 1115A.]

Independent Payment Advisory Board. Section 3403 of the ACA created an Independent Payment Advisory Board (IPAB), administered within HHS, composed of 15 independent members appointed by the President as well as the HHS Secretary, the CMS Administrator, and the Administrator of the Health Resources and Services Administration (HRSA) within HHS, to reduce the per capita rate of growth in Medicare spending. IPAB is intended to be an independent, nonpartisan body of doctors and other health experts. It was envisioned as a way to free Congress from the burdens of dealing with highly technical issues such as Medicare reimbursement rates. [Soc. Sec. Act § 1899A.]

As of December 2015, no members have been appointed to IPAB and the Board has never convened, because Medicare spending has not grown at a high enough rate to require IPAB action. The CMS Actuary publishes its IPAB determinations at https://www.cms.gov/Research-Statistics-Data-and-Systems/Research/ActuarialStudies/IPAB-Determination.html.

Railroad Retirement Board

CMS and the Railroad Retirement Board have agreed on a delegation of important responsibilities to the railroad agency in connection with Medicare Part B. Under this delegation, the Railroad Retirement Board has responsibility for enrolling railroad eligibles in Medicare, for collecting their premiums, and for selecting MACs (see ¶ 705) for railroad enrollees under Part B.

The Railroad Retirement Board applies the same policies and regulations as CMS in determining what expenses are covered and what payments are to be made. [Soc. Sec. Act § 226(a)(2)(B), (b)(2)(B).]

Private Accrediting Organizations

The HHS Secretary contracts with private national accreditation bodies to determine whether hospitals, skilled nursing facilities, home health agencies, ambulatory surgical centers, hospices, organ transplant centers, rural health clinics, laboratories, clinics, rehabilitation agencies (including comprehensive outpatient rehabilitation agencies), psychiatric hospitals, public health agencies, and suppliers of durable medical equipment, prosthetics, orthotics, and supplies meet Medicare requirements. [Soc. Sec. Act §§ 1834(a)(20)(F), 1865(a); 42 C.F.R § 488.6.]

[¶ 703] Role of the State and Local Agencies

The Social Security Act requires the HHS Secretary to enter into agreements with able and willing state agencies to determine whether a provider of services—a hospital, skilled nursing facility, home health agency, hospice, rural health clinic, critical access hospital, comprehensive outpatient rehabilitation facility, clinic, rehabilitation agency, public health agency, or ambulatory surgical center—meets the conditions of participation of federal health care programs. State agencies conduct investigations, called surveys, and certify to the Secretary that a provider meets the conditions of participation. [Soc. Sec. Act § 1864(a), (c).]

State agencies also certify compliance with respect to other health care entities, such as independent laboratories, suppliers of portable x-ray services, and public health agencies providing outpatient physical and occupational therapy or speech-language pathology services under Part B. If the state survey agency determines that a provider or facility is not in substantial compliance with the conditions of participation, it must give written notice of the deficiencies. [42 C.F.R. § 488.18.]

Providers and facilities are surveyed at the following times: on initial application to participate in Medicare; when certification or enrollment is up for renewal; when the provider or facility receives a complaint or allegation of a deficiency; and selectively, on a sample basis. [Soc. Sec. Act § 1864(a), (c).]

Public assistance recipients. State Medicaid agencies also determine eligibility of Medicare beneficiaries for the low-income subsidy, which pays for part or all of the beneficiaries' cost-sharing requirements for prescription drug plans under Medicare Part D (see ¶ 508). [Soc. Sec. Act § 1860D-14.]

If a state enters into an agreement with Medicare to pay the Part B premium on behalf of its public assistance recipients, the agreement may provide for a designated state agency to serve as a Medicare administrative contractor (MAC) on behalf of its public assistance recipients. [Soc. Sec. Act § 1843(f).]

Disclosure of Information

Within 90 days following the state agency's completion of a health facility survey, information from the survey is available to the public, including a statement of deficiencies or the survey report itself and any pertinent written statements furnished by the surveyed facility. [Soc. Sec. Act § 1864(a).]

Adverse fraud and abuse information. The National Practitioner Data Bank (NPDB), which includes the database formerly known as the Healthcare Integrity and Protection Data Bank, collects fraud and abuse data from state agencies and other sources and provides this data to authorized recipients. HHS's Health Resources and Services Administration administers the NPDB as a confidential clearinghouse for fraud and abuse information. The databank is located at http://www.npdb.hrsa.gov/ (see ¶ 720).

[¶ 705] Role of Medicare Administrative Contractors

Private organizations have a considerable role in the administration of Medicare. Medicare administrative contractors (MACs) process and pay both Part A and Part B claims from particular geographic areas of the country. MACs competitively bid on contracts with the federal government to perform administrative and operational tasks for the program. [Soc. Sec. Act § § 1816, 1842(a), 1874A.]

MACs' functions include: (1) determining the amount of Medicare payments required to be made to providers and suppliers; (2) making Medicare payments; (3) providing education and outreach to beneficiaries, providers, and suppliers; (4) communicating with providers and suppliers; (5) having in place an improper payment outreach and education program; and (6) any additional functions as necessary. [Soc. Sec. Act § 1874A(a)(4).]

Requirements for Medicare Administrative Contractors

An entity is eligible to become a MAC only if it: (1) has demonstrated capability to carry out the MAC functions; (2) complies with conflict-of-interest standards as are generally applicable to federal acquisition and procurement; (3) has sufficient assets to financially support the performance of the functions; and (4) meets other requirements as the Secretary may impose. [Soc. Sec. Act § 1874A(a)(2).]

Contract requirements. The HHS Secretary must use competitive procedures when awarding MAC contracts. If a MAC has met or exceeded performance requirements, HHS may renew the contract from term to term without the application of competitive procedures, as long as it recompetes contracts at least once every 10 years. [Soc. Sec. Act § 1874A(b)(1)(B).]

The Secretary is required to develop contract performance requirements and standards for measuring the extent to which a contractor has met the requirements. The Secretary makes contractor performance requirements and measurement standards available to the public. [Soc. Sec. Act § 1874A(b)(3).]

Beginning for contracts entered into or renewed on or after December 28, 2018, the HHS Secretary must provide incentives for MACs to reduce the improper payment error rates in their jurisdictions. [Soc. Sec. Act § 1847A(b)(1)(D).]

MAC Jurisdictions

Out of 15 original MAC jurisdictions, CMS is consolidating MAC workloads into five pairings, to form five consolidated Part A and Part B MAC contracts and its ultimate goal of 10 MAC jurisdictions. Jurisdictions that have already combined are as follows:

- Jurisdictions 2 and 3 were combined to form MAC Jurisdiction F (Alaska, Washington, Oregon, Idaho, North Dakota, South Dakota, Montana, Wyoming, Utah, and Arizona)

- Jurisdictions 4 and 7 were combined to form MAC Jurisdiction H (Louisiana, Arkansas, Mississippi, Texas, Oklahoma, Colorado, and New Mexico)

- Jurisdictions 13 and 14 were combined to form MAC Jurisdiction K (New York, Connecticut, Massachusetts, Rhode Island, Vermont, Maine, and New Hampshire)

CMS intends to keep the following five MAC jurisdictions unchanged:

- Jurisdiction E (formerly known as Jurisdiction 1) (California, Hawaii, Nevada, and Pacific Islands)

- Jurisdiction N (formerly known as Jurisdiction 9) (Florida, Puerto Rico, and U.S. Virgin Islands)

- Jurisdiction J (formerly known as Jurisdiction 10) (Alabama, Georgia, and Tennessee)

- Jurisdiction M (formerly known as Jurisdiction 11) (North Carolina, South Carolina, Virginia, and West Virginia)

- Jurisdiction L (formerly known as Jurisdiction 12) (Delaware, Maryland, Pennsylvania, New Jersey, and Washington, D.C.)

CMS has postponed the consolidation of the following jurisdictions:

- Jurisdictions 5 and 6 will be combined to form Jurisdiction G (Minnesota, Wisconsin, Illinois, Kansas, Nebraska, Iowa, and Missouri)

- Jurisdictions 8 and 15 will be combined to form Jurisdiction I (Kentucky, Ohio, Michigan, and Indiana)

[http://www.cms.gov/Medicare/Medicare-Contracting/Medicare-Administrative-Contractors/A-B_MAC_Jurisdictions.html.]

DME MACs. Durable medical equipment (DME) MACs are responsible for processing Medicare durable medical equipment, orthotics, and prosthetics claims for a jurisdiction. CMS has established four DME MAC jurisdictions. [http://www.cms.gov/Medicare/Medicare-Contracting/Medicare-Administrative-Contractors/DME-MAC-Jurisdictions.html.]

[¶ 710] Quality Improvement Organizations

Quality improvement organizations (QIOs) review the professional activities of physicians and other health care practitioners and providers that furnish health care services and items that may be paid for by Medicare. QIOs are private organizations staffed by professionals, mostly doctors and other health care professionals, who are trained to review medical care, help beneficiaries with complaints about quality of care, and implement improvements in quality of care. CMS contracts with one QIO in each state, the District of Columbia, Puerto Rico, and the U.S. Virgin Islands to serve as that area's QIO; however, CMS may contract with QIOs across state lines. [Soc. Sec. Act §§ 1153, 1154(a)(1); http://www.cms.gov/QualityImprovementOrgs/.]

The term of QIO contracts is five years, with each cycle referenced as an ordinal Statement of Work (SOW). [Soc. Sec. Act § 1153(c)(3).] As a condition of participation in Medicare, all hospitals, critical access hospitals (CAHs), skilled nursing facilities, and home health agencies are required to have an agreement with a QIO. [Soc. Sec. Act § 1866(a)(1)(F).]

Required Review Activities

QIOs review hospitals paid by the hospital inpatient prospective payment system (IPPS), under which hospitals are paid a fixed rate per discharge according to Medicare severity diagnosis-related groups (MS-DRGs) of illnesses (see ¶ 810). QIOs review the care and services provided to a beneficiary to determine the following:

(1) whether the services were reasonable and medically necessary;

(2) whether the quality of the services meets professionally recognized standards of health care;

(3) whether inpatient services could be effectively furnished more economically on an outpatient basis or in an inpatient health care facility of a different type;

(4) the validity of diagnostic and procedural information supplied by the hospital;

(5) the completeness, adequacy, and quality of hospital care provided;

(6) the medical necessity, reasonableness, and appropriateness of hospital admissions and discharges;

(7) the medical necessity, reasonableness, and appropriateness of inpatient hospital care for which additional payment is sought; and

(8) whether a hospital has misrepresented admission or discharge information or has taken an action that results in unnecessary admissions or other inappropriate practices.

[Soc. Sec. Act §§ 1154(a)(1), (d), 1833(i)(1)(A); 42 C.F.R. § 476.71(a).]

The determinations of QIOs on these matters are binding for purposes of determining whether Medicare benefits should be paid, with some exceptions. [Soc. Sec. Act § 1154(a)(2).] If a QIO determines that a hospital has circumvented the IPPS, Medicare payment may be denied or the hospital may be required to take corrective action. [Soc. Sec. Act § 1886(f)(2).]

If a QIO finds that an IPPS hospital engaged in unnecessary admissions, early discharges and subsequent readmissions, or other improper practices to circumvent the IPPS, the Secretary may: (1) deny payment, in whole or in part, for the inappropriate services; or (2) require the hospital to take other corrective action necessary to prevent or correct the inappropriate practice. When a hospital has a pattern of inappropriate admissions and billing practices that has the effect of circumventing the IPPS, the QIO may recommend denying payment to that hospital, as well as other corrective actions, including the exclusion of the provider from Medicare participation. [Soc. Sec. Act § 1886(f)(2); see Soc. Sec. Act § 1128(c)–(g).]

Each QIO assumes review responsibilities in accordance with the schedule, functions, and negotiated objectives specified in its contract with CMS, including the review requirements detailed in the SOW, which are incorporated into the QIO contract. [42 C.F.R. § 476.74.] The SOW establishes specific tasks for QIOs in relation to hospitals, ambulatory surgical centers, clinics, rehabilitation facilities, home health agencies, and physicians. The emphasis is on collaboration with providers to develop and institute processes to improve the quality of care and eliminate unreasonable, unnecessary, and inappropriate care provided to beneficiaries. [*Notice*, 79 FR 46830, Aug. 11, 2014; *Medicare Quality Improvement Organization Manual*, Pub. 100-10, Ch. 1, § 1005.]

The eleventh SOW, which began on August 1, 2014, is scheduled to last five years. As a part of a restructuring of the QIO program in 2014, CMS introduced two new phases aimed at improving patient care and health outcomes and saving taxpayer resources. The first phase of the restructuring allows two Beneficiary and Family-Centered Care (BFCC) QIOs to review and monitor the program separately from the traditional quality improvement activities to ensure consistency in the review process. [*Notice,* 79 FR 43747, July 28, 2014.] In the second phase of the restructuring, CMS will award contracts to Quality Innovation Networks QIOs that will work directly with providers and communities on data-driven initiatives. [*Notice*, 79 FR 46830, Aug. 11, 2014.] More information on the eleventh SOW is posted at https://www.fbo.gov/.

Mandatory Case Review

QIOs must review the following:

Beneficiary complaints. QIOs review all written beneficiary complaints regarding quality of health care and services not meeting professionally recognized standards of health care, as well as oral complaints (see the "Alternative Dispute Resolution Process" discussion below). Written complaints must be received by the QIO not later than three years from the date on which the care giving rise to the complaint occurred. QIOs must treat all information submitted by the beneficiary or his or her representative as confidential. Providers must deliver all medical information requested in response to a Medicare beneficiary complaint within 14 calendar days of the QIO's request. The QIO peer reviewer will complete the review and notify the practitioner and/or provider of the interim initial determination within 10 calendar days of the receipt of all medical information, giving the provider an opportunity for discussion. The QIO peer reviewer then must telephone the beneficiary within three days and issue a written final initial determination to all parties within five days after completion of the review. [Soc. Sec. Act § 1154(a)(14); 42 C.F.R. §§ 476.120, 476.130.]

Beginning with complaints filed after July 31, 2014, a Medicare beneficiary, provider, or practitioner who is dissatisfied with a QIO's final initial determination may request a reconsideration by the QIO. [42 C.F.R. § 476.140.]

Noncoverage notices issued by hospitals. Hospitals issue noncoverage notices to Medicare beneficiaries informing them that Medicare will deny coverage of their continued stay if the hospital determines and the attending physician concurs that inpatient care no longer is required. QIOs are required to review noncoverage notices issued by a hospital on the request of the hospital, the beneficiary, or his or her representative. [Soc. Sec. Act § 1154(e); Pub. 100-10, Ch. 7, § 7000.]

Antidumping violations. QIOs review allegations of hospital emergency rooms turning away or transferring patients without screening for, or stabilizing, emergency medical conditions. [Soc. Sec. Act § 1867(d)(3); 42 C.F.R. § 489.24(h).]

Review of assistants at surgery in cataract operations. QIOs review requests for surgical assistants based on medical necessity. Medicare payment for the services of an assistant at cataract surgery is prohibited unless a QIO approves the services before the surgery based on the existence of a complicating medical condition. [Soc. Sec. Act § 1862(a)(15); Pub. 100-10, Ch. 4, § 4020.]

Requests for upward adjustment of MS-DRG. QIOs perform MS-DRG coding validation reviews of IPPS cases, including hospital requests for higher-weighted MS-DRG adjustments. The purpose of DRG validation is to ensure that diagnostic and procedural information and the discharge status of the patient as coded and reported by the hospital on its claim match the attending physician's description and the information contained in the patient's medical record. [Soc. Sec. Act § 1866(a)(1)(F); 42 C.F.R. § 476.71(a)(4); Pub. 100-10, Ch. 4, § 4130.]

Referrals. QIOs review all cases referred by CMS, HHS, the Office of Inspector General, Medicare contractors, and clinical data abstraction centers. QIOs also review cases referred by Medicare Advantage organization contractors or state Medicaid and survey and certification agencies. [Pub. 100-10, Ch. 4, § 4070.]

CAH patient records. QIOs evaluate CAHs for quality of care, the appropriateness of admissions and discharge, Medicare coverage issues, accuracy of coding, or appropriateness of medical services. [Pub. 100-10, Ch. 3, § 3010.]

Alternative Dispute Resolution Process

QIOs offer an alternative dispute resolution option called "Immediate Advocacy" to quickly resolve an oral complaint a Medicare beneficiary or his or her representative has regarding the quality of Medicare covered health care. This process involves a QIO representative's direct contact with the provider and/or practitioner if:

    (1) the complaint is received within six months from the incident;

(2) after initial screening of the complaint, the QIO makes a preliminary determination that it is unrelated to the clinical quality of health care itself but relates to items or services that accompany or are incidental to the medical care and are provided by a practitioner and/or provider; or the complaint, while related to the clinical quality of health care received by the beneficiary, does not rise to the level of being a gross and flagrant, substantial, or significant quality of care concern;

(3) the beneficiary agrees to the disclosure of his or her name to the involved provider and/or practitioner;

(4) all parties orally consent to the use of immediate advocacy; and

(5) all parties agree to confidentiality limitations on redisclosure.

The QIO or either party may discontinue participation in immediate advocacy at any time. The QIO may determine that a complaint has been abandoned and then inform the parties that immediate advocacy will be discontinued and inform the Medicare beneficiary of his or her right to submit a written complaint. [42 C.F.R. § 476.110.]

Appeals from QIO Coverage Determinations

If a QIO's determination denies coverage or a requested MS-DRG as a result of MS-DRG validation, the beneficiary, provider, or practitioner is entitled to notice and reconsideration of the determination by the QIO. An initial denial determination consists of a finding that the health care services provided were unnecessary, unreasonable, or at an inappropriate level of care. [Soc. Sec. Act §§ 1154(a)(3), 1155; 42 C.F.R. §§ 478.12, 478.15, 478.16.]

The QIO's notice to the beneficiary and the Medicare contractor also must be sent to the provider or practitioner. A dissatisfied party may obtain reconsideration of the initial review by filing a written request within 60 days after the date of the initial denial determination, unless the time is extended for good cause. The date of receipt of the initial denial determination notice is presumed to be five days after the date listed on the notice unless there is a showing to the contrary. [42 C.F.R. §§ 478.20, 478.22.]

If the QIO's reconsidered determination is adverse to the beneficiary and the amount in controversy is at least $200, the beneficiary (but not a provider or practitioner) is entitled to a hearing by an administrative law judge (ALJ). A request for a hearing must be filed within 60 days after the date of receipt of the notice of reconsidered determination. If the amount in controversy is $2,000 or greater, the beneficiary is entitled to judicial review of the ALJ's decision. [Soc. Sec. Act § 1155; 42 C.F.R. §§ 478.12, 478.20, 478.40, 478.46.]

Limitations on Beneficiary Liability

The law prohibits physicians, in the case of assigned claims, from billing beneficiaries for services for which payment has been denied by a QIO on the basis of substandard quality of care. [Soc. Sec. Act § 1842(b)(3)(B)(ii).] CMS also indemnifies the beneficiary in the case of any deductible and coinsurance paid if a QIO has denied Medicare payment for services. [Soc. Sec. Act § 1879(b).]

Sanctions

If a QIO determines that a practitioner or provider has violated its obligations to furnish services that are economical, medically necessary, of proper quality, and properly documented, the QIO may recommend sanctions. Practitioners and providers are entitled to reasonable notice of a sanction determination and must be provided the opportunity for a hearing as well as judicial review. The first step is to give the provider or practitioner the opportunity to meet with three members of the QIO to discuss the potential violation and agree to a corrective action plan approved by the QIO. [Soc. Sec. Act § 1156(a), (b); 42 C.F.R. § 1004.30.]

If the corrective action plan is not completed and the QIO determines that the provider or practitioner has violated the requirements in a substantial number of cases or has violated one or more requirements "grossly and flagrantly," the QIO must submit a report and recommendation to the Secretary on the imposition of sanctions, including exclusion from Medicare and Medicaid participation or assessment of fines. A QIO recommendation of exclusion automatically becomes effective if the Secretary fails to act within a 120-day review period. [Soc. Sec. Act § 1156(b); 42 C.F.R. § § 1004.30, 1004.40; Pub. 100-10, Ch. 9, § 9000.]

[¶ 711] Recovery Audit Contractors

The HHS Secretary is authorized to contract with eligible private entities known as recovery audit contractors (RACs) to perform specified review and audit functions. The RAC program was designed is to identify and correct Medicare improper payments through the efficient detection and collection of overpayments made on claims of health care services provided to Medicare beneficiaries, and the identification of underpayments to providers so that the CMS can implement actions that will prevent future improper payments. [Soc. Sec. Act § 1893(h).]

RACs perform a variety of review and audit functions, including:

(1) review of activities of providers of services or other individuals and entities furnishing items and services for which payment may be made under Medicare, including medical and utilization review and fraud review;

(2) audit of cost reports;

(3) determinations as to whether Medicare payment should not be or should not have been made, and recovery of payments that should not have been made;

(4) education of providers, beneficiaries, and other persons with respect to payment integrity and benefit quality assurance issues;

(5) developing and updating a list of items of durable medical equipment that are subject to prior authorization; and

(6) the Medicare-Medicaid Data Match Program.

[Soc. Sec. Act § 1893(b).]

RACs are paid on a contingency basis from the recovered funds. The amount of the contingency fee is a percentage of the improper payment recovered from, or reimbursed to, providers. [Soc. Sec. Act § 1893(h).]

CMS also has the authority to enter into contracts with RACs to identify and reconcile overpayments and underpayments in Medicare Parts C and D. In addition to their other responsibilities, RACs must: ensure that MA and prescription drug plans (PDPs) have antifraud plans in effect and review the effectiveness of the plans; review PDPs' estimates on enrollment of high-cost beneficiaries; and examine claims for reinsurance payments to determine whether PDPs submitting such claims incurred costs in excess of the allowable reinsurance costs permitted. [Soc. Sec. Act § 1893(h)(9).]

RAC Program Operation

The RAC program originated as a demonstration project in 2005 but was expanded to include all 50 states and the District of Columbia. Four RACs cover specific geographic areas of the nation. [https://www.cms.gov/research-statistics-data-and-systems/monitoring-programs/medicare-ffs-compliance-programs/recovery-audit-program/.]

Requirements. RACs must comply with the following requirements:

    (1) have a medical director;

    (2) look back only three years when reviewing claims;

    (3) not look back for any improper payments on claims paid before October 1, 2007;

    (4) RACs are allowed to review claims during the current fiscal year;

    (5) have certified coders on staff;

    (6) provide credentials of reviewers upon request;

    (7) there is a limit on the number of medical records that a RAC may request in any 45-day period, based on the size and/or volume of the provider or practitioner;

    (8) include the reason(s) for the review on the request for record letters and overpayment demands;

    (9) grant the provider/practitioner a discussion with the medical director on request;

    (10) report frequent problem areas;

    (11) pay back the contingency fee if they lose at any level of appeal;

    (12) have a web-based application that allows providers to customize addresses and contact information or see the status of cases;

    (13) publicly disclose contingency fees; and

    (14) participate in the external validation process, a uniform process among the states.

[*Recovery Auditing in Medicare for Fiscal Year 2014 Report to Congress*, Oct. 15, 2015.]

An entity is eligible to enter into a contract under the RAC program if it meets certain requirements, one of which is to demonstrate to the Secretary that the entity's financial holdings, interests, or relationships will not interfere with its ability to perform as required. Medicare administrative contractors (MACs) (see ¶705) are prohibited from entering into contracts under this provision. [Soc. Sec. Act § 1893(c), (h)(6)(B).]

RACs work with Medicare contractors in determining the amount of any overpayments. RACs collect the overpayments using the same procedures as other contractors, subject to the same requirements and limits on recoupment. [*Medicare Financial Management Manual*, Pub 100-06, Ch. 4, § 100.6.]

Appeals

Appeals of RAC determinations regarding fee-for-service claims are handled with other overpayment determinations under the regular Medicare appeals process, although the MAC must track the RAC appeals separately in its reports to CMS. [Soc. Sec. Act § 1893(h); Pub. 100-06, Ch. 4, § § 100.6, 100.7.]

There are five levels of appeals for claim denials, including those resulting from RAC audits: (1) redetermination by the MAC; (2) reconsideration by a qualified independent contractor; (3) administrative law judge hearing; (4) Medicare Appeals Council review; and (5) judicial review in federal court. [http://www.cms.gov/Outreach-and-Education/Medicare-Learning-Network-MLN/MLNProducts/Downloads/MedicareAppealsProcess.pdf.]

If the Part C or Part D RAC did not apply its stated payment methodology correctly, MA organizations and Part D plan sponsors may appeal the findings of the applied methodology. [42 C.F.R. § § 422.2600, 423.2600.]

See ¶ 924 for a detailed discussion of the claims appeals process.

[¶ 715] Privacy of Health Data

Pursuant to the Health Insurance Portability and Accountability Act of 1996 (HIPAA) (P.L. 104-191), HHS implemented national standards to protect individually identifiable health information. The HIPAA privacy and security standards apply to all health care plans, health care clearinghouses, and health care providers who transmit any health information in electronic form (collectively called "covered entities"). [45 C.F.R. §§ 160.102, 160.103.]

Business associates. Providers are responsible for the use of protected health information (PHI) released to other organizations. Health care providers and other covered entities must have a contract (or other written agreement) with each business associate detailing how the business associate will protect the individually identifiable information. [45 C.F.R. § 164.502(e)(2).] Business associates must provide the same protection to individually identifiable data as health care providers or other covered entities. [45 C.F.R. § 164.504(e).]

Individually Identifiable Health Information

"Individually identifiable health information" is defined as data that is created or received by a health care provider, health plan, employer, or health care clearinghouse that relates to any of the following: (1) the past, present, or future physical or mental health condition of an individual; (2) the provision of health care to an individual; or (3) the past, present, or future payment for the provision of health care that identifies the individual or that could reasonably be used to identify the individual. [45 C.F.R. § 160.103.]

"Protected health information" is defined as individually identifiable health information that is transmitted or maintained in an electronic format or any other medium. The regulations cover all health data, including written records and oral communications, and not just electronically maintained or transmitted data. The disclosure of health information includes the release, transfer, provision of, access to, or divulging of patient health information, in any manner, to others outside of the entity holding the information. [45 C.F.R. § 160.103.]

The term "health care" as it relates to HIPAA means care, services, or supplies related to the health of an individual, including the following services: (1) preventive, diagnostic, therapeutic, rehabilitative, counseling, service assessments, or any other procedure with respect to the physical, mental, or functional condition of a patient; and (2) the sale or dispensing of prescription drugs, equipment, or devices in accordance with a prescription. [45 C.F.R. § 160.103.] For example, the disclosure of information for something as simple as an eyeglass prescription or the cost of services paid by a patient is prohibited under HIPAA.

Patient Notice

Health care providers must issue a notice to patients during the first delivery of service describing the provider's privacy policy. Providers are required to conduct a good faith effort to obtain written acknowledgment from a patient of the receipt of the privacy notice. In an emergency situation, the provider may obtain the acknowledgment as soon as reasonably practicable. The notice also must be available at any time and publicly displayed in a clear and prominent location in the provider's office. [45 C.F.R. § 164.520(c)(2).]

The notice must describe how the patient's medical information will be used and disclosed. The notice is required to inform patients that they have a right to inspect, copy, amend, and receive a list of people and organizations that have requested access to their PHI and must contain the name, title, and telephone number of a contact person in the provider's office, as well as a description of the provider's legal duties with respect to the patient's PHI. [45 C.F.R. § 164.520(a)(1), (b).]

¶715

The notice must contain the following header statement in all capital letters (or otherwise prominently displayed):

"THIS NOTICE DESCRIBES HOW MEDICAL INFORMATION ABOUT YOU MAY BE USED AND DISCLOSED AND HOW YOU CAN GET ACCESS TO THIS INFORMATION. PLEASE REVIEW IT CAREFULLY."

[45 C.F.R. § 164.520(b)(1)(i).] In addition, providers must retain copies of the notices issued and, if applicable, any written acknowledgments of the patient's receipt of the notice, or any other documentation of the provider's good faith efforts to obtain a written acknowledgment of the patient's privacy rights. [45 C.F.R. § 164.520(e).]

Exception for inmates. Inmates do not have a right to notice under the provisions of 45 C.F.R. § 164.520; accordingly, these notice requirements do not apply to a correctional institution that is also a covered entity. [45 C.F.R. § 164.520(a)(3).]

Authorization to Release Individually Identifiable Health Information

Health care providers may not release individually identifiable health information without an authorization unless the information is released: (1) for the provider's own treatment, payment, or health care operations; (2) for treatment activities of another health care provider; (3) for payment activities of another covered entity; (4) to other providers of the patient's care; or (5) to other providers in the provider's organized health care arrangement for the purposes of treating the patient. [45 C.F.R. § 164.506.]

Patients may grant providers authorization to disclose individually identifiable health information for specific purposes. Disclosures of the information must be consistent with the authorization. Providers may not condition the provision of health care based on a patient's signing of such an authorization. [45 C.F.R. § 164.508.] In addition, patients have the right to request that providers restrict the use or disclosure of their personally identifiable health data. The provider, however, does not have to agree to a patient's requested restriction. [45 C.F.R. § 164.522.]

In limited circumstances, oral consent or authorization from a patient is sufficient as long as the patient is informed about how his or her information will be used. [45 C.F.R. § 164.510.]

Marketing. Providers must obtain an authorization from a patient before using the patient's individually identifiable health information for marketing purposes. If the marketing involves financial remuneration to the covered entity from a third party, the authorization must state that such remuneration is involved. [45 C.F.R. § 164.508(a)(3).] "Marketing" means to communicate about a product or service to encourage recipients of the communication to purchase or use the product or service. [45 C.F.R. § 164.501.]

Sale of PHI. A covered entity must obtain an authorization for any sale of protected health information; the authorization must state that the disclosure will result in remuneration to the covered entity. [45 C.F.R. § 164.508(a)(4).]

Psychotherapy notes. Providers also must obtain an authorization from a patient for any use or disclosure of psychotherapy notes, except: (1) to carry out treatment, payment, or health care operations; or (2) for permitted uses by the originator of the psychotherapy notes. [45 C.F.R. § 164.508(a)(2).]

Requirements. Authorizations must contain: (1) a description of the information to be disclosed and how it will be used; (2) the name of the person or organization authorized to make the disclosure; (3) the name of the person or organization or a description of the class of organization to which the information will be disclosed; (4) a description of the purpose of the release ("at the request of the individual" is a sufficient description of the purpose when the patient initiates the authorization); (5) an expiration date or event; (6) a statement of the individual's right to revoke the authorization at any time; (7) a statement about whether the health care provider may condition the provision of treatment based on the individual signing an authorization; (8) a statement that the individually identifiable health information is subject to further disclosure by the recipient of the information; and (9) the dated signature of the patient. [45 C.F.R. § 164.508(c).]

Exemptions to Privacy Rule

Health care facilities may provide a directory of patients that includes the patient's name, location in the facility, the general condition of the patient that does not communicate specific medical information, and the individual's religious affiliation. A patient must be given the opportunity to restrict or prohibit the information placed in this directory. [45 C.F.R. § 164.510(a)(1) and (2).]

Limited use and disclosure. If the patient is unable to agree or object to the use or disclosure of PHI because he or she is not present, incapacitated, or in an emergency circumstance, health care facilities may use their professional judgment to determine whether disclosure is in the best interests of the patient. If so, the facility may only disclose the PHI that is directly relevant. [42 C.F.R. § 164.510(b)(3).]

Disaster relief. Health care facilities may use or disclose PHI to a public or private entity authorized by law or by its charter to assist in disaster relief efforts, for the purpose of coordinating with such entities permitted uses or disclosures of PHI, only to the extent the facility, in the exercise of professional judgment, determines that the requirements do not interfere with the ability to respond to the emergency circumstances. [42 C.F.R. § 164.510(b)(4).]

Deceased patient. If the patient is deceased, a health care facility may disclose the patient's relevant PHI to a family member, or other identified individuals who were involved in the patient's care or payment for health care prior to the patient's death, unless doing so is inconsistent with any prior expressed preference of the patient that is known to the facility. [42 C.F.R. § 164.510(b)(5).]

Public welfare. Health care facilities may use or disclose a patient's PHI without authorization when the use or disclosure is: (1) required by law; (2) for public health activities; (3) to protect victims of abuse, neglect or domestic violence; (4) for health oversight activities; (5) in judicial and administrative proceedings; (6) for law enforcement purposes; (7) about decedents; (8) for cadaveric organ, eye or tissue donation purposes; (9) for research purposes; (10) to avert a serious threat to health or safety; (11) for specialized government functions; (12) for purposes of reporting to the National Instant Criminal Background Check System the identity of an individual who is prohibited from possessing a firearm under 18 U.S.C. § 922(g)(4); or (13) related to workers' compensation. Public welfare exceptions are limited and often require informing the patient about the disclosure. [42 C.F.R. § 164.512.]

Fundraising. Health care facilities may release limited PHI data to a business associate without authorization from the patient for the purpose of raising funds for the benefit of the facility. Health care facilities must remove personally identifiable data from fundraising lists upon request of the individual. [45 C.F.R. § 164.514(f).]

Minors. Health care providers may release PHI regarding a minor to the minor's parents, or individual acting as a parent, only if allowed by state law. If a minor can consent to a medical procedure and does not require the consent of any other individual, then the PHI concerning that procedure may not be released to a parent or individual acting as a parent

¶715

unless the minor agrees or has signed an authorization for the release. [45 C.F.R. § 164.502(g).]

Patients' Rights

Patients may view or request a copy (including electronic copies) of their PHI. A provider may, however, deny access to a patient's records if the provider believes that release of that information will endanger the life or physical safety of the individual. Providers, with the consent of the patient, may provide a summary of the data instead of the actual data itself and may charge a fee for providing access or copies. [45 C.F.R. § 164.524.]

Individuals also have a right of access to PHI when it is held by a laboratory that is either certified or exempt under the Clinical Laboratory Improvement Amendments of 1988 (CLIA) and may access laboratory reports directly from the laboratory. [42 C.F.R. § 493.1291(l).]

An individual has the right to have a covered entity amend PHI or a record about that individual, but the provider does not have to include material submitted by a patient as an amendment if it was generated by another provider, is inaccurate, or is not part of the requested records. [45 C.F.R. § 164.526.] An individual also has a right to receive an accounting of disclosures of protected health information made by a covered entity in the six years before the date on which the accounting is requested. Providers do not have to provide an accounting of the release of individually identifiable health information under certain circumstances, such as pursuant to a valid authorization. [45 C.F.R. § 164.528.]

Breach Notification

HIPAA-covered entities, such as hospitals, doctors' offices, and health insurance plans, are required to notify an individual when his or her unsecured PHI has been or is reasonably believed to have been accessed, acquired, used, or disclosed as the result of a breach. This notice must be sent without unreasonable delay and in no case later than 60 days after the discovery of a breach. [45 C.F.R. § 164.404.] Notification of the HHS Secretary is also required. Covered entities must notify the media for breaches that involve more than 500 residents of a state or jurisdiction. [45 C.F.R. §§ 164.406, 164.408.] Business associates, as defined by HIPAA, are also subject to breach notification procedures. [45 C.F.R. § 164.410.]

16 C.F.R. Part 318 requires vendors of personal health records to notify individuals in the event of a security breach.

HIPAA Complaints

Health care providers must designate a privacy official who is responsible for the development and implementation of privacy policies and procedures and a contact person who is to receive complaints and requests. All staff members must be trained on privacy policies and procedures. [45 C.F.R. § 164.530(a)(1), (b)(1).]

A covered entity must also provide a process for individuals to make complaints concerning the entity's HIPAA privacy policies and procedures or its compliance with such policies and procedures. [45 C.F.R. § 164.530(d).]

A HIPAA complaint must:

- be filed in writing, either on paper or electronically, by mail, fax, or e-mail;

- name the covered entity involved and describe the acts or omissions that violated the requirements of the Privacy, Security, or Breach Notification Rules; and

- be filed within 180 days of when the act or omission complained of occurred.

¶715

The HHS Office for Civil Rights (OCR) may extend the 180-day deadline for complaints if "good cause" is shown. Directions for filing a complaint, including forms, are provided on the OCR website at http://www.hhs.gov/ocr/privacy/hipaa/complaints/.

Penalties

CMS imposes tiered penalties against any person who violates the requirements and standards of HIPAA Administration Simplification (Soc. Sec. Act §§ 1171–1180). Penalties range from $100 to $50,000 per violation. [Soc. Sec. Act § 1176; 45 C.F.R. § 160.404.]

Preemption of State Law

Most states have laws regulating the use and release of PHI. Providers are required to follow the more stringent law if state law differs from HIPAA. State law that provides more stringent regulation on the use and release of PHI preempts the HIPAA regulations; thus, providers must follow the state's laws in these cases. In all other cases, the HIPAA privacy regulations preempt state law. [45 C.F.R. § 160.203.]

Protection of Genetic Information

Title I of the Genetic Information Nondiscrimination Act of 2008 (GINA) (P.L. 110-233) prohibits group health plans and issuers in the group market from increasing premiums for a group based on the results of an enrollee's genetic information, denying enrollment, imposing pre-existing condition exclusions, or doing other forms of underwriting based on genetic information. In the individual health insurance market, GINA prohibits issuers from using genetic information to deny coverage, raise premiums, or impose pre-existing condition exclusions. [45 C.F.R. §§ 146.121, 146.122.]

Further, group health plans and health insurance issuers in both the group and individual markets cannot request, require, or buy genetic information for underwriting purposes or prior to and in connection with enrollment. Plans and issuers are generally prohibited from asking individuals or family members to undergo a genetic test. [45 C.F.R. § 146.122(a)–(c).]

[¶ 717] Electronic Health Records

In addition to requiring increased security for personal health information, the Health Information Technology for Economic and Clinical Health (HITECH) Act (enacted as part of the American Recovery and Reinvestment Act of 2009 (ARRA) (P.L. 111-5)) provided for financial incentives and penalties to encourage the use of electronic health record (EHR) technology by physicians and hospitals to better manage patient care.

Certification

The HHS Office of the National Coordinator (ONC) for Health Information Technology identified the standards and certification criteria for certified EHR technology so that eligible professionals and hospitals can be assured that the systems they adopt are capable of performing the required functions (see 42 C.F.R. §§ 495.2–495.370). Regulations on certification criteria and the certification program for EHR are found at 45 C.F.R. Part 170.

Meaningful Use

To improve the use of EHR technology, CMS developed a three-stage measure known as "meaningful use." Each stage includes a series of specific objectives tied to a measure to allow health care providers providers to demonstrate that they are "meaningful users" of EHR technology. The first stage is data capture and sharing, the second stage is advance clinical processes, and the third stage is improved outcomes. [ARRA §§ 4101, 4102.]

CMS published a final rule on "Stage 1" meaningful use criteria in July 2010, adopting regulations that begin at 42 C.F.R. § 495.2. In the 2010 Stage 1 meaningful use regulations, CMS established an original timeline that would have required Medicare providers who first demonstrated meaningful use in 2011 to meet the "Stage 2" criteria in 2013. [*Final rule,* 75 FR 44314, July 28, 2010.]

CMS has revised the timeline for Stages 2 and 3 several times. It extended Stage 2 through calendar year (CY) 2016 for EPs and through fiscal year (FY) 2016 for eligible hospitals and critical access hospitals (CAHs) that first became meaningful EHR users in either FY or CY 2011 or 2012. [*Final rule,* 79 FR 52910, Sept. 4, 2014.]

Most recently, CMS issued regulations to align Stage 1 and Stage 2 reporting with Stage 3 proposals. In 2015 and 2016, all providers will attest to modified Stage 2 measures, which will no longer include certain redundant, duplicative, and top-down measures. In 2017, providers may choose to report on Stage 2 or Stage 3 measures. All providers will need to report on Stage 3 measures for the full CY beginning in 2018, with the exception of first-time participants in the Medicaid EHR Incentive program, who will report on a 90-day period. The revised timeline and additional information about the meaningful use criteria is available at https://www.cms.gov/Regulations-and-Guidance/Legislation/EHRIncentivePrograms/in-dex.html. [*Final rules*, 80 FR 62762, Oct. 16, 2015; 80 FR 62602, Oct. 16, 2015.]

Incentives and Penalties

Under HITECH, EPs such as physicians that made meaningful use of health information technology (HIT) received incentive payments between 2011 and 2015. Beginning in 2015, doctors who do not make meaningful use of HIT are subject to a payment adjustment to their Medicare physician fee schedule payment of 1 percent in 2015, 2 percent in 2016, and 3 percent in 2017 and 2018. The HHS Secretary may, on a case-by-case basis, exempt an eligible professional from the application of the payment adjustment if compliance with the requirement for being a meaningful EHR user would result in a significant hardship. [Soc. Sec. Act § 1848(a)(7), (o); 42 C.F.R. § 495.102.]

The Medicare Access and CHIP Reauthorization Act of 2015 (MACRA) (P.L. 114-10) consolidates and replaces the EHR meaningful use program, the Physician Quality Reporting System (PQRS), and the value-based payment modifier into the new Merit-Based Incentive Payment System (MIPS) program. MACRA will sunset the three programs at the end of 2018. Under MACRA, starting in 2019, the amounts paid to individual providers will be subject to adjustment through one of two mechanisms, depending on whether the physician chooses to participate in an Alternative Payment Model (APM) program or MIPS. [MACRA § 101(b), (c), (e)(2).]See ¶ 855 for a discussion of MACRA.

CMS maintains a website for providers seeking information on the EHR incentive program at: http://www.cms.gov/Regulations-and-Guidance/Legislation/EHRIncen-tivePrograms/index.html. CMS guidance on EHR incentives and penalties is available at: https://www.cms.gov/Regulations-and-Guidance/Legislation/EHRIncentivePrograms/ FAQ.html.

Eligible hospitals. Eligible hospitals may receive an initial implementation amount of at least $2 million. The total amount of incentive payments eligible hospitals may receive is based on a formula takes into consideration the number of discharges and days in which Medicare pays for individuals' hospital stays as well as a statutory transition factor. [Soc. Sec. Act § 1886(n); 42 C.F.R. § 495.104.]

[¶ 720] Fraud and Abuse Penalties

Several government agencies work jointly to combat waste, fraud, and abuse in the federal health care programs. The Health Care Fraud and Abuse Control Program is under the joint direction of the Attorney General and HHS acting through the Office of Inspector General (OIG). While the statute broadly defines health care fraud to cover fraud in all health care programs, public and private, the OIG's role is limited to Medicare and Medicaid fraud. [Soc. Sec. Act § 1128C.]

Under the Health Care Fraud and Abuse Control Program, the OIG and the Attorney General are required to: (1) coordinate federal, state, and local law enforcement programs to control fraud and abuse with respect to health plans; (2) conduct investigations, audits, evaluations, and inspections relating to the delivery of and payment for health care in the United States; (3) facilitate the enforcement of the provisions of the exclusion provisions, civil money penalties (CMPs) statute, and false statements and anti-kickback provisions, as well as other statutes applicable to health care fraud and abuse; and (4) provide for the establishment and modification of safe harbors and issue advisory opinions and special fraud alerts. [Soc. Sec. Act §§ 1128, 1128A, 1128B, 1128C, 1128D.]

Fraud and Abuse Data Collection Program

HHS's Health Resources and Services Administration (HRSA) acquires, maintains, and releases fraud and abuse data in the National Practitioner Data Bank (NPDB), located at http://www.npdb.hrsa.gov/. [Soc. Sec. Act §§ 1128C, 1128E, and 1921.]

State licensing boards, hospitals, professional societies, and other health care organizations report the following information to the NPDB: providers who are disciplined for engaging in unprofessional behavior; medical malpractice payments (thus restricting the ability of incompetent practitioners to move from state to state without disclosure or discovery of previous medical malpractice payment); and provider adverse action history such as loss of licensure, clinical privileges, and professional society membership, as well as exclusions from Medicare and Medicaid. [Soc. Sec. Act § 1921.]

Anti-kickback Statute

The anti-kickback statute is intended to curb the corrupting monetary influence on a physician's decision as to when and where to refer patients. It forbids the solicitation, receipt, offer, or payment of any kind of remuneration (including any kickback, bribe, or rebate) in return for referring an individual or for recommending or arranging the purchase, lease, or ordering of an item or service that may be wholly or partially paid for under a federal health care program. In addition to criminal prosecution and civil fines, violation of these laws subjects the violator to exclusion from Medicare, Medicaid, and other state health care programs. [Soc. Sec. Act § 1128B.]

Conviction under the anti-kickback statute may be punishable by a fine of up to $25,000 or by imprisonment for not more than five years, or both. [Soc. Sec. Act § 1128B(b).]

Claims that include items or services resulting from a violation of the anti-kickback statute constitute false claims under the federal False Claims Act. [Soc. Sec. Act § 1128B(g).]

Safe harbors. Congress created several exceptions to the anti-kickback prohibitions (referred to as "statutory safe harbors") to address certain permissible activities and carve out exceptions to what can be considered remuneration under the statute. HHS also created regulatory safe harbors that immunize various payment practices and business arrangements from criminal prosecution or civil sanctions under the anti-kickback statute. [Soc. Sec. Act §§ 1128A(i)(6), 1128B(b)(3); 42 C.F.R. § 1001.952.]

Criminal Medicare and Medicaid Fraud

Anyone convicted of a felony related to activities involving federal health care programs may be subject to criminal penalties, including imprisonment and fines between $1,000 and $25,000. Felonies include making false statements and false representations. [Soc. Sec. Act §§ 1107 and 1128B.]

In addition, a physician or supplier who knowingly, willfully, and repeatedly violates Medicare assignment agreement terms (see ¶ 868) by improperly charging beneficiaries will be guilty of a misdemeanor and, when convicted, will be fined a maximum of $2,000 or imprisoned for not more than six months, or both. [Soc. Sec. Act § 1128B(e).] A person need not have specific intent to commit a violation of this section. [Soc. Sec. Act § 1128B(h).]

"Stark" Law: Physician Self-Referral Prohibitions

The "Limitation on Certain Physician Referrals" statute, commonly known as the "Stark" law, prohibits a physician from making referrals for certain designated health care services (DHS) to entities with which the physician (or an immediate family member) has a financial relationship. [Soc. Sec. Act § 1877.] The Stark law is a civil statute, not a criminal statute, and there is no requirement that the government prove unlawful intent of the parties to establish a violation of the law.

If a financial relationship exists between a referring physician and an entity providing a DHS that does not meet an exception, the Stark law is violated and no claims from the referring physician to the entity providing DHS may be submitted to Medicare. [Soc. Sec. Act § 1877.] The Stark law further prohibits an entity from presenting or causing to be presented a Medicare claim or bill to any individual, third-party payer, or other entity, for clinical laboratory services furnished under a prohibited referral. [Soc Sec. § 1877(a)(1)(B).]

Financial relationship. For purposes of the physician self-referral prohibition statute, a "financial relationship" includes a physician's or a physician's immediate family member's ownership, investment interest, or compensation arrangements (i.e., contractual arrangements) in any entity that furnishes DHS. [42 C.F.R. § 411.354.]

Compensation arrangement. A compensation arrangement is any arrangement involving remuneration, direct or indirect, whether cash or in kind, between a physician and an entity. [42 C.F.R. § 411.354(c).]

Exceptions to physician self-referral prohibitions. CMS has provided categories of exceptions to the physician self-referral prohibitions. [42 C.F.R. §§ 411.354–411.357.]

Stark law penalties. The penalties for making prohibited self-referrals include: denial of payment; refund of amounts collected for DHS claims; imposition of CMPs of up to $15,000 for each claim; imposition of CMPs of up to $100,000 for each arrangement or scheme; and exclusion from participation in Medicare. [Soc. Sec. Act § 1877(g)(1)–(5); 42 C.F.R. §§ 411.361(f), 1003.103, 1003.105(a).]

CMS advisory opinions. Any individual or entity may request a written advisory opinion from CMS concerning whether a physician's referral relating to DHS (other than clinical laboratory services) is prohibited. In the advisory opinion, CMS determines whether a business arrangement described by the parties appears to constitute a "financial relationship" that could potentially restrict a physician's referrals and whether the arrangement or the DHS at issue appear to qualify for any of the exceptions to the referral prohibition. [42 C.F.R. § 411.370.] Each advisory opinion issued by CMS is binding as to the Secretary and the party or parties requesting the opinion. [Soc. Sec. Act § 1877(g)(6)(A).]

Other Relevant Criminal Statutes

Title 18 of the United States Code, regarding Crimes and Criminal Procedures, includes the term "federal health care offense," which involves certain offenses or criminal conspiracies to commit such offenses.

The following offenses and sanctions listed in Title 18 pertain to health care crimes:

- knowing or willful defrauding or attempting to defraud a health care benefit program [18 U.S.C. § 1347];

- stealing assets of a health care benefit program [18 U.S.C. § 669];

- knowing and willful concealment of material facts or making false statements in any matter concerning a health care benefit program [18 U.S.C. § 1035];

- obstructing a federal criminal investigation of a federal health care offense [18 U.S.C. § 1518]; and

- laundering of monetary instruments related to a federal health care offense [18 U.S.C. § § 1956(a)(1), 1956(c)(7)(F)].

Civil Money Penalties

Under the provisions of Social Security Act section 1128A, the HHS Secretary is authorized to impose administrative sanctions in the form of CMPs and assessments against any person, organization, agency, or public or private entity that submits or causes the submission of false or improper claims and requests for payment from Medicare, Medicaid, or other federally sponsored health-related programs. [Soc. Sec. Act § 1128A(a).] The law also permits an individual upon whom the Secretary imposes a CMP or assessment to be suspended from participation in the Medicare and Medicaid programs. [Soc. Sec. Act § 1128(b).]

CMPs will not be imposed in connection with certain charitable and other innocuous programs. [Soc. Sec. Act § 1128A(i)(6)(F)–(I).]

Civil Actions Under the False Claims Act

The False Claims Act (FCA) authorizes federal prosecutors to file a civil action against any person or entity that knowingly files a false claim with a federal health care program, including Medicare or Medicaid. [31 U.S.C. § 3729 *et seq.*] The term "claim" refers to an application for payment for items and services under a "federal health care program," such as Medicare or Medicaid. [Soc. Sec. Act § 1128A(i)(2).]

A person or entity may be prosecuted under the FCA for any of the following:

- knowingly presenting, or causing to be presented, a false or fraudulent claim for payment or approval;

- knowingly making, using, or causing to be made or used a false record or statement material to a false or fraudulent claim;

- knowingly making, using, or causing to be made or used a false record or statement, or concealing, avoiding, or decreasing an obligation to pay or transmit money or property to the government; or

- conspiring to commit any of the above violations.

[31 U.S.C. § 3729(a)(1).]

Knowledge. The FCA does not require proof of specific intent to defraud a federal health care program. It is sufficient for the person to (1) have actual knowledge of the information; (2) act in deliberate ignorance of the truth or falsity of the information; or (3) act in reckless disregard of the truth or falsity of the information provided or submitted. [31 U.S.C. § 3729(b).]

***Qui tam* actions.** The FCA authorizes private persons to bring *qui tam* actions (also known as "whistleblower" actions). The FCA's *qui tam* provisions empower private persons to sue on behalf of the government and to share in the recovery of such actions. The amount of recovery for a *qui tam* plaintiff will depend on whether the government decides to intervene in the case and the extent to which the *qui tam* plaintiff contributed to the prosecution of the claim. [31 U.S.C. § 3730.]

Penalties. A party that commits any prohibited acts under the FCA is liable to the federal government for a civil penalty of not less than $5,500 and not more than $11,000, plus three times the amount of damages that the government sustains because of the act of that party (also known as treble damages). [31 U.S.C. § 3729(a).] In addition to CMPs, parties that file false claims may also be subject to criminal prosecution and exclusion from participation in federal and state health care programs.

Exclusion from Program Participation

The OIG has the authority to exclude individuals and entities that have engaged in fraud or abuse from participation in Medicare, Medicaid, and other federal health care programs. The OIG imposes a mandatory exclusionary period for those individuals or entities convicted of a health care-related offense and has the discretion to exclude providers that have engaged in civil fraud, kickbacks, or other prohibited activities, including quality of care deficiencies. [Soc. Sec. Act § § 1128(b)(5), 1128A(a)(1)(D).]

Mandatory exclusion. Under the mandatory exclusion provisions of the Social Security Act, an individual or entity tmust be excluded from participation in *any* federal health care program if convicted of any of the following: (1) a criminal offense related to the delivery of an item of service under title XVIII or under any state health care program; (2) a criminal offense relating to neglect or abuse of patients in connection with the delivery of a health care item or service; (3) a felony relating to fraud, theft, embezzlement, breach of fiduciary responsibility, or other financial misconduct; or (4) a felony relating to the unlawful manufacture, distribution, prescription, or dispensing of a controlled substance. [Soc. Sec. Act § 1128(a).]

In the case of a felony conviction related to a program-related crime, patient abuse, health care fraud, or a controlled substance, the minimum period of exclusion is five years. For a health care provider convicted a second time of a health care-related criminal offense for which the provider is subject to mandatory exclusion, the penalty imposed will be a minimum 10-year exclusion from any federal health care program. For a health care provider convicted of a health care-related criminal offense for which the provider is subject to mandatory exclusion, and who has on two or more previous occasions been subject to exclusion for health care-related criminal convictions, the sanction is a permanent exclusion from any federal health care program. [Soc. Sec. Act § 1128(a), (c).]

Permissive exclusion. The OIG *may* exclude individuals or entities that committed an offense resulting in a conviction under federal or state law in connection with the delivery of a health care item or service or any act or omission in a health care program or other government program, related to:

(1) misdemeanor fraud or financial misconduct;

(2) obstruction of a criminal investigation or audit; or

(3) misdemeanor manufacture, distribution, prescription, or dispensing of a controlled substance.

[Soc. Sec. Act § 1128(b)(1)–(3).] The Secretary may exclude these individuals or entities for a minimum period of three years from any federal health care program, unless the Secretary designates a shorter period on the basis of mitigating circumstances or a longer period based on the presence of aggravating factors. [Soc. Sec. Act § 1128(c)(3)(D).]

The HHS Secretary may exclude any individual or entity whose health care-related license has been revoked or suspended or any individual or entity excluded or suspended from a federal or state health care program. [Soc. Sec. Act § 1128(b)(4), (5).]

Notice of exclusion. When a practitioner is excluded from Medicare participation, notice of the exclusion will be given to: (1) the public; (2) affected beneficiaries; (3) other government agencies; (4) quality improvement organizations; (5) hospitals, nursing homes, managed care organizations, and other providers; (6) contractors; (7) medical societies and other professional organizations; and (8) state and local authorities responsible for licensing and the NPDB. [Soc. Sec. Act § 1128(d), (e); 42 C.F.R. § 1001.2006.]

Payment of claims after exclusion. If a patient submits claims for services furnished by an excluded practitioner, Medicare will pay the first claim submitted. It then will notify the patient that the practitioner is excluded and that, effective 15 days after the date of the notice or after the effective date of the exclusion, whichever is later, no more claims for services furnished by the practitioner will be paid. [42 C.F.R. § 1001.1901(c)(1), (2).]

Secretary's authority to refuse to enter into or renew Medicare agreements. The Secretary has the authority to refuse to enter into Medicare agreements with health care providers who have been convicted of a felony under federal or state law and who the Secretary determines to be detrimental to the Medicare program or its beneficiaries. The Secretary may also refuse to renew or may terminate an existing agreement for the same reasons. [Soc. Sec. Act § 1866(b)(2).] The Secretary's authority to refuse extends to all Medicare-participating providers, including physicians and suppliers. [Soc. Sec. Act § 1842(h)(8).]

Voluntary Self-Disclosure Protocols

The OIG has released a voluntary provider self-disclosure protocol (SDP) intended to encourage providers to make voluntary disclosures that will help resolve possible violations of federal criminal, civil, or administrative laws. Providers should conduct an initial assessment to substantiate that there is noncompliance with program requirements before making a disclosure to the OIG. In addition, a disclosing provider should conduct an internal financial assessment and prepare a report of its findings to estimate the monetary impact of the disclosed matter. Providers that disclose under the SDP should do so with the intention of resolving their overpayment liability exposure for the conduct identified. When FCA liability results from a disclosure, the OIG may be more flexible in considering the terms of a corporate integrity agreement in light of the effectiveness of the provider's compliance program. [*OIG Letter, Recommendations for Provider Self-Disclosure*, April 17, 2013.]

The OIG does not accept disclosure of matters that involve only liability under the Stark law in the absence of a colorable anti-kickback statute violation. With regard to kickback-related submissions to the SDP, the OIG requires a minimum $50,000 settlement amount to resolve the matter. [*OIG Letter to Health Care Providers*, March 24, 2009.]

Open Payments

Manufacturers of covered drugs, devices, biologicals or medical supplies are required to annually submit information regarding payments or other transfers of value made to physicians and teaching hospitals. Applicable manufacturers or group purchasing organizations are also required to disclose all ownership and investment interests in the applicable manufacturer or applicable group purchasing organization that were held by a physician or an immediate family member of a physician. [Soc. Sec. Act § 1128G; 42 C.F.R. § § 403.904, 403.906.] CMS has organized these reporting requirements into an Open Payments program. [http://www.cms.gov/openpayments/index.html.]

[¶ 730] Provider Participation Agreements

To qualify for payment for its services to Medicare beneficiaries, a provider must: (1) undergo a survey and be certified by the state agency or accrediting organization to be in compliance with legal and regulatory requirements; and (2) sign a participation agreement with CMS. The participation agreement includes the conditions required for the provider to maintain compliance and continue certification.

The law defines a "provider of services," for purposes of signing a participation agreement, as a hospital, a critical access hospital, a skilled nursing facility (SNF), a home health agency (HHA), a hospice, a comprehensive outpatient rehabilitation facility, certain funds for payments for physicians and other practitioners provided by hospitals, a clinic, a rehabilitation agency, a public health agency, or a community health center with respect to partial hospitalization services. [Soc. Sec. Act § 1866(e)(1), (e)(2), (u).]

In addition, although they are not "providers of services" as defined above, ambulatory surgical centers (see ¶ 386), rural health clinics (see ¶ 382), freestanding renal dialysis treatment facilities, organ procurement organizations, transplant centers, and histocompatibility laboratories are treated as providers in that they must meet conditions of participation and must sign an agreement in order to participate in the Medicare program. [Soc. Sec. Act § § 1832(a)(2)(F)(i), 1861(aa)(2), 1881(b)(2)(A); 42 C.F.R. § § 405.2402, 413.200(c), 416.2.]

Screening requirements. All Medicare providers are required to undergo screening before initial enrollment and revalidate their compliance with enrollment requirements every five years; suppliers of durable medical equipment, prosthetics, orthotics, and supplies must revalidate every three years. A Medicare contractor is required to screen all initial provider and supplier applications and any applications received in response to a revalidation request and assign them to a level of limited, moderate, or high. [Soc. Sec. Act § 1866(j)(2)(D)(iii); 42 C.F.R. § 424.518.]

Essentials of Provider Agreements

To participate in the Medicare program, a provider of services must sign an agreement with the Secretary:

(1) to limit its charges to beneficiaries to the costs of noncovered services and to the deductible, coinsurance, and other charges allowed under federal law (see "Allowable Charges" below);

(2) to make adequate provision for the refund of amounts incorrectly collected from beneficiaries;

(3) to disclose the hiring of any individual who, at any time during the year preceding employment, was employed in a managerial, accounting, auditing, or similar capacity by the provider's Medicare administrative contractor;

(4) to release, upon request, patient data to a quality improvement organization (QIO) (see ¶ 710) reviewing the provider;

(5) to bill other primary payers before billing Medicare in accordance with statutory and regulatory requirements concerning alternate insurance coverage (see ¶ 636); and

(6) to admit surveyors from the state health agency or accrediting organization to assess their compliance with conditions of participation.

[Soc. Sec. Act § 1866(a)(1); 42 C.F.R. §§ 489.20, 489.30.]

Hospitals. The conditions of participation and provisions of the provider agreement for hospitals include these additional requirements:

- to either furnish directly or make arrangements for all Medicare care and services (other than physician and certain health care practitioner services) (see ¶ 635);

- to maintain an agreement with a QIO for the review of admissions, quality, and diagnostic information and, in the case of SNFs, HHAs, and outpatient hospital services, to maintain an agreement with a QIO for review of services and beneficiary complaints regarding quality (see ¶ 710);

- to participate in TRICARE, CHAMPVA (Civilian Health and Medical Program of the Veterans Administration), and Veterans Administration programs (42 C.F.R. §§ 489.25, 489.26);

- to make available to beneficiaries directories of participating physicians in the area and identify any qualified participating physicians in the area, whenever a referral is made to a nonparticipating physician;

- to provide beneficiaries with a written notice, at the time of admission to the facility, explaining the beneficiary's right to Medicare benefits (see below);

- to provide notice of the right to appeal a discharge from the hospital (42 C.F.R. § 489.27);

- to develop and maintain a quality assessment and performance improvement (QAPI) program (a QAPI focuses provider efforts on the actual care delivered to patients, the performance of the hospital as an organization, and the impact of treatment furnished by the hospital on the health status of its patients) (42 C.F.R. § 482.21); and

- in the case of hospitals with emergency departments, to meet the responsibilities imposed by the law with respect to treating emergency cases (see below under "Treatment of Emergency Cases") (42 C.F.R. § 489.24).

[Soc. Sec. Act § 1866(a)(1).]

Hospitals and SNFs also must agree to accept as payment in full any payments made by risk-basis health maintenance organizations on behalf of their Medicare enrollees if the payments made are at the level traditional Medicare would have paid. [Soc. Sec. Act § 1866(a)(1); 42 C.F.R. § 422.214.]

Treatment of Emergency Cases—Antidumping Rules

Congress enacted the Emergency Medical Treatment & Labor Act (EMTALA) to ensure public access to emergency services regardless of ability to pay. Medicare law requires that each hospital provider agreement include a clause requiring the provider to comply with EMTALA. [Soc. Sec. Act §§ 1866(a)(1)(I), 1867; 42 C.F.R. § 489.20(l).]

Under the EMTALA "antidumping" provision, a hospital must provide for an appropriate medical screening examination (within the capability of the hospital's emergency department) for any individual who comes to the emergency department and requests a medical examination or treatment, regardless of whether that individual is a Medicare beneficiary. The screening examination must be sufficient to determine whether an emergency medical condition exists or whether the individual is in active labor. If a patient has an emergency condition or is in active labor, the hospital must provide the treatment necessary to stabilize his or her condition. For a woman in active labor, stabilization requires delivery of both the newborn and the placenta. [Soc. Sec. Act § 1867(a), (e)(3), (h).]

Transfer. The transfer of an emergency room patient whose condition has not been stabilized is not appropriate unless either: (1) the patient (or a person acting on the patient's behalf) requests a transfer in writing, or (2) a physician has certified that the medical benefits to be obtained from treatment available at the receiving hospital outweigh the risks of transfer and that the receiving facility has the space and personnel necessary to treat the patient. [Soc. Sec. Act § 1867(c); 42 C.F.R. § 489.24(e)(2)(iv), (f).]

Records. Each hospital must post a sign in its emergency department specifying patients' rights with respect to examination and treatment for emergency medical conditions and women in labor. [Soc. Sec. Act § 1866(a)(1)(I), (N)(iii).]

Policies and procedures. A hospital must have written policies and procedures in place to respond to situations in which a particular specialty is not available or the on-call physician cannot respond because of circumstances beyond the physician's control, and to provide that emergency services are available to meet the needs of individuals with emergency medical conditions. [42 C.F.R. § 489.24(j).]

Delay in treatment. Medicare-participating hospitals must not delay required screening and the stabilization of an emergency in order to: (1) obtain insurance information; (2) seek, or direct a patient to seek, authorization to provide screening or stabilizing services from the individual's health plan, managed care organization, or insurance company; or (3) prepare an Advance Beneficiary Notice and obtain a beneficiary signature. Appropriate screening and stabilization must be provided first. [42 C.F.R. § 489.24(d)(4).]

Refusal to consent. If an individual intends to leave the hospital before the screening examination, the hospital should offer the individual further medical examination and treatment, inform the individual of the benefits of such examination and treatment, and take all reasonable steps to obtain the individual's written informed consent to refuse such examination and treatment. Any refusal of treatment and the actions or efforts by the hospital to comply with EMTALA requirements and provide treatment must be documented. [42 C.F.R. § 489.24(d)(3).]

Sanctions. If a hospital knowingly and willfully, or negligently, fails to handle emergency treatment cases, it may have its provider agreement with Medicare terminated. In addition, the Secretary may impose civil money penalties against the hospital and responsible physician, and the law provides for civil actions against a hospital (but not against physicians). [Soc. Sec. Act § 1867(d).]

QIO review. Except in the case where a delay would jeopardize the health and safety of individuals, the Secretary is required to request a QIO review before making a compliance determination that would terminate a hospital's Medicare participation because of EMTALA violations. [Soc. Sec. Act § 1867(d)(3); 42 C.F.R. § 489.24(h).]

Notifying Beneficiaries of Medicare Rights

Within two days of admission, hospitals must provide each Medicare beneficiary with a written statement (using language approved by the Secretary) explaining the beneficiary's Medicare rights, i.e., the "Important Message from Medicare." The explanation of rights must include: (1) rights to inpatient hospital services and post-hospital services; (2) the circumstances under which the beneficiary will and will not be liable for charges for a continued stay at the hospital; (3) the beneficiary's right to appeal a determination that a continued inpatient hospital stay is not covered (including practical steps to initiate such an appeal); and (4) the beneficiary's liability for payment for services if the determination is upheld on appeal. The hospital must give the patient a second copy of the notice not more than two days before discharge. [Soc. Sec. Act § 1866(a)(1)(M); 42 C.F.R. § 405.1205; *Medicare Claims Processing Manual*, Pub. 100-04, Ch. 30, § 200.3.1.]

Advance Directives

Hospitals and other health care facilities must maintain written policies and procedures relating to an advance directive (a written instruction, such as a living will or durable power of attorney for health care), which expresses a patient's wishes relating to the provision of care when the individual is incapacitated. Each facility must: (1) inform Medicare and Medicaid patients of their rights under state law to make an advance directive, and (2) explain the written policies of the organization respecting the implementation of such rights. [Soc. Sec. Act § 1866(a)(1)(Q), (f).]

Allowable Charges

A provider agreement requires a provider of services to limit its charges to beneficiaries to the costs of noncovered services and to the deductible and coinsurance (copayment) charges allowed under federal law and regulations. Under Medicare law and regulations, the provider may charge a beneficiary the following amounts.

(1) Providers may charge beneficiaries for the Part A inpatient hospital deductible and coinsurance, which consist of: (a) the amount of the inpatient hospital deductible or, if less, the actual charges for the services (see ¶ 220); (b) the amount of inpatient hospital coinsurance applicable for each day the individual is furnished inpatient hospital services after the 60th day during a benefit period (see ¶ 224); and (c) the post-hospital extended care services coinsurance amount (see ¶ 242). [42 C.F.R. § § 489.30–489.32.]

(2) Providers may charge beneficiaries for the Part B deductible and coinsurance, which consist of an annual deductible and a coinsurance of 20 percent of the Medicare-approved Part B payment amount in excess of that deductible (see ¶ 335 for further details and exceptions). [Soc. Sec. Act § 1833(b); 42 C.F.R. § 489.30.] For outpatient hospital services, allowable deductible charges depend on whether the hospital can determine the beneficiary's deductible status.

(3) Providers may charge beneficiaries for the blood deductible, which consists of charges for the first three pints of blood or units of packed red blood cells furnished during a calendar year (see ¶ 220). [Soc. Sec. Act § 1833(b).]

(4) Providers may not charge a deductible for certain services not subject to deductible. Many preventive services are not subject to any copayment or deductible (see ¶ 335). [Soc. Sec. Act § 1861.]

(5) For costlier services requested by a beneficiary, the difference between the provider's customary charges for services covered under Medicare and the costlier services may be charged. Whenever a provider is permitted to charge for an item or service, it may not charge the Medicare beneficiary or another person more than the amount customarily charged by the provider for such an item or service. [Soc. Sec. Act § 1866(a)(2)(B).]

Deposits and Prepayment Requests

A provider agreement contains specific requirements concerning prepayment. Under these provisions, the provider agrees not to:

(1) require an individual entitled to hospital insurance benefits to prepay in part or in whole for inpatient services as a condition of admittance, except when it is clear upon admission that payment under Part A cannot be made;

(2) deny covered inpatient services to an eligible individual on the ground of inability or failure to pay a requested amount at or before admission;

(3) evict, or threaten to evict, an individual for inability to pay a deductible or a coinsurance amount required under Medicare; and

(4) charge an individual for: (a) an agreement to admit or readmit the individual on some specified future date for covered inpatient services, (b) the individual's failure to remain an inpatient for any agreed-upon length of time, or (c) the individual's failure to give advance notice of departure from the provider's facilities.

[42 C.F.R. § 489.22.]

Providers must not require advance payment of the inpatient deductible or coinsurance as a condition of admission. Additionally, providers may not require that the beneficiary prepay any Part B charges as a condition of admission, except when prepayment from non-Medicare patients is required. In such cases, only the deductible and coinsurance may be collected. [Pub. 100-04, Ch. 2, § 10.3.]

A hospice is prohibited from discontinuing care to a patient because of the inability of the patient to pay. [Soc. Sec. Act § 1861(dd)(2)(D).]

Termination of Provider Agreements

A provider may terminate its participation in the Medicare program voluntarily, or its participation may be terminated by the Secretary for cause. [Soc. Sec. Act § 1866(b).] A provider whose participation is terminated for cause has the right to administrative appeal and judicial review but has no right to delay of the termination pending the hearing. [Soc. Sec. Act § 1866(h); 42 C.F.R. § § 498.5, 498.20.]

In general, no Medicare payment will be made to a provider after the effective date of the termination. However, in the case of inpatient hospital services (including inpatient psychiatric hospital services) and SNF services, payments may be made for up to 30 days for services furnished to an individual who is admitted to the institution before the effective date of the termination. Similarly, home health services and hospice care furnished under a plan established before the termination date of the participation agreement will be covered for up to 30 days after termination. [Soc. Sec. Act § § 1128(c)(2), 1866(b)(3); 42 C.F.R. § 489.55.]

[¶ 735] Role of Medicaid

Although the Medicaid program is administered separately from Medicare, a provision in the Medicaid law requires Medicaid to pay the Medicare premiums, deductibles, and/or coinsurance amounts for certain Medicare beneficiaries. Medicare beneficiaries eligible for Medicaid cost-sharing assistance are called "qualified Medicare beneficiaries" or "dual eligibles." [Soc. Sec. Act § 1905(p).]

Medicaid pays all Medicare cost-sharing for dual-eligible beneficiaries with incomes up to 100 percent of the federal poverty level (FPL). Medicaid pays the Part B premiums for dual eligibles with incomes between 100 and 120 percent of FPL, referred to as specified low-income beneficiaries. To the extent that funds are available, Medicaid must pay a portion of the Part B premium for Medicare beneficiaries with incomes between 120 percent and 135 percent of FPL, called "qualifying individuals." Section 211 of the Medicare Access and CHIP Reauthorization Act of 2015 (MACRA) (P.L. 114-10) made the qualifying individual program permanent. [Soc. Sec. Act § § 1902(a)(10)(E)(iv), 1933(g).]

States also may pay Medicare Part A and Part B premiums under "buy-in" agreements with Medicare for beneficiaries who do not qualify for qualified Medicare beneficiary status. [Soc. Sec. Act §§ 1818(g), 1843.]

Prescription drug benefit. Medicaid agencies assist in the determination of eligibility for the Medicare low-income subsidies under the prescription drug benefit (see ¶ 508) by notifying CMS of each Medicaid applicant or recipient who is eligible for the low-income subsidy for Medicare Part D cost-sharing. States are required to provide this information as a condition of receiving federal Medicaid assistance. [Soc. Sec. Act § 1935.]

[¶ 740] "Medigap" Insurance

Medicare beneficiaries enrolled in "original Medicare," the traditional fee-for-service Medicare plan, may purchase Medicare supplement policies (also called "Medigap" policies). These policies are private insurance policies used to fill gaps in the coverage provided by Medicare. [Soc. Sec. Act § 1882(g)(1), (o)(1).]

Medicare supplement policies are required to meet certain specified federal standards, as outlined in Social Security Act section 1882. The most important of those standards include:

- a standardized description of policies to avoid confusion when comparing policies from different companies;

- guaranteed renewability of policies to prevent cancellation for any reason other than nonpayment of premiums; and

- elimination of certain "out clauses," such as denial of benefits for preexisting conditions when one Medigap policy is replaced with another.

[Sec. Sec. Act § 1882(o)(3), (o)(4), (q).]

Beginning January 1, 2020, a Medigap plan that provides coverage of the Part B deductible may not be sold or issued to a newly eligible Medicare beneficiary. [Soc. Sec. Act § 1882(z).]

Types of policies. There are several standard types of Medigap policies, each designated with a letter of the alphabet. Each policy type must be the same for every insurance company. For instance, a Medigap policy type A must offer the same coverage no matter which insurance company is offering the plan. Each plan type also has a specific set of benefits, which enables consumers to compare policies on the basis of price and the company's reputation. In Massachusetts, Minnesota, and Wisconsin, however, different standardized Medigap plans are available.

The basic (core) benefits are included in plans with designation A through G as well as plans designated M and N. Plan A covers only the core benefits, and Plan G offers the most benefits. Plans designated M and N are identical to plans designated with a category D except that they pay more of Medicare's copayments. Two plans, K and L, may be sold with a high deductible option (see details below). A free CMS guide, which is updated annually, outlines the various provisions of all of the types of Medigap policies; it is available in print, as described below, and at: http://www.medicare.gov/Publications/Pubs/pdf/02110.pdf.

Minimum Standards

With limited exceptions, Medigap insurers in all states must offer two or more standard benefit packages. Of the standard benefit packages, one, policy A, must cover only a core group of basic benefits; all others must include at least these core benefits:

- Suspension of Medigap premiums and benefits during Medicaid eligibility up to 24 months. [Soc. Sec. Act § 1882(d)(3)(B)(ii)(II), (q)(5).]

- Loss ratio requirements for individual policies and group policies. [Soc. Sec. Act § 1882(b)(1).]

- Preexisting condition limitations. Such conditions may be imposed only in a replacement policy to the extent such conditions were not met under the original policy. There also is a six-month open enrollment period for new Part B enrollees who are age 65 or older. [Soc. Sec. Act § 1882(s)(2)(A).]

- Prohibition of the sale of duplicative coverage. Virtually any sale of duplicative health insurance coverage to Medicare beneficiaries is prohibited. [Soc. Sec. Act § 1882(d)(3).]

Core benefits. Except for policies K and L, discussed below, all Medigap policies must cover: (1) Part A copayments; (2) 365 days of hospital coverage after Part A benefits have been used; (3) payment of Part B copayments after the Part B deductible has been paid; and (4) the first three pints of blood (or the equivalent in packed cells) per calendar year unless the patient or a donor has donated the amount of blood used. Effective for policies issued or renewed on of after June 1, 2010, hospice services must be included as a core benefit. [*Notice*, 74 FR 18807, April 24, 2009.]

Optional benefits. Policies B through G offer varying combinations of: (1) the inpatient hospital deductible; (2) the Part B deductible; (3) coinsurance payments for skilled nursing facility services; (4) Part B excess charges; (5) emergency care during foreign travel; and (6) preventive care not covered under Medicare. Preventive services and at-home recovery are no longer included as optional benefits in policies issued on or after June 1, 2010. [*Notice*, 74 FR 18807, April 24, 2009.]

Benefit packages. Two high-deductible Medigap benefit packages offer less than the core benefits. The first, Policy K, provides: (1) coverage of 50 percent of the cost-sharing obligation (except coverage of 100 percent cost-sharing applicable for preventive benefits); (2) no coverage of the Part B deductible; (3) coverage of all hospital coinsurance for long stays and 365 extra lifetime days of coverage (as in the current core package); and (4) a limitation on annual out-of-pocket costs of $4,960 (increased each year by an appropriate inflation adjustment as specified by the Secretary). The second benefit package, Policy L, has the same benefit structure as the first high-deductible package except that: (1) coverage is provided for 75 percent, rather than 50 percent, of cost-sharing otherwise applicable; and (2) the limitation on out-of-pocket costs is $2,480 rather than $4,960. Medigap issuers are not required to participate as prescription drug plan sponsors under Part D and a state may not impose such a requirement. [Soc. Sec. Act § 1882(s)(3)(C); http://www.medicare.gov/supplement-other-insurance/compare-medigap/compare-medigap.html.]

All issuers of Medigap policies are required to offer either Policy C or F in addition to Policy A. Plan C requires the core services plus the Medicare Part A deductible, skilled nursing facility care, Medicare Part B deductible, and medically necessary emergency care in a foreign country. Plan F covers the same benefits as Plan C except that it also covers 100 percent of the Medicare Part B excess charges. [Soc. Sec. Act § 1882(o)(5).]

The Secretary is authorized to approve states' Medigap regulatory programs and their enforcement efforts. State enforcement efforts, particularly with respect to ensuring that policies comply with minimum loss ratios, are subject to periodic federal review. [Soc. Sec. Act § 1882(b)(1).]

NAIC Standards

The HHS Secretary adopted the National Association of Insurance Commissioners (NAIC) model Medigap regulation. [*Notice*, 74 FR 18807, April 24, 2009.]

¶740

Prescription drug coverage. As of January 1, 2006, when the Medicare prescription drug (Part D) benefit became effective, no new Medigap policies may cover prescription drugs, but Medigap policies that covered prescription drugs before that date may be renewed. Medigap insurers were required to notify their policy holders of the open enrollment period for Part D plans and compare their coverage to the Part D plans available in the same service area. [Soc. Sec. Act § 1882(v)(2)(B).]

Preexisting conditions. Issuance of new Medigap policies is guaranteed without any preexisting condition exclusion for the following Medicare beneficiaries:

(1) persons whose coverage under an employee welfare plan terminates;

(2) persons enrolled in a Medicare Advantage (MA) plan (see ¶ 400 *et seq.*) who disenroll for permissible reasons (plan termination or a move out of the plan area);

(3) persons enrolled in risk- or cost-based health maintenance organizations (HMOs) or other qualifying plans (see below) who disenroll for permissible reasons;

(4) persons whose enrollment in a Medigap policy ceases because of insurer bankruptcy or insolvency;

(5) persons previously enrolled under a Medigap policy who terminate to participate for the first time in MA, an HMO, or other qualifying plan and subsequently terminate within 12 months;

(6) persons previously enrolled in a Medigap policy who are enrolled in MA, are terminated involuntarily within the first 12 months from such an enrollment, and who, without an intervening enrollment, enroll with a similar organization, provider, plan, or program (for whom the subsequent enrollment is considered an initial enrollment, such as in (5)) [Soc. Sec. Act § 1882(s)(3)(F)]; and

(7) persons who enroll in MA or in the Program of All-Inclusive Care for the Elderly (PACE) under section 1894 of the Social Security Act when first reaching Medicare eligibility but then disenroll within 12 months.

[Soc. Sec. Act § 1882(s)(3)(B).]

The preexisting condition exclusion may not be imposed on a beneficiary during the six-month period that begins on the first day of the month in which the individual has reached age 65 and is enrolled in Medicare Part B, if the beneficiary had six continuous months of creditable coverage on the date of application. Persons with fewer than six months of coverage are entitled to have the period of any preexisting condition exclusion reduced by any period of creditable coverage. [Soc. Sec. Act § 1882(s)(2)(A).]

An insurer may not impose an exclusion based on a preexisting condition for individuals enrolling in Medicare Part D (see ¶ 500). Insurers are prohibited from discriminating in the pricing of such policies on the basis of the individual's health status, claims experience, receipt of health care, or medical condition. [Soc. Sec. Act § 1882(s)(3)(A).]

A pamphlet containing Medigap insurance policy information for beneficiaries has been issued jointly by HHS and NAIC. It is entitled "Choosing a Medigap Policy: A Guide to Health Insurance for People with Medicare" and is available free from HHS at http://www.medicare.gov/pubs/pdf/02110.pdf, or it can be ordered by calling 1-800-MEDICARE (1-800-633-4227).

Genetic information. The Genetic Information Nondiscrimination Act of 2008 (GINA) (P.L. 110-233) prohibits Medigap insurers from obtaining or using genetic information for underwriting purposes to make decisions whether to enroll an individual, exclude conditions as preexisting, or set premiums to be charged. Genetic information includes the results of a genetic testing on an individual or family member (dependent or other relative as close as

¶740

great-grandparents and certain cousins) and the manifestation of a disease in a family member of the insured. [GINA § § 102, 104.]

Nominal cost-sharing. The Patient Protection and Affordable Care Act (ACA) (P.L. 111-148) directed the Secretary of HHS to ask the NAIC to develop a new set of standards and benefits that would require nominal cost-sharing from holders of Policies C and F in order to encourage appropriate use of physicians' services. [Soc. Sec. Act § 1882(y).] A December 19, 2012, NAIC letter to the HHS Secretary recommended that no nominal cost-sharing be introduced to benefit packages classified as Medigap plans C and F.

Penalties

It is a criminal offense to engage in fraudulent activities connected with the sale of Medigap policies, including: making false statements and misrepresentations; falsely claiming certification by the federal government; selling policies that duplicate Medicare benefits, including selling to MA beneficiaries; and mailing into a state Medigap policies that have been disapproved by that state. Violation of these provisions is a felony, entailing maximum penalties of $25,000, five years' imprisonment, or both. [Soc. Sec. Act § 1882(d)(3)(A).]

Chapter 8– PAYMENT RULES

[¶ 800] Introduction

Medicare's method of paying for services provided to a beneficiary varies according to whether the services are furnished under Part A, Part B, Part C, or Part D. Providers of most Part A services are reimbursed by Medicare under various prospective payment systems. Providers of most Part B services are reimbursed by Medicare under various fee schedules. Providers of managed care services are paid by Part C organizations, which are funded by Medicare, and providers of prescription drugs are paid by Part D plans, which are also funded by Medicare.

Part A Payment

Payments made to most hospitals are made under the inpatient prospective payment system (IPPS) for services covered by Medicare Part A, which covers institutional services (see ¶ 810). PPS payments are made for a hospital's inpatient operating and capital-related costs at predetermined, specific rates for each hospital discharge. Prospective payment systems also have been established for home health agencies (see ¶ 830), hospital outpatient services (combining elements of Part A and Part B; see ¶ 820), skilled nursing facilities (see ¶ 835), inpatient rehabilitation facilities (see ¶ 837), long-term care hospitals (see ¶ 815), inpatient hospital services furnished in psychiatric hospitals and units (see ¶ 840), and end-stage renal disease facilities (see ¶ 845). Other institutional providers and services not covered by a PPS are paid on the basis of "reasonable costs." Medicare payment is made directly to the provider that furnished the services.

Part B Payment

Part B services provided by physicians and other health care practitioners generally are paid on the basis of a physician fee schedule (see ¶ 855 and ¶ 860). Other suppliers of services and equipment paid under Part B are paid on the basis of different fee schedules (see, for example, the discussions about the clinical laboratory, ambulance, and durable medical equipment fee schedules at ¶ 875, ¶ 880, and ¶ 882) or on a "reasonable charge" basis (not covered in this book). Medicare payment is made to the physician or supplier who furnished the services if assignment has been accepted (see ¶ 868). Otherwise, the payment is made to the beneficiary, who then has the obligation to pay the physician or supplier.

Part C Payment

Medicare Advantage organizations are risk-bearing entities that can issue, within designated geographic areas, health plans offering a specific set of benefits at a uniform premium and uniform level of cost-sharing to each Medicare beneficiary who chooses to enroll in a such a plan under Medicare Part C, which is called the Medicare Advantage (MA) program. The payment rules for MA organizations are at ¶ 407 and ¶ 408. The MA program:

- allows beneficiaries to choose among health maintenance organizations, preferred provider organization plans, fee-for-service plans, and medical savings account plans for their health coverage;

- offers plans designed to provide coverage to people with special needs, i.e., dually eligible for Medicaid and Medicare, institutionalized, or diagnosed with a specified chronic illness or disability;

- provides a wider range of benefit choices available to enrollees, including prescription drug benefits;

- provides for regional plans that provide private plan options to many more beneficiaries, especially in rural areas;

- bases payments for local and regional MA plans on competitive bids rather than administered pricing; and

- establishes uniform grievance and appeals procedures, as well as notice and timeliness procedures to ensure the beneficiary's rights are protected and understood.

[Soc. Sec. Act § 1851.]

Part D Payments

On January 1, 2006, Medicare began to cover the cost of prescription drugs under Medicare Part D. Beneficiaries entitled to Part A and enrolled in Part B, and enrollees in MA private fee-for-service plans or medical savings account plans are eligible for the prescription drug benefit. Medicare Part D is covered at ¶ 500 *et seq.*

Accountable Care Organizations

Medicare services also may be delivered through accountable care organizations (ACOs), groups of service and supplier providers that work together to manage and coordinate care for Medicare fee-for-service beneficiaries. An ACO is typically a network of provider groups, often affiliated with a hospital, that work together and are jointly responsible for the cost and quality of care provided to Medicare beneficiaries. ACOs must meet certain criteria to be designated as an ACO. If an ACO meets specified quality performance standards it may receive a portion of the shared savings. ACOs are discussed at ¶ 853.

[¶ 810] Inpatient Hospital Services

Hospitals have been reimbursed under an inpatient prospective payment system (IPPS) since 1983. Under the IPPS, Medicare provides a single payment amount to hospitals for each hospital discharge, identified by the diagnosis-related group (DRG) into which each discharge is classified. [42 C.F.R. 412.2(a).]

DRG Classifications

Under the IPPS, all patient illnesses and injuries resulting in admission to a hospital are classified into different DRGs, which are clinically coherent and relatively homogeneous with respect to resources used by a hospital. [Soc. Sec. Act § 1886(a); 42 C.F.R. § 412.1 *et seq.*]

Using the DRG classification system, Medicare developed a system of payments to hospitals under which each DRG (each type of illness or injury) is paid at a set rate that is weighted geographically. Cases are classified into DRGs based on a principal diagnosis, additional or secondary diagnoses, surgical procedures, and the age, sex, and discharge status of the patient. The amount paid under the IPPS is based upon the DRG for each discharge, regardless of the number of services received or the length of the patient's stay in the hospital, and includes all inpatient operating costs. The DRG payment covers all items and services provided by the hospital to the patient. If the hospital's costs are less than that payment, the hospital keeps the difference; if the hospital's costs are more than the set rate, the hospital absorbs the loss. Not included in the DRG are services provided by the patient's physician, which are covered under Part B (see ¶ 855). [Soc. Sec. Act § 1886(a); 42 C.F.R. § 412.1 *et seq.*]

Payment Adjustments

The base payment rate to an individual hospital may be adjusted in a number of ways, usually in the form of a percentage add-on payment, including the following:

- If the hospital treats a disproportionate share of low-income patients or is located in an urban area, has 100 or more beds, and can demonstrate that more that 30 percent of its revenue is derived from state and local government payments for indigent care provided to patients not covered by Medicare or Medicaid, it will receive a disproportionate share hospital (DSH) adjustment. [Soc. Sec. Act §1886(d)(5)(F); 42 C.F.R. §412.106(c)(2).] Starting in fiscal year (FY) 2014, hospitals' Medicare DSH payments are reduced to reflect lower uncompensated care costs relative to increases in the number of insured. [Soc. Sec. Act §1886(r).]

• If the hospital is an approved teaching hospital, it will receive an indirect medical education (IME) adjustment. This percentage varies depending on the ratio of residents to beds. [Soc. Sec. Act §1886(d)(5)(B); 42 C.F.R. §412.105.]

• If a particular case involves certain approved new medical technology, additional payments may be made. [Soc. Sec. Act §1886(d)(5)(K); 42 C.F.R. §§412.87, 412.88.]

• If the hospital stay is unusually long or costly, the hospital may be eligible for an additional "outlier" payment. [Soc. Sec. Act §1886(d)(5)(A); 42 C.F.R. §§412.80–412.86.]

See ¶847 for a discussion of payment issues that apply to certain rural hospitals.

Quality Data Reporting

Payments to acute care hospitals are adjusted each year through an increase in the market basket percentage, which is a measure of the inflation rate for the goods and services used by hospitals each year to provide inpatient services. Under the Inpatient Quality Reporting (IQR) program, IPPS hospitals that do not submit required quality data on specific quality indicators to the Medicare program each year have their applicable hospital market basket percentage increase reduced by 2 percent. In the FY 2016 final rule, CMS established three previously finalized quality measures in the IQR program, as well as a fourth previously finalized LTCH functional status measure, which will affect annual payment update determinations for FY 2018 and beyond. [Soc. Sec. Act §1886(b)(3)(B)(viii); 42 C.F.R. §412.140; 80 FR 49325, Aug. 17, 2015.]

Value-Based Purchasing

Under the Hospital Inpatient Value-Based Purchasing (VBP) program, starting with discharges occurring on or after October 1, 2012 (FY 2013), hospitals receive value-based incentive payments if they meet specific performance standards in a given fiscal year. [Soc. Sec. Act §1886(o)(1); 42 C.F.R. §412.162.]

The HHS Secretary must announce performance standards that include levels of achievement and improvement 60 days before the beginning of a performance period. The Secretary will also provide for an assessment for each hospital for each performance period. The assessment must result in an appropriate distribution of value-based incentive payments among hospitals achieving different levels of hospital performance scores, with hospitals achieving the highest hospital performance scores receiving the largest value-based incentive payments. [Soc. Sec. Act §1886(o); 42 C.F.R. §§412.160–412.167.]

Hospital Readmissions Reduction

The Hospital Readmissions Reduction Program (HRRP), which was also effective beginning in FY 2013, reduces reimbursement to certain hospitals that have excess readmissions for certain conditions. For FY 2016, these conditions continue to include: heart attack, heart failure, pneumonia, chronic obstructive pulmonary disease, total hip arthroplasty, and total knee arthroplasty. A "readmission" refers to an admission to an acute-care hospital paid under the IPPS within 30 days of a discharge from the same or another acute-care hospital. For FY 2017 and future years, CMS added a measure of patients readmitted following coronary artery bypass graft surgery. The adjustments for a particular hospital will be calculated with a percentage based on the comparison of the hospital's aggregate payments for excess readmissions with aggregate payments for all discharges. The maximum payment adjustment for FY 2016 is 3 percent. [Soc. Sec. Act § 1886(q); 42 C.F.R. § § 412.152, 412.154; *Final rule*, 80 FR 49325, Aug. 17, 2015.]

Hospital-Acquired Conditions

CMS has implemented a program intended to encourage the prevention of certain avoidable or preventable hospital-acquired conditions (HACs), including infections that may occur during a hospital stay. If a selected condition that was not present on admission (POA) manifests during the hospital stay, it is considered a HAC and the case is paid as though the secondary diagnosis was not present. [Soc. Sec. Act § 1886(d)(4)(D).]

The list of HACs for which CMS does not pay after FY 2015 includes the following:

- foreign object retained after surgery;
- air embolism;
- blood incompatibility;
- stages III and IV pressure ulcers;
- falls and trauma, including fracture, dislocation, intracranial injury, crushing injury, or burn;
- manifestations of poor glycemic control;
- catheter-associated urinary tract infection;
- vascular catheter-associated infection;
- surgical site infection after coronary bypass graft surgery;
- surgical site infection following bariatric surgery for obesity;
- surgical site infection following certain orthopedic procedures;
- surgical site infection following cardiac implantable electronic device;
- deep vein thrombosis and pulmonary embolism following certain orthopedic procedures; and
- iatrogenic pneumothorax with venous catheterization.

[*Final rule*, 79 FR 49854, Aug. 22, 2014.]

Hospital-Acquired Condition Reduction Program. Starting with discharges in FY 2015, hospitals in the top 25th percentile of rates for HACs for certain high-cost and common conditions are subject to a 1 percent payment penalty under Medicare. [Soc. Sec. Act § 1886(p); 42 C.F.R. § 412.172.]

Hospital Closure

To preserve resident positions that would otherwise be lost when a hospital with an approved medical residency program closes on or after March 23, 2008, the HHS Secretary is required to redistribute unused medical resident positions to other hospitals. [Soc. Sec. Act § 1886(h)(4)(H)(vi); 42 C.F.R. § 412.105(f)(1)(ix)(A).] In addition, effective for cost reporting periods occurring on or after July 1, 2011, if a hospital's "reference resident level" is less than the applicable resident limit, the resident limit will be reduced by 65 percent of the difference between the resident limit and the reference resident level. [Soc. Sec. Act § 1886(h)(8); 412.105(f)(1)(iv)(B)(2).]

Three-Day Payment Window

Under the three-day payment window, a hospital (or an entity that is wholly owned or wholly operated by the hospital) subject to the IPPS must include on the claim for a

Medicare beneficiary's inpatient stay the diagnoses, procedures, and charges for all outpatient diagnostic services and admission-related outpatient nondiagnostic services that are furnished to the beneficiary on the date of admission to the hospital and during the three calendar days immediately preceding the date of the beneficiary's admission. This provision does not apply to ambulance services and maintenance renal dialysis services, nor does it apply when the admitting hospital is a critical access hospital. [Soc. Sec. Act § 1886(a)(4); 42 C.F.R. § 412.2(c)(5); *Medicare Claims Processing Manual*, Pub. 100-04, Ch. 3, § 40.3.]

"Two Midnight" Rule

Under the "two midnight" rule, effective for admissions on or after October 1, 2013, if a physician expects a beneficiary's surgical procedure, diagnostic test, or other treatment to require a stay in the hospital lasting at least two midnights and admits the beneficiary to the hospital based on that expectation, it is presumed to be appropriate that the hospital receive Medicare Part A payment. A beneficiary becomes a hospital inpatient if a physician or any other qualified practitioner orders an inpatient admission in accordance with the conditions of participation. The beneficiary's medical record must contain information to justify admission and continued hospitalization, support the diagnosis, and describe the patient's progress and response to medications and services. [42 C.F.R. §§ 412.3(d), 419.22(n); *Final rule,* 78 FR 50496, Aug. 19, 2013.]

Hospital services spanning less than two midnights should be provided on an outpatient basis unless there is clear documentation in the medical record that the procedure is designated by CMS as an inpatient-only service or that the physician's order clearly states an expectation of a stay spanning more than two midnights. [42 C.F.R. §§ 412.3(d), 419.22(n); *Final rule,* 78 FR 50496, Aug. 19, 2013.]

CMS instructed contractors not to focus medical review efforts on stays spanning at least two midnights after admission absent evidence of systematic gaming, abuse, or delays in the provision of care in an attempt to qualify for the two-midnight presumption. The Protecting Access to Medicare Act of 2014 (PAMA) (P.L. 113-93) and Medicare Access and CHIP Reauthorization Act of 2015 (MACRA) (P.L. 114-10) allowed CMS to continue use of the Medicare administrative contractor (MAC) "probe and educate" program to assess provider understanding and compliance with the two-midnight rule, on a pre-payment basis, through September 30, 2015. The legislation allowed CMS to conduct patient status reviews on a post-payment review basis through recovery audit contractors under Soc. Sec. Act § 1893(h) for inpatient claims with dates of admission through September 30, 2015, only if there was evidence of systematic gaming, fraud, abuse, or delays in the provision of care. [MACRA § 521; PAMA § 111.]

Comprehensive Care for Joint Replacement Model

To encourage hospitals to coordinate care with physicians, home health agencies, skilled nursing facilities, and other providers to allow for the best possible outcomes for patients and the best financial outcomes for the Medicare programs, the Comprehensive Care for Joint Replacement (CJR) model provides performance-based payments to acute care hospitals in certain metropolitan statistical areas serving as surgical sites for hip and knee replacements and other major leg procedures. This mandatory program pays such hospitals under the normal fee-for-service system, but the relevant episodes of care will be compared to the target price, which will be adjusted for quality factors, including readmissions, complications, and patient experience reported in surveys. [*Final rule,* 80 FR 73274, Nov. 24, 2015].

Hospitals Excluded from Inpatient PPS

Certain hospitals are exempt from the IPPS, including psychiatric hospitals and units, rehabilitation hospitals and units, pediatric hospitals, long-term care hospitals, and certain cancer hospitals. Hospitals exempt from the IPPS either are reimbursed on a reasonable cost basis but are subject to a ceiling on the rate of increase in inpatient costs or have their own prospective payment system. [Soc. Sec. Act § 1886(b)(1)(C), (j); 42 C.F.R. § 412.23.]

[¶ 815] Long-Term Care Hospitals

Long-term care hospitals (LTCHs) are hospitals that are primarily engaged in providing inpatient services by or under the supervision of a physician to Medicare beneficiaries with medically complex conditions who require a long hospital stay. LTCH facilities must have an average inpatient length of stay greater than 25 days (or 20 days for certain hospitals focusing on cancer treatment) and further meet the requirements for hospitals set forth in Soc. Sec. Act § 1861(e). These facilities generally provide extended medical and rehabilitative care for patients who are clinically complex and may suffer from multiple acute or chronic conditions. [Soc. Sec. Act § 1861(ccc)(1)–(3).]

Requirements for LTCHs

LTCHs are required to do the following:

(1) have a documented patient review process that includes pre-admission screening, validation within 48 hours of admission that patients meet admission criteria, and periodic evaluation of each patient's need for continued care in the LTCH and assessment of the available discharge options;

(2) have active physician involvement with patients through an organized medical staff, with physicians available on-site every day to review patients' progress and consulting physicians on call and able to be at the patient's bedside within a moderate period of time; and

(3) have interdisciplinary teams of health care professionals, including physicians, to prepare and implement an individualized treatment plan for each patient.

[Soc. Sec. Act § 1861(ccc)(4).]

Moratorium on new LTCHs. Section 114(d) of the Medicare, Medicaid and SCHIP Extension Act of 2007 (MMSEA) (P.L. 110-173), as amended by Patient Protection and Affordable Care Act (ACA) (P.L. 111-148) § 3106, imposed a moratorium on the establishment or classification of new LTCH and LTCH satellite facilities and on bed increases for existing facilities from December 29, 2007 to December 28, 2012. [42 C.F.R. § 412.23(e)(6)–(8).]

Section 1206(b) of the Pathways to SGR Reform Act of 2013 (P.L. 113-67), as amended by section 112(b) of the Protecting Access to Medicare Act of 2014 (P.L. 113-93), provides for a new moratorium on the establishment of new Medicare-participating LTCHs, the addition of LTCH satellite facilities to an existing LTCH, and any increase in the number of certified beds in existing LTCHs and LTCH satellites, from April 1, 2014, through September 30, 2017. The new moratorium provides exceptions for the establishment of new LTCHs and LTCH satellite facilities; however, no exceptions are provided for increases in the number of certified beds in existing LTCHs and LTCH satellites. [42 C.F.R. § 412.23(e)(6)–(8); *Letter to State Survey Agency Directors*, S&C: 15-03, Jan. 9, 2015.]

Payment Methodology

CMS publishes the LTCH prospective payment system (PPS) annual update in the *Federal Register* by September 1st of each year. [42 C.F.R. § 412.535; *Final rule*, 80 FR 49325,

Aug. 17, 2015.] The annual update of the Medicare severity long-term care diagnosis-related groups (MS-LTC-DRGs) is linked to the annual adjustments of the inpatient PPS (IPPS) Medicare severity diagnosis-related groups (MS-DRGs), which become effective October 1 of each year. The MS-LTC-DRGs are designed to base compensation to hospitals on the severity of the illness, which affects the resources used in the care of each patient. [42 C.F.R. § 412.513.]

Payment under the LTCH PPS is made on a per-discharge basis. Each patient case is classified according to the principal diagnosis, secondary diagnoses, procedures performed during the stay, and discharge status of the patient. The patient's case is classified by MS-LTC-DRG, based on the relative costliness of treatment for patients in the group, similar to classification under IPPS (see ¶ 810). [42 C.F.R. § 412.513.]

The amount of the prospective payment is based on the standard federal rate, established under 42 C.F.R. § 412.523 and adjusted for the MS-LTC-DRG relative weights, differences in area wage levels, cost of living in Alaska and Hawaii, high-cost outliers, and other special payment provisions.

Productivity adjustment. Section 3401(c) of the ACA amended the annual update to the standard federal rate under Soc. Sec. Act § 1886(m) to add a productivity adjustment for discharges in 2012 and later. The productivity adjustment is the same one applied to inpatient hospital services under Soc. Sec. Act § 1886(b)(3)(B)(xi)(II). The application of this productivity adjustment may result in the annual update being less than 0.0 for a year and may result in payment rates under the LTCH PPS for a year being less than such payment rates for the preceding year. [Soc. Sec. Act § 1886(m)(3).]

Also pursuant to section 3401(c) of the ACA, updates for 2010 through 2019 are subject to an "other adjustment"; the adjustment for 2015 and 2016 is 0.2 percentage point and the adjustment for 2017, 2018, and 2019 is 0.75 percentage point. [Soc. Sec. Act § 1886(m)(3)(A)(ii), (m)(4).]

Section 411(e) of the Medicare and CHIP Reauthorization Act of 2015 (MACRA) (P.L. 114-10) set the the annual update for fiscal year 2018, after the application of these adjustments, at 1.0 percent. [Soc. Sec. Act § 1886(m)(3)(C).]

Site-neutral IPPS payment amount. Effective for discharges in cost reporting periods beginning on or after October 1, 2015, patients with stays longer than three days in an intensive care unit or on a ventilator for more than 96 hours will qualify for the traditional increased rate received by LTCHs. All other cases will be reimbursed at a site-neutral rate, which is the same level as an inpatient facility stay. [Soc. Sec. Act § 1886(m)(6); 42 C.F.R. § 412.522.]

For discharges during cost reporting periods beginning on or after October 1, 2015 and on or before September 30, 2017, payment for discharges under this rule will be paid using a blended payment rate, determined as 50 percent of the site neutral payment rate amount and 50 percent of the standard prospective payment rate amount for the discharge. [42 C.F.R. § 412.522(c)(3).]

Patient shifting and the "25 percent rule." CMS may reduce the payments to an LTCH if more than 25 percent of its Medicare patients were transferred from hospitals co-located with the LTCH or a satellite facility (the "25 percent rule"). Legislative moratoria delayed the full implementation of this rule; CMS adopted a one-year extension on this moratorium through FY 2013, and the Bipartisan Budget Act of 2013 (P.L. 113-67) extended it until cost reporting periods beginning on or after October 1, 2016. Grandfathered LTCHs are permanently exempt from the 25 percent rule under the Bipartisan Budget Act. [MMSEA

§ 114(c) and (d)(1), as amended by Bipartisan Budget Act of 2013 § 1206(b)(1); *Final rule,* 79 FR 49854, Aug. 22, 2014.]

The reduction applies only to discharges beyond the 25 percent threshold, and the adjusted payment is reduced to the amount payable under the IPPS. [42 C.F.R. § 412.534(c)(1).] The threshold for the reduction to apply to rural hospitals is 50 percent, and patients on whose behalf outlier payment was made at the co-located hospital are not counted toward the 50 percent threshold. [42 C.F.R. § 412.534(d).]

One-Day Payment Window

LTCHs under the LTCH PPS are subject to a one-day payment window, the "24-hour rule," for preadmission services related to the patient stay. In other words, outpatient diagnostic services and most nonphysician services provided during the calendar day immediately preceding the date of admission to an LTCH (excluding ambulance services and maintenance renal dialysis services) are included in the standard payment. A preadmission service is related to the patient stay if:

(1) it is diagnostic (including clinical diagnostic laboratory tests);

(2) it is nondiagnostic when furnished on the date of the beneficiary's inpatient admission; or

(3) on or after June 25, 2010, it is nondiagnostic when furnished on the calendar day preceding the date of the beneficiary's inpatient admission and the hospital does not attest that such service is unrelated to the beneficiary's inpatient admission.

[42 C.F.R. § 412.540.]

Outlier Payments

For unusually costly cases, LTCHs under the LTCH PPS receive increased payment. The LTCH PPS outlier policy is modeled after the IPPS outlier policy. The key distinction between the LTCH outlier policy and the IPPS outlier policy is that an LTCH can receive outlier payments for a case that has:

(1) unusually high costs that exceed the typical cost for a MS-LTC-DRG (referred to as a "high-cost outlier");

(2) a length of stay that is considerably shorter than the average length of stay for a MS-LTC-DRG (referred to as a "short-stay outlier"); or

(3) a combination of high-cost and short-stay outlier.

[42 C.F.R. §§ 412.525(a), 412.529(d).]

High-cost outliers. A high-cost outlier under the LTCH PPS is a case with unusually high costs that exceed the typical cost for a MS-LTC-DRG. CMS provides for an additional payment to an LTCH if its estimated costs for a given case exceed the MS-LTC-DRG payment plus a fixed-loss amount. The fixed-loss amount for fiscal year (FY) 2016, which began October 1, 2015, is $22,544, up from $14,972 in FY 2015. The additional payment for high-cost outlier cases is equal to 80 percent of the difference between the estimated cost of the patient's care and the sum of the adjusted LTCH PPS prospective payment and the fixed-loss amount. For each LTCH PPS FY, CMS establishes a fixed-loss amount so that the total high cost outlier payments in a given year are projected to be equal to 8 percent of the total LTCH PPS payments estimated for that year. [42 C.F.R. § 412.525(a)(3); *Final rule,* 80 FR 49325, Aug. 17, 2015.]

Short-stay outliers. LTCHs are paid adjusted rates for outlier patients who have short stays. Short-stay outliers are cases with a length of stay up to and including five-sixths of the geometric average length of stay for each MS-LTC-DRG. The short-stay outlier adjustment allows Medicare to reimburse LTCHs for costly short-stay outlier patients and yet pay less for cases that do not receive a full episode of care at the LTCH and should not be reimbursed at the full MS-LTC-DRG payment rate. [42 C.F.R. § 412.529(a)–(c).]

A short-stay outlier payment may be triggered when an LTCH patient:

(1) is discharged to another facility;

(2) is discharged to his or her home;

(3) expires within the first several days of admission to the LTCH; or

(4) exhausts all benefits during the LTCH stay.

[*Final rule*, 75 FR 50042, Aug. 16, 2010.]

CMS will apply an "IPPS-comparable per diem amount" for very short-stay outlier cases, a generally lowered rate, beginning with discharges occurring on or after December 29, 2012. [42 C.F.R. § 412.529(c)(3); *Final rule,* 77 FR 53257, Aug. 31, 2012.]

Interrupted Stay Policy

Under the LTCH PPS, an interruption of stay occurs when a Medicare inpatient is transferred upon discharge to an acute-care hospital, an inpatient rehabilitation facility (IRF), a skilled nursing facility (SNF), or the patient's home for treatment or services that are not available in the LTCH, and returns to the same LTCH. CMS has divided interruption of stay into two categories, a "three-day or less interruption of stay" and a "greater than three-day interruption of stay." [42 C.F.R. § 412.531(a); *Medicare Claims Processing Manual*, Pub. 100-04, Ch. 3, § 150.9.1.2.]

Three or fewer days. If an interruption of stay of three or fewer days occurs during an episode of care, one MS-LTC-DRG payment is made. Accordingly, the LTCH must provide services either directly or "under arrangements" with the other provider. The LTCH is responsible for paying the other provider for the costs of services and the three or fewer days that the patient is away are included in the patient day count. No other payment may be made by Medicare to the other provider. [42 C.F.R. § 412.531(b)(1)(ii)(A).]

Greater than three-day interruption of stay. A greater than three-day interruption of stay is defined as a stay in a LTCH during which a Medicare inpatient is discharged from the LTCH to an acute care hospital, an IRF, or a SNF for a period of greater than three days but returns to the LTCH within the applicable fixed-day period:

- between four and nine consecutive days for a discharge to an acute care hospital;

- between four and 27 consecutive days for a discharge to an IRF; and

- between four and 45 consecutive days for a discharge to a SNF.

[42 C.F.R. § 412.531(a)(2)(i)–(iii).] In such cases, CMS will make one LTC-DRG payment for all portions of a long-term care stay and will separately pay the acute-care hospital, the IRF, or the SNF in accordance with their respective payment systems. [42 C.F.R. § 412.531(b)(1)(ii)(B), (c).]

If, however, the applicable fixed-day time frames are exceeded, the subsequent admission to the LTCH is considered a new stay and the LTCH will receive two separate PPS payments. [42 C.F.R. § 412.531(b)(4).] For example, if an LTCH patient is discharged to an acute care hospital and is readmitted to the LTCH on any day up to and including the ninth day following the original day of discharge from the LTCH, one MS-LTC-DRG payment will be made. If the patient is readmitted to the LTCH from the acute-care hospital on the tenth day after the original discharge or later, Medicare will pay for the second admission as a separate stay with a second MS-LTC-DRG assignment. [42 C.F.R. § 412.531(b)(4)(i).]

Outlier payments. Interrupted stays at an LTCH are subject to the short-stay and high-cost outlier rules. If the total number of days of a patient's stay before and following an interruption of stay is at or below five-sixths of the geometric average length of stay of the MS-LTC-DRG, CMS will make a short-stay outlier payment. An additional payment will be made if the patient's stay qualifies as a high-cost outlier. [42 C.F.R. § 412.531(b)(2), (3).]

Quality Reporting

Under the LTCH quality reporting program, beginning in FY 2014, LTCHs that fail to provide data on certain quality indicators are subject to a 2.0 percent reduction in their annual market basket update. [Soc. Sec. Act § 1886(m)(5); 42 C.F.R. §§ 412.523(c)(4), 423.560(b)(2).]

CMS adopted the following measures for the FY 2015 payment determination and later years:

(1) catheter-associated urinary tract infections,

(2) central line-associated blood stream infections, and

(3) pressure ulcers that are new or have worsened.

CMS adopted two additional quality measures for LTCH reporting for the FY 2016 payment determination and later years: percent of residents or patients who were assessed and appropriately given the seasonal influenza vaccine (short stay), and influenza vaccination coverage among health care personnel. [*Final rule*, 78 FR 74826, Dec. 10, 2013.]

In the FY 2014 final rule, CMS adopted three additional measures for the FYs 2017 and 2018 payment determinations and subsequent years: (1) facility-wide inpatient hospital-onset *clostridium difficile* infection; (2) unplanned readmission measure for 30 days post-discharge from LTCHs; and (3) percent of residents experiencing one or more falls with major injury (long stay). In the FY 2015 final rule, CMS added three measures for the FY 2018 payment determination: (1) percent of patients with an admission and discharge functional assessment and a care plan that addresses function; (2) change in mobility among patients requiring ventilator support; and (3) Ventilator-Associated Event Outcome Measure. [*Final rule,* 79 FR 49854, Aug. 22, 2014.]

The FY 2016 final rule established three previously finalized quality measures in the IQR Program, as well as a fourth previously finalized LTCH functional status measure. These measures will affect annual payment update determinations for FY 2018 and beyond. [*Final rule*, 80 FR 49325, Aug. 17, 2015.]

The data submitted by a facility is made publicly available on the CMS website after the LTCH has the opportunity to review its data. Any reimbursement reductions due to improperly submitted data will not affect payments in subsequent fiscal years. [Soc. Sec. Act § 1886(m)(5)(E).]

IMPACT Act. Under the Improving Medicare Post-Acute Care Transformation Act of 2014 (IMPACT Act) (P.L. 113-185), the HHS Secretary must require post-acute care (PAC) providers, including LTCHs, to report standardized patient assessment data, data on quality measures, and data on resource use and other measures. Data measures include: (1) functional status, cognitive function, and changes in function and cognitive function; (2) skin integrity and changes in skin integrity; (3) medication reconciliation; (4) incidence of major falls; and (5) accurately communicating the individual's health information and care preferences. [Soc. Sec. Act § 1899B, as added by IMPACT Act § 2.]

This data must be interoperable to allow for its exchange among PAC and other providers to give them access to longitudinal information so as to facilitate coordinated care and improve Medicare beneficiary outcomes. HHS must also modify PAC assessment instruments applicable to PAC providers for the submission of standardized patient assessment data on such providers and enable assessment data comparison across all such providers. LTCHs must begin reporting on most quality measures by October 1, 2016, and patient assessment data no later than October 1, 2018. [Soc. Sec. Act § 1899B, as added by IMPACT Act § 2.] An LTCH that fails to submit the required information will have its market basket update reduced by 2 percent. [Soc. Sec. Act § 1886(m)(5)(F), as added by IMPACT Act § 2(c)(2).]

CMS will begin to publicly report LTCH quality data beginning fall 2016 on a website such as Hospital Compare. [*Final rule*, 80 FR 49325, Aug. 17, 2015.]

[¶ 820] Hospital Outpatient Services

Outpatient services are covered under Medicare Part B and paid under the outpatient prospective payment system (OPPS). Under the OPPS, predetermined amounts are paid for designated services furnished to Medicare beneficiaries. [Soc. Sec. Act § 1833(t); 42 C.F.R. § 419.2.]

The OPPS is applicable to any hospital participating in the Medicare program, except for: critical access hospitals (CAHs); hospitals located in Maryland and paid under the Maryland All-Payer Model; hospitals located outside of the 50 states, the District of Columbia, and Puerto Rico; and Indian Health Service (IHS) hospitals. [42 C.F.R. § 419.20.]

Services subject to the OPPS. CMS makes payment under the OPPS for the following services:

(1) designated hospital outpatient services;

(2) certain Medicare Part B services furnished to hospital inpatients who are either not entitled to benefits under Part A or who have exhausted their Part A benefits but are entitled to benefits under Part B of the program;

(3) partial hospitalization services furnished by community mental health centers (CMHCs);

(4) antigens, splints and casts, and the hepatitis B vaccine furnished by a home health agency (HHA) to patients who are not under an HHA plan or treatment or by a hospice program furnishing services to patients outside the hospice benefit; and

(5) an initial preventive physical examination performed within first 12 months of Part B coverage.

[42 C.F.R. § 419.21.]

Services excluded from the OPPS. The following services are not paid for under the hospital outpatient prospective payment system (except when packaged as a part of a bundled payment):

(1) professional services of physicians and nonphysician practitioners paid under the physician fee schedule;

(2) physical therapy services, speech-language pathology services, and occupational therapy services;

(3) ambulance services;

(4) prosthetic and orthotic devices, except as provided in 42 C.F.R. § 419.2(b)(11);

(5) durable medical equipment (DME) supplied by the hospital for the patient to take home, except as provided in 42 C.F.R. § 419.2(b)(10);

(6) clinical diagnostic tests, except as provided by 42 C.F.R. § 419.2(b)(17);

(7) renal dialysis services for patients with end-stage renal disease (ESRD) that are paid under the ESRD benefit;

(8) services and procedures that the HHS Secretary designates as requiring inpatient care;

(9) hospital outpatient services furnished to skilled nursing facility (SNF) residents as part of the patient's resident assessment or comprehensive care plan (and, thus, included under the SNF prospective payment system (PPS)) that are furnished by the hospital "under arrangements" but billable only by the SNF, regardless of whether the patient is in a Part A SNF stay;

(10) services that are not covered by Medicare by statute;

(11) services that are not reasonable or necessary for the diagnosis or treatment of an illness or disease;

(12) services that are furnished to inpatients of hospitals that do not submit claims for outpatient services under Medicare Part B;

(13) screening and diagnostic mammography;

(14) annual wellness visit providing personalized prevention plan services; and

(15) outpatient diabetes self-management training.

[42 C.F.R. § 419.22.]

Determining a Payment Under OPPS

The unit of payment under the OPPS is the ambulatory payment classification (APC) system. CMS assigns individual services to APCs based on similar clinical characteristics and similar costs. CMS assigns to each APC group an appropriate weighting factor to reflect the relative geometric mean costs for the services within the APC group compared to the geometric mean costs for the services in all APC groups. The APC weights are converted to payment rates through the application of a conversion factor. [Soc. Sec. Act § 1833(t)(3), (5); 42 C.F.R. §§ 419.31, 419.32(c).]

The items and services in an APC group are those that are recognized as contributing to the cost of the procedures or services. Items and services within a group cannot be considered comparable with respect to the use of resources if the highest median cost for an item or service within the group is more than two times greater than the lowest median cost for an item or service within the group, referred to as the "two times rule." The Secretary may make an exception to the two-times limit in unusual cases such as low-volume items and services. [Soc. Sec. Act § 1833(t)(2); 42 C.F.R. § 419.31(a).]

To account for geographic differences in input prices, the labor portion of the payment rate is further adjusted by the hospital wage index for the area where payment is being made. [42 C.F.R. §§ 419.31(c), 419.43(c).]

Items and services included in the APC payment rate. Within each APC, payment for dependent, ancillary, supportive, and adjunctive items and services is packaged into payment for the primary independent service. In general, these packaged costs may include, but are not limited to, the following items and services, the payment for which is packaged or conditionally packaged into the payment for the related procedures or services:

- use of an operating suite, procedure room, or treatment room;
- use of recovery room;
- observation services;

- anesthesia; certain drugs, biologicals, and other pharmaceuticals; medical and surgical supplies and equipment; surgical dressings; and devices used for external reduction of fractures and dislocations;

- supplies and equipment for administering and monitoring anesthesia or sedation;

- intraocular lenses (IOLs);

- ancillary services;

- capital-related costs;

- implantable items used in connection with diagnostic x-ray tests, diagnostic laboratory tests, and other diagnostic tests;

- durable medical equipment that is implantable;

- implantable and insertable medical items and devices, including, but not limited to, prosthetic devices (other than dental) that replace all or part of an internal body organ (including colostomy bags and supplies directly related to colostomy care), including replacement of these devices;

- costs incurred to procure donor tissue other than corneal tissue;

- image guidance, processing, supervision, and interpretation services;

- intraoperative items and services;

- drugs, biologicals, and radiopharmaceuticals that function as supplies when used in a diagnostic test or procedure (including, but not limited to, diagnostic radiopharmaceuticals, contrast agents, and pharmacologic stress agents);

- drugs and biologicals that function as supplies when used in a surgical procedure (including, but not limited to, skin substitutes and similar products that aid wound healing and implantable biologicals);

- certain clinical diagnostic laboratory tests; and

- certain services described by add-on codes.

[42 C.F.R. § 419.2(b).]

Hospitals subject to the OPPS are paid for certain items and services that are outside the scope of OPPS on a reasonable cost or other basis. The following costs are outside the scope of OPPS:

- direct graduate medical education;

- nursing and allied health programs;

- interns and residents not in approved teaching programs;

- teaching physicians' charges for Part B services in hospitals that elect cost-based payment for teaching physicians;

- anesthesia services furnished to hospital outpatients by qualified nonphysician anesthetists such as certified registered nurse anesthetists and anesthesiologists' assistants employed by the hospital or obtained under arrangements;

- bad debts for uncollectible deductible and coinsurance amounts;

- organ acquisition costs paid under Part B; and

- corneal tissue acquisition or procurement costs for corneal transplant procedures.

[42 C.F.R. § 419.2(c).]

Adjustments and Additional Payments Under the OPPS

Hospitals may receive payments in addition to standard OPPS payments.

Outlier payments. Medicare provides for additional "outlier" payments to hospitals when they provide exceptionally costly outpatient services. CMS provides for an additional payment for outpatient services for which a hospital's charges, adjusted to cost, exceed a fixed multiple of the OPPS payment as adjusted by pass-through payments. [Soc. Sec. Act § 1833(t)(5); 42 C.F.R. § 419.43(d).]

To qualify for an outlier payment in calendar year (CY) 2016, the cost of a service must exceed: (1) 1.75 times the APC payment rate, and (2) a fixed dollar outlier threshold of $3,250. The outlier payment for a particular service will equal 50 percent of the amount by which the cost of furnishing the service exceeds 1.75 times the APC payment rate. [*Final rule*, 80 FR 70298, Nov. 6, 2015.]

Transitional pass-through payments. The OPPS provides for additional payments, called transitional pass-through payments, for certain innovative medical devices, drugs, and biologicals for a period of two to three years. CMS makes a transitional pass-through payment for the following drugs and biologicals that are furnished as part of an outpatient hospital service: (1) orphan drugs; (2) cancer therapy drugs and biologicals; (3) radiopharmaceutical drugs and biological products; and (4) new medical devices, drugs, and biologicals. The purpose of transitional pass-through payments is to allow for adequate payment of new and innovative technology until there is enough data to incorporate the costs for these items into the base APC group. [Soc. Sec. Act § 1833(t)(6); 42 C.F.R. §§ 419.64, 419.66.]

Certain cancer hospitals. CMS adjusts OPPS payments to certain cancer hospitals—those exempted by law from payment under the inpatient prospective payment system for covered hospital outpatient services provided in CY 2016. If a cancer hospital has a payment-to-cost ratio (PCR) for CY 2016 that is below a target PCR, the hospital will receive an additional payment so that final payment is equal to the target PCR. The target PCR is defined as the weighted average PCR for other hospitals furnishing services under the OPPS determined from available cost reports. [Soc. Sec. Act § 1833(t)(18); 42 C.F.R. § 419.43(i); *Final rule*, 80 FR 70298, Nov. 6, 2015.]

Hold-harmless status for certain cancer hospitals and children's hospitals. If payments for outpatient department services furnished by cancer hospitals and children's hospitals hospitals are lower than those they would have received under previous policies, CMS provides additional payments to make up the difference. [Soc. Sec. Act § 1833(t)(7)(D)(ii); 42 C.F.R. § 419.70(d)(3).]

Small rural hospital adjustment. Medicare makes an OPPS payment adjustment for rural sole community hospitals and essential access community hospitals. For 2016, the adjustment represents a 7.1 percent payment increase to these small rural hospitals. The adjustment is for all services and procedures paid under the OPPS, excluding separately payable drugs and biologicals, devices paid under the pass-through payment policy, and items paid at charges reduced to costs. [Soc. Sec. Act § 1833(t)(13)(B); 42 C.F.R. § 419.43(g); *Final rule*, 80 FR 70298, Nov. 6, 2015.]

Copayment/Coinsurance

Under the OPPS, coinsurance is defined as the percent of the Medicare-approved amount that beneficiaries pay for a service furnished in the hospital outpatient department (after they have met the Part B deductible—see ¶ 335). Copayment is defined as the set dollar amount that beneficiaries pay under the OPPS and is capped at the Part A deductible

¶820

for that year. In 2016, the Part A deductible will be $1,288 per APC, meaning a beneficiary will never pay more than this amount for any outpatient procedure provided. [42 C.F.R. § 419.41(c)(4); *Notice*, 80 FR 70808, Nov. 16, 2015.]

The coinsurance percentage is calculated as the difference between the program payment percentage and 100 percent. The coinsurance percentage in any year is defined for each APC group as the greater of the ratio of the APC group unadjusted copayment amount to the annual APC group payment rate, or 20 percent. [Soc. Sec. Act § 1833(t)(3)(B), (t)(8)(C); 42 C.F.R. § 419.40.]

The Secretary must reduce the national unadjusted coinsurance amount each year so that the effective coinsurance rate for a covered service in the year does not exceed 40 percent of the APC payment rate. For a covered service furnished in a year, the national unadjusted coinsurance amount cannot be less than 20 percent of the payment rate amount. [Soc. Sec. § 1833(t)(3)(B)(ii) and (t)(8)(C); 42 C.F.R. § 419.41(c)(4)(iii).]

The coinsurance amount for the APC or APCs for a drug or biological furnished on the same day has been aggregated with the coinsurance amount for the APC that reflects the administration of the drug or biological furnished on that day and treated as the coinsurance amount for one APC. [42 C.F.R. § 419.41(c)(4)(i)(B).]

Coinsurance for new procedures. APCs for new procedures may be adopted when the new procedures do not fit well into another APC. When an APC is added that consists of HCPCS codes for which there was no 1996 charge data to calculate the unadjusted coinsurance amount, coinsurance is based on the minimum unadjusted coinsurance, which is 20 percent of the APC payment amount. Additional payments for outlier cases and for certain medical devices, drugs, and biologicals, and transitional corridor payments will not affect the coinsurance amounts. [Soc. Sec. § 1833(t)(3)(B)(iii); *Final rule*, 65 FR 18434, 18487, April 7, 2000.]

Hospital election to reduce coinsurance. A hospital may elect to reduce coinsurance for any or all APC groups on a calendar-year basis by selecting the minimum coinsurance amount; however, it may not reduce coinsurance for some, but not all, services within the same APC group. If a hospital reduces a coinsurance amount, it must notify its Medicare administrative contractor by December 1 of the preceding year by documenting the applicable APCs and the coinsurance amount that the hospital has selected. The reduced coinsurance may not be less than 20 percent of the APC payment rate. The hospital may advertise that it has reduced the level of coinsurance identifying the specific outpatient services to which the reduction is applicable. Coinsurance reductions are not allowed in physicians' offices or other ambulatory settings. [Soc. Sec. Act § 1833(t)(8)(B); 42 C.F.R. § 419.42.]

Coinsurance waiver for preventive services. The Patient Protection and Affordable Care Act (ACA) (P.L. 111-148) required all beneficiary deductibles and copayments for preventive services paid under the OPPS to be waived. Preventive services are defined as: screening and preventive services currently listed in Soc. Sec. Act § 1861(ww)(2); preventive "wellness" physical examinations; and personalized preventive plan services. For coinsurance to be waived, preventive services must be given a grade of "A" or "B" by the United States Preventive Services Task Force. [Soc. Sec. Act § 1833(a), (b)(1).] See ¶ 369 for a discussion of Part B coverage of preventive services.

Reporting of Quality of Care Data

Providers of outpatient services must report quality of care data to avoid a 2.0 percent decrease in their annual market basket payment adjustments as part of the Hospital Outpatient Quality Reporting (OQR) Program. [Soc. Sec. Act § 1833(t)(17)(a)(i).]

¶820

Validation requirement. To ensure that hospitals are accurately reporting quality of care measures for chart-abstracted data, CMS may validate one or more measures by reviewing documentation of patient encounters submitted by selected participating hospitals. CMS requires hospitals to achieve a minimum 75 percent reliability score based on this validation process to receive the full OPPS update. [42 C.F.R. § 419.46(e).]

Quality measures. CMS finalized one new measure for the OQR program for the CY 2018 payment determination and later: percentage of patients (all-payer) with painful bone metastases and no history of previous radiation who receive external beam radiotherapy for bone metastases with an acceptable dosing schedule. CMS finalized the removal of one measure, use of brain computed tomography in the emergency department for atraumatic headache, because the measure does not align with the most updated clinical guidelines or practice. [*Final rule*, 80 FR 70298, Nov. 6, 2015.]

Data submission. Data must be submitted through the QualityNet.org website by specified deadlines. CMS may grant an extension or exception of one or more data submission deadlines and requirements in the event of extraordinary circumstances beyond the control of the hospital, such as when an act of nature affects an entire region or locale or a systemic problem with one of CMS's data collection systems directly or indirectly affects data submission. [42 C.F.R. § 419.46.]

Separately Payable Drugs, Biologicals, and Radiopharmaceuticals

The costs of drugs, biologicals, and radiopharmaceuticals are generally included in the payment for the procedure during which they were administered. For CY 2016, drugs, biologicals, and radiopharmaceuticals with a per-administration cost less than or equal to $100 will be packaged, and items with an estimated per-administration cost greater than $100 will receive separate payment (the packaging threshold was $95 in 2015). [Soc. Sec. Act § 1833(t)(16)(B); *Final rule*, 80 FR 70298, Nov. 6, 2015.]

In CY 2016, CMS will pay for separately payable drugs and biologicals at the average sale price (ASP) plus 6 percent. [*Final rule*, 80 FR 70298, Nov. 6, 2015.]

Specified covered outpatient drugs. Payment for "specified covered hospital outpatient department drugs" must be based on the average acquisition cost of the drug for a certain year, i.e., the adjusted ASP. A "specified covered outpatient department drug" is a covered outpatient drug for which a separate APC has been established and that is (1) a radiopharmaceutical or (2) a drug or biological that qualified for "pass-through" payments on or before December 31, 2002. The term "specified covered outpatient department drug" does not include a drug or biological for which payment was first made on or after January 1, 2003, under the transitional pass-through payment provision in Soc. Sec. Act § 1833(t)(6); a drug or biological for which a temporary HCPCS code has not been assigned; or, during 2004 and 2005, an orphan drug. [Soc. Sec. Act § 1833(t)(14); *Final rule*, 80 FR 70298, Nov. 6, 2015.]

[¶ 825] Ambulatory Surgical Centers

CMS pays for surgical procedures provided in freestanding or hospital-based ambulatory surgical centers (ASCs) using a payment system based on the hospital outpatient prospective payment system (OPPS). Under the system, CMS reimburses ASCs for any covered individual "surgical procedure." ASC covered surgical procedures are those that are separately paid under the OPPS, that would not pose a significant risk to beneficiary safety, and for which standard medical practice dictates that the beneficiary would not typically be expected to require active medical monitoring and care at midnight following the procedure. [Soc. Sec. Act § 1833(i)(1), (2); 42 C.F.R. § 416.166.]

Like the OPPS, the ASC payment system sets payments for individual services using a set of relative weights, a conversion factor (or average payment amount), and adjustments for geographic differences in input prices. Medicare pays ASCs 80 percent of the lesser of: (1) the actual charge for the services, or (2) the geographically adjusted payment rate determined by CMS. The beneficiary pays the remaining 20 percent, as the Part B deductible and coinsurance amount applies to services provided at an ASC. [42 C.F.R. §§ 416.167, 416.171, 416.172.]

Medicare pays for the related physician services under the physician fee schedule (see ¶ 855). [42 C.F.R. § 416.163(b).] See ¶ 386 for a discussion of Medicare coverage of ASC services.

Reporting of ASC Quality Data

Under the ASC quality reporting (ASCQR) program, ASCs must retain and report data on several measures of the quality of care provided. ASCs that do not maintain and report this data as required will have the increase in their payments reduced by 2 percent. [Soc. Sec. Act § 1833(i)(2)(D)(iv), (i)(7)(A); 42 C.F.R. § 416.300.]

For the calendar year (CY) 2017 payment determination and later, ASCs must collect and report quality of care data for the following measures: (1) patient burn; (2) patient fall; (3) wrong site, wrong side, wrong patient, wrong procedure, wrong implant; (4) hospital transfer/admission; (5) prophylactic intravenous antibiotic timing; (6) safe surgery checklist use; (7) ASC facility volume data on selected surgical procedures; (8) influenza vaccination coverage among health care personnel; (9) endoscopy/polyp surveillance: appropriate follow-up interval for normal colonoscopy in average risk patients; (10) endoscopy/polyp surveillance for colonoscopy intervals for patients with a history of adenomatus polyps; and (11) improvement in patients's visual function within 90 days following cataract surgery. The measure addressing improvement in patients' visual function within 90 days following cataract surgery, which was adopted for the CY 2016 payment determination, may be voluntarily rather than mandatorily reported for the CY 2017 payment determination and subsequent years. [*Final rule with comment period*, 80 FR 70298, Nov. 13, 2015.]

For the CY 2018 payment determination and later years, ASCs must collect and report quality of care data on the facility seven-day risk-standardized hospital visit rate after outpatient colonoscopy. [*Final rule with comment period*, 80 FR 70298, Nov. 13, 2015.]

[¶ 827] Hospice Reimbursement

With the exception of payment for physician services, Medicare payment for hospice care is made at one of four predetermined rates for each day that a Medicare beneficiary is under the care of the hospice. Because the rates are prospective, there are no retroactive adjustments other than the application of the statutory "caps" on overall payments made at the end of the fiscal year (FY) and on payments for inpatient care. The rate paid for any particular day varies depending on the level of care furnished to the beneficiary. The four levels of care into which each day of care is classified are:

(1) Routine Home Care—Revenue code 0651;

(2) Continuous Home Care—Revenue code 0652;

(3) Inpatient Respite Care—Revenue code 0655; and

(4) General Inpatient Care (Nonrespite)—Revenue code 0656.

For each day that a Medicare beneficiary is under the care of a hospice, the hospice is reimbursed an amount applicable to the type and intensity of the services furnished to the beneficiary for that day. [42 C.F.R. §418.302(a), (b); *Medicare Claims Processing Manual*, Pub. 100-04, Ch. 11, §30.1.]

The hospice payment on a continuous care day varies depending on the number of hours of continuous services provided. The continuous home care rate is divided by 24 to yield an hourly rate. The number of hours of continuous care provided during a continuous home care day is then multiplied by the hourly rate to yield the continuous home care payment for that day. A minimum of eight hours of care must be furnished on a particular day to qualify for the continuous home care rate. [42 C.F.R. §418.302(e)(4).]

On any day on which the beneficiary is not an inpatient, the hospice is paid the routine home care rate, unless the patient receives continuous care for at least eight hours. Subject to certain limitations, on any day on which the beneficiary is an inpatient in an approved facility for inpatient care, the appropriate inpatient rate (general or respite) is paid depending on the category of care furnished. [42 C.F.R. §418.302(e)(3) and (4), (f).]

Annual update of payment rates. The hospice payment update percentage for FY 2016 is 1.6 percent. This percentage is based on an estimated 2.4 percent inpatient hospital market basket update, reduced by a 0.5 percentage point productivity adjustment mandated by section 3401(g) of the Patient Protection and Affordable Care Act (ACA) (P.L. 111-148), and by 0.3 percentage point FY 2013 through FY 2019. [Soc. Sec. Act §1814(i)(1)(C); *Final rule*, 80 FR 47142, Aug. 6, 2015.]

CMS publishes general hospice payment rates annually to be used for revenue codes 0651, 0652, 0655, and 0656. These rates must then be adjusted by the Medicare administrative contractor based on the beneficiary's locality. [42 C.F.R. §418.306; Pub. 100-04, Ch. 11, §30.2.]

Hospice per diem payment rates for the FY 2016 period from October 1, 2015 through September 30, 2016, for hospices that submit quality data are as follows: continuous home care $944.79, inpatient respite care $167.45, and general inpatient care (non-respite) $720.11. FY 2016 hospice payment rates for routine home care furnished from January 1, 2016, through September 30, 2016, for hospices that submit quality data are $186.84 for days 1 through 60 and $146.83 for days 61 and later. [*Final rule*, 80 FR 47142, Aug. 6, 2015.]

Aggregate cap amount. The total amount of payments made for hospice care provided by (or under arrangements made by) a hospice program for an accounting year may not exceed the "cap amount" for the year multiplied by the number of Medicare beneficiaries in the hospice program in that year. [Soc. Sec. Act §1814(i)(2)(A); 42 C.F.R. §418.309.]

The cap period runs from November 1 of each year through October 31 of the next year. The hospice aggregate cap amount for the cap year ending October 31, 2016, is set at $27,820.75. Any payments in excess of the cap must be refunded by the hospice. [42 C.F.R. §418.309; *Final rule*, 80 FR 47142, Aug. 6, 2015; *Medicare Benefit Policy Manual*, Pub. 100-02, Ch. 9, §90.2.]

Revision of payment methodology. The ACA requires CMS to revise the hospice payment methodology no earlier than October 1, 2013. Starting in 2011, CMS must collect additional data and information to revise payments for hospice care, including data on resource utilization, which can be collected on claims, cost reports, and by other mechanisms. [Soc. Sec. Act §1814(i)(6); *Final rule*, 80 FR 47142, Aug. 6, 2015.]

Quality Reporting

Beginning with FY 2014, CMS will reduce the hospice market basket update by 2.0 percentage points for any hospice that does not comply with quality data submission requirements. CMS did not establish any new quality measures in the FY 2016 final rule.

Hospices are, however, required to complete and submit an admission Hospice Item Set (HIS) and a discharge HIS for each patient admission to hospice, regardless of payer or patient age. [Soc. Sec. Act § 1814(i)(5); 42 C.F.R. § 418.312; *Final rule*, 80 FR 47142, Aug. 6, 2015.]

Physician Reimbursement

The following services performed by hospice physicians and nurse practitioners are included in the hospice rates described above: (1) general supervisory services of the medical director; and (2) participation in the establishment of plans of care, supervision of care and services, periodic review and updating of plans of care, and establishment of governing policies by the physician member of the interdisciplinary group. [42 C.F.R. § 418.304(a).]

For other services, the contractor pays the hospice an amount equivalent to 100 percent of the physician fee schedule for those physician services furnished by hospice employees or under arrangements with the hospice. [42 C.F.R. § 418.304(a).]

Attending physician. Services of the patient's attending physician, if he or she is not an employee of the hospice or providing services under arrangements with the hospice, are not considered hospice services. These services are reimbursed as "physicians' services" under Part B. [Soc. Sec. Act § 1861(dd)(2)(B); 42 C.F.R. § 418.304(c); Pub. 100-04, Ch. 11, § 40.1.3.]

Nurse practitioners. Medicare pays for attending physician services provided by nurse practitioners to Medicare beneficiaries who have elected the hospice benefit and who have selected a nurse practitioner as their attending physician. This applies to nurse practitioners without regard to whether they are hospice employees. Payment for nurse practitioner services are made at 85 percent of the physician fee schedule amount. [42 C.F.R. § 418.304(e).]

Care plan oversight services. Separate payment for physician care plan oversight services is made under the following conditions: (1) the services require recurrent physician supervision of therapy involving 30 or more minutes of the physician's time per month, and (2) payment is made to only one physician per patient for services furnished during a calendar month period. The physician must have furnished a service requiring a face-to-face encounter with the patient at least once during the six-month period before the month for which care plan oversight payment is first billed. [42 C.F.R. § 414.39(b)(1), (b)(2).]

Payment for pre-election evaluation. A physician on staff of a hospice may be paid to evaluate a patient who has not yet elected hospice care to determine the patient's need for pain and symptom management and for hospice care and to help with advance care planning. [Soc. Sec. Act § 1812(a)(5); 42 C.F.R. § 418.304(d).]

[¶ 830] Home Health Agencies

Under the home health prospective payment system (HH PPS), a standardized payment, subject to several adjustments, is made for each 60-day episode of care a beneficiary receives from a home health agency (HHA). [Soc. Sec. Act § 1895; 42 C.F.R. § 484.205(a).] See ¶ 250–¶ 268 for a discussion of Part A coverage of home health services.

Split percentage payment. Generally, payment for a home health episode of care is made in two stages. The HHA may make a request for anticipated payment (RAP) at the beginning of the episode to receive a percentage of the amount expected to be payable for the episode. The balance, including any adjustments, is paid at the end of the episode of care. The anticipated payment is 60 percent for an initial episode of care and 50 percent for each subsequent episode. [42 C.F.R. § 484.205(b).]

If a physician-signed plan of care is not available at the time the HHA requests an initial payment, it can be based on verbal orders from a physician that are copied into the plan of care, including a description of the patient's condition and the services to be provided by the HHA. There must also be an attestation signed and dated by the registered nurse or qualified therapist responsible for furnishing or supervising the ordered service in the plan of care. [42 C.F.R. § 409.43(c).]

The remainder of the adjusted payment will be made when care or the episode is completed. Before submitting that claim, HHAs are required to: (1) have received a physician's certification of the beneficiary's homebound status and need for home care; and (2) have a plan of care signed by a physician. [42 C.F.R. § 409.43(c)(3); *Medicare Claims Processing Manual,* Pub. 100-04, Ch. 10, § 10.1.10.4.]

2016 payment rates. The calendar year (CY) 2016 national standardized 60-day episode payment rate for an HHA that submits quality data is $2,965.12; the rate for an HHA that does not submit quality data is $2,906.92. These rates include rebasing adjustments to the national, standardized 60-day episode payment rate, the national per-visit rates, and the nonroutine medical supply (NMS) conversion factor, as required by Patient Protection and Affordable Care Act (ACA) (P.L. 111-148) section 3131. [Soc. Sec. Act § 1895(b)(3)(A)(iii); *Final rule,* 80 FR 68624, Nov. 5, 2015.]

Adjustments to Standard HH PPS Payment

The base unit of payment under the Medicare HH PPS is a national, standardized 60-day episode payment rate. CMS adjusts the national, standardized 60-day episode payment rate by a case-mix relative weight to explain the relative resource utilization of different patients and a wage index value based on the site of service for the beneficiary. The basic pay rate per 60 days of care is subject to adjustments based on: (1) low utilization, (2) a partial period of care, and (3) outlier visits. [Soc. Sec. Act § 1895(b); 42 C.F.R. §§ 484.205, 484.220.]

Case-mix adjustment. After a home health plan of care is prescribed by a physician, the HHA assesses the patient's condition at the beginning of the episode of care. This assessment must be done for each subsequent episode of care a patient receives. [Soc. Sec. Act § 1895(b)(4); 42 C.F.R. § 484.220.]

Outlier adjustment. The outlier adjustment provides additional payment to an HHA when the cost of providing care to a beneficiary exceeds a threshold amount. The outlier payment is a proportion of the amount of estimated costs beyond a threshold defined by CMS. The total amount of outlier payments to a specific home health agency for a year may not exceed 10 percent of the total payments to the specific agency under the HH PPS for the year. [Soc. Sec. Act § 1895(b)(5); 42 C.F.R. §§ 484.205(e), 484.240.]

Partial episode payment adjustment. A partial period of care adjustment is made if a 60-day episode is interrupted by an intervening event, such as beneficiary-elected transfer or discharge with goals met or no expectation of return to home health and the beneficiary returned to home health during the 60-day episode. The original 60-day episode payment is adjusted to reflect the length of time the beneficiary remained under the care of the original HHA based on the first billable visit date through and including the last billable visit date. [42 C.F.R. §§ 484.205(d), 484.235.]

Low-utilization payment adjustment. A low-utilization payment adjustment (LUPA) applies to beneficiaries who receive four or fewer visits. LUPA episodes that occur as the only episode or as an initial episode in a sequence of adjacent episodes are adjusted by applying an additional amount to the LUPA payment before adjusting for area wage differences. [42 C.F.R. §§ 484.205(c), 484.230.]

Home Health Quality Reporting Program

An HHA must submit data on health care quality to CMS or have its home health market basket update reduced by 2 percentage points for each respective year. The reduction applies to reimbursement for the calendar year for which measures were not reported. [Soc. Sec. Act § 1895(b)(3)(B)(v)(I), (II); 42 C.F.R. §§ 484.225, 484.250(a).]

HHAs that become Medicare certified on or after May 31 of the preceding year are excluded from the Outcome and Assessment Information Set (OASIS) quality reporting requirement and any payment penalty for quality reporting purposes for the following year. Therefore, HHAs that are certified on or after May 31, 2015, are not subject to the 2 percentage point reduction to their market basket update for CY 2016. [*Final rule,* 80 FR 68624, Nov. 5, 2015.]

HHAs submit OASIS assessments and Home Health Care Consumer Assessment of Healthcare Providers and Systems Survey (HHCAHPS) data to meet the quality reporting requirements, and a subset of the home health quality measures is publicly reported on the Home Health Compare website, http://www.medicare.gov/homehealthcompare/. For CY 2016, CMS will continue to use an HHA's submission of the OASIS data as one form of quality data to meet the requirement that the HHA submit data appropriate for the measurement of health care quality. The Home Health Compare website lists six process measures, 10 outcome quality measures, and five HHCAHPS measures, as well as three new measures from the OASIS data set. [*Final rule,* 80 FR 68624, Nov. 5, 2015.]

Pay-for-reporting performance requirement for OASIS quality data. To meet the quality reporting requirements of Soc. Sec. Act § 1895(b)(3)(B)(v) for the reporting period of July 1, 2016 through June 30, 2017, an HHA must score at least 80 percent on the quality assessments only metric of OASIS. An HHA that fails to meet this metric will have its market basket for CY 2017 reduced by 2 percentage points. Further, for the reporting period of July 1, 2017, through June 30, 2018, and later, an HHA must score at 90 percent on the quality assessments only metric. [*Final rule,* 80 FR 68624, Nov. 5, 2015.]

IMPACT Act. Under the Improving Medicare Post-Acute Care Transformation Act of 2014 (IMPACT Act) (P.L. 113-185), the HHS Secretary must require post-acute care (PAC) providers, including HHAs, to report standardized patient assessment data, data on quality measures, and data on resource use and other measures. Data measures include: (1) functional status, cognitive function, and changes in function and cognitive function; (2) skin integrity and changes in skin integrity; (3) medication reconciliation; (4) incidence of major falls; and (4) accurately communicating the individual's health information and care preferences.

HHAs must begin reporting on certain data by January 1, 2017. An HHA that fails to submit the required data will have its market basket update reduced by 2 percent. [Soc. Sec. Act § 1899B.]

Value-based purchasing. Beginning on January 1, 2016, all Medicare-certified HHAs in selected states will be required to participate in a HH value-based purchasing (HHVBP) model, which requires these entities to compete for payment adjustments under the current PPS reimbursement schedule based on quality performance. The HHVBP model allows for the flexibility to incorporate the IMPACT measures in a post-acute care setting. [42 C.F.R. §§ 484.300–484.330.]

Consolidated Billing

All Medicare-covered home health services listed in section 1861(m) of the Social Security Act and ordered by the physician in a plan of care must be billed to Medicare by the

HHA that established a 60-day home health episode of care (see ¶ 250). [Soc. Sec. Act § 1842(b)(6)(F); *Medicare Benefit Policy Manual*, Pub. 100-02, Ch. 7, § 40.]

Home Health Advance Beneficiary Notices and Demand Billing

Whenever an HHA believes that home health services ordered by a physician will not be covered by Medicare, the HHA must give the patient oral and written notice of: (1) the extent to which payment may be expected from Medicare, Medicaid, or any other federally funded or aided program known to the HHA; (2) the charges for services that will not be covered by Medicare; (3) the charges that the individual may have to pay; and (4) any changes with respect to items (1) through (3). [42 C.F.R. § 484.10(e).]

HHAs may seek denials for entire claims from Medicare in cases where the HHA knows that all services will not be covered by Medicare. To inform beneficiaries about possible noncovered charges HHAs must use the ABN of Noncoverage, CMS-R-131, and the Home Health Change of Care Notice (HHCCN). [Pub. 100-04, Ch. 30, § § 50.1, 60.1.]

HHAs must use the HHCCN to provide notice to a beneficiary on the first occasion that a "triggering event" occurs. Triggering events include when the HHA: (1) reduces or stops an item and/or service during a spell of illness while continuing others, including when one home health discipline ends but others continue; or (2) ends delivery of all services. [Pub. 100-04, Ch. 30, § 60.3.]

[¶ 835] Skilled Nursing Facilities

Skilled nursing facilities (SNFs) are paid under a prospective payment system (PPS) on a case-mix adjusted, per diem basis. The payment rates represent payment in full (subject to applicable coinsurance) for all routine, ancillary, and capital-related costs associated with furnishing inpatient SNF services to Medicare beneficiaries, other than costs associated with approved educational activities. [Soc. Sec. Act § 1888(e); 42 C.F.R. § 413.335.]

Services and Items Included in SNF PPS

The SNF PPS covers extended care services furnished to an individual after discharge from a hospital in which he or she was an inpatient for not less than three consecutive days, and transfer to a SNF. A SNF is required to submit consolidated Medicare claims for almost all of the services that a resident receives during the course of a covered Part A stay. SNFs are also responsible for billing for physical and occupational therapy and speech-language pathology services that a resident receives during a noncovered stay. With the below exceptions, all items and services furnished by a SNF are paid under the PPS. [Soc. Sec. Act § § 1842(b)(6)(E), 1861(i), 1862(a)(18), 1888(e)(2)(A).]

Exclusions. The per diem rate does not cover the following costs, for which separate Part B claims must be made:

(1) physician services furnished to individual SNF residents;

(2) certain nurse practitioner, clinical nurse specialist, or physician assistant services;

(3) services of certified nurse-midwives, qualified psychologists, clinical social workers, or certified registered nurse anesthetists;

(4) certain dialysis services (home dialysis supplies and equipment, self-care home dialysis support services, institutional dialysis services and supplies, renal dialysis services), erythropoietin, and ambulance services furnished to an individual in conjunction with renal dialysis services;

(5) telehealth services using the SNF as the originating site;

(6) certain chemotherapy items and administrative services, and radioisotope services;

(7) certain customized prosthetic devices delivered to an inpatient for use during a SNF stay and intended for use after discharge; and

(8) services provided by a rural health clinic (RHC) or a federally qualified health center (FQHC), if the services would have been excluded if furnished by a physician or practitioner who was not affiliated with a RHC or FQHC.

[Soc. Sec. Act § 1888(e)(2)(A)(ii)–(iv).]

FY 2016 Payments

The 2.3 percent SNF market basket update for FY 2016 was adjusted by the forecast error adjustment (0.6 percentage point) and reduced by a 0.5 percent multi-factor productivity (MFP) adjustment required by the Patient Protection and Affordable Care Act (ACA) (P.L. 111-148), resulting in a MFP-adjusted SNF market basket update of 1.2 percent. [*Final rule*, 80 FR 46389, Aug. 4, 2015.]

Payment for residents with AIDS. SNF payment rates include a special adjustment that is intended to cover the additional services required for any SNF resident with HIV/AIDS—a 128 percent increase in the PPS per diem payment. [Soc. Sec. Act § 1888(e)(12)(A); *Final rule*, 80 FR 46389, Aug. 4, 2015.]

Quality Reporting

Starting in FY 2018, SNFs are required to submit quality measures and standardized patient assessment data to CMS. Payment rates will be reduced by 2 percentage points for a SNF in any FY that the SNF that fails to submit this data. [Soc. Sec. Act §§ 1888(e)(6), 1899B.]

Hospital readmission measures. In the FY 2016 SNF PPS final rule, the HHS Secretary specified the SNF 30-Day All-Cause Readmission Measure (SNFRM), which assesses the risk-standardized rate of all-cause, all-condition, unplanned inpatient hospital readmissions of Medicare fee-for-service (FFS) SNF patients within 30 days of discharge from an admission to an inpatient prospective payment system (IPPS) hospital, critical access hospital (CAH), or psychiatric hospital. The SNFRM gives SNFs an incentive to make quality improvements that result in successful transitions of care for patients discharged from the hospital setting to a SNF, and subsequently to the community or to another post-acute care setting; it also reduces unplanned readmission rates of these patients to hospitals and prioritizes safer, better coordinated care and lower costs. [Soc. Sec. Act § 1888(g)(1); *Final rule*, 80 FR 46389, Aug. 4, 2015.]

By October 1, 2016, the HHS Secretary must specify a measure to reflect an all-condition risk-adjusted potentially preventable hospital readmission rate for SNFs. [Soc. Sec. Act § 1888(g)(2).]

Reports. Beginning October 1, 2016, SNFs will receive quarterly confidential reports from the HHS Secretary regarding their performance on the hospital readmission measures. By October 1, 2017, the HHS Secretary must post information on SNFs' performance with respect to these measures on the Nursing Home Compare Medicare website. SNFs will have the opportunity to review and submit corrections to the information before it is made public. [Soc. Sec. Act § 1888(g).]

Value-based purchasing program. The HHS Secretary is required to establish a SNF value-based purchasing (VBP) program effective for payments for services furnished on or after October 1, 2018. The SNF VBP will use the Skilled Nursing Facility 30-Day All-Cause

Readmission Measure (SNFRM) to measure and rank SNF performance. High-measuring SNFs will receive an incentive payment. [Soc. Sec. Act § 1888(h); *Final rule*, 80 FR 46389, Aug. 4, 2015.]

Resource Utilization Groups and Minimum Data Set

Resource Utilization Groups (RUG) is a system used to classify SNF residents into mutually exclusive groups based on clinical, functional, and resource-based criteria. RUGs are the basis for the relative payment weights used both for standardization of the SNF PPS rates and subsequently to establish case-mix adjustments to SNF PPS rates for patients with different service use. Care provided directly to, or for, a patient is represented by an index score based on the amount of staff time associated with each group, weighted by salary levels. Each RUG is assigned an index score that represents the amount of nursing time and rehabilitation (therapy) time associated with caring for patients who qualify for the group. RUG IV was finalized in the SNF PPS update for FY 2011 and became effective October 1, 2010. [*Notice*, 75 FR 42886, July 22, 2010.]

RUG IV includes 66 classification groups based on data collected in 2006 and 2007 during the Staff Time and Resource Intensity Verification (STRIVE) study, which was done to identify the level of staffing resources needed to provide quality care to nursing home patients. To determine the appropriate payment rate, SNFs classify each of their patients into a RUG IV group based on assessment data from the Minimum Data Set (MDS) 3.0. [*Final rule*, 74 FR 40288, Aug. 11, 2009.]

Minimum Data Set. MDS 3.0 is used by nursing homes to conduct functional assessments of SNF residents. To determine appropriate payment rates, SNFs use the functional assessments to classify their residents into RUG IV groups. [*Final rule*, 74 FR 40288, Aug. 11, 2009; *Proposed rule,* 74 FR 22208, May 12, 2009; Medicare and Medicaid Extenders Act of 2010 (MMEA) (P.L. 111-309) § 202.]

Swing-Bed Facilities

Swing-bed hospitals have agreements with HHS that allow their inpatient hospital beds to be used for services that would be considered extended care services if provided by a SNF. Swing-bed facilities, including swing-bed rural hospitals, are reimbursed under the SNF PPS. All updates to rates and wage indices that apply under SNF PPS apply to all swing-bed hospitals. [Soc. Sec. Act § 1888(e)(7).] In addition, all non-critical access hospital (CAH) swing-bed rural hospitals are paid under the SNF PPS, so all rates and wage indexes outlined for the SNF PPS also apply to all non-CAH swing-bed rural hospitals. [Soc. Sec. Act § 1888(e)(7); 42 C.F.R. § 413.114.]

All non-CAH swing-bed rural hospitals are required to complete an MDS 3.0 swing-bed assessment limited to certain demographic, payment, and quality items. [*Final rule*, 74 FR 40288, Aug. 11, 2009.]

[¶ 837] Inpatient Rehabilitation Facilities

An inpatient rehabilitation facility (IRF) is a hospital or hospital unit that has been excluded from the inpatient hospital prospective payment system (IPPS) and serves an inpatient population requiring intensive rehabilitation services for treatment. Patients must require physical and/or occupational therapy, along with other active and ongoing therapeutic intervention of multiple-therapy disciplines such as speech-language pathology or prosthetics/orthotics therapy. [Soc. Sec. Act § 1886(j); 42 C.F.R. §§ 412.23(b), 412.622(a)(3).]

Patient Assessment Instrument

IRFs must use the IRF patient assessment instrument (IRF-PAI) to assess each Medicare Part A fee-for-service and Medicare Advantage IRF patient upon admission and discharge. [Soc. Sec. Act § 1886(j)(2)(D); 42 C.F.R. §§ 412.604(c), 412.606.] The admission assessment is used to place a patient in a case-mix group (CMG). Each CMG is a functional-related group, determined by distinguishing classes of IRF patient discharges on the basis of impairment, age, comorbidities, functional capability of the patient, and other factors that may improve the ability of the functional-related groups to estimate variations in resource use. The CMG determines the base payment rate that the IRF receives for the Medicare-covered Part A services furnished by the IRF during the beneficiary's episode of care. [Soc. Sec. Act § 1886(j)(2); 42 C.F.R. § 412.620.]

IRFs must electronically report patient assessment data for all admission and discharge assessment data, including any interruption in stay data, to CMS. [42 C.F.R. §§ 412.614(b)–(c), 412.618(b).]

Compliance Threshold

One criterion that Medicare uses to classify a hospital or unit of a hospital as an IRF is that a minimum percentage (known as a compliance threshold) of the facility's total inpatient population must require intensive rehabilitative services for the treatment of at least one of 13 medical conditions. The IRF must serve an inpatient population of whom at least 60 percent required intensive rehabilitation services for treatment of one or more of the following conditions:

- stroke;

- spinal cord injury;

- congenital deformity;

- amputation;

- major multiple trauma;

- hip fracture;

- brain injury;

- neurological disorders, including multiple sclerosis, motor neuron diseases, polyneuropathy, muscular dystrophy, and Parkinson's disease;

- burns;

- active, polyarticular rheumatoid arthritis, psoriatic arthritis, and seronegative arthropathies resulting in significant functional impairment of ambulation and other activities of daily living that have not improved after an appropriate, aggressive, and sustained course of outpatient therapy services or services in other less intensive rehabilitation settings immediately preceding the inpatient rehabilitation admission or that result from a systemic disease activation immediately before admission, but have the potential to improve with more intensive rehabilitation;

- systemic vasculidities with joint inflammation, resulting in significant functional impairment of ambulation and other activities of daily living that have not improved after an appropriate, aggressive, and sustained course of outpatient therapy services or services in other less intensive rehabilitation settings immediately preceding the inpatient rehabilitation admission or that result from a systemic disease activation immediately before admission, but have the potential to improve with more intensive rehabilitation;

- severe or advanced osteoarthritis (osteoarthrosis or degenerative joint disease) involving two or more major weight-bearing joints (elbow, shoulders, hips, or knees, but not counting a joint with a prosthesis) with joint deformity and substantial loss of range of motion, atrophy of muscles surrounding the joint, and significant functional impairment of ambulation and other activities of daily living that have not improved after the patient has participated in an appropriate, aggressive, and sustained course of outpatient therapy services or services in other less intensive rehabilitation settings immediately preceding the inpatient rehabilitation admission but have the potential to improve with more intensive rehabilitation; or

- knee or hip joint replacement, or both, during an acute hospitalization immediately preceding the inpatient rehabilitation stay and also meeting one or more of the following specific criteria: (1) the patient underwent bilateral knee or bilateral hip joint replacement surgery during the acute hospital admission immediately preceding the IRF admission; (2) the patient is extremely obese with a Body Mass Index of at least 50 at the time of admission to the IRF; or (3) the patient is age 85 or older at the time of admission to the IRF.

[42 C.F.R. §§ 412.23(b), 412.29(b).]

Payment Rate

Under the IRF PPS, IRFs receive a predetermined amount per discharge for inpatient services furnished to Medicare Part A beneficiaries. PPS rates encompass the inpatient operating costs and capital costs, including routine and ancillary costs, of furnishing covered rehabilitation services. In addition to payments based on prospective payment rates, IRFs receive payments for the bad debts of Medicare beneficiaries and a payment amount per unit for blood clotting factor provided to Medicare inpatients who have hemophilia. Payment rates are calculated using relative weights to account for variations in resource needs in CMGs. [Soc. Sec. Act § 1886(j)(3)(A); 42 C.F.R. § 412.622.]

Payment adjustments. Facility-level adjustments include area wage adjustments, an adjustment for facilities located in rural areas, an adjustment for treating low-income patients, and an adjustment for teaching facilities. CMS makes additional payments for outlier cases that incur extraordinarily high costs, as well as case-level adjustments. [Soc. Sec. Act § 1886(j)(3)(A), (4); 42 C.F.R. § 412.624; *Medicare Claims Processing Manual*, Pub. 100-04, Ch. 3, §§ 140.2.4, 140.2.5.]

2016 update. For fiscal year (FY) 2016, IRF payment rates will increase 1.8 percent, about $135 million. The FY 2016 update reflects a market basket increase of 2.4 percent less a 0.5 percent productivity adjustment and a 0.2 percentage point legislative reduction. Applying the combined budget neutrality factor for the 2016 wage index and the labor-related share results in a standard payment conversion factor of $15,478 for FY 2016, up from $15,198 in FY 2015. The high-cost outlier threshold in FY 2016 is increased to $8,658 from $8,848 in FY 2015, which will maintain outlier payments at 3 percent of all cases. [*Final rule*, 80 FR 47036, Aug. 6, 2015.]

Quality Reporting

Section 3004 of the Patient Protection and Affordable Care Act (P.L. 111-148) (ACA) required CMS to implement a quality data program for providers paid under the IRF PPS. IRFs that fail to successfully participate in the IRF quality reporting program (QRP) receive a 2.0 percent payment reduction in their IRF market basket update, beginning in FY 2014. This could result in payment decreases for non-complying IRFs if the IRF payment update is less than 2.0 percent in any given year. [Soc. Sec. Act § 1886(j)(7); 42 C.F.R. § 412.634; Pub. 100-04, Ch. 3, § 140.2.11.]

¶837

Further, under section 2 of the Improving Medicare Post-Acute Care Transformation Act of 2014 (P.L. 113-185) (IMPACT Act), the HHS Secretary must require IRFs to report standardized patient assessment data, data on quality measures, and data on resource use and other measures. Data measures include: (1) functional status, cognitive function, and changes in function and cognitive function; (2) skin integrity and changes in skin integrity; (3) medication reconciliation; (4) incidence of major falls; and (4) accurately communicating the individual's health information and care preferences. IRFs must begin reporting on most quality measures and data on resource use by October 1, 2016, and patient assessment data no later than October 1, 2018. [Soc. Sec. Act § 1899B.]

Pursuant to the IMPACT Act, in the FY 2016 IRF PPS final rule CMS adopted measures to satisfy three required quality domains: (1) skin integrity and changes in skin integrity; (2) functional status, cognitive function, and changes in function and cognitive function; and (3) incidence of major falls. [*Final rule*, 80 FR 47036, Aug. 6, 2015.]

FY 2018 annual increase factor adjustments. For the FY 2018 adjustments to the IRF PPS annual increase factor, CMS retained the following measures: (1) National Health Safety Network (NHSN) Catheter-Associated Urinary Tract Infection (CAUTI) Outcome Measure; (2) percent of residents or patients who were assessed and appropriately given the seasonal influenza vaccine; (3) percent of residents or patients with pressure ulcers that are new or have worsened; (4) an all-cause unplanned readmission measure for 30 days post-discharge from IRFs measure; (5) influenza vaccination coverage among health care person-nel; (6) facility-wide inpatient hospital-onset MRSA bacteremia outcome measure; and (7) facility-wide inpatient hospital-onset clostridium difficile infection outcome measure. [*Final rule*, 80 FR 47036, Aug. 6, 2015.]

FY 2018 new quality measures. CMS also adopted the following new quality mea-sures for the FY 2018 payment determination and later: (1) percent of residents experiencing one or more falls with major injury (long-stay); (2) percent of long-term care hospital patients with an admission and discharge functional assessment and a care plan that addresses function; (3) change in self-care score for medical rehabilitation patients; (4) change in mobility score for medical rehabilitation patients; (5) discharge self-care score for medical rehabilitation patients; and (6) discharge mobility score for medical rehabilitation patients. [*Final rule*, 80 FR 47036, Aug. 6, 2015.]

One-Day Payment Window

Under the IRF PPS, IRFs are subject to a one-day payment window, or the "24-hour rule," for pre-admission services. In other words, outpatient diagnostic services and most non-physician services provided during the calendar day immediately preceding the date of admission to an IRF are included in the IRF case-mix group payment. Separate payment is not made for outpatient diagnostic services provided during the 24-hour period prior to admission to an IRF. [Pub. 100-04, Ch. 3, § 140.2.]

IRFs and hospitals reimbursed under IRF PPS are not subject to the three-day payment window for pre-admission services. The three-day payment window applies only to acute inpatient hospitals paid under the inpatient prospective payment system (see ¶ 810). [Pub. 100-04, Ch. 3, § 140.2.]

Accreditation Requirements

IRFs must meet accreditation requirements to ensure the quality of suppliers of durable medical equipment, prosthetics, and supplies (DMEPOS). This rule requires that suppliers be accredited by independent accrediting organizations to meet quality standards to bill the Medicare program for items such as walkers, wheelchairs, and hospital beds furnished to Medicare beneficiaries. [42 C.F.R. § 424.57(c).]

[¶ 840] Psychiatric Hospitals and Units

CMS implemented a per diem prospective payment system (PPS) for inpatient psychiatric services that are furnished in a psychiatric hospital, units in an acute care hospitals, or a critical access hospital. The inpatient psychiatric facility (IPF) PPS is designed to ensure appropriate payment for services to patients with severe mental illness, while providing incentives to IPFs for efficient care of Medicare beneficiaries. [Soc. Sec. Act § 1886(s); 42 C.F.R. § 412.400.]

The IPF PPS does not apply to Veterans Administration hospitals, hospitals reimbursed by Medicare under approved state cost-control systems, hospitals in demonstration projects, and nonparticipating hospitals furnishing emergency psychiatric care. Nor does it apply to psychiatric "partial hospitalization" services such as individual and group therapy, which are covered under the outpatient PPS. [Pub. 100-02, Ch. 2, § 10.3.]

For a discussion of Part B coverage of outpatient mental health services, see ¶ 387. For information on lifetime and "spell of illness" restrictions on inpatient psychiatric hospital coverage, see ¶ 225.

Requirements for IPFs

An IPF is certified under Medicare as an inpatient psychiatric hospital, which means an institution that: (1) is primarily engaged in providing, by or under the supervision of a physician, psychiatric services for the diagnosis and treatment of mentally ill patients; (2) maintains clinical records necessary to determine the degree and intensity of the treatment provided to the mentally ill patient; and (3) meets staffing requirements sufficient to carry out active programs of treatment for individuals who are furnished care in the institution. A distinct part psychiatric unit may also be certified if it meets the clinical record and staffing requirements in 42 C.F.R. § 412.27 for a "psychiatric hospital." [42 C.F.R. § § 412.23(a), 412.27; *Medicare Benefit Policy Manual*, Pub. 100-02, Ch. 2, § 10.3.]

For all IPFs, a provisional or admitting diagnosis must be made on every patient at the time of admission, and it must include the diagnosis of comorbid diseases as well as the psychiatric diagnosis. In addition, distinct-part psychiatric units of acute care hospitals are required to admit only those patients whose admission to the unit is required for active treatment of a psychiatric principal diagnosis that is listed in the Fourth Edition, Text Revision of the American Psychiatric Association's Diagnostic and Statistical Manual, or in Chapter Five ("Mental Disorders") of the International Classification of Diseases, Ninth Revision, Clinical Modification and an intensity that can be provided appropriately only in an inpatient hospital setting. [42 C.F.R. § 412.27(a), (c) (1) (ii).]

Services Covered Under the IPF PPS

The IPF must furnish all necessary covered services to an inpatient Medicare beneficiary, either directly or under arrangements. Psychiatric hospital inpatient services payable under the IPF PPS do not include the services of physicians, physician assistants, nurse practitioners, clinical nurse specialists, certified nurse-midwives, qualified psychologists, or certified registered nurse anesthetists. These services are paid by Medicare under applicable provider fee schedule provisions. [42 C.F.R. § 412.404(d).]

Pre-admission services otherwise payable under Medicare Part B and furnished to a beneficiary either on the day of admission or the day preceding admission are paid under the IPF PPS as long as the services are: (1) furnished by the IPF or by an entity wholly owned or wholly operated by the IPF; (2) diagnostic, including clinical diagnostic laboratory tests; or (3) nondiagnostic when furnished on the date of the beneficiary's inpatient admission, nondiagnostic when furnished on the calendar day preceding the date of the beneficiary's inpatient admission and the hospital does not demonstrate that such services are unrelated to the beneficiary's inpatient admission, and are not ambulance services or maintenance renal dialysis services. [42 C.F.R. § 412.405.]

Payment Methodology

Under the IPF PPS, IPFs receive a predetermined federal per diem base rate for inpatient hospital services furnished to Medicare Part A fee-for-service beneficiaries. The federal per diem payment amount is based on the federal per diem base rate plus applicable adjustments. [42 C.F.R. § 412.422.]

Patient- and facility-level adjustments. The federal per diem payment under the IPF PPS is composed of the federal per diem base rate and certain patient- and facility-level payment adjustments that are associated with statistically significant per diem cost differences. Patient-level adjustments include age, diagnosis-related group (DRG) assignment, comorbidities, and variable per diem adjustments to reflect higher per diem costs in the early days of an IPF stay. Facility-level adjustments include adjustments for the IPF's wage index, rural location, teaching status, a cost-of-living adjustment for IPFs located in Alaska and Hawaii, and the presence of a qualifying emergency department. [42 C.F.R. § 412.424(d).]

The IPF PPS provides additional payment policies for outlier cases, interrupted stays, and a per-treatment adjustment for patients who undergo electroconvulsive therapy (ECT). [42 C.F.R. § 412.424(d)(3).]

ACA productivity adjustments. The Patient Protection and Affordable Care Act (ACA) (P.L. 111-148) § 10319(e) amended the annual update to add a productivity adjustment beginning in rate year 2012. The productivity adjustment is the same one applied to inpatient hospital services under Soc. Sec. Act § 1886(b)(3)(B)(xi)(II). [Soc. Sec. Act § 1886(s)(2)(A)(i).]

The ACA also required the application of an "other adjustment" that reduces updates to the IPF PPS base rate from 2010 through 2019. The adjustment for fiscal years (FYs) 2015 and 2016 is 0.2 percent, and the adjustment for FYs 2017, 2018, and 2019 will be 0.75 percent. [Soc. Sec. Act § 1886(s)(2)(A)(ii), (s)(3)(D).]

The application of these adjustments may result in the annual percentage increase being less than 0.0 for a year and may result in payment rates under the IPF PPS being less than such payment rates for the preceding year. [Soc. Sec. Act § 1886(s)(2)(B).]

FY 2016 per diem rates. The standard per diem base rate for FY 2016 is $743.73, up from the per diem base rate of $728.31 for FY 2015. The per-treatment rate for ECT is $320.19 compared to $313.55 for FY 2015. [*Final rule*, 80 FR 46652, Aug. 5, 2015.]

The IPF PPS provides for gradually reduced per diem rates for consecutive days of an IPF stay. The first day of any psychiatric stay provides IPFs with the highest reimbursement due to costly admitting services; the rate is even higher for IPFs with emergency departments. The payments are adjusted downward from day 2 through day 21 of an IPF stay. For day 22 and thereafter, the variable per diem adjustment remains the same each day for the remainder of the stay. [*Final rule*, 80 FR 46652, Aug. 5, 2015.]

Quality Measurement

Beginning in FY 2014, IPFs are required to submit data on specified quality measures that are selected from those endorsed by qualified concensus-based entities or established by a different process. IPFs that do not participate in the program are subject to a 2.0 percent reduction in their annual market basket update. IPFs are required to submit data on specified quality measures to receive a full market basket adjustment. [Soc. Sec. Act § 1886(s)(4); 42 C.F.R. § 412.424(d)(1)(iv).]

Quality measures. CMS added five new measures for the FY 2018 payment determination and later years: (1) Tobacco Use Treatment Provided or Offered at Discharge; (2) Alcohol Use Brief Intervention Provided or Offered; (3) Transition Record with Specified Elements Received by Discharged Patients (Discharges from an Inpatient Facility to Home/Self Care or Any Other Site of Care); (4) Timely Transmission of Transition Record (Discharges from an Inpatient Facility to Home/Self Care or Any Other Site of Care); and (5) Screening for Metabolic Disorders. [*Final rule*, 80 FR 46652, Aug. 5, 2015.]

CMS removed the Patients Discharged on Multiple Antipsychotic Medications measure for the FY 2017 payment determination and later. For the FY 2018 payment determination and later, CMS removed the Post-Discharge Continuing Care Plan and the Post-Discharge Continuing Care Plan Transmitted to the Next Level of Care Provider Upon Discharge measures. [*Final rule*, 80 FR 46652, Aug. 5, 2015.]

Lifetime Limitation

Payment may not be made for more than a total of 190 days of inpatient psychiatric hospital services during the patient's lifetime. [42 C.F.R. § 409.62.] This limitation applies only to services furnished in a free-standing psychiatric hospital. This limitation does not apply to inpatient psychiatric services furnished in a distinct part psychiatric unit of an acute care hospital or critical access hospital. [Pub. 100-02, Ch. 2, § 80.]

[¶ 845] End-Stage Renal Disease

The end-stage renal disease (ESRD) prospective payment system (PPS) provides a case-mix adjusted single payment to ESRD facilities for renal dialysis services provided in an ESRD facility or in a beneficiary's home. [Soc. Sec. Act § 1881(b); 42 C.F.R. § 413.172.]

Under the ESRD PPS, market-based updates are provided annually to all renal dialysis providers. It includes patient-characteristic and facility-level reimbursement adjustments to reflect provider costs, as well as outlier adjustments for particularly costly cases. [42 C.F.R. § 413.170 *et seq.*]

Payment calculation. If the beneficiary has incurred the full Part B deductible before the dialysis treatment, Medicare pays a dialysis facility 80 percent of the prospective rate; if the beneficiary did not incur the full deductible before treatment, CMS subtracts the amount applicable to the deductible from the ESRD facility's prospective rate and pays the facility 80 percent of the remainder, if any. [42 C.F.R. § 413.176.]

Beginning in 2013, the bad debts of ESRD facilities are reimbursed just as they are for all other Medicare providers, suppliers, and other entities, by an allowable bad debt percentage mandated by section 3201 of the Middle Class Tax Extension and Job Creation Act of 2012 (P.L. 112-78). Furthermore, the cap on bad debt reimbursement to ESRD facilities has been removed. [42 C.F.R. § 413.89; *Medicare Benefit Policy Manual*, Pub. 100-02, Ch. 11, § 80.]

Home dialysis. Effective January 1, 2011, all home dialysis claims must be billed by an ESRD facility and paid under the ESRD PPS. [42 C.F.R. § 414.330; Pub. 100-04, Ch. 20, § 30.8.3.]

See ¶ 205 for a discussion of the coverage period for ESRD beneficiaries.

Quality Incentive Program

Under the quality incentive program (QIP), an ESRD facility is required to report to CMS on quality measures. Reimbursement is reduced by up to 2 percent for providers that fail to meet a total score on performance standards for quality measures. Each year, a provider's score is based on reported compliance with quality measures, based on data from two years prior to the reimbursement year (for example, 2016 data affects 2018 reimbursement). [Soc. Sec. Act § 1881(h); 42 C.F.R. § 413.177.]

Measures must include: (1) measures on anemia management that reflect the labeling approved by the Food and Drug Administration for such management and measures on dialysis adequacy; (2) to the extent feasible, such measures of patient satisfaction as the HHS Secretary specifies; (3) for 2016 and subsequent years, measures specific to the conditions treated with oral-only drugs; and (4) such other measures as the Secretary specifies, including, to the extent feasible, measures on iron management, bone mineral metabolism, and vascular access, including for maximizing the placement of arterial venous fistula. [Soc. Sec. Act § 1881(h)(2).]

For ESRD QIP payment year 2017, CMS reinstated the In-Center Hemodialysis Consumer Assessment of Healthcare Providers (ICH CAHPS) Attestation. Further, for payment year 2019 and future payment years, CMS removed four clinical measures: (1) hemodialysis adequacy: minimum delivered hemodialysis dose; (2) peritoneal dialysis adequacy: delivered dose above minimum; (3) pediatric hemodialysis adequacy: minimum spKt/V; and (4) pediatric peritoneal dialysis adequacy. CMS replaced these measures with a single comprehensive dialysis adequacy clinical measure. [*Final rule*, 80 FR 68968, Nov. 6, 2015.]

Reimbursement for Drugs

Most drugs used by dialysis patients, except ESRD-related oral-only drugs, are reimbursed under the ESRD PPS, so they must be billed by the renal dialysis facility. Beginning January 1, 2025, payment for ESRD-related oral-only drugs will be incorporated within the PPS rates and separate payment will no longer be provided. [Soc. Sec. Act. § 1881(b)(14); 42 C.F.R. § 413.174(f); Pub. 100-02, Ch. 11, § 20.3.]

Epoetin alfa (EPO) and darbepoetin alfa (Aranesp) are biologicals that are covered under the Part B benefit for the treatment of anemia associated with ESRD patients who are on dialysis. In addition to coverage incident to a physician service, EPO/Aranesp is covered for the treatment of anemia for ESRD patients who are on maintenance dialysis. Coverage is available regardless of whether the drug is administered by the patient or a caregiver. A dialysis patient who uses EPO in the home must have a current care plan for monitoring home use of EPO, an acceptable hematocrit or hemoglobin level, and be under the care of a responsible physician or renal dialysis facility. [Soc. Sec. Act § 1861(s)(2)(O); Pub. 100-02, Ch. 15, § 50.5.2.]

For patients with chronic renal failure who are not yet on a regular course of dialysis, EPO or Aranesp administered in a hospital outpatient department is paid under the outpatient prospective payment system (OPPS). When ESRD patients come to the hospital for an unscheduled or emergency dialysis treatment, they may also require the administration of EPO or Aranesp. EPO and Aranesp are paid based on the ASP Pricing File. [Pub. 100-04, Ch. 8, §§ 60.4.4.2, 60.4.6.5.]

Physician Reimbursement

Physicians and practitioners managing patients on dialysis are paid a "monthly capitation payment" (MCP) for most outpatient dialysis-related physician services furnished to a Medicare ESRD beneficiary regardless of the volume of the services provided. Under the MCP method, the Medicare administrative contractor (MAC) pays an MCP amount for each patient to cover all professional services furnished by the physician, except those listed below as exclusions from MCP. The payment amount varies based on the number of visits provided within each month and the age of the ESRD beneficiary. [42 C.F.R. § 414.314.]

Exclusions from MCP. The MCP does not apply to the following physician services, which are paid according to the physician fee schedule:

(1) administration of hepatitis B vaccine;

(2) covered physician services furnished by another physician when the patient is not available to receive the outpatient services as usual, for example, when the patient is traveling out of town;

(3) covered physician services furnished to hospital inpatients, including services related to inpatient dialysis, by a physician who elects not to continue to receive the MCP during the period of inpatient stay;

(4) surgical services;

(5) interpretation of tests that have a professional component;

(6) complete evaluation for renal transplantation;

(7) evaluation of potential living transplant donors;

(8) the training of patients to perform home hemodialysis, self-hemodialysis, and the various forms of self-peritoneal dialysis;

(9) non-renal related physician's services; and

(10) all physician services that antedate the initiation of outpatient dialysis.

[42 C.F.R. § 414.314(b)(1); *Medicare Claims Processing Manual*, Pub. 100-04, Ch. 8, § 140.]

"Initial method" of payment. Physicians may elect a different method of reimbursement under a modified version of the former "initial method." Under this method, physicians may be paid for their services to patients in the form of an "add-on" payment. To be eligible for payment under this method, all physicians in a facility must elect this method of payment for all the ESRD facility patients they serve. [42 C.F.R. § § 414.310(e), 414.313.]

Inpatient dialysis services. When a patient requires inpatient dialysis services, the physician can elect to be paid under either the MCP or the Medicare physician fee schedule. If the MCP method is chosen, no additional Medicare payment will be made for the inpatient dialysis services. If the schedule is chosen, the normal MCP payment is reduced accordingly. [42 C.F.R. § § 414.310(b)(1)(ii), 414.314(b)(1)(iii).]

Self-dialysis training services. Physicians are paid for training services furnished to dialysis patients undergoing self-dialysis training. The payment amount is a flat amount that covers all physician services required to create the capacity for self-dialysis and home dialysis. [42 C.F.R. § 414.316; Pub. 100-04, Ch. 8, § 140.2.]

Transplants. Surgeons performing renal transplants on Medicare patients receive a set comprehensive payment from Medicare. The comprehensive payment, which is subject to the Part B deductible and coinsurance, covers all surgical services in connection with a renal transplant and, if the surgeon assumes primary responsibility for post-surgery care, also includes a period of 60 days for post-operative surgical care and a related course of immunosuppressant therapy. Medically necessary services rendered after the 60-day period are paid under reasonable charge criteria. [42 C.F.R. § 414.320.]

[¶ 847] Rural Health Facilities

The Medicare program reimburses rural health facilities for providing health care services to Medicare beneficiaries. Health care entities in low-population rural areas include: (1) critical access hospitals (CAHs), which are rural hospitals with fewer than 25 acute care beds located at least 35 miles from other hospitals; (2) sole community hospitals (SCHs), which are rural hospitals with fewer than 50 acute care beds located at least 50 miles from the nearest hospital; and (3) rural health clinics (RHCs), which are clinics that serve medically underserved communities. Medicare also makes payment adjustments to qualifying low-volume rural hospitals and certain small rural hospitals for which Medicare patients make up a significant percentage of inpatient days or discharges.

Critical Access Hospitals

To qualify as a CAH, a hospital must be located in a county in a rural area or treated as being located in a rural area and (1) located more than a 35-mile drive (or, in the case of mountainous terrain or in areas with only secondary roads available, a 15-mile drive) from a hospital or CAH, or (2) certified before January 1, 2006, by the state as being a necessary provider of health care services to residents in the area. [Soc. Sec. Act § 1820(c)(2).]

CAHs, which are limited to 25 beds, must provide 24-hour emergency services. Generally, they may not provide acute inpatient care for a period longer than, as determined on an annual average basis, 96 hours per patient. In addition to 25 acute beds, CAHs are allowed to have distinct-part 10-bed psychiatric units and 10-bed rehabilitation units; however, these distinct departments of the CAH are paid through Medicare's various prospective payment systems and are not eligible for cost-based reimbursement. [Soc. Sec. Act § 1820(c)(2); *Medicare Claims Processing Manual*, Pub. 100-04, Ch. 3, § 30.1.]

Unlike traditional hospitals, which are paid under the inpatient prospective payment system (IPPS), Medicare pays CAHs based on each hospital's reported costs. Each CAH receives 101 percent of its costs for outpatient, inpatient, laboratory services, and certain ambulance services. [42 C.F.R. § 413.70.]

Sole Community Hospitals

Special reimbursement rules apply to SCHs, hospitals located in rural areas that are the sole source of care available to residents of the area.

Criteria. To qualify for sole community status under the IPPS, a hospital must be the sole source of inpatient hospital services reasonably available to Medicare Part A beneficiaries in the geographic area. CMS classifies a hospital as a SCH if it meets one of the following conditions:

(1) the hospital is located more than 35 miles from other like hospitals;

(2) the hospital is rural and located between 25 and 35 miles from other like hospitals and meets one of the following criteria:

(a) no more than 25 percent of residents who become hospital inpatients or no more than 25 percent of the Medicare beneficiaries who become hospital inpatients in the hospital's service area are admitted to other like hospitals located within a 35-mile radius of the hospital, or, if larger, within its service area;

(b) the hospital has fewer than 50 beds and the Medicare administrative contractor (MAC) certifies that the hospital would have met the criteria in paragraph (2)(a) above were it not for the fact that some beneficiaries or residents were forced to seek care outside the service area due to the unavailability of necessary specialty services at the community hospital; or

(c) because of local topography or periods of prolonged severe weather conditions, the other like hospitals are inaccessible for at least 30 days in each of two out of three years.

(3) the hospital is rural and located between 15 and 25 miles from other like hospitals but because of local topography or periods of prolonged severe weather

conditions, the other like hospitals are inaccessible for at least 30 days in each of two out of three years; or

(4) the hospital is rural and because of distance, posted speed limits, and predictable weather conditions, the travel time between the hospital and the nearest like hospital is at least 45 minutes.

[42 C.F.R. § 412.92(a).]

SCHs are paid based on the rate that results in the greatest aggregate payment to them, using either the federal rate or their hospital-specific rate based on their 1982, 1987, 1996, or 2006 costs per discharge. [Soc. Sec. Act § 1886(d)(5)(D)(i); 42 C.F.R. § 412.92(d)(1).]

Rural Health Clinics

RHCs are facilities located in areas that are not urbanized areas (as defined by the Bureau of the Census) and in which there are insufficient numbers of needed health care practitioners (as determined by HHS). Within the previous three-year period, RHCs must have been designated and certified as being in an area with a shortage of personal health services. [Soc. Sec. Act. § 1861(aa)(2); 42 C.F.R. § 405.2401.] See ¶ 382 for a discussion of coverage of RHC services.

A provider-based RHC that is authorized to bill under the reasonable cost system is paid in accordance with 42 C.F.R. Parts 405 and 413 if it is an integral and subordinate part of a hospital, skilled nursing facility, or home health agency participating in Medicare and operated with other departments of the provider under common licensure, governance, and professional supervision. Independent RHCs that are authorized to bill under the reasonable cost system are paid on the basis of an all-inclusive rate for each beneficiary visit for covered services, as determined by the MAC. [42 C.F.R. § 405.2462(a), (b); Pub. 100-04, Ch. 9, § 20.1.]

Low-Volume Hospitals

Medicare provides an additional payment to qualifying rural hospitals for the higher incremental costs associated with a low volume of discharges. To qualify for the adjustment for fiscal years (FYs) 2011 through 2017, a hospital must have fewer than 1,600 Medicare discharges during the fiscal year, based on the hospital's Medicare discharges from the most recently available MedPAR data, and must be located more than 15 road miles from the nearest subsection (d) hospital. For low-volume hospitals with 200 or fewer Medicare discharges, the adjustment is an additional 25 percent for each Medicare discharge. For low-volume hospitals with Medicare discharges of more than 200 and fewer than 1,600, the adjustment for each Medicare discharge is an additional percent calculated using the formula (4/14)—(number of Medicare discharges/5600). [Soc. Sec. Act § 1886(d)(12), as amended by Medicare Access and CHIP Reauthorization Act of 2015 (MACRA) (P.L. 114-10) § 204; 42 C.F.R. § 412.101.]

To receive the adjustment for FY 2018 and later years, a hospital must have fewer than 200 total discharges, which includes Medicare and non-Medicare discharges, during the fiscal year, based on the hospital's most recently submitted cost report, and must be located more than 25 road miles from the nearest subsection (d) hospital. The adjustment is an additional 25 percent for each Medicare discharge. [Soc. Sec. Act § 1886(d)(12), as amended by MACRA § 204; 42 C.F.R. § 412.101.]

Medicare-Dependent Hospital Program

The Medicare-Dependent Hospital program, which provides increased Medicare reimbursement to certain small rural hospitals for which Medicare patients make up a significant percentage of inpatient days or discharges, has been in existence since 1987. It has been extended a number of times, most recently through October 1, 2017. [Soc. Sec. Act § 1886(d)(5)(G)(i), as amended by MACRA § 205(a); 42 C.F.R. § 412.108.]

A hospital is classified as a Medicare-dependent, small rural hospital if it is located in a rural area and meets the following conditions:

(1) the hospital has 100 or fewer beds during the cost reporting period;

(2) the hospital is not also classified as a SCH; and

(3) at least 60 percent of the hospital's inpatient days or discharges were attributable to individuals entitled to Medicare Part A benefits during at least two of the last three most recent audited cost reporting periods for which the Secretary has a settled cost report. If the cost reporting period is for less than 12 months, the hospital's most recent 12-month or longer cost reporting period before the short period is used.

[42 C.F.R. § 412.108(a)(1).]

[¶ 850] Federally Qualified Health Centers

Section 10501(i)(3)(A) of the Affordable Care Act (ACA) (P.L. 111-148) established a new system of payment for the costs of federally qualified health center (FQHC) services under Medicare Part B based on prospectively set rates. The FQHC prospective payment system (PPS) is based on an average of reasonable costs of FQHCs and pays FQHCs the lesser of their actual charges for services or a single encounter-based rate for professional services furnished per beneficiary per day. [Soc. Sec. Act § 1834(o).] Part B coverage of FQHC services is described at ¶ 382.

Except for preventive services, for which Medicare pays 100 percent, beneficiaries pay a coinsurance amount of 20 percent of the lesser of the FQHC's actual charge or the PPS encounter rate. No deductible is applicable to FQHC services. [Soc. Sec. Act § 1833(a)(1)(Z), (b)(4); 42 C.F.R. § 405.2462(d).]

The PPS transitioned to a calendar year update for all FQHCs, beginning January 1, 2016, to be consistent with many of the physician fee schedule rates that are updated on a calendar year basis. [*Final rule*, 79 FR 25436, May 2, 2014.]

Payment Rates

FQHCs began transitioning to the PPS on October 1, 2014. Beginning January 1, 2016, the payment rates are equal to the prior year's rates increased by the percentage increase in the Medicare Economic Index (MEI) for that year. Beginning January 1, 2017, the previous year's rate will be increased by the percentage increase in a market basket of FQHC goods and services as created by regulations, or if such an index is not created, by the percentage increase in the MEI for the year. [Soc. Sec. Act § 1834(o)(2)(B); 42 C.F.R. § 405.2467.]

FQHCs billing under the PPS receive a single, per diem rate based on the prospectively set rate for each beneficiary visit for covered services. CMS calculates a per diem rate by dividing total FQHC costs by total FQHC daily encounters to establish an average per diem cost. The per diem rate is adjusted for the following:

(1) geographic differences in cost based on the geographic practice cost indices (GPCIs) in accordance with the physician fee schedule (see ¶ 855) during the same period, limited to only the work and practice expense GPCIs;

(2) furnishing care to a beneficiary that is a new patient; and

(3) furnishing care to a beneficiary receiving a comprehensive initial Medicare visit (an initial preventive physical examination or an initial annual wellness visit) or a subsequent annual wellness visit.

[Soc. Sec. Act §1834(o); 42 C.F.R. §§405.2462(c), 405.2464(b).]

Supplemental payments. FQHCs under contract with Medicare Advantage (MA) organizations are eligible for supplemental payments for covered services furnished to enrollees in MA plans to cover any difference between their payments from the MA plan and what they would receive under: (1) the PPS rate if the FQHC is authorized to bill under the PPS; or (2) the Medicare outpatient per visit rate as set annually by the Indian Health Service for grandfathered tribal FQHCs. [Soc. Sec. Act §1833(a)(3)(B); 42 C.F.R. §405.2469; *Medicare Claims Processing Manual*, Pub. 100-04, Ch. 9, §110.2.]

Beneficiary Appeals

A beneficiary may request a hearing by a Medicare administrative contractor (MAC) if he or she:

- is dissatisfied with a MAC's determination denying a request for payment made on his or her behalf by a FQHC;

- is dissatisfied with the amount of payment; or

- believes the request for payment is not being acted upon with reasonable promptness.

[42 C.F.R. 405.2472.]

[¶ 853] Accountable Care Organizations

Accountable care organizations (ACOs) are groups of service and supplier providers that work together to manage and coordinate care for Medicare fee-for-service (FFS) beneficiaries. The program, as required by Patient Protection and Affordable Care Act (ACA) (P.L. 111-148) §3022, is an alternative payment system that rewards provider groups for promoting accountability for patients, coordinating items and services under Medicare Part A and Part B, and encouraging investment in infrastructure and redesigned care processes to ensure high quality and efficient delivery. ACOs are generally networks of provider groups, often affiliated with a hospital, that work together and are jointly responsible for the cost and quality of care provided to Medicare beneficiaries. ACOs must meet certain criteria and specified quality performance standards to receive a portion of the shared savings they create. [Soc. Sec. Act §1899(a)–(b); 42 C.F.R. §§425.10, 425.100.]

Eligibility to participate. The following types of providers of services and suppliers are eligible to participate in the program: (1) ACO professionals in group practice arrangements; (2) networks of individual practices of ACO professionals; (3) partnerships or joint venture arrangements between hospitals and ACO professionals; (4) hospitals employing ACO professionals; (5) critical access hospitals (CAHs) that bill under Method II; (6) rural health clinics (RHCs); and (7) federally qualified health centers (FQHCs). [Soc. Sec. Act §1899(b)(1); 42 C.F.R. §425.102.]

Participation requirements. There are a number of requirements that ACOs must satisfy to participate. ACOs must:

(1) agree to be accountable for the quality, cost, and overall care of Medicare fee-for-service beneficiaries;

(2) agree to participate for at least a three-year period;

(3) have a formal legal structure allowing them to receive and distribute payments;

(4) include enough primary-care ACO professionals to accommodate no fewer than 5,000 beneficiaries;

(5) provide the HHS Secretary with information regarding ACO professionals as deemed appropriate;

(6) have leadership and management in place to support clinical and administrative systems;

(7) define processes to promote evidence-based medicine and patient engagement, report on quality and cost measures, and coordinate care through the use of methods such as telehealth, remote patient monitoring, and other enabling technologies; and

(8) demonstrate to the Secretary that they meet patient-centeredness criteria, such as patient and caregiver assessments and individualized care plans.

[Soc. Sec. Act § 1899(b)(2); 42 C.F.R. §§ 425.104–425.112.]

Providers that participate in models under Soc. Sec. Act § 1115A or any other program or demonstration project that involves shared savings or the independence at home medical practice pilot program under Soc. Sec. Act § 1866E are ineligible to participate as ACOs. [Soc. Sec. Act § 1899(b)(4); 42 C.F.R. § 425.114.] The Secretary assigns beneficiaries to an ACO based on the utilization of primary care services. [Soc. Sec. Act § 1899(c); 42 C.F.R. §§ 425.400–425.404.]

For performance year 2017 and later, the ACO must have an ACO participant agreement with each ACO participant. In addition, an ACO's agreement with an ACO provider/supplier regarding such items and services must satisfy certain requirements. [42 C.F.R. § 425.116.]

Before the start of an agreement period, before each performance year thereafter, and at such other times as specified by CMS, the ACO must submit to CMS an ACO participant list and an ACO provider/supplier list. [42 C.F.R. § 425.118.]

An ACO may be sanctioned if it attempts to keep costs down by avoiding high-risk patients. Furthermore, the Secretary may terminate an agreement with an ACO if the organization does not meet the Secretary's quality-performance standards. [Soc. Sec. Act § 1899(d)(3), (4).]

ACOs, on behalf of their ACO providers/suppliers who are eligible professionals, must submit quality measures using a CMS web interface to qualify on behalf of their EPs for the Physician Quality Reporting System incentive (see ¶ 855) under the Shared Savings Program. [Soc. Sec. Act § 1899(b)(3); 42 C.F.R. §§ 425.500, 425.504.]

Shared Savings and Losses

ACO participants will continue to receive payment under the traditional Medicare FFS program under Parts A and B. Only if an ACO meets certain quality and savings requirements and has per capita costs for beneficiaries that are below specified benchmarks and above a minimum savings rate will the ACO qualify for shared savings, which will be based on the quality score it receives. [Soc. Sec. Act § 1899(d)(1); 42 C.F.R. §§ 425.500–425.506.]

ACOs are able to choose whether to be involved in a one-sided or a two-sided risk model. The one-sided model, referred to as Track 1, allows for the sharing of savings, only, while the two-sided models, Tracks 2 and 3, provide for the sharing of both savings and losses for the duration of an ACO contract with Medicare. [42 C.F.R. §§ 425.600, 425.604, 425.606.]

One-sided model. An ACO may operate under the one-sided model for agreement periods after the initial agreement period; however, it may not operate under the one-sided model for a second agreement period unless the immediately preceding agreement period was under the one-sided model and the ACO meets criteria for ACOs seeking to renew their agreements. [42 C.F.R. § 425.600(b).]

To qualify for shared savings under the one-sided model, an ACO must meet or exceed its minimum savings rate, which is determined on a sliding scale based on the number of beneficiaries assigned to the ACO. An ACO that meets all the requirements for receiving shared savings payments under the one-sided model will receive a shared savings payment of up to 50 percent of all savings under the updated benchmark, as determined on the basis of its quality performance. The amount of shared savings an eligible ACO receives under the one-sided model may not exceed 10 percent of its updated benchmark. [42 C.F.R. § 425.604.]

Two-sided models. Under the two-sided models, for each performance year, CMS determines whether the estimated average per capita Medicare expenditures under the ACO for Medicare fee-for-service beneficiaries for Part A and Part B services are above or below the updated benchmark. To qualify for a shared savings payment under Tracks 2 or 3, or to be responsible for sharing losses with CMS, an ACO's average per capita Medicare expenditures under the ACO for Medicare fee-for-service beneficiaries for Part A and Part B services for the performance year must be below or above the updated benchmark, respectively, by at least the minimum savings or loss rate. [42 C.F.R. § § 425.606(a), 425.610(a).]

Under Track 2, for agreement periods beginning in 2012 through 2015, the ACO's minimum sharing rate (MSR) and minimum loss rate (MLR) were set at 2 percent. For agreement periods beginning in 2016 and later, the ACO must choose from the three options for establishing the MSR/MLR for the duration of the agreement period. An ACO that meets all the requirements for receiving shared savings payments under Track 2 will receive a shared savings payment of up to 60 percent of all the savings under the updated benchmark, and the payment cap is 15 percent of an ACO's benchmark. For an ACO that is required to share losses with the Medicare program for expenditures over the updated benchmark, the amount of shared losses, which may not exceed 60 percent, is determined based on the inverse of its final sharing rate. There is a cap on the amount of shared losses an ACO is liable for: 5 percent of the benchmark for the first performance year of participation in Track 2, 7.5 percent in the second year, and 10 percent in the third and later performance years. [42 C.F.R. § 425.606.]

An ACO that meets all the requirements for receiving shared savings payments under Track 3 will receive a shared savings payment of up to 75 percent of all the savings under the updated benchmark. The sharing loss rate must be between 40 and 70 percent, and the amount of shared losses for which an eligible ACO is liable may not exceed 15 percent of its updated benchmark. [42 C.F.R. § 425.610.]

For performance year 2017 and later, CMS will waive the requirement of a three-day inpatient hospital stay prior to a Medicare-covered post-hospital extended care service (see Soc. Sec. Act § 1861(i)) for eligible beneficiaries prospectively assigned to ACOs participating in Track 3 that receive otherwise covered post-hospital extended care services furnished by an eligible skilled nursing facility that has entered into a written agreement to partner with the ACO for purposes of this waiver. [42 C.F.R. § 425.612.]

[¶ 855] Physician Fee Schedule

Physicians are paid by Medicare on the basis of a national physician fee schedule. The physician fee schedule applies to all "physicians' services" (see ¶ 350 for the meaning of "physician") and certain services performed by other health care professionals. Specifically, the fee schedule applies to the following:

(1) professional services of doctors of medicine and osteopathy (including osteopathic practitioners), doctors of optometry, doctors of podiatry, doctors of dental surgery and dental medicine, and chiropractors (see ¶ 350);

(2) services and supplies furnished as an incident to a physician's professional service (see ¶ 351), excluding drugs, which are separably payable (see ¶ 362);

(3) outpatient physical and occupational therapy services and outpatient speech-language pathology services furnished by a therapist (not a provider such as a hospital, other facility or agency) (see ¶ 381);

(4) diagnostic x-ray tests and other diagnostic tests (see ¶ 353), except diagnostic laboratory tests paid under a separate fee schedule (see ¶ 875);

(5) x-ray, radium, and radioactive isotope therapy, including materials and services of technicians (see ¶ 354);

(6) antigens (see ¶ 362); and

(7) preventive services (see ¶ 369).

[Soc. Sec. Act § 1848(j)(3); 42 C.F.R. § 414.2.]

How the Fee Schedule Works

Under the fee schedule method, Medicare generally pays 80 percent of the lower of: (1) the fee schedule amount or (2) the actual charge billed by the physician or other health care practitioner (the other 20 percent is paid by the patient as coinsurance—see ¶ 335). The fee schedule payment amount for a service is determined by a formula that takes into consideration the relative value unit (RVU) for the service, the conversion factor (CF) for the year, and the geographic adjustment factor (GAF) for the service. The net effect of the physician fee schedule is that, in any particular geographical area, only one fee may be paid for each allowable service. [Soc. Sec. Act § § 1833(a), 1848(a)(1), (b)(1); 42 C.F.R. § § 414.20, 414.21.]

Relative value unit. The Social Security Act requires CMS to establish payments under the physician fee schedule based on national uniform RVUs that account for the relative resources used in furnishing a service. CMS establishes RVUs for three categories of resources:

(1) work required, which reflects the relative time and intensity associated with furnishing a service;

(2) practice expense (PE), which reflects the costs of maintaining a practice (such as renting office space, buying supplies and equipment, and staff costs); and

(3) malpractice insurance expense.

[Soc. Sec. Act § 1848(c)(1)(S); 42 C.F.R. § 414.22.]

Geographic adjustment factor. The GAF compares the relative value of physicians' work effort in each of the different fee schedule areas to the national average of that work effort. CMS uses a geographic practice cost index (GPCI) to establish the GAF for every Medicare payment locality for each of the three components (work, PE, and malpractice). The GPCIs are applied in the calculation of a fee schedule payment amount by multiplying the RVU for each component times the GPCI for that component. [Soc. Sec. Act § 1848(e); 42 C.F.R. § 414.26.]

Soc. Sec. Act § 1848(e)(1)(E) provides for a 1.0 floor for the work GPCIs. Section 102 of the Protecting Medicare Access Act of 2014 (PAMA) (P.L. 113-93) extended the 1.0 work floor for work GPCIs through April 1, 2015, and the Medicare Access and CHIP Reauthorization Act of 2015 (MACRA) (P.L. 114-10) extended it through December 31, 2017. [Soc. Sec. Act § 1848(e)(1)(E).]

Conversion factor. The sum of the geographically adjusted RVUs is multiplied by a dollar CF. Soc. Sec. Act § 1848(d) specifies the formula by which the CF is updated on an annual basis.

Through 2014, the conversion factor update for a year was based on: (1) the estimated percentage increase in the Medicare Economic Index (MEI) for the year, and (2) changes in expenditures for physicians' services, measured by using the Sustainable Growth Rate (SGR). MACRA § 101 repealed the SGR effective April 16, 2015, and changed how the CF is updated. MACRA established that for 2016 through 2019, the CF will be 0.5 percent, and for 2020 through 2025, it will be 0.0 percent. [Soc. Sec. Act § 1848(d); 42 C.F.R. § 414.30.]

Facility-Based Physicians

There are two parts to Medicare payment for the services of physicians who are hospital-based (e.g., radiologists, anesthesiologists, pathologists, teaching physicians, and interns and residents) or otherwise facility-based. The portion of the physician's activities representing services that are not directly related to an identifiable part of the medical care of the individual patient is the "provider component." Payment for provider component services can be made only to a provider and is included in the provider's prospective payment system rate. The "professional component" services, which relate to the portion of the physician's activities that is directly related to the medical care of the individual patient, are generally paid under the physician fee schedule. [*Medicare Claims Processing Manual*, Pub. 100-04, Ch. 6, § 80; Ch. 12, § 60; Ch. 13, § 20.1.]

Another distinction is made between the technical and professional components. The technical component is for nonphysician work, including the taking of a test. The professional component includes the physician's professional services, such as the interpretation of a test. [42 C.F.R. § 414.40(b)(2).]

Medicare pays for physician services furnished to beneficiaries in providers on a fee schedule basis if the following requirements are met: (1) the services are personally furnished for an individual beneficiary by a physician; (2) the services contribute directly to the diagnosis or treatment of an individual beneficiary; (3) the services ordinarily require performance by a physician; and (4) in the case of radiology or laboratory services, the additional requirements in 42 C.F.R. § § 415.120 or 415.130 are met. [42 C.F.R. § 415.102(a); Pub. 100-04, Ch. 12, § 80.]

Anesthesiologists. For anesthesia services performed, medically directed, or medically supervised by a physician, Medicare pays the lesser of the actual charge or the anesthesia fee schedule amount. Payment for anesthesiologists factors in time units as well as relative values. [42 C.F.R. § 414.46; Pub. 100-04, Ch. 12, § 50.]

Radiologists. A radiologist's services are paid under the physician fee schedule if the services are "patient services" and they are identifiable, direct, and discrete diagnostic or therapeutic services furnished to an individual patient, such as interpretation of x-ray plates, angiograms, myelograms, pyelograms, or ultrasound procedures. For interpretations to be paid, a radiologist must prepare a written report for inclusion in the patient's medical record maintained by the hospital. [42 C.F.R. § 415.120(a); Pub. 100-04, Ch. 13, § 20.1.]

Pathologists. A pathologist's services are paid under the physician fee schedule if the services meet the conditions for payment in 42 C.F.R. § 415.102 and are one of the following services: (1) surgical pathology services; (2) specific cytopathology, hematology, and blood banking services that have been identified as requiring performance by a physician and are listed in program operating instructions; (3) clinical consultation services; or (4) clinical laboratory interpretive services meeting some of the same requirements for clinical consultative services. [42 C.F.R. § 415.130(b).]

Physicians in teaching hospitals. A physician in a teaching hospital personally furnishing Part B physician services is paid under the physician fee schedule on the same basis as physicians providing those services in other settings. Payment is made only if a physician in a teaching hospital supervising residents is present during the "key portion" of the service or procedure. [42 C.F.R. § 415.172.]

The services of a resident in an approved teaching program provided as part of that program are covered as inpatient hospital services and not as physician services, even if the resident is licensed as a physician under state law. Consequently, payment for their services is made to the hospital under Part A; however, separate payment may be made for residents for low and mid-level evaluation and management services if the conditions for the non-presence of a teaching physician are met. [42 C.F.R. § 415.200.]

Assistants at surgery. The law permits payment under Part B for a physician assistant at surgery in a teaching hospital only under certain conditions. When payment is authorized for the services of assistants at surgery, Medicare will pay no more than 16 percent of the fee schedule amount otherwise payable to the primary physician for the global surgical service involved. In a teaching hospital setting, Medicare does not pay for assistant-at-surgery services when a resident physician at the hospital could have assisted but did not. [Soc. Sec. Act § § 1842(b)(7)(D)(i), 1848(i)(2); 42 C.F.R. § 415.190(c); Pub. 100-04, Ch. 12, § 20.4.3.]

Payment for "Incident to" Services and Drugs

Services provided by the physician's staff that are incident to the physician's services are paid under the physician fee schedule as if the physician had personally furnished the services. [42 C.F.R. § 414.34(b).]

Office medical supplies are considered to be part of a physician's practice expense, and payment for them is included in the practice expense portion of the payment to the physician for the medical or surgical service to which they are incidental. [42 C.F.R. § 414.34(a)(1).]

Services of certain health care practitioners (e.g., nurse practitioners, physician assistants, etc.) can be billed and paid separately (see ¶ 366). When this occurs, no payment is made to the physician.

Drugs supplied by physician offices are separably payable (see ¶ 885). [42 C.F.R. § § 405.517, 414.36.]

Global Payments for Surgery

The global surgical package includes all necessary services normally furnished by a surgeon before, during, and after a procedure. The Medicare-approved amount includes payment for the following services related to the surgery when furnished by the physician who performs the surgery: (1) pre-operative visits, (2) intra-operative services, (3) complications following surgery, (4) post-operative visits, (5) post-surgical pain management (by the surgeon), (6) supplies (except for splints and casting supplies), and (7) miscellaneous services (changes and removal of tubes, intravenous lines, catheters, and dressings and removal of operative pack, cutaneous sutures and staples, lines, wires, tubes, drains, casts, and splints). [Soc. Sec. Act § 1848(c)(1)(A)(ii); Pub. 100-04, Ch. 12, § 40.1.]

Duration of a global period. The global period for major surgeries includes the day immediately before the day of surgery, the day of surgery, and 90 days following the day of surgery. The period for minor surgeries includes the day of surgery and a post-operative period that varies from 0 to 10 days. [Pub. 100-04, Ch. 12, § 40.1.]

Services not included in the global surgical package. Procedure code modifiers are used to identify the most common services not included in the global fee, such as (1) evaluation and management services on the day before major surgery or the day of major surgery that result in the initial decision to operate, (2) return trips to the operating room during the post-operative period, (3) unrelated procedures or visits during the post-operative period, (4) significant evaluation and management on the day of a procedure (including critical care), and (5) post-operative critical care. [Pub. 100-04, Ch. 12, § 40.2.]

Telehealth Services

Medicare pays a physician or practitioner located at a distant site that furnishes a telehealth service the same amount that would have been paid for the service under the physician fee schedule had it been furnished without the use of a telecommunications system. The consultation may be billed only by the consulting practitioner, and payments made to the practitioner at the distant site may not be shared with the referring practitioner or telepresenter. [Soc. Sec. Act § 1834(m)(2)(A); 42 C.F.R. § 414.65(a).]

The facility fee for the originating site is updated by the Medicare Economic Index. Only the originating site may bill for the originating site facility fee and only on an assignment-related basis. [Soc. Sec. Act § 1834(m)(2)(B); 42 C.F.R. § 414.65(b); Pub. 100-04, Ch. 12, § 190.6.]

The payment for the professional service and originating site facility fee is subject to coinsurance and deductible requirements. [42 C.F.R. § 414.65(c).]

Physician Incentive Programs

CMS increases or decreases payments to physicians to provide various incentives, including:

- physicians that participate in the Medicare program receive a higher amount for the services they provide to Medicare beneficiaries; the physician fee schedule payment amount applicable to nonparticipating physicians, suppliers, and practitioners is 5 percent less than that for participating practitioners or suppliers, pursuant to Soc. Sec. Act § 1848(a)(3);

- under the Physician Quality Reporting System (PQRS), through 2018 a negative adjustment applies for failing to satisfactorily submit data on PQRS quality measures;

- eligible professionals (EPs) that do not meaningfully use certified electronic health record (EHR) technology will have their Medicare physician fee schedule amount reduced for each year from 2015 through 2018 (see ¶ 717);

- the value-based payment modifier, which provides for differential payment under the physician fee schedule is based on the quality of care furnished compared to cost during a performance period; and

- bonus payments for practitioners in underserved areas.

MACRA consolidates and replaces the EHR meaningful use program, PQRS, and the value-based payment modifier into the new Merit-Based Incentive Payment System (MIPS) program. MACRA will sunset the three programs at the end of 2018. [MACRA § 101(b), (c).]

In addition, under MACRA, starting in 2019, the amounts paid to individual providers will be subject to adjustment through one of two mechanisms, depending on whether the physician chooses to participate in an Alternative Payment Model (APM) program or MIPS. [MACRA § 101(c), (e)(2).]

MIPS. Providers who opt to participate in MIPS will receive payments that are subject to positive or negative performance adjustments. The performance adjustment for an individual provider will depend on that provider's performance compared to a threshold. [Soc. Sec. Act § 1848(q), as added by MACRA § 101(c)(1).]

APMs. An APM requires participation in an entity that assumes a meaningful financial risk, reporting of quality measures, and use of certified EHR technology. From 2019 through 2024, eligible professionals receiving a substantial portion of their revenue from APMs will receive a lump-sum payment after each year equal to 5 percent of their Medicare payments in that year. [Soc. Sec. Act § 1833(z), as added by MACRA § 101(e)(2).]

Physician Quality Reporting System. PQRS measures address various aspects of care, such as prevention, chronic- and acute-care management, procedure-related care, resource utilization, and care coordination, and can be reported for measures groups created for specific conditions. Starting with calendar year 2015, a negative adjustment to physician fee schedule payments applies to services for which a professional does not satisfactorily submit data on quality measures. The adjustment in 2016 will result in a 98 percent payment. [Soc. Sec. Act § 1848(a)(8)(A); 42 C.F.R. § 414.90(e).]

An EP or group practice that wishes to participate in the PQRS must report information on the individual PQRS quality measures or measures groups identified by CMS in a form and manner specified by CMS. The details are posted on the CMS website: https://www.cms.gov/PQRS/. Instead of reporting quality measures, an EP may choose to participate in a qualified clinical data registry. [Soc. Sec. Act § 1848(m)(3); 42 C.F.R. § 414.90(c)(5).]

Value-based payment modifier. The value-based payment modifier provides for differential payment starting in 2015 to groups of physicians and starting in 2017 to all physicians and groups of physicians under the physician fee schedule based on the quality of care furnished compared to cost during a performance period. The modifier is based upon a comparison of the composite of quality of care measures and a composite of cost measures. [Soc. Sec. Act § 1848(p); 42 C.F.R. §§ 414.1200, 414.1275.]

Bonus payments for practitioners in underserved areas. Medicare pays a bonus of 10 percent to physicians who furnish covered services to Medicare beneficiaries in areas designated as Health Professional Shortage Areas (HPSAs). The bonus is added to whatever would otherwise be paid under the fee schedule and applies to both urban and rural HPSAs. [Soc. Sec. Act § 1833(m); 42 C.F.R. § 414.67(a).]

A 10 percent bonus also was made for a major surgical procedure furnished by a general surgeon between January 1, 2011, and December 31, 2015 in a HPSA. [Soc. Sec. Act § 1833(y); 42 C.F.R. § 414.67(b).]Medicare also paid a 10 percent bonus for primary care services rendered between January 1, 2011, and December 31, 2015. [Soc. Sec. Act § 1833(x); 42 C.F.R. § 414.80.]

Information on Amounts Paid to Individual Physicians

On January 17, 2014, CMS changed its policy on requests made under the Freedom of Information Act (FOIA) for information on amounts paid to individual physicians under the Medicare program. Effective March 18, 2014, CMS will make case-by-case determinations as to whether exemption 6 of FOIA applies to a given request by weighing the balance between the privacy interest of individual physicians and the public interest in disclosure of such information. [*Notice*, 79 FR 3205, Jan. 17, 2014.]

[¶ 860] Nonphysician Practitioners

As discussed at ¶ 351, separate Medicare coverage is provided for several kinds of nonphysician practitioners. Health care practitioners such as nurse practitioners (NPs) are authorized to bill Medicare separately when they perform specialized services or stand in the place of a physician. At one time, however, the services of nonphysician practitions were covered only as "incident to" a physician's services and payment for their services was included in Medicare's payment to the physician. The Medicare payment amount for nonphysician practitioners is normally a certain percentage of the physician fee schedule for the same services (or less if their actual charges are less).

Assignment. Medicare claims for payment for services of nonphysician practitioners such as PAs, NPs, clinical nurse specialists (CNSs), certified nurse-midwives (CNMs), and certified registered nurse anesthetists (CRNAs) may only be submitted on an assignment basis (see ¶ 868). [42 C.F.R. § § 410.74(d)(2), 410.75(e)(2), 410.76(e)(2), 410.77(d)(2), 414.60(c).]

Physician Assistants, Nurse Practitioners, and Nurse-Midwives

The Medicare payment amount for the services of NPs, CNSs, and PAs (other than assistant-at-surgery services) is based on 85 percent of the fee schedule payment for physicians furnishing the same service. [Soc. Sec. Act § § 1833(a)(1)(O), 1842(b)(18); 42 C.F.R. § § 414.52(d), 414.56(c).]

Physician assistants. PAs must have their own "nonphysician practitioner" national provider identifier (NPI). The NPI is used for identification purposes only when billing for PA services because only an appropriate PA employer or a provider/supplier for whom the PA furnishes services as an independent contractor can bill for PA services. [Soc. Sec. Act § 1842(b)(6)(C); 42 C.F.R. § 410.75(a)(2)(v); *Medicare Claims Processing Manual*, Pub. 100-04, Ch. 12, § 110.4.]

Nurse practitioners and clinical nurse specialists. Payment may be made directly to a NP or CNS for their professional services when furnished in collaboration with a physician. NPs and CNSs must have their own "nonphysician practitioner" NPI number for billing purposes. [Pub. 100-04, Ch. 12, § 120.3.]

Certified nurse-midwives. CNMs services are paid at 80 percent of the lesser of: (1) the actual charge for the services, or (2) 100 percent of the physician fee schedule amount. [Soc. Sec. § 1833(a)(1)(K); 42 C.F.R. § 414.54(b).]

Payment for CNM services is made directly to CNMs for their professional services and for services furnished incident to their professional services. [Pub. 100-04, Ch. 12, § 130.1.]

Global surgical payments. When a PA, NP, or CNS furnishes services to a patient during a global surgical period, Medicare administrative contractors must determine the level of PA, NP, or CNS involvement in furnishing part of the surgeon's global surgical package. PA, NP, or CNS services furnished during a global surgical period are paid at 80 percent of the lesser of the actual charge or 85 percent of what a physician is paid under the physician fee schedule. [Pub. 100-04, Ch. 12, § § 110.1, 120.]

When a CNM is providing most of the care to a Medicare beneficiary that is part of a global service and a physician also provides a portion of the care for this same global service, the fee paid to the CNM is based on the portion of the global fee that would have been paid to the physician for the service provided by the CNM. [Pub. 100-04, Ch. 12, § 130.2.]

Certified Registered Nurse Anesthetists

Anesthesia services furnished by a qualified nonphysician anesthetist (including both certified registered nurse anesthetists (CRNAs) and anesthesia assistants (AAs) are paid at the lesser of the actual charge, the physician fee schedule, or the anesthesia fee schedule. [Soc. Sec. Act § 1833(a)(1)(H), (l); 42 C.F.R. § 414.60.]

Payment may be made to the qualified nonphysician anesthetist who furnished the anesthesia services or to a hospital, physician, group practice, or ambulatory surgical center with which the anesthetist has an employment or contractual relationship. [Soc. Sec. Act § 1842(b)(18); 42 C.F.R. § 414.60; Pub. 100-04, Ch. 12, § 140.2.]

Medicare does not pay for CRNA services when an anesthesiologist is personally involved in the case unless it is determined to be medically necessary for both to be involved. [42 C.F.R. § 414.46(c)(1)(iv).]

Teaching CRNAs. A teaching CRNA is reimbursed 100 percent of the physician fee schedule amount if the teaching CRNA, who is not under medical direction of a physician, is present with the student nurse anesthetist for the pre- and post-anesthesia services included in the anesthesia base units payment and is continuously present during anesthesia time in a single case with a student nurse anesthetist. If the teaching CRNA is involved with two concurrent anesthesia cases, he or she can be involved only with those two concurrent cases and may not perform services for other patients. [Medicare Improvements for Patients and Providers Act of 2008 (MIPPA) (P.L. 110-275) § 139(b); 42 C.F.R. § 414.61.]

Clinical Psychologists and Social Workers

Clinical psychologists are paid 80 percent of the lesser of: (1) the actual charge for the services, or (2) 100 percent of the amount determined for corresponding services under the physician fee schedule. [Soc. Sec. Act § 1833(a)(1)(L); 42 C.F.R. § 414.62.] Direct payment may be made to clinical psychologists under Part B for professional services, and they are required to accept assignment for all Medicare claims for their services. [Pub. 100-04, Ch. 1, § 30.3.1; Ch. 12, § § 170, 170.1.]

Clinical social workers. For therapeutic and other diagnostic services, clinical social workers are paid 80 percent of the lesser of: (1) the actual charge for the services, or (2) 75 percent of the amount determined for payment of a clinical psychologist. [Soc. Sec. Act § 1833(a)(1)(F).]

Physical Therapists, Occupational Therapists, and Speech-Language Pathologists

The Medicare physician fee schedule is the method of payment for outpatient physical therapy, occupational therapy, speech-language pathology services. [Soc. Sec. Act § 1834(k); Pub. 100-04, Ch. 5, § 10.] Outpatient therapists may bill Medicare directly for their services. [Soc. Sec. Act § § 1832(a)(2)(C), 1833(a)(8).]

Functional reporting. Pursuant to § 3005(g) of the Middle Class Tax Relief and Job Creation Act of 2012, therapists must comply with reporting requirements to receive payment for furnished therapy services. At the outset of treatment, therapists are required to report on the projected goal for treatment using modifiers that describe the percentage of impairment. [42 C.F.R. § § 410.59(a)(4), 410.60(a)(4), 410.62(a)(4); Pub. 100-04, Ch. 5, § 10.6.]

Therapy caps. Annual per-beneficiary limitations apply to the amount of expenses that can be considered as incurred expenses for outpatient therapy services under Part B. There is one therapy cap for outpatient occupational therapy services and another separate therapy cap for physical therapy and speech-language pathology services combined. [Soc. Sec. Act § 1833(g).]

The annual therapy cap for 2016 is $1,950 for physical therapy and speech-language pathology services combined; there is a separate cap of $1,950 for occupational therapy services. [*Final rule*, 80 FR 70886, Nov. 16, 2015.]

Therapy caps apply to outpatient therapy services furnished in all settings, including critical access hospitals and the once-exempt outpatient hospital setting. [42 C.F.R.

§§ 410.59 (e) (1) (iv), 410.60 (e) (1) (iv) and (e) (3); *Final rule*, 79 FR 67548, Nov. 13, 2014; Pub. 100-04, Ch. 5, § 10.3.]

Limitations on beneficiary liability. The limitations on beneficiary liability provisions of Soc. Sec. Act § 1879 apply when a claim for services is denied for exceeding the therapy caps. [Soc. Sec. Act § 1833 (g) (5) (D).]

Exceptions to therapy caps. An exceptions process for the therapy caps for when the provision of additional therapy services is medically necessary will be in effect through December 31, 2017. [Soc. Sec. Act § 1833 (g) (5), as amended by Medicare Access and CHIP Reauthorization Act of 2015 (MACRA) (P.L. 114-10) § 202 (a).]

A request for an exception to the therapy cap on claims that are over the cap amount must contain an appropriate modifier (such as the KX modifier) indicating that the services are medically necessary as justified by documentation in the medical record. [Soc. Sec. Act § 1833 (g) (5) (B).]

Requests for an exception to therapy caps with respect to expenses that would be incurred for outpatient therapy services that exceed an annual threshold of (1) $3,700 for occupational therapy services, or (2) $3,700 for physical therapy and speech-language pathology therapy services combined, are subject to a manual medical review. [Soc. Sec. Act § 1833 (g) (5) (C).] MACRA requires the Secretary to implement a process for targeted medical review in place of the manual medical review process. [Soc. Sec. Act § 1833 (g) (5) (E), as added by MACRA § 202 (b).]

[¶ 865] Actual Charge Restrictions

To protect beneficiaries from excessive charges by Medicare physicians and suppliers, the Medicare program has several rules that limit how much beneficiaries can be charged (actual charge restrictions). These rules apply only to physicians and suppliers who do not accept assignment, including "nonparticipating" physicians and suppliers (see ¶ 870 for an explanation of the Participation Program). Payments to physicians and suppliers who accept assignment are governed by separate rules (see ¶ 868). If these actual charge restrictions did not exist, a physician or supplier who does not accept assignment would be free to set any amount as the actual charge and could require the beneficiary to pay that amount. Medicare would, as usual, pay 80 percent of the amount it determines to be allowable, and the beneficiary would have to pay the difference between the Medicare payment amount and the physician's or supplier's actual charge.

The Limiting Charge

As discussed at ¶ 868, when assignment is accepted, a physician agrees to the Medicare-approved charge as the full charge and bills the patient only the 20 percent coinsurance amount not paid by Medicare. Physicians, suppliers, or other practitioners who do not accept assignment, however, are subject to a "limiting charge" that places restrictions on how much they are allowed to charge a Medicare patient. [Soc. Sec. Act § 1848 (g).]

The limiting charge is 115 percent of the fee schedule amount for "nonparticipating" physicians and suppliers, which is 95 percent of the physician fee schedule amount for each service. [Soc. Sec. Act §§ 1834 (b) (5) (B), 1848 (a) (3) and (g) (2) (C); 42 C.F.R. § 414.48.]

In cases when a payment basis other than the physician fee schedule is used, the 115 percent limiting charge is applied to the recognized payment amount for nonparticipating providers, which is defined by the statute as 95 percent of whatever payment basis is utilized. [Soc. Sec. Act § 1848 (g) (2) (D); 42 C.F.R. § 414.48 (b).]

The limiting charge applies to all of the following services/supplies, regardless of who provides or bills for them, if they are covered by the Medicare program:

- physicians' services;

- services and supplies furnished incident to a physician's services that are commonly furnished in a physician's office;

- outpatient physical or occupational therapy services furnished by an independently practicing therapist;

- diagnostic tests; and

- radiation therapy services (including x-ray, radium, and radioactive isotope therapy, and materials and services of technicians).

[*Medicare Claims Processing Manual,* Pub. 100-04, Ch. 1, § 30.3.12.3.]

Example • • • _____

Carla visits Dr. Kent for a series of medical tests and services for which Dr. Kent would charge private-pay patients $800. The physician fee schedule amount for those services, however, is $510. Carla has paid the Part B deductible for the year.

(1) If Dr. Kent is a participating physician, Medicare will pay Dr. Kent $408 and Carla will pay the $102 coinsurance (that is, 20 percent of $510).

(2) If Dr. Kent is a nonparticipating physician, the Medicare-approved amount is 5 percent less than the fee schedule ($485), and the Medicare payment amount is $388 (80 percent of the reduced approved amount).

(a) If Dr. Kent accepts assignment and, thus, agrees to accept the reduced Medicare-approved amount as his full charge, Medicare will pay Dr. Kent $388 and Carla will pay the other $97.

(b) If Dr. Kent does not accept assignment and wants to charge Carla more than the reduced Medicare-approved amount, Dr. Kent may not charge Carla more than 15 percent over the reduced Medicare-approved amount (i.e., 15 percent over $485, or $557.75). The Medicare-approved payment amount ($388) is sent to Carla, and Carla is responsible for paying the other $169.75.

Medicare secondary payments. The rules for calculating Medicare secondary benefits apply regardless of whether the limiting charge applies. However, when the limiting charge is less than the actual charge, the limiting charge will be considered to be the actual charge as well as the plan's allowable charge. [*Medicare Secondary Payer Manual,* Pub. 100-05, Ch. 5, § 40.7.4.]

A nonparticipating physician/supplier that does not take assignment must reduce charges to the beneficiary to reflect the Medicare limiting charge. A physician who charges a patient more than the limiting charge must refund the difference. [Soc. Sec. Act § 1848(g)(1)(A)(iv).]

If a physician knowingly and willfully bills above the limiting charge, the Secretary may apply sanctions, including: (1) barring the physician from participating in the Medicare program for up to five years, and (2) imposing a civil money penalty or assessment. [Soc. Sec. Act § 1842(j)(1)(A), (j)(2).] The Secretary may use any penalties so collected to reimburse the beneficiary for the overcharge. [Soc. Sec. Act § 1842(j)(4).]

Other Actual Charge Restrictions

While a number of limitations on actual charges became obsolete with the adoption of the physician fee schedule and a "limiting charge," other actual charge restrictions affect how much health care providers may charge or bill Medicare beneficiaries.

Services not reasonable or necessary. When a physician furnishes otherwise covered services on an unassigned basis to a Medicare beneficiary and Medicare determines that those services were not covered because they were not reasonable or necessary, the physician is required to refund to the beneficiary any payments collected for those services (including deductible and coinsurance amounts). A program payment, however, may be made to the physician if neither the physician nor the patient knew, nor could reasonably have been expected to know, that Medicare would not pay for the items and services provided. [Soc. Sec. Act § § 1834(a)(18)(A), 1842(l)(1)(A); 42 C.F.R. § 411.408(a).]

Elective surgery on an unassigned basis. When a physician performs an elective surgical procedure on an unassigned basis for a Medicare beneficiary, and the charge for that procedure is at least $500, the physician must refund to the patient any payment collected above the Medicare allowed charge for the procedure unless the physician discloses to the beneficiary in advance the difference between (1) the physician's estimated charge, (2) the estimated Medicare payment, and (3) the excess of the physician's actual charge over the estimated Medicare payment. A physician who knowingly and willfully fails to make a required refund for an elective surgery procedure may be subject to civil money penalties or may be suspended from program participation. The Secretary is required to monitor elective surgery claims to assure that required refunds are being made. [Soc. Sec. Act § 1842(m).]

[¶ 868] Assignment

An assignment is an agreement between a physician or supplier and a Medicare beneficiary. Under the terms of the assignment, the beneficiary transfers to the physician or supplier his right to Medicare benefits for the services received and the physician or supplier accepts the Medicare-approved charge as the full charge for the items or services provided. The physician or supplier submits a claim for payment for the services rendered to the Medicare administrative contractor (MAC). If the MAC approvides the charges, Medicare pays the physician or supplier the Medicare-approved "fee schedule" amount (see ¶ 855) and the beneficiary is responsible for paying the coinsurance and any remaining deductible (see ¶ 335). [Soc. Sec. Act § 1842(b)(3)(B)(ii); 42 C.F.R. § 424.55; *Medicare Claims Processing Manual*, Pub. 100-04, Ch. 1, § § 30.2 and 30.3.]

Some physicians and suppliers do not accept assignment and some beneficiaries may want Medicare to sent payment directly to them. In these situations, a Medicare payment is sent directly to the beneficiary after an itemized bill is submitted to the MAC on the appropriate form (Form CMS-1500). The beneficiary is responsible for paying the physician or supplier (see also ¶ 900). [42 C.F.R. § § 424.50–424.56; Pub. 100-04, Ch. 1, § 30.3.]

Signature of patient. The signature of the patient on the billing form, or that of a person qualified to sign on his or her behalf, is necessary to assign payment of benefits to the physician or supplier. The signature should be obtained on the billing form, on the provider's records, or, in the case of a prolonged illness, on a special statement having the effect of a general consent to assignment. [Pub. 100-04, Ch. 1, § 50.1.3.]

Mandatory Assignment

Certain practitioners who provide services under the Medicare program are required to accept assignment for all Medicare claims for their services. This means that they must accept the Medicare allowed amount as payment in full for their practitioner services. The beneficiary's liability is limited to any applicable deductible plus the 20 percent coinsurance. Assignment is mandated for the following claims:

- Clinical diagnostic laboratory services and physician lab services (see Soc. Sec. Act § 1833(h)(5)(C));

- Physician services to individuals dually entitled to Medicare and Medicaid;

- Services of physician assistants (PAs), nurse practitioners (NPs), clinical nurse specialists (CNSs), nurse-midwives, certified registered nurse anesthetists (CRNAs), clinical psychologists, clinical social workers, registered dietitians/nutritionists, and anesthesiologist assistants (see 42 C.F.R. §§ 410.74(d)(2), 410.75(e)(2), 410.76(e)(2), 414.60(c); Pub. 100-04, Ch. 12, §§ 110–170);

- Mass immunization roster billers (billing only for influenza and pneumococcal vaccinations and administrations, services not subject to the deductible or the 20 percent coinsurance);

- Ambulatory surgical center services (no deductible and 25 percent coinsurance for colorectal cancer screening colonoscopies applies);

- Home dialysis supplies and equipment paid under Method II for dates of service before January 1, 2011 (see Pub. 100-04, Ch. 1, § 30.3.8);

- Drugs and biologicals (see 42 C.F.R. § 414.707(b); Pub. 100-04, Ch. 17, § 50);

- Ambulance services (see 42 C.F.R. § 414.610(b); Pub. 100-04, Ch. 15, § 10.4);

- Competitive bidding items of durable medical equipment, prosthetics, orthotics, and supplies (42 C.F.R. § 414.408) and upgrades from a competitive bid item to a non-bid item; and

- Telehealth services (see 42 C.F.R. § 414.65(d)).

[Pub. 100-04, Ch. 1, § 30.3.1; Ch. 36, §§ 40, 40.11, 40.12.]

The acceptance of assignment is not mandatory for the practitioner services of physicians and independently practicing physical and occupational therapists, or for the suppliers of radiology services or diagnostic tests. [Pub. 100-04, Ch. 1, § 30.3.1.]

Limitation on Physician/Supplier Charges to Beneficiaries

By submitting the claims form with the beneficiary's assignment authorization, the physician or supplier agrees to accept the Medicare-approved charge as the full charge for the items or services provided. A physician or supplier agrees not to charge the beneficiary for services for which Medicare pays 100 percent of the approved amount. In addition, the physician or supplier agrees to collect only: (1) the difference between the Medicare-approved amount and the Medicare Part B payment; (2) any applicable deductible; and (3) any applicable coinsurance amount for which Medicare does not pay 100 percent of the approved amount. [42 C.F.R. § 424.55(b); Pub. 100-04, Ch. 1, § 30.3.2.] If the physician or supplier is dissatisfied with the amount of the Medicare-approved charge, the physician's remedy is to request a review and hearing with the MAC. The physician may not ask the beneficiary for more money. [Soc. Sec. Act § 1842(b)(3)(B)(ii).]

If a beneficiary has private insurance in addition to Medicare (e.g., a Medigap policy— see ¶ 740), the physician or supplier who has accepted assignment is in violation of the assignment agreement if that physician or supplier bills or collects from the beneficiary or the private insurer an amount that, when added to the Medicare benefit received, exceeds the approved charge. [Pub. 100-04, Ch. 1, § 30.3.2.]

Physicians and suppliers who do not accept assignment also are limited on the amount they may charge beneficiaries. This "limiting charge" is 115 percent of the Medicare-approved charge for nonparticipating physicians and suppliers (see ¶ 865).

A physician or supplier who accepts assignment for some services (that is, on a case-by-case basis) is not ordinarily precluded from billing the patient for other services; however, a physician or supplier may not accept assignment for some services and claim payment from the beneficiary for other services he or she performed for that same beneficiary at the same place on the same occasion. [Pub. 100-04, Ch. 1, § 30.3.2.]

Exception. When a physician is required to accept assignment for certain services as a condition for any payment or for Medicare payment to be made (for example, for clinical diagnostic laboratory services (see ¶ 875) and the services of physician assistants (see ¶ 860)), the physician may accept assignment for those services while billing on an unassigned basis for other services the physician furnishes at the same place and on the same occasion. [Pub. 100-04, Ch. 1, § 30.3.2.]

Prohibition Against Reassignment

While a beneficiary may assign his or her right to Medicare payment for Medicare services received, providers, physicians, and suppliers may generally not reassign the right to receive payments assigned to them. [Soc. Sec. Act §§ 1815(c), 1842(b)(6); 42 C.F.R. §§ 424.73(a), 424.80(a); Pub. 100-04, Ch. 1, § 30.2.2.]

The law provides that any person who accepts an assignment of benefits under Medicare and "knowingly, willfully, and repeatedly" violates the assignment agreement shall be guilty of a misdemeanor and subject to a fine of not more than $2,000 or imprisonment of not more than six months or both. Further, if the prohibition against assignment or reassignment is violated, CMS may terminate a provider agreement or revoke the party's right to receive assigned benefits. [Soc. Sec. Act § 1128A; 42 C.F.R. §§ 424.74, 424.82; Pub. 100-04, Ch. 1, § 30.2.15.]

A power of attorney may not be used to circumvent the prohibition against reassignment. [Soc. Sec. Act § 1842(b)(6); 42 C.F.R. § 424.73(a).]

Exceptions. There are several exceptions to the reassignment prohibition. Medicare payment may be made to the employer of a physician or other practitioner providing services if the physician or practitioner is required as a condition of his employment to turn over his fee to his employer and, if the services are provided in a hospital, clinic, or other facility, payment may be made to the facility if there is a contractual arrangement between the physician or other person and the facility under which the facility submits the bill for the services. [Soc. Sec. Act § 1842(b)(6); 42 C.F.R. § 424.80(b)(1); Pub. 100-04, Ch. 1, § 30.2.7.]

There is an additional exception to the prohibition against reassignment—the "indirect payment procedure" for entities that provide payment under a complementary health benefit plan. The coverage that such a plan provides is complementary to Medicare benefits and covers only the amount by which the Part B payment falls short of the approved charge for the service under the plan. ("Medigap" plans are examples of this type of plan.) Under this exception, payment may be made to an entity that provides coverage of the services under a complementary health benefits plan under the circumstances described at 42 C.F.R. § 424.66. [Pub. 100-04, Ch. 1, § 30.2.8.3.]

Medicare payment may be made to a substituting physician when the patient's first physician arranges for substitution services by a second physician because the first physician is unavailable to provide the services and the services are not provided by the second physician over a continuous period longer than 60 days. [Soc. Sec. Act § 1842(b)(6)(D); Pub. 100-04, Ch. 1, § 30.2.11.]

For other exceptions to the prohibition against assignment and reassignment, see regulations beginning at 42 C.F.R. § 424.70 and Pub. 100-04, Ch. 1, § 30.2.1.

[¶ 870] Participation Program for Physicians and Suppliers

Under Medicare's "Participating Physicians and Suppliers Program," physicians and suppliers are encouraged to sign a "participation" agreement with the Secretary of HHS binding them to accept assignment (see ¶ 868) for services provided to all Medicare patients for the following calendar year. [Soc. Sec. Act § 1842(h)(1).]

Participation agreements run on a calendar-year basis and are normally effective for one year. They are automatically renewed unless cancelled. Once the year has begun, physicians and suppliers will not be permitted to enter or drop out of the program until the end of the year. In the case of a newly licensed physician, however, a physician who begins a practice in a new area, or a new supplier who begins a new business, the physician or supplier may enter into a participation agreement for the remainder of the year. [Soc. Sec. Act § 1842(h)(1); *Medicare Claims Processing Manual*, Pub. 100-04, Ch. 1, § 30.3.12.]

WK Note: The "participation" program relates only to how physicians or suppliers are paid; it does not affect whether the services provided are covered. Thus, for coverage purposes, it makes no difference whether the physician or supplier providing the items or services is "participating" or "nonparticipating."

Incentives to Participate

The "participation program" provides incentives to encourage physicians and suppliers to participate. These include the following:

(1) the establishment and free distribution of participating physician and supplier directories (see discussion below); [Soc. Sec. Act § 1842(h)(4)]

(2) toll-free telephone numbers through which beneficiaries may obtain the names, addresses, specialties, and telephone numbers of participating physicians and suppliers; [Soc. Sec. Act § 1842(h)(2)]

(3) electronic transmission of claims to Medicare contractors; [Soc. Sec. Act § 1842(h)(3)]

(4) higher payment rates (nonparticipating physicians are paid 95 percent of the payment rates applied to participating physicians); [Pub. 100-04, Ch. 1, § 30.3] and

(5) limitations on the actual charges that can be billed by nonparticipating physicians, including important refund and disclosure rules (see ¶ 865). [Pub. 100-04, Ch. 1, § 30.3.12.3.]

[Pub. 100-04, Ch. 1, § 30.3.12.1(I).]

Directory of Participating Physicians and Suppliers

At the beginning of each year CMS publishes local directories containing the names, addresses, specialties, and telephone numbers of all local "participating" physicians and suppliers. These directories, called "Medicare Participating Physicians/Suppliers Directories" (abbreviated MEDPARD), are made available at all Social Security and Medicare administrative contractor (MAC) offices and at some senior citizen organization centers. MACs are required to mail directories to beneficiaries at no charge upon request. [Soc. Sec. Act § 1842(h)(2), (4), (5)(A).]

Each time a payment explanation (the Medicare Summary Notice) is sent to beneficiaries with respect to claims made on an unassigned basis, the Secretary is required to remind them about the existence of the participation program, the charge limits applicable to nonparticipants, the local MAC's toll-free telephone number, and an offer to help the beneficiary locate a participating physician or supplier. [Soc. Sec. Act § 1842(h)(7).]

Hospitals and critical access hospitals are required to make available to patients the directory of participating physicians for the area. [Soc. Sec. Act § 1866(a)(1)(N).]

[¶ 872] Private Non-Medicare Contracts with Health Care Practitioners

CMS allows Medicare beneficiaries and their physicians (and certain nonphysician practitioners) to enter into private contracts for health care services outside the Medicare system. A physician or practitioner opts out of Medicare for a two-year period if he or she enters into a private contract with a Medicare beneficiary and submits an affidavit. Services furnished under such private contracts are not covered services under Medicare, and no Medicare payment will be made for such services either directly or indirectly, except in limited cases. [Soc. Sec. Act §§ 1802(b)(1), 1862(a)(19); 42 C.F.R. §§ 405.405, 405.410.]

Physicians who may opt out of Medicare include dentists, podiatrists, and optometrists. Practitioners who may opt out include: (1) physician assistants, nurse practitioners, and clinical nurse specialists; (2) certified registered nurse anesthetists; (3) certified nurse-midwives; (4) clinical social workers; (5) clinical psychologists; and (6) registered dietitians or nutrition professionals. [Soc. Sec. Act § 1802(b)(6).]

Medicare's limiting charge (see ¶ 865) does not apply to private contract arrangements. [Soc. Sec. Act § 1802(b)(4).]Also, a physician or practitioner who opts out is not required to submit claims on behalf of beneficiaries. [*Medicare Benefit Policy Manual*, Pub. 100-02, Ch. 15, § 40.]

Section 106(a)(2) of the Medicare Access and CHIP Reauthorization Act of 2015 (MACRA) (P.L. 114-10) requires the HHS Secretary to post information concerning opt-out physicians and practitioners on the HHS website by February 1, 2016. [Soc. Sec. Act § 1842(b)(5).]

Requirements for Private Physician Contracts

For an opt out to be effective, the contract between the beneficiary and physician/ practitioner must be in writing and signed by the beneficiary before any item or service is provided, and not at a time when the beneficiary is facing an emergency or urgent health care situation. It also must clearly state whether the physician or practitioner is excluded from Medicare under Soc. Sec. Act §§ 1128, 1156, or 1892. [Soc. Sec. Act § 1802(b)(2); 42 C.F.R. § 405.415.]

By signing the contract, the beneficiary:

(1) agrees not to submit a claim (or to request that the physician or practitioner submit a claim) for the items or services, even if they are otherwise covered by Medicare;

(2) agrees to be responsible, through insurance or otherwise, for payment and understands that no reimbursement will be provided;

(3) acknowledges that no limits under Title XVIII (including the limiting charge) apply to amounts that may be charged for such items or services;

(4) acknowledges that Medigap plans under § 1882 do not, and other supplemental insurance plans may elect not to, make payments for the items and services because payment is not made by Medicare; and

(5) acknowledges that the beneficiary has the right to have the items or services provided by other physicians or practitioners for whom payment would be made by Medicare.

[Soc. Sec. Act § 1802(b)(2)(B); 42 C.F.R. § 405.415.]

Opt-out period. Before the enactment of MACRA, Soc. Sec. Act § 1802(b)(3) provided that a physician opt out was effective for two years. [42 C.F.R. §§ 405.400, 405.405(b), 405.410(c).] Under MACRA, effective June 15, 2015, opt outs last two years and are automatically extended for additional two-year periods unless the physician or practitioner provides notice to the Secretary 30 days before the end of the previous two-year period that he or she does not want to exend the contract. [Soc. Sec. Act § 1802(b)(3).]

Physician affidavit. For the private contract to be effective, the physician or practitioner must sign and file with the HHS Secretary an affidavit stating that for the "applicable two-year period" he or she will not submit any claims to Medicare nor receive any payment from Medicare for items or services provided to any Medicare beneficiary. [Soc. Sec. Act § 1802(b)(3); 42 C.F.R. § 405.420.]

Enforcement. A physician or practitioner who knowingly and willfully submits a claim to Medicare or receives any payment from Medicare during the affidavit's two-year period will lose the rights provided under the private contract provision for the remainder of the period and will not be eligible to receive Medicare payments for the remainder of the period. [Soc. Sec. Act § 1802(b)(3)(C); 42 C.F.R. § 405.435(a).]

Medicare payment may be made for the claims submitted by a beneficiary for the services of an opt-out physician or practitioner when the physician or practitioner did not privately contract with the beneficiary for services that were not emergency care services or urgent care services and were furnished no later than 15 days after the date of a notice by the Medicare administrative contractor that the physician or practitioner has opted out of Medicare. [42 C.F.R. § 405.435(c).]

Emergency or urgent care. A physician or practitioner who has opted out of Medicare need not enter into a private contract to furnish emergency care services or urgent care services to a Medicare beneficiary. Accordingly, a physician or practitioner will not be determined to have failed to maintain opt out if he or she furnishes emergency care services or urgent care services to a Medicare beneficiary with whom the physician or practitioner has not previously entered into a private contract. In such circumstances, the physician or practitioner must submit a claim and may collect no more than the Medicare limiting charge, in the case of a physician, or the deductible and coinsurance, in the case of a practitioner. [42 C.F.R. § 405.440; Pub. 100-02, Ch. 15, § 40.28.]

Terminating opt outs and appeals. A physician or practitioner may terminate an opt out by satisfying certain notification and refund requirements. Further, a physician or practitioner who is dissatisfied with a determination by CMS that a physician or practitioner has failed to properly opt out, failed to maintain opt out, failed to timely renew opt out, failed to privately contract, or failed to properly terminate opt out may utilize the enrollment appeals process currently available for providers and suppliers addressed in 42 C.F.R. part 498. [42 C.F.R. §§ 405.445, 405.450(a).]

[¶ 875] Clinical Diagnostic Laboratory Tests

Generally, outpatient clinical diagnostic laboratory tests, except provider-based laboratories performing clinical diagnostic laboratory tests for their own inpatients, are paid according to fee schedules established by the HHS Secretary. This includes clinical laboratory tests performed in a physician's office and by an independent laboratory or a hospital laboratory for its outpatients. [Soc. Sec. Act § 1833(h)(1).]

For services furnished after June 30, 2012, an independent laboratory may not bill the Medicare administrative contractor for the technical component (TC) of physician pathology services furnished to a hospital inpatient or outpatient. [42 C.F.R. § 415.130(d).]

Payment for services furnished before January 1, 2017. For clinical diagnostic laboratory tests furnished before January 1, 2017, that are paid under the clinical laboratory fee schedule pursuant to Soc. Sec. Act § 1833(h)(1), the amount paid is at 80 percent (or 100 percent, in the case of such tests for which payment is made on an assignment-related basis) of the lesser of the fee schedule amount, the limitation amount for that test determined under Soc. Sec. Act § 1833(h)(4)(B), or the actual charges. Part B pays 100 percent of the negotiated rate on the basis of a negotiated rate under Soc. Sec. Act § 1833(h)(6). [Soc. Sec. Act § 1833(a)(1)(D), (a)(2)(D).]

In the case of any diagnostic laboratory test that is not paid on the basis of a fee schedule, the HHS Secretary may negotiate a payment rate with the person or entity performing the test that would be considered the full charge for the test. [Soc. Sec. Act § 1833(h)(6).]

Payment reform after January 1, 2017. Section 216 of the Protecting Access to Medicare Act of 2014 (PAMA) (P.L. 113-93), which added Soc. Sec. Act § 1834A, requires CMS to implement a new Medicare payment system for clinical diagnostic laboratory tests based on private payer rates beginning January 1, 2017. For tests furnished on or after January 1, 2017, that are paid under § 1834A, the amount paid will be 80 percent (or 100 percent, in the case of such tests for which payment is made on an assignment-related basis) of the lesser of the amount determined under § 1834A or the actual charges.

Other methods of payment. Certain outpatient laboratory services can be paid in other ways, including:

- under the physician fee schedule (see *Medicare Claims Processing Manual*, Pub. 100-04, Ch. 16, §§ 100, 100.2);
- at 101 percent of reasonable cost for critical access hospitals only;
- under the outpatient prospective payment system (OPPS) when packaged into the payment for related procedures (see 42 C.F.R. § 419.2(b)); or
- the reasonable charge payment method.

[Pub. 100-04, Ch. 16, § 10.2.]

Mandatory assignment. Payment for clinical diagnostic tests performed by clinical laboratories, excluding tests performed by rural health clinics (RHCs), may be made only on an assignment-related basis. If a person repeatedly bills beneficiaries for clinical diagnostic laboratory tests on other than an assignment-related basis, he or she will be subject to exclusion from the program and civil money penalties. [Soc. Sec. Act § 1833(h)(5)(C), (D).]

Deductibles. The usual Part B deductible does not apply to clinical diagnostic laboratory tests paid (1) under Soc. Sec. Act § 1833(a)(1)(D)(i) or (a)(2)(D)(i) on an assignment-related basis, or to a provider having an agreement under Soc. Sec. Act § 1866; or (2) for tests furnished before January 1, 2017, on the basis of a negotiated rate. [Soc. Sec. Act § 1833(b)(3).]

Calculation of Payment Under the Clinical Laboratory Fee Schedule

Each fee schedule is set at 60 percent of the prevailing charge levels for each area, as adjusted annually to reflect changes in the Consumer Price Index for All Urban Consumers

(U.S. city average), and subject to such other adjustments as the HHS Secretary determines are justified by technological changes or the need to adequately compensate for emergency services or high utilization of sophisticated equipment and skilled personnel. Laboratories in sole community hospitals are paid 62 percent of the prevailing charge level. [Soc. Sec. Act § 1833 (h) (2).]

Fee schedule adjustments. Section 3401 (l) of the Patient Protection and Affordable Care Act (ACA) (P.L. 111-148) provided for a productivity adjustment to the clinical laboratory fee schedule, effective for services in 2011 and later. The productivity adjustment is the same one applied to inpatient hospital services under Soc. Sec. Act § 1886 (b) (3) (B) (xi) (II). The application of this productivity adjustment may not result in the annual percentage increase being less than 0.0 for a year. [Soc. Sec. Act § 1833 (h) (2) (A) (iv) (I).]

Also pursuant to section 3401 (l) of the ACA, updates for 2011 through 2015 were subject to an additional reduction of 1.75 percentage points, which could result in an adjustment to the fee schedule being less than 0.0 for a year and the payment rates for a year being less than the rates for the preceding year. In addition, the Secretary was required to reduce by 2 percent the fee schedules otherwise determined under Soc. Sec. Act § 1833 (h) (2) (A) (i) for 2013, and such reduced fee schedules serve as the base for 2014 and subsequent years. [Soc. Sec. Act § 1833 (h) (2) (A) (iv).]

Fee schedule ceiling. Medicare law imposes a ceiling (called the "national limitation amount") on the amount that may be paid under a fee schedule. The ceiling is set at 74 percent of the median of all fee schedules established for that test for that laboratory setting. In the case of new tests for which no limitation amount has previously been established, the ceiling is 100 percent of the median. [Soc. Sec. Act § 1833 (h) (4) (B).]

Fees for specimen collection and travel. In addition to the fee schedule amount, CMS will pay: (1) a nominal additional fee for the costs in collecting the sample on which a clinical diagnostic laboratory test was performed, and (2) a fee to cover the transportation and personnel expenses for trained personnel to travel to the location of an individual who is homebound or an inpatient in an inpatient facility other than a hospital to collect the sample. [Soc. Sec. Act § 1833 (h) (3) (A); Pub. 100-04, Ch. 16, § § 60.1, 60.2.]

Automated laboratory tests. Clinical laboratory tests are covered under Medicare if they are reasonable and necessary for the diagnosis or treatment of an illness or injury. Because of the numerous technological advances and innovations in the clinical laboratory field and the increased availability of automated testing equipment, no distinction generally is made in determining payment for individual tests because of either (1) the site where the service is performed, or (2) the method of the testing process used, whether manual or automated. Whether the test is performed manually or with automated equipment, the services are considered similar and the payment is the same. [Pub. 100-04, Ch. 16, § 90.1.]

Multiple procedure payment reduction. Effective January 1, 2013, CMS applies the multiple procedure payment reduction (MPRR) to the TC of certain cardiovascular and ophthalmology diagnostic tests. For diagnostic cardiovascular services, full payment is made for the procedure with the highest TC payment, and payment is reduced by 25 percent for the TC for each additional procedure furnished to the same patient on the same day. For diagnostic ophthalmology services, full payment is made for the procedure with the highest TC payment, and payment is reduced by 20 percent for the TC for each additional procedure furnished to the same patient on the same day. [*Final rule*, 77 FR 68891, Nov. 16, 2012.]

Protecting Access to Medicare Act of 2014 Changes

PAMA mandated the modification of reimbursement for clinical laboratories beginning January 1, 2017. [PAMA § 216, adding Soc. Sec. Act § 1834A.]

Reporting of payment rates. Beginning January 1, 2016, and every three years thereafter, each "applicable laboratory" is required to report to CMS, with respect to a laboratory test for the previous 12-month period, the following: (1) the payment rate that was paid by each private payer (health insurance issuers, group health plans, Medicare Advantage plans, and Medicaid managed care organizations) for the test during the period, and (2) the volume of such tests for each such payer for that period. An "applicable laboratory" is defined as a laboratory that derives the majority of its revenues from Soc. Sec. Act §§ 1834A, 1833(h) (the clinical laboratory fee schedule), or 1848 (the physician fee schedule). [Soc. Sec. Act § 1834A(a).]

PAMA required the HHS Secretary to promulgate regulations regarding reporting requirements by June 30, 2015. [Soc. Sec. Act § 1834A(a)(12).] On October 1, 2015, CMS issued a proposed rule that would revise the payment system for clinical diagnostic laboratory tests and implement other changes required by PAMA. [*Proposed rule*, 80 FR 59386, Oct. 1, 2015.]

Payment. For clinical diagnostic laboratory test furnished on or after January 1, 2017, the payment amount under Soc. Sec. Act § 1834A will be equal to the weighted median for the test for the period, as determined by the Secretary based on the information reported under Soc. Sec. Act § 1834A(a). Reductions from the implementation of the private payer rate will be phased in from 2017 through 2022. [Soc. Sec. Act § 1834A(b).]

Different rules will apply to new tests and new advanced diagnostic tests. [Soc. Sec. Act § 1834A(c), (d).]

Who May Bill for Laboratory Tests

In most cases, payment for clinical diagnostic laboratory services may be made only to the person or entity that performed or supervised the performance of the test. Thus, no payment may be made to a physician with respect to such a test unless the physician (or another physician with whom the physician shares his practice) personally performed or supervised the performance of the test. Similarly, payment will not be made in most cases to a laboratory that refers the tests to another laboratory. Payment may, however, be made to a hospital when the tests are performed under arrangements made by the hospital and to a referring laboratory that meets certain conditions and that does not have a financial relationship with the referring physician. [Soc. Sec. Act §§ 1833(h)(5)(A), 1887.]

Payment for clinical diagnostic laboratory tests normally can be made only if the physician ordering the tests is also the physician treating the patient. [42 C.F.R. § 410.32(a).]

When a laboratory bills for a test on the basis of a physician referral, the laboratory is required to include the name and national provider identifier of the referring physician and indicate whether the referring physician is an investor in the laboratory. [Soc. Sec. Act § 1833(q).]

Prohibition on referrals to related labs. Physicians (and their immediate relatives) are generally prohibited from referring laboratory tests to labs with which the physician has a financial relationship. [Soc. Sec. Act § 1877(a)–(g).]

Prohibition on Mark-Up of Clinical Laboratory Services

If a physician bills for a laboratory test performed by an outside laboratory and identifies both the laboratory and the amount the laboratory charged, payment for the test will be based on the lower of the following amounts:

(1) the outside laboratory's reasonable charge for the service; or

(2) the amount that the laboratory charged the physician for the service.

[42 C.F.R. § 405.515(b).]

If the bill or request for payment does not indicate that the test was personally performed or supervised either by the physician who submitted the bill or another physician with whom that physician shares his or her practice and if the outside laboratory and the amount the laboratory charged are not identified, payment will be based on the lowest charge at which the Medicare administrative contractor estimates the test could have been secured from a laboratory serving the physician's locality. [42 C.F.R. § 405.515(c).]

[¶ 880] Ambulance Fee Schedule

Ambulance services, except for services furnished by certain critical access hospitals (CAHs), are reimbursed under a fee schedule payment system. Under the fee schedule, Medicare-covered ambulance services are paid based on the lower of the actual billed amount or the ambulance fee schedule amount. [Soc. Sec. Act § 1834(l); 42 C.F.R. §§ 414.601, 414.610(a).]

The fee schedule payment for ambulance services equals a base rate for the level of service plus a separate payment for mileage to the nearest appropriate facility and applicable adjustment factors. Oxygen and other items and services provided as part of the transport are included in the base payment rate and are not separately payable. [Soc. Sec. Act § 1834(l); 42 C.F.R. § 414.610(a); *Medicare Claims Processing Manual*, Pub. 100-04, Ch. 15, § 20.1.1.]

Ground ambulance service. To compute the fee schedule amount for ground ambulance services, the conversion factor (CF), an amount that serves as a nationally uniform base rate, is multiplied by the applicable relative value units (RVUs) for each level of service to produce a service-level base rate. The service-level base rate is then adjusted by the geographic adjustment factor (GAF) (equal to the practice expense (PE) portion of the geographic practice cost index (GPCI) for the physician fee schedule for each ambulance fee schedule locality area). The lesser of the actual charge or the GAF adjusted base rate amount is added to the lesser of the actual mileage charges or the payment rate per mile, multiplied by the number of miles that the beneficiary was transported. [42 C.F.R. § 414.610(c)(1), (c)(4).]

Air ambulance service. The base payment rate for the applicable type of air ambulance service is adjusted by the GAF and, when applicable, by the appropriate rural adjustment factor, to determine the amount of payment. Air ambulance services have no CF or RVUs. This amount is compared to the actual charge. The lesser of the charge or the adjusted GAF rate amount is added to the payment rate per mile, multiplied by the number of miles that the beneficiary was transported. [42 C.F.R. § 414.610(c)(2).]

Adjustments to Ambulance Fee Schedule Amounts

Soc. Sec. Act § 1834(l)(12)(A) provides for a "super rural bonus," a percent increase in the base rate of the fee schedule for transportation originating in a qualified rural area. The payment amount for the ground ambulance base rate is increased by 22.6 percent where the point of pickup is in a rural area determined to be in the lowest 25 percent of rural population arrayed by population density. Section 203(b) of the Medicare Access and CHIP Reauthorization Act of 2015 (MACRA) (P.L. 114-10) extended this bonus through December 31, 2017. [Soc. Sec. Act § 1834(l)(12)(A); 42 C.F.R. § 414.610(c)(5)(ii).]

Soc. Sec. Act § 1834(l)(13)(A) also provides for temporary increases to ground ambulance services. For covered ground ambulance transports that originate in a rural area or in a rural census tract of a metropolitan statistical area (MSA), the fee schedule amount is increased by 3 percent, and for covered ground ambulance transports that do not originate in a rural area or in a rural census tract of an MSA, the fee schedule amounts are increased by 2 percent. Most recently, MACRA extended these payment add-ons for services furnished through December 31, 2017. [Soc. Sec. Act § 1834(l)(13)(A); 42 C.F.R. § 414.610(c)(1)(ii).]

Productivity adjustment. Section 3401(j) of the Patient Protection and Affordable Care Act (ACA) (P.L. 111-148) amended the annual update under Soc. Sec. Act § 1834(l)(3)(B) to add a productivity adjustment for ambulance services, effective for services in 2011 and later. The productivity adjustment is the same one applied to inpatient hospital services under Soc. Sec. Act § 1886(b)(3)(B)(xi)(II). The application of this productivity adjustment may result in the annual percentage increase being less than 0.0 for a year and may result in payment rates under the ambulance fee schedule for a year being less than such payment rates for the preceding year. [Soc. Sec. Act § 1834(l)(3)(C).]

ESRD beneficiaries. Effective October 1, 2013, the ambulance fee schedule amount normally paid for non-emergency basic life support services to transport beneficiaries with end-stage renal disease for dialysis services is reduced by 10 percent if furnished by a provider or renal dialysis facility. [Soc. Sec. Act § 1834(l)(15); 42 C.F.R. § 414.610(c)(8).]

Transporting more than one patient. The allowable amount per beneficiary for a single ambulance transport when more than one patient is transported simultaneously is based on the total number of patients (both Medicare and non-Medicare) on board:

(1) If two patients are transported at the same time in one ambulance to the same destination, the adjusted payment allowance for each Medicare beneficiary is 75 percent of the single-patient allowed amount applicable to the level of service furnished a beneficiary, plus 50 percent of the total mileage payment allowance for the entire trip.

(2) If three or more patients are transported at the same time in one ambulance to the same destination, the adjusted payment for each Medicare beneficiary is 60 percent of the single-patient allowed amount applicable to the level of service furnished that beneficiary. A single payment allowance for mileage, however, will be prorated by the number of patients on board.

[42 C.F.R. § 414.610(c)(6); *Medicare Benefit Policy Manual*, Pub. 100-02, Ch. 10, § 10.3.10.]

"Patient Transportation"

Ambulance services are separately reimbursable only under Part B. Once a beneficiary is admitted to a hospital, CAH, or skilled nursing facility (SNF), it may be necessary to transport the beneficiary to another hospital or other site temporarily for specialized care while the beneficiary maintains inpatient status with the original provider. This movement of the patient is considered "patient transportation" and is covered as an inpatient hospital or CAH service under Part A and as a SNF service when the SNF is furnishing it as a covered SNF service and Part A payment is made for that service. Because the service is covered and payable as a beneficiary transportation service under Part A, the service cannot be classified and paid for as an ambulance service under Part B. This includes intra-campus transfers between different departments of the same hospital, even when the departments are located in separate buildings. Such intra-campus transfers are not separately payable under the Part B ambulance benefit. [Pub. 100-04, Ch. 15, § 10.4.]

[¶ 882] Payment for Durable Medical Equipment, Prosthetics, Orthotics, and Other Supplies

Medicare pays for durable medical equipment, prosthetics, orthotics, and other supplies (DMEPOS) based on regional fee schedules. Payment for those items equals 80 percent of the lower of the actual charge for the durable medical equipment (DME) or the fee schedule amount. [Soc. Sec. Act §§ 1834(a)(1), 1834(h)(1).]

Productivity adjustment. Pursuant to § 3401(m) of the Patient Protection and Affordable Care Act (ACA) (P.L. 111-148), for 2011 and later, the annual payment update for DME is reduced by the productivity adjustment applicable to hospital inpatient services. The application of this productivity adjustment may result in the annual percentage increase being less than 0.0 for a year and may result in payment rates for DME for a year being less than such payment rates for the preceding year. [Soc. Sec. Act § 1834(a)(14)(L) and (h)(4).]

Fee schedule classes. DMEPOS are categorized into the following classes, with a separate fee schedule for each class:

- inexpensive or routinely purchased items;
- items requiring frequent and substantial servicing;
- certain customized items;
- oxygen and oxygen equipment;
- prosthetic and orthotic devices;
- capped rental items; and
- transcutaneous electrical nerve stimulants (TENS) units.

[Soc. Sec. Act § 1834(a); 42 C.F.R. § 414.210(b).]

Blood-testing strips and glucose monitors. The payment amount for diabetic testing supplies, including test strips, that are not mail-order items are the same as the single payment amounts established under the national mail order competition for diabetic supplies under Soc. Sec. Act § 1847, when such single payment amounts are implemented. [Soc. Sec. Act § 1834(a)(1)(H).]

Maintenance, Servicing, and Replacement of DME

Generally, Medicare pays the reasonable and necessary charges for maintenance and servicing of beneficiary-owned equipment. Reasonable and necessary charges are those made for parts and labor not otherwise covered under a manufacturer's or supplier's warranty. The contractor establishes a reasonable fee for labor associated with repairing, maintaining, and servicing the item. Payment is made for replacement parts in a lump sum based on the contractor's consideration of the item. [42 C.F.R. § 414.210(e)(1).]

Exceptions. No payments are made for maintenance and servicing of the following: (1) items requiring frequent and substantial servicing; (2) capped rental items that are not beneficiary owned; and (3) oxygen equipment. [42 C.F.R. § 414.210(e)(3).]

Replacement. If an item of DME or a prosthetic or orthotic device paid for under the DMEPOS fee schedule has been in continuous use by the patient for the equipment's reasonable useful lifetime (of at least five years) or if the contractor determines that the item is lost, stolen, or irreparably damaged, the beneficiary may elect to obtain a new piece of equipment. If the beneficiary elects to obtain replacement oxygen equipment, payment is made in accordance with 42 C.F.R. § 414.226(a). If the beneficiary elects to obtain a replacement capped rental item, payment is made in accordance with 42 C.F.R. § 414.229(a)(2) or (a)(3). For all other beneficiary-owned items, if the beneficiary elects to obtain replacement equipment, payment is made on a purchase basis. [42 C.F.R. § 414.210(f).]

Prior Authorization Process for Certain DME

Pursuant to section 1834(a)(15) of the Social Security Act, the Secretary developed a list of DMEPOS that she determines, on the basis of prior payment experience, are frequently subject to unnecessary utilization, as well as a prior authorization process for these items. [42 C.F.R. § 414.234; *Final rule*, 80 FR 81674, Dec. 30, 2015.]

The Master List of Items Frequently Subject to Unnecessary Utilization includes items listed on the DMEPOS fee schedule with an average purchase fee of $1,000 (adjusted annually for inflation using consumer price index for all urban consumers (CPI-U)) or greater or an average rental fee schedule of $100 (adjusted annually for inflation using CPI-U) or greater that also meet one of the following two criteria:

(1) the item has been identified as having a high rate of fraud or unnecessary utilization in a report that is national in scope from 2007 or later published by the Office of Inspector General or the General Accountability Office; or

(2) the item is listed in the 2011 or later Comprehensive Error Rate Testing (CERT) program's Annual Medicare Fee-For-Service Improper Payment Rate Report DME and/or DMEPOS Service Specific Reports.

The Master List is self-updating annually, and items remain on it for 10 years. [42 C.F.R. § 414.234(b).]

To balance minimizing provider and supplier burden with CMS's need to protect the Medicare program, CMS is initially implementing prior authorization for a subset of items on the Master List. CMS publishes in the *Federal Register* and posts on the CMS prior authorization website a list of items, the Required Prior Authorization List, which is selected from the Master List, that require prior authorization as a condition of payment. [42 C.F.R. § 414.234(c); *Final rule*, 80 FR 81674, Dec. 30, 2015.]

Before furnishing the item and submitting the claim for processing, a prior authorization requester must submit evidence that the item complies with all applicable Medicare coverage, coding, and payment rules. After receipt of all applicable required Medicare documentation, CMS or one of its review contractors will conduct a medical review and communicate a decision that provisionally affirms or non-affirms the request. A provisional affirmation prior authorization decision is a condition of payment. [42 C.F.R. § 414.234(d), (e).]

Competitive Acquisition Program

For items furnished on or after January 1, 2011, the DME fee schedule amounts may be adjusted, and for items furnished on or after January 1, 2016, the fee schedule amounts must be adjusted, based on information on the payment determined as part of implementation of the competitive bidding programs for certain DMEPOS items, as required by Soc. Sec. Act § 1847(a) and (b) (excluding information on the payment determined in accordance with the special payment rules at 42 C.F.R. § 414.409). If adjustments do occur, inherent reasonableness will not apply. [42 C.F.R. § 414.210(g).]

Inexpensive or Routinely Purchased Items

DME is "inexpensive" if the average purchase price of it did not exceed $150 from July 1986 through June 1987. DME is routinely purchased if it was acquired by purchase on a national basis at least 75 percent of the time from July 1986 through June 1987. Included in the definition of inexpensive or routinely purchased equipment are accessories used in conjunction with a nebulizer, aspirator, or ventilator that is either a continuous airway pressure device or a respiratory assist device with bi-level pressure capability. [Soc. Sec. Act § 1834(a)(2)(A); 42 C.F.R. § 414.220(a); *Medicare Claims Processing Manual*, Pub. 100-04, Ch. 20, § 130.2.]

Payment for inexpensive or routinely purchased items is made on a rental basis or in a lump-sum purchase amount that is based on the national limited payment amount (the cost of purchasing the DME in a national market), as updated by changes in the Consumer Price

Index. If rental rather than lump-sum purchase is chosen, the total amount of rental payments may not exceed the allowed lump-sum purchase amount. [Soc. Sec. Act § 1834(a)(2)(B)(iv), (C); 42 C.F.R. § 414.220(b); Pub. 100-04, Ch. 20, § 30.1.]

Payment for TENS units is made on a purchase basis with the purchase price determined using the methodology for purchase of inexpensive or routinely purchased items. The payment amount for TENS computed under 42 C.F.R. § 414.220(c)(2), however, is reduced. [Soc. Sec. Act § 1834(a)(1)(D); 42 C.F.R. § 414.232(a).]

Customized Items

To be considered a customized item for payment purposes, a covered item (including a wheelchair) must be uniquely constructed or substantially modified for a specific beneficiary according to the description and orders of a physician and be so different from another item used for the same purpose that the two items cannot be grouped together for pricing purposes. [Soc. Sec. Act § 1834(a)(4); 42 C.F.R. § 414.224(a).]According to the *Medicare Claims Processing Manual*, customized items are rarely necessary and rarely furnished. [Pub. 100-04, Ch. 20, § 130.4.]

Payment is made on a lump sum basis for the purchase of a customized item based on the DME Medicare administrative contractor's (MAC) individual consideration and judgment of a reasonable payment amount for each customized item. The MAC's individual consideration takes into account written documentation on the costs of the item including at least the cost of labor and materials used in customizing an item. [Soc. Sec. Act § 1834(a)(4); 42 C.F.R. § 414.224(b).]

Oxygen and Oxygen Equipment

National limited monthly payment rates are calculated and paid as the monthly fee schedule amounts for the following classes of items: (1) stationary oxygen equipment (including stationary concentrators) and oxygen contents (stationary and portable), (2) portable equipment only (gaseous or liquid tanks), (3) oxygen generating portable equipment only, (4) stationary oxygen contents only, and (5) portable oxygen contents only. [42 C.F.R. § 414.226(c)(1).]

Medicare pays for rental of oxygen equipment based on a monthly fee schedule amount during the period of medical need, but for no longer than a period of continuous use of 36 months. Medicare does not pay for purchases of this type of equipment. [Soc. Sec. Act § 1834(a)(5); 42 C.F.R. § 414.226(a)(1), (d)(1) and (2); Pub. 100-04, Ch. 20, §§ 30.6, 30.6.2.]

Medicare pays for purchase of oxygen contents based on a monthly fee schedule amount until medical necessity ends. [42 C.F.R. § 414.226(a)(2), (d)(3) and (4); Pub. 100-04, Ch. 20, § 30.6.3.]

Payment for oxygen equipment after rental cap. A supplier that furnishes oxygen equipment after the 36-month rental cap must (1) continue to furnish the equipment during any period of medical need for the remainder of the reasonable useful lifetime of the equipment in accordance with 42 C.F.R. § 414.210(f)(1); or (2) arrange for furnishing the oxygen equipment with another supplier if the beneficiary relocates to an area outside the supplier's normal service area. [Soc. Sec. Act § 1834(a)(5)(F)(ii); 42 C.F.R. § 414.226(f)(1).]

A supplier that furnishes liquid or gaseous oxygen equipment (stationary or portable) for the 36th continuous month must (1) continue to furnish the oxygen contents necessary for the effective use of the liquid or gaseous equipment during any period of medical need for the remainder of the reasonable useful lifetime established for the equipment in accordance with 42 C.F.R. § 414.210(f)(1); or (2) arrange for furnishing the oxygen contents with another supplier if the beneficiary relocates to an area outside the supplier's normal service area. [Soc. Sec. Act § 1834(a)(5)(F)(ii); 42 C.F.R. § 414.226(f)(2).]

For the first six-month period after the 36-month rental period ends, the contractor makes no payment for maintenance and servicing of oxygen equipment other than liquid and gaseous equipment (stationary and portable). For each succeeding six-month period, payment may be made during the first month of that period for routine maintenance and servicing of the equipment in the beneficiary's home (including an institution used as the beneficiary's home). The supplier must visit the beneficiary's home to inspect the equipment during the first month of the six-month period. [42 C.F.R. § 414.210(e)(5).]

Capped Rental Items

For rented DME not subject to the payment provisions of 42 C.F.R. §§ 414.220 through 414.228, during the first three months of use, payment is limited to 10 percent of the "recognized purchase price"; thereafter, payment is limited to 7.5 percent of the recognized purchase price. [Soc. Sec. Act § 1834(a)(7)(A)(i)(II); 42 C.F.R. § 414.229(b)(2); Pub. 100-04, Ch. 20, § 30.5.1.]

For power-driven wheelchairs, payment equals 15 percent of the recognized purchase price for the first three months and 6 percent of the recognized purchase price for the remaining months. [Soc. Sec. Act § 1834(a)(7)(A)(i)(III); 42 C.F.R. § 414.229(b)(3).]

The purchase price is based on the national limited payment amount (the cost of purchasing the DME in a national market), as updated by changes in the Consumer Price Index. [Soc. Sec. Act § 1834(a)(8); 42 C.F.R. § 414.229(c)(3).]

Replacement. If the reasonable lifetime (five years) of an item has been reached during a continuous period of medical need, or the contractor determines that the item is lost or irreparably damaged, payment for replacement may be made on either a rental or a purchase basis. [Soc. Sec. Act § 1834(a)(7)(C); Pub. 100-04, Ch. 20, § 50.1.]

Complex rehabilitative power-driven wheelchairs. Suppliers must offer beneficiaries the option to purchase complex rehabilitative power-driven wheelchairs at the time the equipment is initially furnished. Medicare pays on a lump-sum purchase basis if the beneficiary chooses this option. [Soc. Sec. Act § 1834(a)(7)(A)(iii); 42 C.F.R. § 414.229(d)(1), (h).]

Ownership after rental. Medicare pays for most capped rental items during the period of medical need, but no longer than a period of continuous use of 13 months. On the first day after the 13th continuous month, the supplier must transfer title of the item to the beneficiary. [Soc. Sec. Act § 1834(a)(7)(A)(i)(I), (ii); 42 C.F.R. § 414.229(f).]

Prosthetic Devices and Prosthetics/Orthotics

Medicare pays for prosthetic devices (excluding parenteral and enteral nutrition, nutrients, supplies, and equipment) and prosthetics and orthotics (excluding intraocular lenses and medical supplies furnished by a home health agency) on a lump sum basis. [Soc. Sec. Act § 1834(h)(1)(A), (4); 42 C.F.R. § 414.228(a); Pub. 100-04, Ch. 20, § 30.4.] Ostomy supplies, tracheostomy supplies, and urologicals are reimbursed as inexpensive or other routinely purchased DME under Soc. Sec. Act § 1834(a)(2). [Soc. Sec. Act § 1834(h)(1)(E).]

The payment rules of Soc. Sec. Act § 1834(h) apply to reimbursement for therapeutic shoes for diabetics. [Soc. Sec. Act § 1833(o)(2); 42 C.F.R. § 414.228(c).]

Parenteral and Enteral Nutrition, Splints, Casts, and Certain Intraocular Lenses

For parenteral and enteral nutrition (PEN) items and services, splints and casts, and intraocular lenses (IOLs) inserted in a physician's office on or after April 1, 2014, Medicare pays for the items and services on the basis of 80 percent of the lesser of: (1) the actual charge for the item or service; or (2) the fee schedule amount for the item or service, as determined in accordance with 42 C.F.R. §§414.104 through 414.108. [Soc. Sec. Act § 1842(s)(2); 42 C.F.R. § 414.102(a).]

CMS or the contractor determines fee schedules for these items, and CMS designates the specific items and services in each category through program instructions. For 2011 and later for PEN items and services and for 2015 and later for splints and casts and IOLs inserted in a physician's office, the fee schedule amounts of the preceding year are updated by the percentage increase in the CPI-U for the 12-month period ending with June of the preceding year. [Soc. Sec. Act § 1842(s)(1)(B)(ii); 42 C.F.R. § 414.102(b), (c).]

PEN. Payment is made in a lump sum for PEN nutrients and supplies that are purchased and on a monthly basis for equipment that is rented. The fee schedule amounts may be adjusted based on information on the payment determined as part of the DME competitive acquisition program using the methodologies described in 42 C.F.R. § 414.210(g). [Soc. Sec. Act § 1842(s)(3); 42 C.F.R. §§414.104(a), 414.105; Pub. 100-04, Ch. 20, § 30.7.]

Splints and casts. Medicare pays for splints and casts in a lump sum. The fee schedule amount for payment for an item or service furnished in 2014 was the reasonable charge amount for 2013, updated by the percentage increase in the CPI-U for the 12-month period ending with June of 2013. [42 C.F.R. § 414.106; Pub. 100-04, Ch. 20, § 170.]

Certain IOLs. Medicare pays for IOLs inserted in a physician's office in a lump sum. The fee schedule amount for payment for an IOL furnished in 2014 was the national average allowed charge for the IOL furnished in calendar year 2012, updated by the percentage increase in the CPI-U for the 24-month period ending with June of 2013. [42 C.F.R. § 414.108.]

[¶ 885] Payment for Drugs and Biologicals

Payment for drugs (other than prescription drugs) furnished by physicians usually is based on the lower of the actual charge or the manufacturer's average sales price (ASP). This payment policy is applicable to drugs furnished to Medicare beneficiaries that are not "paid for on a cost or prospective payment basis." [Soc. Sec. Act §§1842(o), 1847A; 42 C.F.R. §§414.900, 414.904; *Medicare Claims Processing Manual*, Pub. 100-04, Ch. 17, §20.1.]

Drugs furnished incident to a physician's services fall within this category. [42 C.F.R. §§405.517(a)(3), 414.36.]Incident-to services and supplies are defined as services and supplies (including drugs and biologicals that are not usually self-administered by the patient) furnished as an incident to a physician's professional service that commonly are furnished in physicians' offices and either rendered without charge or included in the physicians' bills. [Soc. Sec. Act § 1861(s)(2)(A).] See ¶ 855 for an explanation of Part B payment for incident-to items and services.

Outpatient surgery. Beginning January 1, 2014, the following are packaged into the outpatient prospective payment system (OPPS) rate:

- drugs, biologicals, and radiopharmaceuticals that function as supplies when used in a diagnostic test or procedure (including, but not limited to, diagnostic radiopharmaceuticals, contrast agents, and pharmacologic stress agents); and

- drugs and biologicals that function as supplies when used in a surgical procedure (including, but not limited to, skin substitutes and similar products that aid wound healing and implantable biological).

[42 C.F.R. § 419.2(b).]

Assignment. All billing for drugs and biologicals covered under Part B must be on an assignment-related basis. Sanctions may be imposed against violators. [Soc. Sec. Act § 1842(o)(3).]

Use of Average Sales Price Methodology

The payment allowance limit for Medicare Part B drugs and biologicals that are not paid on a cost or prospective payment basis is 106 percent of the ASP. [42 C.F.R. § 414.904(a)(2).]

The payment allowance limits for end-stage renal disease (ESRD) drugs when separately billed by freestanding and hospital-based ESRD facilities, specified covered outpatient drugs, and drugs and biologicals with pass-through status under the OPPS are paid based on 106 percent of the ASP. [42 C.F.R. § 414.904(d)(2); Pub. 100-04, Ch. 17, § 20.1.2.]

Except for infusion drugs, payment limits are updated quarterly. The payment amount is subject to coinsurance and deductibles. [Soc. Sec. Act § 1847A(b)(5); 42 C.F.R. § 414.904(f), (h).]

Price substitution. When the Inspector General finds that the ASP exceeds the widely available market price (WAMP) or the average manufacturer price (AMP) by an applicable threshold percentage, CMS must substitute the payment amount for the drug or biological. [42 C.F.R. § 414.904(d)(3).]

Payment at 103 percent of the AMP for a billing code will occur when the following conditions are met:

(1) the ASP for the billing code has exceeded the AMP for the billing code by 5 percent or more in two consecutive quarters, or three of the previous four quarters immediately preceding the quarter to which the price substitution would be applied;

(2) the AMP for the billing code is calculated using the same set of National Drug Codes used for the ASP for the billing code;

(3) 103 percent of the AMP is less than the 106 percent of the ASP for the quarter in which the price substitution would be applied; and

(4) the drug and dosage form represented by the Healthcare Common Procedure Coding System (HCPCS) code are not reported by the Food and Drug Administration (FDA) on its Current Drug Shortage List to be in short supply at the time the ASP payment limits are finalized.

[42 C.F.R. § 414.904(d)(3).]

The applicable percentage threshold for AMP price comparisons is 5 percent. [42 C.F.R. § 414.904(d)(3)(iv).]

Exceptions to the ASP. The following exceptions to the ASP apply:

• The payment limits for hepatits B vaccine furinshed to individuals at high or intermediate risk of contracting hepatitis B, pneumococcal vaccine, and influenza vaccine are calculated using 95 percent of the AWP.

• The payment limits for infusion drugs furnished through a covered item of durable medical equipment (DME) is calculated using 95 percent of the AWP in effect on October 1, 2003.

• For blood and blood products (other than clotting factors), the payment limits are determined in the same manner as they were determined October 1, 2003.

• For an initial period, if data on the sale prices for drugs is not sufficiently available to compute the ASP, the payment limit is based on the wholesale acquisition cost or the applicable Part B drug methodology in effect on October 1, 2003.

[Soc. Sec. Act § 1847A(b)(4); 42 C.F.R. § 414.90(e); Pub. 100-04, Ch. 17, § 20.1.3.]

¶885

Chapter 9– CLAIMS, PAYMENTS, AND APPEALS

[¶ 900] Claims and Payments

Medicare defines a claim as a filing from a provider, supplier, or beneficiary that includes or refers to a beneficiary's request for Medicare payment and furnishes the Medicare administrative contractor (MAC) with sufficient information to determine whether payment of Medicare benefits is due and the payment amount. [42 C.F.R. §§ 424.5(a)(5), (6).] A claim must contain sufficient identifying information about the beneficiary to allow any missing information to be obtained through routine methods, such as a file check, microfilm reference, mail, or telephone contact based on an address or telephone number in the file. [*Medicare Claims Processing Manual*, Pub. 100-04, Ch. 1, § 50.1.7.]

Payments under Part C Medicare Advantage (MA) plans and Part D prescription drug plans are not subject to the same requirements for submitting claims for payment and appeals that apply to services provided under Parts A and B. For a detailed discussion of payment and appeals under Part C and Part D, see Chapter 4 and Chapter 5, respectively.

Beneficiary Notices

Providers, physicians, and suppliers are required to notify beneficiaries when they believe that Medicare will not cover charges or when services may be terminated. An Advance Beneficiary Notice (ABN) is evidence of beneficiary knowledge about the likelihood of Medicare denial for the purpose of determining financial liability for expenses incurred for services furnished to a beneficiary, and for which Medicare may not pay. An ABN must: (1) be in writing, using approved notice language; (2) cite the particular service or services for which payment is likely to be denied; and (3) cite the notifier's reasons for believing Medicare payment will be denied. [42 C.F.R. § 411.408(f)(1).]

Beneficiaries may select one of several billing options they prefer when notified by the provider that it anticipates that Medicare will not cover a service. If the beneficiary signs a request for payment using the ABN, the provider is required to submit a claim. The beneficiary becomes fully responsible for payments after being notified that Medicare may not pay the claim. [Pub. 100-04, Ch. 1, § 60.4.1; Ch. 30, § 50.]

Medicare summary notice. After the MAC processes and either approves or denies the claim, it sends the results to the beneficiary in the form of a Medicare summary notice (MSN). The MSN explains which charges were allowed, any deductible or coinsurance amount, and what Medicare paid on the claim and why. It also explains various features of the Medicare program of interest to the beneficiary. If the claim is denied in whole or in part, the MSN provides the procedures for an appeal (see ¶ 924). The beneficiary is responsible for any applicable deductible or coinsurance (for Part A, see ¶ 220). [Soc. Sec. Act § 1806(a); Pub. 100-04, Ch. 21, §§ 10, 10.1.]

Beginning January 1, 2016, beneficiaries can elect to receive MSNs electronically. [Soc. Sec. Act § 1806(c), as added by Medicare Access and CHIP Reauthorization Act of 2015 (MACRA) (P.L. 114-10) § 508(a).]

Submission of Claims

All initial claims for Medicare reimbursement, except claims from small providers, must be submitted electronically (with limited exceptions). Initial Medicare claims are those claims submitted to the appropriate MAC for payment under Part A or Part B for initial processing, including claims sent to Medicare for the first time for secondary payment purposes, resubmitted previously rejected claims, claims with paper attachments, demand bills, claims in situations in which Medicare is secondary and there is only one primary payer, and nonpayment claims. Initial claims do not include adjustments submitted to MACs on previously submitted claims or appeal requests.[Soc. Sec. Act § 1862(a)(22), (h); 42 C.F.R. § 424.32(d)(1)–(3).]

The Secretary may waive the electronic claims submission requirement in unusual cases as the Secretary finds appropriate. Unusual cases are deemed to exist in the following situations: (1) the submission of dental claims; (2) there is a service interruption in the mode of submitting the electronic claim that is outside the control of the entity submitting the claim, for the period of the interruption; (3) the entity submitting the claim submits fewer than 10 claims to Medicare per month, on average; (4) the entity submitting the claim furnishes services outside of the U.S. territory only; or (5) other extraordinary circumstances precluding submission of electronic claims. [42 C.F.R. § 424.32(d)(4); Pub. 100-04, Ch. 24, § 90.]

Every entity that submits electronic claims to the Medicare program is required to complete an Electronic Data Interchange (EDI) Enrollment Form. New electronic billers must sign and submit the enrollment form before their first billing will be accepted. A provider must obtain a National Provider Identifier (NPI) and furnish that NPI to its MAC prior to completion of an initial EDI Enrollment Agreement and issuance of an initial EDI number and password by the MAC. [Pub. 100-04, Ch. 24, § 30.1.]

Part A benefits. Hospitals, skilled nursing facilities (SNFs), home health agencies, hospices, and other providers submit claims for payment for items and services rendered under Part A to the MAC. As discussed at ¶ 730, providers charge beneficiaries for applicable deductible and coinsurance amounts as well as for any noncovered or extra services requested by the beneficiary. When a provider knows or believes that no Medicare payment will be made because of the lack of medical necessity or the service or item is excluded from coverage, the provider must notify the beneficiary in writing in the form of an ABN.

Part B benefits. Physicians, practitioners, durable medical equipment suppliers, or outpatient facilities (physician or supplier) that furnish items or services to beneficiaries covered under Part B are required to complete and submit a claim for payment to a MAC. Beneficiaries may not be charged for this service. [Soc. Sec. Act § 1848(g)(4)(A).] Payment will be made to the physician or supplier if the physician or supplier has accepted assignment (see ¶ 868). Payment will be made to the beneficiary directly if the physician or supplier does not accept assignment. If payment is made to a physician or supplier that is entitled to receive payment on the beneficiary's behalf, the beneficiary is responsible for any applicable deductible or coinsurance requirements (see ¶ 330 and ¶ 335).

Claims forms. Form CMS-1490S, "Patient's Request for Medicare Payment Form," is used only by beneficiaries (or their representatives) who complete and file their own claims. It contains only the first six comparable items of data that are on Form CMS-1500 (provider form). When Form CMS-1490S is used, an itemized bill must be submitted with the claim. Form CMS-1490S is used by beneficiaries to submit Part B claims only if the service provider refuses to do so. [42 C.F.R. § 424.32(b); Pub. 100-04, Ch. 1, § 70.8.4.]

Under Part B, a claim can be any writing submitted by or on behalf of the beneficiary; however, when the writing constituting a Part B claim is not submitted on a claim form, there must be enough information about the nature of the medical or other health service to enable the MAC to determine that the service was furnished by a physician or supplier. [Pub. 100-04, Ch. 1, § 50.1.7.]

Physicians and suppliers (except ambulance suppliers) normally submit requests for payment on Form CMS-1500, the "Health Insurance Claim Form," whether or not the claim is assigned. The form is identical to forms used by other health insurance plans in addition to Medicare. Form CMS-1500 contains a patient's signature line or reference to the patient signature incorporating the patient's request for payment of benefits, authorization to release information, and assignment of benefits. When the billing form is used as the request for payment, there must be a signature, except in limited circumstances. [42 C.F.R. § 424.32(b); Pub. 100-04, Ch. 1, § § 50.1.1, 70.8.4; Ch. 26, § 10.]

Request for Payment Signature Requirements

For an eligible provider of services to receive payment from Medicare for services furnished to a beneficiary under either Part A or Part B, a written request for payment must be signed by the individual who receives the services. [Soc. Sec. Act § § 1814(a)(1); 1835(a)(1); 42 C.F.R. § § 424.32(a)(3), 424.36.]

Signature of beneficiary's representative. If the beneficiary is physically or mentally unable to sign the claim, it may be signed by the following individuals: (1) the beneficiary's legal guardian; (2) a relative or other individual that receives Social Security or other governmental benefits on behalf of the beneficiary; (3) a relative or other person that arranges for the beneficiary's treatment or takes responsibility for the beneficiary's affairs; (4) a representative of an agency or institution that did not furnish the care in question but that did furnish other care for the beneficiary; (5) a representative of the provider or of the nonparticipating hospital providing the services in question if the provider is unable to have the claim signed in another way outlined above after making reasonable efforts; or (6) an ambulance provider or supplier that provided emergency or non-emergency transport services if certain conditions are met. [42 C.F.R. § 424.36(b).]

Beneficiary not present for the service. If a provider, nonparticipating hospital, or supplier files a claim for services that involved no personal contact between the provider, hospital, or supplier and the beneficiary (for example, a physician sent a blood sample to the provider for diagnostic tests), a representative of the provider, hospital, or supplier may sign the claim on the beneficiary's behalf. [42 C.F.R. § 424.36(c); Pub. 100-04, Ch. 1, § 50.1.3.]

Refusal to sign. A patient on admission to a hospital or SNF may refuse to request Medicare payment and agree to pay for the services out of his or her own funds or from other insurance. If the patient refuses to request Medicare payment, the provider should obtain a signed statement of refusal whenever possible. If the patient is unwilling to sign the statement of refusal, the provider should record that the patient refused to file a request for payment and was unwilling to sign the statement of refusal. [Pub. 100-04, Ch. 1, § 50.1.5.]

Death of beneficiary. If the patient dies before the request for payment is signed, it may be signed by the legal representative of the estate or by any of the persons or institutions (including an authorized official of the provider) who could have signed it had the patient been alive and incompetent. [Pub. 100-04, Ch. 1, § 50.1.3.]

Time Limits

Claims must be submitted no later than one calendar year after the date of service. Claims with dates of service received later than one calendar year beyond the date of service will be denied by Medicare, unless an exception applies. [Soc. Sec. Act § § 1814(a)(1), 1835(a)(1); 42 C.F.R. § 424.44(a)(1).]

Exceptions to the one-year time limit. Medicare regulations allow for the following exceptions to the one calendar year time limit for filing fee-for-service claims: (1) administrative error; (2) retroactive Medicare entitlement; (3) retroactive Medicare entitlement involving state Medicaid agencies; and (4) retroactive disenrollment from a Medicare Advantage

(MA) plan or Program of All-inclusive Care for the Elderly (PACE) provider organization. [42 C.F.R. § 424.44(b).]

When a provider or supplier makes the initial request for an exception to the timely filing limit, the MAC must determine whether a late claim may be honored based on all pertinent documentation submitted by the provider or supplier. [Pub. 100-04, Ch. 1, § 70.7.]

Prompt Payment of Claims

MACs are required to pay not less than 95 percent of all "clean claims" within 30 days after the clean claims are received. A clean claim is a claim for which payment is not made on a periodic interim payment basis, and one that has no defect, impropriety, or particular circumstance requiring special treatment that prevents timely payment from being made. [Soc. Sec. Act §§ 1816(c)(2)(A) and (B), 1842(c)(2)(A) and (B); Pub. 100-04, Ch. 1, § 80.2.]

If a clean claim payment is not issued, mailed, or otherwise transmitted within the specified time period, the government will be required to pay interest on the amount of payment it should have made, beginning with the day after the required payment date and ending on the date on which the payment is made. [Soc. Sec. Act §§ 1816(c)(2)(C), 1842(c)(2)(C); Pub. 100-04, Ch. 1, § 80.2.2.]

MACs are prohibited from paying electronic claims within 13 days after their receipt. As an incentive to encourage health care providers to submit claims electronically, this prohibition on payment is expanded to 28 days for all other claims. [Soc. Sec. Act §§ 1816(c)(3)(A) and (B), 1842(c)(3)(A) and (B).]

[¶ 902] Certification and Recertification

Medicare requires, as a condition of coverage, that the physician who ordered the services certify on the claim form that the services were medically necessary and, in some instances, recertify that the services continue to be required. [42 C.F.R. §§ 424.10(a), 424.13.]

When a certification or recertification is required, it is the responsibility of the provider to obtain the physician's certifying statement. [42 C.F.R. § 424.5(a)(4).] In the case of services furnished by an institutional provider, the provider must have available on file a written description that specifies the time schedule for certifications and recertifications and indicates whether utilization review of long-stay cases fulfills the requirement for second and subsequent recertifications. [42 C.F.R. §§ 424.13(g), 424.14(e), 424.20(g).]

In certain instances, nonphysician practitioners such as nurse practitioners, clinical nurse specialists, or physician assistants may certify as to medical necessity. The content requirements and time factors related to certifications and recertifications vary according to the items or services furnished and the facility or institution furnishing them. [Soc. Sec. Act § 1814(a)(2).]

Requirements for Part A

Various certification and recertification requirements apply to Part A providers.

Psychiatric hospitals. For psychiatric hospital services, a physician must certify that inpatient services under the supervision of a physician were required and that (1) such treatment can or can be reasonably expected to improve the condition; or (2) inpatient diagnostic study is or was necessary and such services were necessary for such purposes. [Soc. Sec. Act § 1814(a)(2)(A).]

Inpatient hospital services. For inpatient hospital services other than psychiatric hospital services, a physician must certify that such services were required to be given on an inpatient basis for the individual's medical treatment or that inpatient diagnostic study is required and such services are necessary for those purposes. However, such certification should be limited to only such cases and accompanied by supporting materials. The certification for such services must be furnished no later than the 20th day of such services. [Soc. Sec. Act § 1814 (a) (3).]

Skilled nursing facilities. Certification and recertification for skilled nursing facility (SNF) services must indicate that the services are or were required to be given because the individual needs or needed, on a daily basis, skilled nursing care (provided directly by or requiring the supervision of skilled nursing personnel) or other skilled rehabilitation services that, as a practical matter, can be provided only in a SNF or a swing-bed hospital on an inpatient basis, for any of the conditions with respect to which the individual received covered inpatient hospital services. [Soc. Sec. Act § 1814 (a) (2) (B); 42 C.F.R. § 424.20.]

Home health. For home health services, a physician must certify that such services were required because the individual is or was confined to the home (except when receiving items or services pursuant to Soc. Sec. Act § 1861 (m) (7)) and needs or needed skilled nursing care (other than solely venipucture for the purposes of obtaining a blood sample) on an intermittent basis or physical or speech therapy, or in the case of an individual who has been furnished home health services based on such a need and who no longer has such a need for such care or therapy, continues or continued to need occupational therapy. [Soc. Sec. Act § § 1814 (a) (2) (C), 1835 (a) (2) (A); 42 C.F.R. § 424.22.]

No payment can be made for covered home health services unless the physician who established the plan of care documents that a face-to-face encounter has occurred no more than 90 days before the home health start of care or within 30 days of the start of home health care and certifies to the necessity for home health services and, when services are to continue for a period of time, recertifies as to the continued need for services. The face-to-face encounter may occur through telehealth. [Soc. Sec. Act § 1835 (a) (2) (A); 42 C.F.R. § 424.22.] See ¶ 260.

Hospice. For hospice care to be covered by Medicare, the beneficiary's attending physician and the medical director of the hospice must each certify in the first 90-day period that the beneficiary is terminally ill, i.e., that the medical prognosis is that the individual's life expectancy is six months or less if the terminal illness runs its normal course. For a subsequent 90- or 60-day period, the medical director or physician must recertify at the beginning of the period that the individual is terminally ill. [Soc. Sec. Act § 1814 (a) (7) (A); 42 C.F.R. § 418.22.]

A hospice physician or hospice nurse practitioner must have a face-to-face encounter with each hospice patient whose total stay across all hospices is anticipated to reach the third benefit period. The face-to-face encounter must occur prior to, but no more than 30 calendar days prior to, the third benefit period recertification, and every benefit period recertification thereafter, to gather clinical findings to determine continued eligibility for hospice care. [Soc. Sec. Act § 1814 (a) (7) (D); 42 C.F.R. § 418.22 (a) (4).]

Critical access hospital. A physician must certify that an individual is reasonably expected to be discharged from a critical access hospital (CAH) or transferred to another hospital within 96 hours of the date of admission to the CAH for the services to be covered under Medicare Part A. That certification is required no less than one day before the claim for payment for such services is submitted. [42 C.F.R. § 424.15.]

Requirements for Part B

Generally, a physician's certification and recertification is required for all Part B medical and other health services except: (1) hospital services and supplies incident to physicians' services rendered to outpatients, including drugs and biologicals that cannot be self-administered, and (2) outpatient hospital diagnostic services, including necessary drugs and biologicals ordinarily furnished or arranged for by a hospital for the purpose of diagnostic study. [Soc. Sec. Act § 1835(a)(2)(B); 42 C.F.R. § 424.24(a), (g).]

Blood glucose. For each blood glucose test the physician must certify that the test is medically necessary. A physician's standing order is not sufficient to order a series of blood glucose tests payable under the clinical laboratory fee schedule. [42 C.F.R. § 424.24(f).]

Partial hospitalization services. The physician must certify that the individual would require inpatient psychiatric care if the partial hospitalization services were not provided and that the services were furnished under an individualized written plan of treatment while the individual was under the care of a physician. The plan sets forth: (1) the physician's diagnosis; (2) the type, amount, duration, and frequency of the services; and (3) the treatment goals. [Soc. Sec. Act § 1835(a)(2)(F); 42 C.F.R. § 424.24(e).]

Physical and occupational therapy and speech-language pathology services. The physician must certify (and recertify, when appropriate) that the patient needs or needed physical therapy (including occupational therapy) or speech-language pathology services while the patient is under the care of a physician, nurse practitioner, clinical nurse specialist, or physician assistant, and that the services were furnished under a plan of treatment. [Soc. Sec. Act §§ 1835(a)(2)(C), (D); 42 C.F.R. § 424.24(c).]

Comprehensive outpatient rehabilitation facility services. For payment to be made for comprehensive outpatient rehabilitation facility services, a physician must certify (and recertify, when appropriate) that: (1) the services were required because the individual needed skilled rehabilitation services; (2) the services were furnished while the individual was under the care of a physician; and (3) a written plan of treatment has been established and is reviewed periodically by a physician. [Soc. Sec. Act § 1835(a)(2)(E); 42 C.F.R. § 424.27.]

Durable medical equipment. For durable medical equipment (DME) items that appear on a list of specified covered items that CMS updates annually in the *Federal Register*, the physician must document that the physician, a physician assistant, a nurse practitioner, or a clinical nurse specialist had a face-to-face encounter (including through telehealth) with the individual within six months before an order for DME is written. [42 C.F.R. § 410.38(g).]

[¶ 904] Guarantee of Payment to Hospitals

Under the guarantee of payment provisions, if a hospital or critical access hospital (CAH) acted reasonably and in good faith and did not have knowledge that an individual was not entitled to Medicare benefits but instead assumed that entitlement existed, the hospital or CAH may be paid for: (1) inpatient hospital services furnished to a beneficiary whose eligibility for inpatient hospital benefit days has been exhausted, or (2) inpatient psychiatric hospital services after the 190-day psychiatric lifetime benefit has been exhausted. [Soc. Sec. Act § 1814(e); *Medicare Benefit Policy Manual*, Pub. 100-02, Ch. 5, § 10.1.]

The guarantee provisions are not applicable until the individual has exhausted his or her 60-day lifetime reserve days for inpatient hospital services except in situations in which the beneficiary is deemed to have elected not to use lifetime reserve days. In these cases, the guarantee of payment generally applies because the reserve days cannot be used. [Soc. Sec. Act § 1814(e); Pub. 100-02, Ch. 5, § 10.1.]

Conditions for payment. Payment may be made for inpatient hospital or inpatient CAH services furnished to a beneficiary after he or she has exhausted the available benefit days if the following conditions are met:

(1) The services were furnished before CMS or the Medicare contractor notified the hospital or CAH that the beneficiary had exhausted the available benefit days and was not entitled to have payment made for those services.

(2) At the time the hospital or CAH furnished the services, it was unaware that the beneficiary had exhausted the available benefit days and could reasonably have assumed that he or she was entitled to have payment made for these services.

(3) Payment would be precluded solely because the beneficiary has no benefit days available for the particular hospital or CAH stay.

(4) The hospital or CAH claims reimbursement for the services and refunds any payments made for those services by the beneficiary or by another person on his or her behalf.

[42 C.F.R. § 409.68.]

Limitation on payment. Payment cannot be made if the hospital has received prior notification that all days of entitlement have been used and, in any event, payment cannot be made beyond the sixth day after the day of admission to the hospital (excluding Saturdays, Sundays, and legal holidays). [Soc. Sec. Act § 1814(e); 42 C.F.R. § 409.68(b).] Benefits paid to a hospital under the guarantee provision are subject to recovery from the beneficiary or third-party payers in the same way as other overpayments are subject to recovery. [Soc. Sec. Act § 1870; 42 C.F.R. § 409.68(c).]

The guarantee of payment provisions extend to inpatient services furnished to individuals who have exhausted their eligibility for inpatient hospital services, but they do not extend to individuals who have no coverage for other reasons; for example, hospitals are not guaranteed payment by Medicare when an individual is not entitled under hospital insurance or when entitlement has been terminated. [Pub. 100-02, Ch. 5, § 10.1.]

[¶ 905] Payments on Behalf of a Deceased Beneficiary

When a beneficiary dies after receiving covered Part B services for which reimbursement is due but before reimbursement has been made, if the beneficiary has assigned the right to payment before his or her death, the provider or supplier of such services may be reimbursed under the agreement. [42 C.F.R. § 424.64.]

Beneficiary dies and bill has been paid. If a beneficiary has received covered services for which he or she could receive direct payment under 42 C.F.R. § 424.53 but dies without receiving Medicare payment and the bill has been paid, Medicare pays the following people in the specified circumstances:

- The person or persons who, without a legal obligation to do so, paid for the services with their own funds, before or after the beneficiary's death.

- The legal representative of the beneficiary's estate if the services were paid for by the beneficiary before he or she died, or with funds from the estate.

- If the deceased beneficiary or his or her estate paid for the services and no legal representative of the estate has been appointed, the survivors, in order of priority.

- If none of the specified relatives survive, no payment is made.

- If the services were paid for by a person other than the deceased beneficiary, and that person died before payment was completed, Medicare does not pay that person's estate. Medicare pays a surviving relative of the deceased beneficiary in accordance with the priorities referenced above. If none of those relatives survive, Medicare pays the legal representative of the deceased beneficiary's estate. If there is no legal representative of the estate, no payment is made.

[Soc. Sec. Act § 1870(e); 42 C.F.R. § 424.62(b), (c).]

For a payment to be made to the person other than the beneficiary, the person who claims payment must: (1) submit a claim on a CMS-prescribed form and include an itemized bill; (2) provide evidence that the services were furnished if the Medicare contractor requests it; and (3) provide evidence of payment of the bill and the identity of the person who paid it. Evidence of payment includes: a receipted bill or a properly completed "Report of Services" section of a claim form showing who paid the bill; a cancelled check; a written statement from the provider or supplier or an authorized staff member; or other probative evidence. [42 C.F.R. § 424.62(e), (f).]

Request for payment signed on behalf of a deceased beneficiary. If a patient dies before he or she can sign the request for payment for Part A or Part B services, the request may be signed on his or her behalf by the legal representative of his or her estate or by a representative payee (a person designated by the Social Security Administration or other governmental agency to receive an incompetent beneficiary's monthly cash benefits), relative, friend, representative of an institution providing him or her care or support, or by a governmental agency providing assistance. Claims for Part B services may be filed by physicians and suppliers without a request for payment signed by the beneficiary when the beneficiary is deceased, the bill is unpaid, and the physician or supplier agrees to accept the Medicare-approved amount as the full charge. [42 C.F.R. § 424.62; *Medicare Claims Processing Manual*, Pub. 100-04, Ch. 1, §§ 50.1.3 and 50.1.6.]

[¶ 906] Overpayments and Underpayments

Overpayments are Medicare payments a provider or beneficiary has received in excess of amounts due and payable under the statute and regulations. Overpayments are defined as "any funds that a person receives or retains under Medicare or Medicaid to which the person, after applicable reconciliation, is not entitled under such title." [Soc. Sec. Act § 1128J(d)(4)(B).]

Providers, suppliers, Medicare Advantage organizations, prescription drug sponsors, and Medicaid managed care organizations that receive an overpayment from Medicare or Medicaid must, by the later of 60 days after the date the overpayment was identified or the date any corresponding cost report is due: (1) report and return the overpayment to the Secretary of HHS, CMS, the state, or Medicare administrative contractor (MAC), as appropriate, and (2) provide written notification of the reason for the overpayment. [Soc. Sec. Act § 1128J(d).]

The report, return, and notice must be made by the later of 60 days after the date the overpayment was identified or the date any corresponding cost report is due. [Soc. Sec. Act § 1128J(d)(3).]

Once a determination of an overpayment has been made, the amount is a debt owed by the debtor to the United States government. [Soc. Sec. Act § 1128J(d); *Medicare Financial Management Manual*, Pub. 100-06, Ch. 3, § 10.]

The requirement to report and return overpayments is enforced under the False Claims Act (FCA), which means that the retention of an overpayment beyond the 60-day period exposes a provider to civil money penalties plus treble damages and penalties, even if the provider voluntarily discloses and repays the overpayment after the 60-day period has elapsed. Exposure to the penalties under the FCA exists only if the provider "knew" of the overpayment for more than 60 days. Under the FCA, "knowingly" is defined to include reckless disregard and deliberate ignorance. [Soc. Sec. Act § 1128J(d)(3); 31 U.S.C. § 3729; 28 C.F.R. § 85.3.] In addition, the Office of Inspector General's (OIG) permissive exclusion authority has been expanded to include individuals or entities that know of an overpayment and do not report and return it. [Soc. Sec. Act § 1128A(a)(10).]

Examples of individual overpayment cases include: (1) payment for provider, supplier, or physician services after benefits have been exhausted, or when the individual was not entitled to benefits; (2) incorrect application of the deductible or coinsurance; (3) payment for noncovered items and services, including medically unnecessary services or custodial care furnished to an individual; (4) payment based on a charge that exceeds the reasonable charge; (5) duplicate processing of charges or claims; (6) payment to a physician on a nonassigned claim or to a beneficiary on an assigned claim (payment made to wrong payee); (7) primary payment for items or services for which another entity is the primary payer; and (8) payment for items or services rendered during a period of nonentitlement. [Pub. 100-06, Ch. 3, § 10.2.]

Beneficiary Liability for Overpayments

The law provides that any Medicare payment made for a beneficiary's benefit will be considered a payment to the beneficiary, even if the payment is received by someone other than the beneficiary. Accordingly, if the MAC determines that the overpayment cannot be recouped from the provider, physician, or supplier or that provider the provider, physician, or supplier was without fault with respect to the overpayment, the beneficiary then becomes liable. A provider is deemed to be without fault if, in the absence of evidence to the contrary, more than the correct amount was paid was made subsequent to the fifth year following the year in which notice was sent to such individual that such amount had been paid. [Soc. Sec. Act § 1870(a), (b); 42 C.F.R. § 405.350.]

If payment is made directly to the beneficiary, liability always lies with the beneficiary unless recovery is waived under the limitation of liability provision. [Pub. 100-06, Ch. 3, § 70.]

Recovery from beneficiary. In a recovery action, the Secretary will make the proper adjustment by: (1) decreasing any Social Security (or Railroad Retirement) benefits to which the individual is entitled; (2) requiring the individual or his estate to refund the amount in excess of the correct amount; (3) decreasing any Social Security payments to the estate of the individual or to any other person on the basis of the wages and self-employment income (or compensation) that were the basis of the payments to the individual; or (4) applying any combination of these adjustments. [Soc. Sec. Act § 1870(b); 42 C.F.R. § 405.352; Pub. 100-06, Ch. 3, § 110.]

If an individual who is overpaid dies before the overpayment has been recovered, the Secretary may initiate a recovery action, as necessary, against any other individual who is receiving cash Social Security benefits on the same earnings record as the deceased overpaid beneficiary. [Soc. Sec. Act § 1870(b).]

Waiver of beneficiary liability. The Secretary may not pursue recovery of the overpayment if the (1) overpaid beneficiary is without fault (or the survivor of the deceased overpaid beneficiary who is liable for repayment of a Medicare overpayment is without fault), and (2) the recovery would be against equity and good conscience or defeat the purposes of titles II or XVIII the Social Security Act. Adjustment or recovery of an incorrect payment against an individual who is without fault is deemed to be against equity and good conscience if the Secretary's determination that such payment was incorrect was made subsequent to the fifth year following the year in which notice of such payment was sent to such individual; the Secretary may, however, reduce such five-year period to not less than one year.[Soc. Sec. Act § 1870(c); 42 C.F.R. §§ 405.355, 405.358; Pub. 100-06, Ch. 3, §§ 70.3, 110.10.]

When collection of a beneficiary overpayment is from a provider (or physicians or other persons who have accepted assignments), after three years the provider (or the physician or other person) is prohibited from charging the beneficiary for services found by the Secretary to be medically unnecessary or custodial in nature, in the absence of fault on the part of the individual who received the services. Again, the Secretary is authorized to make the presumption before the three years have expired (but not before one year) if to do so would be consistent with the objectives of the Medicare program. [Soc. Sec. Act §§ 1842(b)(3)(B)(ii), 1866(a)(1)(B).]

Interest Charges on Overpayments and Underpayments

When a final determination is made that a provider of services under Part A or a physician or supplier that has accepted assignment under Part B has received an overpayment or underpayment from Medicare, and payment of the excess or deficit is not made within 30 days of the determination, interest charges will be applied to the balance due. The interest rate on overpayments is determined in accordance with regulations promulgated by the Secretary of the Treasury and is the higher of the private consumer rate or the current value of fund rates prevailing on the date of final determination. No interest is assessed for a period of less than 30 days; interest is calculated in full 30-day periods. Interest is assessed on the principal amount only and is calculated on a simple rather than a compound basis. [Soc. Sec. Act §§ 1815(d), 1833(j); 42 C.F.R. § 405.378.]

Suspension, Offset, and Recoupment of Overpayments

Under the Federal Claims Collection Act of 1966, each agency of the federal government must attempt collection of claims for the federal government for money arising out of the activities of the agency in a timely and aggressive manner. The MAC will not be liable for overpayments it makes to debtors in the absence of fraud or gross negligence on its part; however, once the MAC determines an overpayment has been made, it must attempt recovery of overpayments in accordance with CMS regulations. [31 U.S.C. §§ 3701–3720A; Pub. 100-06, Ch. 3, § 10.] CMS may, under certain circumstances, suspend, offset, and recoup Medicare payments to providers and suppliers of services to recover overpayments. [42 C.F.R. § 405.371(a).]

Suspension of payments. CMS or a MAC may suspend, in whole or in part, Medicare payments to providers and suppliers: (1) if CMS or the MAC possesses reliable information that an overpayment exists or that the payments to be made may not be correct, although additional information may be needed for a determination; or (2) in cases of suspected fraud, if CMS or the MAC has consulted with the OIG, and, as appropriate, the Department of Justice, and determined that a credible allegation of fraud exists against a provider or supplier, unless there is good cause not to suspend payments. [42 C.F.R. § 405.371(a)(1), (2).]

Once the determination has been made that a suspension of payments should be put into effect, notice ordinarily will be given to the provider or supplier along with a written statement of the reasons for the suspension. Notice to the provider or supplier is not necessary if: (1) the intended suspension involves fraud or misrepresentation; (2) CMS or the MAC determines that the Medicare Trust Fund would be harmed by giving prior notice; or (3) the intended suspension is the result of the provider's or supplier's failure to submit requested information necessary to determine amounts due the provider or supplier. [42 C.F.R. § 405.372(a).]

If prior notice is required, the MAC must give the provider or supplier 15 days to submit a statement of rebuttal. If, by the end of the period specified in the notice, no rebuttal has been received, the suspension will go into effect automatically. With certain exceptions, the period of suspension is limited to 180 days. [42 C.F.R. §§ 405.372(b), (d), 405.374.]

¶906

Offset or recoupment. CMS or a MAC may offset or recoup Medicare payments, in whole or in part, if it determines that the provider or supplier to whom payments are to be made has been overpaid. An offset is the recovery by Medicare of a non-Medicare debt by reducing present or future Medicare payments and applying the amount withheld to the indebtedness. A recoupment, on the other hand, refers to the recovery by Medicare of outstanding Medicare debt by reducing present or future Medicare payments and applying the amount withheld to the indebtedness. [42 C.F.R. §§ 405.370(a), 405.371(a)(3).]

When CMS or the MAC determines that an offset or recoupment should be put in place, the provider or supplier must receive notice and an opportunity for rebuttal. If no rebuttal statement is received within the time period specified in the notice, the recoupment or offset will go into effect immediately and remain in effect until the earliest of the following: (1) the overpayment and any assessed interest are liquidated; (2) the MAC obtains a satisfactory agreement from the provider or supplier for liquidation of the overpayment; or (3) the MAC, on the basis of subsequently acquired evidence or otherwise, determines that there is no overpayment. [42 C.F.R. § 405.373.]

Rebuttals. The rebuttal process occurs before the appeals process and permits the provider a vehicle to indicate why the recoupment or offset should not take place. If the provider or supplier submits a statement as to why a suspension, offset, or recoupment should not be put into effect, CMS or the MAC must, within 15 days from the date the statement is received, consider the statement and determine whether the facts justify the suspension, offset, or recoupment. CMS or the MAC must send written notice of the determination to the provider or supplier, including an explanatory statement of the determination and: (1) in the case of offset or recoupment, the rationale for the determination, or (2) in the case of suspension of payment, specific findings on the conditions upon which the suspension is initiated, continued, or removed. Suspension, offset, or recoupment is not delayed beyond the date stated in the notice to review the statement. Such a determination is not an initial determination and, therefore, is not appealable. [42 C.F.R. § 405.375.]

Requests for reconsideration and redetermination. When a provider or supplier seeks a redetermination by a MAC or reconsideration by a qualified independent contractor (QIC) on an overpayment determination, CMS may not recoup or demand a Medicare overpayment until the decision on the redetermination or reconsideration is rendered. When a valid request for a redetermination or reconsideration has been received from a provider, the MAC will cease recoupment or not begin recoupment at the normally scheduled time (41 days from the date of the initial overpayment demand for the redetermination and 76 days for the reconsideration). Interest paid to a provider or supplier whose overpayment is reversed at subsequent levels of appeal will accrue from the date of the original determination. [Soc. Sec. Act § 1893(f)(2); 42 C.F.R. §§ 405.379(a), (d); Pub. 100-06, Ch. 3, §§ 200, 200.3.]

Once both the redetermination and reconsideration are completed and CMS prevails, collection activities, including demand letters and internal recoupment, may resume. [Pub. 100-06, Ch. 3, § 200.]

Extended repayment schedule. If the repayment of an overpayment within 30 days would constitute a hardship, a provider or supplier can enter into a plan with the Secretary to repay the overpayment over a period of six to 36 months (or, in the case of extreme hardship, no longer than five years). [Soc. Sec. Act § 1893(f)(1); 42 C.F.R. §§ 401.607(c)(2), 405.379(h).]

[¶ 915] Limitation of Liability

Medicare law provides financial relief to beneficiaries, providers, practitioners, physicians, and suppliers by permitting Medicare payment to be made, or requiring refunds to be made, for certain services and items for which Medicare payment would otherwise be denied. This is referred to as "the limitation on liability provision." The purpose of this provision is to protect beneficiaries and other claimants from liability in denial cases under certain conditions when services they received are found to be excluded from coverage for one of the reasons specified below. [Soc. Sec. Act § 1879; *Medicare Claims Processing Manual*, Pub. 100-04, Ch. 30, § § 20, 20.1.1.]

Services for which the limitation on liability provisions apply. The limitation on liability (LOL) of claims payment and beneficiary indemnification provisions are applicable only to claims for beneficiary items or services submitted by providers or suppliers, including physicians or other practitioners, or entities other than providers, that furnish health care services under Medicare and that have taken assignment. The LOL provisions are triggered by two factors: (1) the provider, practitioner, physician, supplier, or beneficiary must not have known or could not reasonably have been expected to know that items or services were not covered, and (2) the claims for items or services must have been denied for the following statutory reasons:

(1) services and items or additional preventive services that are found not to be reasonable and necessary for the diagnosis or treatment of illness or injury or to improve the functioning of a malformed body member under section 1861(a)(1)(A) of the Social Security Act;

(2) pneumococcal vaccine and its administration, influenza vaccine and its administration, and hepatitis B vaccine and its administration, furnished to an individual who is at high or intermediate risk of contracting hepatitis B, which are not reasonable and necessary for the prevention of illness;

(3) in the case of hospice care, services and items that are not reasonable and necessary for the palliation or management of terminal illness;

(4) clinical care items and services provided with the concurrence of the Secretary and, with respect to research and experimentation conducted by, or under contract with, the Medicare Payment Advisory Commission or the Secretary, that are not reasonable and necessary;

(5) services and items that, in the case of research conducted pursuant to Soc. Sec. Act § 1142, are not reasonable and necessary to carry out the purposes of the governing law;

(6) screening mammography that is performed more frequently than is covered under Soc. Sec. Act § 1834(c)(2) or that is not conducted by a facility described in Soc. Sec. Act § 1834(c)(1)(B), and screening pap smears and screening pelvic exams performed more frequently than is provided for under Soc. Sec. Act § 1861(nn);

(7) screening for glaucoma that is performed more frequently than is provided under Soc. Sec. Act § 1861(uu);

(8) prostate cancer screening tests that are performed more frequently than is covered under Soc. Sec. Act § 1861(oo);

(9) colorectal cancer screening tests that are performed more frequently than is covered under Soc. Sec. Act § 1834(d);

(10) the frequency and duration of home health services (see ¶ 250) that are in excess of normative guidelines established by the Secretary;

(11) a drug or biological specified in Soc. Sec. Act § 1847A(c)(6)(C) for which payment is made under Part B that is furnished in a competitive area that is not furnished by an entity under a contract under Soc. Sec. Act § 1847B;

(12) an initial preventive physical examination that is performed more than one year after the date the individual's first coverage period begins under Part B;

(13) cardiovascular screening blood tests that are performed more frequently than is covered under Soc. Sec. Act § 1861 (xx) (1);

(14) a diabetes screening test that is performed more frequently than is covered under Soc. Sec. Act § 1861 (yy) (1);

(15) ultrasound screening for abdominal aortic aneurysm that is performed more frequently than is provided for under Soc. Sec. Act § 1861 (s) (2) (AA);

(16) kidney disease education services that are furnished in excess of the number of sessions covered under Soc. Sec. Act § 1861 (ggg);

(17) personalized prevention plan services that are performed more frequently than is covered under Soc. Sec. Act § 1861 (hhh) (1);

(18) custodial care under Soc. Sec. Act § 1862 (a) (9) (see ¶ 625);

(19) inpatient hospital services or extended care services if payment is denied solely because of an unintentional, inadvertent, or erroneous action that resulted in the beneficiary's transfer from a certified bed in a skilled nursing facility (SNF) or hospital (Soc. Sec. Act § 1879 (e));

(20) home health services determined to be noncovered because the beneficiary was not homebound or did not require intermittent skilled nursing care; and

(21) hospice care (see ¶ 270) determined to be noncovered because the beneficiary was not "terminally ill" (as required by Soc. Sec. Act § 1861 (dd) (3) (A), as referenced by Soc. Sec. Act § 1879 (g) (2)).

[Soc. Sec. Act §§ 1862 (a) (1) and (a) (9), 1879; Pub. 100-04, Ch. 30, §§ 20, 20.1.1.]

Services not subject to the LOL provisions. Medicare payment under the LOL provision cannot be made when Medicare coverage is denied on any basis other than one of the provisions of the law specified above. There are certain claims that may appear to involve a question of medical necessity, as described in section 1862 (a) (1) of the Social Security Act, but Medicare payment denial is based on a different statutory provision. Under these circumstances, Medicare payment under the limitation on liability provision cannot be made because the denial is not based on one of the statutory provisions specified above. [Pub. 100-04, Ch. 30, § 20.2.]

Third-party payers. The waiver of liability provision applies to third-party payers. Accordingly, a provider, practitioner, or supplier that is determined liable may not seek payment from a third-party payer without being subject to recovery action that could occur if it sought payment from the beneficiary. [Pub. 100-04, Ch. 30, § 30.2.2.]

Determination of Liability

The Medicare administrative contractor determines whether the provider, physician, or beneficiary is liable for the overpayment and whether to waive liability. [*Medicare Financial Management Manual*, Pub. 100-06, Ch. 3, § 70.] In addition, quality improvement organization determinations (see ¶ 710) are conclusive for payment purposes as to whether the provider and the beneficiary knew or could reasonably be expected to have known that services were excluded because of the reasonableness, medical necessity, and appropriateness of placement at an acute level of patient care. [42 C.F.R. § 476.86 (a) (4).]

There are three possible outcomes of a determination of liability. If the beneficiary had knowledge (or could have been expected to know) of the noncoverage of services for the reasons specified above, the ultimate liability will rest with the beneficiary. When neither the beneficiary nor the provider, practitioner, or supplier knew or reasonably could have been expected to know that services were not covered, the government will accept liability. When the beneficiary did not have such knowledge, but the provider, practitioner, or supplier knew, or could have been expected to know, of the exclusion of the items or services, the liability for the charges for the denied items or services rests with the provider, practitioner, or supplier. [Pub. 100-04, Ch. 30, § 20.]

If the Medicare program accepts liability and makes payment, CMS will put the provider and beneficiary on notice that the service was noncovered and, in any subsequent cases involving similar situations and further stays or treatments (or similar types of cases in the instance of the provider), will consider that the provider and beneficiary had knowledge that payment would not be made. [Soc. Sec. Act § 1879(a).]

If the provider did not exercise due care but there was good faith on the part of the beneficiary, liability will shift to the provider. The provider can appeal the contractor's decision as to coverage of the services and whether it exercised due care. If the provider received reimbursement from the beneficiary, the program will indemnify the beneficiary (although deductibles and coinsurance apply). Medicare treats the indemnification as an overpayment against the provider and recoups the amount of the payment through an offset against any amounts otherwise payable to the provider. [Soc. Sec. Act § 1879(b), (d); Pub. 100-04, Ch. 30, § § 20, 30.1.1, 30.2.2.]

Waiver of Beneficiary Liability

The waiver of liability provision provides that the beneficiary will not have to pay for noncovered services if the beneficiary did not know, and did not have reason to know, that the services were not covered. The contractor presumes that the beneficiary did not know that services are not covered unless the evidence indicates that written notice was given to the beneficiary by the QIO, the Medicare contractor, the utilization review committee responsible for the provider that furnished the services, or the provider, practitioner, or supplier that furnished the service. [Soc. Sec. Act § 1879(a); 42 C.F.R. § § 411.404, 411.408(f); Pub. 100-04, Ch. 30, § § 30.1, 30.1.1, 30.1.2.]

If the beneficiary's liability for the services is waived by the contractor, liability shifts either to the government or to the provider—depending upon whether the provider utilized due care in applying Medicare policy in its dealings with the beneficiary and the government. [Soc. Sec. Act § 1879(a), (b), and (c); 42 C.F.R. § 411.402; Pub. 100-04, Ch. 30, § 30.2.1; Pub. 100-06, Ch. 3, § § 70, 70.1.]

Waiver of Provider Liability

The issue of whether a practitioner or other supplier is liable for payment for services not covered by Medicare arises only when the beneficiary has been found not liable. A physician's or supplier's liability will not be waived for noncovered services unless the physician or supplier accepted assignment for the services (see ¶ 868). [42 C.F.R. § 411.400(a); Pub. 100-06, Ch. 3, § § 70.3, 90.]

For the initial determination, the practitioner or other supplier is presumed to have had the requisite knowledge of likely Medicare denial of payment for denied services or items and will be liable unless the practitioner or supplier gave the beneficiary a proper Advance Beneficiary Notice (ABN) that Medicare will likely deny payment for the service or item to be furnished. A provider, practitioner, or supplier will not be held liable when the provider, practitioner, or supplier indicates on the claim (via Occurrence Code 32 or the Healthcare Common Procedure Coding System (HCPCS) code modifier "GA" on contractor claims) that the beneficiary has been given an ABN before the items or services were furnished. In that case, the Medicare contractor will hold the beneficiary liable for the denied services or items at the initial determination because the notice constitutes proof that the beneficiary and the practitioner or supplier had prior knowledge that Medicare payment would be denied for the service or item in question. When the beneficiary and the practitioner or other supplier are found to have had the requisite knowledge of likely Medicare denial, the beneficiary is held liable. [Pub. 100-04, Ch. 30, §§ 30.2.1, 40.1.1.]

A provider, practitioner, or supplier that furnished services that constitute custodial care or are not reasonable and necessary is considered to have known that the services were not covered if:

- the Medicare contractor had informed the provider, practitioner, or supplier that the services furnished were not covered, or that similar or reasonably comparable services were not covered;

- the utilization review committee for the provider or the beneficiary's attending physician had informed the provider that these services were not covered;

- before the services were furnished, the provider, practitioner, or supplier informed the beneficiary that the services were not covered or the beneficiary no longer needed covered services; or

- the provider, practitioner, or supplier could have been expected to have known that the services were excluded from coverage based on the receipt of CMS notices, including manual issuances, bulletins, or other written guides or directives from Medicare contractors, including: (1) QIO screening criteria and preadmission review; (2) *Federal Register* publications containing notice of national coverage decisions or of other specifications regarding noncoverage of an item or service; and (3) knowledge of acceptable standards of practice by the local medical community.

[42 C.F.R. § 411.406.] A provider, practitioner, or supplier that is determined liable for all or a portion of the charges for noncovered items and services furnished a beneficiary may appeal such a decision by the contractor. [Pub. 100-04, Ch. 30, § 30.2.2.]

[¶ 920] Medicare Entitlement and Enrollment Appeals

The Social Security Administration (SSA) makes an initial determination on an application for Medicare benefits and entitlement of an individual to receive Medicare benefits. Entitlement concerns whether an individual has a right to Medicare benefits, not whether a particular item or service is covered or how much Medicare pays for it. Any individual dissatisfied with the SSA's initial determination as to whether he or she is *entitled to* or *enrolled in* Medicare may request reconsideration of the determination in the same manner provided for Social Security (or Railroad Retirement) benefit claims if the requirements for obtaining a reconsideration are met. [20 C.F.R. §§ 404.909, 405.904(a).]

Written notice of the government's determination that an individual is not eligible for Medicare is mailed to the individual at his or her last known address. An initial determination becomes final and binding on the parties unless reconsideration is requested or the determination is reopened and revised within the specified time limits. [20 C.F.R. §§ 404.904, 404.905.]

The claimant (or his or her representative) may request a reconsideration of this determination by letter or on a special form available at any district Social Security office. The request for a reconsideration should be in writing and filed at a district office within 60 days from the date of receipt of the original adverse determination. [20 C.F.R. § 404.909.]

The SSA reviews the evidence considered in making the initial determination and any other evidence received and makes its determination on the preponderance of the evidence. The reconsideration is binding unless a request for a hearing is made within the stated time period and a decision is made, the expedited appeals process is used, or the determination is revised. The SSA mails a written notice of the reconsidered determination stating the specific reasons for the determination and the right to a hearing before an administrative law judge (ALJ). [20 C.F.R. § § 404.900(b), 404.913(a), 404.920, 404.921, 404.922.]

Following the reconsideration, the individual may request a hearing before an ALJ under the Medicare appeal rules. If the individual is dissatisfied with the ALJ decision, he or she may request the Medicare Appeals Council to review the case. If dissatisfied with the Medicare Appeals Council decision, the individual is entitled to file a suit in federal district court. [42 C.F.R. § 405.904(a).]

[¶ 924] Medicare Part A and B Claims Appeals

There are four levels of administrative appeals to challenge a coverage or payment decision under Part A or Part B. The first level of appeal is a redetermination made by the Medicare administrative contractor (MAC). The second administrative appeal, a "reconsideration," is conducted by a qualified independent contractor (QIC). The third level of appeal is to an administrative law judge (ALJ), and the final administrative review is conducted by the Medicare Appeals Council. [Soc. Sec. Act § § 1869(b)–(d).]

For beneficiaries that have enrolled in Medicare Advantage plans, specific requirements have been established with respect to administrative determinations, reconsiderations, appeals, and judicial review. These requirements are outlined at ¶ 403. For beneficiaries enrolled in Part D, the voluntary prescription drug benefit, administrative determinations, appeals, grievances, and judicial review are discussed at ¶ 515–¶ 516.

Initial Determinations

When a medical service provider or supplier or a beneficiary submits a bill containing a request for payment for benefits, the MAC will make an initial determination approving, denying, or partially denying the claim. The MAC will notify the beneficiary of its initial determination with a Medicare summary notice (MSN) and the provider or supplier with an electronic or paper remittance advice (RA) describing the action taken. The MSN states in detail the basis for the determination, informs beneficiaries of the right to appeal the determination if they are dissatisfied, and provides instructions on how to obtain, on request, information on the specific provision of the policy, manual, or regulation used in making the determination or redetermination. [Soc. Sec. Act § 1869(a)(4); 42 C.F.R. § § 405.920, 405.921.]

An initial determination on claims made by or on behalf of a beneficiary includes, but is not limited to, determinations with respect to:

(1) coverage of furnished items and services;

(2) if the beneficiary, physician, or supplier who accepts assignment knew or could reasonably be expected to know that the items or services were not covered;

(3) whether the deductible is met;

(4) computation of the coinsurance amount;

(5) the number of inpatient hospital days used for inpatient hospital, psychiatric hospital, or post-hospital extended care;

(6) periods of hospice care used;

(7) requirements for certification and plan of treatment for physician services, durable medical equipment, therapies, inpatient hospitalization, skilled nursing care, home health, hospice, and partial hospitalization services;

(8) the beginning and ending of a spell of illness;

(9) the medical necessity of the services, or the reasonableness or appropriateness of placement of an individual at an acute level of patient care made by the quality improvement organization (QIO) on behalf of the MAC;

(10) any other issues affecting the amount of benefits payable, including underpayments;

(11) a determination with respect to the waiver of liability provision;

(12) if a particular claim is not payable to Medicare based on the application of Medicare Secondary Payer (MSP) provisions;

(13) under MSP provisions, that Medicare has a recovery claim against a provider, supplier, or beneficiary for services or items that were already paid by the Medicare program, except when the recovery claim is based on failure to file a proper claim;

(14) if a claim is not payable to a beneficiary for the services of a physician who has opted out; and

(15) under the MSP provisions, that Medicare has a recovery claim if Medicare is pursuing recovery directly from an applicable plan (defined as liability insurance, no-fault insurance, or a workers' compensation law or plan).

[42 C.F.R. § 405.924(b).]

An initial determination also includes a determination made by a QIO that: (1) a provider can terminate services provided to an individual when a physician certified that failure to continue the provision of those services is likely to place the individual's health at significant risk, or (2) a provider can discharge an individual from the provider of services. [42 C.F.R. § 405.924(c).] See ¶ 926 for a discussion of expedited appeals of provider service terminations to QIOs. See also ¶ 710 for a discussion of beneficiary complaints and appeals to QIOs regarding quality of care issues.

Parties to initial determinations. The parties to the initial determination are: (1) the beneficiary who files a claim for payment under Medicare Part A or Part B or has had a claim for payment filed on his or her behalf, or in the case of a deceased beneficiary, when there is no estate, any person obligated to make or entitled to receive payment, except that payment by a third-party payer does not entitle that entity to party status; (2) a supplier who has accepted assignment for items or services furnished to a beneficiary that are at issue in the claim; (3) a provider of services who files a claim for items or services furnished to a beneficiary; and (4) an applicable plan for an initial determination under 42 C.F.R. § 405.924(b)(16) where Medicare is pursuing recovery directly from the applicable plan. [42 C.F.R. § 405.906(a).]

Deadlines for making initial determinations. Initial determinations must be concluded no later than the 45-day period beginning on the day the claim is received. [Soc. Sec. Act § 1869(a)(2)(A).]

Parties to Redeterminations, Reconsiderations, ALJ Hearings, and Medicare Appeals Council Reviews

Parties to a redetermination, reconsideration, hearing, and Medicare Appeals Council review are: (1) the parties to the initial determination, except when a beneficiary has assigned appeal rights pursuant to 42 C.F.R. § 405.912; (2) a Medicaid state agency (see 42 C.F.R. § 405.908); (3) a provider or supplier that has accepted an assignment of appeal rights from the beneficiary pursuant to 42 C.F.R. § 405.912; (4) a nonparticipating physician not billing on an assigned basis who may be liable to refund monies collected for services furnished to the beneficiary because those services were denied due to their exclusion from coverage; and (5) a nonparticipating supplier not billing on an assigned basis who may be liable to refund monies collected for items furnished to the beneficiary. [42 C.F.R § 405.906(b).]

Except for an initial determination with respect to an applicable plan under 42 C.F.R § 405.924(b)(16), if a provider or supplier is not a party to an initial determination, it may appeal an initial determination related to services it rendered to a beneficiary who subsequently dies if there is no other party available to appeal the determination. [42 C.F.R § 405.906(c).]

Redeterminations

A person or entity that may be a party to a redetermination in accordance with 42 C.F.R. § 405.906(b) that is dissatisfied with an initial determination may request a redetermination by a MAC. [Soc. Sec. Act § 1869(a)(3); 42 C.F.R. § 405.940

A request for redetermination must be filed with the MAC indicated on the notice of the initial determination. The request for redetermination must be in writing and should be made on a standard CMS form. A written request that is not made on a standard form is accepted if it contains the required elements, i.e., the beneficiary's name, health insurance claim number, the specific services or items for which the redetermination is being requested and the dates the services or items were furnished, and the name and signature of the party or the party's representative. [42 C.F.R. § 405.944(a), (b).]

The request for redetermination must be filed within 120 calendar days after receipt of an initial determination (presumed to be five days after the date of the notice), unless the MAC grants the appellant an extension to the filing deadline. [Soc. Sec. Act § 1869(a)(3)(C)(i); 42 C.F.R. § 405.942(a), (b).]

The request for redetermination must include an explanation of why the party disagrees with the MAC's determination and should include any evidence that the MAC should consider in making the redetermination. If parties cannot submit relevant documentation along with their redetermination requests, then they can provide later submissions. When a party submits additional evidence after filing the request for redetermination, however, the MAC's 60 calendar-day decision-making time frame is automatically extended 14 calendar days for each submission. [42 C.F.R. § 405.946.]

MACs are required to process all redeterminations within 60 calendar days. The time frame may be extended when: a MAC grants an extension of the 120-day deadline for filing a request for redetermination, multiple parties request a redetermination, or a party submits evidence after the request for redetermination is filed. [Soc. Sec. Act § 1869(a)(3)(C)(ii); 42 C.F.R. § 405.950.]

Written notice of the redetermination affirming, in whole or in part, the initial determination must be mailed to the parties. For decisions that are affirmations, in whole or in part, of the initial determination, the redetermination must be written in a manner calculated to be understood by a beneficiary and contain, among other explanations and information, a summary of the rationale of the redetermination, rules for submitting evidence and missing documentation, and the right to a reconsideration and the procedures to request a reconsideration. For decisions that are full reversals of the initial determination, the redetermination must be in writing and contain a clear statement indicating that the redetermination is wholly favorable and any other requirements specified by CMS. [Soc. Sec. Act § 1869(a)(5); 42 C.F.R. §§ 405.954, 405.956.]

The redetermination is binding on all parties unless a timely appeal is filed, the redetermination is revised, or the expedited appeals process is used. [42 C.F.R. § 405.958.]

¶924

Reconsiderations

A person or entity that is a party to a redetermination made by a MAC and is dissatisfied with that determination may request a reconsideration, regardless of the amount in controversy. A reconsideration is an independent, on-the-record review of an initial determination, including the redetermination and all the issues related to payment of the claim, performed by a QIC. An initial determination may be reconsidered by a QIC only after the MAC has performed a redetermination of the initial determination. [Soc. Sec. Act § 1869(c)(3)(B); 42 C.F.R. §§ 405.960, 405.968(a).]

A reconsideration is final and binding on all parties unless a timely appeal is filed and a higher appeal overturns the reconsideration decision or the reconsideration is reopened and revised by the QIC. [42 C.F.R. §§ 405.974(b)(3), 405.978.]

If the initial determination involves a finding as to whether an item or service is reasonable and necessary, the QIC's reconsideration must involve consideration by a panel of physicians or other appropriate health care professionals and be based on clinical experience, the patient's medical records, and medical, technical, and scientific evidence of record to the extent applicable. When the claim pertains to the furnishing of treatment by a physician, or the provision of items and services by a physician, the reviewing professional must be a physician. National coverage determinations (NCDs), CMS rulings, and applicable laws and regulations are binding on the QIC. [42 C.F.R. § 405.968.]

Request for reconsideration. A request for reconsideration must be in writing and filed with the QIC indicated on the notice of redetermination within 180 calendar days after receipt of the notice of redetermination (presumed to be five days after the date of the notice). It should be on a standard CMS form; a written request that is not made on a standard CMS form is accepted if it contains the beneficiary's name, Medicare health insurance claim number, specific services and items for which the reconsideration is being requested, name and signature of the party or the representative of the party, and the name of the MAC that made the redetermination. [42 C.F.R. §§ 405.962(a), 405.964; Pub. 100-04, Ch. 29, § 320.1.]

Time frame for reconsideration. QICs must complete their reconsiderations within 60 calendar days of receiving a timely filed request. [42 C.F.R. § 405.970(a).] Note, however, that when a party submits additional evidence after filing the request for redetermination, the QIC's 60 calendar-day decision-making time frame is automatically extended by up to 14 calendar days for each submission. [Soc. Sec. Act § 1869(c)(3)(C); 42 C.F.R. §§ 405.966(b), 405.970(b)(3).]

Escalation. If the QIC does not issue its decision within the 60-calendar-day deadline, the parties may submit a written request directing the QIC to escalate the appeal to the ALJ. When a QIC receives an escalation request, it has five days to complete its reconsideration and notify the parties of its decision or acknowledge the escalation request and forward the case file to the ALJ. [42 C.F.R. § 405.970(d),(e).]

Expedited access to judicial review. A beneficiary, provider, or supplier may obtain expedited access to judicial review (EAJR) after the QIC completes a reconsideration if the review entity determines that the Medicare Appeals Council does not have the authority to decide the question of law or regulation relevant to the matters in controversy and there is no material issue of fact to dispute. The requester has 60 calendar days from the date of certification to bring a civil action in federal court. [42 C.F.R. § 405.990(a), (c), (h).]

¶924

Administrative Law Judge Review

The third level of the claims appeal process, which follows a QIC reconsideration, is a review by the ALJ. [42 C.F.R. § 405.1000.]

Parties to an ALJ hearing. Any party to the QIC's reconsideration may request a hearing before an ALJ. The party who filed the request for hearing and all other parties to the reconsideration are parties to the ALJ hearing. [42 C.F.R. § 405.1008.]

CMS or its MAC may enter an appeal at the ALJ level as a party unless an unrepresented beneficiary brings the appeal. CMS will have all the rights of a party, including the right to call witnesses, submit additional evidence within the time frame specified by the ALJ, and seek review of a decision adverse to CMS. The ALJ may not require CMS or a MAC to enter a case as a party or draw any adverse inferences if CMS or a MAC decides not to enter as a party. [42 C.F.R. § 405.1012.] CMS or a MAC also will be allowed to participate in an ALJ hearing, including oral hearing, at the request of an ALJ, CMS, or a MAC. [42 C.F.R. § 405.1010.]

Amount-in-controversy requirement. To be entitled to a hearing before an ALJ, the party must meet the amount-in-controversy requirements. Claims may be aggregated to meet the amount in controversy if they involve common issues of law and fact and delivery of similar or related services. Effective for requests for ALJ hearings filed on or after January 1, 2016, the amount-in-controversy threshold amount is $150. [Soc. Sec. Act § 1869(b)(1)(E); 42 C.F.R. § 405.1006(b); *Notice*, 80 FR 57827, Sept. 25, 2015.]

Request for an ALJ hearing. ALJ hearing requests must be in writing and include: (1) the name, address, and Medicare health insurance claim number of the beneficiary whose claim is being appealed; (2) the name and address of the appellant, when the appellant is not the beneficiary; (3) the name and address of designated representatives; (4) the document control number assigned to the appeal by the QIC; (5) the dates of service; (6) the reasons the appellant disagrees with the QIC's reconsideration or other determination being appealed; and (7) a statement of any additional evidence to be submitted and the date it will be submitted. [42 C.F.R. § 405.1014(a).]

Requests for ALJ review must be filed with the entity specified in the QIC's reconsideration within 60 calendar days of receipt of the notice of the reconsideration. [42 C.F.R. § 405.1014(b).]

Evidence. Generally, parties must submit all written evidence they wish to have considered at the hearing with the request for hearing (or within 10 calendar days of receiving the notice of hearing). Any evidence submitted by a provider, supplier, or beneficiary represented by a provider or supplier that is not submitted prior to the issuance of the QIC's reconsideration determination must be accompanied by a statement explaining why the evidence was not previously submitted to the QIC or to a prior decision maker. However, these requirements do not apply to oral testimony given at a hearing or evidence submitted by an unrepresented beneficiary. [42 C.F.R. § 405.1018.]

The hearing. The ALJ hearing results in a new decision by an independent reviewer and a decision based on the hearing. The ALJ conducts the hearing in person, by video-teleconference, or by telephone. The ALJ will conduct a *de novo* review (i.e., an in-depth review conducted as if for the first time) and issue a decision based on the hearing record. If the beneficiary or his or her representative waives the right to appear at the hearing, the ALJ will make a decision based on the evidence that is in the file and any new evidence that may have been submitted for consideration. [42 C.F.R. § 405.1000(b), (d), (e).]

The issues before the ALJ include all the issues brought out in the initial determination, redetermination, or reconsideration that were not decided entirely in a party's favor. In addition, the ALJ may consider a new issue at the hearing if he or she notifies all of the parties about the new issue any time before the start of the hearing. The new issues may result from the participation of CMS at the ALJ level of adjudication and from any evidence and position papers submitted by CMS for the first time to the ALJ. The ALJ may consider a new issue only if its resolution could have a material impact on the claim or claims that are the subject of the request for hearing and is permissible under the rules governing reopening of determinations and decisions. [42 C.F.R. § 405.1032(a), (b).]

ALJs are bound by all NCDs whether based on Soc. Sec. Act § 1862(a)(1) or on other grounds, as well as the Medicare Act, applicable regulations, and CMS rulings. ALJs also must give substantial deference to nonbinding CMS and MAC policies such as local coverage determinations, manual instructions, and program memoranda, and if the ALJ declines to follow a policy in a particular case, his or her decision must explain the reasons. [42 C.F.R. §§ 405.1060(a)(4), (b), 405.1062.]

Time frame for ALJ's decision. The ALJ must issue a decision, dismissal order, or remand to the QIC within 90 calendar days of when the request for hearing is received by the entity specified in the QIC's notice of reconsideration. When an appellant escalates an appeal from the QIC level to the ALJ level, the proceedings before the ALJ are not subject to the 90-calendar-day limit. In these cases, ALJs must complete their action within 180 calendar days of receipt of the escalation request, unless the 180-calendar-day period has been extended. When CMS is a party to the hearing and a party requests discovery against another party, these adjudication periods are tolled. [42 C.F.R. § 405.1016.]

Notice of ALJ's decision. The notice of the ALJ's decision must be in writing in a manner that is understood by the beneficiary and must include: (1) the specific reasons for the determination, including, to the extent appropriate, a summary of the clinical or scientific evidence used in making the determination; (2) the procedures for obtaining additional information concerning the decision; and (3) notification of the right to appeal the decision and instructions on how to initiate the appeal. [42 C.F.R. § 405.1046(b).]

Escalation. If the ALJ does not issue a decision within the deadline, the parties may escalate the case to the next level of appeal. A party may request Medicare Appeals Council review if: (1) the party files a written request with the ALJ to escalate the appeal to the Medicare Appeals Council after the adjudication period has expired, and (2) the ALJ does not issue a decision, dismissal order, or remand order within the later of five calendar days of receiving the request for escalation or five calendar days from the end of the applicable adjudication period. [42 C.F.R. § 405.1104.]

If the ALJ is not able to issue a decision, dismissal order, or remand order within the time period, he or she sends notice to the appellant acknowledging receipt of the request for escalation and confirming that the ALJ is not able to issue a decision, dismissal order, or remand order within the statutory time frame. If the ALJ does not act on a request for escalation within the time period or does not send the required notice to the appellant, the QIC decision becomes the decision that is subject to Medicare Appeals Council review. [42 C.F.R. § 405.1104, 405.1106(b).]

Escalation affects the next level's deadlines for making a decision. For example, although the decision-making deadline for the Medicare Appeals Council is generally 90 days, if a case is escalated from the ALJ to the Medicare Appeals Council, the Medicare Appeals Council has 180 calendar days from receipt of a request for escalation to complete its action. [42 C.F.R. § 405.1100(d).]

Medicare Appeals Council Review

A party to the ALJ hearing may request a Medicare Appeals Council review by filing a written request for review with the Medicare Appeals Council or appropriate ALJ office within 60 calendar days after receiving the ALJ's decision. The request should be made on a standard form but will be accepted if it contains the required elements. [42 C.F.R. §§405.1102(a), 405.1106(a), 405.1112(a).]

In addition, any time within 60 calendar days after the date of an ALJ decision or dismissal, the Medicare Appeals Council may decide on its own motion to review the ALJ's action. CMS or any of its MACs also may refer a case to the Medicare Appeals Council for it to consider reviewing under this authority any time within 60 calendar days of an ALJ's decision or dismissal. [42 C.F.R. §405.1110(a).]

The review. The Medicare Appeals Council conducts a *de novo* review of an ALJ decision and limits its review to the evidence contained in the record of the proceedings before the ALJ. If the hearing decision identifies a new issue that the parties were not afforded an opportunity to present at the ALJ level, the Medicare Appeals Council considers any evidence related to that issue that is submitted with the request for review. If the Medicare Appeals Council determines that additional evidence is necessary to resolve the issues in the case and the hearing record indicates that the previous decision-makers have not attempted to obtain the evidence, it may remand the case to an ALJ to obtain the evidence and issue a new decision. [42 C.F.R. §§405.1108(a), 405.1122(a), 405.1126(a).] A party also may request to appear before the Medicare Appeals Council to present oral argument. [42 C.F.R. §405.1124.]

If the Medicare Appeals Council is reviewing a case that was escalated from the ALJ level, it will decide the case based on the record constructed by the QIC and any additional evidence that was entered into the record by the ALJ before the case was escalated. The Medicare Appeals Council may remand the case to an ALJ to consider or obtain evidence and issue a new decision if it receives additional evidence with the request for escalation that is material to the question to be decided or determines that additional evidence is needed to resolve the issues in the case, and the record provided to the Medicare Appeals Council indicates that the previous decision makers did not attempt to obtain the evidence before escalation. [42 C.F.R. §§405.1122(b), 405.1126(a).]

Final action. Subject to the limitations on Medicare Appeals Council consideration of additional evidence, it issues a final action or remands a case to the ALJ for further proceedings within 90 calendar days of receipt of the appellant's request for review, unless the 90-day period is extended. [42 C.F.R. §405.1100(c).] The Medicare Appeals Council may adopt, modify, or reverse the ALJ hearing decision or recommended decision. It mails a copy of its decision to all the parties. [42 C.F.R. §405.1128.]

The Medicare Appeals Council's decision is final and binding on all parties unless a federal district court issues a decision modifying the decision or it is revised as the result of a reopening. [42 C.F.R. §405.1130.]

Escalation. If the Medicare Appeals Council does not issue a decision or dismissal or remand the case to an ALJ within the applicable time frame, the appellant may request that the appeal, other than an appeal of an ALJ dismissal, be escalated to the federal district court. If the Medicare Appeals Council is unable to issue a decision or dismissal or remand within five calendar days of the receipt of the request or five calendar days of the end of the applicable adjudication period, it will send a notice to the appellant acknowledging receipt and confirming that it is not able to issue a decision, dismissal, or remand within the statutory time frame. A party may file an action in a federal district court within 60 calendar days after it receives the Medicare Appeals Council's notice. [42 C.F.R. § 405.1132.]

Judicial Review

A party dissatisfied with the Medicare Appeals Council review may request court review of the decision if the amount in controversy meets the threshold and all of the above administrative remedies have been exhausted. For requests filed on or after January 1, 2016, the minimum amount-in-controversy required for beneficiaries to qualify for judicial review of determinations by an ALJ is $1,500; the requirement for 2015 was $1,460. [Soc. Sec. Act §§ 1155(b)(4), 1869(b)(1)(E); *Notices*, 80 FR 57827, Sept. 25, 2015; 79 FR 57933, Sept. 26, 2014.]

The party must file the complaint in the U.S. district court for the judicial district in which the party resides or where the individual, institution, or agency has its principal place of business, within 60 calendar days after the date it receives notice of the Medicare Appeals Council's decision or within 60 calendar days after the date it receives notice that the Medicare Appeals Council is not able to issue a final decision, dismissal order, or remand order. If the party does not reside within any judicial district, or if the individual, institution, or agency does not have its principal place of business within any such judicial district, the civil action must be filed in the District Court of the United States for the District of Columbia. [42 C.F.R. §§ 405.1130, 405.1132, 405.1134, 405.1136.]

Standard of review. In general, federal courts will liberally construe the Medicare Act to include rather than exclude coverage and any doubts are resolved in favor of coverage. The courts, however, are required to give deference to CMS's actions. The federal court may hold unlawful or set aside agency action, findings, and conclusions that are found to be: (1) arbitrary or capricious; (2) an abuse of discretion; (3) not in accordance with the law; or (4) not supported by substantial evidence. [Administrative Procedure Act, 5 U.S.C. § 706.] Judicial review of administrative determinations of Medicare cases is limited by the substantial evidence rule. The finding of the Secretary as to any fact, if supported by substantial evidence, is considered conclusive. [Soc. Sec. Act § 205(g); 42 C.F.R. § 405.1136(f).]

Assignment of Appeal Rights

Only a provider or supplier that is not a party to the initial determination and that furnished an item or service to the beneficiary may seek assignment of appeal rights from the beneficiary for that item or service. An individual or entity that is not a provider or supplier may not be an assignee. [42 C.F.R. § 405.912(a), (b).]

The assignee must waive the right to collect payment for the item or service for which the assignment of appeal rights is made. If the assignment is revoked, the waiver of the right to collect payment remains valid. In addition, a waiver of the right to collect payment remains in effect regardless of the outcome of the appeal decision. The assignee, however, is not prohibited from recovering payment associated with coinsurance or deductibles or when an Advance Beneficiary Notice (ABN) is properly executed. [42 C.F.R. § 405.912(d).]

When a valid assignment of appeal rights is executed, the assignor transfers all appeal rights involving the particular item or service to the assignee. These rights include, but are not limited to, obtaining information about the claim to the same extent as the assignor; submitting evidence; making statements about facts or law; and making any request, or giving or receiving any notice about, appeal proceedings. When an assignment of appeal rights is revoked, the rights to appeal revert to the assignor. [42 C.F.R. § 405.912(f)–(g).]

Appointment of Representatives

An appointed representative may act on behalf of an individual or entity in exercising his or her right to an initial determination or appeal. Appointed representatives do not have party status and may take action only on behalf of the individual or entity that they represent. [42 C.F.R. § 405.910(a).]

If the requestor is the beneficiary's legal guardian, no appointment is necessary, and the requestor is defined as the authorized representative. [*Medicare Claims Processing Manual*, Pub. 100-04, Ch. 29, § 270.1.1.]

A representative may be appointed at any point in the appeals process. To file an appeal, the representative must file a copy of the Appointment of Representative (AOR) form or other written instrument with the appeal request. [42 C.F.R. § 405.910(c); Pub. 100-04, Ch. 29, § 270.1.2.]

Duration of appointment. Unless revoked, an appointment is considered valid for one year from the date that the AOR form or other conforming written instrument contains the signatures of both the party and the appointed representative. If the initial determination involves a MSP recovery, an appointment signed in connection with the party's efforts to make a claim for third-party payment is valid for the duration of any later appeal. [42 C.F.R. § 405.910(e); Pub. 100-04, Ch. 29, § 270.1.5.]

Authority and responsibilities of appointed representative. An appointed representative has an affirmative duty to inform the party of the scope and responsibilities of the representation and of the status of the appeal and the results of actions taken, including, notification of appeal determinations, decisions, and further appeal rights. The representative must also disclose to the beneficiary any financial risk and liability of a non-assigned claim that the beneficiary may have. An appointed representative may, on behalf of the party, obtain appeals information about the claim to the same extent as the party, submit evidence, make statements about facts and law, and make any request, or give or receive, any notice about the appeal proceedings. [42 C.F.R. § 405.910(g) and (h).]

Fees. An appointed representative may charge a fee, if approved by the Secretary, for an appeal before the Secretary; however, no fees may be charged against the Medicare trust funds, and services rendered below the ALJ level are not considered proceedings before the Secretary. [42 C.F.R. § 405.910(f)(1)–(2).]

Representation by provider or supplier. A provider, physician, or supplier cannot represent a beneficiary if there is a conflict of interest under the waiver of liability provision (i.e., if there is a question as to who knew or had reason to know that the services would not be covered) (see ¶ 915). A provider, physician, or supplier cannot impose any financial liability on the beneficiary in connection with such a representation. [Soc. Sec. Act § 1869(b)(1)(B); 42 C.F.R. § 405.910(f)(3).]

An appeal request filed by a provider or supplier must include a signed statement that no financial liability is imposed on the beneficiary in connection with the representation. If applicable, the appeal request also must include a signed statement that the provider or supplier waives the right to payment from the beneficiary for services or items regarding issues related to items and services considered under the limitation on liability provisions. [42 C.F.R. § 405.910(g)(2).]

[¶ 926] Expedited Appeals of Provider Service Terminations

Expedited determination and reconsideration procedures are available to beneficiaries when a home health agency, skilled nursing facility, hospice, or comprehensive outpatient rehabilitation facility informs them of a decision that Medicare coverage of their services is about to end. [42 C.F.R. § 405.1200(a)(1).]

Termination of Medicare-covered service is considered a discharge of a beneficiary from a residential provider of services or a complete cessation of coverage at the end of a course of treatment, regardless of whether the beneficiary agrees that the services should end. A termination does not include a reduction in services, nor does it include the termination of one type of service by the provider if the beneficiary continues to receive other Medicare-covered services from the provider. [42 C.F.R. § 405.1200(a)(2).]

The provider of the service must deliver valid written notice to the beneficiary of the decision to terminate covered services no later than two days before the proposed end of the services. The provider must use a standardized notice as specified by CMS and include the date the services are to terminate and the date financial liability is to begin as well as a description of the beneficiary's right to an expedited determination. Quality improvement organizations (QIOs) conduct the expedited determination, and qualified independent contractors (QICs) conduct the expedited reconsideration. [42 C.F.R. §§ 405.1200(b), 405.1202, 405.1204.]

QIO's Expedited Redetermination

A beneficiary has a right to an expedited determination by a QIO for services furnished by a nonresidential provider if he or she disagrees with the provider that services should be terminated and a physician certifies that failure to continue the provision of the services may place the beneficiary's health at significant risk. For services furnished by a residential provider or a hospice, a beneficiary has a right to an expedited determination if he or she disagrees with the provider's decision to discharge him or her. Coverage of provider services continues until the date and time designated on the termination notice, unless the QIO reverses the provider's service termination decision. [42 C.F.R. § 405.1202(a), (c).]

A beneficiary must submit a request for an expedited determination to the QIO in the state in which he or she is receiving the services, in writing or by telephone, no later than noon of the calendar day following receipt of the notice of termination. The beneficiary or his or her representative must be available to answer questions or supply information that the QIO may request to conduct its review. The beneficiary may, but is not required to, submit evidence to be considered by a QIO in making its decision. [42 C.F.R. § 405.1202(b).]

When a beneficiary requests an expedited determination by a QIO, the burden of proof rests with the provider to demonstrate that termination of coverage is the correct decision, based either on medical necessity or other Medicare coverage policies. [42 C.F.R. § 405.1202(d).]

Within 72 hours of receiving the request for an expedited determination, the QIO must notify the beneficiary, the beneficiary's physician, and the provider of services of its determination of whether termination of Medicare coverage is the correct decision. [42 C.F.R. § 405.1202(e)(6).]

QIC Expedited Reconsiderations

A beneficiary who is dissatisfied with a QIO's expedited determination may request an expedited reconsideration by a QIC. The request for reconsideration must be submitted to the appropriate QIC in writing or by telephone no later than noon of the calendar day following initial notification of receipt of the QIO's determination. When a beneficiary requests an expedited reconsideration in accordance with the required deadline, the provider may not bill the beneficiary for any disputed services until the QIC makes its determination. [42 C.F.R. § 405.1204(a), (b), (f).]

On the day the QIC receives the request for reconsideration, it must notify the QIO that made the expedited determination and the provider of services of the request. When a QIC notifies a QIO that a beneficiary has requested an expedited reconsideration, the QIO must supply all information that the QIC needs to make its expedited reconsideration as soon as possible, but no later than by close of business of the day that the QIC notifies the QIO of the request for an expedited reconsideration. At a beneficiary's request, the QIO must furnish the beneficiary with a copy of, or access to, any documentation that it sends to the QIC. A provider may, but is not required to, submit evidence to be considered by a QIC in making its decision. If a provider fails to comply with a QIC's request for additional information beyond that furnished to the QIO for purposes of the expedited determination, the QIC makes its reconsideration decision based on the information available. [42 C.F.R. § 405.1204(c)–(e).]

QICs must provide their reconsideration decisions no later than 72 hours after receiving the appeal request and related medical records. The decisions must be provided by telephone and in writing to the provider of services, the beneficiary requesting the appeal, and the attending physician of the beneficiary. [42 C.F.R. § 405.1204(c).]

See ¶ 710 for a discussion of QIO coverage determinations and reconsideration determinations related to: (1) reasonableness, medical necessity (including the need for using assistants at cataract surgery), and appropriateness of the services furnished or proposed to be furnished (for example, whether treatment was appropriate for the condition); (2) appropriateness of the setting in which the services were, or are proposed to be, furnished; (3) financial liability for the services; and (4) diagnosis-related group (DRG) validation reviews.

Hospital Inpatient Expedited Determinations

A beneficiary has a right to request an expedited determination by the QIO when a hospital, acting directly or through its utilization review committee, with physician concurrence, determines that inpatient care is no longer necessary. [42 C.F.R. § 405.1206(a).] If the hospital acting directly or through its utilization review committee believes that the beneficiary does not require further inpatient hospital care but is unable to obtain the agreement of the physician, it may request an expedited determination by the QIO. [42 C.F.R. § 405.1208(a).]

A beneficiary who wishes to exercise his or her right to an expedited determination must submit a request in writing or by telephone to the QIO that has an agreement with the hospital no later than the day of discharge. Upon request by the QIO, the beneficiary, or his or her representative, must be available to discuss the case and may, but is not required to, submit written evidence to be considered by a QIO in making its decision. [42 C.F.R. §§ 405.1206(b)(1)–(b)(3).]

When the QIO issues an expedited determination, it must notify the beneficiary, physician, and hospital of its decision by telephone, followed by a written notice that includes: (1) the basis and rationale for the determination; (2) an explanation of the Medicare payment consequences of the determination and the date a beneficiary becomes fully liable for the services; and (3) information about the beneficiary's right to a reconsideration of the QIO's determination, including how to request a reconsideration and the time period for doing so. [42 C.F.R. §§ 405.1206(d)(8), 405.1208(d).] When the hospital requests a determination, the QIO must make a determination and notify the beneficiary, hospital, and physician within two working days of the hospital's request and receipt of any pertinent information submitted by the hospital. [42 C.F.R. § 405.1208(c)(4).]

¶926

The QIO determination is binding upon the beneficiary, physician, and hospital, except: (1) if the beneficiary is still an inpatient in the hospital and is dissatisfied with the determination, he or she may request a QIC reconsideration (see discussion above), or (2) if the beneficiary is no longer an inpatient in the hospital and is dissatisfied with this determination, the determination is subject to the general claims appeal process (see ¶ 924). [42 C.F.R. §§ 405.1206(g), 405.1208(e).]

[¶ 928] NCD and LCD Appeals

The term "national coverage determination" (NCD) means a determination by the HHS Secretary with respect to whether a particular item or service is covered under the Medicare program (see ¶ 390), but it does not include a determination of what code, if any, is assigned to a particular item or service covered or a determination with respect to the amount of payment made for a particular item or service so covered. The term "local coverage determination" (LCD) means a determination by a contractor under Part A or Part B concerning whether a particular item or service is covered on a Medicare administrative contractor-wide basis in accordance with Social Security Act section 1862(a)(1)(A), which sets the reasonable and necessary standard for covered services. [Soc. Sec. Act § 1869(f)(1)(B), (f)(2)(B).]

Avenues of appeals. The right to challenge NCDs and LCDs is distinct from the existing rights that beneficiaries have for appealing Medicare claims (see ¶ 924). [42 C.F.R. § 426.310(a).] The Secretary established specific procedures for filing a written complaint for a review of an LCD and separate procedures for filing a written complaint for a review of an NCD (see 42 C.F.R. §§ 426.400 *et seq.*; 426.500 *et seq.*).

There are two avenues of appeals for LCDs and NCDs: reconsideration and review. The main differences between an LCD/NCD review and an LCD/NCD reconsideration are the avenue an individual chooses to take to initiate a change to a coverage policy and who may initiate the review. The reconsideration process allows any individual, not just an aggrieved party, to submit new evidence for reconsideration of an LCD or NCD. The review process permits only an "aggrieved party" to file a complaint to initiate the review of an LCD or NCD. [*Final rule*, 68 FR 63692, Nov. 7, 2003.]

Mediation for disputes related to LCDs. CMS established a mediation process to mediate disputes between groups representing providers of services, suppliers, and the medical director for a Medicare administrative contractor whenever the regional administrator involved determines that there is a systematic pattern and a large volume of complaints from such groups regarding decisions of the director or there is a complaint from the co-chair of the advisory committee of that contractor to the regional administrator regarding the dispute. [Soc. Sec. Act § 1869(i).]

LCD/NCD Reviews

Under CMS's appeals process for NCDs and LCDs, beneficiaries who qualify as aggrieved parties can challenge NCDs and LCDs by filing a complaint. An aggrieved party is defined as a Medicare beneficiary who is entitled to benefits under Part A, enrolled under Part B, or both (including an individual enrolled in fee-for-service Medicare, a Medicare Advantage plan, or another Medicare managed care plan), and is in need of coverage for a service that is the subject of an applicable LCD (in the relevant jurisdiction) or an NCD, as documented by the beneficiary's treating physician. The HHS Departmental Appeals Board (DAB) conducts NCD reviews and administrative law judges (ALJs) review LCDs. [Soc. Sec. Act § 1869(f)(1), (2), (5); 42 C.F.R. §§ 426.110, 426.300, 426.320.]

Only LCDs or NCDs (including deemed NCDs) that are currently effective may be challenged. The following items are not reviewable:

(1) pre-decisional materials, including draft LCDs, template LCDs or suggested LCDs, and draft NCDs, including national coverage decision memoranda;

(2) retired LCDs or withdrawn NCDs;

(3) LCD or NCD provisions that are no longer in effect due to revisions or reconsiderations;

(4) interpretive policies that are not an LCD or NCD;

(5) contractor decisions that are not based on Soc. Sec. Act § 1862(a)(1)(A);

(6) contractor claims processing edits;

(7) payment amounts or methodologies;

(8) procedure coding issues, including determinations, methodologies, definitions, or provisions;

(9) contractor bulletin articles, educational materials, or website frequently asked questions;

(10) any Medicare Advantage organization or managed care plan policy, rule, or procedure;

(11) an individual claim determination; or

(12) any other policy that is not an LCD or an NCD as set forth in 42 C.F.R. § 400.202.

[42 C.F.R. § 426.325.]

LCD review. An aggrieved party may initiate a review of an LCD by filing a timely written complaint that meets the requirements and includes all the necessary elements with the office designated by CMS on the Medicare website. [42 C.F.R. § 426.400.]

After a complete review of a coverage challenge, the applicable adjudicator is required to issue a description of the appeal rights or provide notice that the decision is pending. An ALJ's decision must include one of the following findings: (1) the provision of the LCD is valid under the reasonableness standard; (2) the provision of the LCD is not valid under the reasonableness standard; (3) the complaint regarding the LCD is dismissed, with a rationale for the dismissal; or (4) the LCD record is complete and adequate to support the validity of the LCD provisions under the reasonableness standard. [42 C.F.R. §§ 426.447, 426.450, 426.462, 426.482.]

An aggrieved party, CMS, or a CMS contractor may appeal the ALJ's decision if it states that a provision of the LCD is valid under the reasonableness standard or the complaint is dismissed. If the DAB determines the appeal is acceptable, it will permit the party that did not file the appeal an opportunity to respond, hear oral arguments, review the LCD record and the parties' arguments, and issue a written decision either upholding, modifying, or reversing the ALJ decision, or remanding the ALJ decision to the ALJ for further proceedings. [42 C.F.R. §§ 426.465, 426.476(a).]

NCD review. An aggrieved party may initiate a review of an NCD by filing with the DAB a timely written complaint that meets the requirements and includes all the necessary elements. [42 C.F.R. § 426.500.] The DAB's decision must include one of the following: (1) a determination that the provision of the NCD is valid under the reasonableness standard; (2) a determination that the provision of the NCD is not valid under the reasonableness standard; (3) a statement dismissing the complaint regarding the NCD and a rationale for the dismissal; or (4) a determination that the NCD record is complete and adequate to support the validity of the NCD provisions under the reasonableness standard. [42 C.F.R. § 426.550.]

¶928

After the DAB makes a decision regarding an NCD complaint, it sends a written notice of the decision to each party stating the outcome of the review and informing each party to the determination of his or her rights to seek further review if he or she is dissatisfied with the determination, and the time limit under which an appeal must be requested. CMS may not appeal a DAB decision. [42 C.F.R. §§ 426.562, 426.566.]

A decision by the DAB constitutes a final agency action and is subject to judicial review. DAB review may be bypassed in favor of judicial review if a party alleges an absence of material issues of the facts in dispute and the only issue concerns the constitutionality of the law or the validity of the regulation. [Soc. Sec. Act § 1869(f)(3); 42 C.F.R. § 426.560(a).]

NCD Reconsiderations

When an NCD currently exists, any individual or entity may request that CMS reconsider any provision of that NCD by filing a complete formal request for reconsideration. CMS will consider accepting a request for reconsideration if the requestor submits evidence of one of the following:

- additional scientific evidence that was not considered in the most recent review;

or

- plausible arguments that the conclusion reached in the last review along with a sound premise that new evidence may change the conclusion.

[*Notice*, 78 FR 48167, Aug. 7, 2013.]

CMS considers a request to complete and formal only if the following conditions are met:

- the requester provides a final letter of request and clearly identifies the request as a "Formal Request for NCD Reconsideration";

- the requester identifies the scientific evidence that he or she believes supports the request for reconsideration; and

- the written request includes and supports any additional Medicare Part A or Part B benefit categories in which the requester believes the item or service falls.

The request for reconsideration must be submitted electronically. CMS will usually make a decision within 60 days. [*Notice*, 78 FR 48167, Aug. 7, 2013.]

[¶ 930] Recovery Audit Contractor, Cost Report, Status, Exclusion, and Suspension Appeals

Provider and supplier appeals include appeals of recovery audit contractor (RAC) determinations, provider status determinations, and suspension and exclusion from participation in Medicare and other federal health care programs. Cost report reviews pertain to only certain providers, such as hospitals, critical access hospitals, and skilled nursing facilities, because those providers are required to submit annual cost reports.

Recovery Audit Contractor Appeals

Although RACs do not make initial determinations, as Medicare contractors, they are able to reopen claims based on their audits of providers' claims to detect improper payments. [*Final rule*, 74 FR 65296, Dec. 9, 2009.] Appeals of RAC determinations regarding fee-for-service claims are handled with other overpayment determinations under the fee-for-service Medicare appeals process (see ¶ 924), although Medicare administrative contractors (MACs) must track the RAC appeals separately in their reports to CMS. [*Medicare Financial Management Manual*, Pub. 100-06, Ch. 4, §§ 100.6, 100.7.] For a discussion of RAC responsibilities, see ¶ 711.

Administrative Review of Disputed Cost Reports

Hospitals and certain other providers that participate in the Medicare program are required to submit an annual accounting of the costs they incur to operate their facilities, including direct patient costs for Medicare and non-Medicare patients and operating costs such as depreciation, capital-related costs, and other expenses. The cost report is the vehicle for reporting costs and income to CMS.

Section 1878 of the Social Security Act and its implementing regulations (42 C.F.R. § 405.1801 *et seq.*) give providers of services and other entities, such as managed care organizations, the right to request a hearing on disputed cost reports submitted to their contractors. [Soc. Sec. Act § 1878(a).]

When the amount in controversy is $1,000 or more, but less than $10,000, a dissatisfied provider or other entity may request a MAC hearing. [42 C.F.R. § 405.1809(b)(2).]

If a provider disagrees with the hearing officer's interpretation of the law, regulations, rulings, or general instructions relied on in the decision, it may request a review of the decision by a CMS special review officer. CMS also may review a hearing officer's decision on its own motion. [42 C.F.R. § 405.1834(a).]

PRRB review. Any provider of services that has filed a timely cost report may appeal an adverse final decision of the MAC to the Provider Reimbursement Review Board (PRRB) if the amount at issue is $10,000 or more. The appeal must be filed within 180 days after the provider receives notice of the MAC's or Secretary's final determination. [Soc. Sec. Act § 1878(a); 42 C.F.R. § 405.1835(a)(2), (a)(3).]

Groups of providers may appeal adverse final decisions of the MAC to the PRRB when the matters at issue share a common question of fact or law and the total amount in controversy, in the aggregate, is $50,000 or more. Providers also may appeal to the PRRB on a late cost report decision by the MAC if the amount involved is $10,000 or more. Implementation of the MAC's determinations will not be suspended pending the PRRB's decision. [Soc. Sec. Act § 1878(a), (b).]

CMS review. A party to a PRRB appeal or CMS may request a CMS Administrator review, or the CMS Administrator, at his or her discretion, may immediately review any decision of the PRRB related to: (1) a hearing decision; (2) a dismissal of a request for hearing; (3) a decision for an expedited judicial review, but only to the question of whether there is PRRB jurisdiction over a specific matter at issue in the decision (the Administrator may not review the PRRB's determination in a decision of its authority to decide a legal question relevant to the matter at issue); or (4) any other final decision of the PRRB. [42 C.F.R. § 405.1875(a), (c).]

Judicial review. A provider has a right to obtain judicial review of a final decision of the PRRB, or of a timely reversal, affirmation, or modification by the Administrator, by filing a civil action within 60 days of receipt of the decision. When judicial review is sought, the amount in controversy is subject to annual interest beginning on the first day of the first month that begins after the 180-day period following the notice of the Medicare contractor's final determination. [Soc. Sec. Act § 1878(f)(1), (2); 42 C.F.R. § 405.1877.]

Providers also have the right to obtain judicial review of any action of the MAC involving a question of law or regulations relevant to the matters in controversy, whenever the PRRB determines (on its own motion or at the request of the provider) that it is without authority to decide the question. [Soc. Sec. Act § 1878(f)(1).]

¶930

Provider Status Determinations

CMS will make the initial determinations with respect to whether a provider or supplier meets the conditions for participation or coverage in the Medicare program. Adverse decisions may be appealed to an administrative law judge (ALJ) and the Departmental Appeals Board (DAB). [Soc. Sec. Act § 1866(h); 42 C.F.R. § 498.5.] The determinations and appeals procedures are outlined in 42 C.F.R. Part 498 and are applicable to these and other status determinations.

Appeals Concerning Suspensions and Fines

The law contains provisions, discussed at ¶ 720, granting the Secretary authority to exclude from participation in the Medicare program or impose sanctions upon entities or individuals if they are determined to have committed certain program abuses. The Secretary delegated this authority to the HHS Inspector General. An excluded entity or individual is entitled to reasonable notice of an opportunity for hearing by the Secretary. Any practitioner, provider, or supplier who has been suspended, whose services have been excluded from coverage, or who has been sanctioned is entitled to a hearing before an ALJ. Any suspended or excluded practitioner, provider, or supplier dissatisfied with a hearing decision may request a DAB review and has a right to seek judicial review of the DAB's decision by filing an action in federal district court. [Soc. Sec. Act § 1128(f); 42 C.F.R. § 498.5(i).]

Any person adversely affected by a determination of the Secretary with respect to the imposition of a civil money penalty may obtain review of the determination in a U.S. Court of Appeals (see ¶ 720). [Soc. Sec. Act § 1128A(e).]

Topical Index

→ *References are to paragraph numbers*

C

EMT

END

IRO